ENGLISH GRAMMAR
AND
TRANSLATION

Comprehensive
BETTER
ENGLISH GRAMMAR
AND
TRANSLATION

[For all Board/University Courses & Competitive Exams]

By
K.D. UPADHYAY

M.A. (Eng. and Hindi), B.Ed.

Ex-Lecturer
Deptt. of English
L.D. Inter College, Ballia (U.P.)

LAXMI PUBLICATIONS (P) LTD

BANGALORE ● CHENNAI ● COCHIN ● GUWAHATI ● HYDERABAD
JALANDHAR ● KOLKATA ● LUCKNOW ● MUMBAI ● RANCHI
NEW DELHI

Published by :

LAXMI PUBLICATIONS (P) LTD
22, Golden House, Daryaganj,
New Delhi-110002.

Phones : {
011-23 26 23 68
011-23 26 23 70
}

Faxes : {
011-23 25 25 72
011-23 26 22 79
}

Branches :

- 129/1, IIIrd Main Road, IX Cross Chamrajpet, **Bangalore** (*Phone :* 080-26 61 15 61)
- 26, Damodaran Street, T. Nagar, **Chennai** (*Phone :* 044-24 34 47 26)
- St. Benedict's Road, **Cochin** (*Phone :* 0484-239 70 04)
- Pan Bazar, Rani Bari, **Guwahati** (*Phones :* 0361-254 36 69, 251 38 81)
- 4-2-453, Ist Floor, Ramkote, **Hyderabad** (*Phone :* 040-24 75 02 47)
- Adda Tanda Chowk, N.D. 365, **Jalandhar City** (*Phone :* 0181-222 12 72)
- 106/A, Ist Floor, S.N. Banerjee Road, **Kolkata** (*Phones :* 033-22 27 37 73, 22 27 52 47)
- 18, Madan Mohan Malviya Marg, **Lucknow** (*Phone :* 0522-220 95 78)
- 128A, Block 3, First Floor, Noorani Building, L.J. Road, **Mumbai** (*Phone :* 022-24 46 39 98)
- Radha Govind Street, Tharpagna, **Ranchi** (*Phone :* 0651-230 77 64)

EMAIL : colaxmi@hotmail.com

WEBSITE : www.laxmipublications.com

T12-8934-145-BETTER ENG GRAMMAR & TRANSL

New Edition

Price : **Rs. 145.00** *Only.*

C—983 9/05/02

Laser Typesetting at : Goswami Printers, Delhi.   ***Printed at :*** Akashdeep Printers, Delhi.

PREFACE

The present effort on **English Grammar** and **Translation** is meant to meet the purposes of college students and those who aspire to appear at the various competitive examinations. Here important and necessary topics are deeply and widely touched and explained so that they may fulfil the requisite demands of the candidates. Besides it, copious exercises are given with a view to improve and increase their knowledge and make them able to write better English. Nonetheless, I dare not profess that this endeavour is altogether free from defects and drawbacks. However, if the book proves a little useful for the students, the effort will be accounted successful.

K.D. Upadhyay

CONTENTS

3. There and It.
4. Can, Could, May, Might
5. Should, Must, Ought to, Would
6. Degree of Comparison
7. Interrogative Sentence
8. Imperative, Optative and Exclamatory Sentences
9. Tenses (Active Voice)
10. Tenses (Passive Voice)
11. Non-Finites
12. Conditional Sentences
13. Complex Sentences
14. Compound Sentences
15. Miscellaneous Sentences
16. Passages for Practice
17. Vocabulary

Part
GRAMMAR

Part I
GRAMMAR

Chapter 1

Important Grammatical Terms
—Definitions and Descriptions

1. Adjective (विशेषण)–वह शब्द जो Noun की विशेषता (गुण, मात्रा, संख्या इत्यादि) बताए। जैसे–An *honest* man. *All* creatures must die. *Some* men are born *great*.

2. Adverb (क्रिया विशेषण)–जो शब्द किसी verb (क्रिया), adjective (विशेषण) अथवा अन्य adverb की विशेषता बताए। जैसे–He walks *slowly*. John is a *very clever* boy. The Rajputs fought *very bravely*.

3. Affix–अर्थात् prefix (उपसर्ग) तथा suffix (प्रत्यय) : prefix शब्द के पूर्व जोड़कर नया शब्द बनाया जाता है। जैसे–ex-student में *ex* prefix हुआ। Childish में *-ish* suffix हुआ। शब्द के बाद में जो जोड़ा जाय उसे suffix कहते हैं। *Unheard ; disgrace, restless* इत्यादि।

4. Agent–Passive voice (कर्म वाच्य) में जिसके द्वारा कार्य सम्पन्न हो agent कहा जाता है। The letter was written by *me*. The candle was blown out by *the child*. यहाँ me तथा child agents हैं।

5. Alphabet (वर्णमाला)–The set of letters used in a language (Concise Oxford Dictionary—C.O.D.). जैसे–A से Z तक Alphabet कहा जाएगा a, e, i, o तथा u—vowels 19 letters—consonants एवं 2 (*w, y*) semi-vowels.

6. Analysis (वाक्य विश्लेषण)–यह verb 'analyse' का Noun है। अर्थ है–To resolve (sentence) into its grammatical elements. प्रयोगों को दृष्टिगत करते हुए वाक्य के प्रत्येक पद या उपवाक्य (clause) की व्याकरणीय मीमांसा करना।

7. Antecedent (पूर्वगामी शब्द या कर्ता)–उस Noun/pronoun को कहा जाता है जिसके तुरन्त बाद Relative pronoun से बने clause से उसकी विशेषता बताई गई हो। जैसे–*The book* which I bought yesterday is lost. I do not know *the time* when the boat leaves. यहाँ book तथा time antecedents हैं।

8. Antonyms (विलोम या विपरीतार्थक शब्द)–शब्दों के विपरीत अर्थ वाले शब्द जैसे–New का old या Wide—*narrow* ; alive—*dead* ; bad—*good*.

9. Apposition (समानाधिकरण, एकान्वय)–अर्थात् placing side by side. जब कोई Noun किसी अन्य Noun का वर्णन या परिचय बताए तो वह परिचयांश Apposition कहलाता है।

His brother, *a renowned physician*, arrived here yesterday. His belief *that he will stand first*, is reasonable. यहाँ *a renowned physician* जो brother का परिचय देता है तथा *that he will stand first* जो belief का स्पष्टीकरण देता है, Appositions हैं।

10. Articles–A, *An*, तथा *The* तीनों Articles कहे जाते हैं। Definite Article—*The* तथा Indefinite Articles—*A, An*.

11. Attribution–Quality, Quantity etc. ascribed to any person, thing or place. जैसे–*A talkative* boy, *A shy* girl ; *Womanish* nature इत्यादि। यहाँ *talkative, shy* तथा *Womanish* Attributes हैं। ये प्राय: qualified word के पूर्व रखे जाते हैं।

3

12. Auxiliary (सहायक)—इसे helping verbs, special, defective, या anomalous verbs भी कहते हैं जो कुल 24 हैं। One used to form tenses, moods, voices of other verbs. जो finite verbs या principal verbs की सहायता करे।

Shall, will, must, can, may, has, have, had, do, does, did, should, would, could, might, ought to, verbs to be, need, dare, used (to).

13. Bare Infinitive (नग्न क्रियात्मक संज्ञा)—जब Infinitive बिना to का रहे। जैसे—Let them *laugh*. I heard him *say*. यहाँ *laugh* तथा *say* infinitives without to हैं अत: bare infinitives हैं।

14. Case (कारक, विभक्ति)—(*a*) Nominative case (कर्ता कारक)—वाक्य के subject (कर्ता) को कहते हैं।

(*b*) Objective case or Accusative case (कर्मकारक)—वाक्य के object (कर्म) को कहते हैं।

प्रस्तुत वाक्य के verb में who या what (कौन, किसने) से प्रश्न करने पर जो उत्तर आएगा वह वाक्य का subject (अत: nominative case) होगा यदि whom या what (किसको, किसे) से प्रश्न किया जाय तो जो उत्तर आएगा वह वाक्य का object (अत: objective case) होगा। जैसे—Govind kicked the ball. Who kicked the ball ? answer—*Govind*. अत: *Govind* वाक्य का subject और nominative case हुआ। पुन: whom did Govind kick ? answer—*ball*. अत: *ball* object तथा objective case हुआ।

(*c*) Possessive या Genitive case (सम्बन्ध कारक)—Noun/pronoun का ऐसा स्वरूप जिससे possession, authorship, origin, kind etc. का बोध हो। इसकी प्रमुख पहचान Apostrophe ('s) है। The *king's* crown, *Ram's* book, *Man's* destiny इनमें *king's, Ram's, Man's* possessive case में हैं।

(*d*) Nominative of Address या Vocative case (सम्बोधन)—जैसे—*O* World ! *O* Life ! *O* Time ! *O* Death ! Where is thy charm ?

(*e*) Dative case (द्विकर्मक कारक)—Direct object (प्रत्यक्ष कर्म) तथा Indirect object (परोक्ष कर्म) जो person हुआ करता है। Thing direct object होता है, person dative case.

(*f*) Case in Apposition—Apposition का अर्थ है 'Placing of word in syntactic parallelism with another especially addition of one noun to another'. Apposite *i.e.,* well put. जब कोई वाक्य अपने पूर्व Noun के वर्णन, परिचय, व्याख्या इत्यादि के लिए उसके बाद प्रयुक्त होता है तो वह Apposition कहलाता है।

Milton, *the greatest poet of English literature*, was blind. His belief *that he would succeed*, was true. यहाँ *The greatest poet of English literature* तथा *that he would succeed* क्रमश: Milton तथा belief के appositions हैं।

15. Clause (उपवाक्य)—शब्दों का वह सार्थक समूह जिसमें subject तथा predicate हों। ऐसे अनेक वाक्य परस्पर conjunctions से सम्बद्ध रहते हैं। जैसे—He noticed a girl *whose eyes were blue*. He promised *that he would come*. इनमें *whose* तथा *that* से सम्बद्ध वाक्य clauses हैं। उक्त दोनों वाक्यों में दो-दो Clauses हैं।

More About Clauses :

Complex sentence को दो भागों में विभाजित किया जा सकता है :–

(*a*) Principal clause (Main clause मुख्य उपवाक्य) तथा

(*b*) Subordinate clause (आश्रित उपवाक्य)

पुन: Subordinate clause के तीन प्रकार–

(I) Noun clause (संज्ञा उपवाक्य)—जो मुख्यत: *that* तथा *Wh* word से प्रारम्भ होता है। हिन्दी में इनका प्रथमाक्षर 'क' हुआ करता है। जैसे–

I believe *that he will come*.

Do you know *where he lives* ?

(II) **Adjective clause** (विशेषण उपवाक्य)—जो अपने antecedent के तुरन्त पश्चात् that, as या Wh से प्रारम्भ होते हैं और भाषान्तर करने पर इनका प्रथमाक्षर 'ज' से प्रारम्भ होता है। जैसे—

The house *that is on the hill* is seen by all.

He *who climbs high* is sure to fall.

(III) **Adverb clause** (क्रिया विशेषण उपवाक्य)—जैसे—

As soon as they noticed me, they took to their heels.

Although he is very rich, he is not contented.

(c) **Coordinate clause**—एक compound sentence (यौगिक वाक्य) में Main clause तथा उसी के समानान्तर Coordinate clause होता है। ये Clauses प्राय: *and, as well as, but, still, so, for, neither .... nor, either ..... or* आदि से सम्बद्ध रहते हैं।

(d) Main तथा Coordinate clause से बना वाक्य **Double sentence** कहलाता है। जैसे—

He came *and* sat down quietly.

(e) Main clause तथा Coordinate clauses से जुटे अनेक वाक्यों को **Multiple sentence** कहा जाता है। जैसे—

He was badly injured *so* he went to hospital *but* the physicians were not there.

(f) **Eliptical clause**—संक्षिप्त Adverb clause जिसके subject/verb/or part of the verb का लोप कर दिया गया हो। जैसे—

When young, I thought so.

When young—When I was young—eliptical clause.

16. Cognate object— (Latin—cognatus *i.e.* akin) जो intransitive verbs के पश्चात् उसी के समानार्थी (Similar or akin in meaning) रूप में प्रयुक्त होता है—

He laughed *a hearty laugh*.

I dreamt *a strange dream*.

He ran *a race*.

17. Complement (पूरक)—वाक्य का वह भाग जो subject, object के बारे में अधिक सूचना दे। Complement means 'that which completes the meaning of a verb of incomplete predication. जैसे—

He appears *to be mad*.

My wish is *to amass money*.

18. Conditional sentence (शर्तवाला वाक्य)—जो if, unless, until, provided, in case आदि से शर्त की ध्वनि प्रगट करे। जैसे—

If you work hard, you will succeed.

I may help you *provided* you come to me.

Unless you speak the truth, I will not forgive you.

19. Conjunction (योजक)—वह शब्द या शब्द-संवर्ग जो सामान्यतया शब्दों या वाक्यों को जोड़े। जोड़ने वाले उस word या group of words को connectives कहते हैं। जैसे—and, but, or, either....or, not only...but also, so, therefore, because, since as आदि। जैसे—

You can explain it *because* you are clever.

Speak the truth *and* do not fear.

He abused me *still* I was quiet.

20. Consonant (व्यंजन)–अंग्रेजी के 26 letters में से *a, e, i, o* तथा *u* एवं *w* और *y* को छोड़कर कहे जाते हैं, alphabet के शेष 19 letters consonants होते हैं।

21. Contraction—Subject, verb, auxiliary verb तथा not के संक्षिप्त स्वरूप को कहते हैं। जैसे–*Couldn't, Wasn't, Won't, Shan't, You'll, I'm* etc.

22. Finite verb (मुख्य क्रिया)–वाक्य में जिस verb को उसका subject प्रतिपादित (सम्पादित) करे उसे finite verb कहा जाता है। अन्य शब्दों में, जिसका number, tense इत्यादि उसके subject के अनुसार निश्चित हो सके।

He *broke* the jug.
A wild wind *blew* against the tree.
Success often *depends* upon time.

यहाँ *broke, blew, depends* finite verbs हैं।

23. Gender (लिंग)–Masculine gender (पुलिंग), feminine gender (स्त्रीलिंग), Common gender (उभय लिंग) तथा Neuter gender (निर्जीव)। Gender, sex distinction बताता है। जैसे–*He, She, it* इत्यादि।

24. Gerund (क्रियात्मक संज्ञा)–यह verb का ऐसा स्वरूप होता है जिसके अन्त में ing होता है तथा Noun का कार्य करता है। सामान्यतया हिन्दी की ना, ने, नी से समाप्त हुई क्रिया को यह प्रगट करता है। जैसे–

Walking is a good exercise.
Sticking bills on the wall is forbidden.

25. Homonym—Word of same form as another but different sense. 'Homo' means same or similar in sound, origin, descent etc. वे शब्द जो मूल रूप में बनावट तथा उच्चारण-ध्वनि में समान हों किन्तु अर्थ अनेक हों। जैसे–Temple—मन्दिर, कनपटी ; cricket—झींगुर, एक खेल का नाम ; foot–पैर, बारह इंच, बिल भुगतान करना।

26. Homophone (समध्वन्यात्मक शब्द)–वे शब्द जिनकी उच्चारण ध्वनि समान हो किन्तु spelling तथा meaning में भिन्नता हो।'Phone' means sound. *Break*–तोड़ना *Brake*–गत्यावरोधक *Rage*—anger ; *raise*–to lift ; *raze*—to destroy. *Human*—of man ; *humane*—beneficent.

27. Idiom—It is an expression peculiar to a language. (Wren) किसी भाषा के शब्द समूह की प्रयुक्त शब्दों से पृथक् विशिष्ट अभिव्यक्ति। जैसे–*A black sheep, at daggers drawn, to get rid of* इत्यादि।

28. Infinitive (क्रियात्मक संज्ञा)–सामान्यतया इसका स्वरूप to + verb हुआ करता है और यह हिन्दी की उस क्रिया को प्रगट करता है जो, ना, ने, नी से समाप्त हो। मूल रूप से यह verb से बनता है किन्तु कार्य Noun Adjective का करता है। जैसे–

He came *to see* me.
To please all is *to please none*.
This medicine is bitter *to take*.

29. Interjection (विस्मयादि बोधक)–वह शब्द जो संवेगों या उमंगों को अभिव्यक्त करे। जैसे–*Alas* ! *Hurrah* ! *Oh* ! *Bravo* ! etc.

30. Imperative sentence (आज्ञा सूचक वाक्य)–ऐसे वाक्य जिनसे आज्ञा (order), आदेश (command), सलाह (advice), निवेदन (request) इत्यादि का बोध हो। इसमें You छिपा रहता है और सामान्यतया इसे verb से प्रारम्भ किया जाता है। जैसे–

Speak loudly.
First *deserve* then *desire*.
Do not look a gift horse in the mouth.

31. Impersonal–It को Impersonal pronoun कहा जाता है प्राय: इसे निर्जीव वस्तु (छोटे-छोटे जीवों के लिए भी) के लिए प्रयोग किया जाता है। इसे **Introductory, provisional** या **Temporary subject** भी कहा जाता है। जैसे–

> *It* was blowing hard.
> *It* is Monday today.

32. Modal Auxiliary verbs–*Can, could, may, might, must, will, would, shall, should, ought (to), need, dare, used to* modal verbs हैं।

33. Mood–Mood is the mode or manner in which the action denoted by the verb is represented (P.C. Wren) क्रिया द्वारा प्रगटित कार्य के अभिव्यक्ति का ढंग, तरीका या शैली। जैसे–

> He became a laughing stock.
> Have you abandoned the scheme ? (Indicative mood)
> Come into the garden. Be honest. (Imperative mood)
> He talks as if he were my officer.
> May God save them. (Subjunctive mood)

34. Narration–Direct and Indirect speech (प्रत्यक्ष तथा परोक्ष कथन)–

> St. Francis said *"It is my turn, little birds !"* (Direct)
> St. Francis told little birds lovingly *that it was his turn*. (Indirect)

35. Noun (संज्ञा)–It is a word used as the name of a person, place or thing. Besides formal meanings, it also includes something that we can think of but cannot perceive by the senses.

इसके पाँच भेद हैं–

(*a*) **Proper Noun** (व्यक्तिवाचक संज्ञा)–नाम विशेष को कहते हैं, जैसे–Hari, Allahabad etc.

(*b*) **Common Noun** (जातिवाचक संज्ञा)–सम्पूर्ण जाति का बोध कराता है। जैसे–Student, servant, town etc.

(*c*) **Material Noun** (द्रव्य वाचक संज्ञा)–माप-तौल की वस्तु का नाम। जैसे–Iron, coal, wheat etc.

(*d*) **Collective Noun** (समूह या झुंडवाचक संज्ञा)–समूह का बोध कराता है। जैसे–Crowd, class, team etc.

(*e*) **Abstract Noun** (गुण या भाववाचक संज्ञा)–जो *Quality, state* or *action* का संकेत दे। अर्थात् जो अनुभवजन्य हो जिसका स्पर्श आदि न हो सके, जो स्वरूपहीन हो। सामान्य पहचान–ऐसे शब्द के अन्त में प्राय:

-ness (kindness),	*-ty* (Honesty),
-dom (wisdom),	*-ery* (bravery),
-ment (Movement),	*-er* (laughter),
-hood (childhood),	*-th* (Youth) आदि रहा करते हैं।

आधुनिक व्याकरणाचार्यों ने इसे निम्नस्थ रूप में विभाजित किया है–

(*a*) **Proper Noun**–(व्यक्तिवाचक संज्ञा)।

(*b*) **Common Noun**–(जातिवाचक संज्ञा)–जिसके countable तथा uncountable दो भेद हैं।

(*i*) **Countable Noun**–(गणनीय संज्ञा)–जिसके पूर्व *A/An* लगाया जा सके अथवा जिनका plural number बन सके। जैसे–Man, Class, beast etc.

(*ii*) **Uncountable (or mass) Noun**–(अगणनीय संज्ञा)–जिसके पूर्व *A/An* न लग सके तथा जिसका plural form न हो। जैसे–Success, poverty, kindness etc.

36. Non-finite verb–Infinitive, Gerund तथा Participle जैसे–

Better *to reign* in hell than to serve in heaven.

He is afraid of *going* in the dark.

A *rolling* stone gathers no moss.

Borrowed garments never fit well.

37. Number (वचन)–(*a*) Singular Number (एक वचन) जैसे–Child, elephant तथा (*b*) Plural Number (बहुवचन)–जैसे–Children, elephants इत्यादि।

38. Parenthetical clause (असम्बद्ध शब्द/अप्रासंगिक उपवाक्य)–इसे parenthesis भी कहा जा सकता है। वाक्य में प्रयुक्त उस भाग को कहते हैं जो उसके अर्थ के प्रति अप्रासंगिक होता है तथा व्याकरणीय दृष्टि से अनावश्यक भी। प्राय: वाक्य में इसे कोष्ठ, विराम या अल्प विराम में देखा जाता है।

'Parenthesis is a word, clause or sentence, inserted into a passage to which it is not grammatically essential and usually marked off by brackets, dashes or commas'.

(Concise Oxford Dictionary)

जैसे–

This is, *as far as I know*, the whole truth.

Mr. Patel, *I am not sure*, is said to be a man of hot temper.

इनमें *as far as I know* तथा *I am not sure*—parentheses हैं।

39. Participle (क्रियात्मक विशेषण)–यह verb से बनता है किन्तु Adjective का काम करता है। इसके तीन भेद होते हैं–

(*a*) Present participle–Verb + ing. जैसे–

Authority forgets a *dying* king.

(*b*) Past participle–Verb को किसी Noun के पूर्व रखकर। जैसे–

A *retired* teacher.

'(Home) they brought her warrior *dead*'. (Tennyson)

(*c*) Perfect participle–Having + verb जैसे–

Having drawn his sword, he jumped over the lion.

40. Parts of speech–Words according to their uses in a sentence, have been classified into several parts. Those are called 'Parts of speech'. वाक्य में प्रयोग को दृष्टिगत करते हुए शब्दों का अनेक भागों में वर्गीकरण किया गया है, उन्हें parts of speech कहते हैं।

Noun, pronoun, adjective, verb इत्यादि इनके अन्तर्गत आएँगे।

41. Phrase–'A group of words, which makes sense, but not complete sense, is called a phrase. सामान्यतया बिना predicate (विधेय) के शब्दों का एक संक्षिप्त समूह जो अपूर्ण भाव रखे। जैसे–

(*i*) *A humorous page*—a page full of humours. (full of humours). (Adj. phrase)

(*ii*) *He answered rudely*—he answered in a rude manner. (Adverb phrase)

(*iii*) *They went to see a man in prison*—a prisoner (Noun phrase)

इनका और भी वर्गीकरण किया जा सकता है–

Verbal phrase (*blow out*) ; Phrase preposition (*by dint of*) ; Phrasal conjunction (*as if*) ; participle, Infinitive, Gerund, Absolute phrase इत्यादि।

42. Positive degree–Adjective/Adverb का तुलनात्मक स्तर–(a) Positive degree, (b) Comparative degree and Superlative degree. प्राय: Positive में -er जोड़ने पर comparative तथा -est जोड़ने पर superlative degree बनता है।

Tall	taller	tallest
Wise	wiser	wisest
Easy	easier	easiest
Difficult	More difficult	Most difficult.

43. Predicate (विधेय)–प्रत्येक Simple sentence के दो भाग होते हैं–(a) वह भाग जिसमें उस व्यक्ति, वस्तु इत्यादि का संकेत रहता है–जिसके विषय में कुछ कहा जाने को हो–उद्देश्य अर्थात् subject part और (b) वह भाग जो पूर्व संकेतित व्यक्ति या वस्तु के बारे में कहा गया हो predicate part (विधेय) कहा जाता है, जैसे–

> The boys ran after the butterflies.

The boys—subject part ; *ran after the butterflies*—predicate part है।

Predicative use *i.e.,* जिसे qualified/governing word के पश्चात् रखा जाय *viz.* a man *bold and sober*, left the ship *afloat.*

44. Prepositions (समुच्चयबोधक अव्यय)–pre (पूर्व) + position (स्थिति)। 'It is a word placed before a noun or a pronoun to show in what relation the person or thing is.' (P.C. Wren) जैसे–*In, to, of, with, for, about, without, in lieu of, for want of* इत्यादि।

45. Pronoun (सर्वनाम)–pro *i.e.,* substitute for, favouring or siding with + Noun (संज्ञा) hence pronoun means for -a- noun. इसके अनेक भेद हैं जिनमें से कुछ प्रमुख इस प्रकार हैं–

(I) Personal pronoun (पुरुषवाचक सर्वनाम)

Person पुरुष	Nominative case कर्ता कारक–ने	Objective case कर्म कारक–को	Possessive case सम्बन्ध कारक– का, के, की, रा, रे, री
First person (उत्तम पुरुष)	I (Singular) We (Plural)	me Us	my, mine our, ours
Second person (मध्यम पुरुष)	You (pl.) Thou (s.)	You	Your, Yours
Third person (अन्य पुरुष)	He She (s.) It They (pl.)	him her it them	his her, hers its their, theirs
Indefinite pronoun (अनिश्चयवाचक सर्वनाम)	One (s.)	One	One's
Interrogative/Relative pronoun प्रश्नवाचक/सम्बन्धवाचक सर्वनाम	Who	Whom	Whose

(II) Reflexive pronoun (or Emphatic pronoun) (निजवाचक सर्वनाम)—जब my, your, him, her, it, one के साथ -self लगा हो और our, your, them के साथ -selves जैसे—

> He wrote *himself*. (Reflexive pronoun)
> He *himself* wrote it. (Emphatic pronoun)

(III) Relative pronoun (सम्बन्धवाचक सर्वनाम)—that, as तथा wh प्रश्नवाचक शब्द जिनसे प्रारम्भ हुए वाक्य Antecedent के तुरन्त बाद से शुरू किए जाते हैं।

ऐसे वाक्य (wh वाले) प्रश्नवाचक वाक्य नहीं होते। उनकी हिन्दी 'ज' वर्ण से प्रारम्भ हुआ करती है और ये subordinate adjective clauses कहे जाते हैं जैसे—

> I noticed a girl who was rushing against the violent wind.
> The ideas that moved the world... .

(IV) Interrogative pronoun (प्रश्नवाचक सर्वनाम)—प्रश्नवाचक शब्द जो W या H से प्रारम्भ हो इन्हें W/h question words भी कहा जाता है जैसे—Who, When, Which, How इत्यादि। इनसे प्रारम्भ वाक्य के अन्त में Note of interrogation (?) रहा करता है और इनकी हिन्दी 'क' से प्रारम्भ होती है।

(V) Reciprocal pronoun (परस्पर बोधक सर्वनाम) अर्थात् each other and one another.

46. Quasi-Agent—Quasi means not real or practical, half. Passive voice में कभी-कभी पारम्परिक *'By'* agent का प्रयोग न करके उसके स्थान पर किसी स्वाभाविक प्रयुज्य—preposition का प्रयोग किया जाता है उसे Quasi-agent कहते हैं।

> The news surprised me. (Active)
> I was surprised at the news. (Passive)
> Everyone knows Shivaji. (Active)
> Shivaji is known to every one (Passive)

47. Question Tag—कथन के अन्त में प्रयुक्त प्रश्न को कहते हैं। जैसे—

> You have bought a scooter, *haven't you* ?
> She did not speak, *did she* ?

48. Rhetorical Question (उदात्त प्रश्न)—*i.e.*, expressed with a view to persuasive or impressive effect. यह Information seeking न होकर प्रभावोत्पादक होता है। जैसे—

> Who does not know Shivaji ? Who cares ?
> Where is God not present ?

49. Reported speech—वक्ता के वास्तविक कथन को Inverted commas में उद्धृत किया जाता है उसे Reported speech कहते हैं। Inverted commas के बाहर के clause को Reporting clause कहा जाता है और उसके verb को Reporting verb. जैसे—The hermit preached, "Better to light up a lamp than curse darkness." The hermit preached *i.e.*, Reporting clause and "Better .... darkness" Reported speech है।

50. Retained object—Double object वाले वाक्य को passive voice में बदलते समय जिस object को subject रूप में प्रयोग नहीं किया जाता उसे Retained object कहा जाता है। जैसे—Who taught you English ? (Active) By whom was English taught to you ? (Passive) or By whom were you taught English ? (Passive) प्रथम Passive में you और द्वितीय में English Retained objects हैं।

51. Sentence—A group of words or a single word that sounds complete sense or meaning is called a sentence. एक शब्द या शब्दों का समूह जो पूर्ण भाव या अर्थ प्रगट करे, वाक्य कहा जाता है। जैसे—

> His pages sparkle with lustrous beauty.

Sentence के भेद–

1. According to construction (or clause) बनावट की दृष्टि से Sentence के तीन भाग (a) simple sentence (सामान्य वाक्य)–जिसमें एक subject तथा अन्य predicate भाग हो।

(b) Complex sentence (मिश्रित वाक्य)–जिसमें एक Principal clause (मुख्य उपवाक्य) तथा अन्य उसका subordinate clause या clauses हो।

Subordinate clause के अन्तर्गत तीन भाग–

(a) Noun clause (संज्ञा उपवाक्य), (b) Adjective clause (विशेषण उपवाक्य) तथा (c) Adverb clause (क्रिया विशेषण उपवाक्य)।

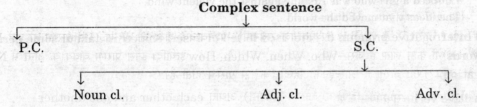

जैसे–

> Whenever he heard the question the old man who lived in that house, exclaimed that the earth was flat.

Compound sentence (यौगिक वाक्य)–जिसमें एक P.C. या Main clause हो और अन्य co-ordinating conjunction से जुड़ा समानान्तर स्तर का co-ordinate clause. जैसे–

> The horse jumped *and* threw the rider off.

2. According to meanings (अर्थानुसार) वाक्य के निम्नस्थ भेद होते हैं–

Assertive sentence—सामान्य वाक्य

Affirmative sentence—स्वीकारात्मक वाक्य

Negative sentence—नकारात्मक वाक्य

Interrogative sentence—प्रश्नवाचक वाक्य

Imperative sentence—आज्ञासूचक वाक्य

Optative sentence—अभिलाषा बोधक वाक्य

Exclamatory sentence—विस्मयादिबोधक वाक्य

आधुनिक Grammar में इनकी संख्या चार कर दी गई है :

1. Statement (Assertive)

2. Question (Interrogative)

3. Imperative

4. Exclamatory.

52. Substitution (स्थानापन्न शब्द)–अर्थात् One word for a group of words. जैसे–Born after the death of one's father *i.e., posthumous.* Which may cause death *i.e., fatal.*

53. Synonym (पर्यायवाची शब्द)–*i.e.,* word equivalent to another in meaning, or denoting the similar meaning. जैसे–Savage—*rude* ; Uncivilized—*wild* ; Abandon—*give up* ; forsake—*renounce.*

54. Syntax (वाक्य रचना या विन्यास)–वाक्य में शब्दों के व्याकरणीय दृष्टि से उचित प्रयोग को कहते हैं।

55. Synthesis (वाक्य संश्लेषण)–अर्थात् to join or combine the divided parts. अनेक simple sentences को जोड़कर एक simple, complex या compound sentence बनाना। जैसे–

> Her husband died. She heard the news. She fainted—
> On hearing the news of her husband's death, she fainted. (Simple)

56. Tense (काल)–Verb का वह स्वरूप जो व्यापार के घटना-काल को अभिव्यक्त करे। इसके तीन भेद–
Present tense (वर्तमान काल) ; past tense (भूतकाल) तथा **future tense** (भविष्यत् काल)।

> Man *proposes*, God *disposes*.   (Present)
> We *heard* sweet notes of birds.   (Past)
> He *will help* you.   (Future)

57. Verb (क्रिया)–'A verb is a word used to tell or assert something about some person or thing.' (Wren)

इसके दो भेद–

Transitive verb–सकर्मक क्रिया

Intransitive verb–अकर्मक क्रिया

इनके अतिरिक्त प्रयोग की दृष्टि से दो प्रकार के भेद–

Progressive verb (गत्यात्मक क्रिया) तथा Stative verb (स्थिर क्रिया)–जो verbs progressive or dynamic force वाली हो अथवा जो Activity बताएँ उन्हें **progressive verbs** कहेंगे। जैसे–jump, run, play, write, grow इत्यादि।

जो verbs किसी activity या motion को न व्यक्त करे अर्थात् जो अनुभवजन्य या संवेगात्मक हो उन्हें stative verbs कहेंगे। जैसे–Hope, believe, know, desire इत्यादि। जहाँ तक संभव हो stative verbs का प्रयोग continuous tense में नहीं करना चाहिए। जैसे–

> I *am knowing* you.   (Incorrect)
> I *know* you.   (Correct)

58. Verb to be (होना , बनना)–अर्थात् is, am, are (Present tense), was, were (Past tense), be, being, been. कुछ व्याकरणाचार्यों ने इन्हें Auxiliary verbs भी माना है।

> 'It is that form of a verb which shows whether what is denoted by the subject does something or has something done to it.' (Wren)

59. Voice (वाच्य)–(*a*) Active voice (कर्तृ वाच्य)–जिसमें verb का सम्पादन स्वयं उसके subject द्वारा हो। जैसे–

> He *bought* a horse.

(*b*) Passive voice (कर्मवाच्य)–जिसमें object की प्रधानता हो। जैसे–

> A horse *was bought* by him.

60. Weak verb–जिस verb का second form 'd' या 't' से समाप्त हो उसे weak verb कहते हैं। किन्तु जिसका वैसा न हो उसे strong verb कहते हैं। जैसे–

> Laugh–laughed–laughed–weak verb.   (Regular verb)
> See–Saw–Seen–strong verb.   (Irregular verb)

61. Some Abbreviations :

C.O.D.–Concise Oxford Dictionary.

etc.—et cetera—इत्यादि,

i.e.—id est—that is to say अर्थात्

viz.—Videlicet—namely अर्थात्

M.E.U.—Fowler's 'Modern English Usage'.

cf.—compare. (confer)

a—Adjective

n.—Noun

V.—verb

Adv.—Adverb

esp—especially

Semi Vowels—W तथा Y Semi vowels कहे जाते हैं।

Chapter 2

Articles

1. Articles

A, An तथा *The* को Articles कहा जाता है। वस्तुतः ये Demonstrative Adjectives हैं जिन्हें Noun के पूर्व रखा जाता है। इसके दो भेद होते हैं–(*i*) Indefinite Articles (*A and An*) और (*ii*) Definite Article (*The*). Definite *i.e.*, precise, not vague (निश्चित) क्योंकि यह निश्चित व्यक्ति या वस्तु का संकेत देता है जब कि *A, An* अनिश्चित। जैसे–

Call *a* doctor *i.e.*, any doctor.

Call *the* doctor *i.e.*, refers to a particular doctor.

2. Position of Articles

(1) Countable Noun (Singular) के पहले articles का प्रयोग करें। जैसे–

He is *a* teacher. (and not he is teacher).

That is *a* fox. Here is *a* pen.

That is *the* house.

(2) जब Countable Noun (Singular) के साथ कोई Adjective हो तो उस Adjective के पूर्व और यदि Adjective के साथ कोई Adverb हो तो उस Adverb के पूर्व Articles का प्रयोग करें। जैसे–

That is *the* best book. *An* unforgetable humour.

Balu is *a* tall boy. *A* precise remark.

She was *a* beautiful girl. She was *a* very beautiful girl.

An immensely black lady. *The* seemly bright garb.

(3) जाति/समुदाय के सर्वसामान्य विशेषता के सन्दर्भ में Articles का प्रयोग करें। जैसे–

An elephant is *a* wise animal.

The rose is *the* sweetest of all flowers.

The dog is *a* faithful animal.

(4) व्यक्तियों/वस्तुओं को पृथक्-पृथक् मानते समय प्रत्येक के पहले Articles का प्रयोग करें।

A black and white cow. (*i.e.*, only one cow)

A black and *a* white cow. (*i.e.*, two cows)

The president and secretary has come.

(But) I have studied *the* Tamil and *the* Bengali languages.

(5) Comparison अर्थात् तुलना या समता करते समय Proper Noun के पूर्व Articles का प्रयोग करें।

Kalidas is *the* Shakespeare of Sanskrit language.

He is *a* Hercules in power.

(6) Exclamation में a, an का प्रयोग करें। जैसे–

What *a* piece of work is man !

14

What *an* arresting sight !

Many *a* man has said so.

Have you ever seen such *a* sight ?

(7) सामान्यतया *all, both, such, how, so, as, too* आदि के पश्चात् तथा Adjective के बाद Article आता है।

All the boys.	So fine *a* man.
As good *a* book.	Too good *an* attempt etc.

Use of A/An

किसी शब्द के पूर्व A/An लगाने का आधार उस शब्द की उच्चारण-ध्वनि हुआ करता है। भाव यह है कि यदि उस शब्द की उच्चारण-ध्वनि का प्रारम्भ हिन्दी के स्वर (vowel) से हो तो उसके साथ An और यदि व्यंजन (consonant) से हो तो उसके साथ A का प्रयोग करें। Semi Vowels (W तथा Y) से प्रारम्भ शब्दों के साथ भी A का प्रयोग करें। जैसे—

A historian	*A* useful metal	*A* river
A university	*A* year	*A* yard
A woolen cloth	*A* brave man	*A* one rupee note
A European	*An* elephant	*An* honest man
An M.A	*An* M.P.	*An* answer
An umbrella	*An* hour before	*An* island
An owl	*An* Egyptian	*A* headache, *A* cold

No Articles

1. Proper Nouns तथा Uncountable Nouns जैसे—*news, mischief, business, health, work, homework, bread, information, luggage, advice, poetry, furniture* इत्यादि के साथ *a/an* का प्रयोग न करें। इसके पहले piece of, article of, act of का प्रयोग किया जा सकेगा।

Incorrect	**Correct**
He is a Mohan.	He is Mohan.
My ring is made of a gold.	My ring is made of gold.
He took a pity.	He took pity.
A fine advice.	A fine piece of advice.

2. कुछ व्यवस्थित prepositional phrases or idioms के साथ किसी articles का प्रयोग नहीं किया जाता। जैसे—

At school	*By* train	*On* foot	*In* bed
At home	*By* letter	*By* hand	*By* telegram
By mistake	*On* duty	*By* day	*To* send word
At fault	*In* fault	*At* dinner etc.	

3. किसी post/job/rank तथा Proper Noun के Apposition स्वरूप Titles के साथ कोई article न रखें।

Mr. Bahuguna is promoted to *the* rank of colonel. (not the colonel)

Dr. Rajendra Prasad, President of India, was a great scholar. (not the President of India)

He has applied for *the* post of Inspector of schools. (not the Inspector of schools)

4. निम्नस्थ Nouns के साथ the का प्रयोग न करें—

Church, market, school, college, hospital, court, bed

He went to *school*.

My neighbour went to *prison*.

She went to *bed*.

इनके पूर्व the का प्रयोग करने पर अर्थ भिन्न हो जाएगा।

I know English—अंग्रेजी जानता हूँ।

I know *the* English—अंग्रेजों को जानता हूँ।

He went to *the* school. (*i.e.,* not to read but for other purposes)

Kalu went to *the* prison. (*i.e.,* not for any crime)

5. Countable nouns (plural) जब subject रूप में आए तो उनके पूर्व प्राय: the नहीं लगता।

Birds like to sing. (not the birds ......)

Poets are the greatest liars (not the poets ......)

Men must work and *women* must talk.

6. बीमारियों के नाम, भोज्यपदार्थ तथा *Heaven ; Hell* के साथ कोई article न लगाएँ।

He has been suffering from the Malaria. (Incorrect)

He has been suffering from *Malaria*. (Correct)

We have taken the breakfast. (Incorrect)

We have taken *breakfast*. (Correct)

Better to reign in hell than serve in *heaven*. (Milton)

7. भाषा तथा खेल (*languages, games*) के नाम के साथ कोई article न लगाएँ।

I can speak *English*.   We like to play *cricket*.

8. *Nature, science, mankind* इत्यादि जब सामान्य या व्यापक भाव में रहें तो article न लगाएँ। यदि उस पर बल दिया गया हो (emphasis) तो the लगाया जा सकता है।

Science has moved *mankind* widely.

Life is a walking shadow.   *Man* is mortal.

(But) *Civics* is the science of citizenship.

9. *Appoint, declare, elect* इत्यादि के साथ article न लगाएँ।

The commission appointed him *Police Inspector, Principal* etc. (not the Police Inspector)

The court declared him *guilty*.

Use of 'The'

1. निश्चित व्यक्ति/वस्तु का संकेत रहने पर तथा वर्णनात्मक सन्दर्भ में दूसरी बार प्रयोग करते समय the का प्रयोग करें।

Bring *the book*.   I recollect *the scene*.

Where is *the stick* ?   Once there was *a king*.

The king was very kind.

2. Superlative Degree के पूर्व the का प्रयोग करें।

The smallest boy.   *The noblest* man.

The most beautiful sight.   (But) *My greatest* desire.

Imitation is *the sincerest* flattery.

3. जब 'The' Adjective (positive) के पूर्व रहेगा तो वह स्वयं Countable Noun (plural number) हो जाएगा। उसे plural बनाने के लिए उसमें -s या -es न लगाएँ।

Incorrect	Correct
The poors are happy.	*The poor* are happy.
The riches are unhappy.	*The rich* are unhappy.

4. जितना ही उतना ही के भाव में Comparative Adverb के पूर्व the का प्रयोग करें।

  The sooner, the better. The more, the merrier.

5. जब Uncountable Noun पर विशेष बल (Emphasis) दिया गया हो तो the लगाया जा सकता है।

  The peace of the grave.

  The kindness that he showed was beyond admiration.

6. विशाल पर्वत (उपभाग नहीं), नदियाँ, ऐतिहासिक भवन, प्रसिद्ध ग्रन्थ, भौगोलिक नाम, विशिष्ट प्राकृतिक वस्तुएँ, दिशाएँ, वाद्य यंत्र, शारीरिक अंग, धार्मिक समुदाय, समाचार-पत्र के नाम के साथ the का प्रयोग करें।

The Himalayas. (not the Everest)	*The* Ganga ; *The* Amazon
The Red Fort	*The* Ramayan
The Bible	*The* Bay of Bengal
The Strait of Zibralter	*The* Indian ocean
The sun	*The* moon
The earth	*The* world
The sky	*The* east
The west	*The* face
The arm	*The* Hindus
The Sikh	To play *the* violin, *the* harmonium
The Times of India ; *The* shining path etc.	

7. Political parties, empire, dynasty, armed forces, historical events के साथ the का प्रयोग करें।

The Bhartiya Janta Party.	*The* Moghal Empire.
The Behamini Dynasty.	*The* battle of Khanwa.
Where is *the* Roman Empire now ?	He has not retired from *the* Navy.

8. कुछ विशेष Idioms के साथ the का प्रयोग करें।

  To go to *the* pictures or *movies* or *theatre*, *cinema*, *circus* etc.

The sum and substance.	*The* gift of the gab.

Exercise 1

Fill up the blanks with appropriate articles :

1. ...... servant has ...... hand in it.
2. Passion is ...... abuse of power.
3. ...... union is ...... symbol of unity.
4. Here is ...... one-rupee note.
5. He founded ...... university.
6. ...... dog is ...... useful animal.
7. She pronounced ...... eulogy on him.
8. Mukul came ...... year ago.
9. The cloth is sold by ...... yard.
10. Let ...... matter drop now.
11. Even ...... cat may look at ...... king.
12. ...... poor are blessed but poverty is not.
13. ...... bad carpenter quarrels with his tools.
14. ...... poor man never praises poverty.

15. ...... one world is dead ...... other powerless to be born.
16. ...... world of today is not ...... world of yesterday.
17. ...... fashion has became ...... order of the day.
18. ...... beauty and ...... balm of nature caught our fancy.
19. He is as wise as ...... owl.
20. Who does not like ...... calm and quiet life ?
21. ...... able bodied man is always successful.
22. ...... Ramayan is ...... epic of epics.
23. She had to undergo ...... untold misery.
24. ...... hand that rocks in ...... cradle rules over ...... world.
25. English is ...... language of ...... English.
26. ...... moon was shining in ...... clear sky.
27. ...... Ganga ...... holy river, is also ...... goddess of ...... Hindus.
28. He used to play ...... flute.
29. ...... more you get ...... merrier you feel.
30. ...... live ass is better than ...... dead lion.
31. Do not be in such ...... hurry.
32. What ...... fool he is !
33. How could you leave him at such ...... time ?
34. What ...... partial judge we are !
35. ...... friend in need is ...... friend indeed.
36. My master is ...... thorough jew.
37. Your scheme is ...... wild goose chase.
38. ...... good deed always shine in ...... wicked world.
39. O, for ...... drop of water, for ...... piece of bread !
40. Do ...... little wrong in order to do ...... great right.
41. Where there is ...... will ...... there is ...... way.
42. ...... whole forest was filled with ...... melody of teeming birds.
43. Today flattery is ...... key to success.
44. ...... honest man speaks ...... truth.
45. ...... dying man never tells ...... lie.
46. ...... good and ...... noble always survive.
47. Give me ...... robe, I must go.
48. What is ...... use of going there ?

Answers

1. The, a	2. an	3. A, a	4. a	5. a
6. The, a	7. a	8. a	9. a	10. the
11. a, a	12. the	13. A	14. A	15. The, the
16. the, the	17. The, the	18. The, the	19. an	20. a
21. An	22. The, an	23. An	24. The, a, the	25. a, the
26. The, the	27. The, a, the, the		28. the	29. the, the
30. A, a	31. a	32. a	33. a	34. a
35. A, a	36. a	37. a	38. A, the	39. a, a
40. a, a	41. a, a	42. the, the	43. an, a	44. An, the
45. A, a	46. The, the	47. the	48. the.	

Exercise 2

Correct the following sentences, if necessary :

1. That is boy who got first prize.
2. I can read and write the English.
3. My teacher is M.Sc. in the physics.
4. Peacock is national bird of our country.
5. He was a face in the crowd.
6. The gold is very precious metal.
7. Honesty is the best policy.
8. It is no use to cry over a spilt milk.
9. Preference will be given to the deafs and the dumbs.
10. More you get, more you want.
11. The suspiciousness is mark of ignorance.
12. Our life is a satire on our religion.
13. What genius he is !
14. So good man is he that all respect him.
15. Once there was man in moon.
16. Communal disharmony is more harmful than helpful.
17. Mukesh was man of parts.
18. What is not in Mahabharat is not in the Bharat.
19. He was confined to the bed.
20. We went to the school.
21. Account for downfall of Moghal Empire.
22. He has been suffering from the high blood pressure for two years.
23. The God is in the heaven and everything is good in world.
24. Authority forgets a dying king.
25. Better to go by a bus.
26. Kabir, the social reformer, was a great poet.
27. The science has shaken us from our dated beliefs.
28. He was Shylock of his province.
29. Umesh is the author of the whole quarrel.
30. Umbrella that you bought is lost.
31. My ring is made of the silver.
32. All world was gay.
33. We shall take the tea at station.
34. The childhood is gem of life.
35. Silver is a second rated metal.
36. The poet and the playwright is dead.
37. Call first and last boy.
38. The union is strength.
39. Uranium is heavy substance.
40. Discretion is a better part of valour.
41. He got highest praise.
42. Two negatives make affirmative.
43. He gave us song and sentiment.

44. Section of opposition defied speaker's ruling.
45. The historians should be impartial.
46. It is ill wind that blows nobody good.
47. Good customs may also corrupt world.
48. His poverty is a testimony of his honesty.
49. The cleanliness is next to the godliness.
50. Sardar Patel was man of iron will.

Exercise 3

Fill up the blanks with appropriate articles :

1. Life is ...... tale told by ...... idiot.
2. I have ...... scooter.
3. Yesterday we met ...... European.
4. His father is ...... engineer.
5. ...... novel you gave is very interesting.
6. ...... poet leads us towards ...... unknown land.
7. ...... team of my college has won ...... match.
8. Sahara is ...... great desert.
9. ...... picture was painted by ...... famous painter.
10. ...... good will prosper, ... bad will suffer.
11. He is ...... Inspector of schools.
12. Govind is ...... good player.
13. It was ...... longest battle.
14. He bought ...... woolen cloth.
15. .... gang of robbers looted ...... bank.
16. ...... news climbed up ...... city early in ...... morning.
17. ...... thief was rounded up by ...... people.
18. His statement opened ...... mystery of ...... case.
19. Ali Baba saw ...... treasure in ...... forest.
20. Urmila is ...... clerk in ...... Bank of Baroda.
21. We noticed ...... girl carrying ...... pitcher on her head.
22. ...... horse reared and threw ...... rider off.
23. Once ...... grocer received ...... anonymous letter.
24. She put ...... kettle on ...... oven.
25. He came of ...... high family.
26. Time is ...... greatest teacher.
27. His experiment opened .... eyes of ...... scientists.
28. ...... Ramcharit Manas and ...... Vinaya Patrika are Goswami's eminent works.
29. ...... water in ...... jug is filthy.
30. Such ...... sight can only be described in ...... extraordinary language.
31. ...... Shepherd aroused us in ...... dawn.
32. ...... aweful sight frightened us.
33. ...... Urban life is worse than ...... rural one.
34. ...... Battle of Talikot decided ...... fate of ...... Vijaya.Nagar dynasty.
35. Rana Pratap was ...... unique example of fortitude.

36. There is ...... rumour abroad.
37. ...... book on ...... table is ...... fine model of wit and wisdom.
38. ...... storm uprooted ...... trees.
39. ...... bill caused ...... great hue and cry in ...... parliament.
40. He had ...... hen that laid ...... gold egg daily.
41. Oxygen is ...... odourless and colourless gas.
42. Kashmir is ...... Switzerland of India.
43. ...... rate at which ...... population is increasing gives ...... impression of ...... explosion.
44. To day ...... United Kingdom is ...... prosperous country.
45. Julius Caesar is ...... historical drama.
46. We shall go to ...... movies tomorrow.
47. .... true politician always thinks about ...... well-beings of ...... people.
48. ...... city looked like ...... fairy land.
49. ...... lion is ...... king of forest.
50. He gave us ...... song and ...... sentiment that caught ...... fancy of all ...... listeners.

Chapter 3

The Noun

1. निम्नलिखित Nouns केवल Singular माने जाते हैं अतः इनके साथ Singular verb का प्रयोग करें Plural का नहीं। जैसे–

Advice	*bread*	*business*	*furniture*	*ground*
hair	*information*	*luggage*	*electricity*	*food*
fruit	*music*	*progress*	*nonsense*	*coffee*
tea	*work*	*machinery*	*mischief*	*poetry*
scenery etc.				

पुनः plural प्रतीत होनेवाले इन शब्दों को भी singular माना जाता है–*news*, (विषयों के नाम जिनके अन्त में s हो), *civics, economics, physics* (*physic—medicine*), *innings* etc.

Incorrect	Correct
Her hairs were curly.	Her *hair* was curly.
Milton's poetries are sublime.	Milton's *poetry* is sublime.
The sceneries were attractive.	The *scenery* was attractive.
Mind your businesses.	Mind your *business*.
Physics are my favourite subjects.	*Physics* is my favourite subject.

2. *Advice, bread, furniture, information, luggage, poetry, mischief, business* etc. को plural बनाने के लिए इनके पहले *pieces of* ; *items of* ; *acts of* ; *articles of* का प्रयोग किया जा सकता है। जैसे–

He gave many *pieces of advice*.
Give me two *pieces of bread*.
Your son did *many acts of mischief*.
Have all *articles of luggage* been thieved ?
He bought *two cakes of soap*.
I have *some pieces of work*.

Note. Poetry—poem—poems and
Bread—loaf—loaves.
Advice—commercial news from abroad.

3. Dozen, score, hundred, thousand, Million etc. के पूर्व कोई number रहने पर singular हुआ करते हैं किन्तु number न रहने पर plural में प्रयोग किए जा सकते हैं।

He bought *five dozen eggs*.
Two hundred people died.
Thousands of citizens were marching.

4. निम्नस्थ collective Nouns plural माने जाते हैं–

Artillery	*infantry*	*cattle*	*elergy*	*company*
gentry	*military*	*offspring*	*people*	*police*

public   *deer*   *sheep*   *poultry*   *fish*
vermin etc.

Incorrect	Correct
Cattles are grazing.	*Cattle* are grazing. *Or*
	Many heads of cattle are grazing.
Police has come.	*Police* have come.
He has many offsprings.	He has *offspring*.
Peoples were gathered.	*People* were gathered (peoples—nations)

5. *Annals, bowels, riches, scissors, thanks, spectacles, tongs, trousers, alms, glasses, vegetables, fetters, parts, premises, measels, mumps, tidings* etc. plural हुआ करते हैं।

Riches has wings.	*Riches* have wings.
I can't see without spectacle.	I cannot see without *spectacles*.
Your scissors is sharp.	Your *scissors* are sharp.
The tiding is false.	The *tidings* are false.

6. Collective Nouns *i.e., committee, club, audience, class, family, government* etc. के साथ आशय के अनुसार singular or plural verb लगाया जा सकता है।

The *committee* has (or have) decided.
The *audience* was (or were) applauding.
The *public* was (or were) of different opinions.

7. निम्नस्थ collective nouns के पश्चात् of + plural noun रहने पर verb singular हुआ करती हैं–
Company, group, crowd, herd, team etc.

A group of students was there.
A crowd of angry men is shouting.
A team of players has arrived.

An army	(of soldiers)	A flock	(of sheep)
A bouquet	(of flowers)	A herd	(of cattle)
A team	(of players, inspectors etc.)	A crowd or mob	(of people)
A crew	(of ship, aircraft)	A sheaf	(of corn)
A gang	(of robbers)	A company	(of men)
A pack	(of hounds, cards)	A band	(of robbers, musicians)
A hand	(of bananas)	A bundle	(of goods, articles)
A bunch	(of key, grapes etc.)	A fleet	(of ships, boats esp. of naval)
A jury	(of judges)	A swarm	(of insects, birds)
A galaxy	(of beauties, talent, milky way etc.)	A cluster	(of honey-bee, stars)

8. Uncountable Nouns (material and abstract nouns) का plural नहीं होता। जैसे–

Incorrect	Correct
He showed many kindnesses.	He showed many acts of *kindness*.
Knowledges are power.	*Knowledge* is power.
Magics are interesting.	*Magic* is interesting.
Charities begin at home.	*Charity* begins at home.
Honesties are the best policy.	*Honesty* is the best policy.

किन्तु कुछ Material nouns में s, es जोड़ देने पर उनका अर्थ भिन्न हो जाता है–

Wood—woods *i.e.,* forests ; *irons*—fetters

golds—rings made of gold ; *tins*—cans

9. *Means, pains, wages ...... means* यदि income बताए तो plural verb, यदि साधन बताए तो singular verb रखता है। Pains के साथ आशय के अनुसार कभी singular, कभी plural verb लगता है। Wages कुछ phrases में fruits/reward के भाव में singular verb रखता है।

> *My means* were much reduced. (income)
> *The means* does not justify the end.
> *All means* were or every means was adopted.
> *Much pains* has (or have) been taken.
> *The wages* of sin is death. *A wage* or *wages* of Rs. ten a day.

10. निम्नस्थ nouns जो s से समाप्त हैं, plural माने जाते हैं और verb भी plural होती हैं किन्तु भिन्न अर्थों में इनमें से कुछ singular माने जा सकते हैं।

Alphabets (languages)	Manners (dealings)
Arms (weapons)	Pains (sorrow, worry)
Arrears (of pay)	Particulars (details)
Clothes (tailored)	Regards (respect)
Dresses (of females)	Remains (ruins, leavings)
Customs (duty)	Riches (wealth)
Earnings (earned money)	Spirits (courage)
Goods (articles, language)	Surroundings (healthy atmosphere)
Letters (learning, literature)	Works (machines, factories)
Lodgings (abode)	Advices (information)
Parts (ability)	Colours (flag of army)
Forces (troops)	Morals (courage)
Fruits (reward)	Quarters (residence)
Effects (property)	Numbers (verses)
Premises (buildings)	Black-bird (cuckoo)
Grounds (reasons)	Repairs (restorming to sound condition)
Matter-of-fact (unimaginative, prosaic).	Circumstances (condition).

11. Hyphen (-) के पश्चात् आनेवाला Noun singular होता है। Hyphen न रहने पर वह plural हो सकता है।

> I have *a fifty-rupee note.*
> I have *two fifty-rupee notes.*
> Have you *twenty rupees* ?
> A *three-hour* examination. (not three-hours)

Money का plural नहीं होता यद्यपि C.O.D. में इसे Moneys कहा गया है।

12. Possessive case (Genitive case)—के अन्तर्गत आनेवाले apostrophe's का प्रयोग निम्नस्थ स्थितियों में करेंगे–

(*a*) केवल persons के साथ things के साथ नहीं।

> *Ram's* book. A *child's* play. *Shelley's* poems.
> *Children's* park. *Mr. Khanna's* mill. *Animal's* hide.

(b) *Lifeless objects* (निर्जीव वस्तुओं) के साथ भी 's लगाया जा सकेगा यदि उसे personify (मानवीकरण) किया गया हो।

India's hero. *Nature's* law. *Fortune's* favour. *Death's* door.

(c) *Time, distance, weight* तथा collective nouns के साथ, जैसे–

A day's mark. *A stone's* throw. *Mob's* voice. *Nation's* unity. *A pound's* flesh.

(d) *Abbreviation* तथा *Arithmetic* में 's लगाया जा सकता है।

M.P.'s, W.H.O's, V.C.'s, 7's, I's

There are more *t's* than *r's* in this sentence.

(e) जिन शब्दों का अन्त ts, ce या s के उच्चारण से हों उनमें Apostrophe's का केवल चिह्न लगाया जाता है। जैसे–

Keats' poetry. *Girls'* school. For *justice'* sake. For *goodness'* sake.

(f) *Idioms and phrases* में, जैसे–

At one's wit's end. For mercy's sake. To heart's content.

Yeoman's service. A bird's eye view.

(g) *Compound nouns* के अन्त में apostrophe's लगता है।

Mother-in-law's residence.

Brother-in-law's village.

किन्तु मुख्य शब्द के साथ भी उसे लगाया जा सकेगा–

Commander's-in-chief order.

Passer's-by luggage. *Looker's* on. *Solicitor's* general.

(h) जब कोई proper noun या ऐसा noun जो *trade, profession*, or *relationship* का संकेत देते हुए किसी विशेष भवन, स्थान, व्यापार (*church, house, school, shop, theatre* etc.) से सम्बन्ध व्यक्त करे तो बहुधा उसे हटा देते हैं, जैसे–

St. Paul's. I shall lodge at my *uncle's*. He taught at *Queen's*.

(i) जब अनेक nouns subjects हो तो 's अन्तिम के साथ लगाएँ–

Beaumant and Fletcher's drama.

Shankar and Jaikishan's music.

Patrich and Pill's tyre.

The Nawab of Rampur's library.

किन्तु जब possession एक से अधिक का हो तो दोनों के साथ 's लगाना चाहिए।

Marlow's and *Sidney's* plays.

(j) *Things (lifeless objects)* के साथ 's न लगाकर of का प्रयोग करें।

Incorrect	Correct
Chair's leg.	The *leg of the chair*.
Ink's colour	The *colour of the ink*.
House's roof.	The *roof of the house*.

(k) **Double apostrophe** का प्रयोग न करें–

| My wife's sister's result. | The result of my *wife's sister*. |
| My brother's son-in law's marriage. | The marriage of my *brother's son-in-law*. |

(l) *Anyone, everyone, anybody, somebody* etc. के साथ else रहने पर apostrophe's *else* में लगाएँ।

Somebody else's help can be expected.

Anybody else's umbrella can be taken.

13. Number

(a) *A lot of, lots of, a great deal of, plenty of, most of, some of, part of, two thirds of, half of, heap of, heaps of* इत्यादि के पश्चात् जब plural countable noun रहेगा तो verb भी plural होगी किन्तु singular uncountable noun रहेगा तो verb singular होगी।

Incorrect	Correct
Most of the student are without uniforms.	*Most of the students* are without uniforms.
A lot of wealth were amassed.	*A lot of wealth* was amassed.
Heaps of humour were illustrated.	*Heaps of humours* were illustrated.
There are a plenty of milk.	There is a *plenty of milk.*
Half of the mango are rotted.	*Half of the mangoes* are rotted.
Half of the milk are split.	*Half of the milk* is split.

(b) प्राय: collective nouns singular माने जाते हैं। अत: इनके बाद of + plural noun रहे तो singular verb का प्रयोग करें। वह वस्तु जो दो भाग वाली होकर भी एक ही वस्तु का बोध कराती है तो अकेले वह plural मानी जाती है। किन्तु a pair of उनके पहले रहे तो verb singular होती है।

इसी प्रकार *a series of, a bunch of, a chair of, a fleet of, a team of, a batch of, a class of, a flock of,* etc. समझें *A pair of shoes* (or *scissors, trousers, socks,* etc) is bought.

कभी-कभी *group after group, day after day* जैसी singular noun + after + singular noun बनावट हुआ करती है। इसमें दोनों nouns singular होते हैं तथा verb भी singular होती है। इनके साथ article का प्रयोग नहीं होता।

A team of officers have arrived for enquiry.	*A team of officers* has arrived for enquiry.
A flock of birds were twittering.	*A flock of birds* was twittering.
A crew of mariners were sailing.	*A crew of mariners* was sailing.
A pair of socks have been lost.	*A pair of socks* has been lost.
This *pair of shocks* are mine.	This *pair of shocks* is mine.
Villages after villages were destroyed.	*Village after village* was destroyed.
Forests after forests were felled.	*Forest after forest* was felled.

(c) *Kinds of, sorts of, types of*—इनके पश्चात् countable noun (plural) or uncountable noun का प्रयोग करें।

Incorrect	Correct
I do not like this kind of men.	I do not like these *kinds of men.*
	Or
	I do not like the *men of this kind.*
Bring here all sort of food.	Bring here *all sorts of food.*

14. Gender

(a) *Collective nouns, small creatures* and *organs* (treated separately)—सभी Neuter gender माने जाते हैं। Neuter *i.e.* neither male nor female.

The team has chosen his captain.	*The team* has chosen *its* captain.
The bird hopped and wounded her feather.	*The bird* hopped and wounded *its* feather.
This is my arm. He is strong.	This is *my arm. It* is strong.

(b) जो वस्तुएँ *strength, violence* के प्रतीक हों उन्हें Masculine gender माना जाता है।

Winter has her charms.	*Winter* has *his* charms.
Death lays its icy hands on kings.	*Death* lays *his* icy hands on kings.

Summer is on **her** climax.	*Summer* is on *his* climax.

(c) *Beauty*, *gentleness*, *grace* वाली वस्तुएँ feminine gender मानी जाती है।

Autumn now shows **his** face.	*Autumn* now shows *her* face.
Spring displays **its** beauty.	*Spring* displays *her* beauty.
Liberty demands prizes from **his** lovers.	*Liberty* demands prizes from *her* lovers.
Justice knows **its** ways.	*Justice* knows *her* ways.

(d) किसी Noun का feminine बनाने के लिए (i) नए शब्द का प्रयोग करके (ii) -ess, -ine, -trex इत्यादि suffix जोड़कर या (iii) शब्द में prefix लगाकर, विधि प्रयुक्त की जाती है।

Masculine	Feminine	Masculine	Feminine
Sir	Madam	Negro	Negress
Lord	Lady	Abbot	Abbess
Nephew	Niece	Emperor	Empress
Gentleman	Lady	Hero	Heroine
Uncle	Aunt	Administrator	Administratrix
Author	Authoress	Bull-calf	Cow-calf
Heir	Heiress	Land lord	Land lady
Poet	Poetess	Milkman	Milkmaid
Lion	Lioness	He-bear	She-bear
Actor	Actress	Peacock	Peahen
Master	Mistress	Washerman	Washerwoman
Prince	Princess		

15. कुछ Nouns के भिन्न अर्थों में दो plural हुआ करते हैं–

Singular	Plural
Brother	brothers (sons of the same parents)
	bretheren (members of a society).
Die	dies (stamps for counting)
	dice (small cubes)
Fish	fishes (taken separately)
	fish (collectively)
Cloth	cloths (pieces of cloth)
	clothes (garments)
Genius	geniuses (man of **uncommon talent**)
	genii (spirits)

Exercise 1

Correct the following sentences :

1. His advices ruined me.
2. The poetries of Wordsworth are blended with natural sceneries.
3. All machineries have turned out of order.
4. Mathematics make man shrewd.
5. Where are our real annal ?
6. The peoples of India are mostly religious.
7. Silvers are a second rated metal.
8. Suspiciousnesses are marks of ignorances.

9. New York Times are a leading daily.
10. Popularities are not a great measure of merit.
11. His brother-in-law's have come.
12. Can you give me a five-rupees note ?
13. The chair's leg is broken.
14. She is a famous actor.
15. Time knows her ways.
16. A fleet of ships are sinking.
17. Where is the Maharaja's of Bikaner kingdom now ?
18. Most of Keat's odes sound a note of melancholy.
19. Golds are precious.
20. Will you like this sort of men ?
21. What were the causes of the decline of the Tugloque Dynasty ?
22. Whose is these cattles ?

Answers

1. pieces of advice
2. poems, scenery
3. parts of machinery
4. makes
5. annals
6. people
7. silver is
8. Suspiciousness is a mark of ignorance
9. is
10. popularity is
11. brother-in-law
12. a five-rupee note
13. The leg of the chair
14. actress
15. his/its
16. is
17. Maharaja of Bikaner's
18. Keats'
19. Gold is
20. These sorts
21. reasons
22. Whose heads of cattle are these ? *Or* Whose cattle are these ?

Exercise 2

Rewrite these sentences in their correct forms :

1. Alexanders' invasion was a turning point in our history.
2. The moon is quoted for his beauty.
3. My books's pages are torn.
4. He was married to his cousin sister.
5. The mob has taken his decision.
6. I have a lot of works.
7. I have to do homeworks.
8. The farmer has driven ten cattles.
9. She has some urgent works.
10. The princes has given away the prize.
11. A heap of gold were discovered by the police.
12. Plenty of tears was trickled.
13. We do not like that kinds of fancy.
14. Men after men were attacked.
15. The house's roof is leaking.
16. The sons-in-laws examination is near.
17. We should do every work for the upliftment of the society.

18. The soldiers were full of spirit.
19. Mr. Kumar practises doctory.
20. The whole surrounding was healthy.
21. The Rajputs took up arm.
22. His dress was attractive.
23. My teacher is a man of letter.
24. One must taste the fruit of one's deeds.
25. He could not bear the insulty.

Answers

1. Alexander's	2. her	3. The pages of my books
4. omit sister	5. its	6. work or pieces of work
7. homework	8. ten heads of cattle	9. pieces of work
10. princess	11. was	12. were
13. those	14. was	15. the roof of the house
16. son-in-law's	17. uplift	18. spirits
19. doctorship	20. surroundings were	21. arms
22. Her dress or his clothes (or garments)		23. letters
24. fruits	25. insult	

Exercise 3

Fill up the blanks with appropriate words given in brackets :

1. Portia is the ...... of the play. (hero/heroine)
2. Dhandu is a good ...... (cooker/cook)
3. Pratap is his .... (cousin/cousin brother)
4. He got the job of .... (lecturer/lecturership/lectureship)
5. A .... of robbers came at night (gang/company)
6. Beasts live in the .... (wood/woods)
7. The patriot was enchained with .... (irons/iron)
8. A .... of insects was flying. (flock/swarm)
9. .... runs faster than .... (light/lights ; sounds/sound)
10. The van was packed with .... (goods/good)
11. His ...... always stands first in the class. (girl/daughter)
12. Her ...... is well groomed. (hair/hairs)
13. ...... were grazing in the field. (sheep/sheeps)
14. ...... have wings. (riches/rich)

Exercise 4

Rewrite the following sentences in their correct forms :

1. The team was defeated by an inning.
2. What tiding have you brought.
3. Phatik's mischiefs are incalculable.
4. Villages after villages were turned to ashes.
5. The beggar asked for alm.
6. I extended him thank.

7. Will you keep your word ?

8. She could not obtain good mark.

9. There was a lot of errors in the essay.

10. Please pay my regard to your brother.

11. The merchant was a man of rupees.

12. How many offsprings have you ?

13. He talks as if he had no brain.

14. The son of Mr. Sinha's is a man of part.

15. The arear is not paid.

16. The pair of scissor was blunt.

17. Phillipines are a nation of many islands.

18. There are a plenty of time for gossip.

19. No more furnitures are required.

20. They brought their luggages from Varanasi.

21. Lamb's 'Essays of Eliah' carry us in the past.

22. Who will go to the picture with me ?

23. Franci's 'Hounds of Heaven' present a mysterious picture.

24. The gentries were angry.

25. Be kind to the poors.

26. These news are not reliable.

27. Two third of his informations are false.

28. Officer's order must be obeyed.

29. He has disease.

30. He is a deafy man.

31. Shelley's poetries give a note of dismay and dejection.

32. Your scissors is sharp.

33. Ten thousands I saw at a glance.

34. She bought five dozens bananas.

35. Good night ! take your seat.

36. We shall start yesterday.

37. She is the author of the novel.

38. Lots of reasonings was given.

39. M.Ps decisions were praised.

40. The sceneries of Kashmir are charming.

41. There is no place in the bus for you.

42. My family members are not rich.

43. He took troubles to do his work.

44. Put your sign here.

Chapter 4

The Pronoun

Personal Pronoun

1. Pronoun का number, person तथा gender उसके antecedent (पूर्ववर्ती कर्ता) के अनुसार होना चाहिए। जैसे—

You should give up *your* bad habits.

They work hard for *their* living.

Boys have brought *their* books.

One should do *one's* duty honestly.

2. जब collective noun पृथक् इकाइयों का संकेत दे तो plural pronoun का प्रयोग करें।

The committee have taken *their* decision.

The jury were divided in *their* opinions.

3. जब दो singular nouns 'and' से जोड़े गए हों तो उनका pronoun plural होगा किन्तु यदि उनके पहले each या every आए तो pronoun singular होगा।

Usha and Asha have brought *their* kettles.

Balu and Sudesh have broken *their* relation.

Each day and *each night* brings *its* message.

Every soldier and sailor was on *his* duty.

4. जब दो singular nouns 'and' से जोड़े गए हों किन्तु एक ही व्यक्ति, वस्तु, या विचार को बताते हों तो pronoun singular होगा।

The president and *secretary* has control over *his* office.

The treasurer and *clerk* is not on *his* chair.

5. जब दो या तीनों persons subject रूप में रहें तो वाक्य में उनका position 231 के अनुसार होगा किन्तु 'अपना' के भाव में आनेवाला genitive case 123 के अनुसार (plural) होगा। 2 *i.e.*, second person, 3 *i.e.*, third person and 1 *i.e.*, first person.

You, he and I stick to *our* views.

You and he are pleading for *your* cause.

You and I have *our* own way.

He and I should fight for our interests. किन्तु अपराध स्वीकारोक्ति के भाव में पहले first person रखें।

I and *you* are partly to blame for this.

6. जब दो या दो से अधिक singular nouns *either ... or, neither ... nor, or* या *nor* से जोड़े गए हों तो pronoun singular होगा।

Either Ram or Hari has lost *his* watch.

Neither Kamla nor Nilu has done *her* lesson.

31

7. किन्तु उपरोक्त स्थिति (Rule-6) में *nor, or* आदि से जोड़े जानेवाले subjects में से कोई plural रहे तो pronoun plural होगा।

> *Neither the principal nor the teachers* left *their* chairs.
> *Sohan or his sisters* have left *their* pens.

8. यदि उक्त स्थिति में subjects भिन्न persons के हों तो pronoun अन्तिम subject के अनुसार होगा।

> *Either you or he* has to relinquish *his* post.
> *Neither you nor I am* to blame.
> > *Or*
> *Neither you are* to blame *nor I am*.

9. Genitive case के अन्तर्गत आनेवाले *my, our, your, his, her, their* possessive adjectives होते हैं और *mine, ours, yours, hers, theirs* possessive pronouns जो verb के पूर्व या पश्चात् (predicative or elliptical uses में) प्रयुक्त होते हैं।

> This is *my* book. (possessive adjective)
> This book is *mine*. (possessive pronoun)
> He is a friend of *mine*.
> *Ours* is a great country.
> My hat is cheaper than *yours*.

इनमें apostrophe का चिह्न (') न लगाएँ।

10. *Me, us, you, him, her, them, thee* (thou का) ये objective case कहे जाते हैं। जब and, for, between आदि से pronoun जोड़े गए हों तो objective case का प्रयोग करें। किन्तु noun/pronoun पर emphasis रहे तो it + to be + nominative case + Adjective clause .... जैसी बनावट करें।

यदि objective case में noun/pronoun रहे तो उसके बाद to be + objective case रखें। जैसे–I know the man to be him.

> It was meant for *you* and *me*. (not I)
> There is no dispute between *you* and *him*. (not he)
> It was *I* who helped you. (not it was me)
> It is *he* who has stolen the watch. (not him)

11. *Than, as* से यदि तुलना या समता रहे तो उसके पश्चात् pronoun को प्रसंगानुसार nominative या objective case में रखें।

> He is taller than *I* (am).
> You are as gentle as *she* (is).
> He likes you more than *me*. (*i.e.,* than he likes me.)

12. Let के पश्चात् objective case रखें। जैसे–

Incorrect	Correct
Let I go.	*Let me* go.
Let they say what they say.	*Let them* say what they say.
Let he speak first.	*Let him* speak first.

Indefinite Pronouns

13. *Anybody, everybody, everyone, anyone,* etc. के लिए pronoun को सन्दर्भानुसार possessive case में रखें।

> *Everybody* has *his* failings.
> Has *anyone* brought *his* original testimonials ?

इस प्रसंग में कुछ आचार्य–Everyone should love his/her country जैसी बनावट के पक्ष में हैं तो कुछ–their के प्रयोग के पक्षधर हैं अर्थात्

    Everyone should love their country.

14. One subject रहने पर *one's* का प्रयोग करें his, her का नहीं। One should discharge one's duty honestly.

किन्तु one + of + plural noun or pronoun के साथ singular verb रखें–

    One of the robbers was arrested.
    One of my servants is ill.
    Here is a red *horse*. I want a black *one*.
    Here are red *horses*. I want black *ones*.

15. All .... जब *all* एक unit रूप में कल्पित हों तो उसके साथ singular verb अन्यथा plural verb का प्रयोग करें।

    But *all* is not lost. (Milton)
    That is *all*.
    All is well that end's well.
    All were agreed.
    All are aggrieved.

16. None (*i.e.* not one)–इसके प्रयोग में व्याकरणाचार्यों में काफी कुछ मतभेद हैं। कुछ लोग इसके साथ singular verb रखने के पक्ष में हैं तो कुछ लोग plural verb.

    None is happy. *None of them* were wise.

अत: none के पश्चात् यदि of + plural noun/pronoun रहे तो plural verb अन्यथा singular verb रखें।

    None is immortal.
    None of the girls were tall.
    None but fools have ever believed it.
    This is *none but the house* of God.

Distributive Pronouns

17. *each, every* .... *each* दो या दो से अधिक व्यक्तियों/वस्तुओं के लिए किन्तु every दो से अधिक के लिए प्रयोग करें। पुन: each का प्रयोग तब करें जब एक इकाई या निश्चित संख्या (सम्पूर्ण वर्ग में) बताए तथा every सम्पूर्ण वर्ग या अनिश्चित संख्या बताने पर प्रयुक्त करें। संक्षेप में each छोटा हिस्सा किन्तु every कहीं अधिक सम्पूर्ण बताता है। दोनों ही singular number हैं।

    Each of the students got good marks.
    He came here *every day*.
    Each man had to play his part.
    Every man had to play his part.

18. Reciprocal pronouns ... *each other* दो व्यक्ति/वस्तु के लिए और one another दो से अधिक के लिए आते हैं। कुछ लोग इस नियम का उल्लंघन करते हुए भी देखे जा सकेंगे।

    Both the brothers loved *each other*.
    All the boys liked *one another*.

19. *Either*, *neither* दो व्यक्ति या वस्तु के लिए किन्तु *anyone*, *none*, *no one*, all दो से अधिक के लिए प्रयोग किए जाते हैं।

Either—anyone, Neither—none ; Both—all पुन : Either.... or, neither .... nor जिनके लिए आया हो उन्हीं के निकट रखना चाहिए।

> *Either of the two sisters* is intelligent.
> *Neither of these two books* can solve my purpose.
> *None of the boys* could do well.
> Neither he is wise nor honest. (Incorrect)
> He is *neither wise nor honest*. (Correct)

Relative Pronouns

20. (*i*) *who, whom, whose, which, when, where, why, that, as* आदि से जब adjective clause शुरू किया जाय इनका अर्थ हिन्दी के "ज" वर्ण से प्रारम्भ होगा तो ये Relative pronouns कहे जाएँगे। इस प्रकार के वाक्यों को उनके Antecedent (पूर्ववर्ती कर्ता) के पश्चात् से प्रारम्भ किया जाना चाहिए। जैसे :-

I have read Nehru's writings. (incorrect)   I have read *the writings of Nehru*. (correct)
Who was a great statesman ? (incorrect)   Who was a great *statesman* ? (correct)

यहाँ who से प्रारम्भ clause Nehru के लिए आया है, न कि writings के लिए। अतः प्रथम वाक्य त्रुटिपूर्ण है।

(*ii*) *Who, Whom* केवल person के लिए–जो, जिसने, जिसे, जिसको

Whose–person/thing सभी के लिए–जिसका, जिसके, जिसकी के भाव में।

Which–केवल thing के लिए–जो, जिसने, जिसको, जिसे।

When–time के लिए–जब

Where–place के लिए–जहाँ

Why–Reason के लिए–जिस कारण

That–जो, जिसने, जिसको, जिसे–इसे who तथा which के बदले पूर्व में *superlative degree, idea, none, same, nothing, only, all, the only, who, what* या दो *antecedents* (एक person तथा अन्य animal) के रहने पर प्रयोग किया जाता है। *such* के बाद *as* से clause प्रारम्भ करें।

> The ideas *that* moved the world, will never die.
> It was the best model *that* he could present.
> That is the same boy *that* got the prize.
> All *that* glitters is not gold.
> You will say nothing *that* I do not know.
> None *that* was there took pity.
> He is *such* a man as we all respect.
> His answer was *such as* could not be said precise.
> Who *that* met him laughed at him.
> What is it *that* troubles you.
> Uneasy lies the head *that* wears the crown.
> Those (not they) who climb too high are sure to fall.

Note. (*a*) What things का संकेत देता है और कभी-कभी बिना antecedent के भी प्रयुक्त होता है।

> What cannot be cured must be endured.
> What I have said, I have said.

(b) Negative के बाद but से प्रारम्भ clauses Relative pronoun का संकेत देते हैं। जैसे—

There was none but would sympathise with him (but—who would not sympathise ...)

There is no rose but has a thorn.

(but—which has no ....)

There is none but wishes to become wealthy.

(iii) चूँकि Relative pronouns किसी noun/pronoun (antecedent) के लिए हुआ करते हैं अतः उनसे प्रारम्भ clause का verb उसके antecedent के अनुसार होना चाहिए।

Incorrect	**Correct**
I who is your friend will help you.	I who *am* your friend will help you.
The flowers which grows in my garden is not for sale.	The *flowers* which *grow* in my garden are not for sale.
He who are honest do not fear.	*He* who is honest *does* not fear.
Those (not they) who lives in glass-houses must be noble.	*Those* who live in glass-houses *must* be noble.

21. Reflexive pronouns—ये कभी subject नहीं हुआ करते।

Incorrect	**Correct**
Myself did it.	I *myself* did it.
Himself says so.	He *himself* says so.

22. *Absent, acquit, apply, avail, betake, drink, enjoy, exert, pride, resign, revenge* आदि transitive verbs के साथ Reflexive pronoun का प्रयोग करें किन्तु *Begin, break, burn, gather, keep, move, melt, open, refrain, burst, close, dash, disperse, draw, feed, set, spread, steal, stop* आदि के साथ Reflexive pronoun का प्रयोग न करें। Enjoy के साथ object रहे तो Reflexive pronoun का प्रयोग लुप्त किया जा सकता है।

He resigned to his fate.	He *resigned himself* to his fate.
They pride on their achievements.	They *pride themselves* on their achievements.
The Rajputs revenged on their enemy.	The Rajputs *revenged themselves* on their enemy.
The rider drew the sword himself.	The rider *drew* the sword.
He stopped himself on the way.	He *stopped* on the way.
We enjoyed ourselves the picnic.	We *enjoyed* the picnic.

23. It, This, that—this निकटता बताता है, जबकि **that** दूरी। **This** पहचान तथा परिचय भी बताता है। जैसे—

This is my horse. *That* is my garden.

It (Impersonal pronoun) कर्ता के रूप में ऋतु, मौसम, समय, दूरी, छोटे जीवों या प्राकृतिक घटनाओं का संकेत देता है। इस कथन पर बल देने के लिए भी प्रयोग किया जाता है।

It was *winter*. It is *ten o'clock*. It *blew* hard. *It was he* who helped me.

24. Both के साथ नकारात्मक भाव वाला शब्द (not, never) न रखें। इस हेतु neither ... nor का प्रयोग करें।

Both he and his brother were not tall. (Incorrect)

Neither he *nor* his brother *was* tall. (Correct)

Exercise 1

Correct the following sentences :

1. He that excuses himself accuses himself.
2. He is not among those which submit easily.

3. Each hour and each moment is important for I.
4. I and he have fought well.
5. It is you that has rescued me.
6. We are such who has come here to suffer.
7. Let he and I test the machine.
8. Let they play to the gallery.
9. Ours life is a satire on ours religion.
10. This is the boy who I gave a pen.
11. Myself revenged on him.
12. The two gentlemen noticed one another.
13. People are not ready to cooperate with each other.
14. He reaps the field who does not fear death.
15. He is more generous than her.
16. Neither of the roads lead to home.
17. One should be proud of his motherland.
18. This story is such which reminds our childhood.
19. This is the same watch which I bought yesterday.
20. One of the beasts were chosen the leader.
21. He is one of those who has seen better days.
22. Have you read Mr. Verma's story who is a unique story teller ?
23. Whoever does best he will get a prize.
24. Nobody was there but I.
25. Both brothers were not gentle.

Answers

1. who	2. who	3. me
4. He and I	5. Who have	6. as have
7. him and me.	8. them	9. our ... our
10. whom I gave a pen	11. I myself	12. each other
13. One another	14. He who does not fear death reaps the field	
15. than she	16. None	17. of one's motherland
18. as reminds	19. that I ...	20. was chosen
21. have seen	22. The story of Mr. Verma who ...	
23. does best will get	24. but me	
25. Neither of the brothers was.		

Exercise 2

Correct the following sentences :

1. Everyone must think what they think best.
2. He is wiser than me.
3. Neither Ram nor Mohan were liked.
4. He is one of the best leaders who has lately appeared on the scene.
5. I should like to avail the opportunities.
6. I like my friend's dog who is a good man.
7. It is I who is your best friend.

8. Neither of the students got the prize they expected.
9. We enjoyed during the holidays.
10. His answer was such which I expected.
11. It is not for I but for he and she to decide.
12. It is one of those questions that is often raised.
13. Some men in our society get his chance.
14. Your's fault does not admit any excuse.
15. You and myself can do it.
16. One should keep his promises.
17. I, he and you were present there.
18. What did make you sad ?
19. He and you have their own ends.
20. Any of these two beasts can help us.
21. Your's faithfully.
22. Your horse is swifter than that of mine.
23. My shirt is whiter than that of yours.
24. How many have you books ?
25. Who does recognise you ?

Answers

1. What he thinks
2. than I
3. was liked
4. who have
5. avail myself
6. I like the dog of my friend who ...
7. Who am
8. he expected
9. enjoyed
10. such as
11. for me, for him, for her
12. that are
13. their
14. your fault
15. you and I
16. one's promises
17. you, he and I
18. What made
19. you and he .... your
20. Either
21. yours
22. than mine
23. than yours
24. How many books have you ?
25. Who recognises you ?

Exercise 3

Correct these sentences :
1. He asked the servant whether either of the ladies were at home.
2. This is one of the best models who has come in the market.
3. One must mind his own business.
4. The reason that I was silent was clear.
5. One of the members have voted against the bill.
6. This is a unique opportunity for he.
7. He is a man whom I know is trustworthy.
8. She went with a policeman on one side and I on the other.
9. Either the step taken was right or wrong.
10. Neither his action was just nor unjust.
11. It is one of the most interesting cases that has come before I.
12. He will help anyone in whatever subject they choose. (he chooses).
13. None of the two reasons were allowed.
14. What your aim of life is ?

15. I know that man to be he. (... to be him)
16. He believed his statement, he did not ? (did't he ?)
17. He asked me that what do I mean.
18. I asked him where did he live.
19. Everybody rested in their own shelter.
20. There are thieves in the street—is it ?
21. All what he said came true.
22. One cannot be always careful of his good manners.
23. It is selfish to enjoy what others are suffering.
24. One should eat when he is hungry.
25. This is between he and I.
26. John was a man whom we believed would win the race.
27. The reason that he failed is clear.
28. I wish to know who they will choose their leader.
29. The ox has two horns on each side of its head.
30. I am one of those who cannot describe what I think.
31. The man who I saw yesterday was a teacher.
32. He asked me why was I late.
33. He that is down need not fear to fall.
34. The umbrella whom handle is broken is mine.
35. Who is he who should speak like this ?
36. The hands who rock in the cradle reigns over the world.
37. They invited my friend and I to tea.
38. He is one of the greatest leader that has ever lived.
39. Why you did not answer my question ?
40. Did you like the house whom I built last year ?

Chapter 5

The Adjective

1. Adjective of Quality (Descriptive adjective) के दो प्रयोग—

(a) Attributive use (उद्देश्यात्मक प्रयोग)

(b) Predicative use (विधेयात्मक प्रयोग)

A *smooth and steadfast* mind.	Attributive use
It is an *easy question*.	
She shall be *sportive as the fawn*.	Predicative use
That student was *tall*.	
Art is *long*, life *short*.	

निष्कर्ष यह कि सामान्यतया Adjective को अपने qualified word के पूर्व या पश्चात् रखा जाता है।

2. *A born fool, a bosom friend, a close relation, a certain, a complete, a real, a strong, a great* आदि का प्रयोग केवल attributively होता है, जबकि *asleep, afraid, awake, alike, alone, ashamed, alive, afloat, ashore, away, aloof, aground, ahead* आदि predicatively प्रयोग किए जाते हैं। prefix 'a' *i.e.,* on, to, in.

In a *certain forest* ; a *real beauty* ; a *close friend* ; a *great man* ; the ship sank and went *aground*.

I found the baby *asleep* ; went *ahead* ; wandered *alone* etc.

3. जब किसी noun के अनेक adjectives हों तो सामान्यतया उन्हें उस noun के पश्चात् रखा जाता है। जब adjectives समान महत्त्व के हों तो जो अधिक अक्षरों से बना होगा उसे noun के निकटतम रखेंगे और सबसे छोटे को सबसे दूर। Predicative use में यह क्रम उलट जाएगा। जैसे—

He was a man *noble*, *honest* and *truthful*.

The captain was *bold*, *brave* and *valiant*.

It is a *beauteous* evening *calm* and *free*.

Most of his works are *wayward*, *puerile*, *eccentric* and *commonplace*.

Coal is *hard*, *black*, *bright* and *brittle*.

A *tall handsome* lad. The lad was *tall* and *handsome*.

4. Titles और poems में तथा जब phrase को adjective से अर्थ जताने हेतु जोड़ा गया हो तो उसे noun के पश्चात् रख सकते हैं।

Ashoka, *the great*, Yudhisthir, *the just*,

Accountant *general*, God, *Almighty* ; Time *immemorial*.

He was a man *honest* in dealings.

This is a matter too *urgent* to be neglected.

Home they brought her warrior *dead*.

Children *dear* !

39

5. *Sick* तथा *ill* का attributive/predicative दोनों प्रयोग भिन्न अर्थों में हो सकेगा। Enough, noun के पूर्व या पश्चात् किसी ओर भी आवश्यकतानुसार रखा जा सकता है।

Attributive use	Predicative use
Ill intention (*i.e.,* evil intention.)	He is *ill* (*i.e.,* unwell).
A *sick* man	I am *sick* of the whole business or *sick* for a sight (*i.e.,* perturbed, disgusted).
We have *enough* time to do it.	We have time *enough* to do it.

6. Incorrect	Correct
My all friends.	All *my* friends.
His all books.	All *his* books.
Two first boys.	First *two* boys.
My these friends.	*These* friends of mine.
Your those pens.	*Those* pens of yours.
Three times heavier than the other.	*Three* times as *heavy* as the other.
Ten times larger than Ballia.	*Ten* times as *large* as Ballia.

7. Degrees of comparison. तुलना, समता अथवा सर्वाधिक गुण/दोष को अभिव्यक्त करने के लिए Adjective of quality का स्तरीय विभाजन किया गया है, उन्हें Degree of comparison कहा जाता है। सामान्य या प्राथमिक गुण–अवस्था को positive degree कहते हैं जिसमें प्रायः -er जोड़कर comparative तथा -est जोड़कर superlative degree बनाया जाता है। comparative degree तुलना/समता के लिए तथा superlative degree सर्वाधिक गुण बताने के लिए प्रयोग किया जाता है।

Positive	Comparative	Superlative
Small	smaller	smallest
Young	younger	youngest
Great	greater	greatest
Fine	finer	finest
Noble	nobler	noblest
wise	wiser	wisest
Happy	happier	happiest
Easy	easier	easiest
Big	bigger	biggest
Beautiful	more beautiful	most beautiful
Difficult	more difficult	most difficult
Intelligent	more intelligent	most intelligent

कुछ Irregular forms द्रष्टव्य करें–

Positive	Comparative	Superlative
Good, well	better	best
Bad, ill, evil	worse	worst
Little	less, lesser	least
Much (quantity)	more	most
Many (number)	more	most
Late	later	latest-time
	latter	last-position.
Old	older, elder	oldest, eldest
Fore	former	foremost, first
	further	furthest

8. जब तुलना -*er* से समाप्त रहे तो than + nominative case रखें। कुछ Adjective -*or* से समाप्त रहते हैं, उनके साथ to + objective case रखें। किन्तु modern English grammar than + objective case को भी उपयुक्त मानता है। He is wiser than me.

> I am *taller* than he.
> Govind is *cleverer* than his friend.
> She is *more beautiful* than her sister.
> I am *senior* to him.
> She is *junior* to me.

-*or* से समाप्त कुछ अन्य adjectives–*superior, inferior, prior, major, minor, interior, anterior, posterior.*

9. Comparison किन्हीं दो के मध्य होता है। दो से अधिक के लिए superlative degree का प्रयोग किया जाता है। यदि comparison दो से अधिक के बीच हो तो *any other/all other* का प्रयोग करें। किन्तु superlative के साथ other का प्रयोग न करें।

> This picture is *better* of the two.
> My horse is *swifter* than any other horse of the village.
> His house is *higher* than all other houses of the village.
> He was *cleverest* boy in the class.

10. एक ही व्यक्ति या वस्तु के दो गुणों की परस्पर तुलना हो तो -*er* का प्रयोग न करके more... than का प्रयोग इस विधि से करें–

> Ashok was *more wise* than brave.
> He is *more noble* than *kind.*

11. Compared word को वाक्य में स्पष्ट प्रयोग करें अथवा *than that of* or *than those of* का प्रयोग करें–

> The climate of Ranchi is *better than that of* Patna. (not than Patna)
> The roads of Kanpur are *wider than those of* Allahabad. (not than Allahabad)

12. समान गुण बताते समय as (so) + positive degree + as का प्रयोग करें। (not रहने पर so अन्यथा as का प्रयोग होगा)।

> She is *as beautiful as* her sister.
> This book is not *so interesting as* that.
> The Yamuna is not *so wide as* the Ganga.

13. Than के पश्चात् noun रहने पर other तथा pronoun रहने पर else का प्रयोग करें–anyother man, anyone else, someone else, all other beasts etc.

14. सर्वाधिक गुण बताने के लिए दो से अधिक के साथ Superlative degree का प्रयोग करें जिसके पूर्व the का प्रयोग करें।

> He was *the strongest* of all boys.
> Mr. Gandhi was *the greatest* man of his time.
> This is *the best* that I can do.
> The fox was *the cleverest* of all beasts.
> This is one of *the best* books on this subject.

15. *Elder, prefer* के साथ to लगाएँ than नहीं। ध्यान रहे कि prefer verb है adjective नहीं और *elder, upper, inner, outer, utter* अब comparative नहीं माने जाते। अतः इनके साथ than न लगाएँ–

My sister is *elder* to me. (not older than I)

Milk is *preferable* to tea.

Note. Elder परिवारिक प्रयोग के लिए केवल person के लिए तथा older परिवार के अन्य person और things दोनों के लिए प्रयोग किया जाता है।

Rahim is *elder* to Karim. (Incorrect)

Rahim is *older* than Karim. (Correct)

16. Double comparative या superlative का प्रयोग न करें। इसी प्रकार यदि एक ही व्यक्ति या वस्तु के लिए अनेक adjectives हो तो उन्हें एक ही degree में रखें, भिन्न-भिन्न में नहीं।

Incorrect	Correct
He is the most wisest man.	He is *the wisest* man.
Hari is more smaller than Ram.	Hari is *smaller* than Ram.
A noble, wealthier and happiest man.	A *noble*, *happy* and *wealthy* man.
	Or The *noblest*, *happiest* and *wealthiest* man.

17. निम्नस्थ adjectives का comparative or superlative degree में प्रयोग न करें क्योंकि ये स्वयं में गुण की अन्तिम सीमा बताते हैं।

Chief	complete	empty	extreme	full
ideal	infinite	impossible	perfect	unanimous
unique	universal	eternal	perpetual	round
dead	square	golden	entire	free
blind etc.				

A most unique dawn. (Incorrect)

A *unique* dawn. (Correct)

The most perfect gentleman. (Incorrect)

A *perfect* gentleman. (Correct)

Similarly–*round* (not more round) ; *dead* (not more dead) ; *entire* (not more entire) etc.

18. *Bounden, cloven, drunken, gotten, dead, olden, shrunken, sunken, stricken* etc. केवल adjective रूप (past participle) में प्रयोग किए जाते हैं।

Dead men tell no tales.

To respect our parents is our *bounden* duty.

We caught a storm *stricken* bird.

The *olden* time (*i.e.,* old time, of a former age).

19.

Incorrect	Correct
The poor child could not get father love.	The poor child could not get *fatherly* love.
Moti is a proudy boy.	Moti is a *proud* boy.
He dead.	He died, he has died, he was *dead*.
My family members are considerate.	The members of my family are *considerate*.
He played a well part.	He played a *better* part.
He is beautiful.	He is *handsome*. *Or* She is *beautiful*.
They were mutual friends.	They were *common* friends.

Dead अब adjective माना जाता है। Well positive degree का रूप है और better उसका comparative.

Father, mother, coward nouns हैं। इनका adjective तथा adverb *fatherly, motherly, cowardly* होता है।

20. जब verb के action की अपेक्षा subject के गुण को उससे प्रगट किया जाय तो adjective का प्रयोग किया जाएगा, adverb का नहीं। वैसे कुछ verbs हैं–

Smell, taste, look, sound, feel etc. ये verbs transitive हैं किन्तु कभी-कभी passive voice में प्रयुक्त होते हैं।

These mangoes taste *sourly*.   These mangoes taste *sour*.

The flowers smell *nicely*.   The flowers smell *nice*.

The version sounds *peculiarly*.   The version sounds *peculiar*.

(प्रथम उदाहरण का अर्थ होगा–These mangoes are sour when they are tasted. (Wren)

(But)

He sounded the bell *loudly*.

She smelt the gas *immediately*.

21. निम्नस्थ Indefinite numeral adjectives–*quantity, bulk, size, number* (मात्रा, परिमाण, आकार, संख्या) का बोध कराते हैं–*all, any, certain, enough, little, no, same, several* etc. किन्तु *much, less, sufficient* केवल मात्रा/परिमाण बताते हैं। *few, many, all, several* इत्यादि संख्या बताते हैं किन्तु *some* दोनों ही।

Some *natural* sorrow, loss or pain.

Some are born *great*.

His *certain* lyrics are blended with *high* morality.

No idea is so *vivid* as this.

Most men eddy about here and there.

Incorrect	Correct
Give me a few milk.	Give me *some* milk.
There are much boys in the class.	There are *many* boys in the class.
Empty vessels sound many.	Empty vessels sound *much*.

Note. Proper noun के साथ whole के पूर्व The और बाद में of लगेगा। जैसे–
The whole of India was on surge.

22. Oral तथा verbal दोनों का अर्थ है–''मौखिक''। Verbal means concerned with words as verbal distinctions, criticism etc. वाचिक, मौखिक Oral means spoken, by word of *mouth*, as *oral examination, exercise*. Most of our 'Shastras' were oral in the beginning. अर्थात् मुख सम्बन्धी बोला हुआ वचन द्वारा। Verbal—adjective of *word*. Oral—adjective of *mouth*.

23. *Few, a few, the few*—यह number बताता है, quantity नहीं। इसके विपरीत *little, a little* तथा *the little* quantity बताता है number नहीं। *few* तथा *little* नकारात्मक भाव में (शायद ही कुछ) *a few, a little* (कुछ थोड़ा) तथा *the few, the little* (जो कुछ थोड़ा बताते हैं)

Few came to help him. (*i.e.*, no person...)

There are *a few* exceptions of this rule. (*i.e.* limited)

The few instances that have been cited, may be enough.

I have *little* knowledge of surgery. (*i.e.* no knowledge)

He has *a little* time to worship.

The little time that we have must be utilised in exercise.

24. Later, latter

Late—*latter, last*—denote place or position oppo. to *former*.

Late—*later—latest*—denote time.

Between John and Jack, the *latter* (Jack) is wise while the former (John) is lazy.

Call the *last* witness.

Open your book at the *last* page.

This trend was criticised by the *later* generations.

What is the *latest* news ?

Dr. Murshall's latest, but we hope not his *last* contribution. (M.E.U.)

25. Farther, further

Far   farther   farthest—denote distance

further   furthest—denote moreover, additional.

His wings of poetry soared to the *farthest* land unknown.

I am loath to give *further* remarks.

Kolkata is *farther* from the equator than Colombo.

He refused to give *further* help.

26. Nearest, next. *Nearest denotes* distance ; *next* denotes *position*.

Nigh   nigher   nighest, next.

near   nearer   nearest.

Next अर्थात् क्रम से सबसे निकट का, उस के बाद दूसरा।

Give the *nearest* translation of the passage.

Call the *next* worker.

My house is *next* to Information Bureau.

Ghaziabad is *nearest* to Delhi.

27. Both ... Adjective के रूप में both के पश्चात् the का प्रयोग करें।

He came on *both the* days.

You have to take *both the* ways.

28. Comparative के पहले the ... का प्रयोग जितना ही ...... उतना ही के भाव में हुआ करता है—

The *sooner*, the *better* (adverb)

The *more*, the *better*.

The *more* you think, the *less* you feel happy.

The *rarer* it is, the *more* it is worth.

29. Complex तथा compound sentences में प्रत्येक उपवाक्य के grammatical construction उपयुक्त ढंग से प्रस्तुत करना आवश्यक है—

Incorrect	Correct
Govind Rai was as brave, if not braver than, his brother.	Govind Rai was as brave as, *if not braver than,* his brother.
He has and will quit well.	He has quitted and will *quit well.*

यहाँ as brave तथा braver than से brother के साथ समता/तुलना की गई। Positive degree हेतु as (so) + positive + as होता है, अत: as brave as हुआ। Has के साथ present perfect में verb[3] होगा जबकि will (simple future) के साथ verb[1]. अत: has quitted तथा will quit जैसा लिखना तार्किक है।

30. Worth, worthwhile ... (*i.e.* of value equivalent to योग्य, उचित, पात्र) worth के साथ एक ही object रखना चाहिए, बिना object के इसका प्रयोग उचित नहीं।

This is worth. (Incorrect)

This is *worth saying*. (Correct)

"But one such object satisfies its requirements, 'This is worthwhile saying, with the separate objects. 'While' and 'saying' is ungrammatical."

>It is worth saying this. (Incorrect)

>This is worth saying or it is worth while to say. (Correct)—M.E.U.

Saying तथा this दो objects it की भूमिका से संभव हुए जिसे शुद्ध किया जा सकता है।

>A bird in hand is worth two in bush.

>To reign is worth while ambition.

31. Whole, all–Whole संख्या नहीं बताता जबकि all संख्या का संकेत देता है। Adjective के साथ रहने पर whole के पूर्व प्राय: the रहता है। Proper noun के रहने पर उसके बाद of लगेगा।

>The golden rule contains the *whole* of morality.

>The *whole* christendom sank into mourning.

>He visited the *whole* of India.

>This is the *whole* truth.

>*All* whom I saw were laughing.

>He renounced *all* connections.

Exercise 1

Fill in each blank with the appropriate adjective given in the brackets :

1.	Many tried but ...... succeeded.	(few, a few)
2.	...... the queen begot a son.	(Later, Latter)
3.	The building was erected	(late, lately)
4.	They had ...... chance to escape.	(least, a little)
5.	The ...... chapters are full of humours.	(two first, first two)
6.	Ram is ...... Sohan.	(older than, elder to)
7.	...... day, I wrote the letter hurriedly.	(Next, Nearest)
8.	...... books were at sixes and sevens.	(His all, all his)
9.	He gave no ...... remarks.	(farther, further)
10.	Mix ...... sugar in tea.	(any, some)
11.	We noticed even ...... a single man there.	(no, not)
12.	...... chemist will tell you.	(Any, Some)
13.	Call the ...... boy.	(latest, last)
14.	...... fool has locked the door.	(Any, Some)
15.	The sailors were ...... to their goal.	(nearest, next)
16.	My brother is ...... me.	(elder to, older than)
17.	The ...... students are intelligent.	(first five, five first)
18.	...... tall talks are to beguile others.	(All his, His all)
19.	My house is not ...... than this place.	(further, farther)
20.	He has after all ...... sense of decency.	(any, some)
21.	Have you ...... sense ?	(not, no)
22.	This table is ...... that.	(older than, elder to)
23.	...... knowledge is a dangerous thing.	(A little, Little)
24.	What are you doing ...... ?	(laterly, latterly)
25.	The ...... message was vague.	(oral, verbal)

Exercise 2

Correct or justify the following sentences :

1. Ashok was more greater than Prithwiraj.
2. That was the most boldest action.
3. The Red Fort is an elder fort.
4. The jackal was a cunning and the cleverest among them.
5. This incident is more former than that.
6. Khadag has got more minor injury than Ramlal.
7. Rajan is superior to Kamal.
8. Health is preferable than wealth.
9. This work of art seems to be more perfect.
10. He is junior than I.
11. Give me a few milk.
12. The whole boys were making a noise.
13. There was few water in the jug.
14. Several senses tore my mind.
15. Passion is the most harmful than helpful.
16. No less than fifty students failed to get a pass in English.
17. Of two boys, he was the most intelligent.
18. I prefer milk to tea.
19. He is superior than me.
20. This is the best of the two books.
21. This is a more better proposal.
22. He is one of my best friends.
23. The flowers smell sweetly.
24. Agha palace is the most best palace.
25. It is the best and cheap pen.
26. A live ass is better than a dead lion.
27. That is a man poor.
28. His sanskrit knowledge is deep.
29. Her dog dead at night.
30. This carpet is better than all carpets I have ever seen.
31. He was a famous dacoit.

Exercise 3 (Unsolved)

Correct the following sentences :

1. He is a dwarf man.
2. Mr. Brown is senior than all other officers.
3. He has cold.
4. This set is the best of the two sets.
5. The population of Delhi is larger than Calcutta.
6. He has been sick for three days.
7. As I have little money, I can give you Rs. 50 only.
8. The owl was wiser than all.

9. Which is easiest—English or Sanskrit ?
10. You are older than me.
11. He is kinder than upright.
12. This book is more preferable than that.
13. He is more taller than me.
14. Which is best—milk or butter ?
15. It is one of the best model that is seen latterly.
16. I have no any enemy.
17. He has ahead gone in the domain of science.
18. I found the asleep baby.
19. His all geese are swans.
20. I am confidence in winning.
21. He is very beneficial.
22. This umbrella is much more cheaper than that.
23. Milton was one of the greatest poet that had ever lived.
24. He came to me every five hour.
25. They were alike all.
26. You are well acquainted with my family members.
27. His command of language is as good if not better than any teacher.
28. This is the most unique illustration.
29. There was no other alternative but resignation.
30. We met at the house of a mutual friend.
31. He never has, and never will, take such strong measures.
32. They returned quicker than they hoped.
33. Shelley was an imaginary poet.
34. I am not one of those who believes every thing I hear.
35. They were drank in fun and frolic.
36. Tom spent money lavishly with both hands.
37. The poorer woman lives in a dirty hut.
38. What is the last news ?
39. The later chapters of the novel are prosaic.
40. His older sister is a lecturer.
41. The climate of Ceylone is hotter than India.
42. He is a coward man.
43. The child was deprived of father affection.
44. The vessel is more empty.
45. Your all remarks were precise.
46. No less than three maskers were in disguise.
47. The few men are free from faults.
48. Little care would have prevented it.
49. He spoke few words.
50. I have a little time to go the pictures.
51. Heard melodies are sweet but that unheard are sweeter.

Answers (Exercise 1)

1. a few	**2.** Later	**3.** lately	**4.** a little	**5.** first two
6. older than	**7.** Next	**8.** All his	**9.** further	**10.** some
11. not	**12.** Any	**13.** last	**14.** Some	**15.** nearest
16. elder to	**17.** first five	**18.** All his	**19.** farther	**20.** some
21. no	**22.** older	**23.** A little	**24.** latterly	**25.** verbal.

Answers (Exercise 2)

1. omit more	**2.** omit most	**3.** old	**4.** The most cunning
5. omit more	**6.** omit more	**7.** No error	**8.** preferable to
9. omit more	**10.** junior to	**11.** a little	**12.** All the boys
13. a little water	**14.** some senses	**15.** more harmful	**16.** No fewer
17. more	**18.** No error	**19.** to and not than	**20.** better
21. omit more	**22.** No error	**23.** sweet	**24.** omit most
25. cheapest	**26.** No error	**27.** a poor man	**28.** knowledge of Sanskrit
29. died	**30.** all other	**31.** notorious.	

Chapter 6

The Adverb

1. Adverb किसी verb, adjective या अन्य adverb की विशेषता बताता है। जैसे–

The Rajputs fought *bravely*.

He was a *very rich* merchant.

She got up *very sadly*.

यहाँ प्रथम वाक्य में *bravely*, verb 'fought' को, दूसरे में *very* adjective 'rich' को और तीसरे में *very* adverb 'sadly' को modify करता है।

Adverb के तीन भेद होते हैं–(a) Simple Adverb, (ii) Interrogative Adverb तथा (iii) Relative Adverb. पुनः Simple adverb के निम्नस्थ भेद हैं–

(*a*) **Adverbs of time**–*Now, never, formerly, lately, late, daily, already, yesterday* etc.

(*b*) **Adverbs of place**–*Here, there, away, out, in*, etc.

(*c*) **Adverbs of frequency**–*Always, often, again, once, seldom* etc.

(*d*) **Adverbs of manner**–जो प्रायः Adjective में *-ly* (*i.e.,* like) जोड़ने से बनते हैं। जैसे–*slowly, clearly, rapidly, badly, hard, well*, etc.

(*e*) **Adverbs of degree**–*Fully, almost, quite, too, partly* (or quantity), *very, rather* etc.

(*f*) **Adverbs of affirmation and negation**—*Certainly, surely, not*, etc.

(*g*) **Adverbs of reason**–*Hence, therefore*, etc.

2. Adverbs of manners को समान्यतया उसके modified verb या object के पश्चात् रखा जाता है।

He walks *slowly*.

I wrote the letter *hurriedly*. ⎫ **Manners**

She played *well*. ⎭

बहुधा Adjective में *-ly* लगाने पर Adverb किन्तु कुछ Nouns में *-ly* जोड़ने पर Adjectives बनते हैं। Mother—*motherly* (Adj.) ; slow—*slowly* (Adv.) ; coward—*cowardly* ; silent—*silently* etc.

3. Adverbs of frequency–*always, often, generally, usually, never, quite, just, almost, nearly, hard*, etc. का प्रयोग finite verbs के पूर्व किन्तु to be or helping verbs के पश्चात् किया जाता है। Presently (शीघ्र) का प्रयोग Future Tense में करना चाहिए अन्य में नहीं।

Incorrect	Correct
He boasts always of his bravery.	He *always* boasts of his bravery.
They never will accept this proposal.	They will *never* accept this proposal.
The train has arrived just.	The train has *just* arrived.
Here I am alone quite.	*Here* I am quite alone.
I never have seen her.	I have *never* seen her.

4. इसी तरह Time तथा place बताने वाले Adverbs (*now*, *then*, *today*, *daily*, *here*, *there*, etc.) को प्रायः उनके verb या object के पश्चात् रखा जाता है।

God is *everywhere*.

He came *daily*.

The result comes *tomorrow*.

Bring the chair *here*.

Note. जब दो या दो से अधिक Adverbs अपने verb या object के पश्चात् हों तो उन्हें manner, place तथा time के क्रम में रखना चाहिए।

She got up *tenderly* at the meeting today.

The meeting went *peacefully* yesterday.

A magician lived there two years *ago*.

5. जब कोई Adverb किसी अन्य Adverb या Adjective को Modify करे तो वह उनके पूर्व रखा जाता है। इसी प्रकार उसे have to तथा used to को भी पूर्व रखना उचित होगा।

Her answer was *quite* correct.

The river was flowing *very* rapidly.

The question was *rather* easy.

He *always* used to yawn at night.

We *again* have to put a model.

6. Only सामान्यतया modified word के अति निकट रखा जाता है। किन्तु कभी-कभी इसमें असावधानी होने पर अर्थ में भ्रम हो जाया करता है। जैसे–

He *only* died a week ago. यहाँ only का position उचित नहीं। *Only* he died a week ago कहना उचित होगा।

We can *only* form a sound opinion. (for 'form')

Only we can form a sound opinion. (for 'we')

We can form *only* a sound opinion. (for 'opinion')

7. Two negatives make an affirmative.

He did not go *nowhere*.

He did not go *anywhere*.

Or He went *nowhere* लिखें।

I have not got no chance. (Incorrect)

I have not got *any* chances. (Correct)

Or I have got *no* chance. (Correct)

8. Adverb 'enough' को अपने द्वारा modify किए जाने वाले शब्द के पश्चात् रखना चाहिए।

He was clever enough to play the trick.

You have done more than enough.

She sings well enough.

9. Very, much, too ....

(*a*) Very का attributive use, Adjective (positive), Adverb, Superlative degree तथा Present participle के साथ होता है। जैसे–very wise ; very easy ; very slowly ; very soon ; very best ; a very interesting boy ; a very dazzling effect etc.

(b) कुछ Past participles का प्रयोग (noun तथा very के साथ) attributive एवं complement जैसा हुआ करता है। pained, pleased, puzzled, troubled, vexed, annoyed, surprised, tired, satisfied, concerned, disappointed, interested, etc.

> He wore a *very* puzzled expression.
> We discussed a *very* complicated case.
> We were *very* tired, *very* disappointed.
> He is *very* confused etc.

(c) Very का प्रयोग जब superlative के साथ करें तो sense fullest होना चाहिए। जैसे–

> I did the *very* best I could ; did my *very* utmost.

Very तथा much का प्रयोग Adjective की तरह। जैसे–

> There is *much* sugar in the cup.
> That is the *very* boy who abused you yesterday.

(d) Very का प्रयोग comparative degree के साथ न करें। यह किसी verb को modify नहीं करता और निम्नस्थ adjectives के साथ (जिसका predicative use हो) इसका प्रयोग नहीं किया जाता।

Afraid, asleep, awake, alone, alive, around, aboard, etc. इस तरह very alone, very alive, very prefer आदि जैसा लिखना त्रुटिपूर्ण है।

Conclusion–Positive degree, superlative degree, present participle तथा कुछ past participles के साथ very का प्रयोग उचित होगा।

Much–(a) यह किसी verb को modify करता है। जैसे–

> I *much* regret the mistake.

(b) अत्यधिक मात्रा के संकेत रहने पर adjective जैसा प्रयोग। जैसे–*much* trouble, *too much* noise, not *much* rain etc.

(c) Past participle के साथ passive voice में much/very much का प्रयोग, जैसे–

> Were *much* pleased ; am *much* delighted to see you ; was *much* ashamed ; *very much* improved etc.

(d) Comparative degree में attributive use. जैसे–

> A *much* easier question.
> A *much* greater contribution etc.

(e) वाक्य के मध्य में much (very के बिना) किन्तु object के साथ

वाक्य के अन्त में very much. जैसे–

> They *much* suffered.
> She loved me *very much*.
> We enjoyed the movies *very much*.

Conclusion–Verb को modify करने की स्थिति में past participle (passive) के साथ एवं comparative degree के साथ much का प्रयोग करें।

Too–*Too* means in a higher degree than is admissible for a *purpose, standard, more than enough* etc. अर्थात् उचित या आवश्यकता से अधिक।

यह Adverb तथा Adjective दोनों ही है। Adverb के रूप में negative भाव में–

> He is *too* fat to run easily.
> You are *too* weak to walk.

She is *too* shy to raise her face.

This is really *too* much.

Too large for me ; *too* long intervals, etc.

'He never came a wink *too* soon,

Nor brought *too* long a day'. (T. Hood)

10. Else के पश्चात् adverb *'but'* का प्रयोग करें, than का नहीं। किन्तु no other के साथ *than* का प्रयोग करें।

Give me anything else but beggary. (not than beggary)

I have nothing else but affection for you.

It is nothing else but mockery.

No other than she solved all the sums. (not but she)

11. Quite–*Quite* means completely, wholly, entirely, altogether इसे very के भाव में प्रयोग नहीं करना चाहिए। पुन: इसके पूर्व almost जैसे qualifying word का प्रयोग नहीं किया जाता और नहीं इसे adjective के रूप में व्यक्त किया जाता।

It is not *quite* proper.

It took *quite* a long time.

Your answer is *quite* correct.

Similarly–*Quite* young ; *quite* so ; is *quite* other ; is *quite* too delightful ; *quite* absurd, etc.

12. यदि Adverb पूरे वाक्य को modify करे तो उसे वाक्य के प्रारम्भ में प्रयोग किया जाता है।

And *slowly* answered Arthur from the barge. (Tennyson)

Fortunately, some people came there.

13. जब Adverb किसी Intransitive verb को modify करे तो वह उस verb के पश्चात् रखा जाता है।

She slept *soundly*.

We ran *fast*. (fastly कोई बनावट नहीं)

They laughed *loudly*.

14. *Hardly* तथा *Scarcely* का अर्थ होता है with difficulty (शायद ही, मुश्किल से, करीब करीब नहीं) इनके साथ no/not न लगाएँ क्योंकि ये स्वयं ही negative sense रखते हैं। इनके साथ when, before आ सकता है than नहीं।

I could *hardly* recognise him.

He *scarcely* comes here.

(But)

The stone hit me *hard*. (not hardly)

A *hard* test. (not hardly)

15. जैसा कि Adjective के chapter (Rule-20) में संकेत दिया जा चुका है, *look, smell, taste, seem, sound*, etc. के पश्चात् Adjective रखना चाहिए Adverb नहीं।

The flower *smelt* sweet. (not sweetly)

He *appears* sad. (not sadly)

16. Comparatively शब्द का प्रयोग निम्न स्थिति में इस प्रकार करें–

Incorrect	Correct
The patient is comparatively better today.	The patient is *better* today.
	Or (comparatively good today.)

Comparatively *more* methodical.   More methodical. (Or comparatively much methodical.)

17. उम्र बताते समय या तो केवल number बताएँ अथवा number के साथ years old करें।

She is sixteen or she is sixteen years old.

18. Seldom–*i.e.*, rarely, not often.

'Seldom or never ; very seldom ; not seldom' (C.O.D.). अत: Seldom or never or seldom if ever .शुद्ध है, किन्तु seldom or ever अशुद्ध।

Barking dogs *seldom* (or never) bite.

19. Ago–**(Adjective and Adverb)**–'Adjective always following noun as ten years ago ; long ago (Adv.) (C.O.D.). If 'ago' is used and the event to be dated is given by a clause, it must be by one beginning with 'that' and not 'since'.

He died twenty years ago. (no clause)

It is twenty years since he died. (not ago)

It was twenty years ago that he died. (Fowler-M.E.U.)

Before तथा *ago*–*before* past तथा future दोनों में प्रयोग किया जा सकता है लेकिन *ago* केवल past tense में। पुन: *ago*–period of time बताता है, *before*–point of time.

20. जैसा कि नियम 4 में निर्दिष्ट है, यदि कोई विशिष्ट परिस्थिति न हो तो सामान्यतया भिन्न-भिन्न Adverbs को manner, place, time के क्रम में रखना चाहिए–

He behaved *gently* in the *meeting yesterday*.

इसी तरह Adverbs of time या place के रहने पर पहले छोटे अंश का और तब क्रमश: बड़े अंश का प्रयोग करना उचित होगा।

... *at eight A.M.* on Sunday in March 1994.

... *in my room* at Nai Basti in Ballia.

P.M.—per mensem (not per month) ; P.D.—per diem (not per day) ; P.A.—per annum (not per year).

Exercise 1

Correct the following sentences :

1. The milk is enough pure to drink.
2. Success is a question of time merely.
3. This answer is correct certainly.
4. You are late almost.
5. Brightly the moon was shining in the sky.
6. He has opposed strongly the bill.
7. Happily he helped to lift the log.
8. He frankly told me.
9. You now are right.
10. He formerly was a minister for Information and Broadcasting.
11. Bhavtosh plays truant always.
12. He was harassed often.
13. Our leader timely arrived.
14. The prince dismounted suddenly from the horse.
15. Never we have heard such improbability.

16. He almost is at fault.
17. The candidate must be twenty one years.
18. He seldom or ever comes here.
19. The poem sounds occultly.
20. The apple tastes sourly.
21. The patient could speak hard.
22. Your friend did not scarcely came to school.
23. He ran fastly.
24. The newcomer is a coward fellow.
25. He escaped fortunately.

Answers

1. pure enough	2. is merely	3. is certainly
4. are almost	5. shining brightly	6. has strongly
7. the log happily	8. told me frankly	9. are now or now you
10. was formerly	11. always plays	12. was often
13. arrived timely	14. suddenly dismounted	15. have never
16. is almost	17. twenty one	18. or never
19. occult	20. sour	21. could hardly
22. omit 'did not'	23. fast	24. cowardly
25. begin with 'fortunately'.		

Exercise 2

Correct or justify the following sentences :

1. She said to her mate. 'Much silly'.
2. Why do you wear a much worried look ?
3. Rohan's face is much inviting.
4. His habit is daily to exercise in the morning.
5. Unfortunately he got no chance.
6. What day is to day it ?
7. They boldly fought but unluckily fell.
8. The sailors walked to the deck peacefully.
9. The allusions were given differently.
10. The battle was won nearly.
11. We everywhere looked anxiously.
12. The traveller left soon the inn.
13. Temples are found mostly in India.
14. The wild wind blew often in the coastal area.
15. Lead me from this sordid world away.
16. What was the event lately happened here ?
17. She had not gone nowhere.
18. The mother tenderly got up and embraced affectionately him.
19. My watch was fastly going.
20. Why have you again come here ?

Exercise 3

Correct the following sentences :

1. Your son is enough wise to adjust in his life.
2. The play was much amusing.
3. The news seems to be very fabricated.
4. They wandered very alone.
5. This point is very discussed latterly.
6. She was very annoyed at her husband's behaviour.
7. This is a much best example.
8. I am too glad to see you.
9. We are very sorry to say anything.
10. The world is much too with us.
11. The seldom or ever speaks the truth.
12. You seem to be a cowardly.
13. The evidence was true falsely.
14. We are very blessed.
15. It may be not true probably.
16. Many facilities are to be offered yet.
17. Are you in doubt still ?
18. He late came but well did.
19. His much utmost skill is his simple truth.
20. He was ruined completely.
21. People mournfully went on the deck.
22. Why did foolishly you behave ?
23. We were aback taken.
24. The first athlete was comparatively faster than the second.
25. The painting was done artistically.
26. I cannot but praise her too highly.
27. Aeroplanes now are common but half a century ago they rarely were seen.
28. It is time to immediately take the work in hand.
29. They only work when they have not any money.
30. He carefully investigated the case.
31. Hardly was the order given than two guards shot at the mob.
32. It was five years ago when he left this place.
33. Scarcely I had arrived than all the visitors departed.

Chapter 7

The Preposition

'The preposition governs a noun or pronoun or its equivalent, usually indicating relationship of place or time.' (An A.B.C. of English usage)

Preposition (*i.e.,* placed in front of) is a 'word serving to mark relation between the noun or pronoun it governs.' (C.O.D.)

Kinds of Prepositions

1. Simple prepositions—*At, by, down, for, from, in, like, near, of, off, on, over, past, round, since, than, through, till* (until), *to, under, up, out, worth, with.*

2. Compound prepositions—*About, above, across, after, against, along, amidst, among, around, before, behind, below, beneath, beside, besides, between, beyond, despite, except, inside, unto, outside towards, underneath, unlike, upon, within, without.*

3. Phrase (or complex) prepositions

According to	In accordance with (thing)	In quest of
Along with	In addition to (person)	In (with) reference to
As for	In (on) behalf of	In spite of
As to	In case of	Instead of
Apart from	In comparison to (with)	In the event of
Away from	In compliance with	next to
Because of	In consequence of	on account of
By dint of	In course of	out of
By means of	In favour of	owing to
By reason of	In front of	such as
Due to	In lieu of	up to
for the sake of	In order to	with a view to
for want of	In place of	with regard to

इनके अतिरिक्त निम्नस्थ शब्द जो participles जैसे लगते हैं, prepositions के रूप में भी प्रयुक्त होते हैं। इनके साथ कोई अन्य preposition नहीं लगता। ये participial prepositions से भी ज्ञात किए जाते हैं।

Concerning	considering	during	following	including
excepting	regarding	respecting	barring	touching
pending	notwithstanding etc.			

Note. कभी-कभी verbs के पूर्व prepositions रखकर नए verbs बना लिए जाते हैं।

Overcome	overflow	overlook	overtake	overvalue
understand	undertake	uphold	upset	withdraw
withhold etc.				

56

1. Prepositions किसी Noun, pronoun या gerund के पूर्व रखे जाते हैं।

The travellers were attacked *by* the robbers.

My friend called *on* me.

The child is afraid of going *in* the dark.

I am sorry *for* the mistake.

We were prevented *from* going there.

Suddenly he spoke *to* me.

2. निम्नस्थ परिस्थितियों में prepositions अन्त में रखे जाते हैं–

(*a*) Wh words से प्रारम्भ हुए question के अन्त में–

Where do you come *from* ?

What is he *after* ?

Which way shall we go *through* ?

What are you laughing *at* ?

Which word are you going to look *up* ?

(*b*) Relative clauses, passive clauses तथा Infinitive phrases के अन्त में preposition आता है।

Here is the book I was talking *of*.

Avoid such persons as you mix *with*.

He is the man she is married *to*.

It was his success they were envious *of*.

People do not like her to be deprived *of*.

Give me a pen to write *with*.

1. Some Prepositions Distinguished

(1) **On, At**–दिन तथा दिनांक (Day and date) के लिए *on* तथा निश्चित समय (बजे से) के लिए *at* का प्रयोग करें।

The meeting will be held *on* Sunday.

They will go *on* second July.

He went out *at* 8 o'clock.

Will you see me *at* 7 o'clock *on* Monday ?

(2) **For, At**–कुल कीमत के लिए *for* तथा प्रति दर के लिए *at* का प्रयोग करें।

I sold my scooter *for* seven thousand rupees.

Rice is sold *at* Rs. ten per kg.

(3) **From (से) To (तक)**–दोनों ही place तथा time बताते हैं।

We travelled *from* Delhi *to* Kolkata.

Their race was driven *from* pillar *to* post.

They lived there *from* March *to* July.

They will go *to* the end *of* this road.

(4) **In, into**–*In* स्थिरता (thing at rest) बताता है जबकि *into* गति, दिशा (motion, direction) बताता है।

The physician is *in* his room.

The angry workers rushed *into* the room.

Into the valley of death, rode the six hundred.

In the country of the blind. *In* anger. Fell *into* a deep trance. Come *into* the garden Maud.

(5) **Between, Among, Amongst**—*Between* दो व्यक्ति या वस्तु के लिए तथा *among/amongst* दो से अधिक के लिए प्रयोग करें। आधुनिक व्याकरण में कही-कहीं between का प्रयोग दो से अधिक के लिए भी देखने को मिल जाएगा।

> There were differences of ideas *between* them.
> *Between* Scylla and Charybdis.
> *Between* the devil and the deep sea.
> *Between* wind and water.
> They quarrelled *among* themselves.
> Divide all the sums *among* us.
> He fell *among* thieves.

Among तथा *amongst* में अन्तर यह है कि vowel से प्रारम्भ हुए शब्द के साथ प्राय: amongst का प्रयोग होता है किन्तु इनके बाद the आए तो किसी का भी प्रयोग किया जा सकता है—

> *Amongst* elephants ; *amongst* the boys ; *among* the jackals.

(6) **In, Within**—*In* को समय समाप्ति (at the end of) के भाव में प्रयोग किया जाता है। *Within* समय-समाप्ति से (before the end of) पूर्व का संकेत देता है। *In*—period of time भी बताता है तथा माह, वर्ष के नाम के साथ भी प्रयुक्त होता है।

> He will return the book *in* an hour.
> He will return the book *within* an hour.
> It is a task well *within* his powers.
> Keep it *within* bounds.
> *In* spring, *In* the morning, *In* August, *In* 1994 etc.

(7) **In, At**—देश या बड़े नगर के लिए *in* का प्रयोग तथा गाँव या छोटे स्थान के लिए *at* का प्रयोग करें।

> He lives *at* Nag Vasuki *in* Allahabad.
> *In* Europe, *In* India, Wait *at* the corner.
> *At* school, *At* sea, *At* an arm's length.

(8) **With, By**—*With* साधन (instrument) का संकेत देता है जबकि *by* कर्ता (doer or agent) का—

> We write *with* a pen.
> The novel is written *by* Thomas Hardy.
> Cut it *with* a knife.
> Walks *with* a crutch. (*i.e.*, a staff, stick).
> Travel *by* train, *By* dint of, *By* reason of. Caught him *by* the neck etc.

(9) **Till, to, Until**—*Till* समय (तक) बताता है जबकि *to* स्थान—

> They will return *till* 8 o'clock.
> She hurried *to* post office.
> Wait *till* evening. Waited *till* his arrival.
> Was true *till* death. Fled *to* Rome. *On* his way *to* the station.

Till तथा *until* दोनों का अर्थ समान है किन्तु till को प्राय: point of time के लिए और until को Duration of time के लिए प्रयोग किया जाता है।

> *Until* he finished the work. *Till* tomorrow.

(10) **Since, For, From**—Perfect tense में *since* का प्रयोग निश्चित समय (point of time, speci-fied past time or event) जैसे—बजे से, निश्चित दिन, माह, वर्ष, दिन तथा जीवन का अनुभाग आदि के लिए प्रयोग किया जाता है। *for* समय की अवधि (Period of time) बताता है, जैसे दो घंटे से, चार दिनों से, तीन माह से, दस वर्षों से आदि,

from का प्रयोग since की ही तरह point of time के लिए सभी tenses में होता है। since का प्रयोग इस सन्दर्भ में future tense में नहीं करना चाहिए।

> She has eaten nothing *since* yesterday.
> It has been raining *since* Sunday.
> He has been serving in this institution *for* ten years.
> *Since* two o'clock (but) *for* two hours.
> *Since* Friday (but) *for* four days.
> *Since* July (but) *for* six months.
> *Since* 1993 (but) *for* five years.
> *Since* arrival. *Since* departure. *Since* childhood etc.
> *From* 2nd July. Will join *from* Monday.

(11) **Beside, Besides**—*Beside* means close, near, by the side of (निकट, बगल में). *Besides* means in addition (to) moreover (अतिरिक्त, साथ ही)।

> She was sitting *beside* me.
> *Besides* a scooter, he has a car also.
> *Beside* the question, *beside* the mark etc.

(12) **In, Among**—*In* का प्रयोग Collective noun (singular) के साथ और *among* का प्रयोग plural के साथ होता है।

> *In* the meeting, in the team, *among* the thieves, *among* the classes.

(13) **Throughout, Around**—*Throughout i.e.,* right, through, from end to end of (लगातार) throughout the 18th century, throughout the life, throughout the year ; *Around i.e.,* the circuit of, about (आसपास) around 5 o'clock.

(14) अनेक transitive verbs के बाद objects आते हैं, preposition नहीं। *Need*, *obey*, *oppose*, *serve*, *trust*, *use*, *stop*, *teach*, *treat*, *approach*, *attack*, *discuss*, *answer*, *accept*, *help*, *give*, *join*, *take*, *enjoy*, *ask*, *describe*, *visit*, *confuse*, *reach* etc. Answer to—for person only (for anything)

> He helped to me. (Incorrect)
> He helped me. (Correct)

(15) **On, Upon, Over, Above**—*On* स्थिरता, *upon* गति, *over* सिर से कुछ ही ऊपर तथा *above* बहुत दूर ऊपर बताता है।

> A monkey is sitting *on* the roof.
> He threw the book *upon* the table.
> The fan was oscillating *over* my head.
> Clouds rose *above* the hills.

2. Different Uses of Prepositions

(1) **About**—(बारे में, विषय में, चारों ओर, लगभग, आसन्न–*i.e.,* in connection with, of, somewhere round, Quarrels about trade.

> What do you know *about* radio-activity ?
> Went *about* the world ; fields *about* the university ; *about* ten feet high ; talked *about* the world affairs.
> The man is *about* to rise.

(2) Above—(Oppo. to below)—Over, on the top of, higher than, superior—ऊपर, सिरा पर, अधिक ऊँचाई पर, श्रेष्ठतर।

The glow-worms were flying *above* the banyan tree.

Above a hundred ; head *above* water ; heard *above* the tumult ; not traced *above* 3rd-century. *above* criticism or understanding ; the passage quoted *above* etc.

(3) Across—From the side to side (of), on the other side (of) आर पार, एक ओर से दूसरी ओर, अन्य ओर।

Ran *across* the road ; *by* this time ; he is *across* the stream ; came *across* the tiger ; house *across* the lake.

(4) After—In pursuit of or in quest of ; later than ; about ; concerning ; in view of ; according to ; in imitation to खोज या प्रयास में, पश्चात्, विषय में, सम्बन्धित, उद्देश्य से, के अनुसार या अनुकरण में, अन्तत:।

Looked *after* him ; hankered *after* riches ; ran *after* him ; enquired *after* him ; *after* his departure ; *after* a fashion ; a picture *after* 'Chitralekha' ; Salim was named *after* 'Jahangir'–*after* all what does it matter ? You have come *after* all.

(5) Against—(*a*) In opposition to–प्रतिकूल, विरूद्ध–I am *against* reform ; spoke *against* the authority.

(*b*) In contrast to–तुलना में–The light was shining *against* a dark background.

(*c*) In anticipation of–पूर्व या प्रत्याशा में–*Against* his coming ; *against* a rainy day.

(*d*) In preparation for–तैयारी में, के लिए, प्रतिकूल–The police had warned *against* pickpockets.

(*e*) Into collision with–टक्कर या भिड़न्त में A violent wind blew *against* the rock ; ran *against* a friend (*i.e.*, chanced to meet)।

(*f*) Opposite to–विमुख ओर–*Against* the horesepond.

(6) Along—(*a*) from end to end of–प्रारम्भ से अन्त तक, साथ–
Two friends were walking *along* the road.
To get *along* ; *along* with ; *all along*.

(*b*) Through any part of the length of–
Along the shore (by the shore).

(7) At—(*a*) Exact place, time or work–नियत स्थान, समय या कार्य पर–
At the top ; *at* school ; *at* ten o'clock ; *at* dinner ; *at* death's door.

(*b*) Per value–प्रति दर sold *at* a low price ; bought *at* a cheap rate.

(*c*) Towards–की ओर He threw the letter *at* her face.

(*d*) Position–स्थिति–*At* his mercy ; *at* dagger's drawn ; *at* a disadvantage ; clever *at* mathematics.

(*e*) In any degree किसी सीमा तक–*At all* ; *at* best ; *at* worst.

(8) Before—(*a*) In front of–सामने–There was a vast landscape *before* us. She appeared *before* the judge.

(*b*) Earlier than–समय से पूर्व–He had left a will *before* he died. Look *before* you leap.

(c) Rather than–की अपेक्षा, बल्कि–He would die *before* lying. To prefer death *before* disgrace.

(9) **Behind**–(a) At the back of–पीछे–Went *behind* the curtain. She was standing *behind* me.

(b) In support of–समर्थन में–My friends were *behind* me in that case. He left three children *behind* him.

(c) Below standard–स्तर से भिन्न, कम, हीन–

Her dress is *behind* the fashion.

(d) Hidden–छिपा हुआ–The moon hid her face *behind* the hills.

(e) To refuse to consider–मुकरना–You should not go *behind* your words.

(10) **Below**–(Opp. to above)–

(a) Lower than–अपेक्षाकृत नीचे–*Below* the bridge ; *below* the roof ; *below* the surface ; to hit *below* the belt (*i.e.*) to fight unfairly).

(b) Lower in amount, degree–मात्रा या मानक से न्यून–

Your son is *below* the general average ; *below* standard etc.

Below तथा above के प्रसंग में Fowler का दृष्टिकोण–

'The distinction is that below is concerned with superstition and subjection and suggests some interrelation. Below the bridge means with it higher up the stream, under the bridge, with it overhead.'

उनके कुछ उदाहरण–

Men below 45 ; below one's breath ; no one below a bishop ; income below Rs. 500.

But for under as–under the sun ; under the table ; under the circumstances etc.

Beneath–*i.e.,* too mean (ly) or low for as he married beneath him ; it is beneath contempt ; it would be beneath me to notice it. Apart from this it is now little more than a poetic, rhetorical or emotional substitute for under (neath) or below. (M.E.U.)

(11) **Between**–In or into space, time/line or route–किन्हीं दो के मध्य–A space *between* two compartments ; see me *between* 7 A.M. to 8 A.M. ; *Between* the devil and the deep sea. Plies *between* London and Brighton. *Between* you and me. *Between* wind and water.

(12) **Beyond**–(a) Fall ahead, excelling–बहुत आगे, अति बढ़कर–Seeking the holy city beyond the rim of the sky. (Masefield)

Beyond the end of the road.

Beyond description ; *beyond* praise ; *beyond* one's doubt.

(b) Out of–से अधिक–He tried beyond his power.

Beyond the horizon ; *beyond* one's reach.

(13) **By**–(a) Near, at, to side of, along–से, निकट, बगल, साथ–Come here by me ; stand by her ; passed by him.

(b) In passive voice–कर्म वाच्य में–

The lamb was chased *by* the dog.

Steam-engine was invented *by* James Watt.

Character is revealed *by* manners.

(c) Measure, rate, standard, value–तौल, दर, मानक, कीमत–

Cloth is sold *by* the yard. He is taller than you *by* one inch ; *by* auction.

(d) Through the agency, means, owing to, in such a manner—साधन द्वारा, कारण से, रीति से—

It is ten o'clock by my watch   sent the parcel by post
known by the name of   by means of beggary
live by bread, travel by train   made by a carpenter
caught him by his neck.

(e) Till, during—तक—

The train will arrive by two o'clock.
I shall return by Sunday. By day etc.

(14) **For**—(a) In place of, on behalf of, in contrast with—के स्थान पर, लिए, की तुलना में—For one enemy, he has a hundred friends ; chose this for that ; Minister for Education ; exchanged the camera for a radio ; did it for her good ; For all his wealth, he is not content.

(b) In favour of—के पक्ष में—Take my word for it ; am for tariff reform ; vote for.

(c) With a view to—उद्देश्य से—Go for a walk ; would do it for the world ; for amusement ; a longing for praise ; He undertook his journey for Bareily ; married for wealth.

(d) To affect beneficially or revenge—लाभ या बदले के अभिप्राय में—

They live for each other ; things look bad for you ; It is bad for him to smoke.

(e) In the character of—Mistaken for him ; take for granted ; I for one do not believe it ; did it for the second time.

(f) By reason of—कारण से—Did it for pure wontonness ; avoid it for fear of accidents ; fie for shame ; suffered for his evil deeds.

(g) In spite of—बावजूद—For all, he seems to dislike me ; I still like him ; for all you say.

(h) Regarding—सम्बन्धित—For my part ; hard up for money ; wants for nothing.

(i) Price, distance—कीमत, दूरी—Bought for Rs. 500/- sold the horse for ten thousand ; walked for two miles.

(j) Period of time—कालावधि—He has been serving in this office for ten years ; for long ; for centuries.

(15) **From**—(a) Separation and starting point, origin—पृथक्त्व, प्रारम्भ बिन्दु, मूल स्रोत—Rain comes from the clouds.

Light emanates from the sun ; worked from dawn to dusk ; set out from the village ; fell from the sky ; diseases spring from dirt ; will open from 7 A.M.

(b) Distance or remoteness—Ten miles from Delhi ; far from home ; apart from its moral aspect.

(c) Get rid of—छुटकारा पाना, उपेक्षा—Released him from prison ; cannot refrain from laughing ; dissuade from folly.

(d) Place of vantage, giver—Saw it from the roof ; a shelter from the rain and storm ; from his point of view ; gifts from providence.

(e) Reason, motive—कारण, प्रेरणा Died from fatigue ; suffering from blood pressure.

(16) **In**—(a) Purpose—उद्देश्य—In quest of ; in reply to ; in honour of ; in search of ; in crossing the river.

(b) Time—In the day ; in three months, in five minutes ; in march ; in 1994.

(c) Capacity—सामर्थ्य—As far as in me lies ; did not think he had it in him.

(*d*) Position and place–स्थिति तथा स्थान–*In* America ; *in* a good condition ; *in* the universe ; *in* my opinion ; *in* haste.

(*e*) Of dress and means–पोशाक, साधन सम्बन्धी–Dressed *in* muslin ; *in* white ; printed *in* yellow ; write *in* ink or pencil.

(*f*) Of number or dimension–संख्या तथा विस्तार–Seven *in* number ; four feet *in* width.

(*g*) In adverbial phrases–*In* fact, *in* truth ; *in* any case, *in* so far as.

(17) **Into**—(*a*) Motion or direction–गति या दिशा–Came *into* the garden, throw it *into* the fire ; look *into* the box ; get *into* trouble ; peep *into* the life of things.

(*b*) Change, condition, result–Turn stone *into* gold ; collect them *into* heaps ; divide them *into* three classes ; flogged *into* submission ; translate *into* English ; Turned *into* a cat.

(18) **Of**—(*a*) belonging, connection, possession–सम्बन्ध, अधिकार–We *of* the middle class ; the manners *of* today, a thing *of* the past ; the master *of* the house ; a topic *of* conversation.

(*b*) Origin, cause, authority–उद्गम, कारण, ग्रन्थकार–Came *of* a high family ; take ill *of* ; die *of* ; ashamed, afraid, proud *of* ; it was kind *of* you to say so ; the works *of* Shakespeare ; deprive one *of* one's property.

(*c*) Material, identity–पदार्थ जनित समानता–House *of* cards ; the class *of* idiots ; a family *of* eight ; built *of* brick.

(*d*) Reference, about–सन्दर्भ, बारे में–Think well *of* him ; never heard *of* it ; was informed *of* the fact ; blind *of* an eye ; confident, fond, guilty *of*.

(*e*) Quality–गुण–Man of tact ; the hour of prayer ; girl of ten years or ten years old ; hard of hearing.

(*f*) Classification, selection–वर्गीकरण, चुनाव–Some *of* us ; the most dangerous *of* enemies ; song *of* songs ; holy *of* holies ; a friend *of* mine.

(*g*) Objective relation–सम्बन्ध–In search *of* ; knowledge, capable, sensible, desirous ; impatient *of* etc.

(19) **Off**—From, away, distant from, no longer on–से, दूर आदि–

Drove them *off* the sea ; is *off* the beaten track ; fell *off* a ladder ; is *off* duty, work ; *off* the map (vanish) ; *off* the point (irrelevant) ; from *off*.

(20) **On, Upon**–पर, ऊपर–'Upon is perhaps preferred when the preposition follows its object, as has no evidence to go upon ; nothing to depend upon ; not enough to live upon ; upon my word ; fell upon him.' (C.O.D.)

(*a*) Basis of, supported by, attached to or close to–आधार, सम्बद्धता, निकट–Sat *on* the table ; floats *on* the water ; is *on* the horns of dilemma ; birds live *on* insects ; *on* the wing of the wind ; put a ring *on* his finger ; a town *on* the border ; imprisoned *on* suspicion ; borrowed money *on* his jewels.

(*b*) Touching, arrived at, against–स्पर्श, आगमन, विरुद्ध–Hit him *on* the head ; serve a notice *on* ; arrived *on* Monday ; drew his knife *on* me.

(*c*) (of time) Duration or after–समय के मध्य या पश्चात्–*On* the next day ; *on* time ; *on* my arriving, I found that ....

(*d*) In manner–*On* fire ; *on* lease ; *on* sale ; *on* strike ; *on* guard.

(*e*) Concerning, about—सम्बन्धित, विषय में—Court martial was held *on* him ; my opinion *on* free trade ; title was conferred *on* him.

(*f*) Added to—Ruin *on* ruin ; heaps *on* heaps.

(**21**) **Through**—(*a*) From end to end, between the parts of—प्रारम्भ से अन्त तक, दो के बीच, से होकर—

Marched *through* the town ; *through* the forest ; arrow went *through* his arm ; look *through* the window ; swam *through* the waves ; pass *through* misfortune ; *through* thick and thin.

(*b*) By means of, by agency—साधन से—It all came about *through* his not knowing the way ; it was all *through* you that we were late.

(*c*) To read—Went *through* the novel ; came to know *through* an article.

(*d*) To complete—When I was *through* ; I reported to the teacher.

(**22**) **To**—(*a*) With infinitive—Declines *to* go ; wants *to* know ; failed *to* understand ; the matter is difficult *to* understand.

(*b*) With indirect object, person or thing—परोक्ष व्यक्ति या वस्तु हेतु—

Apply *to* the Secretary ; seems *to* me absurd ; pleasant *to* the taste ; unkind *to* him ; not a rupee *to* his name ; there is no end *to* it. Wrote *to* me.

(*c*) for, comparison, reference etc.—के लिए, तुलना या सन्दर्भ में—

Equal *to* the occasion, not *to* the point ; will speak *to* that question later.

(*d*) As far as, not short of—Fought *to* the last gasp ; hit it *to* the boundary; drank himself *to* death.

(*e*) In the direction of—ओर, स्थान, व्यक्ति, वस्तु, हालात का संकेत रहने पर—

On his way *to* the station ; throw it *to* me ; hand *to* hand, appointed *to* a place, born *to* a great fortune.

(**23**) **Under**—(*a*) To a position lower than—नीचे—fell *under* the table ; nothing is new *under* the sun ; struck him *under* the left eye ; *under* the tree ; *under* the nose.

(*b*) Within, on the inside of (surface)—Was seen to blush *under* his dusky skin ; *under* the lee (shelter) of.

(*c*) Inferior to, less than—तुच्छ, न्यूनतर—Income *under* Rs. two thousand ; speak *under* one's breath (in a whisper).

(*d*) में, के नीचे, अधीनता, अवस्था—Groaning *under* tyranny ; is now *under* repair ; country prospered *under* his rule ; was *under* the impression ; lived *under* the Stuarts ; *under* the circumstances.

(**24**) **With**—(*a*) Despite—बावजूद—*With* all his learning, he is the simplest of men.

(*b*) In regard to, in the view of—What do you want *with* me ? *With* God, all things are possible.

(*c*) In favour of or against—पक्ष या विपक्ष में—All were *with* him ; heard it *with* calmness ; fought *with* courage ; fought *with* him.

(*d*) Owing to—कारण से—Trembles *with* fear ; is down *with* fever.

(*e*) In same direction—उसी ओर—Changes *with* the seasons, rise *with* the lark.

(*f*) By addition or possession, in charge of—वृद्धि में, आश्रित—Overflowing *with* water ; blessed *with* beauty ; have no money *with* him ; it rests *with* you to decide.

(g) **By means of**—साधन से—Have no pen to write *with* ; walks *with* a stick.

(h) **Having, carrying**—Vase *with* a handle ; man *with* sinister expression ; went out *with* no hat on.

(i) **In harmonious relation to**—अनुकूलता के भाव में—I sympathise *with* you ; I disagree *with* you ; He that is not *with* me is against me.

(j) **In company of or relation to**—साथ में, सम्बन्ध—Spent the day *with* me ; have nothing to do *with* ; king is expected *with* queen ; experience grows *with* the growth of age.

3. One word with many Prepositions

(1) **Abhorrent**—(Hateful)—to (person) ; (Inconsistent) असंगत—from ; (feeling disgust) of, *abhorrent to* drunkards, *abhorrent from* flattery, the Greeks were *abhorrent of* excess.

(2) **Abound**—Overflow परिपूर्ण—In (be plentiful or rich), with (teem or be infested).

A country *abounded in* minerals ; a house *abounded with* vermin.

(3) **Accompany**—(साथ देना)—By or with (a person) to (a place).

The prince was *accompanied by* some attendants, *accompanied to* the station.

(4) **Account**—(consider, regard)—No preposition if followed by object—as account him wise or a gentleman.

> *Account for* (show cause). *Account for* the decline of the Gupta's dynasty. Present true *account to* God. *On account of* (due to) starvation. *On account of* drought.

(5) **Act**—Act upon (execute सम्पादन करना)—Acted upon the suggestion or acted upto the principle.

> *Act on* (perform special function) ; Alcohol *acts on* brain.

(6) **Agree**—Agree to (proposal) with (person).

> *Agreed to* the scheme ; does not *agree with* him.

(7) **Angry**—angry at, about (thing) with, at (person).

> My mother became *angry with* me at my uncivil behaviour.

(8) **Appeal**—Appeal to (person) for (something).

> Against (a thing, authority)
>
> *Appealed to* the country for restoring peace and maintaining unity ; *appealed against* the decision.

(9) **Argue**—With, against (person) for, against, about (thing).

> *Argues with* them for nothing or about the problem.

(10) **Arrange**—With (person) about, for (thing).

> *Arranged with* the members. *Arrange for* the car to be there. *Arranged about* the situations.

(11) **Blind**—In, of (without sight) to (without foresight).

> *Blind of* (in) one eye. He is *blind to* his well beings.

(12) **Compare**—'Compare to especially with negative, as not to be compared to' (C.O.D.)

> Compare to (between different classes). Her cheeks have been *compared* to a rose. Compare with (of the same class). Kalidas is often *compared with* Shakespeare.

(13) **Compete**—Compete with another for thing in doing or in quality. I do not want to *compete with* him for that post. Cannot *compete in* wisdom or in technical skill.

(14) **Complain**—Complain of (a thing) to (an authority) against (a person). The people have *complained to* the authority against the officer. The *complain of* scarcity of sugar was proper.

(15) **Differ**—Differ *with* (a person) *on* (a point) *from* (thing). He differs *with* me *on* some points. Her nature differs *from* her husband.

(16) **Disqualify**—For (unfit). Disqualified for the post. From (thing) disqualified *from* discharging his duty.

(17) **Distinguish**—*i.e.,* divide–Distinguished *into* several classes. Point out the difference of thing *from* another as distinguished virtue *from* vice, right *from* wrong. Be known as Kashi is distinguished *from* its temples. Be famous or eminent for as Columbus is distinguished *for* his discovery of America.

(18) **Deal**—Do business with person in goods.

> He deals honourably *with* his customers. My neighbour deals *in* Plastic goods. The company is dealt *by* several partners.
>
> I deal the cards *i.e.,* distribute the cards.

(19) **Eager**—Eager to (impatient) as eager *to* see his friend. For (desirous) as eager *for* fame, eager *after* getting a job.

(20) **Enter**—Entered the room but not entered in the room. Entered *into* a conversation. Enter (up) *on*—To deal with subject or work as enter *upon* a new lease of life ; *upon* a happy bargaining. Entered *for* the contest.

(21) **Entrust**—With (thing, duty) to (person).

> He is entrusted *with* a serious task. Do not entrust it *to* me.

(22) **Familiar**—With (in close friendship or acquainted with).

> The clerk is not familiar *with* the office work.
>
> Familiar *to* (person) Shivaji is familiar *to* all.

(23) **Fear**—of (used as a noun) as the fear *of* God, in fear *of* his life. (No preposition when used as a verb) as need not fear. He feared *to* go there.

(24) **Fight**—With (a person) against (a country, or an evil) for (for the sake of).

> The Rajputs fought *with* their enemy bravely.
>
> Fought *against* slavery, dowry system. Fought *against* the English for liberty. Fought *off i.e.,* repel with effort.

(25) **Free**—From (something undesirable) as free *from* danger, worry, free *with* duty being levied on.

(26) **Grateful**—To (a person) for (a thing). He is grateful *to* me *for* the help I rendered to him.

(27) **Impatient**—For (a thing) as the employees turned impatient *for* non-payment. At (manner, behaviour) Being impatient *at* this behaviour, he went away. Under (intolerant). The truck operators became impatient *under* the heavy customs.

(28) **Impress**—On (person, his mind) with (Stamp). The teacher impressed *on* us *with* his deep learning combined with high character.

(29) **Interest**—In (a thing) with (a person) for (concern) as has no interest in such hollow affairs ; made personal interest *with* those men. This has no interest *for* me.

(30) **Interfere**—In (thing, affair) with (person). A gentleman never interferes *with* any body in his personal affairs.

(31) **Jump**—For (excitement) jumped for joy. At (accept) jumped *at* the bargain eagerly. To (a conclusion).

> Never jump *to* a conclusion in sentiment.
>
> With (agree with a person) cannot jump *with* all.

(32) **Laugh**—In (secretly amused). They laughed *in* their sleeves. *At* (person or thing). Do not laugh at their homely joy.

(33) **Oblige**—To (a person) I am obliged *to* you. *By, with* (an oath, a song etc.) *for* (a small service)–for your sympathy.

(34) **Originate**—from or in (a thing or a place).

> With or from (a person. The fancy originated in me in the dawn.
>
> Originates *from* the Himalayas.

(35) **Part**—from (a person) with (to give up a thing).

> Both the friends parted *from* each other.
>
> He parted *with* all his belongings *for* a noble cause.

(36) **Proof**—of (evidence). What is the proof *of* your honesty ? against as proof *against* the severest weather, proof *against* mischief.

(37) **Quarrel**—with (a person) about or over (a thing).

> I never quarrel *with* providence. Quarrel *over* (or about) nothing.

(38) **Reason**—with (a person) of, upon, about (a thing), a subject.

> He reasoned *with* me *about* what was *beyond* our ability.
>
> Out of, into (persuade by argument) as tried to reason him *out* of his fears, reasoned himself *into* perplexity.

(39) **Reputation**—for (character). Reputation *for* nobility. Of (credit, distinction) as has the reputation *of* being a learned man.

(40) **Rest**—(up) on (based, rely). Science rests *on* phenomena ; I rest *upon* your promise. With (person) it rests *with* you to decide.

(41) **Result**—from (causes). Hope often results *from* dismay ; in (a specified manner) as resulted badly *in* failure.

> of (consequence) This is the result *of* his hard labour.

(42) **Slave**—of (dominating influence). The youngmen to day are the slaves *of* fashion.

> to (victim) as a slave *to* drink.

(43) **Smile**—at (ridicule) as smiles *at* the claims of, *at* his rustic manners. Up (on) (in favour of) success smiled *on* him.

(44) **Struggle**—with (a person) for (a thing) against (difficulties)–Struggled *with* the authority ; struggled *for* existence ; struggled *against* the forces of nature.

(45) **Succeed**—to (came next to) in (doing).

> The princess succeeded *to* the throne, succeeded *in* his effort.

(46) **Suitable**—for (the purpose) to (the occasion).

> The climate is suitable *for* his health. Clothes suitable *to* the function.

(47) **Supply**—to (a person) with (a thing) as supplied *to* the storm stricken people *with* ample foodstuff.

(48) **Tired**—with (exhausted) of (fed up with).

> I am tired *with* riding (as a result of) ; I am tired *of* riding (with the business of riding).

(49) **Use**—of (right or power) as taught him the use *of* voting, the globes etc. Use for (utility).

> I have no use *for* a scooter.

(50) **Victim**—(of prey) as the victims of a railway accident.

To (as result of circumstances) fell a victim *to* his own ambition.

(51) **Warn**—a person of (danger or consequences).

Against (a thing or doing) as warned him *of* the danger *against* smoking.

(52) **Watch**—for (opportunity) over (protecting care).

I am watching *for* the events ; have a watch *over* those children.

4. Some Appropriate Prepositions

(1) The following words take the preposition 'To' after them :

Nouns :

Alternative	Enmity	Preface
Antipathy	Gratitude	Reaction
Approach	Exception	Reference
Attachment	Indifference	Reply
Attention	Invitation	Resemblance
Concession	Key	Response
Correspondence	Likeness	Stranger
Disgrace	Limit	Supplement
Dislike	Obedience	Thanks
Duty	Objection	Witness
Encouragement	Opposition	

Adjective and participles :

Acceptable	Due	Opposite
Accountable	Entitled	Painful
Accustomed	Equal	Parallel
Addicted	Essential	Polite
Affectionate	Faithful	Preferable
Agreeable	Fatal	Prior
Alien	Favourable	Profitable
Alive	Foreign	Prove
Answerable	Harmful	Reduced
Applicable	Hurtful	Related
Appropriate	Indebted	Respectful
Averse	Indifferent	Responsible
Beneficial	Insensible	Sacred
Blind	Liable	Serviceable
Common	Limited	Similar
Comparable	Loyal	Subject
Contrary	Natural	Suitable
Creditable	Necessary	Supplementary
Deaf	Obedient	True
Devoted	Obliged	

Verbs :

Agree	Complian	Speak
Attach	Contribute	Stick
Appeal	Entrust	Submit
Appoint	Lead	Supply
Apply	Listen	Surrender
Attend	Object	Take
Attain	Occur	Talk
Belong	Prefer	
Bring	Refer	

(2) The following words take the preposition 'For' after them :

Nouns :

Ability	Fine	Punishment
Affection	Fitness	Qualification
Ambition	Fondness	Regard
Anxiety	Genius	Regret
Appetite	Gratitude	Remedy
Blame	Guarantee	Remorse
Candidate	Leisure	Reputation
Capacity	Liking	Request
Care	Love	Reward
Competition	Lust	Suggestion
Concern	Match	Sympathy
Cure	Opportunity	Taste
Desire	Passion	Thirst
Distaste	Pity	
Facility	Preparation	

Adjectives and participles :

Answerable	Fit	Proper
Bound	Good	Qualified
Designed	Grateful	Ready
Disqualified	Greedy	Responsible
Eager	Mad	Sorry
Essential	Notorious	Sufficient
Famous	Prepared	Useful

Verbs :

Appeal	Ask	Care
Apply	Beg	Complete
Argue	Call	Die

Feel	Pine	Start
Hope	Prepare	Wait
Look	Provide	Wish
Mourn	Search	

(3) The following words take 'with' after them :

Nouns :

Accordance	Contact	Interest
Agreement	Correspondence	Quarrel
Comparison	Disagreement	Relations
Competition	Enmity	

Adjectives and participles :

Acquainted	Contrasted	Inspired
Angry	Delighted	Mad
Annoyed	Disappointed	Moved
Associated	Displeased	Occupied
Blessed	Endowed	Overcome
Busy	Exhausted	Overwhelmed
Charged	Familiar	Popular
Complaint	Fired	Satisfied
Concerned	Gifted	Tired
Contemporary	Honoured	Touched
Contented	Ill	Vexed

Verbs

Agree	Comply	Fill
Argue	Consult	Part
Associate	Credit	Quarrel
Bear	Differ	Side
Charge	Disagree	Sympathise
Compete	Fall	

(4) The following words take 'of' after them :

Nouns :

Appreciation	Danger	Impression
Assurance	Distrust	Method
Care	Doubt	Proof
Cause	Experience	Result
Charge	Expression	Victim
Control	Failure	Want

Adjectives and participles :

Accused	Desirous	Lame
Afraid	Devoid	Negligent
Ashamed	Doubtful	Proud
Assured	Dull	Regardless
Aware	Easy	Sensible
Born	Envious	Short
Capable	Fearful	Sick
Careful	Fond	Slow
Caution	Full	Sure
Certain	Greedy	Suspicious
Characteristic	Guilty	Tolerant
Confident	Hopeful	Vain
Conscious	Informed	Weary
Convinced	Innocent·	Worthy
Deprived	Jealous	

Verbs :

Beware	Die	Relieve
Boast	Disapprove	Remind
Complain	Dream	Repent
Deprive	Inquire	Taste
Despair	Judge	Think

(5) The following words take the preposition 'From' after them :

Verbs :

Alight	Differ	Prevent
Borrow	Distinguish	Prohibit
Buy	Escape	Protect
Cease	Free	Recover
Derive	Preserve	Save

(6) The following words take the preposition 'In' after them :

Adjectives and participles :

Accomplished	Experienced	Skilful
Accurate	Fertile	Slow
Backward	Honest	Wanting
Correct	Interested	Weak
Defective	Ready	
Engaged	Rich	

Verbs :

Believe	Enlist	Interfere
Confide	Fall	Involve
Delight	Glorify	Succeed
Die	Increase	
Employ	Indulge	

Note. (*a*) Write—I will write you the result.

              result—Direct object

              you—Indirect object

'If a direct object is wanting, the person written to must be introduced by 'to' as I will write to you about it.' (Fowler)

(*b*) Home—जब home के पूर्व या पश्चात् कोई वर्णनात्मक शब्द न रहे तो उसके पूर्व the नहीं लगता।

come, go, arrive, get, send, take, bring के पश्चात् home रहने पर उसके पूर्व preposition नहीं लगता।

(*c*) Marry—Passive voice रहने पर to लगाएँ with नहीं। किन्तु active voice में कोई preposition नहीं।

              He was married to my sister.

              He married my sister.

Exercise 1

Supply suitable prepositions in the following blanks :

1. Your friend is taller than you ...... one inch.
2. May you entrust ...... me ...... that box ?
3. He arrived here ...... 6 o'clock ...... Sunday.
4. Are you confident ...... your success ?
5. Open your book ...... page 51.
6. You can appeal ...... the decision ...... the upper court.
7. We were prohibited ...... going ahead.
8. We have a duty ...... our elders.
9. Why are you always short ...... money ?
10. His father is ...... The Board of Education.
11. She was deprived ...... her husband and son.
12. Do you want to speak ...... me ...... any point ?
13. His son is appointed ...... the post ...... probationary officer.
14. The criminal was sentenced ...... two years' imprisonment ...... theft.
15. I never hanker ...... getting honour.
16. I caught him ...... the neck and threw him ...... the ground.
17. You will have to answer ...... me ...... your misconduct.
18. Do not try to take advantage ...... his poverty.
19. The child is attached ...... fever.
20. The teacher was popular ...... his pupils.
21. We are not totally free ...... superstitions ...... our life.
22. Fifty young men are enlisted ...... the army ...... the captain.
23. She always dreamt ...... better days ...... her family.
24. It is useless to mourn ...... the past.
25. She pounced ...... me ...... anger.

Answers

1. by	2. to ; with	3. at ; on	4. of	5. at
6. against ; in	7. from	8. to	9. of	10. on
11. of	12. to ; on	13. to ; of	14. to ; for	15. after
16. by, upon	17. to ; for	18. of	19. with	20. with
21. of	22. in, by	23. of, for	24. for	25. upon, in.

Exercise 2

Insert suitable prepositions in the following blank spaces :

1. The soldiers fought ...... courage.
2. When they were going ...... the forest, the king's eyes fell ...... a beautiful deer.
3. We were surprised ...... her rudeness.
4. What grudge do you have ...... me ?
5. His disease is ...... cure.
6. The waves dashed ...... the shore.
7. She excels ...... dancing.
8. I am thankful ...... you ...... your kindness.
9. He yielded ...... his son's request.
10. He acted contrary ...... my wishes.
11. It is not wise to be inimical ...... a neighbour.
12. One should have freedom ...... action ...... his field.
13. He longs ...... returning ...... his country.
14. You are not eligible ...... the post.
15. Keats is known ...... his love ...... beauty.
16. The meeting has been adjourned ...... a week.
17. Cruelty is alien ...... his nature.
18. I am not allowed ...... her conduct.
19. He attributed his failure ...... hard marking.
20. Refrain yourself ...... smoking.
21. They were astonished ...... my success.
22. The thieves broke ...... the house.
23. The manager is not satisfied ...... his work.
24. He congratulated me ...... my success.
25. Who is knocking ...... the door ?

Answers

1. with	2. through, upon	3. at	4. against	5. beyond
6. against	7. in	8. to, for	9. to	10. to
11. to	12. of in, of	13. for, to	14. for	15. for, of
16. for	17. to	18. from	19. to	20. from
21. at	22. into	23. with	24. on	25. at.

Exercise 3

Fill in the blanks with suitable prepositions given in the brackets :

1.	Thank you ...... the drink.	(at, for, of)
2.	My opinions on this subject are different ...... yours.	(with, from, to)
3.	I cannot agree ...... you.	(to, with, about)
4.	I am conscious ...... my shortcomings.	(to, by, of)
5.	Many people died ...... the battle field.	(from, of, in)
6.	Get your feet ...... the chair.	(below, under, over)
7.	Can you swim ...... the current ?	(into, in, against)
8.	You are always ...... fault.	(at, in, under)
9.	He proceeded ...... the work.	(to, with, on)
10.	You always boast ...... your wealth.	(of, for, about)
11.	Need I remind you ...... your promise ?	(to, of, for)
12.	Many people waited ...... their favourite leader.	(for, on, to)
13.	Hard work is the key ...... success.	(of, to, for)
14.	He is interested ...... hockey.	(in, with, to)
15.	I rely ...... you for help.	(for, on, with)
16.	Listen ...... what he says.	(to, of, about)
17.	He prefers milk ...... tea.	(upon, to, over)
18.	The work must be completed ...... the end of the week.	(by, to, after)
19.	It has been raining heavily ...... morning.	(for, since, till)
20.	This ring is made ...... gold.	(with, of, for)

Note. At fault—be puzzled.

> In fault—be guilty
> Proceed with—continue
> Proceed to—make one's way
> Wait for—in the hope of
> Wait (up) on—serve as attendant.

Exercise 4

Fill in the blanks with suitable prepositions given in the brackets :

1.	Newton is famous ...... his discovery.	(from, with, for)
2.	He is ashamed ...... his behaviour.	(for, of, at)
3.	My brother takes care ...... his books.	(to, of, for)
4.	He bought a fountain pen ...... a shop.	(to, in, from)
5.	Please listen ...... me.	(to, for, of)
6.	I bought this cycle ...... Rs. 1200/-	(in, for, on)
7.	She has been suffering ...... **fever for a week**.	(for, with, from)
8.	Do not depend ...... others.	(upon, with, to)
9.	They live ...... Allahabad.	(in, at, beside)
10.	He is true ...... his word.	(in, for, to)
11.	I want a pen to write	(with, from, by)
12.	He has no taste ...... art.	(of, for, in)
13.	He arrived ...... 9 o'clock.	(on, at, to)
14.	The frogs jumped ...... the tank.	(into, in, over)

15. The train arrived ...... platform in time.   (on, upon, at)
16. Look ...... the black-board.   (at, on, upon)
17. It is four o'clock ...... my watch.   (in, at, by)
18. She is fond ...... dancing.   (in, from, of)
19. Why are you afraid ...... going in the dark ?   (to, of, from)
20. She spoke ...... her husband.   (with, from, to)

Exercise 5

Fill in the blanks with suitable prepositions given in the brackets :

1. The stranger cried ...... anger.   (with, from, in)
2. Whom have you invited ...... dinner ?   (on, at, to)
3. He takes ...... his father.   (to, after, on)
4. The boys dived ...... the water.   (into, in, at)
5. He is sure ...... his success.   (of, in, to)
6. Your progress ...... mathematics is very slow.   (at, in, on)
7. One should be careful ...... one's health.   (to, for, of)
8. The key is made ...... iron.   (of, from, in)
9. He tried ...... all his might.   (from, with, of)
10. The train departs ...... 2 o'clock.   (on, from, at)
11. He is ...... the opinion that we should go.   (of, to, in)
12. He died ...... cancer.   (from, of, with)
13. Sohan is the leader ...... all the boys.   (of, to, among)
14. Our success depends ...... chance.   (on, upon, with)
15. Milk is necessary ...... health.   (for, of, about)
16. Some teachers have no control ...... their class.   (over, on, upon)
17. We shall never see her match ...... any other lady.   (for, of, to)
18. She is married ...... my cousin.   (with, from, to)
19. We agreed ...... them.   (to, with, from)
20. I am not envious ...... his success.   (from, of, with)

Exercise 6

Fill in the blanks with suitable prepositions given in the brackets :

1. He quarrelled with me ...... a trivial matter.   (on, for, into)
2. I had no knowledge ...... this accident.   (to, of, in)
3. He is very sincere ...... me.   (with, for, to)
4. He felt ashamed of himself ...... doing so.   (on, for, with)
5. We hurried home ...... school.   (to, from, at)
6. It is difficult ...... me to foretell anything.   (for, with, to)
7. ...... the way, I met his father.   (By, On, In)
8. She longs ...... her father's arrival.   (for, after)
9. The crew fell short ...... food.   (in, of, by)
10. He has reputation ...... honesty.   (for, of, in)
11. The patient is now free ...... danger.   (from, of, with)
12. He has a special liking ...... red garments.   (of, for, to)
13. We are proud ...... his deeds.   (of, for, to)

14. This is the book I was talking ....   (of, to, about)
15. The sparrow prevented her child ...... going outside.   (from, by, with)
16. He put the purse ...... his pocket.   (under, into, in)
17. He has been ill ...... three months.   (since, from, for)
18. She is afraid ...... going alone.   (to, from, of)
19. I am senior ...... him.   (than, from, to)
20. There is no cure ...... this disease.   (of, from, to)

Exercise 7

Insert suitable prepositions in the blanks in the following sentences :

1. They set out ...... six ...... the morning.
2. I prefer milk ...... coffee.
3. Do not jump ...... a decision in emotion.
4. Your fault does not admit ...... any excuse.
5. Never laugh ...... those rustic people.
6. We do not go ...... school ...... Sunday.
7. Wait ...... me ...... the bus-stop.
8. We arrived ...... Delhi ...... exactly six o'clock.
9. He spoke ...... me ...... his hands ...... his pockets.
10. Later on she was named ...... Noor-Jahan.
11. The prince alighted ...... the horse.
12. Antonio borrowed money ...... Shylock.
13. My home is ...... Lucknow but I was born ...... a small village ...... Ballia.
14. They went ...... the seaside ...... car.
15. I shall call ...... you ...... a more convenient time.
16. A girl ...... blue eyes has just gone ...... the door.
17. Here is a present ...... you.
18. The teacher was sitting ...... a desk ...... the class.
19. They were standing ...... the two houses.
20. We had to go ...... the hill ...... a small house ...... the top.

Exercise 8

Put in suitable prepositions :

1. She was looking ...... the window ...... the busy street.
2. Read ...... line ten ...... line twenty ...... page seven.
3. The stream ran ...... a little tunnel ...... the roadway.
4. I walked ...... one end of the street ...... the other.
5. You can reach the station ...... bus ...... ten minutes.
6. I shall bring an old book ...... leather covers ...... you ...... the evening ...... dinner.
7. Do not look ...... me like that.
8. A brick has fallen ...... the well.
9. I fell ...... a rock when I was climbing ...... a mountain.
10. I am staying ...... friends not far ...... the station.
11. Please come ...... me ...... the theatre to night.
12. Whom did you give the money ...... ?

13. Children ...... four years ...... age do not often go ...... school.
14. My school was founded ...... a sage ...... 1916.
15. Come and sit ...... this chair ...... the sunshine.
16. Do you want to speak ...... me ...... anything ?
17. There is a knock ...... the door. Who can be calling ...... us ...... this late hour ?
18. Do not go out ...... the rain ...... an umbrella.
19. The cat is hiding ...... us ...... the table.
20. When we get back ...... our walk, we sit ...... the fire ...... our books.

Exercise 9

Insert suitable prepositions in the following blank spaces :

1. Smoking is injurious ...... health.
2. Portia appealed ...... mercy ...... the jew.
3. The acquaintance ...... the jackal landed the deer ...... disaster.
4. He was born ...... a high family ...... Calcutta.
5. The ox died ...... harness.
6. The nightingale reminded ...... the designs ...... the crow.
7. Hard work is a key ...... success ...... a young man.
8. The manager conceded the demands ...... the workers ...... factory.
9. He was endowed ...... beauty and bliss.
10. We all are accountable ...... our deeds done ...... this world.
11. His passion ...... pleasure brought disgrace ...... many occasions.
12. Are you worried ...... hearing all assurances ...... help ?
13. The access ...... anything is undesirable.
14. I am obliged ...... you ...... the help ...... a rainy day.
15. The teacher impresses ...... us ...... his noble thoughts.
16. Are you disqualified ...... the post because you showed the negligence ...... duty ?
17. Everybody was familiar ...... him because he supplied the poor ...... free medicines.
18. They condoled ...... him for his sudden departure ...... the world.
19. His abhorrence ...... flattery made him popular ...... the people.
20. Suddenly a wild wind blew ...... the tree and took ...... the kite ...... the unknown sky.

Exercise 10

Supply suitable prepositions :

1. Are you not eligible ...... the post ?
2. I was filled ...... pity ...... the poor lady.
3. The boys were trembling ......fear.
4. They felled the tree ...... an axe.
5. Decision taken ...... haste results ...... failure.
6. If you have a little faith ...... me, you should leave the matter ...... me.
7. The whole mountain was covered ...... snow.
8. The forest was filled ...... the melody of birds.
9. May you tell me something ...... the case ?
10. The fox jumped ...... the lazy dog.
11. You are capable ...... doing this work.

12. The leader appealed ...... the audience ...... help.
13. Are you blind ...... your own interests ?
14. This book is written ...... my teacher.
15. The villagers were shouting ...... joy.
16. The cottager arouses us ...... the dawn.
17. I heard the sweet notes of a cuckoo ...... mango trees ...... the garden.
18. The crow was sitting ...... the branch.
19. She is very eager ...... her result.
20. Boys ...... their school are very obedient ...... their teachers.
21. Are you ...... need ...... money ?
22. He was displeased ...... me ...... my behaviour.
23. Do not derive victory ...... defeat.
24. We have no command ...... our destiny.
25. The lion pounced ...... the lame ox.
26. What are the qualifications ...... the post ?
27. Come and sit ...... me ...... the shade.
28. ...... a scooter, he has car also.
29. ...... him, life is full ...... tears and fears.
30. Are you acquainted ...... me ?

Exercise 11

Supply suitable prepositions :

1. ...... account ...... his love ...... God, he got spiritual deliverance ...... the sordid earth.
2. We rescued a woman ...... drowning ...... the river.
3. Sympathy ...... all living creatures is a mark ...... greatness.
4. Now it rests ...... you to decide.
5. His son is addicted ...... drugs.
6. They laughed ...... his remarks.
7. Do not interfere ...... my personal business.
8. He derived inspiration ...... his teacher ...... the domain of poesy.
9. There was an unshakable friendship ...... the camel and the dunkey.
10. His house is adjacent ...... the station.
11. Early rising is beneficial ...... health.
12. The doctor left the handkerchief ...... the stomach.
13. The influence ...... the Buddh spread ...... and wide.
14. Adverse ...... his pieces of advice, he did not appear ...... the examination.
15. Most of us are afraid ...... superstitions.
16. This house is adequate ...... my requirements.
17. Give explanation ...... your act of mischief.
18. The teacher was debarred ...... examinership.
19. Contentment is the guarantee ...... happiness.
20. Your reasoning is irrelevant ...... the fact.
21. His indifference ...... his friends isolated him ...... a good company.
22. Do not be envious ...... those who are risen high ...... ability.
23. He was acquitted ...... the charges framed ...... him ...... his neighbours.

THE PREPOSITION

24. The idea dawned ...... him ...... his visit ...... a natural spot.
25. Smoking proved fatal ...... his health.
26. The land was abound ...... natural resources.
27. You cannot compete ...... him ...... magic.
28. A bird ...... hand is worth two ...... the bush.
29. Always bear ...... mind that to bear ...... in hardship results ...... happiness.
30. Instead of finding fault ...... others, we should peep ...... our deeds and ways.

Chapter 8

The Conjunction

Conjunction उस शब्द को कहा जाता है जो वाक्यों या शब्दों को जोड़े। इसे दो वर्गों में बाँटा जा सकता है—(i) co-ordinating conjunction and (ii) subordinating conjunction.

(i) कुछ प्रमुख co-ordinating conjunctions—*And ; both ... and, as well as ; besides, not only but... also ; either .... or, neither ... nor, or, nor, otherwise, else, so, therefore, hence, for, still ; yet, but etc.*

(ii) Subordinating conjunctions—*that, when, while, who, where, wh words, if, though, although, unless, till, because, after, before, as, just as, lest, than, since etc.* इनसे subordinate clauses को जोड़ा जाता है। इनके अतिरिक्त कुछ compound conjunctions भी हुआ करते हैं।

The Uses of Conjunctions

1. And, But, Or ...... And दो समान भाव, अतिरिक्त योग या एक के पश्चात् दूसरे कथन वाले वाक्यों को जोड़ता है। But परस्पर विपरीत भाव वाले वाक्यों को जोड़ता है। *Or* विकल्प (Choice or selection) बताता है।

> I came, I saw *and* I conquered.
> He worked hard *and* passed.
> Art knows *but* science does.
> They fought bravely *but* failed.
> The battle was won *but* the leader was lost.
> Do *or* die.
> Either keep-quiet *or* go out.
> She must weep *or* she will turn mad.

2. Both के साथ and आता है, as well as नहीं। इसके साथ not/never भी न रखें बल्कि इसके लिए neither .... nor का प्रयोग करें।

> *Both* he and his brother took to their heels.
> *Both* the crow and the deer were fast friends.
> *Both* Pal and Bal are not guilty. (Incorrect)
> *Neither* Pal *nor* Bal is guilty. (Correct)

3. Though के साथ yet आता है but नहीं। yet को छिपाया भी जा सकता है। Although clauses के प्रारम्भ में तथा though पश्चात् में प्रयोग करना चाहिए।

> *Although* he is poor, he is honest. (not but he is...)
> I can run *though* I am weak.
> *Though* he earned a lot of money yet he was not happy.
> *Though* he worked hard *yet* he could not get intended result.

4. As if, as though (मानों) के पश्चात् present verb नहीं रखना चाहिए। इनके संदर्भ में सभी प्रकार के subjects के साथ were के प्रयोग का प्रचलन है। "As if, as though, these should ordinarily be followed by the past form of the conditional, and not by the present indicative." (Fowler-M.E.U.)

> He spoke *as if* he were (or was) mad.
>
> They behave *as if* they were my masters.
>
> It looks *as if* the party is bringing pressure on Dr. Adenawer. (Incorrect)
>
> It is not *as though* a sound liquor is supplied. (Incorrect)

अन्तिम दो उदाहरणों को Fowler ने नियम विरुद्ध दृष्टान्त बताया है। इनमें क्रमश: as if the party were bringing तथा as though a sound liquor were supplied होना चाहिए।

5. Adjective 'other' तथा Adverb 'no sooner' के पश्चात् than का प्रयोग करें but का नहीं।

Incorrect	Correct
He has no other remedy but to escape.	He has no *other* way *than* to escape.
The Hermit has no other aim but to get spiritual deliverance.	The Hermit has no *other* aim *than* to get spiritual deliverance.
No sooner I had entered the hall when the music stopped.	*No sooner* had I entered the hall *than* the music stopped.
No sooner I got up to set out when it began to rain.	*No sooner* did I get up to set out *than* it began to rain.

6. Not only .... but also ... ध्यान रहे कि एक ही parts of speech के शब्द इनके साथ होने चाहिए। पुन: not only .... but also, तथा either ... or, neither ... nor को उन्हीं शब्दों के निकट रखने चाहिए जिनसे ये सम्बद्ध हों।

'Not only' out of its place is like at intack loose on the floor, it might have been most serviceable somewhere else.' (Fowler-M.E.U.)

इस प्रसंग में कुछ उदाहरण–

Incorrect	Correct
Not only had she now a right to speak, but to speak with authority also.	She had now a right *not only* to speak *but* ......
Not only does the proportion of suicides vary with the season of the year, but also with different races.	The proportion of suicides varies *not only* with ...
Not only he is truthful, but also honest.	He is *not only* honest *but also* truthful.
Not only he is a teacher, but a preacher also.	He is *not only* a teacher *but* a preacher *also*.
Neither he eats nor he drinks.	He *neither* eats *nor* drinks. *Or* *Neither* does he eat *nor* does he drink.

7. Because, so that, in order that .... (ताकि, जिससे कि Because कारण (reason or cause) बताता है, जबकि so that/in order that *purpose* बताता है।

> I could not come because I was ill.
>
> They sailed *because* the wind was favourable.
>
> We eat *that* (or so that) we may live.
>
> I helped *so that* he might rise above.

8. Since...जब since conjunction का कार्य करे तो उसके पूर्व present perfect और बाद में simple past रखें।

> What have you done *since* we met ?
> Nothing has happened *since* we parted.
> We have not seen him *since* he came.

9. As (चूँकि, क्योंकि because, since) के पश्चात् so से clause न बनाएँ।

Incorrect	Correct
As he was unable to come so I did not invite him.	*As* he was unable to come, I did not invite him.
As you are clever so you can do it.	*As* you are clever, you can do it.

किन्तु emphasis रहने पर या जैसा-वैसा के भाव में so लग सकता है। जैसे–*As* you sow, *so* will you reap.

10. जब किसी Wh word से subordinate clause प्रारम्भ होगा तो उसे सामान्य वाक्य (assertive sentence) जैसा बनाएँ, प्रश्नवाचक नहीं। पुनः उसके साथ अन्य कोई conjunction न रखें। बनावट होगी Wh + subject + verb.

Incorrect	Correct
I know that where he lives.	I know *where* he lives.
I cannot say that why he came.	I cannot say *why* he came.
He noticed how did she behave.	He noticed *how* she behaved.
Can you say who is he ?	Can you say *who* he is ?

अन्तिम वाक्य Interrogative इसलिए हुआ क्योंकि Principal clause Interrogative है।

11. Regard, describe, treat, represent, define, mention, depict etc. के बाद as आएगा किन्तु think, consider, make, elect, choose, call, name, term, appoint के साथ as का प्रयोग न करें।

Regard all ladies your mothers and sisters.	Regard all ladies as your mothers and sisters.
Should you describe it serious ?	Should you describe it as serious ?
People call him as a Saint.	People call him a Saint.
It is not thought as fair.	It is not thought fair.

12. Until point of time बताता है, जबकि so long as or as long as से period of time का बोध होता है।

Till को until के स्थान पर प्रायः उस समय प्रयोग करते हैं जब उसका clause या phrase पहले प्रयुक्त हो। जैसे–Wait till he returns. Walk on till you come to the gate.

> 'When the clause or phrase precedes the main sentence, until is perhaps actually the commoner as until his accession, he had been unpopular'. (Fowler)
> *Until* you told me I had no 'idea of it.'

कभी-कभी unless and until का एक साथ प्रयोग leisurly or dignified style में देखने को मिलता है।

> There is no use of your statement *unless* and until he accepts.
> *So* long *as* it rains, I shall not go out.
> I had never seen him *until* he arrived.
> *As* long *as* the strike continues, the factory will remain closed.

13. If, unless, until, till, when, whenever, while, just as, as soon as, because, etc. के पश्चात् so, then, therefore का प्रयोग वांछनीय नहीं है।

Incorrect	Correct
When you come, then I shall go.	*When* you come, I shall go.
If you are ill, then you should take complete rest.	*If* you are ill, you should take complete rest.
While she was singing, then we were playing.	*While* she was singing, we were playing.
Just as he reached there, then it began to rain.	*Just as* he reached there, it began to rain.
As you are very wise, so you can do it.	*As* you are very wise, you can do it.
Because you repent, therefore I forgive you.	*Because* you repent, I forgive you.

14. Hardly तथा scarcely (मुश्किल से) के पश्चात् का clause when or before से शुरू होगा। शब्दों का क्रम कुछ इस प्रकार करें–Hardly/scarcely + helping verb या to be + sub. + main verb + ... when/ before + sub. + ... बाद में than/that भी न रखें। पुनः इनके साथ कोई negative न रखें।

> *Scarcely* had he moved a step or two when he fell down. (not than he fell down)
> *Hardly* did I enter the room when the light was off.
> He cannot hardly solve this sum. (Incorrect)
> He can *hardly* solve this sum. (Correct)

Exercise 1

Fill in the blanks with appropriate conjunctions :

1. Speak the truth ...... you may keep your head aloft.
2. He cannot rise to eminence ...... hard he endeavours.
3. ...... you call me, I must come.
4. ...... he could not prepare well, he did not take the examination.
5. The teacher is younger ...... he looks.
6. I will not move ...... he comes.
7. The passer-by was tired ...... hungry.
8. My servant is slow in work ...... right in dealings.
9. ...... Caesar is ambitions, I slay him.
10. He stood first ...... he was very intelligent.
11. The plant dried up ...... it was not watered.
12. Control your self ...... you should spoil.
13. ...... the work goes, he will not come.
14. He tried his best ..... in vain.
15. Follow him ...... he goes.
16. I must come ...... I am not well.
17. We are ready ...... the country calls.
18. Come ...... you wish.
19. Laugh ...... you will be beaten.
20. ...... kind is he ...... everybody loves him.
21. Your neighbour is ...... honest ...... gentle.
22. I will not return ...... you weep.
23. The burglar was jailed ...... he had committed many crimes.

24. Mend your ways ...... you will suffer.
25. Do ...... die.
26. ...... there is life, there is hope.
27. ...... there is a will, there is a way.
28. Make hay ...... the sun shines.
29. Gather courage ...... you will do the best.
30. They fought bravely ...... failed.

Answers

1. so that	2. however	3. Whenever
4. Because	5. than	6. till
7. and	8. but	9. Since
10. because	11. because	12. lest
13. So long as	14. but	15. wherever
16. though	17. Whenever	18. if
19. and	20. So .... that	21. neither ... nor
22. even if or however or whether	23. because	24. otherwise/or
25. or	26. While	27. Where
28. while	29. and	30. but.

Exercise 2

Join each pair of the following sentences by means of suitable conjunctions :

1. He is not a bad man. He is not a good man.
2. He was ill. He was hopeful to recover.
3. The king won the battle. He became sad.
4. You earn money to deposit. I earn money to enjoy.
5. Begin your dance. She sings.
6. The leaves are falling. It is autumn.
7. James stood first. John stood second.
8. My friend left no stone unturned. All was of no avail.
9. I prefer milk. I do not prefer coffee.
10. God is in heaven. Everything is good on the earth.
11. The stranger ate too much. He was very hungry.
12. I went in the garden. A scorpion stung me there.
13. The merchant was a man of money. He was unhappy.
14. Rohan is flying a kite. His friends are playing tennis.
15. This apple is sweet. That apple is sour.
16. He is not a mere dreamer. He is also a practical man.
17. His enemies are not here. His enemies are not there.
18. The wearer knows. The shoe pinches.
19. Nero was playing the flute. Rome was burning then.
20. You were in Bombay. She was in Poona.
21. He was injured. He was smiling.
22. They made haste. They missed the bus.
23. The train arrived. The coolies began to run to and fro.

24. His answer was in brief. It was quite precise.
25. I wrote the letter hurriedly. I went out to post it.
26. Do you know ? A man will across the Ganga on foot.
27. It began to rain. We had arrived before.
28. She is beautiful. Her sister is not like her.
29. Heard melodies are sweet. Unheard melodies are sweeter.
30. The boy cried. He was frightened by a shadow.
31. The horse reared. It threw the rider off.
32. I wish. I were a millionaire.
33. Say you are sorry. I will forgive you.
34. He lay under the tree. He was tired.
35. It is a matter of life. It is a matter of death.
36. Open the window. Sweet breeze is blowing.
37. He was agitated. He sat down for relaxation.
38. The old man whispered. No one heard.
39. The boy may be Ajay. The boy may be Kanak.
40. I have a small shadow. It walks with me.

Exercise 3

Correct the following sentences :

1. He looks as if he is in a dream.
2. Do not treat me a stranger.
3. As the weather was fine so we decided to go out.
4. As you are not ready so we abandon the scheme.
5. He asked me that the train was late.
6. Our teacher narrated that how we got freedom.
7. When you are in need then you should call me.
8. If the extremists submit then peace will be restored.
9. You will have arrived before I shall finish the work.
10. Many years passed since I saw him.
11. Nothing new happened since he left the place.
12. Mr. Peter has been appointed as Solicitor General.
13. Antonio named Shylock as a dog.
14. His theme has been treated false, faked and fictitious.
15. It was such an event which none could imagine.
16. This is the same pair who we saw yesterday.
17. No sooner did she utter a word but fell.
18. Did you see no other fellow but Mr. Peel ?
19. I did not hardly arrive than I was informed to quit the place.
20. She could scarcely smile that she heard a sad news.
21. He was not hardly seventeen years old than he became blind.
22. Though I was loath but I attended the meeting.
23. Both Raghu as well as Manohar are intelligent.
24. Both contentment and avarice cannot go side by side.
25. She talks as if she is a great scholar.

26. Though the train was late but I failed to catch it.
27. Both of them have no patience.
28. Hardly was it dark than the sky was covered with clouds.
29. He doubts that you will favour him.
30. As the pilgrims were tired so they rested in an inn.
31. It seems as though she has lost some treasure.
32. He could do nothing else than laugh.
33. I would not come until he does not invite.
34. This poem is either didactic nor pedantic.
35. Not only he is a liar but also a cheat.
36. She looks as if she is innocent.
37. Such was her condition as everyone was moved.
38. Both Rohan as well as Sohan are not responsible for that.
39. Though he is fat still he runs fast.
40. Not only he will go but also he will stay there.

Chapter 9

Syntax

Syntax (वाक्य विन्यास)

Syntax means sentence-construction ; the grammatical arrangement of words in speech or writing. Syntax treats of the relations of words or group of 'Words to one another in sentences.' (Curme).

Syntax व्याकरणीय दृष्टि से शब्दों के उचित प्रयोग द्वारा वाक्य की उचित रचना पर प्रकाश डालता है। इसके तीन मुख्य अंग हैं–

(*i*) Concord (समन्वय) अर्थात् number, person, tense इत्यादि के आधार पर वाक्य में शब्दों का परस्पर समन्वय।

(*ii*) Government–शब्दों का case, mood सम्बन्धी अनुशासन।

(*iii*) Order–अर्थात् वाक्य में शब्द-क्रम।

1. किसी भी sentence का verb उसके subject के number और person के अनुसार होता है। यदि subject singular है तो verb singular, और plural है तो verb भी plural होगी। ध्यान रहे कि सामान्य वाक्य S + V + E *i.e.,* subject + verb + extension of the predicate जैसा बनाया जाता है जबकि Interrogative sentence सामान्यतया Wh + helping verb + subject etc. जैसा हुआ करता है। Imperative sentence verb[1] से तथा negative में Do not/Never + verb[1] जैसा हुआ करता है। जब दो subjects and से जोड़े गए हों तो verb plural होगी।

John and Jack *were* friends.

Light *travels* faster than sound.

I *am* the monarch or all I *survey*.

Most of the diseases *proceed* from dirt.

Are you sad ? When will he *return* ?

Do not *beat* about the bush.

First *deserve* then *desire*.

Forgive and *forget*.

Blessed are they that *mourn*.

2. यदि दो या दो से अधिक singular nouns एक ही व्यक्ति/वस्तु/भाव को व्यक्त करें तो verb singular होगी।

Time and tide *waits* for none.

The clerk and treasurer *has* arrived.

Kabir the poet and reformer *was* a weaver.

Bread and butter *is* his favourite food.

यदि a, an or the दोनों के पूर्व रहेगा तो **verb plural** होगी।

The lyrist and the lawyer *were* **present**.

The lyrist and lawyer *was* **present**.

3. Either .... or, neither ... nor, or, nor से (a) यदि singular subjects (3rd person) जोड़े गए हों तो verb singular होगी।

> Neither Hari nor Mohan *is* in fault.
> Either he or his brother *has* beaten my dog.

(a) यदि subjects भिन्न number के हों तो प्राय: plural बाद में रखकर verb को plural रखते हैं।

> Neither the officer nor the soldiers *were* on the spot.
> Either Israiel or Arabian countries *are* aggressors.

(b) यदि subjects भिन्न persons के हों तो verb अन्तिम subject के अनुसार होगी—

> Neither you nor he *is* innocent.
> Either you or I *am* wise.
> *Or*
> Either you *are* wise or I *am*.
> Neither *did* he come, nor *did* he send any message (for emphasis).

4. यदि singular subject के पूर्व each/every आए तो verb singular होगी।

> Each day and each night *was* a great promise for him.
> Every man, woman and child *was* present.

5. Each of, everyone of, either of, neither of आदि से यदि वाक्य प्रारम्भ रहे तो इनके बाद plural noun/pronoun आएगा किन्तु verb singular होगी क्योंकि each, every etc. subject होंगे जो singular हैं।

> Each of the girls *was* tall.
> Neither of the two beasts *was* ready to second the fox.
> Everyone of them *was* gentle.

6. यदि अनेक subjects with, together with, along with, in addition to, as well as, besides से जोड़े जाएँ तो verb प्रथम subject के अनुसार होगी।

> She with her brothers, *was* seen on the strand.
> The leader as well as his followers, *has* been arrested.
> Descretion besides patience, *is* a better part of valour.

7. Subordinate clause में जब subject कोई Relative pronoun रहे तो उसका verb उसके antecedent के अनुसार होगा।

> I who *am* your mentor will help you against a rainy day.
> You who *are* a man of good sense may decide the case.
> He is not among those who are easily persuaded.

8. Rule-1 में Assertive sentence के नियम S + V + E के विपरीत कथन पर बल देने के लिए (for emphasis) प्राय: verb को subject के पूर्व या helping verb तथा principal verb के बीच में रखा जाता है।

> Sweet *are* the uses of adversity.
> Down *went* the ship.
> *Do be* quiet, please. (Imperative)
> Rightly *have* our forefathers said.
> So bravely *did* they fight that the enemy ran away. (Complex)
> Hardly *had* he entered the room when the clock struck.
> Neither *did* he accept nor did refuse the proposal.
> Seldom *have* you spoken to me.
> Here *comes* the leader.

There *was* a king in Saket.

Beauty and bliss *have* I none.

9. Not only ... but also से जब दो subjects जोड़े जाएँ तो verb अन्तिम subject के अनुसार होगी।

Not only the principal but also the teachers *were* laughing.

Not only the officials but also the manager *was* against the strike.

10. Sequence of tenses (कालों का अनुक्रम)—यह नियम मुख्यत: Noun clause तथा Adverb clause of purpose पर लागू होता है।

(*a*) जब principal clause present या future tense में होगा तो भावानुसार उसका subordinate clause किसी भी tense में रखा जा सकता है।

He *says* (or *will say*) that he *has* not *done* the work or he *did* not *do* the work or he *could* not *do* the work.

We *suppose* that she *has come* or she *had come* or she *will come*.

(*b*) किन्तु जब principal clause past tense में रहे तो उसका subordinate clause भी past tense में होगा।

He *spoke* loudly that his father *might come*.

They *thought* that it *would* be a fine day.

She *denied* that she *had written* the letter.

Exceptions (अपवाद)—यदि उक्त स्थिति में subordinate clause में कोई universal truth, prevailed idea or idiom (सार्वभौम सत्य, प्रस्थापित नियम या आदर्श सूत्र) जैसा कथन हो तो उसे present tense में रखा जाएगा यदि clause than से हो तो उसे आशय के अनुसार किसी भी tense में रखा जा सकता है।

The teacher *said* that one swallow *cannot bring* a summer.

Galileo *maintained* that the earth *moves* round the sun.

Mr. Bose *observed* that even plants *have* life.

The father *said* that borrowed garments never *fit* well.

He *was* older than he *looks*.

She *loved* him more than she *loves* me.

He *thought* more than he *thinks* to day.

11. More than one and many a ... इनके पश्चात् singular noun आएगा और verb भी singular होगी। 'More than one' though its sense is necessarily plural, is treated as a sort of compound of 'one', it agrees with a singular noun and takes a singular verb. (M.E.U.) किन्तु यदि more than + plural subject रहे तो verb plural होगी।

More than one worker *was* killed.

More than thirty sailors *were* drowned.

यही नियम Many a के साथ भी लागू होगा—

Many a man *has* said so.

(But)

Many men *desire* to amass money quickly.

12. A number of, The number of इनके पश्चात् noun or pronoun plural होगा लेकिन A number of के साथ plural verb तथा The number of के साथ singular verb रखें—

A number of students *were* on strike.

The number of birds *was* singing.

यही नियम A variety of तथा the variety of के साथ लागू होगा–

A great variety of subjects *distract* the mind.

13. Conditional sentences (शर्त वाले वाक्य)–Present तथा future में if के साथ shall/will न रखें। Past में if के साथ past perfect और बाद में should or would have + verb³ रखें। काल्पनिक या अवास्तविक भाव में if के साथ किसी भी subject हेतु were, पश्चात् should or would के साथ verb¹ रखें। इसमें then का प्रयोग वर्जित है।

If you *weep*, I *will* not give sweets.

If he *had worked* hard, he *would have passed*.

Or   Had he *worked* hard, he *would have passed*.

If he *were* to go there, he *would inform* you.

If I *were* a bird, I *should fly* in the sky.

Or   Were I a bird, I *should fly* in the sky.

I *wish* I *were* a millionaire.

Unless, when, while, as soon as, just as, whenever, if, after, before, until, till etc. के साथ future tense का प्रयोग न करें। Unless, until, till के साथ not भी न रखें। Then के प्रयोग से बचें। Unless you try hard, you cannot succeed.

14. Collective nouns and verbs ......

(*a*) कुछ collective nouns–*gentry, police, people, poultry,* etc. स्वयं ही plural होते हैं।

(*b*) *Scenery, luggage, baggage, information, poetry* etc. singular हुआ करते हैं।

(*c*) *Public, committee, jury, parliament* etc. singular or plural हुआ करते हैं।

(*d*) *Class, group, batch, swarm* etc. singular से plural भी बनते हैं।

इस प्रकार (*a*) वर्ग के साथ plural verb (*b*) वर्ग के साथ singular verb तथा (*c*) वर्ग के साथ भावानुसार singular/plural कोई भी verb हो सकती है।

People *differ* in their feelings.

The poetry of Keats *is* charged with sensual beauty.

The committee *has* (or *have*) decided.

All the classes *are* suspended.

The jury *was* (or *were*) unanimous.

Several groups of the students *were* made.

A lot of ; a team of, a pair of, kinds of, के लिए Noun के chapter में नियम 13 देखें।

15. Optative sentence (अभिलाषा बोधक वाक्य) में प्राय: subject को verb के बाद या helping verb तथा main verb के बीच में रखते हैं।

May *you* live long !

Long live *our democracy* !

और यह भी

O, that I were a king !

i.e., I wish (that) I were a king.

16. The verb of a subject must be appropriately used—

Incorrect	Correct
The man who helped you, he must be praised.	The man who helped you *must* be praised.

The rider who *is* tired with riding let him   Let the rider who *is* tired with riding *take* rest.
take rest.

17. Lie के साथ tell तथा truth के साथ speak का प्रयोग करें। झूठ बोलने के भाव में lie transitive तथा intransitive दोनों हैं–

     lie   lied   lied (झूठ बोलना)

     lie   lay   lain (Intransitive पड़ा रहना, विश्राम करना)

     Lay   laid   laid (Transitive/Intransitive पड़ जाना, डालना, बैठाना place, set, prostrate)

         Never *tell* a lie.

         Always *speak* the truth.

         The remedy *lies* in education.

         He *lay* asleep under the tree.

         She *laid* the child on the table.

         The hen *laid* a gold egg daily.

18. जब मात्रा, दूरी, राशि आदि के भाव में plural subject के पूर्व कोई संख्या रहे तो verb singular होगी।

         Ten miles *is* a long distance.

         Twenty thousand rupees *is* a handsome amount.

         Ten years *is* a long time.

         Two quintals *is* a heavy load.

लेकिन पृथक् पृथक् units का भाव रहने पर उसे plural माना जा सकेगा।

         Two years *have* passed since he came here.

         There *were* fifteen rupees in my pocket.

19. Most, most of के पश्चात् plural subject रहे तो verb plural और most of + uncountable noun रहे तो verb singular होगी।

         Most students *do* not work hard.

         Most of the work *is* tiresome.

         Most of the chemists *sell* false medicines.

         Most of the bread *has* gone bad.

20.   He spoke as *follows*.

         His words were as *follows*.

         The main things are as *follows*.

As follow न लिखकर प्रत्येक स्थिति में as follows लिखें। In all such contexts, *as follows* should be written. The O.E.D. ruling is : 'The construction in as follows is impersonal and the verb should always be used in the singular.' (M.E.U.)

21. Nothing but के साथ verb हमेशा singular होगी भले ही इसके बाद का noun singular हो या plural।

         Nothing but tears *was* on her part.

         Nothing but fog *was* seen.

         Nothing but sign and sob *was* heard there.

22. As if and as though (मानो) के बाद were तथा lest के बाद should का प्रयोग करें।

         He talks as if he *were* my officer.

         The stranger behaved as if he *were* a millionaire.

         Walk carefully lest you *should* fall.

         Watch lest you *should* enter into temptation.

23. Discover (खोज करना) *i.e.,* to make known, disclose. जो पहले से विद्यमान किन्तु अज्ञात हों उस सन्दर्भ में discover का प्रयोग करें। Invent (आविष्कार करना) इसका प्रयोग जो न तो विद्यमान है और न हीं किसी को ज्ञात है के भाव में करना चाहिए।

Deny (असत्य बताना to declare untrue or non-existent–दोष अस्वीकारना) Refuse (अस्वीकार करना–not to accept, grant, give or submit).

> Captain Cook *discovered* sandwich Islands. (not invented)
> Columbus *discovered* the new world. (not invented)
> Steam-engine was *invented* by James Watt. (not discovered)
> Who *invented* television ? (J.H. Baird)
> I do not *deny* but he may have thought so.
> The priest *refused* the gift.
> The manager *refused* the candidate.

Incorrect	Correct
He said me a liar.	He *called* me a liar.
The criminal was hung.	The criminal *was hanged*.
She hanged the frock from the hook.	She *hung* the frock from the hook.
They have given the examination.	They *have taken* the examination or *appeared* at the examination or *sat* for the examination.
Babar found the Moghal Empire.	Babar *founded* the Moghal Empire.
I founded no sense in it.	I *found* no sense in it.
The wind blowed against the tree.	The wind *blew* against the tree. (Blow—blew—blown)
The river flew under the bridge.	The river *flowed* under the bridge. (flow—flowed—flowed)
The dacoits flew.	The dacoits *fled*. (flee—fled—fled)
Ali flowed the kite.	Ali *flew* the kite. (fly—flew—flown)
He felled to qualify in English.	He *failed* to qualify in English. (fail—failed—failed—असफल होना)
A leaf failed from the tree.	A leaf *fell* from the tree. (fall—fell—fallen गिरना)
They failed a big tree.	They *felled* a big tree. (fell—felled—felled काटकर गिराना)
We maked a picture.	We *made* a picture. (make—made—made)
He admitted his son into the college.	He *got* his son admitted in the college.
He knowed me well.	He *knew* me well. (Know—knew—known)
The teacher ordered to me to enter.	The teacher *ordered* me to enter.
He gave a speech.	He *made* a speech.
She said me good-bye.	She *bade* me goodbye or *bade* goodbye to me.
Shut the radio.	*Switch* the radio *off*.
Open the T.V.	*Switch on* the T.V. or *Switch* the T.V. *on*.
Burn the lamp.	*Light up* the lamp or *Kindle* the lamp.
When do you go to sleep.	When do you go *to bed* ?
Blow (बुझाना) out the light.	*Put* out the light. (But) *Blow out* the candle.

The more you teach, the more you will   The more you *teach*, the more *will* you
experience.   *experience.*

24. जब किसी वाक्य के Nominative (subject) तथा nominative predicate अपने number में भिन्न-भिन्न हो तो उसका verb प्रथम nominative के अनुसार होगा न कि predicate nominative (complement) के अनुसार।

> The fact *was* of different intentions.
>
> His reputation *is* his eminent works.

25. जब complex sentence में कोई subordinate clause Wh word से प्रारम्भ हो तो वह Interrogative sentence न होकर Assertive होगा। जैसे—

> He knows *where his friend lives.*

(.... Where does his friend live ? नहीं)

> I do not know *who he is.*

(Who is he ? नहीं). जब P.C. प्रश्नवाचक होगा तो वह sentence प्रश्नवाचक होगा।

> Do you know *when the train departs* ?

Exercise 1

Fill up the following blank spaces with the verbs agreeing with their subjects :

1. Five rupees ...... nothing for this article.
2. Rice and curry ...... good to eat.
3. I am not among those who ...... not face the challenge.
4. Each of the criminals ...... sentenced to rigorous imprisonment.
5. Either of them ...... committed the sin.
6. Two thirds of the population ...... unacquainted with the matters and factors.
7. Seven and three ...... equal to ten.
8. His each line and phrase ...... endowed with imperishable value.
9. I am sure that you as well as he ...... my well-wishers.
10. None of the suggestions ...... devoid of faults and failings.
11. Many a man ...... unknown. (die)
12. Even kings and conquerors ...... subject to perish away.
13. Most of the ideas and ideals ...... impracticable.
14. Feasts and festivals ...... their aims and ambitions.
15. Slow and steady ...... the race.
16. Either cure or curse ...... the choice.
17. Neither great nor good things ...... their likings.
18. Each of the solutions ...... unjust and ungenerous.
19. Invaders besides adventurers ...... equally fated to die.
20. Those who ...... high ...... sure to fall.

Answers

1. is	2. is	3. can	4. was/is	5. has
6. are	7. is	8. is/was	9. are	10. was/were
11. dies	12. are	13. are	14. are/were	15. wins
16. is/was	17. are/were	18. is/was	19. are	20. are ... are.

Exercise 2

Correct the following sentences :

1.   Each of his words have rendered me an insult.
2.   Neither the realm of fancy nor abound wealth have given him relief and relaxation.
3.   Neither of the songs mirror beauty and balm.
4.   A number of plans is chalked out by us.
5.   Fifty rupees are not sufficient for me.
6.   Sight along with sounds, were the main feature.
7.   I who is your best adviser will never mislead you.
8.   The army have launched a furious attack.
9.   Each of the pages were sparkling with wit.
10. Every bud and every flowers were torn by the storm.
11. I, he and you is the candidates for the same.
12. If I have courage, I should have answered him.
13. If it will rain, you will get wet.
14. What will happen if the bridge broke ?
15. Unless you do not have a dog, your house will not remain safe.
16. People speaks against him.
17. You may get success.
18. The teacher who teaches you, he must be regular.
19. Most of the papers is torn.
20. A lot of money were lavishly spent.
21. A pair of shoes were lost.
22. A team of players have arrived.
23. Villagers after villagers were deserted.
24. I do not believe in this type of happenings.
25. Do not speak lies.

Answers

1. has	2. has	3. mirrors	4. are	5. is
6. was	7. who am	8. has	9. was	10. was
11. you, he and I are	12. If I had (or had I)		13. If it rains	14. breaks
15. Omit 'do not'	16. speak	17. May you	18. teaches you must be	
19. are	20. was	21. was	22. has	
23. villager after village was		24. these types	25. tell lies.	

Exercise 3

Rewrite these sentences in their correct forms :

1.   Twenty years were a long gap.
2.   The rest of the papers is kept in the safe.
3.   Half of the sugar were scattered.
4.   I shall go through the matter yesterday.
5.   Nothing but repentance are destined to him.
6.   He speaks to me as if he is my well-wisher.
7.   Be careful lest you will lose.

8. Vasco-de-gama invented the Cape of Good Hope.
9. Who discovered the electric lamp ?
10. Did he refused his guilt ?
11. Much water has flown in the Ganga.
12. He met me in the street tomorrow.
13. Did your son fell to qualify in English ?
14. Suddenly a wild wind blowed against the tree.
15. Have you hanged my stick ?
16. Blow out the light.
17. Has he maked the picture precisely ?
18. He lay the bundle on the floor.
19. O, that I am a wealthy man !
20. We swimmed in the river.
21. None will speak when you will dance.
22. The bird flied away.
23. Explain these passages as follow.
24. A number of instances was given by him.
25. He does not use to wear a sweater.

Chapter 10

Tenses and Modals

Natures of Tenses

Tense को तीन भागों में विभाजित किया गया है–Present Tense (वर्तमान काल) ; Past Tense (भूतकाल) तथा Future Tense (भविष्यत् काल) (i) पुनः इन्हें भी verbs के forces को दृष्टिगत करते हुए चार भागों में वर्गीकरण किया गया है। Indefinite, continuous, perfect, and perfect continuous.

1. Present Indefinite (Simple Present)–(a) यह वर्तमान में घटित कार्य को बताता है, (b) शाश्वत तथ्य को प्रतिपादित करता है, (c) आदत प्रगट करता है, (d) भविष्य में घटित होनेवाले कार्य का संकेत देता है, (e) भूतकाल में घटित नाटकीय घटना का चरित्रांकन या वर्णन करता है।

(a) He *is* in the garden.

Someone *knocks* at the door.

(b) The sun *rises* in the east.

The hot air *rises* upwards.

(c) My uncle often *comes* here.

The teacher always *takes* a nap in the class.

(d) Mr. Lal *retires* next week.

The train *departs* at 6.15 A.M.

(e) Then Caesar *says*, 'Cowards die many times before their deaths.'

Brutus *is* noble in character. He *sits* high in all the people's heart.

2. Present Continuous (Progressive)

(a) यह अस्थायी रूप से कार्य की गतिशीलता बताता है।

(b) कार्य की निरन्तरता का संकेत देता है।

(a) The boys *are* playing in the field.

It *is* raining heavily.

(b) He *is* always playing to the gallery.

The child *is* always weeping.

We *are* leaving for Allahabad tomorrow.

Note. सभी verbs progressive force नहीं रखतीं।

अतः ऐसे verbs को continuous tense में प्रयोग से बचना चाहिए। अच्छा हो कि इन्हें simple present में रखा जाय। जैसे–

I am knowing you. (not admissible)

I *know* you. (admissible)

इस तरह से verb को दो भागों में बाँट सकते हैं–

I. **Progressive verbs** (गत्यात्मक क्रियाएँ) अर्थात् जिनसे progressive, activity (क्रियाशीलता) का बोध हो, जो स्वयं में dynamic force रखती हो, जैसे–

> read, write, jump, run, play, work, change, kick, knock etc.

II. **Stative verbs** (स्थिर क्रियाएँ)–जिनसे सक्रियता (क्रियाशीलता) का बोध न हो। ऐसे verbs चित्त की स्थिति, भावना, संवेग बताते हैं। इनसे किसी प्रकार की गति का संकेत नहीं मिलता, जैसे–

> know, hope, desire, doubt, like, see, love, belong, contain, remember, own etc.

He is hoping ; You are desiring न करके He *hopes* ; You *desire* आदि जैसा लिखना तर्क संगत है। कभी-कभी कुछ stative verbs activity भी बताती हैं, जैसे–

> I *am thinking* latterly to start a factory.

3. Present Perfect–(*a*) यह बताता है कि कार्य भूतकाल में तो समाप्त हो गया किन्तु वर्तमान से इसका सम्बन्ध है। इसके साथ भूतकाल बताने वाला कोई समय न रखे।

> The Express *has arrived*.
>
> We *have played* the game.

(But)

> I *have passed* B.A. long ago.

यहाँ long ago भूतकाल बताता है किन्तु इसे present perfect में प्रयोग किया गया है जो काल दोष है। अत: I passed B.A. long ago (or had passed) स्वीकार्य है।

(*b*) Present perfect हाल ही में, शीघ्र पूर्व कार्य को घटित बताता है जिसका प्रभाव वर्तमान तक है।

> They *have* just *finished* their work.
>
> I *have* lately *read* 'Gone with the Wind'.
>
> What *have* you *discovered* up-to-now ?

(*c*) चूँकि यह past से प्रारम्भ कार्य को एक अवधि से present तक जारी रहने का संकेत देता है, इसमें point of time के लिए since (or from) तथा period of time के लिए for का प्रयोग कर सकते हैं।

> I *have walked* for an hour.
>
> The wind *has shaken* the trees since morning.
>
> They *have hidden* the letter since morning.

ऐसी स्थिति को Indefinite अथवा continuous से प्रगट नहीं किया जा सकता। अब इन वाक्यों को लें–

He *has come*. (i.e., the act is completed आया है।)

He *is come*. (i.e., he has come and is here आया हुआ है।)

Note. दिन, माह तथा वर्ष का नाम, बजे से, दिन तथा जीवन के अनुभाग, Yesterday, arrival, departure etc. के साथ since का प्रयोग (point of time) के लिए करें। कालांश, अवधि (portion or period of time) के लिए for का प्रयोग करें।

Since four o' clock.	for four hours.
Since Sunday.	for two days.
Since July.	for five months.
Since morning, childhood etc.	

4. Present Perfect Continuous—इसमें वैसे कार्य का संकेत रहता है जो भूतकाल से प्रारम्भ हुआ अभी तक चल रहा है या उसका प्रभाव है। इस प्रकार यह tense continuous तथा perfect का मिश्रण है। यह सीमित समय तक चलते हुए व्यापार का संकेत देता है, जबकि perfect पूर्ण हो चुका (कार्य का)

Continuous के साथ समय-संकेत (for, since) नहीं रहता।

> It *has been raining* since Wednesday.

We *have been living* in Lucknow since 1980.

Which picture *have* you *been drawing* for an hour ?

Why have the farmers not *been threshing* for two days ?

For what has she *been weeping* bitterly since yesterday ?

5. Past Perfect–इस tense में प्रायः दो कार्यों का संकेत रहता है। जो कार्य पहले सम्पन्न हो गया था उसे past perfect (had + verb³) में तथा बाद वाले को Simple past verb² में रखा जाता है।

वैसे एक कार्य के लिए भी इसका प्रयोग दर्शनीय होगा। ध्यान रहे कि past perfect का समय simple past से अधिक दूर का भूतकाल बताता है, जैसे–

He *wrote* a letter.

He *had written* a letter.

The train *had departed* before we reached the station.

The postman *had* not *come* before you went.

Where *had* he *gone* before the guests came ?

Why *had* you not *solved* the sum before the teacher came ?

Had I not *warned* you before you went there ?

6. Future Perfect–Past perfect की तरह इसमें भी दो कार्यों का बहुधा संकेत रहता है। प्रथम कार्य को future perfect में (shall/will + have + verb³) तथा द्वितीय को present indefinite में रखा जाता है क्योंकि दो future tenses एक ही वाक्य में नही रहा करते। Have का प्रयोग इसमें सभी के साथ होगा।

The enemy *will have fled* before they come.

The bell *will* not *have gone* before he reaches.

Shall we not *have set* out before it dawns ? or (before dawn)

Whom *will* the dog *have teased* before the master comes ?

7. Like–I would like/I should like.... "If anything it (I should like) makes the matter worse ; would is properly used without 'like' because it contains the idea of volition ; to use it with 'like' is equivalent to saying I should like. I would like is no better than any of the wills and woulds ..... it is not English English." (Fowler—M.E.U.)

भाव यह कि इस स्थिति में would का प्रयोग अन्य verbs के साथ तो कर सकते हैं। जैसे–I would refer to ; we would ask किन्तु I would like जैसे प्रयोग से बचना चाहिए यद्यपि कि इसका प्रचलन सर्वाधिक है।

8. Modal Auxiliary Verbs—(a) (i) **Can/could**–यह power, ability तथा capacity (योग्यता, क्षमता बताता है। could, can का past tense है।

I will do what I *can*.

Can you run against the violent wind ?

He *can* control the furious mob.

She *could* work out this sum.

(ii) **Can, permission, request तथा possibility** (अनुमति, निवेदन, संभावना) का संकेत देता है।

You *can* go. (Emphasis)

You *cannot* make a noise when I am reading.

Can you give some room to sit in ?

Could you kindly grant me a leave ?

The college *can* give him free studentship.

The physician *can* come.

(b) *(i)* **May/might**—यह permission तथा possibility बताता है। Might, may का past tense है।

You *may* take my pen.

The sky *may* rain to day.

You *may* not talk in this way.

The prices *may* increase in future.

Your team *might* do well.

Might he do so ?

(ii) यह optative sentence में अभिलाषा (wish) को व्यक्त करता है।

May you succeed in your attempt !

May you be happy !

May your race grow !

cf.—It *cannot* be true. It *may* be true.

(c) **Must**—यह obligation (बाध्यता), duty (कर्तव्य), necessity (आवश्यकता) तथा possibility (संभावना) बताता है।

She *must* weep or she will die.

You *must* quit this place.

We *must* work hard to get first class.

A judge *must* be honest.

You *must* have heard the name of Shivaji.

(d) **Should** (चाहिए)—Shall का past tense है। यह duty, suggestion तथा probability (कर्तव्य, सलाह, संभावना) व्यक्त करता है। Condition हेतु 1st person के साथ भी इसका प्रयोग होता है।

We *should* respect our elders.

You *should* apply for the post.

She *should* be there.

If we had gone there, we *should* have seen him.

If I were a bird, I *should* fly at large.

(e) **Ought (to)**—(चाहिए था, चाहिए owe का पूर्व में past tense हुआ करता था।) यह morality, advice, possibility and unfulfilled obligation (नैतिकता, सलाह, संभावना तथा अपूर्ण बाध्यता) का संकेत देता है।

He *ought to* respect him.

You *ought to* die for the noble cause.

You *ought to* read good books.

She *oughtn't* bring disgrace to the family.

You *ought to* bring him home.

Note. संक्षेप में सामान्य 'चाहिए' हेतु should ; 'चाहिए' पर यदि बल दिया गया हो तो must और 'चाहिए था' के रहने पर ought to का प्रयोग करना चाहिए।

(f) *(i)* **Shall**—सामान्य भविष्य बताने के लिए shall का प्रयोग first person के subject के साथ होता है। यदि कथन पर बल दिया गया हो तो इसे अन्य persons के साथ भी (must के भाव में) प्रयोग किया जा सकता है, जैसे—

He *shall* (*i.e.,* must) pay the penality.

You *shall* not go.

(ii) **Shall, intention/will** भी बताता है—

You *shall* not catch me again.

Shall I give you some help ?

Trespassers *shall* be arrested. (Legal notice)

(g) (i) **Will**—सामान्य भविष्य (simple future) के अतिरिक्त यह willingness, truth तथा first person के साथ obligation बताता है। यह Request का भी संकेत देता है।

> I *will* consider your case.
> I *will* see it afterward.
> What is your *will* ?
> Water *will* boil now.
> The moon *will* rise after sometime.
> I *will* go. (*i.e.*, must go)
> We *will* face the challenge. (*i.e.*, must face)
> *Will* you please give me support and sustenance ?

(ii) इसके अतिरिक्त will कभी-कभी fixed intension का भी संकेत देता है।

> Where there is a *will*, there is a way.
> My poverty but not my *will*, consents.

(iii) **Would**—यह will का past tense है। Conditional sentence में (2nd तथा 3rd person के साथ) ; habit के लिए (often तथा sometimes के साथ) तथा Requests हेतु would का प्रयोग देखा जा सकेगा।

> If he had worked hard, he *would* have passed.
> Had he tried, he *would* have succeeded.
> If you were (or were you) a jackal, you *would* howl at night.
> They *would* often go to the woods.
> She *would* sometimes burst into tears.

(h) **Need**—इसका प्रयोग do के साथ तथा do के बिना भी हो सकता है। बिना do के इसके साथ -s या -ed का प्रयोग Interrogative तथा negative और semi negative (Hardly, scarcely) के साथ नहीं होगा। Infinitive का to हट जाएगा।

> He *need not* trouble himself.
> Why *need* he have come to night ? (C.O.D)
> She *need not* speak to me.
> He *need* scarcely speak to you.
> They *needn't* be counted or they did not need to be counted.

किन्तु do के प्रयोग में need के साथ -s या -ed लग सकता है।

> Does it *need* to be done with care ?
> I do not *need* your help.
> It *needs* to be done with care. (C.O.D.)

(i) **Dare** (साहस करना)—Third person, singular number (simple present) के साथ -s का प्रयोग इसके साथ नहीं होगा तथा Infinitive के to का भी लोप हो जाएगा।

> He *dare* not fight with me (not does not)
> *Dare* she go in the dark ?

किन्तु do के साथ Infinitive का to रखा भी जा सकता है, हटाया भी जा सकता है।

> She does not dare call me.

(j) **Used to**—आदत (Habit) के लिए इसका प्रयोग past tense में किया जाता है।

> I *used to* take the bus.
> The bell *used to* ring at one.
> What *used* he *to* say ?
> She *used to* sigh.

इस आशय को Simple past से भी प्रगट किया जा सकता है।

       They *said*. He *played* truant.

       He *did* not *use* to sit under the tree. (Colloquial)

       Did it *happen* always ? (Archaic)

'Use is now confined to the past tense. We may say—He used to live in London. The proper negative form is therefore–He used not to–but–He did not use to–Should be regarded as an archaism.' (Fowler-M.E.U.)

प्रश्नवाचक में Used he go by bus ? किन्तु Did he use to come here ? (Archaic)

Exercise 1

Supply the correct tenses :

1. He (not arrive) when I (post) the letter.
2. They just (decide) that they must (leave) the place.
3. He usually (write) in green ink.
4. Where (to be) my tooth brush ?
5. She (play) the piano when our guests (arrive) last night.
6. (Helping verb) you please show me the way ?
7. Never (lose) your heart.
8. O, that I (to be) a child again !
9. I never (forget) what you just (tell) me.
10. Have you in your hand (W/h) ?
11. Hurrah ! we all (secure) first class.
12. I (finish) the work before my next birth day.
13. Hello ! you (make) a cake ?
14. She said, "You have a feather in your cap." (May)
15. The house (to be) much smaller than we (think) at first.
16. The little girl (ask) what (happen) to her toys.
17. When he (grow) old he often (think) of all the things he (do) when he (to be) young.
18. Yesterday I (buy) a new watch as my old one (be stolen).
19. Whose stick you (break) ?
20. The child cried as if (frighten).
21. We (study) English for six years.
22. He (visit) his friend yesterday and (find) that he (to be) out.
23. He (walk) very quickly when I (meet) him yesterday.
24. If I (to be) a ghost, I (try) to frighten all the people.
25. She (to be) sure that better days (come).
26. The beggar said, "You (go) to hell." (May)
27. They were (fascinate) by the scenery as though they (to be) in the seventh heaven.
28. Hi ! how jolly you (appear).
29. So daring (to be) he that he (jump) into the horrid current.
30. Just as he (hear) the news, he (write) to me.

Exercise 2

Supply the proper forms of verbs in the following sentences :

1. Everyone of the gamblers (be arrest) red handed.
2. Jack with John (to be) sitting on the tree.
3. Not only the fox but also all the beasts (be assemble) there.
4. She denied that she (write) the letter.
5. It is believed that he (speak/tell) the truth.
6. She (be lie) down on the cushion.
7. Most of us (desire) to amass money quickly.
8. Two thirds of the property (be give) to the elder brother.
9. Man after man (to be slay).
10. They (refuse/deny) to submit.
11. Shivaji (find/found) the Hindu dynasty.
12. Heaps of grains (be rot).
13. If dinner is not ready, I (go) without it.
14. I should not have thought it possible unless I (see) it.
15. If she (to be) cunning, he (divorce) her.
16. The child (be kill) if the train had not (stop).
17. Do not (disturb) while she (sing).
18. So quickly did they (attack) that the enemy (can do) nothing.
19. Do not speak lest you (be arrest).
20. I feel as though my head (to be) aloft.
21. I thought that the day (will) be fine.
22. With whom have you met yesterday ?
23. He came here the next day.
24. Yesterday will be the day of glory.
25. Our democracy long live !

Chapter 11

Verbs : Non-finites

1. Infinitive

1. Infinite verb से बनता है किन्तु प्राय: Noun का कार्य करता है। इसे To + verb[1] से प्रगट किया जाता है। जैसे—

To forgive is divine.	*Subject of the verb 'is'*
Children like *to play*.	*Object of the verb 'like'*
Her habit is *to sing*.	*Complement of the verb 'is'*
The ripe mango is about *to fall*.	*Object of the preposition 'about'*
We heard him *say*.	*Objective complement.*

Noun के रूप में इस प्रकार के प्रयोग को **simple infinitive** कहा जाता है।

2. Infinitive का to निम्नस्थ परिस्थितियों में छिप जाता है—

(a) Auxiliary verbs (ought को छोड़कर)। जैसे—

He will *try* again.
We should *go* there.
They *can* cross the river.
I shall *do* it tomorrow.
She may *win*.

(But)

You *ought to fight* for the noble cause.

(b) Let, bid, make, see, watch, feel, hear, know के साथ infinitive का to हट जाता है।

Let them *say* what they say.
I saw him *go*.
We found her *sleep*.
She made the boys *laugh*.

Need तथा Dare जब Negative or Interrogative में प्रयुक्त हों तो उनके साथ to लुप्त हो जाता है।

You need not *speak* thus.
He dare not *come* here.
They do not *need* our help.
Dare he *speak* so ?

(c) Rather than, had rather, would rather, sooner than, had better जैसे **phrases** के साथ Infinitive का to हट जाता है।

He would rather *die* than beg.
You had better *decide* not to go there.

(But)

He would rather have died than *refused*.

(*d*) Prepositions but तथा than के साथ infinitive का to हट जाता है।

He does nothing but *weep*.

They did no more than *play*.

(*e*) जब एक ही वाक्य में अनेक Infinitives आएँ तो प्रथम के साथ ही to रखें, अन्य के साथ नहीं—

To travel hopefully is better than arrive.

Better *to light* up a lamp than curse darkness.

I came here *to see* and talk with you.

Perfect Infinitive को सामान्यतया unfulfilled hope के लिए प्रयुक्त किया जाता है, जैसे—

I hoped *to have seen* you before now.

We meant *to have stayed* there a week.

3. Noun के अतिरिक्त Infinitive किसी verb, adjective या सम्पूर्ण sentence को भी qualify करने का कार्य करता है। इस अवस्था को Gerundial infinitive कहा जाता है। जैसे—

She came *to see* her ailing brother. (Qualifies a verb)

This medicine is bitter *to take*. (Qualifies an adjective)

To speak clearly, he will never come. (Qualifies a sentence)

4. Too तथा enough के साथ Infinitive का प्रयोग क्रमश: negative तथा sufficiency के भाव में किया जाता है। Too को Adjective Adverb के पूर्व तथा enough को बाद में रखा जाता है। Enough किसी Noun के पहले भी आ सकता है या बाद में भी—

I have enough time *to do* it.   *Or*

I have time enough *to do* it.

He is too fat *to run* easily.

I am too weak to walk.

She is clever enough *to explain* it.

You are lucky enough to get the prize.

5. जब कोई Infinitive किसी Noun को qualify करे तो उसके preposition को वाक्य में स्पष्ट करना चाहिए।

Give me a pen *to write* with. (not to write)

Here is a chair *to sit* on.

Bring the horse *to ride* on.

He built a house *to live* in.

6. Split Infinitive—जहाँ तक संभव हो Infinitive को to से पृथक् करके कोई Adverb/adverbial phrase का प्रयोग नहीं करना चाहिए।

I request you *to kindly* grant me leave. (Incorrect)

I request you *to grant* me leave kindly. (Correct).

Similarly—to considerably improve ; to still be allowed ; to strongly favour ; to once more try—in these examples infinitives are wrongly separated.

7. Infinitive का Active voice में present तथा perfect रूप हुआ करता है। अत: इनका passive voice present में to be + verb^3 तथा perfect में to have + been + verb^3 जैसा बनेगा।

Active	**Passive**
She is *to type* a letter.	A letter is *to be typed* by her.
He is *to teach* the boys.	The boys are *to be taught* by him.

Roads have *to be repaired* or have got *to be repaired*.

Boys could have been taught.

Seem, appear के साथ seems to be ill/seems to have been ill जैसी बनावट sense की दृष्टि से भिन्न है किन्तु grammar के अनुसार उपयुक्त। जैसे—

He seems *to be ill*. (*i.e.*, this time only)

He seems *to have been ill*. (*i.e.*, not this time but before)

8. Wh word के साथ Infinitive का प्रयोग Noun clause के लिए किया जाता है। इसमें मूल verb का लोप हो जाया करता है। इस विषय में W.S. Allen का note द्रष्टव्य करें—

'A very odd but important idiom, particularly in spoken English, is the habit of finishing a phrase (usually a response) with the infinitive particle 'to' leaving the verb to be implied.'

Will you show me how *to do* it properly ?

कुछ लोग किसी art or technique के जानने या न जानने से इसे जोड़ते हैं, यद्यपि इसके अपवाद भी दर्शनीय हो सकेंगे।

I do not know how *to swim*. (But teach him to swim.–C.O.D.)

Do you know how *to play* the piano ?

We could hardly decide what *to do*.

Where *to find* him was the problem.

9. Introductory 'It' के साथ infinitive का प्रयोग—

To take exercise in the morning is useful.

Or   It is useful *to take* exercise in the morning.

To sleep in day is harmful.

Or   It is harmful *to sleep* in day.

To fly in the sky was a day-dream.

Or   It was a day-dream *to fly* in the sky.

To row a boat at night is pleasant.

Or   It is pleasant *to row* a boat at night.

2. Gerund

1. Gerund को verb में -ing लगाकर बनाया जाता है। यह Noun का काम करता है, अत: यह verb–noun है।

'A gerund is that form of the verb which ends in -ing and has the force of a noun and a verb.' (P.C.Wren)

Gerund के पूर्व the और बाद में of आने पर उसे verbal noun कहा जाता है जो Adjective द्वारा qualify होता है, Adverb द्वारा नहीं।

The making of a plan carelessly brings failure. (Incorrect)

The careless *making* of a plan brings failure. (Correct)

2. Noun के रूप में Gerund—

Walking is a good exercise.	(*Subject of the verb 'is'*)
Stop *writing*.	(*Object of the verb 'stop'*)
I am tired of *riding*.	(*Object of the preposition 'of'*)
Seeing is *believing*.	(*Complement of the verb 'is'*)
Walking stick.	(*i.e., a stick for walking*)
Writing table.	(*i.e., a table for writing*)

3. चूँकि Gerund तथा Infinitive दोनों ही verb से बनकर Noun का काम करते हैं, वे दोनों रूपों में व्यक्त किए जा सकते हैं–

> To *say* is easier than to *do*.
> *Saying* is easier than *doing*.
> To *give* is better than to *take*.
> *Giving* is better than *taking*.

दोनों में अन्तर यह है कि verbs or participles etc. के पश्चात् जब उनके स्वाभाविक prepositions रहें तो उनके बाद Gerund आएगा, Infinitive नहीं। इस प्रकार fond of, afraid of, insist upon, aim at, succeed in, prevent from, think of etc. के पश्चात् gerund आएगा। इस नियम का अब उल्लंघन होने लगा है। जैसे–He aims to overpower you.

Incorrect	Correct
He is fond to ride.	He is fond of *riding*.
She is afraid to go in the dark.	She is afraid of *going* in the dark.
We succeeded to persuade him.	We succeeded in *persuading* him.

4. जब कोई Noun/pronoun gerund को govern करे तो वह noun or pronoun possessive case में होगा–

Incorrect	Correct
I do not like the teacher coming late.	I do not like the teacher's *coming* late.
He insists on me being present.	He insists on my *being* present.
It depends on you joining the service.	It depends on your *joining* the service.
Do you object us smoking ?	Do you object our *smoking* ?

5. Gerund and passive voice–इसके present form को being + verb^3 तथा perfect form को **having** been + verb^3 जैसा करके passive forms बनाते हैं। Participle का passive voice भी इसी रूप में होगा।

Being tired, being harassed, being teased, having been done, having been punished etc.

3. Participle

1. 'A participle is that form of the verb which partakes of the nature both of a verb and **of an Adjective.'** (Wren)

संक्षेप में participle verb से बनता है किन्तु Adjective का कार्य करता है। इसके तीन भेद हैं–

(*a*) **Present participle**–verb + ing

> A *barking* dog seldom bites.
> A *rolling* stone gathers no moss.
> Newton saw a *falling* apple.

(*b*) **Past participle**–verb^3 के द्वारा संकेतित वस्तु के पूर्ण कार्य या स्थिति का भाव प्रगट किया जाता है। यह passive का force व्यक्त करता है। जैसे–

> A *dead* soldier.   A *retired* teacher.
> A *broken* fortune.   A *burnt* child.
> *Driven* by hunger, I stole a piece of bread.
> *Delighted* by his behaviour, we accepted the invitation.

(*c*) **Perfect participle**–Having + verb^3. इसे प्रायः Noun के पूर्व रखा जाता है। जैसे–

> *Having drawn* the sword, he pounced upon the enemy.
> *Having lost* his fortune, he is now a beggar.

2. Participles मुख्यत: तीन रूपों में प्रयुक्त हुआ करते हैं–

(a) **Attributively**–A pressing problem is before us. (*i.e.,* there is a pressing problem...)

    The *frowned* king rose from the seat.

    Spoken words are like dry leaves.

    Authority forgets a *dying* king.

(b) **Predicatively**

    Home they brought her warrior *dead*.

    I found the child *sleeping*.

    She broomed the leaves *drifted* by the storm.

(c) **Absolutely with a noun or pronoun**

    The weather *being* fine, we went out to walk.

    The school *being* over, the boys went home.

    The sun *having* set, the birds flew to their nests.

    The sky *being* clear, I opened my window.

3. Unattached participles–चूँकि participles Adjectives हुआ करते हैं, अत: किसी noun या pronoun से इनका सम्बन्ध होना आवश्यक है, संक्षेप में इन्हें बिना proper agreement के प्रयोग नहीं करना चाहिए। जैसे–

    Handing the whisky, his face broke into smile.

    Being Sunday, I went to the pictures.

    Entering the room, a dog bit me.

ध्यान से देखें तो ज्ञात होगा कि एक कार्य का subject अस्पष्ट है।

'In all doubtful cases it is best to put off recognition.'–Fowler. इसे स्पष्ट करने के लिये when, while आदि से सहायता ली जा सकती है।

    While he was handing the whiskey, his face broke into smile.

    It *being* Sunday, I went to the pictures.

    When I was entering the room, a dog bit me.

4. Regarding, considering, owing to, taking, speaking etc. को बिना proper agreement के भी प्रयोग किया जा सकता है।

    I have nothing to say *regarding* his case.

    Owing to illness, he could not take the examination.

    Considering my capacity, I left the idea of crossing the river.

Exercise 1

Rewrite the following sentences into their correct forms :

1. The messenger could to reach early.
2. Let me to take rest.
3. You need not to worry.
4. They ought die for the noble cause.
5. He is the proper man to talk.
6. Is there any morality to draw ?
7. My father advised me to hopefully go on the business.
8. The Buddha was possessed with the idea to liberate mankind.
9. He tried his utmost to narrowly escape from the danger.

10. Please excuse calling you by your first name.
11. I am afraid of John losing the way.
12. Would you mind me opening the window ?
13. Bid him to go.
14. Are you not incapable to handle it ?
15. We should all aim to do excellence.
16. Are you not ashamed to do such a mean act ?
17. I heard him to call a spade, a spade.
18. He needs not come here.
19. She dares not to have a dialogue with me.
20. He would rather die than to submit.
21. These sums are to work out by us.
22. He is instructed to slowly go.
23. You do nothing but to play the flute.
24. He is enough beneficent to help you.
25. The article is to sing and to dance to day.

Answers

1. could reach
2. omit 'to'
3. omit 'to'
4. ought to die
5. to talk to or with
6. to draw from
7. to go hopefully
8. of liberating
9. to escape narrowly
10. excuse our
11. John's
12. mind my
13. omit 'to'
14. of handling
15. aim at doing
16. of doing
17. omit 'to'
18. need not
19. dare not
20. than submit
21. to be worked out
22. to go slowly
23. but play
24. beneficent enough
25. and dance.

Exercise 2

Correct the following sentences :

1. Being a hot day, we did nothing.
2. I went for seeing my friend.
3. We tried our best except to request him.
4. They agreed observing the rule.
5. Clothes are only to wear and to tear.
6. She is too sorry for doing this.
7. The mangoes are good to eating.
8. He had better to go now.
9. We noticed a girl to carry a pitcher on her head.
10. The rider tired sat under the tree.
11. Being a rainy season, we should take an umbrella.
12. Sitting at the bridge, a man noticed me.
13. The work having finished, the workers went home.
14. Boys are prevented to go there.
15. I saw the dog to cross the river.
16. A lived ass is better to a died lion.

17. Garments borrowed never fit well.
18. Writing a letter, he called me in.
19. To be glad, he gave a handful of coins.
20. A man died tells no lie.
21. A rose faded has less smell.
22. The wander gipsy found his son to miss.
23. I objected him knocking at the door.
24. He is afraid to peep into the dark room.
25. Where is her doll painted ?
26. He is abstained to drink liquor.
27. He is insisted to go.
28. He has a passion to be a face in the crowd.
29. Being a holiday, we went to our village.
30. Please forgive me asking such a personal question.

Exercise 3

Replace clauses with Infinitives or its phrases :

Example : I was glad when I heard of your success.
I was glad to hear of your success.

1. It seems that it is impossible.
2. Do you understand what you have to do ?
3. She was told that she must not dirty her frock.
4. He hopes that he will know by tomorrow.
5. She asked if she might leave the room.
6. I shall be delighted if I could join your company.
7. Bob was pleased when he heard he had been promoted.

Re-write the following using 'too' or 'enough' :

8. This coffee is so hot that I cannot drink it.
9. He is quite well, and can go out again now.
10. She is quite old and she ought to know better.
11. The accident was so terrible that we could not talk about it.
12. This room is so small that we all cannot get in.
13. She was very foolish and she believed everything.
14. This problem is so difficult that I cannot explain it.
15. He was not rich so he did not marry him.

Complete the following sentences by putting the given verbs into the gerund forms :

16. They had started (write) the lesson before the teacher came in.
17. I began (read) a novel yesterday.
18. We did not like to (do) homework.
19. Do you mind (speak) to John and (ask) him to help us.
20. Thank you for (lend) us the book.
21. It has stopped (rain).
22. My uncle has given up (smoke).
23. (Climb up) mountains is also a sport.

Complete the following sentences by putting the given verbs into the participle forms :

24. (Open) the window, I peeped out.
25. Do not recollect the (forget) story.
26. (Drive) by thirst, the prince went near a stream.
27. We went on (see) the rain (fall) gently from the sky.
28. The umbrella with (break) handle is mine.
29. (Come) from the school, she saw a snake.
30. (Come) events cast their shadows before.

Chapter 12

Active and Passive Voice

Active voice को Passive voice में परिवर्तित करते समय यहाँ निम्नस्थ नियमों का उल्लेख करना आवश्यक है–

1. Passive voice का verb हमेशा to be + past participle हुआ करता है। to be *i.e.,* is, an, are, was, were, be, being, been.

2. Active voice के subject को passive voice में object के स्थान पर प्रयोग किया जाता है। उसे **Agent** कहा जाता है और सामान्यतया उसे **by** से जोड़ते हैं। जैसे–

Active	Passive
He *threw* the book.	The book *was thrown* by him.
The peon *has rung* the bell.	The bell *has been rung* by the peon.

Passive voice का verb उसके subject (Active का object) के अनुसार व्यक्त किया जाता है।

3. कुछ निम्नस्थ verbs के prepositions उनके साथ स्वभावतः प्रयुक्त रहा करते हैं। अतः इनके साथ **by** का प्रयोग न करके उन prepositions का प्रयोग करना अधिक तार्किक होगा। तब उन्हें Quasi-Agent कहा जाता है। जैसे–alarmed (at), interested (in), delighted (with), astonished (at), displeased (with), **worried** (about), disappointed (with), surprised (at), annoyed (at), known (to), dissatisfied (with) इत्यादि।

Active	Passive
His explanation *satisfied* me.	I was *satisfied with* his explanation.
The news *surprised* us.	We *were surprised* at the news.
Death *knows* me well.	I *am* well *known* to death.
He *looks after* his nephew.	His nephew *is looked after* by him.

4. सामान्यतया Transitive verb का passive voice हुआ करता है, Intransitive का नहीं। अन्य शब्दों में passive बनाने के लिए वाक्य में object का रहना आवश्यक है। किन्तु have, contain, lack, suit, fit, resemble जैसे कुछ verbs का objects रहने पर भी उनका passive संभव नहीं है। पुनः जब Active का object कोई Reciprocal pronoun अथवा Reflexive pronoun रहे तो उसका भी Passive voice संभव नहीं है।

I have a cow.	A cow is had by me. (Not admissible)
He loves himself.	passive not possible.
Both the friends loved each other.	passive not possible.

5. जब Active voice में Somebody, someone, **one, none, they, people, everyone** इत्यादि जैसे Indefinite या Vague pronouns subject रूप में रहें तो **Passive** में इनका लोप कर दें। जैसे–

They *chose* him Captain.	He *was chosen* Captain.
Someone *has picked* my pocket.	My pocket *has been picked.*
People *understand* Hindi all over India.	Hindi *is understood* all over India.

That से प्रारम्भ Noun clause वाले वाक्य की बनावट कुछ इस प्रकार करें—

Dummy subject (It) + to be + thought ; known, considered, believed, felt, found, said ; maintained इत्यादि + that से Noun clause.

People say that he is mad.	He *is said* to be mad.
	Or It is said that he is mad.
People felt that better days were ahead.	Better days *were felt* to be ahead. *Or*
	It was felt that better days were ahead.

इस प्रकार या तो Dummy subject मानकर अथवा Noun clause में प्रयुक्त subject को passive में subject मानकर दो तरह से Passive voices बनाए जा सकते हैं।

6. He is come, He is arrived, He is gone जैसे वाक्य को Passive नहीं मानना चाहिए क्योंकि इनमें प्रयुक्त verbs Intransitive verbs है। ऐसे ही *It is believed, it is felt, it is thought* etc.—impersonal passive के रूप में ज्ञात होंगे। किन्तु The glass is broken—passive है क्योंकि glass object है जो किसी के द्वारा तोड़ा गया है।

7. वाक्य में Double objects रहने पर (Direct तथा Indirect objects) किसी भी object से Passive voice बनाया जा सकता है। जिस object को subject रूप में प्रयोग नहीं किया जाएगा उसे Retained object कहा जाएगा।

Mr. Gupta teaches us English.	English *is taught* to us by Mr. Gupta. *Or*
	We *are taught* English by Mr. Gupta.
I have given Hari a pen.	A pen *has been given* to Hari by me. *Or*
	Hari *has been given* a pen by me.

1. Tenses (Passive Voice)

1. Present and Past Indefinite—Assertive तथा Affirmative में Object + to be + verb³ .... जैसे–

Govind plants a tree.	A tree *is planted* by Govind.
The incident melted her heart.	Her heart *was melted* by the incident.

यहाँ Interrogative तथा Negative sentences के do, does तथा did का लोप कर दिया जाता है। यदि Wh word रहे तो उसे to be के पूर्व रखकर निम्नस्थ सूत्रानुसार Passive में बदलें—Wh + to be + object + not, never + verb³....

Do you not help him ?	*Is* he not *helped* by you ?
Did he write a letter ?	*Was* a letter *written* by him ?
When does he beat you ?	When *are* you *beaten* by him ?
Why did you not trust him ?	Why *was* he not *trusted* by you ?

Who से Question प्रारम्भ रहे तो Passive में उसे By whom से प्रारम्भ करें। जैसे–

Who prevented you ?	By whom *were* you *prevented* ?
Who does not oppose the bill ?	By whom *is* the bill not *opposed* ?

2. Present and Past Continuous

Assertive Negative हेतु–Object + to be + not, never + being + verb³ + ...

Interrogative—Wh + to be + object + not, never + being + verb³ + ...

Boys are not gathering the grapes.	The grapes *are* not *being gathered* by boys.
Am I not writing the letter.	*Is* the letter not *being written* by me ?
The teachers were praising Ram.	Ram *was being praised* by the teachers.

When were they catching butterflies ?	When *were* butterflies *being caught* by them ?
Who is teasing the pig ?	By whom *is* the pig *being teased* ?

3. Present and Past Perfect

Assertive Negative—Object + has, have or had + not, never + been + verb³

Interrogative—Wh + has, have or had + object + not, never + been + verb³ + ...

He has asked a question.	A question *has been asked* by him.
The workers had not demanded bonus.	Bonus *had* not *been demanded* by the workers.
Where had the Rajputs defeated the enemy ?	Where *had* the enemy *been defeated* by the Rajputs ?
Why have you not done your work ?	Why *has* your work not *been done* by you ?

4. Shall, should, Will, Would, Can, Could, May, Might, Must, Ought to इत्यादि Anomalous Verbs रहने पर उन्हें इस प्रकार Passive में बदलें–

Assertive Negative हेतु–Object + anomalous verb + not, never + be + verb³......

Interrogative—Wh + anomalous verb + object + not, never + be + verb³ + ...

I shall draw a map.	A map *will be drawn* by me.
They cannot work out this sum.	This sum *cannot be worked* out.
We should look after him.	He *should be looked* after by us.
Why could they not win the match ?	Why *could* the match not *be won* ?

5. Future Perfect

Assertive Negative हेतु–Object + shall or will + not, never + have been + verb³ + ...

Interrogative– Wh + shall or will + object + not, never + have been + verb³ + ...

The boys will have flown the kites.	The kites *will have been flown* by the boys.
Who will have knocked at the door ?	By whom *will* the door have been knocked at ?

Note. तीनों Tenses के perfect continuous तथा future continuous का passive नहीं होता है।

6. Imperative Sentences (Passive Voice)

(*a*) सामान्य Imperative sentence को Let + object + be + verb³ से Passive में बदलें। जैसे–

Arouse him.	*Let* him *be aroused.* Or
	You are *ordered* to arouse him.
Respect your elders.	*Let* your elders *be respected.* Or
	Better say—You are *advised/instructed* to *respect* your elders.
Bring a glass.	*Let* a glass *be brought.*

(*b*) यदि वाक्य Do not/never से प्रारम्भ रहे तो do को हटा दें तथा–Let + object +not or never + be + verb³ के रूप में वाक्य को Passive में बदलें। जैसे–

Do not fan the fire.	*Let* the fire not *be fanned. Or*
	You are advised not to fan the fire. *Or*
	You are forbidden to fan the fire.
Never tell a lie.	*Let* a lie never *be told. Or*
	You are advised never to tell a lie.

Do not lose the sense of duty.

Let the sense of duty not *be lost.*   *Or*
You are advised not to lose the sense of duty.

(c) यदि वाक्य में Please or kindly रहे तो इनका लोप करके You are requested + Infinitive जैसी बनावट द्वारा उसे Passive voice में बदलें। जैसे—

Please help him.

You are requested to help him.

Kindly, give a pen.

You are requested to give a pen.

7. Infinitive, Gerund and Participle (Passive Voice)

यहाँ प्रस्तुत तालिका का अध्ययन करें–

Voice		Active	Passive
Infinitive	Present	To drive	To be driven.
	Perfect	To have driven	To have been driven.
Gerund (n)/	Present	Teaching	Being taught.
Participle	Perfect	Having taught	Having been taught.
(Adj.)	Past		Taught (participle)

इन्हें Object + is, am, are, was or were + to be + verb³ ....जैसा बदलें। अथवा has, have or had की स्थिति में object + has, have or had + to be + verb³ के आधार पर Passive voice में बदलें। जैसे—

We are to start a game.

A game is *to be started* by us.

The farmers were to plough the fields.

The fields were *to be ploughed* by the farmers.

It is the time to shut the shops.

It is the time for the shops *to be shut*.

I have to convey a message.

A message has *to be conveyed* by me.   *Or*
has got *to be conveyed*

He had to preach his disciples.

His disciples had *to be preached* by him.   *Or*
had got *to be preached*.

She has/to buy a frock.

A frock has *to be bought* by her.

People believed him to have been murdered.

He was believed *to have been murdered*.
(M.E.U. 439)

Note. जब किसी Passive voice को Active voice में बदलना हो और उसका Agent वाक्य में अस्पष्ट हो तो सन्दर्भानुसार उसके Agent को परिकल्पित करें–

He *was chosen* the President of the Union. (Passive)

The employees *chose* him the President of the Union. (Active)

Exercise 1

Change the Voice in the following sentences :

1. The hunter kills the lion.
2. The horse is fed by me.
3. The ghost has frightened the children.
4. James Watt invented the steam-engine.
5. The teacher has been pleased by the boys.
6. My uncle is building a house.
7. He had abandoned the scheme.
8. I am taking leave of smoking.
9. The Rajputs expected to seize the fort.
10. The captain was commanding the troops.
11. Birds were catching the insects.
12. A strange cry was heard by the Shepherd.
13. The enemy had created havoc.
14. Adversity gives us lessons.
15. They conquered the city.
16. One man cannot serve two masters.
17. Our country should be served.
18. The committee had not elected him manager.

19. They ought to respect you.	20. He might win the field.
21. The pig is not teased by the dog.	22. It is not taken amiss by me.
23. He did not produce a good impression.	24. An imless effort does not bring success.
25. Stone walls cannot make a prison.	

Exercise 2

Rewrite the following sentences into Passive voice :

1. Do you know him ?	2. Have you not satisfied your officers ?
3. Did he never recognize you ?	4. Have you accounted him a fool ?
5. Has the beauty not arrested our eyes ?	6. Does the story give us a lesson ?
7. Were you not making a false notion ?	8. Had the accident dislocated your joints ?
9. Did they make you a laughing stock ?	10. Do the birds not sing a song today ?
11. Where did you find this ?	12. Does phosphorus produce light ?
13. Did they beat you ?	14. Had the wild wind destroyed the nests ?
15. Is the medicine not giving any relief ?	16. Can you explain this passage ?
17. Should you not discharge your duty honestly ?	
18. Will you do me a service ?	19. Would you not like it ?
20. Shall we overcome our broken lot ?	

Exercise 3

Put these sentences into Passive voice :

1. Why did they not fight the battle bravely ?	2. Who insulted you ?
3. When does the servant bring the newspaper ?	
4. Where had you kept the stick ?	5. How many books did you buy ?
6. Who has obtained the highest marks ?	7. Why did the news surprise you ?
8. When does he teach you English ?	9. Did the news disappoint you ?
10. Has the novel interested you ?	11. How will you solve the problem ?
12. When will the gipsy awake us ?	13. How can we forget this story ?
14. Why did his friends laugh at him ?	15. When will he bring the message ?

Exercise 4

Change the Voice in the following sentences :

1. Do it just now.	2. Do not kill the bird.
3. Please, give him shelter.	4. Do not make gossips.
5. Let wine not be drunk.	6. Explain the stanza clearly.
7. You are requested to help me.	8. Never throw mud upon others.
9. Control your passions.	10. You are advised never to lose your heart.
11. Let the book be showed to me.	12. Do not give the order in haste.
13. Never account him inferior.	14. Open the door.
15. Watch their activity.	16. You are forbidden to run in the sunshine.

Exercise 5

Change the Voice in the following sentences :

1. People always talk ill of others.	2. They believed that he would come one day.
3. Promises should be kept.	4. My watch has been stolen.

5. Everyone knows him.
6. They feel that he has made a mistake.
7. Everyone claimed that Balu would win.
8. Somebody has seen him lamenting.
9. Many men account him a man of good sense.
10. They maintained the event historic.
11. She will be obliged to weep.
12. We expected to bring a good result.
13. By whom was the chair broken ?
14. All desire to be rich.
15. He was refused admittance.
16. The committee appointed him principal.
17. One cannot hope good results with bad means.
18. Our fleet has been sunk.
19. What cannot be cured must be endured. (You must endure ... .)
20. This is the chance for us to avail.
21. The car could have knocked me down.
22. His pages were flashed with lustrous beauty.
23. He has to perform a holy duty.
24. He is to decorate the house.
25. We have to sell the articles by auction.
26. By whom were you annoyed ?
27. Which thing did startle you ?
28. Will the audience have been amused by the talisman ?
29. Whence had you gathered the grapes ?
30. Who would trust a traitor ?
31. He was thought to be a happy man.
32. The demands were to be conceded by the company.
33. People conceived that peace would be restored.
34. Alas ! I cannot see her face again.
35. My wealth has been thieved.
36. Do not long for future.
37. Teach us to see beauty in objects.
38. Someone has put out the light.
39. Never snatch victory from defeat.
40. Do not throw cold water on his success.
41. Battles are fought and forgotten ; books are written and remembered.
42. He pretended to be a scholar.
43. Promises should be kept. (One.... one's ... .)

Chapter 13

Direct and Indirect Speech

वक्ता के कथन को दो प्रकार से प्रस्तुत किया जाता है–(*a*) वास्तविक रूप में (ज्यों का त्यों) उद्धृत करके (Direct speech) जिसे Inverted commas " " के अन्तर्गत रखा जाता है। इसे Reported speech या clause कहते हैं।

He said, "The climate does not suit me." (Direct)

(*b*) वक्ता के कथन को कुछ परिवर्तनों के साथ अन्य द्वारा प्रस्तुत या वर्णित करने को Indirect speech कहा जाता है। ऊपर के वाक्य में said—Reporting verb (R.V.) तथा "The climate does not suit me"—Reported speech (R.S.) कहा जाएगा। He said—Reported clause होगा। उक्त वाक्य का Indirect narration होगा–He said that the climate did not suit him.

इसी तरह–

Direct	Indirect
She said, "*Usha has taken the book.*"	She said *that Usha had taken the book.*
The teacher said, "*Ajay is a gentle boy.*"	The teacher said *that Ajay was a gentle boy.*
The old man said to me, "*I know the boy.*"	The old man told me *that he knew the boy.*

इस प्रकार Direct से Indirect में बदलने के लिए–

(*a*) R.V. के verb को said, told, ordered इत्यादि में प्रसंगानुसार बदलते हैं तथा उसके बाद के commas हटा देते हैं।

(*b*) सामान्य तथा स्वीकारात्मक वाक्य (Assertive तथा Affirmative) में Indirect करते समय RV/RS को परस्पर 'that' conjunction से जोड़ते हैं।

(*c*) आवश्यकतानुसार–R.S. के verbs तथा persons इत्यादि का परिवर्तन करते हैं।

(*d*) R.S. के प्रथम शब्द को capital letter से न लिखकर small से प्रगट करते हैं।

(*e*) R.V. में object रहने पर said to को told में बदलते हैं।

अब हम विभिन्न प्रकार के वाक्यों को Indirect में करने के लिए अलग-अलग विचार करें।

1. Assertive and Affirmative Sentences

सामान्यतः परिवर्तनों को तीन वर्गों में विभाजित किया जा सकता है :

(*a*) Change of pronoun, (*b*) Change of tenses और (*c*) other changes.

1. Change of Pronoun

(*a*) R.S. के first person को R.V. के subject के number, gender तथा person के अनुसार बदलें।

जैसे–

Direct	Indirect
I said, "*I have done my work.*"	I said *that I had done my work.*
You said, "*I did not post the letter.*"	You said *that you had not posted the letter.*

117

They said, "*We shall not take part in the picnic.*"

They said *that they would not take part in the picnic.*

(*b*) R.S. के second person को R.V. के object के number, gender तथा person के अनुसार बदलें। यदि R.V. में कोई object न रहे तो R.S. के second person को सन्दर्भानुसार first या third person में बदलेंगे। किन्तु अच्छा हो यदि R.V. में कोई object कल्पित कर लिया जाय जिसके अनुसार R.S. के second person को बदला जा सके।

He said, "*You cannot cheat me.*"

He said *that he could not cheat him.*

But better say :

He told (me) *that I could not cheat him.*

The old mother said to her son, "*You have tried your best.*"

The old mother told her son *that he had tried his best.*

I said, "*You cannot leave me in the lurch.*"

I told (him) *that he could not leave me in the lurch.*

Note. (*a*) कभी-कभी R.V. का subject तथा object दोनों Third person में प्रयुक्त मिलेंगे। Indirect करते समय R.S. में उन्हें स्पष्ट कर देना चाहिए।

John said to James, "*You can help me.*"

John told James *that he (James) could help him (John).* Or

John told James *that the latter could help the former.*

(*b*) R.S. के We को उस स्थिति में अपरिवर्तित रखा जाता है जब तथ्य वक्ता तथा श्रोता दोनों पर समान रूप से लागू हो अर्थात् उसमें सभी सम्मिलित हों।

The preacher said to us, "*We are subject to die and decay.*"

The preacher told us *that we are subject to die and decay.*

Conclusion (निष्कर्ष)–R.S. का First person—R.V. के subject(S) के अनुसार ; R.S. का Second person—R.V. के object (O) अनुसार तथा R.S. का Third person—No change (N) *i.e.,* SON सूत्रानुसार बदलेंगे।

(*c*) R.S. के Third person का change नहीं होता।

She said, "*He is a black sheep in the family.*"

She said *that he was a black sheep in the family.*

2. Change of Tense

चूँकि Indirect speech के सभी वाक्य complex या compound sentences हुआ करते हैं अतः se-quence of tenses (कालों के अनुक्रम) के नियम उनमें भी लागू होंगे। इस प्रकार—

(*a*) यदि R.V. का verb (principal clause/main clause का) present या future tense में रहे तो R.S. के tense का परिवर्तन नहीं होता, persons पूर्व नियमानुसार बदल सकते हैं।

I say, "*Govind can explain it.*"

I say *that Govind can explain it.*

He says, "*People have now turned money minded.*"

He says *that people have now turned money minded.*

You will say, "*I do not know even the A B C of Latin.*"

You will say *that you do not know even the ABC of Latin.*

He says to me, "*We have entered the space-age.*"

He tells me *that we have entered the space-age.*

(*b*) R.V. यदि past tense में रहे तो R.S. का present tense अपने वर्ग के past tense में बदल जाता है। अर्थात्—

Present Indefinite

Past Indefinite

Present Continuous

Past Continuous

| Present Perfect and Present Perfect continuous | Past Perfect Past perfect Continuous होगा। |

He said,

"I follow the footsteps of my noble father."	He said that he followed the footsteps of his noble father.
"You are beating about the bush."	He told (me) that I was beating about the bush.
"We have patched up the quarrel."	He said that they had patched up the quarrel.
"I have been living there for ten years."	He said that he had been living there for ten years.
He said to me, "Thank you."	He thanked me.

(c) R.V. अगर past tense में रहे तो 13/24 के अनुसार R.S. के tense को बदलें। 1—3 *i.e.*, past indefinite into past perfect, and 2—4 *i.e.*, past continuous into past perfect continuous. However the past perfect and perfect continuous of R.S. remain unchanged.

(1)	(2)	(3)	(4)
Past tense—Indefinite	Continuous	Perfect	Perfect Continuous

Balu said, "Kalu broke the jug."   Balu said that Kalu had broken the jug.

He said,	**He said that**
"The horse was running in the field."	the horse had been running in the field.
"We had reached safe and sound."	they had reached safe and sound.
"It had been raining since yesterday."	it had been raining since the previous day.
"I did not beat Govind."	he had not beaten Govind.

(d) **Shall is changed into should**

Will is changed into Would

May is changed into Might

and **Can is changed into Could.**

Indirect करते समय I, We के लिए **should** तथा शेष persons के लिए **would** का प्रयोग करें। इस स्थिति में **verb** को first form में रखें।

He said,	**He said that**
"I shall go there."	he would go there.
"The mother will teach me."	the mother would teach him.
"I can lift the box."	he could lift the box.
"She may win."	she might win.
The teacher said to me, "You will make the best of it."	The teacher told me that I should make the best of it.
He said, "If I had money, I could buy the house."	He said (or wished) that if he had had money, he could have bought the house.
He said, "I had a dog."	He said that he had had a dog.

(e) **Other Changes**

Direct को Indirect करते समय निम्नस्थ शब्द जो निकटता (nearness) का बोध कराते हैं, दूरी के भाव में (*i.e.*, into corresponding words expressing remoteness) बदल दिए जाते हैं—

This is changed into *that*

These is changed into *those*

Here is changed into *There*

Now is changed into *Then*

Today is changed into *That day*

Tonight is changed into *That night*

Tomorrow is changed into *The next day* (or the following day)

Yesterday is changed into *The previous day* (or the day before)

Next week is changed into *The following week*

Last night/week/year is changed into *The following night/week/year*

Thus is changed into *so*

Ago is changed into *Before*.

(f) Some Special Rules

(a) जब R.S. का verb केवल *was/were* रहे तो उसे *had been* में बदलें।

He said, "I was sad and downcast."	He said that he had been sad and downcast.

(b) R.V. का object जब R.S. में प्रयुक्त हो तो Indirect करते समय उसे R.V. में प्रयोग करें।

The boy said, "I am going to school, mother."	The boy told mother that he was going to school.
The physician said, "You will soon recover child."	The physician told child lovingly that he would soon recover.
The leader said, "Friends and gentlemen, we should restore peace and bring prosperity in the country."	Addressing as friends and gentlemen, the leader said that they should restore peace and prosperity in the country.

(c) जब R.S. से कोई **सर्वकालिक सत्य (universal truth), कहावत (proverb)**, अतीत की ऐतिहासिक घटना (Historical fact जो प्रायः Past Indefinite में रहती है) या used to से आदतजन्य तथ्य (Habitual fact) का बोध हो तो उसका परिवर्तन नहीं किया जाता।

He said, "The servant always used to nap."	He said that the servant always used to nap.
He said, "The earth is round."	He said that the earth is round.
Money said, "I go from pocket to pocket."	Money said that it goes from pocket to pocket.
He said, "A live ass is better than a dead lion."	He said that a live ass is better than a dead lion.
Dr. Sarkar wrote, "The Sepoy Mutiny in 1857 opened the eyes of the people."	Dr. Sarkar wrote that the Sepoy Mutiny in 1857 opened the eyes of the people.

(d) **Must** (i) यदि must से **(morality)** नैतिकता का बोध हो तो उसे ज्यों का त्यों रखें और (ii) यदि (objection) बाध्यता का बोध हो तो उसे *had to* या *would have to* में बदलें।

The teacher said, "A judge must be upright."	The teacher said (or maintained) that a judge must be upright.
The stranger said, "I must go."	The stranger said that he had to go.
His son said, "I must obtain the degree for a better future."	His son said (or thought) that he would have to obtain the degree for a better future.

सामान्यतः R.S. के must का परिवर्तन नहीं होता।

The king said, "I must reach the place by sunset."	The king said that he must reach the place by sunset.

(e) R.S. में व्यक्त *should, would, could, might, ought to*—Indirect में अपरिवर्तित रहते हैं। Could को यदि चाहें तो अनुमति (permission) के भाव में to be + allowed (to) or had been allowed (to) या भूतकालीन क्षमता (past ability) का बोध होने पर had been able (to) में बदल सकते हैं।

My friend said to me, "In my youth, I could cross the river."	My friend told me that in his youth, he had been able to cross the river.

इसी प्रकार *need not* भी अपरिवर्तनीय है किन्तु present के लिए उसे *did not have to* तथा future obligation हेतु *would not have to* में बदला जा सकता है। जैसे—

"I need not go."	He did not have to go. (Past)
"I need not go next week."	He would not have to go the following week. (future)

—(W.B. Allen)

(f) (1) R.S. में प्रयुक्त *Sir, Madam* जैसे आदरसूचक शब्दों को हटाकर उनके स्थान पर *respectfully* या *politely* का प्रयोग करें।

The student said to the teacher, "Sir, I have not bought the book."	The student told the teacher respectfully that he had not bought the book.
Usha said to her mistress, "Madam, due to illness, I could not come to school yesterday."	Usha told her mistress politely that due to illness she could not come to school the previous day.

(g) *Said* तथा *told* के अतिरिक्त R.S. के भाव को दृष्टिगत करते हुए R.V. को Indirect करते समय *maintained, hoped, believed, replied, remarked, promised, assured, added, thought* आदि में भी बदला जा सकता है।

He said, "Better days will come."	He believed that better days would come.
My friend said to me, "I will help you against a rainy day."	My friend promised me that he would help me against a rainy day.
The old man said, "Every dog has his day."	The old man maintained that every dog has his day.

(h) (1) जब R.S. में *When, While, as soon as, just as* इत्यादि से एक ही समय में घटित दो व्यापार (Time clause) का संकेत रहे तो उसका simple past तथा past continuous नहीं बदलता।

(2) इसी तरह *If* से अवास्तविक शर्त (Unreal conditions) अपूर्ण शर्त (Unfulfilled condition) अथवा असम्भाव्य घटना (Improbable happenings) का बोध हो तो R.S. का काल परिवर्तन नहीं होता।

(i) He said, "When I called on the doctor, he was reading a novel."	He said that when he called on the doctor, he was reading a novel.
He said, "When I asked the old man, he nodded his head."	He said that when he asked the old man, he nodded his head.
(ii) My neighbour said, "If I had won the lottery, I should have bought a car."	My neighbour said (or wished) that if he had won the lottery, he would have bought a car.
He said, "If a tiger came into the room, what would I do ?"	He asked what he would do if a tiger came into the room.
He said to me, "Just as I entered the room, the clock struck."	He told me that just as he entered the room, the clock struck.

(3) *Has / Have / Had + to + verb¹*—यदि R.S. में *has / have + to + verb¹* रहे तो Indirect करते समय उन्हें *had to + verb¹* जैसा करें और *had to + verb¹* रहे तो *had had to + verb¹* जैसा बदलें।

She said, "I have to do an urgent piece of work."	She said that she had to do an urgent piece of work.
The student said, "I had to cross the river daily."	The student said that he had had to cross the river daily.

Exercise 1

Change into Indirect speech :

1. He says, "She wears a worried look."
2. You will say, "I can do it."
3. He has said, "I shall not blow out the candle."
4. She is confessing, "I have broken the cups."
5. The fox says to the jackal, "I am also not a riff-raff."
6. I will say to him, "I care a fig for you."
7. People say, "The school master is abroad."
8. He says to all, "Corruption is the order of the day."
9. He will say, "You have run amuck."
10. He writes, "His days are numbered."
11. I thought, "My days and dreams have gone with the wind."
12. My friend said, "I do not like the mangoes of this kind."
13. The boys said, "We shall play a match today."
14. The servant said to me, "I request you to grant me leave for tomorrow."
15. She said to her mates, "It is time now to set out from here."
16. He said, "I left Poona yesterday."
17. Govind said to Mohan, "I do not lead you astray."
18. The teacher said, "I was busy in writing a novel yesterday."
19. The boy said, "The father was angry so he did not speak to me."
20. The physician said to the patient, "Now, you have, recovered your health."
21. The mother said, "A miss is as good as a mile."
22. They said, "The battle is won but the leader is lost."
23. He thought, "The workers will have completed the work."
24. They said, "We are toiling hard for a bright future."
25. He said, "Caesar's wife must be above suspicion."

Exercise 2

Change into Indirect speech :

1. The teacher said, "Battles are fought and forgotten, books are written and remembered."
2. Becon remarked, "Some books are to be chewed, some are to be swallowed and some are to be digested."
3. The old man said, "One swallow cannot bring a summer."
4. He said, "The sun sets in the west."
5. The hermit said, "A rolling stone gathers no moss, my pupils."
6. He said, "She is dead and there is none to look after the child."
7. The electrician said, "The fuse has blown, I have to mend it just now."

8. The candidate said, "Today is the day of examination I hope to leave tomorrow."
9. John said, "I can tell you, Tom, what strikes me as the most ridiculous."
10. The lawyer said to the client, "Since you have not submitted the requisite papers, the case will be postponed."
11. "But all is not lost," said Satan.
12. "I am afraid I cannot marry you," she said to me, "I know that you are very rich."
13. He said, "I am very glad to see you, friend."
14. "It is time to call a meeting," the lion said to the fox.
15. The mother said, "The boy used to sit under the tree and sing a song."
16. He said to me, "You need not help me."
17. The student said, "When I entered the room, the teacher was teaching."
18. The servant said to the master, "Sir, I must start now, otherwise my family may suffer."
19. He said, "As soon as she heard the news, she fainted."
20. The driver said, "When the car stopped, the people fell on it angrily."
21. Sarandha said to her brother, "You ought to die in the battlefield instead of returning the palace."
22. They said, "The teacher used to nap in the class."
23. "Fools rush in where angels fear to tread"—Pope.
24. "I am," the old man said, "not as weak as people think me to be."
25. "Children, you must remember what I told you," said the father.

Exercise 3

Change into Indirect speech :

1. The preacher said, "We must try to become a man."
2. He said, "Where ignorance is bliss, it is folly to be wise."
3. They said, "We do not play truant."
4. The clown said, "The mistress took me in yesterday."
5. The passengers said, "The train might arrive late."
6. "Thank you," said Govind, "But I am very well here. I shall, if you please, argue the point from where I am."
7. She said, "This is not the sort of place where you will get rich in a hurry."
8. The traveller said, "I have lost my way and shall be glad if you give me a night's lodging."
9. The old lady said, "You ought to keep a cat in your house to get rid of all these mice."
10. "That is my horse," said he, "and if I do not prove it, I will give up my claim.
11. The teacher instructed, "No candidate is allowed to bring unfair papers in the hall nor ask me question about what has been asked to do."
12. "I can extend no other mercy to you," said the king, "except permitting you to choose what kind of death you wish to die."
13. "It was not love that made me turn back to this little inn," said the stranger, "The truth is that I found here something without which love and wealth and power and everything are but dust and ashes."
14. Duke said, "Shylock, the world thinks, and I too think so, that you are exercising your malice against Antonio too far. I trust you will give up your claim in the name of mercy."
15. The coin said, "I thus moved from pocket to pocket. It would be tedious to relate all my adventures. Soon I grew old and was disfigured by constant use. Then came the fatal end of my life. Along with many other coins, I was thrown into a furnace. But strangely enough, I rose out of the furnace with greater beauty and brightness than I ever was."

2. Interrogative Sentences

जब किसी Direct question को Indirect speech में बदला जाता है तो वह Indirect question हो जाता है। उसके अन्त का Note of Interrogation (?) हटाकर full stop अंकित किया जाता है। यदि वाक्य Wh से प्रारम्भ हो। तो उसकी बनावट ऐसी होगी Wh + subject + verb.... अर्थात् उसे Assertive sentence में परिवर्तित कर दिया जाता है। शेष परिवर्तन इस प्रकार करें—

(a) Reporting verb को *asked, enquired (of), wanted to know* or *wondered* में बदलें।

(b) यदि Question किसी Verb to be या helping verb से प्रारम्भ हो तो *If or whether* connective का प्रयोग करें। किन्तु यदि Question किसी Wh word से प्रारम्भ हो तो उस Wh को ही connective मानें if आदि नहीं। इनके बाद उल्लिखित सूत्रानुसार परिवर्तन करें।

(c) यदि Question में do, does या did रहे तो उनका लोप कर दें और do/does .... Wh/if + subject + verb^2 ..... जैसा बदलें।

यदि इनके साथ not रहे तो ..... Wh/if + subject + did not + verb^1 .... जैसा करें। Did रहे तो उसको subject + past perfect.... के क्रम में परिवर्तन करें।

He said to me, "*Am I not your friend ?*"	He asked me *if he was not my friend.*
The police said to Kalu, "*Have you hidden the thief in your house ?*"	The police enquired of Kalu *if he had hidden the thief in his house.*
The teacher said to the newcomer, "*What is your name ?*"	The teacher asked the newcomer *what his name was.*
I said to my brother, "When are you going ?"	I asked my brother when he was going.
He said, "Is your father in ?"	He wanted to know if, my father was in.
The audience said, "How does the talisman do all these tricks ?"	The audience wondered how the talisman did all those tricks.
The teacher said, "Do you know me ?"	The teacher asked (me) if I knew him.
She said, "Does the boy not bring tea ?"	She asked (or wanted to know) if the boy did not bring tea.
The father said to me, "Did you not foot the bill ?"	The father enquired of me if I had not footed the bill.

The Change of Yes/No

1. यदि R.S. में Yes or No रहे तो—

(a) इनका लोप कर दें तथा इनके लिए क्रमशः replied in the affirmative or replied in the negative करें। Or (b) Yes/no के लिए क्रमशः agree या disagree करें। Or (c) इनके स्थान पर subject + helping verb जैसा करके इन्हें short answers का रूप दें। (a) में निर्दिष्ट नियम पुराना अतः त्याज्य है। ऐसे प्रयोग से बचें।

He said to Radha, "*Will you dance* ?" Radha said, "*Yes.*"	He asked Radha *if she would dance and she said that she would. Or* When he asked Radha *if she would dance. She replied in the affirmative.*
I said to my friend, "*Can you run with me ?*" My friend said, "*No.*"	I asked my friend *if he could run with me but he said he could not. Or* When I asked my friend *if he could run with me, he replied in the negative.*
He said, "Is this problem very difficult ?" I said, "No."	He asked me if that problem was very difficult and I said that it was not.
Hari said, "Have you brought your books ?" Ram—"Yes."	Hari asked Ram if he (Ram) had brought his books and he said that he had.

Note. (*a*) R.S. में प्रयुक्त well, you see, all right तथा कथन पर बल देने के लिए do जैसे अनावश्यक कथन को Indirect करते समय हटा दिया जाता है।

He said, "Well, what service can I do to you ?"	He wanted to know what service he could do to him (or me).
James said to me, "Do post the letter very shortly."	James asked (or requested) me to post the letter very shortly.

(*b*) यदि R.S. में कोई question tag रहे तो Indirect speech में उसका लोप कर दें।

She said to her son, "You spoiled your career, did you not ?"	She asked her son if he had spoiled his career.
He said to me, "You have forgiven me, haven't you ?"	He asked me if I had not forgiven him.

Exercise 1

Change into Indirect speech :

1. I said to Mohan, "Is it raining heavily ?"
2. He said to his brother, "Have you received the letter ?"
3. The stranger said, "Are you coming from India ?"
4. My room-mate said, "Was that book very interesting ?"
5. The king said to his courtiers, "Am I a good king ?"
6. I said to the gardener, "Are there many flowers in your garden ?"
7. I said to the boy, "Do you know Mr. Lall ?"
8. Hari said, "Did my friend come here ?"
9. The youngman said, "Do you not account me a gentleman ?"
10. The old man said, "Did they not bury the hatchet ?"
11. The fellow traveller said to the lady, "Madam, have you taken it amiss ?"
12. The child asked, "Mother, has the angel gone ?"
13. The falcon said, "Dear sparrow, had all the birds not flocked together ?"
14. She said to me, "Had you an extra pen ?"
15. Ravi said to her, "Can I pocket an insult ?"
16. The student said to the teacher, "May I come in, Sir ?"
17. The old man asked, "Has every man not his price today ?"
18. The leader said to the audience, "Will the rank and file bear such situation ?"
19. She said, "Shall I hear from you soon ?"
20. The clerk said to the old man, "Did you not open an account yesterday ?"
21. The soldier said, "Should we lay down arms ?"
22. Tom said to Jack, "Do you not blackmail me ?"
23. He said, "Do the old rules hold good today ?"
24. King Arthur asked, "Does authority not forget a dying king ?"
25. The manager said, "Do you find it easy ?"

Exercise 2

Change into Indirect speech :

1. The officer said to the clerk, "Why are you late ?"
2. He said, "Whose horse have you bought ?"
3. She said to her husband, "What will people say ?"

4. The teacher said to Ram, "What do you really mean by it ?"
5. I asked, "What sort of man is he ?"
6. The mentor said, "When did I suggest such a thing ?"
7. The reformer said to the audience, "Whence do these evils spring ?"
8. I said to my sister, "Where did you read this ?"
9. The manager said, "Where does it touch our interests ?"
10. The innkeeper said to the passerby, "Where do you come from and where are you going ?"
11. I said, "What is he after ?"
12. The prince said to his secretary, "How will you solve this problem ?"
13. "Which is the proper way to answer this question, father ?" the boy said.
14. "What will you like to eat ?" said Flemin to guests.
15. "How do you desire to be treated ?" Alexander said to Porus, "Have you nothing else to request ?"
16. The cottager said, "Who are you to speak to me like this ? Why should I help you ?"
17. The lawyer said to the witness, "Are you acquainted with the facts of the case ?"
18. Shylock—Who can force me to show mercy ?
19. "Ungrateful man !" roared the beast, "Did I not feed you when you were hungry, and shelter you for the night ? Remember, ingratitude is a sin, I cannot pardon."
20. "What is your name, O Statue ?"

    "I am called opportunity."

    "Why have you wings on the feet ?"

    "To show how quickly I pass by."

    "But why is your hair so long on the forehead ?"

    "That men may seize me, when they meet me."

    "Then why is the head so bald behind ?"

    "To show that when I once pass, I cannot be caught."
21. Alexander—Have you nothing else to request ?

    Porus—No
22. Shylock—Is that the law ?

    Portia—Yes.
23. Prince—Shall we return the palace ?

    Attendant—No.
24. John—Is the college closed today ?

    Jack—No
25. I said—Can you run in the dark ?

    He said—Yes.

3. Imperative Sentences

1. R.V. के said को R.S. के भावानुसार ordered, commanded, begged, advised, यदि R.S. में *please, kindly, madam or sir* रहे तो इनका लोप करके *requested (asked)* विशेषत: समवयस्क, समान पद वाले व्यक्ति के object रहने पर, *entreated, prayed, implored* इत्यादि में बदलें।

2. इसमें R.V. के पश्चात् Inverted commas के स्थान पर connective that का प्रयोग न करके R.S. के finite verb को infinitive में बदल दिया जाता है, अर्थात् to + verb[1]

3. यदि R.S. *Do not* या *never* से प्रारम्भ हो तो do को हटा दें और not to/never to + verb[1] ... के अनुसार परिवर्तन करें।

Do not को हटाकर R.V. को forbade/prohibited जैसा करके भी वाक्य को Indirect में बदला जा सकता है किन्तु इनके साथ not न रखें। Never हेतु forbade का प्रयोग न करें।

The master *said* to his servant, *"Bring a cup of tea."*	The master *ordered* his servant *to bring a cup of tea.*
The teacher *said*, *"Work hard, my pupils."*	The teacher *advised* his pupils *to work hard.*
The colonel *said* to the soldiers, *"Fire."*	The colonel *commanded* the soldiers *to fire.*
The rider said to the villager, "please give me a glass of water."	The rider requested the villager to give him a glass of water.
He said to his friend, "Accompany me."	He asked his friend to accompany him.
The father said, 'Do not think of past, my son."	The father advised (asked) his son not to think of past.
The mother said to the boys, "Do not run in the sunshine."	The mother ordered (asked or advised) the boys not to run in the sunshine. *Or* The mother forbade the boys to run in the sunshine.
He said to me, "Never look at the dark side of life."	He advised (or asked) me never to look at the dark side of life.

4. Direct speech में Request or advice को कभी-कभी can, could, will, would इत्यादि से question में भी प्रगट किया जाता है। Indirect करते समय इनका लोप कर दें और R.V. को to के द्वारा R.S. के verb[1] (main) से जोड़कर उन्हें इस प्रकार बनाएँ–

Balu said to me, "Will you please look after my house in my absence ?"	Balu requested me to look after his house in his absence.
The passerby said to him, "Can you show me the way of the nearest inn ?"	The passerby requested him to show him (the passerby) the way of the nearest inn.
"Would you mind leaving the seats for the guests ?" the manager said to the subordinates.	The manager requested the subordinates to leave the seats for the guests.

5. Change of 'Let'

(*a*) यदि *let* द्वारा प्रारम्भ वाक्य से सलाह या प्रस्ताव का बोध हो तो R.V. को *proposed / suggested to* में बदलें। Let को should में बदलकर R.S. को... that + subject + should + verb[1] जैसा करें।

(*b*) जब let से *permission / wish* का भाव रहे तो R.V. को *requested / asked / ordered / wished* में बदलें तथा R.S. को *to let* or *to allow* or *might be allowed* जैसा परिवर्तित करें।

(*c*) Let से यदि इरादा का भाव रहे तो however/even if इत्यादि से बदलें।

The players said, *"Let us start the match."*	The players *proposed* (or *suggested*) *that they should start the match.*
He said to his friend, *"Let us alone do it."*	He *suggested* (or *proposed*) to his friend *that they should alone do it.*
The teacher said to the peon, *"Let the boys enter the campus."*	The teacher ordered the peon *to allow* (or *to let*) *the boys enter the campus.*
The inspector said, "Let the miscreants go home."	The inspector ordered to let (or to allow) the miscreants go home. *Or* The inspector ordered that the miscreants might be allowed to go home.
My mother said, **"Let it rain ever** so heavily, I must come."	My mother said that she must come however heavily it might rain.

Exercise 1

Put the following into Indirect speech :

1. The captain said to the troop, "Beat back the enemy."
2. The father said to me, "Give a wide berth to bad companions."
3. The teacher said, "Forgive and forget, my boy."
4. We said to the villager, "Arouse us at dawn."
5. "Hurry up" he said to his servant, "Do not waste time."
6. Socretese said, "Be quiet and have patience."
7. The policeman said, "Stand up and follow me."
8. The boy said, "Tell me how you will solve the question."
9. Mother said, "Children, remember what I told you."
10. I said to the servant, "Open the window."
11. The physician said to the patient, "Do not eat too much."
12. The warden said to the boys, "Do not burn the midnight oil."
13. "Do not run amuck," said the mother to her son.
14. He said, "Never smoke."
15. The nurse said, "Do not make a noise."
16. My friend said to me, "Do not fling mud upon others."
17. He advised, "First deserve then desire."
18. I said to him, "Do not play to the gallery."
19. I said to the fellow traveller, "Please look after my luggage for a while."
20. The head clerk said, "Do not gossip. Prepare the draft in time."
21. The blind man said to Alen, "Kindly help me."
22. The neighbour said to them, "Please stop loud music. Let the patient sleep."
23. I said to the angry man, "Please do not beat him black and blue."
24. The crow said to the fox, "Do not take advantage of friendship."
25. The uncle said to his nephew, "Do not long for a windfall."
26. The preacher said to his disciples, "Never wish for worldly wealth."
27. I said to the mechanic, "Kindly do it very soon."
28. He said, "Thank you." (He thanked me.)
29. The man cried, "Please do not unveil the mystery."
30. The lawyer said to the culprit, "Liar." (said—called)
31. We said, "Curse the darkness."
32. The master said to the people, "Do be quiet please."

Exercise 2

Turn the following sentences into Indirect speech :

1. The student said to the teacher, "Would you mind my coming late ?"
2. The old man said, "Let the boys play."
3. I said to the passenger, "Will you please give your glass ?"
4. The boy said to his friends, "Let us play a game."
5. I said, "Let me have a cup of tea."
6. He said, "Let it be ever so dark, I must go."
7. "Can you accompany me to the college ?" said the newcomer.

8. The flower said, "Let me laugh and dance with the flowers."
9. I said to the servant, "Let the milkman come in."
10. He said to Radha, "Could you lend me your book for one night ?"
11. She said to her husband, "Let bygones be bygones."
12. He said to me, "Let us start tomorrow."
13. The gentleman said to Rohit, "Will you please come with me ?"
14. The villagers said, "Let her weep or she will turn mad."
15. He said, "Let the cat not go out of the bag."
16. She said to us, "let us hear some sweet music."
17. Ramesh said to me, "Do inform me immediately."
18. The two cats cried, "Let the case be closed."
19. The beggar said to me, "Can you give me a piece of bread ?"
20. The saint said to the farmers, "Let us go on a pilgrimage."

4. Optative Sentences

1. ऐसे वाक्य प्राय: May से प्रारम्भ होते हैं जिनके साथ Mark of exclamation (!) रहा करता है। इनसे प्रार्थना, कामना, आशीर्वाद, श्राप का बोध होता है।

(a) Reporting verb को R.S. के भावानुसार *wish, curse* (श्राप देना), *pray* (प्रार्थना करना R.S. में God रहने पर) आदि में बदलते हैं। प्राय: इसमें R.V. के object का लोप कर दिया जाता है।

(b) R.V. तथा R.S. को that connective से जोड़ते हैं।

(c) R.S. का शब्द-क्रम इस प्रकार रखें—... that + subject + might + verb[1]. R.S. में May न रहने पर भी might का प्रयोग होगा।

The mother said to me, *"May you live long !"*	The mother *wished that I might live long.*
The hermit said to him, *"Go to the dogs !"*	The hermit *cursed that he might go to the dogs.*
The crowd said, "Long live Netaji !"	The crowd wished that Netaji might live long.
The poor widow said, "May God, save my child !"	The poor widow prayed that God might save her child.

2. यदि R.S. में Good morning ; good-bye ; good night इत्यादि रहे तो R.V. के said को bade good morning, bade good-bye इत्यादि जैसा करते हैं। Hi, Hallo को greeted में बदलेंगे।

I said, *"Good morning, my friend ! What news have you brought ?"*	I *bade good morning* to my friend (or bade my friend good morning) and asked *what news he had brought.*
She said, *"Good night ! My mate !"*	She *bade good night* to her mate. *Or* She bade her mate good night.
He said, "Good-bye my friend ! We shall see again."	He bade good-bye to his friend and wished that they would see again.
He said to her, "Hallo ! Where are you living these days ?"	He greeted her and asked where she was living those days.

Exercise 1

Turn the following into Indirect speech :

1. The sailors said to the voyagers, "May God make your passage happy !"
2. The mother said to her son, "May you obtain first class !"
3. The people said, "May our country be prosperous !"
4. Princess Sita wished, "May God help Ram to break the bow !"
5. I said to John, "May you be successful !"
6. The women said, "May the terrorists be ruined !"
7. The mob cried, "Long live our king and queen !"
8. The minister said, "Long live Indo-Russian friendship !"
9. The spectators said, "May our team win the match !"
10. The poor mother said, "May God save my ailing child !"
11. He said to the wretch, "May you go to hell !"
12. My friend said to me, "Good morning ! I am happy to see you."
13. The holy sage said to me, "May your future be bright !"
14. The brother said, "Good-bye, sister !"
15. I said to my friend, "Hallo ! How are you ?"
16. The captain said, "Good-night ! I shall see you in the field tomorrow."
17. He said, "May God show you broken days !"
18. My friend said, "May you succeed in your venture !"
19. He said, "May God bless you !"
20. The father said to me, "May you top the list of successful candidates !"

5. Exclamatory Sentences

विस्मय, खेद, प्रसन्नता आदि का भाव व्यक्त करते हुए ऐसे वाक्य *Hurrah, Alas, Ah, Oh, Bravo, O (that),* *What, How* इत्यादि से प्रारम्भ हुआ करते हैं और इनमें Note of Exclamation (!) रहता है।

1. Said—Reporting verb 'said' को exclaimed में बदलें और R.S. में प्रयुक्त-

    Hurrah—exclaimed with joy (or delight)

    Alas—exclaimed with sorrow (or grief)

    Bravo, Well done—applauded (or shouted with applause)

    Good gracious, Good Heavens—exclaimed with surprise/regret

    O—eagerly wished.

2. Indirect speech को That से प्रारम्भ करके सामान्य वाक्य जैसा बदलेंगे, अर्थात् + ... that + subject + verb इत्यादि। वाक्यांत में full stop दें।

3. What/How से प्रारम्भ वाक्य के लिए R.V. को शोक, खेद का भाव रहने पर exclaimed with regret में बदलेंगे और आश्चर्य की स्थिति में exclaimed with surprise करेंगे। What/How का लोप कर देंगे और that से R.S. को प्रारम्भ करके सामान्य वाक्य जैसी उसकी बनावट करेंगे जिसमें very/great का भी प्रयोग करेंगे।

She said, "*Alas ! I am ruined.*"	She *exclaimed with sorrow that she was ruined.*
They said, "*Hurrah ! Our team has won the match.*	They *exclaimed with joy that their team had won the match.*
The father said, "*Bravo ! Well done ! My son.*"	The father *applauded* (or *shouted with applause*) *that his son had done well. Or*
	The father *applauded his son that ....*

I said, "Nonsense !"	I exclaimed that it was nonsense.
He said, "O, that I were very rich !"	He eagerly wished (or longed) that he were very rich.
He said, "What a fine morning it is !"	He exclaimed with surprise that it was a very fine morning.
The deer said, "What a fool I am !"	The deer exclaimed with regret that he was a great fool.
We said, "How horrid !"	We exclaimed (with awe) that it was very horrid.
"Oh dear !" cried the prince.	The prince exclaimed with profound dismay.
"What a pity !" the queen said.	The queen exclaimed that it was a great pity.

Exercise 1

Put the following sentences into Indirect speech :

1. He said, "Alas ! I have lost the field."
2. The soldiers said, "Bravo !"
3. He said, "Curse it !"
4. "How pretty you are !" said the fox to the crow.
5. The people cried, "Hurrah ! Our candidate is returned."
6. The girls said, "How sweet the music is !"
7. The old man said, "What a stupid fellow you are !"
8. The boys said, "Tut, tut !"
9. The members cried, "Shame ! Shame !"
10. The mother said, "How foolishly you behaved !"
11. She said, "What a sight !"
12. Shelly repented, "Alas ! I have neither hope, nor health."
13. The guests said, "Happy birthday." (wished me ...)
14. She said, "O, that I were able to see better days !"
15. The guest said, "Enough !"
16. The spectators said, "Bravo ! A good shot !"
17. He said, "fie, fie !"
18. I said, "What an idea !"
19. Democles said, "O, that I were a king !"
20. The worker said, "Oh ! For a breathing-space !"
21. They said, "How tiresome !"

जब Dialogues या किसी लम्बे passage को जिसमें अनेक प्रकार के वाक्य हों Indirect speech में बदलना हो तो भिन्न-भिन्न वाक्यों को जोड़ने के लिए वाक्य के भावानुसार *further* or *again + subject + verb (i.e. said)—ordered, added, remarked, reminded, warned, asked* etc.) जैसा करते हैं। अन्तिम वाक्य को Lastly (or finally) + subject + verb जैसा कर सकते हैं। कभी-कभी and, but, for, so इत्यादि conjunctions से भी सहायता ली जा सकेगी। यदि R.S. में किसी को सम्बोधित किया गया हो तो R.V. से पूर्व Addressing as, calling as, remarking as का प्रयोग कर वाक्य प्रारम्भ करें।

He said, "Brothers and sisters ! God is immanent."

Addressing as brothers and sisters, he said that God is immanent.

Some Solved Models

(From Intermediate General English)

1. "Friends, where are you coming from and what has brought you to this place ?" the villager asked the strangers. The strangers said, "We have come from the neighbouring city and want to start an adult literacy programme. Don't you think we ought to eradicate illiteracy from our country ?"

   Addressing as friends, the villager asked the strangers where they were coming from and what had brought them to that place. The strangers replied that they had come from the neighbouring city and wanted to start an adult-literacy programme. Lastly they enquired of him if he did not think they ought to eradicate illiteracy from their country.

2. "Is it your own composition ?" asked the editor. The writer said, "Yes, of course. Why do you ask this ?" "No offence," "said the editor." I just wanted to confirm that it wasn't borrowed from any other source."

   When the editor enquired of the writer if it was his own composition the latter firmly replied that of course it was and asked why the former asked that. The editor convinced that it was no offence for he had then wanted to confirm that it had not been borrowed from any other source.

3. Duke   : Shylock must execute the deed of gift or I shall revoke the pardon.

   Portia   : Are you satisfied Shylock ? What do you say ?

   Shylock : I am satisfied.

   Portia   : Clerk, please draw up a deed of gift.

   Shylock : Kindly permit me to go away, I am not well. Send the deed to my house and I will sign it.

   When the Duke pronounced that Shylock had to execute the deed of gift or he would revoke the pardon, Portia asked Shylock if he was satisfied and when she again enquired what he said, Shylock replied that he was satisfied. Then Portia requested the clerk to draw up a deed of gift. Finally, Shylock requested to permit him to go away because he was not well. He asked to send the deed to his house and assured that he would sign it.

4. The teacher became angry with the student and said, "Why have you disturbed the class in this way ? I have told you not to make a noise while I am teaching. Get out of the class and do not come again today."

   Becoming angry with the student, the teacher asked why he had disturbed the class in that way. He reminded that he had told him not to make a noise while he was teaching. Lastly he ordered to get out of the class and not to come again that day.

Exercise 1

Report the following into Indirect speech :

1. The teacher said, "Ram, have you done your home-work ? Bring the exercise book."
2. He said, "I am very tired. May I take a little rest ? I cannot walk anymore."
3. Ram said to Shyam, "Please take your seat. I am very glad to see you. Where had you been so long ?"
4. "How pretty you are !" said the fox to the crow. "I am sure that so beautiful a bird must have a beautiful voice. Will you not sing a few notes for me ?"
5. He said, "When do you intend to leave Mumbai ?" I said, "Today is the day of examination. I cannot leave now. I hope to do so tomorrow."
6. But the sea-god cried, "Do not be afraid, noble prince, I have taken pity on you and will help you."
7. Dashrath said to Vishwamitra, "Please do not insist on taking Ram and Lakshman with you. I am prepared to send my whole army with you."
8. "Thank you," said Jack, "but I am very well here, I will, if you please, argue the point from where I am."

9. Duke : "You are welcome. Take your seat. Are you acquainted with the facts of the case ?"

10. "I believe,'" said he, "that we are in this country among the people whom we like and who like us."

11. He said, "Take that bird away. Its gilded cage reminds me of my father whom I imprisoned."

12. "Friends," said the old man," sit down and rest yourselves here on this bench. My good wife Baucis had gone to see what you can have for super."

13. "Little sisters" he said, "it is my turn to speak. Keep silent and be very quiet till I have finished." He said to his companions. "Wait for me here and I will go and preach to my little sisters."

14. Virvar said to the woman, "Can nothing save our king ?" The woman said, "Yes, one thing can save the king's life. Give your life for the king just now and he will live."

15. "I can extend no other mercy to you," said the king, "except permitting you to choose what kind of death you wish to die. Decide immediately, for the sentence must be carried out."

16. "If you kill me," she cried, "I will say no other thing. If I were in the fire, I would say no more, and till death I will hold that what I have said is truth. I have done nothing against God or the faith."

17. "Have you finished your lesson, Mohan ?" said Ramesh to his son. "No, father," replied Mohan hanging down his head. "Why not my son ?" "Because it is so difficult, father I am sure I shall never learn it."

18. "You are wiser than you were, King Midas !," said the stranger, looking seriously at him. "Your own heart, I perceive has not entirely changed from flesh to gold. Were it so, your case would indeed be desperate. Tell me if you sincerely desire to rid yourself of this Golden Touch."

19. When the lords laughed he cried, "Wait, and I will bring the king such a gift as no man has ever seen. I will bring him the head of the Gorgon". "Go then," said the king, "and do not return till you bring it."

20. "Pardon me, dear master," said Ariel, "I will obey your commands." "Do so," said the master, "and I will set you free."

21. Her voices very plainly said, "Before the feast of saint John, Midsummer Day. You will be taken prisoner, but have no fear, be strong and of good courage, and God will help you."

22. Portia   : Mercy is never forced. It comes naturally. We should all show mercy to one another.

    Shylock   : I will have nothing to do with mercy. I ask for justice.

    Portia   : But justice should always be softened by mercy.

    Shylock   : I know of that. I must have what is due to me on my bond.

23. An old woman said, "Why do you come here ? And where are you going ?" "I am going to the queen," said the young man, "to whom I was to have taken a letter, but I have lost my way, and shall be glad if you give me a night's lodging."

24. Abou said to the Angel, "What are you writing ?" The Angel replied, "The names of those who love the lord." Abou said, "Is mine one ?" "Nay, not so," said the Angel.

25. Miranda : Heaven thank you, my dear father : Now pray tell me, Sir, your reason for raising this storm.

    Father   : Know then that by means of this storm my enemies are cast ashore upon this island.

26. "Forward, my men," said the General, "and face the foe bravely. It is true that they are more in numbers than we are, but what of that ? If we retreat now, Or women will scorn us and we shall be branded forever with the name of coward."

27. "I hope you are up in time." said the earth. "Every time I run round the sun, you must run thirteen times round me, else there will be a mistake in the almanac." "I have been running here long enough to know what I have to do, you ill tempered old planet," said the Moon.

28. Nal said to Damyanti, "The gods want to marry you. So choose one of them as your husband." Damyanti replied, "Please tell the gods that I have already chosen you." Nal said, "Don't choose me otherwise the gods will be angry." Damyanti said, "An Indian woman chooses her husband only once and I have chosen you."

29. The merchant said, "Young man ! Pardon me the liberty which I take in asking you how it happens that you always make use of your left hand, never your right. Has some accident happened to it ?"

30. When Phatik entered the house his mother called out angrily, "So you have been hitting Makhan again ?" Phatik answered indignantly, "No, I haven't. Who told you that ?" His mother shouted, "Don't tell lies. You have." Phatik said sullenly, "I tell you I haven't. You ask Makhan."

31. Shyam said, "Well Hari, how did you fare in the examination ?" "Oh I please do not talk about it." "But why ?" "I have done very badly. I am afraid I won't pass."

32. "Let me hire as a nurse for my poor children," said a butterfly to a quiet caterpillar, "See these little eggs. I don't know how long it will be before they came to life, and if I should die, who will take care of my baby butterflies ?"

33. She said to me, "I am afraid I cannot marry you. I know that you are very rich. But you are fifteen years older than I. Do you really think that I shall be happy with you ? I am doubtful of that."

34. "Naughty boy," said his mother, "You've been fighting again." "But I didn't start it, mother," said the boy protestingly, "he hit me first."

35. Mr. Sinha's secretary told the client, "You have come well in time. Please wait a bit. Mr. Sinha is dictating a plaint at the moment. He will be free very soon. Have you got your documents with you ? Let me see them if they are here."

36. The ant said to the cricket, "What were you doing all the summer ? Why do you beg from others instead of earning your food ? If you can while away the summer in singing and dancing, you can pass the autumn in the same way."

37. "Mother," replied Aladin, "keep your cotton for another time and give me the lamp I brought home with me yesterday. I will go and sell it, and will buy both breakfast and dinner, and perhaps supper too."

Chapter 14

Common Errors

जब किसी Incorrect sentence को correct करने के लिए दिया जाय तो सम्पूर्ण वाक्य के स्वरूप को बदलने के बजाय उसमें निहित सूक्ष्म त्रुटि को दूर करना चाहिए। सम्पूर्ण वाक्य को परिवर्तित करना सूक्ष्म त्रुटि को न समझने का संकेत देता है।

दृष्टान्त स्वरूप निम्नस्थ वाक्यों का अध्ययन करें—

Incorrect	Correct
1. Ram told Mohan that his brother met with an accident.	Ram told Mohan that his brother had met with an accident.
2. Necessary knows no law.	Necessity knows no law.
3. If I was you, I would do this.	If I were you, I should do this.
4. It is one of those questions that is often set in the examination.	It is one of those questions that are often set in the examination.
5. Many a soldier die in the battle field.	Many a soldier dies in the battlefield.
6. The thieves ran away before the constables reached.	The thieves had run away before the constables reached.
7. I told to him that I am not well.	I told him that I was not well.
8. I prevented him to beat the child.	I prevented him from beating the child.
9. Everyone of the boys were interested in cricket.	Everyone of the boys was interested in cricket.
10. I aim to get the first position in the class.	I aim at getting the first position in the class.
11. If I knew this before, I would have surely told you.	If I had known this before, I should have surely told you.
12. I want to avail this opportunity.	I want to avail myself this opportunity.
13. He is senior than you.	He is senior to you.
14. I hope you will excuse me leaving early.	I hope you will excuse my leaving early.
15. Lights travel faster than sounds.	Light travels faster than sound.
16. These news have disturbed the peace of my mind.	This news has (or these pieces of news have) disturbed the peace of my mind.
17. If he will come here I shall help him.	If he comes here, I shall help him.
18. He has come here yesterday.	He came here yesterday.
19. All the furnitures of my room are sixes and sevens.	All the articles of furniture of my room are at sixes and sevens.
20. Being a hot day, I could not go out.	It being a hot day, I could not go out.

21. He jumped in the river.   He jumped into the river.

22. I shall order for the book at once.   I shall order the book at once.

23. He wants to dispose his cycle off.   He wants to dispose of his cycle.

24. Your fault does not admit any excuse.   Your fault does not admit any excuses.

25. I like my friend's dog who is a good man.   I like the dog of my friend who is a good man.

26. Neither of the students got the prize they expected.   None of the students got the prize they expected.

27. It is I who is your best friend.   It is I who am your best friend.

28. The poet and scholar are dead.   The poet and scholar is dead.

29. How a foolish plan it is !   What a foolish plan it is !

30. Either the step is right or wrong.   The step is either right or wrong.

31. You need not to worry.   You need not worry.

32. I have been knowing her since her childhood.   I have known her since her childhood.

33. Who did go with you to movie ?   Who went with you to the movies ?

34. Kindly tell me where can I meet him.   Kindly tell me where I can meet him.

35. He is laid down with fever.   He is laid up with fever.

36. They have left the town last year.   They had left the town last year.

37. He is waiting for you since morning.   He has been waiting for you since morning.

38. The flowers smell sweetly.   The flowers smell sweet.

39. Walk slowly lest you may not fall.   Walk slowly lest you should fall.

40. He looks never sad.   He never looks sad.

41. No sooner I reached the station, the train left.   No sooner did I reach the station than the train left.

42. If you worked hard, you would have passed.   If you had worked hard, you would have passed.

43. He is the member of an union.   He is the member of a union.

44. It is not me who is in love with you.   It is not I who am in love with you.

45. We enjoyed during the holidays.   We enjoyed ourselves during the holidays.

46. My brother married with his cousin sister.   My brother married his cousin.

47. I saw many dead soldiers riding across the battlefield.   Riding across the battlefield, I saw many dead soldiers.

48. She is a famous actor.   She is a famous actress.

49. I asked him where did he live.   I asked him where he lived.

50. I went for seeing my friend.   I went to see my friend.

51. He looks at me from suspicion.   He looks at me with suspicion.

52. He is a M.A. in English.   He is an M.A. in English.

53. He suffered from cold.   He suffered from a cold.

54. His answer was such which I expected.   His answer was such as I expected.

55. He is the most best boy in the class.   He is the best boy in the class.

56. This nut is hard to be cracked.   This nut is hard to crack.

57. He is too weak that he cannot walk.

He is so weak that he cannot walk.
Or He is too weak to walk.

58. I advised him to not make noise.

I advised him not to make a noise.

59. Your teacher is enough pleased with you.

Your teacher is much pleased with you.

60. On which of these chairs did you sit ?

Which of these chairs did you sit on ?

61. He soon will return home.

He will soon return home.

62. That is the man for whom we were look-ing.

That is the man whom we were looking for.

63. He not only built a house but a garage also.

He built not only a house but a garage also.

64. It is not for I but for he and she to decide.

It is not for me but for him and her to decide.

65. Listen what I say.

Listen to what I say.

66. He left this place with bag and baggage.

He left this place bag and baggage.

67. Burn the lamp, it is getting dark.

Light up the lamp, it is getting dark.

68. I do not know who are you ?

I do not know who you are.

69. Neither of them saw one another.

None of them saw one another.

70. What do speak of helping me, he did not even speak to me.

Not to speak of helping me, he did not even speak to me.

71. Unless you do not labour hard, you will not pass.

Unless you labour hard, you will not pass.

72. He came on both days.

He came on both the days.

73. He is a right man in the right place.

He is right man in the right place.

74. He fought with tooth and nail.

He fought tooth and nail.

75. His house is better than I.

His house is better than mine.

76. Tell me when are you going.

Tell me when you are going.

77. Either he or his friend have done this work.

Either he or his friend has done this work.

78. His all works proved fruitful.

All his work proved fruitful.

79. The gamblers saw a police and ran away.

The gamblers saw a policeman and ran away.

80. The gentries of his kingdom were happy.

The gentry of his kingdom were happy.

81. All posts are reserved for the poors.

All posts are reserved for the poor.

82. Keat's work are charged with sensual beauty.

Keats' works are charged with sensual beauty.

83. Will you keep your words ?

Will you keep your word ?

84. Two-third of your informations are fab-ricated.

Two-third of your information are fabricated.

85. As I felt out of sort, I did not go out of door.

As I felt out of sorts, I did not go out of door.

86. We must carry out the order of the teacher who taught us the English alpha-bet.

We must carry out the orders of the teacher who taught us the English alphabet.

87. She has now gone to sleep.

She has now gone to bed.

88. His family members are very gentle. — The members of his family are very gentle.

89. I have an urgent work in the office. — I have an urgent piece of work in the office.

90. He borned in 1975. — He was born in 1975.

91. He failed in English. — He failed to get a pass in English or to qualify in English.

92. The physician found the patient living. — The physician found the patient alive.

93. Do you like to swim ? — Do you like swimming ? or (how to swim ?)

94. A lot of men was going in the fair. — A lot of men were going in the fair.

95. Lots of sugar were in the cup. — Lots of sugar was in the cup.

96. Half of the mango are rotten. — Half of the mangoes are rotten.

97. A pair of shoes were torn. — A pair of shoes was torn.

98. More than one workers were on strike. — More than one worker was on strike.

99. A number of boys was absent. — A number of boys were absent.

100. The number of beasts were assembled there. — The number of beasts was assembled there.

101. He returned to the home. — He returned home.

102. What is your birth day ? — What is the date of your birth ?

103. Either of the two sisters are tall. — Either of the two sisters is tall.

104. There is no place in this bus. — There is no room in this bus.

105. Service is more preferable than business. — Service is preferable to business.

106. One should love his country. — One should love one's country.

107. I know him a truthful man. — I know him to be a truthful man.

108. Always he boasts his achievements. — He always boasts of his achievements.

109. We shall discuss to the matter tomorrow. — We shall discuss the matter tomorrow.

110. The reason of his success is owing to diligence. — The reason of his success is diligence.

111. I am too glad to see you. — I am very glad to see you.

112. He talks English well. — He speaks English well.

113. Your brother is the most perfect gentleman. — Your brother is a perfect gentleman.

114. He believed me a scholar. — He believed me to be a scholar.

115. No one cared for him after he came home. — No one took care of him after he had come home.

116. He has given the examination. — He has taken (or sat for) the examination or appeared at the examination.

117. The condition of the patient is comparatively better to day. — The condition of the patient is better to day (or comparatively good to day).

118. Ten years passed since I saw you. — Ten years have passed since I saw you.

119. The climate of Ceylone is hotter than India. — The climate or Ceylone is hotter than that of India.

120. There was no other alternative but fight. — There was no alternative other than fight.

121. I congratulated him for his good fortune. — I congratulated him on his good fortune.

122. The boat drowned and fifty men sank in the river.

The boat sank and fifty men drowned in the river.

123. I said to him that why he was sad.

I asked him why he was sad.

124. Edison discovered the electric bulb.

Edison invented the electric bulb.

125. He hanged the stick on the hook.

He hung the stick from the hook.

126. Sita the wife of Ram she also went with him in the forest.

Sita the wife of Ram also went with him in the forest.

127. I am ill of the whole business.

I am sick of the whole business.

128. He said me a liar.

He called me a liar.

129. People should not throw stones who live in glass houses.

People who live in glass houses should not throw stones.

130. He hurriedly wrote the letter.

He wrote the letter hurriedly.

131. The wind was calm, the path clear.

The wind was calm ; the path was clear.

132. He never has, and never will take wrong steps.

He has never taken and will never take wrong steps.

133. He advised us to slowly go ahead.

He advised us to go ahead slowly.

134. Sitting at the gate, a dog jumped over me.

While I was sitting at the gate a dog jumped over me.

135. He returned quicker than I expected.

He returned more quickly than I expected.

136. I never remember having met him.

I do not remember having met him ever.

137. His dress was bright and beautiful.

Her dress was bright and beautiful.

138. The post of a lecturer in English has fallen empty in the college.

The post of a lecturer in English has fallen vacant in this college.

139. Five men lost their life in the incident.

Five men lost their life in the accident.

140. Descretion is a better part of bravery.

Descretion is a better part of valour.

141. Sketch the conduct of Julius Caesar.

Sketch the character of Julius Caesar.

142. He is sick these days.

He is ill these days.

143. O God, excuse me for my sins.

O God, forgive me for my sins.

144. He denied to appoint him.

He refused to appoint him.

145. Reply any five questions.

Answer any five questions.

146. The wrestler had ability to lift the heavy box.

The wrestler had capacity to lift the heavy box.

147. I am not among those who believes everything I hear.

I am not among those who believe everything they hear.

148. He suggested me a new style of writing.

He suggested to me a new style of writing.

149. Until the world lasts, the story will go.

So long as the world lasts, the story will go.

150. We have five fingers in each hand.

We have five fingers on each hand.

151. Scarcely had I arrived that it began to rain.

Scarcely had I arrived when it began to rain.

152. He runs faster than me.

He runs faster than I.

153. He was always sitting near the temple.

He always sat near the temple.

154. I feel as if I am swimming in the sky.

I feel as if I were swimming in the sky.

155. He thought he will reach in time.   He thought he would reach in time.
156. They went through a thick forest.   They went through a dense forest.
157. Neither he comes nor helps.   He neither comes nor helps.
158. Not he was hungry but also thirsty.   He was not only hungry but also thirsty.
159. Seeing is to believe.   Seeing is believing.
160. Which do you think about it ?   What do you think about it ?
161. Where your father has gone ?   Where has your father gone ?
162. The house was reduced in ashes.   The house was burnt to ashes.
163. The road was well cemented.   The road was well metalled.
164. Your help is next for nothing.   Your help is next to nothing.
165. We should follow on the footsteps of mighty minds.   We should follow the footsteps of mighty minds.
166. They failed a victim of superstitions.   They fell a victim of superstitions.
167. He has died yesterday.   He died yesterday.
168. He refused that he had made a mistake.   He denied that he had made a mistake.
169. No lady was more beautiful than her.   No lady was more beautiful than she.
170. He is a coward fellow.   He is a cowardly fellow.
171. We should try for the upliftment of the villagers.   We should try for the uplift of the villagers.
172. I cannot tell where he lives.   I cannot say where he lives.
173. He will accompany with us.   He will accompany us.
174. He tried his best that he may get through.   He tried his best so that he might get through.
175. I wish I may be a child again.   I wish I were a child again.
176. No less than fifty boys were present.   No fewer than fifty boys were present.
177. As you are clever so you can explain it.   As you are clever, you can explain it.
178. He can speak the English fluently.   He can speak English fluently.
179. His face resembles with his father.   His face resembles the face of his father.
180. The selection of poems are praiseworthy.   The selection of poems is praiseworthy.
181. He is fond of ride.   He is fond of riding.
182. I did not find no one in the field.   I did not find anyone in the field.
183. Walking is an useful exercise.   Walking is a useful exercise.
184. He is a good player of the hockey.   He is a good player of hockey.
185. Much water has flown.   Much water has flowed.
186. He was sent to the prison.   He was sent to prison.
187. I am ill for four days.   I have been ill for four days.
188. Switch the candle off.   Blow out the candle.
189. Unless you do not work hard, you will not succeed.   Unless you work hard, you will not succeed.
190. He had come yesterday.   He came yesterday.
191. The work was completed tomorrow.   The work was completed yesterday.
192. I have to do many homeworks.   I have to do much homework.
193. The weather of U.P. is beneficial for health.   The climate of U.P. is beneficial for health.

194. Your girl is clever at mathematics.	Your daughter is clever at mathematics.
195. Good night, the news is as follow.	Good evening, the news is as follows.
196. He arrived here by a car.	He arrived here by car.
197. He looks sadly.	He looks sad.
198. The five first lessons are didactics.	The first five lessons are didactic.
199. I do not know to swim.	I do not know to swim.
200. He gave a speech.	He made a speech.
201. I am sorry at what I have done.	I am sorry for what I have done.

Exercise 1

Correct the following sentences :

1. He fears from walking alone in the night.
2. Tell me where have you kept the umbrella.
3. Balu is taller to all other boys.
4. Listen what I say.
5. Give me a pen to write.
6. Nothing but detective novels delight me.
7. Close the light.
8. Fill water in the jug.
9. My foot is paining.
10. I have bought a horse yesterday.

Answers

1. fears to walk ...... at night	2. Where you have	3. taller than
4. listen to	5. Write with	6. delights
7. put out (or put off, switch off)	8. fill the jug	9. is aching
10. I bought (or to day in place of yesterday)		

Exercise 2

1. John is the smallest of the two boys.
2. Every man and every child were lost in the storm.
3. Do you know the man which came to see you ?
4. He told me that he will come.
5. Have you not applied for the mastery ?
6. The number of the candidates are large.
7. Either of those three boys have hidden my handkerchief.
8. He is ill since a week.
9. The iron is an useful metal.
10. He is too beneficent to help me.

Answers

1. smaller	2. was lost	3. man who
4. would	5. (the post of master)	6. is large
7. Anyone of ..... has	8. has been ill for	9. Iron ...... a useful
10. is beneficent enough.		

Exercise 3

1. It is a nice poetry.
2. Which is best ...... milk or tea ?
3. The teacher as well as the boys were laughing.
4. Neither of the two sisters are intelligent.
5. It is one of the best medicine that is efficacious for health.
6. It is not my way to deserting people's interests.
7. How will I do it ?
8. I did not see him since he came.
9. Lay down because you are tired.
10. They were awaiting for me at the station.

Answers

1. poem
2. better
3. was
4. is
5. medicines that are
6. office to desert (or province to desert)
7. Shall
8. have not seen
9. lie down
10. awaiting me (or waiting for).

Exercises 4

1. He ran fastly.
2. He drunked two glasses of water.
3. He maked a pitcher.
4. Tooking my stick, he chased the cat.
5. His father was died long ago.
6. Many a man run after wealth.
7. The horse and carriage are at the door.
8. His family members are happy.
9. Do you know the alphabets of English ?
10. Many sheeps were grazing in the meadow.

Answers

1. fast
2. drank
3. made
4. taking
5. father had died
6. runs
7. is
8. The members of his family
9. alphabet
10. Many heads of sheep.

Exercise 5

1. Either he is innocent or guilty.
2. He is slow and sure.
3. He tried his best but stood first.
4. It is a five-member's committee.
5. I reached there before it rained.
6. Why you did not reply ?
7. I was discouraged to read English by my friend.
8. This pen is much more cheaper than that.

9.   They invited my friend and I to tea.
10. He came to me every five hour.

Answers

1. is either
2. but sure
3. and stood
4. five-member
5. had reached
6. did you
7. from reading
8. Much cheaper
9. and me
10. fifth.

Exercise 6

1.   When he entered in the room then he noticed a snake.
2.   If you will come to me then I will help you.
3.   Although he is strong yet he has no courage.
4.   As you are tall so you can catch the broken kite.
5.   He was found guilty so he was sent to the prison.
6.   Do you like the way she will smile ?
7.   Which way is he looks going ?
8.   I have no any friend.
9.   You will hear enough soon.
10. He said he will never manage it.

Answers

1.   entered the room
2.   you come to me I
3.   is strong, he has
4.   are tall you can
5.   to prison
6.   she smiles
7.   looking
8.   no friend (or not any friends)
9.   soon enough
10. that he would.

Exercise 7

1.   He can had three wins and no defeats.
2.   While there is a life there is a hope.
3.   He believed that there is something in the wind.
4.   The voluntary organizations have and will rescue the people from the debris.
5.   He struck him with the sword.
6.   Fifty miles are a long distance.
7.   When will he come yesterday ?
8.   His all books are at sixes and sevens.
9.   Science knew but art did.
10. It is only the donkey who brays.

Answers

1.   has had
2.   is life .... is hope
3.   there was
4.   have rescued
5.   He killed
6.   miles is
7.   When did (or write tomorrow in place of yesterday)
8.   All his books
9.   knows ...... does
10. that brays.

Exercise 8

1.   Her son is an efficient mechanic man.
2.   His behaviour was an insulty to me.

3. Are you doubting my ability ?
4. I heard him to say.
5. The outermost walls are to be painted.
6. She has not taken some food for two days.
7. Bring five dozens bunches of bananas.
8. The poor man squeezed to death in the crowd.
9. His poetries are spontaneous overflow of powerful feelings.
10. His was the most ardent spirits of his time.

Answers

1. mechanic	**2.** insult	**3.** Do you doubt
4. him say	**5.** outer	**6.** any food
7. dozen hands of	**8.** was squeezed	**9.** poems
10. spirit.		

Exercise 9

1. He has pronounced an eulogy on him.
2. Send an immediate answer.
3. Our motoes are small profit and quick return.
4. He braked the jug in pieces.
5. Stick not bill here.
6. Not only he repented but also wept bitterly.
7. She is a poet of no mean repute.
8. A company of robbers was attacked by a flock of hounds.
9. I have read this novel more than one.
10. Once meat is another man's poison.

Answers

1. a eulogy	**2.** reply	**3.** profits returns
4. broke into	**5.** no bills	**6.** He not only
7. poetess	**8.** gang (or band) of robbers, pack of hounds	
9. than once	**10.** One's meat.	

Exercise 10

1. She sat besides me.
2. His all informations are precise.
3. He is a hard worked man.
4. A black bird in the spring is lovable to all.
5. He has no word to express my gratitude.
6. We were out of the woods.
7. To all his learning, he is the simplest of men.
8. The deer ran fastly.
9. I and he were fast friends.
10. The fox together with all the beasts were assembled there.

Answers

1. beside
2. All his pieces of information
3. hard working
4. black-bird
5. words
6. wood
7. with all
8. fast
9. He and I
10. was.

More Exercises Without Answers

Exercise 1

Correct the following sentences if necessary :

1. The water is colourless.
2. Only the remain of the civilization can be seen there.
3. The table's leg is broken.
4. The soldiers were in high spirit.
5. The whole surrounding appeared occult and woeful.
6. He has no brain.
7. The brother of Ram's was very faithful.
8. The United States are a rich country.
9. Where are you going Mr. ?
10. My girl can speak the English fluently.
11. The mangoes taste sourly.
12. She plays on piano.
13. I bought a soap rich in fragrance.
14. There were a lot of trouble.
15. Pages after pages are charged with lots of humours.
16. Lots of tear was trickled by her.
17. Most of the plan was not implicated.
18. A great deal of food grains was rotted.
19. He looked sadly.
20. Your radio is more cheaper than me.
21. We walked the end of the road.
22. We ate our heart content.
23. Your hair need cut.
24. The scooter requires service.
25. When you will repent then I shall forgive you.
26. We had finished our work before you will come.
27. It's high time that you try.
28. Do you like to coming here ?
29. Be careful lest you will lose.
30. He died of a shock.

Exercise 2

Put these sentences in their correct forms :

1. I shall no go out until it rains.
2. She will not eat, not drink.

3. A group of students were standing there.
4. A crowd of angry mob were crying.
5. A series of lectures were not sufficient.
6. Many a child do not go to school.
7. More than one chairs were in the corner.
8. I do not like these kind of men.
9. Heaps of broken furnitures were kept there.
10. Your scissors is blunt.
11. We stayed there for few days.
12. My sister is older than I.
13. This umbrella is the cheapest of the two.
14. The fox is a cleverer beast.
15. No less than five boys were making noises.
16. The man is mortal.
17. Light travels move fastly than sound.
18. The honesty is a best policy.
19. He arrived by the bus.
20. The letter was written by the mistake.
21. He is a man of letter but your father is a man of part.
22. The child is now out of the danger.
23. It was an unique dawn.
24. Dog is faithful animal.
25. The building was made of bricks and stones.
26. The Everest is a highest peak in Himalayas.
27. It is me who is your best mentor.
28. I and you have not done your duty.
29. Either of the three sisters are wise.
30. What is the day to day ?

Exercise 3

Correct each of the following sentences if necessary :

1. What a ravishing sight is it !
2. Alas ! I am blessed with a windfall.
3. The hermit said to me, "Your race may survive !"
4. He resigned to his fate.
5. I saw a delightful dream last night.
6. Let you and me sit here for a while.
7. Where have you loosed your pen ?
8. What did cause the fire ?
9. Come, if you wished.
10. Who did accompany you in the woods ?
11. This is one of the best models which I have found.

12. How much this tonic costs these days ?
13. He is fallen evil days.
14. Now what you mean by it ?
15. Myself solved all the sums.
16. Why you are not going there ?
17. Hardly the teacher had left the room than the boys began to make noises.
18. Shall you please do me a service ?
19. You need not to speak to me.
20. No one did not help her.
21. Only he has come yesterday.
22. He dare not to come here.
23. Who is owning this car ?
24. He has already footed the bill.
25. Had you helped me I should have succeeded.
26. It has been thought for long.
27. She carried it in a fold of his dress.
28. I for one, does not believe it.
29. The pathetic sight forced tears from his eyes.
30. He founded a solution.

Exercise 4

Correct these Sentences :

1. Crown was the fountain of honour.
2. I will make him to lick the dust.
3. The window will not opened.
4. The teacher said that a miss was as good as a mile.
5. He is fond to play cards.
6. Stop to write.
7. She got a letter write by me.
8. I have had already a chance.
9. God is called to be immanent by them.
10. We were surprised by his behaviour.
11. Who saw him go out ?
12. How many have you books ?
13. The sight was really much enchanting.
14. We were very amused by his talks.
15. He always are happy.
16. The room is enough specious for us.
17. He had to eat to a humble pie.
18. The dog was faithful with his master.
19. Unless you will not try, you will not succeed.
20. Do not go in the rain lest you will fall ill.

21. He is very intelligent and careless.
22. Most of us desires to make money quickly.
23. More is meant than met the ear.
24. He was more frightened than hurted.
25. It will go hard to him.
26. He believed in the philosophy of happy go lucky.
27. You are much reduced since I saw you recently.
28. He was very annoyed at her decision.
29. You must have known well quite what did I meant.
30. The whole atmosphere of the play is wrapped in mysterious.
31. He is a man of beneficial character.
32. Nearer it resembles him less I like it.
33. He was sure that his hope will come to fulfilment.
34. The necessary of protecting life and property are felt today.
35. He felt very ashamed.
36. He was Shylock of his province.
37. Saint and sinner is rewarded alike.
38. The weather was fairly cold.

Exercise 5

Correct the mistakes, if necessary, in the following sentences :

1. His clothe was shabby.
2. The child hankered after the affectation of the mother.
3. Are you illegible for the post ?
4. His economical condition was much concerning.
5. He was a populous man.
6. We have all ready done it.
7. Though I was loath but I attended the meeting.
8. Both contentment and avarice cannot go side by side.
9. You will have arrived before I shall finish the work.
10. His theme has been treated false, faked and fictitious.
11. I asked him that when he had came.
12. I came, I saw but I conquered.
13. He that excuses himself, accuses himself.
14. It is him that has spoiled her life.
15. Myself revenged on him.
16. I have gone through Gokhale's speeches who was the disciple of Ranaday.
17. One should be proud of his native land.
18. Neither of the roads lead to eternity.
19. Where is our real annal ?
20. Popularities are not great measures of merit.
21. Most of Keats' odes sound a note of sadness.

22. Francis 'The Hounds of Heaven' present occult and nebulous pictures.
23. I got the portrait hang on the cross-road.
24. The horrid drought caused us starve.
25. He made the boys laughed.
26. Villages after villages were destroyed.
27. Let me to sleep.
28. Is there any morality to draw ?
29. You might try if I advise.
30. Success is a question of time merely.
31. He suddenly dismounted from the horse.
32. Never have we heard such improbability.
33. The moon was gliding silently in the sky.
34. Happily give me your helping hand.
35. The milk is enough pure.
36. Our lives are satire on our religion.
37. All world was gay.
38. The silver is second rated metal.

Exercise 6

Correct the following Sentences :

1. Till you account him a noble man, you will be deceived.
2. Wait until it rains.
3. Though my purse is empty but my patience is ample.
4. Although she shed copious tears yet no body took pity on her.
5. Till he thrashes we should unfold the sheaves.
6. Many a men have tried.
7. The quality of these guavas are nice.
8. The number of application was limited.
9. The horse and carriage were at the door.
10. Each of the boys were rewarded.
11. Open at the latest page.
12. He gave no farther remarks.
13. What is the last news ?
14. He has read only few books of Bernard Shaw.
15. Several senses tore my mind.
16. There is few water in the jug.
17. He was an unsuccessful and the most unfortunate king.
18. This specimen is superior than that.
19. It is a calm and free beauteous evening.
20. It proved a blanket much small for the bed.
21. The lady that eyes are blue is a spy.
22. This is the same case which has been discussed.

23. They never fail who die in a great cause.
24. The table whom you bought is broken.
25. Blessed are they that mourn.
26. Neither the realm of fancy nor abound wealth have any truth.
27. The army have launched his furious attack.
28. Each of the pages were sparkling with wit.
29. More than one planes were downed.
30. The editor and essayist are dead.
31. Every flower and every bud were trampled.
32. Judge not lest you will be judged.
33. Lots of misfortunes awaits for him.
34. Leave none stone unturned, not corner unsought.
35. There was a heaps of broken images.
36. He does nothing than laugh.
37. When their glory faded ?
38. What I am a good king ?
39. What fool he is !
40. They also serve who only stands and waits.

Chapter 15

Synthesis of Sentences

Synthesis means combination, putting together (opp. to analysis) अर्थात् संश्लेषण, समन्वय, समीकरण। अनेक छोटे-छोटे वाक्यों को मिलाकर एक लम्बा वाक्य बनाना synthesis कहलाता है। इस तरह से बने वाक्य simple, complex or compound हो सकते हैं। इसमें यथासंभव कम-से-कम finite verb का प्रयोग करना चाहिए।

1. Combination of Simple Sentences into a Simple Sentence

Simple sentence बनाते समय यह ध्यान रखें कि इसमें एक ही subject तथा एक ही finite verb रहे। एक से अधिक रहने पर वह complex or compound sentence हो सकता है, simple नहीं। Simple sentence बनाने के लिए निम्नस्थ नियमों की सहायता ली जा सकती है।

1. By Using a Participle

Participle के तीन भेद–

(i) Present Participle i.e., verb में ing लगाकर

(ii) Past Participle i.e., verb³ को qualified word के साथ रखकर

(iii) Perfect Participle i.e., having + verb³

(a) जब प्रस्तुत वाक्यों का subject एक हो किन्तु finite verb भिन्न भिन्न हों। इसमें एक कार्य पूर्व में (पूर्वकालिक क्रिया) तथा अन्य पश्चात् में सम्पन्न हुआ रहता है। ऐसी स्थिति में जो क्रिया पहले हो चुकी हो उसे present या perfect participle में बदलकर वाक्य प्रारम्भ करें और बाद की क्रिया वाले वाक्य को यथावत् रखें। जैसे–

He drew the sword. He killed the lion.

इसमें sword को draw करने का कार्य पहले और lion को kill करने का काम बाद में हुआ है। अतः

Drawing the sword, he killed the lion.

Or

Having drawn the sword, he killed the lion.

प्रथम कार्य की समाप्ति पर comma का प्रयोग करें।

Note. Present तथा Perfect participle में अन्तर यह है कि यदि कार्य वर्तमान काल का हो या सभी क्रियाएँ लगभग एक ही समय में सम्पन्न हुई हों तो Present participle का प्रयोग उचित होगा किन्तु एक क्रिया के पहले ही यदि दूसरी क्रिया हो चुकी हो तो Perfect participle का प्रयोग करें, जैसे–

I took my pen. I began to write.

—Taking my pen, I began to write.

He had finished his work, he returned home.

(प्रथम कार्य पहले हो चुका था। अतः)

—Having finished his work, he returned home.

(b) यदि subjects भिन्न हो जाएँ एवं दूसरी क्रिया प्रथम कार्य के object द्वारा सम्पन्न हो तो उसे पश्चात् वाली क्रिया से जोड़ें–

> I noticed a girl. She was carrying a pitcher on her head.

Pitcher को carry करने का काम प्रथम वाक्य का object (girl) कर रहा है, अत:

> I noticed a girl carrying a pitcher on her head.

(c) By Past Participle–

> He found his pen. It was lost.
> —He found his lost pen.
> I met the teacher. He was retired.
> —I met the retired teacher.

(d) जब प्रथम क्रिया Passive Voice में हो तो being + verb³ etc. or having been + verb³ etc. से वाक्य बनाएँ।

> He was driven by thirst. He went near the brook.
> —Being driven by thirst, he went near the brook.
> I was deceived by my friend. I left his company.
> —Being deceived by my friend (or having been deceived by my friend), I left his company.
> He entered the room. He opened the window.
> He sat down to read.
> —Entering the room and opening the window, he sat down to read.

Exercise 1

Combine each set of sentences into one simple sentence by using participles :

1. Turn to the right. You will then find the house.
2. The hermit took pity on the mouse. He turned it into a cat.
3. She was tired of reading. She lay down in bed.
4. He jumped up. He ran away.
5. He lost his book. He searched for it.
6. The physician finished his work. He went to hospital.
7. The warrior drew his sword. He attacked his foe.
8. I wrote the letter hurriedly. I went out to post it.
9. She put out the lamp. She began to take a nap.
10. The old man blazed up in anger. He pounced upon the man.
11. They noticed an occult shadow. They took to their heels.
12. She went home. She had a cup of tea.
13. I bought a table. It was made of fine wood.
14. He was laughed at. He felt ashamed.
15. The children were frightened. They began to weep.
16. She entered into the flames. She took away her burning child.
17. My uncle caught the kite. It was torn.
18. He was taught well. He became a scholar.
19. He raised his gun. He took aim. He shot the deer.
20. He took the ball. He put it in the centre. He kicked it.

Exercise 2

1. We reached the foot of the hill. We aroused the shepherd.
2. I stood eastward. I noticed a unique dawn.
3. The deer heard a murmur in the forest. It ran away.
4. She went in. She found some magazines. They were lying on the table.
5. She gathered the figs. They were fallen from the tree.
6. Bharat went near the mother. She was bereft.
7. We were disappointed. We abandoned the scheme.
8. The boys saw a butterfly. They ran after it.
9. The two foxes saw an ox. The ox was lying wounded by the path.
10. The king heard a strange sound. He shot an arrow straight.
11. The child broke the toy. He began to weep.
12. The manager became angry. He threw the papers.
13. We were walking along the road. We noticed a scorpion.
14. He built a luxurious house. He is now living in it.
15. The soldier fought for the noble cause. He sacrificed his life.
16. A man jumped up from his seat. He went on the stage. He began to speak in emotion.
17. The boy set his books aside. He locked the door. He went to the pictures.
18. The lion came near the river. He gazed at a deer. He chased it.
19. We saw many kinds of birds in the forest. They were hopping upon the twigs. They were singing sweet songs.
20. The king was defeated. He was bereft of his kingdom. He escaped from the capital.

2. By Using an Infinitive

(a) जब प्रस्तुत वाक्यों में से किसी में Infinitive (to + verb[1]) रहे तथा किसी purpose (उद्देश्य) का संकेत दे। ऐसी स्थिति में पहले बिना infinitive वाले वाक्य को चुनें और बाद में उसे infinitive से जोड़ दें।

I went to the station. I was to see off my sister.

यहाँ station जाने का purpose see off करना था। अत:

—I went to the station to see off my sister.

I bought the book. I wished to read it thoroughly.

—I bought the book to read thoroughly.

(b) जब प्रस्तुत वाक्यों में से किसी में ... very, too, much आदि के साथ Adjective या Adverb रहे तथा अन्य में इसके परिणामस्वरूप सामर्थ्य के भाव में can/helping verb तथा असमर्थता के भाव में cannot/helping verb के साथ negative भाव (नकारात्मक, अशक्यता) रहे तो ... too + adj/adv + infinitive जैसा करें। सामर्थ्य के लिए adj/adv + enough + infinitive के क्रम में वाक्य को इस प्रकार बनाएँ–

He was very weak. He could not walk easily.

—He was too weak to walk easily.

She is very kind. She can help you.

—She is kind enough to help you.

He is too miserly. He cannot help you.

—He is too miserly to help you.

Exercise 1

Combine the following sets of sentences into a single simple sentence :

1. He bought a bicycle. He wanted to do his work quickly.
2. I went to Allahabad. My purpose was to see my son.
3. He sent his son to England. He wanted to educate him.
4. He took a rod. He intended to beat his enemy.
5. She has two daughters. She must provide for them.
6. I have appointed a servant. He will cook my food.
7. They heard the news of my success. They were much pleased.
8. Mr. Gandhi was a great man. It was accounted by all.
9. I went to my aunt's house. I wanted to see my ailing cousin.
10. Hari ran fast. He wanted to get the first prize.
11. He could not prepare well for the examination. He had not sufficient time.
12. He keeps a fierce dog. His purpose is to guard his house.
13. You cannot do this job. You have no time for it.
14. She wished to stand first. She worked hard.
15. He thinks seriously. He desires to amass money.
16. This coffee is very hot. One cannot take it.
17. He is very tall. He can catch the broken kite.
18. You are a great coward. You cannot face your enemy.
19. This room is too small. We all cannot get in.
20. I have got very fat. I cannot wear this dress now.
21. The student was very clever. He could solve all sums.
22. I am much excited. I cannot think.
23. The accident is too terrible. We cannot talk about it.
24. She is quite old. She cannot do better.
25. You are very strong. You can lift this trunk.
26. The river was very narrow. We could cross it.
27. The light is much dim. I cannot read easily.
28. The current was very strong. One could not swim against it.
29. He is very wise. He can decide the case properly.
30. The orange was too sour. They could not taste it.

3. By Using a Noun or a Phrase in Apposition

Apposition means 'placing side by side (समानाधिकरण, पार्श्वबद्धता) 'Placing of word in syntactic parallelism with another, especially addition of one noun to another.' (C.O.D.) अर्थात् वाक्य-रचनानुसार किसी Noun के समानान्तर अन्य Noun को रखना। इसका प्रयोग उस समय करें जब एक ही Noun का अनेक वाक्यों में वर्णन, व्याख्या या परिचय दिया गया हो अर्थात् उसके बारे में कुछ और बातें वर्णित हों। ऐसी स्थिति में Noun के पश्चात् उसकी व्याख्या या परिचय वाले भाग को रखें जिसके दोनों ओर commas का प्रयोग करें। यही भाग Apposition कहलाता है। जैसे—

(a)   Milton was a great poet. He was the writer of the 'Paradise Lost.'

यहाँ दूसरा वाक्य प्रथम वाक्य के Noun (Milton) के विषय में कुछ विशेष परिचय प्रस्तुत करता है। अत:

—Milton, the writer of the 'Paradise Lost', was a great poet.

Or

Milton, a great poet, was the writer of the 'Paradise Lost.'

(b)   My brother is a famous scholar. He is a man of talent.

—My brother, a man of talent, is a famous scholar.

Or

My brother, a famous scholar, is a man of talent.

(c)   Sikri was once a prosperous town. It is now a place of resort.

—Sikri, once a prosperous town, is now a place of resort.

(d)   I met my old friend. He is a reputed physician.

—I met my old friend, a reputed physician.

(e)   Columbus was a famous sea man. He discovered The New World.

—Columbus, a famous sea man, discovered The New World.

Or

Columbus, the discoverer of The New World, was a famous sea man.

Note. ध्यान रखें कि प्रस्तुत वाक्यों में से किसी एक ही के verb का चयन हो। इस सन्दर्भ में verb to be का लोप करना सुविधाजनक होगा, जैसा कि अन्तिम उदाहरण में है।

This is my friend. His name is Balu. He is the son of Bhola.
Bhola is a rich farmer of my village.

—This is my friend Balu, the son of Bhola, a rich farmer of my village.

Pandit Nehru was a great man. He was the son of Moti Lal Nehru. He was the first Prime Minister of India.

—The first Prime Minister of India, Pandit Nehru, the son of Moti Lal Nehru, was a great man.

Exercise 1

Combine each set of sentences into one sentence by using Noun or Phrase in Apposition :

1.   He has murdered many innocent people. He is a notorious robber.
2.   Wordsworth was a great poet. He was the devotee of Nature.
3.   Homer was a blind poet. He was the writer of 'The Iliad'.
4.   Education is an instrument of power. It has been the guiding factor of civilization.
5.   The Ramlila is played near the temple. It is a fine display of stage-craft.
6.   Kalidas was a great Sanskrit poet and dramatist. He wrote 'Abhigyan Shakuntalam'.
7.   Kalumal is the richest merchant in the town. He is known for his honesty and nobility.
8.   Allahabad is our pilgrimage. It is an eminent seat of learning.
9.   Chaucer was the first English poet. He wrote 'Canterbury Tales'.
10. Iron is a very important metal. It fulfils our many needs.
11. The Ganga is a sacred river to the Hindus. It originates from the Himalayas.
12. The elephant is a wise animal. It is a symbol of peace and prosperity.
13. Tagore's masterpiece work is the 'Gitanjali'. It is a collection of short poems.
14. My horse is a great helper. I love it.
15. His hermitage was situated in a dense forest. It gave him inner peace.
16. Ashok was the king of Maurya dynasty. He fought a horrid war. The war was fought in Kalinga.
17. Delhi is the capital of India. It is thickly populated. It is situated on the bank of the Yamuna.
18. The map of this city was designed by an engineer. He was very famous. He was a Russian.
19. Mr. Duglas saw a girl. She was nine years old. She was a refugee girl.

20. I bought a watch. It is very beautiful. I bought it last month. I bought it from a famous shop. It cost eight hundred rupees.

4. By Using the Nominative Absolute Construction

Nominative absolute का प्रयोग उस समय किया जाता है जब प्रस्तुत वाक्यों के subjects तथा functions (कार्य) पृथक्-पृथक् हों और उनसे (cause and effect) कारण तथा परिणाम का बोध हो। इसे Nominative absolute इसलिए कहा जाता है क्योंकि ये बिना finite verb के nominative हुआ करते हैं अर्थात् उसके verb को having + verb³ करके Perfect participle कर दिया जाता है।

(a) यदि प्रथम कार्य में केवल Finitive verb हो तो subject + having + verb³ पश्चात् comma देकर दूसरा वाक्य ज्यों का त्यों रखें। जैसे–

The sun set. The birds flew to their nests.

यहाँ sun के set होने का कार्य पहले हुआ है जिसमें finite verb-set है, अत:

—The sun having set, the birds flew to their nests.

(b) जब प्रथम कार्यवाले वाक्य में केवल verb to be (is, am, are, was, were) + Adjective आदि रहे तो to be को being में बदलकर subject + being + adjective आदि जैसा करें। जैसे–

The game was over. We returned home.
—The game being over, we returned home.

(c) जब प्रथम कार्य Passive voice में रहे तो प्रथम कार्य का subject + having been (or being) + verb³ आदि जैसा करें। जैसे–

The mice were killed. The house holder felt relief.
—The mice having been killed (or being killed), the house holder felt relief.

Some more examples :

(a)   Their father died. The children landed into hardship.
      —Their father having died, the children landed into disaster.

(b)   The police arrived. The crowd dispersed.
      —The police having arrived, the crowd dispersed.

(c)   The novel was very interesting. Many people read it.
      —The novel being very interesting, many people read it.

(d)   The night was dark. No one could go out.
      —The night being dark, no one could go out.

(e)   The city was conquered. The inhabitants ran away in fear.
      —The city having been conquered, the inhabitants ran away in fear.

(f)   My pocket was picked. I sank into worry.
      —My pocket having been picked, I sank into worry.

Exercise 1

Combine each set of sentences into a single simple sentence by the help of Nominative Absolute construction :

1.   The day dawned. The forest began to hum with the sweet notes of birds.
2.   The fog was dense. No one could look through it.
3.   It is very cold to day. I have not taken my proper bath.
4.   The earthquake was very terrible. It brought about untold devastation.
5.   The sky is cloudy. It may rain to day.

6. The teacher entered the class. The boys became silent.
7. The leader was slain. The followers ran away.
8. It was a holiday. We did not go to school.
9. The storm passed. We opened our window.
10. The master arrived. The dog began to wag its tail.
11. The cruel king died. Nobody trickled tears at his death.
12. The train was cancelled. All the passengers returned.
13. The team won the match. The spectators exclaimed in joy.
14. A wild wind blew against the ruins. All the birds flew away out of fear.
15. He failed in the examination. His father displeased with him.
16. The price of gold reduced. Many people began to buy jewels.
17. A bus fell into the river. Many persons lost their lives in it.
18. The physician was absent. The patients were in great trouble.
19. The court dismissed the case. The employees resumed their duty.
20. It was the advent of spring. The migratory birds began to arrive.
21. The rain was scanty. The harvest was poor.
22. The job was lucrative. Many young men applied for it.
23. A fire broke out in the village. The fire Brigade reached in no time.
24. Many butterflies swarmed over the flowers. The boys ran after them to catch.
25. An industrial fair was held in Delhi. Many nations participated in it.

5. By Using Preposition with Nouns or Gerunds

यदा कदा दो या दो से अधिक simple sentences को Preposition + Noun or Gerund (verb में ing) के अनुसार एक simple sentence में परिवर्तित किया जाता है। Preposition के स्थान पर कभी-कभी phrase preposition or (participial preposition) से भी काम लिया जाता है। इस प्रसंग में for, on, besides, in spite of, instead of, due to, by, of, with, without, after, before आदि कुछ prepositions विशेष उल्लेखनीय हैं।

(a) Her husband died. She heard the news. She fainted.
   —On hearing the news of her husband's death, she fainted.

(b) He is a man of property. He is discontented.
   —In spite of his property, he is discontented.

   Or

   In spite of being a man of property, he is discontented.

(c) He consoled me. He also helped me.
   —Besides consoling me, he also helped me.

(d) He sent a letter. He ought to come here.
   —Instead of sending a letter, he ought to come here.

(e) An old man was going along the road. He had a stick in his hand.
   —An old man with a stick in his hand, was going along the road.

(f) The volunteers helped many persons. They would have otherwise died.
   —Many persons would have died without the volunteers' help.

(g) She failed. She tried again.
   —She tried again after failure.

(h) He opened a small shop. He earned his living in this way.
   —He earned his living by opening a small shop.

Exercise 1

Combine the following groups of sentences into one simple sentence by the methods over mentioned :

1. He got success. He earned name and fame.
2. An old hermit came here today. His hair was white. His beard was long.
3. A few people now like to buy new books. The reason is their high prices.
4. He was talking with me. That time his hands were in his pocket.
5. He cannot walk. He has no stick in his hand.
6. It is strange. It is yet true.
7. He went to Allahabad. On his way he met his friend.
8. I heard the news. I went to see him. He was injured in an accident.
9. He is ill. He appears to be so.
10. The hunter saw a deer. He ran after him.
11. He succeeded. He was overjoyed.
12. He walked ten miles on foot. He was not tired.
13. She must weep. Otherwise she may turn mad.
14. You helped me. Otherwise I would have been ruined.
15. I was going along the road. I met a man. He was a drunkard.
16. He got failure. He still thinks to try.
17. I consoled him. Still he wept bitterly.
18. The accident occurred. It was the result of carelessness of the driver.
19. I bought a scooter. I bought it from Mohan's shop. It cost me Rs. fifteen thousand.
20. Virvar entered the palace. His sword was stained with blood.

6. By Using an Adverb or an Adverbial Phrase

जब प्रस्तुत वाक्यों में से किसी वाक्य के verb को दूसरा वाक्य विशेषता प्रगट करता हो तो इस प्रसंग में ध्यान रखें कि ऐसे वाक्यों को जोड़कर एक simple sentence बनाने के लिए Adverbs of Manner जो अधिकतर Adjective + ly से समाप्त रहते हैं, अधिक सहायक सिद्ध हो सकेंगे। इन्हें Adverbial phrases द्वारा भी जोड़ा जा सकता है। उदाहरणार्थ—

Carelessly—without care. Rudely—in a rude way.

Hurriedly—in a hurry. Undoubtedly—without doubt.

Very immediately—in no time etc. (Nouns में -ly जोड़ने पर Adjectives बनाए जाते हैं—Manly, fatherly, etc. किन्तु Adj. + -ly—Adverb. जैसे—slow—slowly, etc.)

(*i*) Prithvi Raj was a brave warrior.

There is no doubt in it.

—Prithvi Raj was undoubtedly a brave warrior.

(*ii*) They occupied the land. It was not legal.

—They occupied the land illegally.

(*iii*) They laid him down. They did so sadly and slowly.

—They laid him down sadly and slowly.

(*iv*) His novel was published. It was done lately.

—His novel was lately published.

(*v*) You spent the money. You spent it lavishly.

—You spent the money lavishly.

(vi)   The servant returned from the market. He made no delay.
        —The servant returned from the market without delay.
(vii)   The fox wandered in the woods. She wandered all day long.
        —The fox wandered in the woods all day long.
(viii) The prince saw an ugly man. It was unfortunate.
        —Unfortunately the prince saw an ugly man.
(ix)   He left the school. He did not want to leave the school.
        —He left the school unwillingly. (or reluctantly)

Exercise 1

Combine each set of sentences into a simple sentence by using Adverbs or Adverbial phrases :

1.   He answered all the questions. His answers were correct.
2.   The river was flowing. Its flow was rapid and graceful.
3.   He left the examination. It was his foolish decision.
4.   The jackal talked with the deer. He talked in a cunning way.
5.   The old man gave the judgement. The judgement was not impartial.
6.   The climate ruined his health. The ruin was complete.
7.   The sailors sailed on. They sailed on without aim.
8.   Your son will stand first. This is certain.
9.   He will return. His return will not take a long time.
10. I have read the Gita. It has greatly influenced me.
11. Her dress was bright. Her dress was elegant.
12. Aashis scored a goal. He did this in a clear way.
13. He admitted his fault. He admitted it with regret.
14. The passer-by slept under the tree. The sleep was sound.
15. The manager rejected the proposal. He did this in anger.
16. He quitted the duty. He did it like a man.
17. The child cried in fear. He cried in a loud voice.
18. He gazed at me. He did so in suspicion.
19. Clym went to see his mother. It was his frequent practice.
20. I park my car near the office. I park it in a usual manner.
21. They went to her grave. They were silent. They were sad. They were slow.

7. By Using 'And' an Adjective or by Dropping a Verb

(a) यदि प्रस्तुत वाक्यों में से किसी में प्रयुक्त Noun का अन्य वाक्य में कोई Adjective दिया गया हो तो उस Adjective को उस Noun के निकट रखें जिसकी वह विशेषता बताता हो। जैसे—

        A beggar came to my house. He was blind.

यहाँ दूसरे वाक्य में प्रयुक्त blind (adjective) प्रथम वाक्य में प्रयुक्त beggar के लिए आया है, अत :

        —A blind beggar came to my house.
        He took pity on the boy. The boy was orphan.
        —He took pity on the orphan boy.

(b) यदि दिए गए वाक्यों के subjects भिन्न हों किन्तु बनावट एक जैसी हो तो उन subjects को and, as well as, with, alongwith आदि से जोड़ें।

        Balu was present there. His brother and sisters were also with him.
        —Balu with his brother and sisters, was present there.

(c) यदि प्रस्तुत वाक्यों की बनावट समान हो, केवल **complement or object** भिन्न हों तो उन्हें **and** से जोड़ें। अधिक **complements** या **objects** हों तो अन्य के साथ **comma** रखें, अन्तिम दो को **and** से जोड़ें।

> I saw a lamb. I saw a dog. I saw a cow.
>
> —I saw a lamb, a dog and a cow.
>
> He bought a book. He bought a pen. He bought a pencil.
>
> —He bought a book, a pen and a pencil.

(d) दिए गए वाक्यों में से अनावश्यक **verb** का लोप करके—

> Once there was a crow. It was very thirsty.
>
> —Once there was a thirsty crow.
>
> A man was hungry. He stole a piece of bread.
>
> —A hungry man stole a piece of bread.

Exercise 1

Combine the following sets of sentences into a single simple sentence :

1. Raghu found a pen on the road. The pen was costly.
2. He beat the boy. The boy was naughty.
3. Mr. Harish is a teacher. He is very learned.
4. He is a physician. He is very renowned in his domain.
5. Tolstoy was a Russian. He was a great story teller.
6. I bought a shoe yesterday. It was black.
7. Shivaji was a warrior. He was very brave.
8. I met a man. He was wise. He was upright.
9. I saw her face. It was sad.
10. He solved the sum. The sum was difficult.
11. I ate a biscuit. I ate a cake.
12. He bought a brush. He bought a cake of soap.
13. There are novels on the table. There are magazines on the table.
14. We saw him sad. We saw him morose. We saw him downcast.
15. I met a girl. Her eyes were blue.
16. We visited the Agha Khan palace. It is historical.
17. The manager was absent. The cashier was absent. The clerk was absent.
18. He went to America. His wife also went with him.
19. There lived a man in Ujjain. He was a great talisman.
20. A falcon noticed a young bird. It chased the bird.

Some Solved Examples

1. There was an old man. He was dying. He had four sons. He called all his sons near him. He advised them to live with unity after his death.

   —A dying old man, calling his four sons near him, advised them to live with unity after his death.

2. Ashok fought a battle. He was a great king of the Maurya dynasty. The battle was fought in Kaling. The battle was very fearful. It moved the mind of the king .

   —The fearful battle of Kaling moved the mind of Ashok a great king of the Maurya dynasty.

3. Swami Vivekanand was born in Calcutta. He renounced his home. He did so under the influence of Swami Ram Krishna. The latter was the preceptor of the former.

—Swami Vivekanand, born in Calcutta, renounced his home under the influence of his preceptor Swami Ram Krishna.

निष्कर्ष यह कि simple में combine करने के लिए प्रस्तुत वाक्यों के प्रमुख तथ्यों को चुनकर उनमें से किसी एक आवश्यक verb को मूल subject के साथ प्रयोग करें।

Exercise 1

Combine each of the following sets of sentences into one simple sentence :

1. A man was strolling on the road. He was old. He was weak.
2. I bought a novel. It is very interesting.
3. Jaddu was a famous cricketer. He invented a new stroke in cricket.
4. He won the world cup. He won it under his captaincy.
5. He built a house. The house was airy. It was also specious.
6. The principal fined the boy. He also expelled him.
7. He planted a rose. He planted it in his garden. The rose was red and fragrant.
8. Mr. Gardiner felt ashamed. He developed a human relationship with the mosquito.
9. He was vexed with his life. He left the village for good.
10. Birbal was the gem of Akbar's court. He was notable for his wit and wisdom.
11. The saint called the people of the village. He wanted to preach them.
12. He is very clever. He may play a dirty trick.
13. The storm was over. The fishermen rowed their boats.
14. Shakespeare was a great playwright. He wrote a number of extraordinary plays.
15. He fell among the robbers. He fell by chance.
16. I have gone through the report. I have done so in hurry.
17. Your conduct is good. Your conduct is noble. Your conduct is praiseworthy.
18. Once there was a swallow. It was hungry. It went near the ant. It wanted some food from the ant.
19. He is very obstinate. He cannot submit to your terms and conditions.
20. Your sin is unforgivable. It must yield bitter fruit.
21. He was punished. He repented.
22. The earthquake devastated the city. The inhabitants became homeless.
23. Endurance is a good quality. We should cultivate this quality.
24. He amassed a lot of money. He broke his health.
25. Flattery is the business of the day. We should condemn it.
26. She struck out a novel plan. She wished to get rid of the robbers.
27. The swimmer tried his best. He could not save the drowning child.
28. I received the news of his success. I congratulated him.
29. You have power. You can make impossible possible.
30. He taught us. His purpose was to enable us to see into the life of the things.
31. He rowed the boat. It was moonlight. He heard the silent music of life.
32. Smoking is injurious to health. It must be seriously avoided by all.
33. A story goes about an emperor. The emperor was generous. His character was peculiar.
34. Once there was a barber. He was jealous of the secretary of the king. The secretary was wise. The barber fell a victim of his own trick.
35. Prithvi Raj was a king. He was valiant. He fought against Mohammad Gori. The battle took place in the field of Tarain.

36. He saw a ghost. The ghost was moving in the dark. He ran away out of fear.

37. A doctor came there. He was clad in a white robe. He came there to examine the patient.

38. He bought a cow. The cow was black. He bought it for Rs. four thousand.

39. Life is serious. Life is earnest. It should be devoted to attain perfection.

40. There was a lion. He was old. He had a gold bangle in his hand. He intended to deceive other beasts with the bangle.

2. Combination of Simple Sentences into a Compound Sentence

अनेक simple sentences को जोड़कर एक compound sentence बनाने के लिए co-ordinating conjunctions से सहायता ली जाती है। उनका वर्गीकरण निम्नस्थ रूपों में द्रष्टव्य होगा।

(a) By Cumulative (or copulative) conjunctions... viz. and, besides, as well as, both ... and, not only ... but also. यदि प्रस्तुत वाक्यों के भाव एक समान हों और एक के पश्चात् दूसरा कथन हुआ हो तो उन्हें उपरोक्त conjunctions से जोड़ेंगे। ध्यान रहे कि इसमें एक से अधिक verb हों।

He went to market. He bought a book.

—He went to market and bought a book.

Or

—He was marked absent. He was fined.

Or

—He was marked absent and fined.

Or

—He was marked absent as well as fined.

Or

—He was not only marked absent but was fined also.

(b) By Adversative conjunctions (विरोधाभासक संयोजक)–viz. but, still, yet, however, only, nevertheless. जब प्रस्तुत वाक्यों से परस्पर विरोध का आभास हो तो उन्हें उल्लिखित conjunctions से जोड़ेंगे।

He tried his best. He could not succeed.

—He tried his best but could not succeed.

Or

He tried his best yet he could not succeed.

Or

He tried his best however he could not succeed.

He is rich. He is miserly.

He is rich only he is miserly.

Or

He is rich but he is miserly.

Or

He is rich still he is miserly.

(c) By Illative conjunctions (परिणामबोधक संयोजक)–viz. so, therefore, hence, consequently, for (क्योंकि), यदि प्रस्तुत वाक्यों से कारण तथा परिणाम का बोध हो तो उन्हें उल्लिखित conjunctions से जोड़ें।

He was down with fever. He could not appear at the examination.

—He was down with fever so (or hence or therefore or consequently) he could not appear at the examination.

Or

He could not appear at the examination for he was down with fever.

Note. Consequence + for + reason or reason + so/hence/therefore + consequence जैसी विधि प्रयोग करें।

Aashis was intelligent. He stood first.

—Aashis stood first for he was intelligent.

Or

—Aashis was intelligent so he stood first.

(*d*) By **Alternative conjunctions** (विकल्पबोधक संयोजक)–*viz.*, Either ... or, neither ... nor, or, nor, otherwise, else (नहीं तो, अन्यथा, या तो)–यदि दिए गए simple sentences से choice or selection (विकल्प, चयन) का बोध हो तो उन्हें उल्लिखित conjunctions से जोड़ेंगे।

Mend your ways. You will have to repent.

—Mend your ways or (otherwise, else) you will have to repent.

He may not be a liar. He may not be a deceiver.

—He may be neither a liar nor a deceiver.

Do not be a borrower. Do not be a lender.

—Neither be a borrower nor a lender be.

Keep quiet. Go out.

—Either keep quiet or go out.

Or

Keep quiet otherwise go out.

(*e*) कभी-कभी Non-defining clause में जब progressive sense (निरन्तरता का बोध हो, तो) Relative pronoun/Adverb का प्रयोग करके वाक्यों को जोड़ा जाता है। जैसे–who, which, where, when etc. के द्वारा जबकि इनसे antecedent (पूर्ववर्तीकर्ता) का परिचय/विशेषता/गुण आदि का बोध न होता हो क्योंकि तब वह–

Adjective clause हो जाएगा जो complex sentence का अंग है।

I met Sandhu. He gave me your message.

—I met Sandhu, who gave me your message (who—and he)

He will go to Varanasi. He will see his ailing brother.

—He will go to Varanasi, where he will see his ailing brother. (where—and there)

Note. कभी-कभी बिना conjunctions के छोटे छोटे वाक्यों को comma या semi-colon के द्वारा जोड़ा जाता है।

The way was long. The night was dark.

—The way was long, the night was dark.

I came I saw I conquered.

—I came ; I saw ; I conquered.

Exercise 1

Combine each of the following sets of simple sentences into a compound sentence :

1. The world is full of pomp. The world is full of vanity.
2. Some books are to be chewed. Some books are to be swallowed. Some books are to be digested.
3. Art is long. Life is short.
4. Some are born great. Some achieve greatness.
5. To err is human. To forgive is divine.
6. I went to the school. The teachers recognised me soon.
7. He want to market. He bought a watch.
8. Speak the truth. Do not fear.
9. He was harassed. He was discouraged.

10. Cowards die many times before their death. The valiant die but once.
11. He has a lot of pelf. He is parsimonious.
12. He was immensely fed up. He went to a ball-room for rest and relief.
13. Minerva is the goddess of wisdom. Diana is the goddess of chastity.
14. I took my stick and hat. I got down from the train.
15. She went to her relatives. They did not help her.
16. Submit yourself. Be ready to fight either.
17. Work hard. You may fail.
18. He may be a teacher. He may be a preacher. He may not be both.
19. He was not invited. He came here.
20. The sky is cloudy. It may rain to day.
21. He was a man of parts. He occupied an eminent post.
22. The police was vigilant. The incident happened.
23. It was very cold. I put on my coat.
24. He took the gun. He shot the tiger.
25. Admit your fault. In either case you cannot be forgiven.
26. Somewhere ignorance is bliss. It is folly for one to be wise there.
27. The train was late. I caught it.
28. Smoking should be abstained. Drinking should be abstained.
29. Caesar was ambitious. He was murdered.
30. He did not invite me. I did not partake in his ceremony.
31. Do not move. You will be killed.
32. Say you are sorry. I shall forgive you then.
33. The sea was calm. The wind was favourable.
34. He deserved the post. He failed.
35. You did the best. You got the prize.
36. Let me take breath. I have recovered a long track.
37. He was found guilty. He was punished.
38. She cried for help. Nobody went near her.
39. He has failed many times. He is not disheartened. He hopes to succeed.
40. A child was drowning in the river. He saw him. He jumped into the river. He saved the child.

3. Combination of Simple Sentences into a Complex Sentence

Complex sentence में एक से अधिक वाक्य हुआ करते हैं। इसमें एक principal clause (main clause मुख्य उपवाक्य) तथा शेष उसके subordinate clause या clauses (आश्रित उपवाक्य) हुआ करते हैं। Combination करते समय प्रस्तुत वाक्यों में से जो प्रमुख हो उसे main clause बनाकर शेष को subordinate में परिणत कर देना चाहिए। Subordinate clause तीन प्रकार के होते हैं।

(a) Subordinate Noun Clause (संज्ञा उपवाक्य)

(b) Subordinate Adjective Clause (विशेषण उपवाक्य)

(c) Subordinate Adverb Clause (क्रिया विशेषण उपवाक्य)

(a) Subordinate Noun Clause

ये जिन connectives से जोड़े जाते हैं उनकी हिन्दी 'क' अक्षर से प्रारम्भ होती है। जैसे–कि, कहाँ, कैसे, कब आदि और वे conjunctions हैं–that (कि) ; when (कि कब) ; why (कि क्यों-कारण हेतु) ; who (कि कौन

someone somebody आदि के भाव में) ; where (कि कहाँ somewhere के भाव में) ; what (कि क्या something के भाव में), which (कि कौन सा, कौन), if/whether (कि-अस्पष्टता, अनिश्चितता की स्थिति में) ; How (कि कैसे-विधि, शैली के भाव में) sometime—when ; why इत्यादि।

He will pass. It is certain.

—That he will pass is certain.

Or

It is certain that he will pass.

He did not appear at the examination. Can you say its reason ?

—Can you say why he did not appear at the examination ?

I advised you recently. You should rely on it.

—You should rely on what I advised you recently.

He lives somewhere. I cannot say where.

—I cannot say where he lives.

Someone knocked at the door. I do not know him.

—I do not know who knocked at the door.

He may be guilty. I do not know.

—I do not know if he is guilty.

ध्यान रहे कि Wh से प्रारम्भ हुआ subordinate clause प्रश्नवाचक वाक्य नहीं हुआ करता बल्कि सामान्य वाक्य होता है। अत: उनका स्वरूप Wh + subject + verb आदि जैसा होगा। जब main clause प्रश्नवाचक होगा तभी complex sentence प्रश्नवाचक हो सकेगा। noun clause वाक्य में noun का कार्य करता है जो मुख्यत: पाँच प्रकार के हैं। प्राय: noun clauses (P.C.) के verb के पश्चात् से प्रारम्भ हुआ करते हैं, जैसे—

I know that he is a noble man.

Can you say when he will come ?

His belief is that he will succeed.

Listen to what I say. etc.

Exercise 1

Combine each set of simple sentences into one complex sentence containing a Noun clause :

1. The war may break out at any time. Nobody knows it.
2. He has topped the list of successful candidates. Do you know it ?
3. You helped me. I cannot forget it.
4. She said something. I did not hear.
5. Better days will come. It is her belief.
6. You are in fault. I am sure of it.
7. She will get over the difficulties. This is her statement.
8. You lost the field. This is a fact.
9. Is it the time to come out of the pitcher ? One of the robbers asked so.
10. Is it not proper to go there ? I think so.
11. When will the train depart ? A passenger asked the guard.
12. His behaviour was uncivilised. He was sorry for it.
13. My friend lives somewhere. Please tell me where.
14. He became angry. I want to know the reason.
15. Someone has stolen my watch. Do you know him ?

16. One day Tom declared. His decision was that he would not work.
17. The bus will arrive at sometime. I cannot say the time.
18. The condition is very concerning. I am aggrieved to see this.
19. You will deceive me. I never thought so.
20. Gambling will destroy him. This is certain.

(b) Subordinate Adjective Clause

Adjective clauses जिन connectives से प्रारम्भ किए जाते हैं वे हैं–Wh words (who, when, where etc. अर्थात् Relative pronouns) ; that, as etc. इनकी हिन्दी 'ज' अक्षर से प्रारम्भ हुआ करती है अर्थात् जो, जिसने, जिसको, जहाँ, जब आदि। ध्यान रहे कि उक्त connectives से Adjective clause को उसके antecedent के तुरंत पश्चात् से शुरू करना चाहिए अन्यथा वाक्य भ्रमास्पद हो सकता है।

> This is the pen. I bought it yesterday.
> —This is the pen which I bought yesterday.
> His brother is a physician. He is my friend.
> —His brother who is a physician is my friend.
> He will not come. I know the reason.
> —I know the reason why he will not come.
> This is the house. He lives here.
> —This is the house where he lives.
> The boat leaves at sometime. Can you tell me the time ?
> —Can you tell me the time when the boat leaves ?
> This is the boy. You beat him yesterday.
> —This is the boy whom you beat yesterday.
> The boy is my friend. His shirt is red.
> —The boy whose shirt is red is my friend.
> It is an old game. I am tired of it.
> —It is an old game of which I am tired.
> Some men are incredible. They must be avoided.
> —Such men as are incredible must be avoided.
> *Or*
> Some men who are ......

Exercise 1

Combine the following sentences in a complex sentence containing an Adjective clause :

1. The boy got the first prize. Do you know him ?
2. This is the place. An accident recently occurred here.
3. He has destroyed the papers. The papers were confidential.
4. People live in glass houses. So they should not throw stones.
5. This is the story. He told me this.
6. The car is red. It belongs to my uncle.
7. He will not help you. Do you know the reason ?
8. We proceeded towards the foot of the hill. We saw there a lady. She was advancing against the wind.
9. I noticed a girl. Her eyes were blue.
10. This is the road. It leads to the university.

11. That is the man. All respect him.
12. This is the proper time. We should undertake our passage.
13. I am your friend. I cannot beguile you.
14. Where is the umbrella ? Tell me the place.
15. He laughs last. He laughs best.
16. I have a magic stick. It strikes the onlookers with surprise.
17. Tom brought disgrace to his family. He was a black sheep.
18. The hands rock in the cradle. The same hands rule over the world.
19. I met a hermit. He blessed me.
20. Some burglars broke into the house. The police have arrested them.

(c) Subordinate Adverb Clause

यदि दिए गए वाक्यों से Time, place, purpose, cause, condition, result, camparison, manner, concession आदि का भाव व्यक्त हो तो उन्हें Adverb clause में बदलकर combine किया जा सकता है। इस प्रसंग में इनके मुख्य connectives का अध्ययन करें।

Time—When, whenever, while, after, before, since, till, as, just as, as soon as, etc.

Place—Where, wherever, whence.

Purpose—That, so that (ताकि, जिससे कि) ; lest (कही ऐसा न हो अन्यथा)।

Cause—Because, as, since (चूँकि, क्योंकि)।

Condition—If, unless, etc.

Result—So.... that (इतना कि अर्थात् that) से result प्रगट होता है।

Comparison/manner—Than as

Concession—Although, though, even if, etc.

    The cat is away. The mice will play then.
    —When the cat is away, the mice will play. (Time)
    He returned. It began to rain just then.
    —Just as (or as soon as) he returned, it began to rain. (Time)
    I went to the place. My friend lived there.
    —I went where my friend lived. (Place)
    He drew his sword. He wished to defend himself (Purpose)
    —He drew his sword that he might defend himself.
    Walk carefully. You may fall.
    —Walk carefully lest you should fall. (purpose)
    He left the school. He did so due to his illness. (cause)
    —He left the school because he was ill.
    He was very intelligent. He did his best.
    —As (since or because) he was very intelligent, he did his best. (Cause)
    Try again. You must succeed. (Condition)
    —If you try again, you must succeed.
    The Rajputs fought very bravely. Consequently the enemies ran away. (Result)
    —So bravely did the Rajputs fight that the enemies ran away.
    He is tall. His brother is equally tall.
    —He is as tall as his brother (is). (Comparison)

It was late. Still we decided to go.

—Although it was late we decided to go. (Concession)

Exercise 1

Combine the following sentences in a complex sentence containing Adverb Clause :

1. Take a torch. It is very dark.
2. She cried very loudly. The child woke up.
3. He is young in age. He is old in brains.
4. Usha is tall. Her sister is not so tall.
5. He came out of the cinema hall. His father saw him then.
6. It was very hot yesterday. I felt much uneasiness.
7. The horse reared on hind legs. The rider fell down.
8. He was surrounded by his foes. He escaped unbeaten.
9. Play the piano. Meanwhile I bring a cup of coffee for you.
10. Do not start the scooter. You may get hurt.
11. Your health is not sound. You cannot get the job.
12. He had gone from there. I reached there afterward.
13. Patience is the use of power. Passion is the abuse of power.
14. The warden checked the hostel. The students were sleeping then.
15. He could not succeed. He did not lose his heart.
16. We saw a snake. We ran away then.
17. I went to the place. My friend lived there.
18. Take balanced diet. Otherwise you may break your health.
19. We are poor. Even then we cannot lower down our dignity.
20. The leader stood to speak. Just then the audience began to cry against him.
21. This sum is very easy. Even a child can solve it.
22. Make haste. Otherwise it will get dark.
23. He was angry. He refused to see me.
24. The news shocked her too much. The result was that she fainted.
25. Let it rain heavily. I must come.

More About Synthesis

(*i*) अनेक प्रस्तुत Simple sentences को आवश्यकतानुसार simple, complex or compound sentence किसी में भी या तीनों में परिणत किया जा सकता है। जैसे–

She heard the news. She began to weep.

On hearing the news, she began to weep.   (*Simple*)

When she heard the news, she began to weep.   (*Complex*)

She heard the news and began to weep.   (*Compound*)

(*ii*) Complex का Simple में परिणत करना–

He could not appear at the examination because he was ill.   (*Complex*)

Owing to illness, he could not appear at the examination.   (*Simple*)

(*iii*) Compound sentence को Complex बनाना–

He was wounded in an accident so he went to hospital. But the doctor was not available.

                                                           (*Compound*)

Being wounded in an accident, he went to hospital where the doctor was not available.
(Complex)

(*iv*) Complex तथा Compound sentences का एक दूसरे में परिवर्तन–

So good a man is he that all respect him. *(Complex)*

He is a very good man therefore all respect him. *(Compound)*

He is very weak still he wants to go to office. *(Compound)*

Although he is very weak he wants to go to office. *(Complex)*

(*v*) यदि कम से कम finite verb का प्रयोग करना हो तो प्राथमिकता का क्रम Simple, Complex तब Compound sentence होना चाहिए।

He saw the boy in the street. He stopped to speak to him. He gave him a book.

—Seeing the boy in the street, he stopped him to give a book. *(Simple)*

His parents are poor. They cannot afford him education. He has to discontinue his studies. It is very unfortunate.

—Unfortunately he has to discontinue his studies because his parents being poor, cannot afford him education. *(Complex)*

सुविधा के लिए निम्नस्थ तालिका में Complex तथा Compound sentences के कुछ मुख्य connectives पृथक् रूप में प्रस्तुत किए गए हैं। इन्हें ध्यान से देखें।

Complex Sentence (Subordinating Conjunctions)	Compound Sentence (Co-ordinating Conjunctions)
That, Wh-words, if, just as, as soon as, lest, after, before, than, though, although, even if, unless, till, until, so ... that, because, as, since, etc.	And, as well as, not only ... but also, or, nor, either ... or, neither ... nor, otherwise, so, therefore, for (क्योंकि) but, still, yet, etc.

Exercise 1

Combine each of the following groups of sentences into a Simple, Complex or Compound sentence :

1. A man was strolling on the road. He was old. He had a stick in his hand.
2. They played the game very skilfully. No one could have played it so skilfully. They had been thoroughly well trained.
3. I was standing near the gate. A motor car suddenly came up. The motor car was being driven by a young man.
4. Your son has been ill during the greater part of this session. His studies have fallen into arrears. I am unable to give him promotion.
5. There was a rumour. It was about his death. It was false.
6. The master was out of the room. The door was shut. The boys made a lot of noise.
7. You may like it. You may not like it. In either case you shall have to marry. You are already thirty years old.
8. The lion was let out of the cage. It came up quietly to Androcles. A dog does like that. He had been kind to it. It remembered this.
9. He turned over the cradle. He found his child unhurt. He found a big snake lying dead on the floor. The snake had been killed.
10. A fox wanted to quench his thirst. He tried to get at the grapes. He failed in his attempts. The grapes were beyond his reach. He went away disappointed. He remarked that the grapes were sour.

11. Once there was a king. He was a famous archer. He went to forest. He noticed a fairy queen there.

12. Self-confidence is a power. It is precious. It makes impossible possible. It inspires man to remain immovable against a massive rock.

13. Man is a social animal. He cannot live without society. Society fulfills his necessities. The necessities are essential for his survival.

14. A child was drowning in the river. He saw him. He jumped into the river. He saved the child.

15. Gafur set out. His daughter Amina was with him. He had nobody to call him his own. He had nothing to say to anybody.

16. He saw me. He came running to me. He carried a gun in his hand. It was a big gun.

17. A traveller was crossing a desert. He was starving. He found a bag. He opened the bag. He found only gold in it.

18. The obligation is mutual. It is found on a fact. The fact is that we are fellow mortals. We are just like ghosts. This time is ; that time is not.

19. This is a business. It is based on being good. It has something to do with civilization. It means making beautiful things, thinking freely and keeping the rules.

Chapter 16

Transformation of Sentences
(वाक्यों का रूपान्तरण)

Transformation का अर्थ है changing the form. संक्षेप में, किसी वाक्य के अर्थ को यथावत् रखते हुए उसे वांछित रूप में परिवर्तित करना। जैसे—

She is beautiful.
—She is not ugly.
Everybody will remember him.
—No body will forget him.

1. Interchange of One Part of Speech for Another

1. He *abhorred* flattery.   (*Verb*)
   Flattery was his *abhorrence*.   (*Noun*)
   He was *abhorrent* of flattery.   (*Adjective*)

2. Nature made lucy *beautiful*.   (*Adjective*)
   Nature *beautified* lucy.   (*Verb*)
   Nature bestowed *beauty* upon lucy.   (*Noun*)

3. The company *supplied* the raw material *regularly*.   (*Verb, Adverb*)
   The *supply* of raw materials by the company was *regular*. (*Noun, Adjective*)

4. His *arrival* is *certain*.   (*Noun, Adjective*)
   He will *certainly arrive*.   (*Adverb, Verb*)

5. He was *fortunate* to get the job.   (*Adjective*)
   Fortunately he got the job.   (*Adverb*)

6. He was a man of *influence*.   (*Noun*)
   He was an *influential* man.   (*Adjective*)

7. The clown *pleased* everybody.   (*Verb*)
   Everybody took *pleasure* from the clown.   (*Noun*)

8. His success *surprised* us.   (*Verb*)
   His success caused *surprise* in us.   (*Noun*)

9. He *departed* suddenly.   (*Verb, Adverb*)
   His *departure* was sudden.   (*Noun, Adjective*)

10. This T.V. set *differs* from that.   (*Verb*)
    This T.V. set is *different* from that.   (*Adjective*)

171

Exercise 1

Rewrite the following sentences by replacing the underlined words in their forms indicated in the brackets :

1. Mr. Henry was the *president* of the Board of Trade.   (Verb)
2. His *preparation* for the competition was *satisfactory*.   (Verb, Adverb)
3. He *helped* me joyfully.   (Noun)
4. You have *to choose* between them.   (Noun)
5. Answer the question in *brief*.   (Adverb)
6. She *was married* in June.   (Noun)
7. His *action* was *quick*.   (Verb, Adverb)
8. The *comparison* is made between the sun and the wind.   (Verb)
9. He was a young man of *sound* *health*.   (Adjective)
10. This medicine is not out of *harm*.   (Adjective)
11. Life is full of *mystery*.   (Adjective)
12. To live in *darkness* was his liking.   (Adjective)
13. He *tried* for the best in his life.   (Noun)
14. His *achievement* made him noble.   (Verb)
15. The country *was abounded* with minerals.   (Adjective)
16. His *behaviour amused* the people.   (Verb, Noun)
17. The troops *advanced rapidly*.   (Noun, Adjective)
18. He *gave* me some useful kits.   (Noun)
19. Have you no *confidence* in your ability ?   (Verb)
20. The train was running in a *slow* speed.   (Adverb)
21. They buried him with *sadness*.   (Adverb)
22. The news made me *sad*.   (Verb)
23. We felt *extreme happiness*.   (Adverb, Adjective)
24. She was very *anxious* for her child.   (Noun)
25. He behaved as a *child*.   (Adjective)

2. The Removal of 'Too'

(a) जब emphasis (कथन पर बल) के रूप में too का अर्थ 'भी' हो तो उसे also में बदलें, जैसे–

    Thorium is found in India too.

    —Thorium is found in India also.

(b) जब too + adjective + or adverb + infinitive रहे तो too को so में बदलकर उसकी बनावट इस प्रकार करें–

so + adjective + that से ऐसा clause जिसमें cannot/could not/should not आदि रहे। जैसे–

    He is too fat to run easily.

    —He is so fat that he cannot run easily.

    This scooter is too costly to be bought.

    —This scooter is so costly that it cannot be bought.

    Ravi is too clever not to see through your tricks.

    —Ravi is so clever that he will see through your tricks.

(c) यदि प्रस्तुत वाक्य में too + adjective रहे। जैसे–He is too virtuous or being too virtuous तो ऐसे प्रयोग में too का भाव होता है more than enough अर्थात् अत्यन्त अधिक।

अत: too को extremely/beyond the proper limit etc. में बदलें। Adjective के साथ over भी रखा जा सकता है।

He is being too virtuous.
—He is being extremely virtuous.
She was too busy.
—She was over busy.
Or
She was busy beyond the proper limit.
Or
She was extremely busy.
The crowd was too noisy.
The crowd was over noisy.
Or
The crowd was extremely noisy.

(*d*) जब too + adjective + objective case रहे तो too को हटाकर so + adjective + that से subordinate clause बनाएँ।

He is too strong for me.
—He is so strong that I am no match for him.
The house is too small for me.
—The house is so small that it cannot serve my purpose.
Much too—so very. The climate is much too harmful for me. The climate is so very harmful that I cannot live here.
The tree was too high for him to climb.
—The tree was so high that he could not climb.
It is never too late to mend.
—It is never so late that one cannot mend.
The amount is much too petty for you.
—The amount is so very petty that it cannot serve your needs.
Her sigh was too profound for tears.
—Her sigh was so profound that she could not express it in tears.

Exercise 1

Rewrite the following sentences removing 'too' :

1. And you too Brutus !
2. Cassius thinks too much.
3. His father too was a partner.
4. He is too good to be a successful businessman.
5. He was too tired to work.
6. The results were too bad to be published.
7. He speaks too fast to be understood.
8. The box is too heavy for me to lift.
9. Do not make yourself too inferior.
10. His uncle is too old to work hard.
11. This cup of coffee is too hot for me.

12. He is too old to run the race.
13. The fact is too evident to require proof.
14. He is too wise to solve the problem.
15. I too was present there.
16. The flower is too tender to be touched.
17. The water was too clear.
18. He was too much distressed to hear all this.
19. The manager is too lenient.
20. You are too prudent to handle the situation.

Exercise 2

Rewrite the following sentences adding 'too' :

1. The sheaf is so heavy that she cannot carry it.
2. The current was so fast that I dared not cross it.
3. The medicine is so bitter that he cannot take it.
4. She was extremely eager to hear the news.
5. You are so little that you cannot follow me.
6. He is powerful enough to help you.
7. The blanket is extremely small for me.
8. He is so old that he is not fit for this job.
9. The way was extremely long.
10. The atmosphere was so quiet that it could not be described.
11. He was bold enough to speak against the furious mob.
12. It was so dark that one could not see through it.
13. The story is so false that we cannot believe it.
14. He is popular enough to be recognised.
15. She was so frightened that she was unable to speak.
16. The land was woody beyond the proper limit.
17. He is over gentle.
18. My friend is so worldly that he has no trust in anybody.
19. This shirt is so small that I cannot get into it.
20. One is never so old that one cannot learn.

3. Interchange of Assertive and Interrogative Sentences

Assertive को Interrogative में परिवर्तित करते समय ध्यान रखना चाहिए कि जिस tense में वाक्य दिया गया है, परिवर्तनीय वाक्य का tense भी वही रहे। सभी प्रकार के Interrogative sentences को Assertive में बदलना संभव नहीं है। जैसे–Information seeking questions को नहीं बदला जा सकता। परिवर्तन केवल rhetorical questions का होता है। वाक्य के स्वरूप को दृष्टिगत करते हुए note of interrogation तथा full stop का ध्यान रखें।

यदि प्रस्तुत वाक्य में not रहे तो परिवर्तनीय वाक्य में उसका प्रयोग न करें और not न रहे तो not का प्रयोग करें। Double negatives का भी प्रयोग हो सकेगा।

        Who—Everyone, Everybody, etc.

        Who has not heard the name of Shivaji ?

        —Everyone has heard the name of Shivaji.

                Or

        There is nobody who has not heard the name of Shivaji.

Where is coal not found ?

—Coal is found everywhere.

(b) can—cannot

When can their glory fade ?

Their glory can never fade.

Can the sun rise in the west ?

The sun cannot rise in the west.

(c) जब What ; Why से ऐसा प्रश्नवाचक वाक्य प्रारम्भ रहे जिससे उद्बोधन या व्यर्थता का भाव रहे तो उसे क्रमश: It does not matter. Or It is useless जैसा जोड़कर बनाएँ।

What does it matter if we lose the field ? (or   what though we ...)

—It does not matter if we lose the field.

Why help him ?

—It is useless to help him.

(d) No one, nobody, none—anyone, anybody.

Can anyone speak against him ?

—No one can speak against him.

Were you not sure that he would pass ?

—You were sure that he would pass.

What is that to you ?

—That is nothing to you.

Is this a way to treat a servant ?

—This is not a way to treat a servant.

निष्कर्ष यह कि प्रश्नवाचक वाक्य में यदि negative verb रहे तो सामान्य में उसे affirmative या double negatives में बदल देते हैं। यदि negative न रहे तो not, no का प्रयोग करते हैं। यही प्रक्रिया assertive को interrogative में बनाते समय विपरीत रूप में प्रयोग की जाती है।

I can solve this sum.

—Can I not solve this sum ?

It is very strange.

—Is it not very strange ?

Everybody has his likes and dislikes.

—Who has not his likes and dislikes ?

It is useless to invite him.

Why invite him ?

It does not matter if the way is long.

—What though the way is long ?

Exercise 1

Transform the following sentences into assertive :

1. Who can control the wind ?
2. Is honesty not the best policy ?
3. Can there be smoke without fire ?
4. Why waste time in hearing such nonsensical talk ?
5. Who is not afraid of death ?
6. Is it not an irony of life ?

7. Who has found peace and pleasure in this life ?
8. Why talk to him ?
9. What does it matter if he insults me ?
10. Had I not forbidden you to do so ?
11. Can time leave anyone untouched ?
12. Did I not help you ?
13. If winter comes, can spring be far behind ?
14. Can a dog change its nature ?
15. If gold cannot do, why must we try silver ?
16. Is this the way to teach a child ?
17. Why derive victory from defeat ?
18. What did it matter if you failed in your attempt ?
19. Can you gather grapes from thorns ?
20. Is there any places so sweet like home ?

Exercise 2

Transform the following sentences into interrogative :

1. Nobody would like to be called a fool.
2. Everybody loves his homeland.
3. Nobody likes to be a slave.
4. No one can put up with such an insult.
5. It did not matter if you failed to stand first.
6. It matters very little if I live with her.
7. Anyone will grow wise through experience.
8. Our life is a satire on our religion.
9. Nature pleases everyone.
10. Alcohol is injurious to health.
11. No one likes to die.
12. Everybody would like to be free.
13. Honest men are honoured everywhere.
14. Time and tide wait for none.
15. Wealth is not a guarantee of happiness.
16. It matters little if we miss the train.
17. Nobody would like to be poor.
18. It cannot be true.
19. This is not an example to be followed.
20. Forgiveness cannot be named after cowardice.

4. Interchange of Affirmative and Negative Sentences

(a) दिए गए Affirmative sentence को Negative में बदलने के लिए उसके verb, adjective आदि के विपरीतार्थक शब्द का Negative भाव रखकर परिवर्तन करें। जैसे—always—never ; sometimes—not always ; doubtful—not sure ; all—none ; without ; not fail, double negatives आदि द्वारा।

    I will always remember you.
    —I will never forget you.

Everyone is imperfect.
—No one is perfect.
He is wealthy.
—He is not without wealth.
Man is mortal.
—No man is immortal.
He is sometimes sad.
—He is not always happy.
I did my duty.
—I did not fail to do my duty.
Every rose has a thorn.
—There is no rose without a thorn.
Every man has his price.
—There is no man who has no price.
I was sure about his success.
—I was not doubtful about his success.
He helped me against a rainy day.
—He did not fail to help me against a rainy day.

(b) Only, alone—nothing but, none but तथा as soon as—no sooner ... than just as.

Only Deepak could do well.
—None but Deepak could do well.
Balu alone was successful.
—None but Balu was successful.
As soon as I heard, I wrote to him.
—No sooner did I hear than I wrote to him.

(c) Imperative sentence में दिए गए वाक्य को negative बनाने के लिए उसे do not से प्रारम्भ करें।

Think well before you decide.
—Do not decide before you think well.
Do it before you go.
—Do not go before you do it.

(d) Degree of comparison—यदि comparative में वाक्य affirmative है तो so + positive + as जैसा उसे negative में बदलें।

She is cleverer than her sister.
—Her sister is not so clever as she.
I am as tall as you.
—You are not taller than I.

इसी तरह दिए गए negative sentence को affirmative में परिवर्तित करने के लिए उल्लिखित नियमों के विपरीत बनावट करनी चाहिए। जैसे—

(a) I was not sure of his arrival.
—I was doubtful of his arrival.
(b) He is not so wise as you. (are)
—You are wiser than he. (is)
(c) None but the brave deserve the fair.
—Only the brave (or the brave alone) deserve the fair.

(d)   There was none but appreciated his behaviour.
       —Everybody appreciated his behaviour.
                          Or
       There was none who did not appreciate his behaviour.

(e)   There is no smoke without fire.
       —Fire always causes smoke.

(f)   Do not smoke.
       —Abstain from smoking. (abstain ......)

(g)   He does not drink.
       —He refrains from drinking.

(h)   He did not make many tables.
       —He made a few tables.

(i)   No fool like an old fool.
       An old fool surpasses all fools.

Exercise 1

Transform the following sentences into negative :

1.   Dashrath loved Ram.
2.   As soon as he cried his father came.
3.   Calcutta is the largest city of India.
4.   He is stronger than I.
5.   He goes to bed after midnight.
6.   Only a little child would talk like this.
7.   I went to see my ailing uncle.
8.   He was doubtful in his son's success.
9.   Everyone desires to make money quickly.
10. Enevy begets enevy.
11. He is seldom punctual.
12. He tried every means.
13. Abstain from alcoholic drink.
14. Look before you leap.
15. Every cloud has a silver lining.
16. You are sometimes nervous.
17. I will always love you.
18. The fact is fabricated.
19. Everyone will admit that he left no stone unturned.
20. He alone deserves the post.

Exercise 2

Transform the following sentences into affirmative :

1.   No sooner did he see the tiger than he fled.
2.   None but Ram was selected in the college.
3.   We should not disobey our parents.
4.   He is not cruel.
5.   He did not accept the request.

6. Nothing but a miracle can save him.
7. He was not dishonest.
8. Life did not seem easy to him.
9. You are not always earnest.
10. We were not sure that the day would be fair.
11. They never fail who die in a great cause.
12. The house on a hill is never hidden.
13. No man in the city is so rich as he.
14. God does not forget the tears of the poor.
15. They are slept never to awake.
16. Nobody can bear his such act.
17. He is not a man of mean repute.
18. He did not fail to bring the medicine.
19. We should never be cruel.
20. He is not always impartial.

5. Different Ways of Expressing Condition

एक conditional sentence (शर्तवाले वाक्य) को अनेक प्रकार से conditional sentences में बदला जा सकता है। इसके लिए कुछ प्रमुख conjunctions/phrases निम्नस्थ रूप में देखे जा सकेंगे—

If, unless, in case, provided, but for, supposing, should, had, were, and, or, one more, etc.

(a)   If you are clever, you can explain it.

Or

You can explain it provided you are clever.

Or

Should you be clever, you can explain it.

Or

In case you are clever, you can explain it.

Or

Supposing that you are clever, you can explain it.

Or

Be clever and you can explain it.

Or

Unless you are clever, you cannot explain it.

(b)   If he had worked hard, he would have passed.

Or

Had he worked hard, he would have passed.

Or

In case (or provided that) he had worked hard, he would have passed.

(c)   Move and you will be killed.

Or

If you move, you will be killed.

(d)   **Abuse me and you will be beaten.**

Or

If you abuse me, you will be beaten.

(e)   Be careful or you will lose.

Or

Unless you are careful, you will lose.

Or

If you are not careful, you will lose.

(f)   If he had not warned, I should have fallen.

Or

But for his warning, I should have fallen.

(g)   If I were an angel, I should arouse the fairies.

Or

Were I an angel, I should arouse the fairies.

Exercise 1

Change into conditional sentences :

1.   If I were at your place, I should never think so.
2.   If you go to Prayag, you will see the famous fort.
3.   In case it rains, I will not go to the pictures.
4.   Had you come here, I should have told you all.
5.   Speak one word and you will be punished.
6.   Say you are sorry and I will forgive you.
7.   If you were to do so, why would you invite me ?
8.   Were you there, you would break your heart.
9.   Unless you go there, he cannot help you.
10.   I can help you, provided you accept it.

6. Ways of Expressing Concession or Contrast

इसमें concession वाले clause को *although, though, even if, despite, however, indeed, notwith-standing, in spite of, as*, etc. से प्रगट किया जाता है तथा contrast हेतु *but, yet, all the same, nonetheless*, etc. का प्रयोग किया जाता है।

Though the way was long the day was fine.

Or

Although the way was long the day was fine.

Or

In spite of (or despite) the way being long, the day was fine.

Or

Long as the way was, the day was fine.

Or

Even if the way was long, the day was fine.

Or

The way was long yet (nonetheless/but/all the same/nevertheless) the day was fine.

Exercise 1

Express the following sentences in different ways of concession or contrast :

1.   Although he was slow he was sure.
2.   He began late nevertheless he finished first.

3. Despite being late, we decided to go.
4. For all my unwillingness, I helped him.
5. Notwithstanding his best effort, he could not succeed.
6. Rich as he was, he was not happy.
7. You are clever indeed but you failed to compete.
8. Even if it rains heavily, I must come.
9. In spite of favourable wind, the sailors did not go to sea.
10. Though he has nothing he has all.

7. Interchange of Exclamatory and Assertive Sentences

यदि Exclamatory sentence Hurrah आदि से आनन्दबोधक संकेत दे तो It + verb + joyful के पश्चात् that से बनाकर उसे Assertive sentence में बदलें। यदि Alas आदि के द्वारा खेद/शोक का संकेत दे तो regretful/ sorrowful रखें। यदि Bravo, how, what से वाक्य रहे तो इनका लोप करके सामान्य वाक्य बनाएँ जिसमें very/great + adjective/noun etc. का प्रयोग करें। यदि O, would से लालसा का बोध हो तो इनके लिए I wish के पश्चात् that से clause बनाएँ। यही प्रक्रिया विपरीत रूप में Assertive को Exclamatory में परिवर्तित करने के लिए करें। जैसे—

(a) Hurrah ! I have got the prize.
 —It is very joyful that I have got the prize.
(b) Alas ! my dog is no more !
 —It is regretful (sorrowful or a matter of sorrow) that my dog is no more.
(c) Bravo ! he hit a lucky shot !
 —He hit a very lucky shot.
(d) What a fine morning it is !
 —The morning is really very fine.
   Or
 It is really a very fine morning.
(e) O, that I were a prince !
 —I wish that I were a prince.
(f) It is very joyful that we have done well.
 —Hurrah ! we have done well.
(g) I wish that I were a millionaire.
 —O, that I were a millionaire !

Exercise 1

Transform these sentences into assertive sentences :

1. O, that I were a child again !
2. Alas ! I have lost my pen.
3. Hurrah ! you stood first.
4. Bravo ! a good running between the wickets.
5. How beautiful the rain is !
6. What a charming landscape !
7. O, that I were always young !
8. Ah ! for a drop of water !
9. Hurrah ! I have won the lottery.
10. Alas ! my child is kidnapped.

11.   Oh ! for the wing of a dove !
12.   What a piece of work is man.
13.   How tiresome !

8. Interchange of Degrees of Comparison

1. यदि प्रस्तुत वाक्य superlative degree में हो तो positive में बदलने के लिए No से वाक्य प्रारम्भ करके as (so) + positive + as जैसी बनावट करें और comparative हेतु comparative + than + other जैसा परिवर्तन करें।

He is the richest man in the town. (s)
—No man in the town is so rich as he. (p)
He is richer than any other man in the town. (c)
John is not the cleverest student of the class. (s)
John may be cleverer than most students of the class. (c)
There are a few students cleverer than John. (c)
There are some students who are atleast as clever as John. (p)

Note. Comparison केवल दो के मध्य होता है। दो से अधिक के लिए other का प्रयोग करें। Superlative degree दो से अधिक में प्रयुक्त होती है, केवल दो में नहीं।

He is not so wise as his brother (is). (p)
He is less wise than his brother. (c)
His brother is wiser than he (is). (c)

इसका superlative संभव नहीं।

2. यदि प्रस्तुत वाक्य में one of the + adjective(s) + countable noun (plural) रहे तो positive के लिए very few से वाक्य प्रारम्भ करके उसमें as(so) + positive + as जैसा प्रयोग करें तथा comparative के लिए a few से प्रारम्भ करके पश्चात् में comparative-degree तथा than का प्रयोग करें। जैसे—

Ashok is one of the greatest kings of India. (s)
i.e., Ashok is not the greatest Indian king. (s)
Very few Indian kings are as great as Ashok. (p)

Or

Ashok is not so great as some other Indian kings. (p)
A few Indian kings are greater than Ashok. (c)

Or

Ashok is greater than most Indian kings. (c)

निष्कर्ष यह है कि इन स्थितियों में नियमबद्धता कम, तर्क अधिक है, जैसे—

A horse is not more useful than a cow. (c)
i.e., A cow is (probably) more useful than a horse. (c)
i.e., A cow is (undoubtedly) as useful as a horse. (p)

Exercise 1

Change the degrees of comparison of the following in as many ways as possible :

1.   Mumbai is the busiest sea-port of India.
2.   June is the hottest month.
3.   Thorium is as useful as uranium.
4.   This pen is cheaper than that.

5. She is as tall as her brother (is).
6. Milton was the greatest English poet.
7. No lady was so beautiful as Helen of Troy.
8. Very few countries are as hot as Ceylone.
9. Calcutta is not larger than Delhi.
10. A few Hindi poets are greater than Tulsidas.
11. This tree is higher than any other tree in the garden.
12. This is not the smallest T.V. set in the town.
13. It is easier than most questions.
14. A live ass is better than a dead lion.
15. It is better to reign in hell than serve in heaven.
16. Words are as empty as dry leaves.
17. Discretion is better than valour.
18. Australia is the largest island in the world.
19. This newspaper has a wider circulation than any other newspaper.
20. 'Shakuntalam' is one of the masterpieces of the world literature.

9. Conversion of Simple Sentence to Complex and Vice-versa

जैसा कि पूर्व में संकेत दिया जा चुका है, Simple sentence में एक ही subject, verb etc. हुआ करते हैं जब कि Complex sentence में एक principal clause तथा एक या एक से अधिक subordinate clauses हुआ करते हैं। Simple को Complex में परिवर्तित करने के लिए Simple sentence के किसी प्रमुख word or phrase को Complex sentence के अन्तर्गत आने वाले noun, adjective or adverb clause में बदल देते हैं। इस हेतु कुछ निम्नस्थ शब्दों की सहायता ली जा सकती है—

That, if, who, whom, whose, which, why, where, when, lest, unless, till, before, after, though, because, as, since, just as, as soon as, than, so ... that, etc. Complex को Simple में बदलने के लिए विपरीत प्रक्रिया का प्रयोग करें।

Simple	Complex
1. He is said to be a talisman.	It is said that he is a talisman.
2. Tell me the time of his arrival.	Tell me when he arrives.
3. I know his birth place.	I know where he was born.
4. We saw a blue eyed girl.	We saw a girl whose eyes were blue.
5. The tall man is John's father.	The man who is tall is John's father.
6. Can you show me his residence ?	Can you show me the place where he lives (or resides) ?
7. A high climber certainly falls.	A man who climbs high-certainly falls.
8. You cannot succeed without hard work.	You cannot succeed unless you work hard.
9. A rolling stone gathers no moss.	A stone that rolls gathers no moss.

Complex	Simple
1. Although he is wealthy, he is not happy.	In spite of his wealth, he is not happy. *Or* In spite of being wealthy he is not happy.
2. If you walk in the morning, your health will improve.	Walking in the morning will improve your health.
3. He cannot continue his study because he is poor.	Due to poverty, he cannot continue his study.
4. He is a man who has power.	He is a man of power.
5. I hope that better days will come.	I hope for better days to come. *Or* I hope for the coming of better days.
6. A learned man is respected wherever he goes.	A learned man is respected everywhere.
7. Can you count why he failed ?	Can you count the reason of his failure ?
8. The garments that are borrowed never fit well.	Borrowed garments never fit well.
9. Blessed are they that mourn.	The mourners are blessed.

Exercise 1

Transform the following simple sentences into complex sentences :

1. He thinks of getting a lucrative job.
2. I noticed a girl with a basket of flowers in her hand.
3. Barking dogs seldom bite.
4. He worked hard to earn his living.
5. Only the honest will prosper.
6. Because of heavy rain I could not go out.
7. Tell me your achievement.
8. Despite being old, he works as a young man.
9. You will find despiteful persons everywhere.
10. I want you to join the army.
11. A lost moment never returns.
12. He is too unable to express his feelings.
13. I found my lost book.
14. I gave a rupee to a blind man.
15. Good wine needs no bush.
16. Never think of the past.
17. Will you help me in my need ?
18. The dog without tail is mine.
19. He was returned because of popularity.
20. His conception of life in objects is meaningful.

Exercise 2

Transform the following complex sentences into simple sentences :

1. I cannot say if he will succeed this year.
2. The birds that were little were singing melodious songs.
3. The whole forest was filled with the fragrance that was ravishing.
4. She cast a charm that was bewitching.
5. I noticed a girl whose hair was curly.
6. Can you tell me when he comes ?
7. Tell me what the price of this book is.
8. What is his aim of life is uncertain.
9. He asked me why I was late.
10. All that glitters is not gold.
11. He who amasses wealth loses health.
12. She is older than she looks.
13. We believe that he is a man of good sense.
14. His poverty testifies that he is honest.
15. Since you are weak you should take rest.
16. Can you guess what after your refusal will happen ?
17. I cannot see unless I wear glasses.
18. I thanked him because he did a yeoman's service.
19. Just as I entered the room I saw a snake.
20. Where you live I will live.

10. Interchange of Simple and Compound Sentences

Complex sentence की तरह compound sentence में भी एक से अधिक वाक्य हुआ करते हैं किन्तु वे main clause के समानान्तर या समकक्ष हुआ करते हैं। उन्हें Co-ordinate clauses कहा जाता है। ऐसे clauses निम्नस्थ Co-ordinating conjunctions से जोड़े जाते हैं–

And, as well as, not only ... but also, either ... or, neither ... nor, or, nor, otherwise, so, therefore, for, but, still, yet, etc. यदि अनेक subordinate clauses से बने sentence में कोई co-ordinate clause आ जाएगा तो उस स्थिति में वह compound sentence होगा।

इस प्रकार उपरोक्त conjunctions से बने (main clause और co-ordinate clause के) compound sentence का simple के लिए विपरीत अवस्था में रूपान्तरण करना पड़ेगा अर्थात् उन conjunctions का लोप करके उस compound sentence का संक्षिप्तीकरण करें जिसमें एक ही verb रहे। जैसे–

Simple	Compound
1. Taking a pen, he wrote a poem.	He took a pen and wrote a poem.
2. You secured first class by dint of hard labour.	You laboured hard so you secured first class.
	Or
	You secured first for you laboured hard.
3. Besides defeating the enemy, Shivaji seized many forts.	Shivaji not only defeated the enemy but also seized many forts.
4. Being driven by hunger, he stole a piece of bread.	He was driven by hunger so he stole a piece of bread.

5. He must not escape at the cost of his life.	He must not escape or he will lose his life.
6. Owing to poverty, he left the village bag and baggage.	He was poor so he left the village bag and baggage.
7. Having completed homework, I went to bed.	I completed homework and went to bed.

Compound	Simple
1. He is weak still he is not disheartened.	Inspite of weakness, he is not disheartened.
2. We must eat or we cannot live.	We must eat to live.
3. He had a lot of money yet he had to undergo an untold misery.	Inspite of a lot of money, he had to undergo an untold misery.
4. He organised a strong army and recovered his kingdom.	Having organised a strong army, he recovered his kingdom.
5. First deserve then desire.	Do not desire undeservedly.
6. The physician made the best effort but he could not save the patient.	Inspite of the best effort, the physician could not save the patient.
7. You are the head of the family hence you should be reserved.	Being the head of the family, you should be reserved.

Exercise 1

Rewrite the following sentences as compound ones :

1.   Seeing the sky cloudy, I took an umbrella.
2.   Besides giving my son the formal education, I also taught him manners.
3.   The book being torn, he is to buy a new one.
4.   Mr. Gardiner, seizing his hat and stick, got down from the train.
5.   Being chased by hounds, the deer ran off the dense forest.
6.   Inspite of popularity, he cannot be accounted a man of merit.
7.   Seeing the crow, the fox began to praise it.
8.   For all his learning, he was not proud.
9.   Due to dark and stormy night I abandoned the idea of coming to you.
10. Notwithstanding his ability, he failed.
11. His personality, being inviting, many people liked him.
12. On account of long strike, the factory was permanently closed.
13. Being disappointed, he left their company.
14. For all his wealth, he is discontented.
15. Seeing the youngones of the swallow, the falcon pounced upon it.
16. People admire him because of his simplicity.
17. Despite its capacity, the machine does not work properly.
18. The sun, having set, the birds flew to their nests.
19. Besides making a promise, he kept it.
20. The fog, being dense, nothing was clearly visible.

Exercise 2

Convert the following double sentence into simple sentences :

1. He helped the disabled man and went away.
2. He was late so he failed to reach in time.
3. He is a learned man but in practical life he fails.
4. Ask pardon or you will suffer.
5. The parliament passed the bill but the people voiced against it.
6. He was not only harassed but was also left heedless.
7. The earthquake came and devastated a large area.
8. The aircraft clashed with a vulture and crashed.
9. The child is either kidnapped or drowned.
10. I sent the telegram but he did not came.
11. She opened the window and peeped out.
12. You are sinful so you must suffer.
13. He is poor still he preserves prestige.
14. The ship sank and went aground.
15. I went to Allahabad where I bathed in the confluence.
16. The coat is tattered and it needs mending.

11. Interchange of Complex and Compound Sentences

Complex sentence को double sentence अथवा double को complex में बदलने से पूर्व एक बार पुन: दोनों के कुछ मुख्य connectives का अवलोकन करें–

Complex Sentence (Subordinating Conjunctions)	Compound Sentence (Co-ordinating Conjunctions)
That, who, which, whom, whose, when, where, how, before, after, just as, as soon as, while, as, lest, than, because, unless, till, until, if since, though, so ... that etc.	And, as well as, not only ... but also, or, nor, either ... or, neither ... nor, otherwise, so, therefore, for, but, still, yet, etc.

Complex को compound में परिवर्तित करने के लिए उसके main clause को co-ordinating conjunction से जोड़ें तथा complex के subordinate clause को compound में main clause बना दें। यही प्रक्रिया compound को complex में बदलने के लिए विपरीत रूप में करें अर्थात् compound के co-ordinate clause को complex में main clause बना दें तथा उसके main clause को complex में subordinating conjunction से जोड़कर subordinate clause बनाएँ। संक्षेप में–

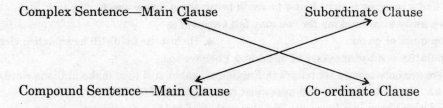

Complex Sentence	Compound Sentence
1. If you spare the rod, you will spoil the child.	Spare the rod and you will spoil the child.
2. Though he is a learned man, he is not a good teacher.	He is a learned man yet he is not a good teacher.
3. If you do not do, you will die.	Do or die.
4. If you prick me, I must cry.	Prick me and I must cry.
5. People liked him because he was handsome.	He was handsome therefore people liked him.
6. When we saw the storm coming, we took shelter in a hut.	We saw the storm coming and took shelter in a hut.
7. You are not strong though you are tall.	You are tall but you are not strong.
8. We went to a restaurant because the train was late.	The train was late so we went to a restaurant.
9. The Rajputs failed though they fought bravely.	The Rajputs fought bravely still they failed.
10. I am sure that you have stolen my pen.	You have stolen my pen and I am sure of it.

Exercise 1

Convert the following complex sentences into compound sentences :

1. I had tried my best before I got this job.
2. It is a matter of regret that he has lost all decencies.
3. If you are aimless, you will not succeed. 4. You desire because you deserve.
5. Since you speak the truth, I forgive you.
6. The patient dies because there was no physician.
7. Her condition was so pathetic that everybody took pity on her.
8. Although we are strong, we have no courage.
9. They settled at a place where they could find the living easily.
10. He who laughs last laughs best.
11. Take a torch because it is very dark.
12. You must be reserved lest you should suffer.
13. While all the races declined we survived.
14. He fell into deep worries because he had lost all hopes of success.
15. His book was widely recognised because it sparkled with the flashes of lustrous beauty.

Exercise 2

Rewrite the following compound sentences as complex ones :

1. He had a piercing insight hence he could bring about a new epoch.
2. Keep away from smoking for you may fall victim of it.
3. Keep quiet or go out. 4. He lost the field still he snatched victory from it.
5. Popularity is a bad measure of merit and I believe so.
6. There are only twenty six letters in English alphabet still they make millions words.
7. Dawn turns into dusk so darkness must turn into dawn.
8. I had never been in a large city and this rather added to my misery.

9. We fear to get into rows so we observe the rules seriously.
10. I tried but I became almost discouraged.
11. Hunting with a camera is the best sport for it does not involve killing.
12. Make haste otherwise we shall miss the train.
13. I persuaded him but he could not be convinced.
14. He was intelligent so he stood first.
15. The weather was wretched but the night was clear.

Exercise 3

Change the following sentences as directed in the brackets :

1. Iron is the most useful of all metals.   (Positive degree)
2. The Taj is a very beautiful monument.   (Exclamatory)
3. No one can put up with such conduct.   (Interrogative)
4. Only a little child would talk like this.   (Negative)
5. Nepolean was the Greatest general of his time.   (Positive degrees)
6. None but Ram was selected in the college.   (Affirmative)
7. No one ever saw a greater misfortune.   (Interrogative)
8. Samudra Gupt was one of the greatest kings of India.   (Positive and Comparative Degrees)
9. You are not as good as I.   (Comparative Degree)
10. Nobody would like to be called a fool.   (Interrogative)
11. The box is too heavy for me to lift.   (Remove 'too')
12. Who has seen death ?   (Assertive)
13. Some grains are at least as nutritious as rice.   (Superlative Degree)
14. O, that I were a bird !   (Complex)
15. It is impossible that he may recover.   (Simple)
16. I have not seen him for ten years.   (Replace 'for' by 'since')
17. How sweet the moonlight is !   (Assertive)
18. He rejected our proposal.   (Negative)
19. It is no joke.   (Affirmative)
20. Just as I reached there it began to rain.   (Change Main Clause into Subordinate)
21. There is none but will agree with me.   (Affirmative)
22. You appear to be ill.   (Negative)
23. He was so beneficent that he helped me.   (Use enough)
24. He asked me a question which I could not answer.   (Interchange Clauses)
25. It was a very narrow escape.   (Exclamatory)
26. You are not the tallest boy in the village.   (Change the Degree)
27. Tell me why you did it.   (Simple)
28. He has none to look after him.   (Adjective Clause)
29. What though they were indifferent to you ?   (Assertive)
30. Who has not seen you crossing the bar ?   (Assertive)
31. Very few men are as rich as he.   (Change the Degree)
32. We are sure that you are honest.   (Compound)
33. He was more to blame than anyone else.   (Negative)
34. She is thought to be a witch.   (Noun Clause)
35. I will live with you.   (Adverb Clause)

Chapter 17

Figures of Speech
(अलंकार)

'A figure of speech' is a recognized form of abnormal expression giving variety, force etc.'

—C.O.D.

'A figure of speech is a deviation from the ordinary use of words with a view to increase their effect.'

—Nesfield

1. Simile (उपमा)

'In simile a comparison is made between two objects of different kinds which have however at least one point in common.' It is introduced by such words as like, as, so.

उपमा अलंकार दो भिन्न वस्तुओं की समता या तुलना को कहते हैं जिनमें कम से कम एक समान धर्म हो और जिसे like, as या so जैसे वाचक शब्द से व्यक्त किया गया हो। ध्यान रहे कि एक ही जाति की वस्तुओं की समता simile नहीं होता।

1. Her face was beautiful as the full moon.
2. Thy soul was like a star and dwelt apart.
3. Life is like a dome of many coloured glass.
4. I wandered lonely as a cloud.
5. O, my love is like a red, red rose.
6. But life's way is like the wind's way.
7. She falls like a tear from the eyes of a bride.
8. She walks in beauty, like the night the of cloudless climes and starry skies.

Some common similes—as wise as an owl ; as mad as a March Hare ; as proud as a peacock ; as bold as brass ; as innocent as a lamb ; as clear as crystal ; as good as gold ; as pale as death, etc.

2. Metaphor (रूपक)

A metaphor is an implied simile (an abridged simile) without like, as or so as introducing words. Metaphor संक्षिप्त simile हुआ करता है जिसमें simile के वाचक शब्द like, as या so का लोप हो जाता है।

1. Whose armour is his honest thought.
2. Life is but a walking shadow.
3. Revenge is a kind of wild justice.
4. The camel is the ship of the desert.
5. The news was a dagger to his heart.
6. Rana Pratap was a lion in the battlefield.
7. Variety is the spice of life.
8. Whose simple truth is his utmost skill.

190

Note. A metaphor can be turned into a simile by introducing the words like, as or so and a simile can be turned into a metaphor by omitting those words, *viz.*

> Life is a dream. (Metaphor)
>
> Life is like a dream. (Simile)

3. Personification (मानवीकरण)

A personification mirrors some dead, lifeless things or abstract notions as a living being. किसी मृत, निर्जीव या स्वरूपहीन वस्तु को जीवित व्यक्ति के रूप में कल्पित करना personification कहलाता है। The personified object or image is often written in a capital letter, *e.g.*

1. But Patience, to prevent that murmur, soon replies.
2. Authority forgets a dying king.
3. Death lays his icy hands on kings.
4. Let not Ambition mock their useful toil.
5. Pride goeth forth on horseback, gay and grand.
6. The Moon veiled her face.
7. Worry sits at his face.
8. Avarice has a long unquenchable thirst.

4. Apostrophe (सम्बोधन)

'An apostrophe is a direct address to the dead, to the absent or to a personified object or idea.' (Wren). किसी अमूर्त वस्तु, विचार अथवा मृत व्यक्ति को सम्बोधित करना Apostrophe कहलाता है। जैसे–

1. O World ! O life ! O Time !
2. O solitude ! where art thy charms ?
3. Death ! where art thou ?
4. O captain ! my captain ! our fearful trip is done.
5. Exult, O shores ! and ring, O bells !
6. For me, O my master ! the rapture of love.
7. Roll on ! thou deep and dark blue ocean-roll.
8. Milton ! thou shouldst be living at this hour.

5. Hyperbole (अतिशयोक्ति)

A hyperbole is an overstatement or some kind of exaggeration, not meant to be taken literally. जहाँ वास्तविक वस्तु/व्यक्ति/स्थिति को अतिशयोक्ति रूप में अभिव्यक्त किया जाय Hyperbole होता है। जैसे–

1. He sneezed and the Himalayas reduced to dust.
2. Ten thousand saw I at a glance.
3. Belinda smiled and all the world was gay.
4. All the perfumes of Arabia can not sweeten this little hand.
5. She wept oceans of tears.
6. The waves rose mountains high.
7. The sky shrank upward with unusual dread.
8. He stopped the furious river in one thunder.

6. Oxymoron (विरोधाभास)

It is an expression of two words or phrases containing contradictory (opposite) meanings. परस्पर विरोधी अर्थों वाले शब्दों की अभिव्यक्ति को Oxymoron कहते हैं। जैसे–

1. Life is a sweet pain.
2. Lord of himself, though not of lands, and having nothing he hath all.
3. I heard the silent music of life.
4. Never we saw such a holy sinner.
5. His honour rooted in dishonour stood, and faith unfaithful kept him falsely true.
6. Our sweetest songs are those that tell of saddest thoughts.
7. He fell victim of her kind cruelty.
8. He is regularly irregular.

7. Onomatopoeia (ध्वन्यालंकार)

'It is a formation of names or words from sounds that resemble those associated with the object or action to be named, or that seem naturally suggestive of its qualities ; e.g., Cuckoo.' (C.O.D.) जब शब्द की ध्वनि से उसका भाव अभिव्यक्त हो जाय Onomatopoeia figure of speech होगा।

1. And beauty born of murmuring sound shall pass into her face.
2. Grunt, grunt goes the hog.
3. The curfew tolls the knell of parting day.
4. We heard twittering of numerous birds.
5. I heard the hissing of a snake.
6. The humming of countless bees.
7. The shrill screaming of birds.
8. Canon to right of them.
   Canon to left of them.
   Canon in front of them.
   Volleyed and thundered.

Exercise 1

Name the figures of speech in the following :

1. As shines the moon in clouded sky.
   She in her poor attire was seen.
2. Life is a funeral march.
3. Blow, blow thou winter wind !
4. Experience is the best teacher.
5. Sardar Patel was the iron man of India.
6. Self-excuse is like self-accuse.
7. Like the dew on the mountain.
   Like the foam on the river.
   Like the bubble on the fountain.
   Thou art gone and forever.
8. How far that little candle throws his beam !
9. James first was the wisest fool.
10. Sweet Thames ! run softly, till I end my song.
11. It droppeth as the gentle rain from heaven.
12. Whose armour is his honest thought.
13. As old Time makes these decay
    so his flames must waste away.

14. The swallow was twittering from the straw-built shed.
15. She shall be sportive as the fawn.
16. I see the waves upon the shore
    like light dissolved in star-showers thrown.
17. I see a lily on thy face.
18. Expanding like the petals of young flowers.
19. I see fame in the mirror of futurity.
20. Wherefore, let thy voice
    Rise like a fountain for me night and day.
21. I hear the lake water lapping with low sounds.
22. She sways like a flower in the wind of our song.
23. The noon is a mystic dog with paws of fire.
24. The sea that bares her bosom to the moon.
25. Thus, idly busy rolls the world away.
26. Break, break, break
    on thy cold grey shores, O sea !
27. I chatter, chatter as I flow
    To join the brimming river.
28. He has a heart of stone.
29. She is as fresh as dew.
30. She floats like a laugh from the lips of a dream.
31. Death lays his icy hands on kings.
32. They build the nation's pillars deep.
    And lift them to the sky.
33. Thy soul was like a star and dwelt apart.
34. Great lord of all things yet a prey to all.
35. Ten thousand saw I at a glance.
36. O heavy lightness, serious vanity.
37. Errors like straws upon the surface flow.
38. Our sweetest songs are those.
    That tell of saddest thoughts.
39. She walks in beauty, like the night
    of cloudless climes and starry skies.
40. The Wind lies asleep in the arms of the dawn.
41. Revenge is a kind of wild justice.
42. Hasten slowly.
43. Charity suffereth long, and is kind.
44. Humour is a seamy side of life.
45. Exult, O shores ! and ring, O bells !
46. The Moon borrowed beauty from her.
47. Where ignorance is bliss, it is folly to be wise.
48. Heard melodies are sweet but those unheard are sweeter.
49. As you sow, so will you reap.
50. Like water we came, like wind we go.

Some More Figures of Speech

8. Alliteration (अनुप्रास)

It is a commencement of words in close connection with the same letter or sound.
1. The field of freedom, faction, fame.
2. He died unseen, unwept, unheard, unknown.
3. Leave love for love of lovers, for woe's sake.
4. A load of learning lumbering in his head.
5. Since pleasures end in pain,
   And love in loss, and life in hateful death.
6. Life is a moan, a sigh, a sab, a storm, a strife.

9. Antithesis (विरोधालंकार)

It is a contrast of words or ideas expressed by parallelism of strongly contrasted words.
1. To err is human, to forgive divine.
2. Give everyman thy ear, but few thy voice.
3. Science knows but art does.
4. Not that I loved Caesar less, but that I loved Rome more.
5. United we stand, divided we fall.

10. Assonance (ध्वनिसाम्यता)

Assonance means resemblance of sound between two syllables or rhyming of one word with another in the accented vowel and those that follow.
1. Bear your tears and fears.
2. He was a pioneer and prophet born in a palace.
3. Equality, liberty and fraternity.
4. Rest and relief, recreation and relaxation.
5. Glad, sad and bad aspects of life.

11. Climax (चरमोत्कर्ष)

It is the arrangement of a series of sentiments in the order of increasing importance.
1. I came ; I saw ; I conquered.
2. Some are born great, some achieve greatness
   and some have greatness thrust upon them.
3. He fought, he flew, he fell.
4. Some books are to be tasted, others swallowed and some few to be chewed and digested.

12. Anti Climax

It is opposite of climax—a sudden descent from higher to lower. It is chiefly used for the sake of satire, ridicule or humour.
1. He was noble, upright, kind and would often steal loaves.
2. The earthquake damaged his all property and his cup too.
3. Here thou, great Anna, whom three realms obey,
   Dost sometimes counsel take and sometimes tea.

13. Epigram (चुटकुला)

It is a short poem ending in witty, turn of thought or pointed saying or mode of expression.

1. The child is the father of man.
2. Fools rush in where angels fear to tread.
3. Art lies in concealing art.
4. Open rebuke is better than secret love.
5. Our sweetest songs are those that tell of saddest thoughts.
6. He makes no friend, who never made a foe.

14. Euphemism (मधुरोक्ति)

It is a substitution of mild or vague expression for harsh or blunt one. 'Queer' is an euphemism for 'mad'.

1. You are telling me a fairy tale. (*i.e.*, a lie)
2. This car is a white elephant. (*i.e.*, a burdensome possession)
3. He fell into the arms of orpheus. (*i.e.*, slept soundly)
4. He was in the seventh heaven. (*i.e.*, in a state of extreme delight.)

15. Irony (व्यंगोक्ति)

Irony is a mode of speech in which the real meaning is exactly the opposite of that which is literally conveyed.

1. No doubt but you are the people, and wisdom shall die with you.
2. Yet Brutus says he was ambitious, and Brutus is an honourable man.
3. Fair sir, you spat on me last Wednesday,
   and at another time you called me dog, and
   for these acts of courtesy, I shall lend you this much money.

16. Paradox (विरोधाभास)

It is a statement contrary to the received opinion or seemingly absurd though perhaps really well-founded statement.

1. I have never known so young a body with so old a head.
2. Do a little wrong in order to do a great right.
3. There is no one so poor as a wealthy miser.
4. The child is the father of man.

17. Pathetic Fallacy (संवेदनाभास)

It means crediting Nature with human emotion.

1. The sky shed tears at her woeful state.
2. The rude sea grew cold at her song.

18. Pun (श्लेष)

Pun is a humorous use of words to suggest different meanings.

1. Is life worth living ? That depends on liver.
2. An ambassador is an honest man who lies abroad for the good of his country.

3. Hostess, I took you in last night, I say.
    Dr. Syntax : 'Tis true, and if this bill I pay
    you'll take me in again today.
    [Take in *i.e.,* (*i*) receive into house as a guest. (*ii*) to cheat.]

19. Sarcasm (कटाक्ष)

It is a bitter or wounding remark especially one ironically worded.

1. There are three sexes : men, women and clergymen.
2. How these Christians love one another !

20. Tautology (पुनरूक्ति)

It means the use of two or more words or phrases having the grammatical situation.

1. He may again regain his property.
2. Life is a sob, a sigh, a strife.
3. Slavery and drudgery lagged the country far behind.

21. Transferred Epithet (विशेषण विपर्यय)

Here an epithet is transferred from its proper word to another that is closely associated with it in the sentence.

1. He spent a sleepless night.
2. He spent an anxious night on a restless pillow.

Chapter 18

Precis-Writing

The word 'precis' means summary, abstract. It is related to 'precise'. But it would be better to mean as a brief, orderly and clear expression of the given passage. In order to make a summary of the passage, we must follow these instructions :

(a) To find out the essential idea, you must read the passage fairly, quickly and carefully. You may do so twice or thrice.

(b) Make a rough draft arranging the important matters logically. Then make the draft more abridged. It should be noted that your precis should not exceed one-third of the original passage. Besides these, no important point should be left out.

(c) A precis should be written in your own language simple, clear and precise. No personal comments or quotations should be given in the precis. Do not mention the examples of the passage in your precis nor use its illustrations.

(d) A precis must be written in indirect or reported speech i.e., in the past tense, third person. Avoid the use of figurative and flowery languages.

(e) In order to choose a suitable title you should focus your attention on the main theme of the passage. The title should reflect the subject precisely.

Model Passages with Their Precis
(From Intermediate General English)

1.   A book is essentially not a talked thing, but a written thing ; written not with the view of mere communication, but of permanance. The book of talk is printed only because its author cannot speak to thousands of people at once, if he could, he would—the volume is mere multiplication of his voice. You cannot talk to your friend in India, if you could, you would, you write instead : that is mere conveyance of voice. But a book is written, not to multiply the voice merely, not to carry it merely, but to preserve it. The author has something to say which he perceives to be true and useful, or helpfully beautiful. So far as he knows, no one has yet said it, so far as he knows, no one else can say it.

He is bound to say it, clearly and melodiously if he may, clearly, at all events. In the sum of his life he finds this to be the thing, or group of things, manifest to him—this the piece of true knowledge or sight. Which his share of sunshine and earth has permitted him to seize.

(a) The title of the passage would be : 'The Secret of Book.'

(b) The precis of the passage—A book is the voice of the author written and meant to attach permanance to his faith that he accounts to be true and useful for the mass. His object is to preserve his knowledge for the time to come. His book works as an agent to convey his thoughts to teeming readers living at home and abroad. He is

197

sure that he alone has designed and invented such an idea as is quite novel, clear and splendid.

2. In order to speak well you must know your subject. Speakers acquire their information from books, others from experience, and others, the best from both.

It is useless to endeavour to explain how would-be speakers should acquire power and shot for their speeches. Any such explanation would involve a discussion of the whole question of education. In short if a speaker has got very little in his head, he can get very little out of it.

Knowing a subject does not, however, imply the power of expressing what we know is a lucid and attractive form. Socrates was of opinion that everyone can speak sufficiently well about what he understands, but, as Cicero remarked, it would be more true to say that no one can speak well on a subject which he does not understand, and that even if he understands a subject he cannot speak well unless he knows how to express himself.

1. The suitable title of the passage should be—'The Art of Speaking.'

2. Summary of the passage—It is necessary for a good speaker to acquire a command over the subject of his speech. Such ability can be obtained either by books or by experience or by both. Besides these, his style must be clear, well-arranged and charming. He must know how to express his feelings.

3. The man who has not the habit of reading is imprisoned in his immediate world, in respect of time and space. His life falls into a set routine ; he is limited to contact and conversation with a few friends and acquaintances and he sees only that what happens in his immediate neighbourhood. From this prison there is no escape. But the moment he takes up a book, he is immediately put in touch with one of the best talkers of the world. This talker leads him on and carries him into a different country or a different age, or unburdens to him.

Some of his personal regrets, or discourses with him. Some special line or aspect of life that the reader knows nothing about. An ancient author puts him in communion with a dead spirit of long ago, and as he reads along, he begins to imagine what that ancient author looked like and what type of person he was.

(a) The suitable title of the passage should be—'The Blessing of Book.'

(b) Summary of the passage—A man untouched with books, is like an imprisoned man. But as soon as he comes into the contact of books, his mind soars away into the far past and abroad. He gets relief and relaxation. His communion with ancient authors widens his knowledge and charges power in order to enable him to have a novel outlook of life.

4. The modern age has witnessed a phenomenal rise in literacy. Cheap books, magazines, papers etc. have been pouring out in their tens of thousands with the result that the spread of education has been almost universal. However, there has been a visible decline in quality. The old culture of the people expressed in folk-song, dance, rustic craft etc. has been destroyed. The cinema, the radio, the popular literature, full of crime or love stories, have exploited the people for commercial purposes.

There has been an increase in vulgarity, brutality and coarseness. Human relationship has been coarsened and cheapened ; man has become incapable of finer and subtle emotional responses. Further, the cinema, the television and the cheap novel, have fostered a kind of day-dreaming and a proportionately weakened the grasp of reality. This lowering of tastes has had adverse effect on art and literature. Bad art and cheap literature have become the bone of the new age. Vigorous experiments are being made in the field of music and other fine arts, and literature, but this is a symptom of the breakdown of cultural continuity rather than of cultural vigour.

(a) The suitable title of the passage would be—'The Decline of Literature.'

(b) Precis of the passage—The tendency of modern young readers mostly rests on buying cheap and mediocre books and magazines. They get little taste and interest in reading popular literature. The result is that literature has to suffer a great loss. Secondly, the commercial movies full of love and crimes are mostly appreciated. Television and radio have also weakened the quality of literature. Consequently, literature has gone to waning.

5. He that loves a rosy cheek,

or a coral lip admires,

or from star like eyes, doth seek,

fuel to maintain his fires ;

As old time makes these decay,

so his flames must waste away.

But a smooth and steadfast mind,

Gentle thoughts and calm desires,

Hearts with equal love combined,

Kindle never-dying fires.

Where these are not I despise

lovely cheeks or lips or eyes.

(a) The suitable title of the poem would be—'The True Beauty'.

(b) Precis of the poem—Physical beauty is subject to perish away with the passage of time and the love born of it, also declines as soon as it fades. But the beauty endowed with unshakable thought, gentleness and serenity never dies.

Summarise the following passages and suggest suitable titles :

1. The advantage which punctually brings to man is manifold. A punctual man is never in want of time and hence he is never in a hurry. Whatever he does, he can do with perfect calmness and so his work has no defect and is perfect. He is never late in his work or in his appointments and consequently men can safely rely upon his promises and engagements. By his habit of punctuality he never puts others to inconvenience and accordingly wins the respect and confidence of all who come in contact with him. Further a punctual man has confidence in his own powers and knows that he cannot but be successful in any undertaking where time is an essential factor. One who attends office regularly and finishes his work punctually, is sure to come in good graces of his superior and secure promotion in service.

2. Man's worth cannot be evaluated in terms of wealth. He acquires value only through the cultivation of character. Therefore, he should not remain satisfied with the attainment of mere physical and mental powers ; he must strive to develop good character so that he may shine in all walks of life. The old Indian tradition proclaims the importance of character-building for religious fulfilment. That religion which does not stress the importance of character is no religion at all. Several people today attach importance to external practices and make a show of religion in a parade of pomp. They care little for internal purity. Outward show is no sign of good character. The development of good character consists not in practices external but in exercises internal. Inner purity is a must for cultivation of character.

3. Ashok's title to greatness was not only territorial but moral, not merely the geographical extent of his empire, but rather the principles of its administration. He stands out as the pioneer of peace, peace between man and man and between man and every sentient creature, for the sanctity of life and for the abolition of violence in every sphere, domestic and foreign, internal and international. He organised measures for the relief of suffering of men and animals by provision of medical treatment with medicine derived from sources such as herbs, roots and fruits, obtained by import where necessary and also by cultivation in the country of medicinal plants in specialised botanical gardens or plantations. In his Rock Edicts he reports that humanitarian measures were making good progress in the country and also in the states on its frontiers, while his religion of universal brotherhood impelled him to despatch to the more prominent foreign western countries fully equipped medical missions charged with the duty of introducing to them— these measures of social service and welfare. The kings of these Western countries, who were his contemporaries are mentioned by him in various inscriptions.

4. Human actions are modified by circumstances. A burnt child dreads the fire; if a parent arranged conditions so that every time a child touched a certain toy he got burnt, the child would learn to avoid that toy as automatically as he avoids touching fire. So far, however, we are dealing with what may be called training in distinction from educative teaching. The changes considered are in outer action rather than in mental and emotional dispositions of behaviour. The distinction is not, however, a sharp one. The child might conceivably generate in time a violent antipathy, not only to that particular toy, but to the class of toys resembling it. The aversion might even persist after he had forgotten about the original burn ; later on he might even invent some reason to account for his seemingly irrational antipathy. In some cases, altering the external habit of action by changing the environment to affect the stimuli to action will also alter the mental disposition concerned in the action. Yet this does not always happen ; a person trained to dodge a threatening blow, dodges automatically with no corresponding thought or emotion. We have to find, then, some differential of training from education.

5. It is the fashion now-a-days to bewail poverty as an evil, and to pity the young man who is not born with a silver spoon in his mouth, but I heartily subscribe to President Garfield's doctrine that 'the richest heritage a young man can be born to is poverty.' I make no publication when I say that it is the class from whom the good and the great will spring. It is not from the sons of millionaires on the nobles that the world receives its teachers, its martyrs, its inventors, its statesmen, its poets or even its men of affairs. It is from the cottage of the poor that all these spring. We can scarcely read one among the few immortal names that were not born to die or who have rendered exceptional service to our race, who had not the advantage of being cradled, nursed and reared in the stimulating school of poverty.

6. Every man reaps the result of his own actions. If he is active, he will be rewarded for his activity and if he is idle, he will have to suffer for his idleness. Many men have a tendency to sit idle, for they say it is impossible to do anything against fate. But there can be nothing so foolish as to believe that luck or destiny makes one's fortune.

We all know that 'Fortune favours the brave', and there is no exaggeration in this. Fortune comes only to those who have the capacity to face dangers without shrinking and who are not disheartened by failure. To trust fate and remain inactive, is nothing but cowardice, and it is idle to expect that fortune will ever favour such cowards.

Chapter 19

Idioms and Phrases

Idiom means form of expression peculiar to a language. Phrase means an idiomatic expression or small group of words usually without predicate. Phrases can be divided into three parts (i) Noun phrase (ii) Adjective phrase and (iii) Adverbial phrase.

Besides these, more classifications of phrases are possible, viz. (iv) Prepositional phrases (v) Participial phrases (vi) Infinitive phrases (vii) Gerund phrases (viii) Absolute phrases etc.

Part I

Noun Phrases

ABC (elementary knowledge प्रारम्भिक ज्ञान)—He does not know even the ABC of physics.

Apple of discord (bone of contention विवाद की जड़)—The paternal property was the apple of discord among them.

A black sheep (mean fellow कुल कलंकी)—Tom was a black sheep in the family of Ramsay.

Bed of roses (a luxurious thing सुख शय्या)—Life is not a bed of roses.

Broad daylight (during daytime दिन दहाड़े)—The robbers came in broad daylight.

Bosom friend (the dearest friend सर्वप्रिय मित्र)—A real bosom friend will never leave you in the lurch.

A burning question (an important topic प्रमुख प्रश्न)—Terrorism is a burning question of today.

Castles in the air (imaginary scheme हवाई किला)—Be practical and never build castles in the air.

Casting vote (decisive vote निर्णायक मत)—The bill totally depends on the casting vote.

Crocodile tears (Showy tears दिखावटी या घड़ियाली आँसू)—Md. **Tuglaque** shed crocodile tears over the death of his uncle.

Clarion-call (दुन्दुभी नाद)—The voice of Rana Pratap was a clarion-call for the Rajputs.

A cock and bull story (false story झूठी कहानी)—His report is a cock and bull story.

A cry in the wilderness (a heedless voice अरण्य रोदन)—All protests of the opposition turned to be a cry in the wilderness.

A dead letter (obsolete कालातीत नियम)—The Hindu code Bill has now become a dead letter.

A fancy price (मुँहमाँगा दाम)—That grocer always demands a fancy price for his articles.

A fish out of water (person out of his element जल बिना मछली)—After retirement his condition has become as a fish out of water.

A fresh lease of life (a renewed life नवजीवन)—The long waited rain gave a fresh lease of life to the farmers.

Gift of the gab (fluency of speech भाषण का वरदान)—Mr. A.B. Bajpayee is endowed with gift of the gab.

A good samaritan (a kind-hearted person दयालु व्यक्ति)—St. Francis was a good samaritan.

A hard nut to crack (difficult to solve टेढ़ी खीर)—The problem of Kashmir is a hard nut to crack.

Hallmark (mark of eminence)—The splendid dignity of expression is the hall mark of Milton's poetry.

A jaundiced eye (prejudical attitude पक्षपातपूर्ण प्रवृति)—A judge must not have a jaundiced eye.

A jack of all trades (हरफन मौला)—His son must succeed in all domains of life because he is a jack of all trades.

A man of letters (a literary man साहित्यिक व्यक्ति)—Nehru was a man of letters.

A man of parts (an able man गुणवान व्यक्ति)—He is a man of parts and can try his fate in any field.

Man in the street (common man)—Today even a man of street desires to have a scooter.

A maiden speech (first speech प्रथम भाषण)—He felt nervous in his maiden speech.

An oily tongue (smooth tongue)—Today a man of oily tongue occupies an eminent post in the society.

Palmy days (flourishing period समृद्धि के दिन)—It is often seen that in his palmy days man forgets his kiths and kins.

A pandora's box (a cursed gift अभिशप्त वरदान)—The boon of Shiva to the demon proved a pandora's box.

Part and parcel (inseparable part अविभाज्य अंग)—Kashmir has been and will remain the part and parcel of India.

The pros and cons (points in favour and against पक्ष तथा विपक्ष में तथ्य)—We should pass the bill after examining its pros and cons.

A red letter day (a memorable day स्मरणीय दिवस)—The 15th of August is a red letter day in the History of India.

Ups and downs (rise and fall उत्थान पतन)—Our history is a history of many ups and downs.

Adjective Phrases

All in all (सर्वेसर्वा)—My uncle is all in all in my family.

At hand (near)—Work hard because the examination is at hand.

At large (freely)—The birds were twittering in the garden at large.

At sixes and sevens (Scattered तितर बितर)–His books were at sixes and sevens on the table.

Fair and square (clear hearted निर्मल अन्तर का)–We should be fair and square in all walks of life.

In black and white (in writing लिखित रूप में)–Give your explanation in black and white.

In vogue (rampant प्रचलित)–In those days idolatory was in vogue.

Null and void (illegal अवैध)–The previous decision has fallen null and void.

Of no avail (Useless व्यर्थ)–He made many efforts but of no avail.

Adverbial Phrases

At arm's length (far away दूर)–Keep the bad boys at arm's length.

At all costs (किसी भी कीमत पर)–I will support you at all costs.

At daggers drawn (on the point of fighting कट्टर दुश्मनी)–India and Pakistan have long been at daggers drawn.

At home (comfortable चैन)–He felt at home after paying the debt.

At a loss (at fault किंकर्तव्यविमूढ़)–He was at a loss when he heard the news of his father's demise.

At once (very soon)–The relief for the injured should at once be started.

At random (without aim or purpose उद्देश्यहीन)–He let his gun off at random.

By fair means and foul (by hook or by crook उचित या अनुचित रूप से)–Most of the candidates intend to win the election by fair means or foul.

Beyond question (undoubtedly निसन्देह)–His only son is the owner of the whole property beyond question.

By leaps and bounds (with startling speed दिन दूना रात चौगुना)–He is flourishing by leaps and bounds.

Few and far between (rare दुर्लभ)–The pure eatable things today are few and far between.

For good (forever हमेशा के लिए)–Henchard left his village for good.

From head to foot (completely सिर से पैर तक)–The beggar was shivering from head to foot.

Heart and soul (हृदय से)–He devoted himself to the mission heart and soul.

In cash or in kind (नकद या अन्य रूप में)–People may donate for the relief fund in cash or kind.

In cold blood (knowingly जानबूझकर)–He resigned himself from the post in cold blood.

In a nutshell (in a word, in brief)–Account, in a nut shell, for the decline of the Tuglaque Dynasty.

In the meantime (meanwhile इसी बीच)–She had lost all hopes of her son's return ; in the meantime his letter came.

In time (on time, not late समय पर)–We reached the station in time.

In full swing (fully active जोर शोर से)—The construction of the new bridge was going on in full swing.

In no time (rapidly, in the twinkling of an eye पलक मारते)—I returned from the market in no time.

In the same breath (एक ही साँस में)—Antony put his point and in the same breath appreciated Brutus also.

On the verge of (on the brink of कगार पर)—She was on the verge of death.

To and fro (hither and thither इधर-उधर)—Wandering to and fro, the jackal saw a beautiful deer.

To one's heart's content (जी भर कर)—The beggar was very hungry so he ate to his heart's content.

To the last farthing (पाई पाई भर)—I have paid off my debts to the last farthing.

Through and through (completely पूर्णरूपेण)—He got failure through and through.

Under one's breath (दबे जबान से)—No one could hear what he spoke under his breath.

And what not (और क्या नहीं, सब कुछ)—

Without rhyme and reason (अकारण ही)—The teacher chid him without rhyme and reason.

Prepositional Phrases

At home in (expert निपुण)—He is at home in technical work.

At home with (familiar परिचित) Many people are not at home with this problem.

For the sake of (कि लिए)—They fought for the sake of the country.

For want of (in lack of कमी से)—Many children die for want of nutritious food.

In the wake of (behind, following के पीछे)—Fatal diseases prevailed in the wake of the earthquake.

On the eve of (just before ठीक पूर्व)—People were busy in feast and festivity on the eve of independence day.

With a view to (in view of मंशा से)—He worked hard with a view to secure first class.

Phrases Composed of Pairs of Words

Again and again (frequently, every now and then, time and again बार-बार बहुधा)—He was attacked with fever again and again.

Bag and baggage (with all belongings बोरिया-बिस्तर सहित)—Being dissatisfied, he left the village bag and baggage.

Bread and butter (livelihood आजीविका)—The house on rent was her bread and butter.

By and by (presently, gradually शीघ्र, धीरे-धीरे करके)—He unveiled the whole mystery by and by.

Cheek by jowl (close together, intimate)—Very soon both the friends began to live cheek and jowl.

Ducks and drakes (to play) (to spent money lavishly)—Many mills play ducks and drakes on publicity.

Fair and square (just and honest न्याय परायण ईमानदार)—A judge must be fair and square.

Far and wide (दूर-दूर तक)—His fame spread far and wide.

Fast and loose (to play) (कथनी कुछ, करनी कुछ)—Today many leaders play fast and loose so people look askance at them.

Fire and water (through) (through all sorts of difficulties)

Fits and starts (irregularly अनियमित रूप से)—It is not good for a student to attend his classes by fits and starts.

Hard and fast (strict) Some rules are hard and fast.

Kith and kin (blood relations सगे सम्बन्धी)—It is very regretting that even his kith and kin left him in the lurch.

Thick and thin (through) (in spite of all obstacles सभी बाधाओं के बावजूद)—He remained brave through thick and thin.

Warp and woof (the central theme मुख्य कथ्य)—The emptiness of the sordid world is the warp and woof of the novel.

Weal and woe (pleasure and pain सुख-दुख)—Life is full of weal and woe.

Some More Phrases

A bird's eye view (to take a general glance सरसरी निगाह से)—I have read your poem in a bird's eye view.

A bold from the blue (a sudden danger वज्राघात)—The death of his father was a bolt from the blue for the family.

A bull in a china shop (a red rag to a bull, unintended person अवांछित व्यक्ति)—Keep him away from the department because he is a bull in a china shop.

A feather in one's cap (an honour प्रतिष्ठा)—Gyan Peeth Award is a feather in one's cap.

A storm in a tea-cup (raise)—(to make mountains of mole hills. (बात का बतंगड़ या तिल का ताड़)—Her complaint is a storm in a tea-cup.

A dog in the manger (a selfish person स्वार्थी व्यक्ति)—He neither enjoys himself nor let others enjoy. He is a dog in the manger.

A fabian policy (of delaying matters विलम्ब की नीति)—Today many office clerks adopt a fabian policy.

Halcyon days (peaceful and prosperous time शान्ति समृद्धि के दिन)—The age of Vikramaditya was an age of Halcyon days.

A utopian scheme (हवाई किला)—A utopian scheme is an empty scheme because it is quite impractical.

A wet blanket (a thing or person to weaken the courage)—Do not throw a wet blanket upon his ambition.

A white elephant (an expensive possession एक खर्चीली वस्तु)—The poor man won a car in the lottery. It became a white elephant for him.

A flowery style (अलंकारिक भाषा)—A literary work written in a flowery style is appreciated by all.

Hush money (bribe घूस)—The officer was caught red handed while he was taking hush money.

A gala day (day of festivity आनन्द उत्सव का दिन)—Diwali is a gala day for the Hindus.

To cut the Gordian knot (to solve a difficult problem कठिन समस्या हल करना)—We may have to cut the Gordian knot to solve the problem.

On the horns of a dilemma (between scylla and charybdis दुविधा में)—The old Brahmin was on the horns of a dilemma when he could not decide whether the kid was a kid or puppy.

To dine with Duke Humphrey (to remain hungry भूखे रहना)—It is not a gentleman's behaviour to cause a guest to dine with Duke, Humphrey.

A hair breath escape (a narrow escape बाल बाल बचना)—The minister had a hair breath escape when his car clashed with a tree.

To make faces (मुँह बनाना)—He makes faces whenever his father advises him.

To catch the fancy of (to attract आकर्षित करना)—The whole natural landscape caught the fancy of the onlookers.

To go to rack and ruin (to spoil नष्ट होना)—A very wide area went to rack and ruin due to the flood.

To smell a rat (to suspect something संशय करना)—His attitudes and behaviours caused us to smell a rat.

Standing order (permanent order स्थायी आदेश)—No one was allowed to defy the standing order.

At a stone's throw (very near निकट)—The university is not away. It is at a stone's throw.

Tight fisted (a miser कंजूस)—A tight fisted man is never happy.

To turn a deaf ear (to pay heedless अनसुना करना)—The people turned a deaf ear to her woeful tale.

To draw a veil over (to conceal परदा डालना, छिपाना)—The police tried to draw a veil over that case.

Of the first water (उच्च श्रेणी का)—Your father is a gentleman of the first water.

From A to Z (from the beginning to the end आदि से अन्त तक)—All boys from A to Z were dull minded.

A wind fall (unexpected good fortune अप्रत्याशित सौभाग्य)—When the farmer unearthed the mound in his field, he found a lot of gold. It was really a wind fall for him.

Caesar's wife (beyond doubt) Caesar's wife must be above suspicion.

Idioms

To be in abeyance (in doubt सन्देहावस्था में)—He was arrested in abeyance.

To beat about the bush (to approach subject slowly)—Please do not beat about the bush because I have a little time.

Above board (fair and square)–Today India needs the leaders who are above board in their character.

Above one's understanding (समझ से परे)–My reasoning is above your understanding.

To account for (to show reasons कारण बताना, हिसाब किताब देना)–Account for the decline of the Moghal Empire. We must have to account for our deeds.

To take into account (to keep in mind ध्यान में रखना)–While writing a precis, important points should be taken into account.

On no account (not in any condition किसी हालत में नहीं)–I will pardon you on no account.

Man of action (कर्मवीर)–Rana Pratap was a man of action.

What is he after ? (वह क्या चाहता है)–He is often seen loitering about here. What is he after ?

To come of age (बालिग होना)–When lucy came of age, she died.

All agog (anxiously उत्सुकता तथा उमंग से)–The last ball was watched all agog.

To take amiss (to feel bothered बुरा मानना)–Excuse me. Do not take my remark amiss.

To run amuck (to go mad पागल हो जाना)–He behaved as if he were run amuck.

Animal spirits (यौवन की चंचलता)–He is young still he lacks animal spirits.

To set apart (to set aside पृथक् रखना)–Set the rest of the papers apart I shall see them hereafter.

With open arms (whole heartedly हार्दिक रूप से)–Both the friends met with open arms after along time.

To take up arms (हथियार उठाना)–The Naga-rebels took up arms against hill-tribes.

To lay down arms (to surrender हथियार डालना)–The outcome of the battle was that the enemy had to lay down arms.

Without avail (of little avail, of no avail, in vain सब व्यर्थ)–He left no stone unturned but without avail.

To beat back (to retreat पीछे हटना, हटाना)–The militants were beaten back.

To go bad (सड़ जाना)–The food has gone bad. Do not serve it.

To let the cat out of the bag (to unveil a secret unknowingly अनजाने में रहस्य खोलना)–Your talkative nature may let the cat out of the bag.

To be the be-all and end-all (चरमोद्देश्य)–In those days, to achieve liberty was the be-all and end-all for our countrymen.

To bear in mind (to keep in mind ध्यान में रखना)–Always bear in mind that a rolling stone gathers no moss.

To beard the lion in his den (to challenge a dangerous person in his own house)–He is a notorious dacoit and the police dare not beard the lion in his den.

To be brought to bed (प्रसव करना)–His wife was brought to bed last night.

To die in bed (to die in a natural way स्वाभाविक रूप से मरना)–He died in bed when he was ninety years old.

A beggar description (beyond description वर्णनातीत होना)—He was very rich but now his economic condition is a beggar description.

Beginning of the end (clear sign of result)—The first fifteen overs are the beginning of the end.

To bell the cat (बिल्ली के गले में घंटी बाँधना)—The proposal of the mouse was accepted by all but the question was who would bell the cat.

Bend upon (determine इरादा रखना)—He is bent upon punishing his rivals.

To give a wide berth to (कोसों दूर रहना)—Good boys always gave a wide berth to a bad company.

To fall between two stools (दुविधा में पड़ना)—The terrorists, in the mosque, fell between two stools.

Birds of a feather (एक ही डाल के पंछी)—Birds of a feather flock together.

To bite the dust (to lick the dust धूल धूसरित होना)—Many soldiers had to bite the dust in the battlefield.

Black mail (बदनाम करने की धमकी)—Russia warned China not to black mail him.

Blue blood (of high family कुलीन या अभिजात्य)—Milton belonged to blue blood.

Blood is thicker than water (खून का रिश्ता सबसे श्रेष्ठ है)—Despite many objectionable acts of her son, the mother pardoned him. Really blood is thicker than water.

To blow hot and cold (क्षणे रुष्टा, क्षणे तुष्टा)—He cannot be a sociable man for he always blows hot and cold.

To be in one's black book (in disfavour with)—He cannot get promotion because he is in officer's black book.

To blow one's own trumpet (अपना ही राग अलापना)—On the issue of Kashmir, Pakistan always blows his own trumpet.

To keep body and soul together (to make both ends meet जीवन निर्वाह करना)—With his petty salary he keeps body and soul together.

To bring to book (to punish)—A criminal must be brought to book.

Born yesterday (कल का बच्चा)—He talks to me as if I were born yesterday.

To be born with a silver spoon in one's mouth (born in a rich family धनी परिवार में जन्म लेना)—Pt. Nehru was born with a silver spoon in his mouth.

To be in the wrong box (or boat) (to be in fault गलती पर होना)—Everybody accounts that you are in the wrong box.

To cudgel one's brains (to think hard सिर खुजलाना)—I cudgelled my brains to find out a solution but in vain.

To breath one's last (to die)—After a glorious rule king Arthar breathed his last in an unknown island.

To bring home to (to persuade, to make know समझाना, जानकारी देना)—Who can bring home to a prejudical man ?

To bring to mind (to recollect स्मरण करना)—We must bring to mind that we all are the offspring of God.

To nip in the bud (to destroy in the outset प्रारम्भ में ही नष्ट कर देना)—A disease must be nipped in the bud.

To take the bull by the horns (to face difficulty with courage कठिनाई का साहसपूर्वक सामना करना)—We should not break our heart rather take the bull by the horns.

To burn the candle at both ends (not husband energy किसी कार्य में शक्ति क्षीण करना)—One should make proper use of one's energy and not burn the candle at both ends.

To burn the midnight oil (to work late देर रात तक काम करना)—To burn the midnight oil is injurious to health.

To bury the hatchet (to cement the old enmity पुरानी शत्रुता मिटाना)—Both China and India should bury the hatchet for common good.

To let bygones be bygones (बीती ताहि बिसारी दे)—Let bygones be bygones and do your duty entrusted to you.

To call in question (to express doubt संशय करना)—He is a noble man so he must not be called in question.

To call a spade a spade (to tell roundly दो टूक कह देना)—Either help me or call a spade a spade.

To carry the day (to win जीतना)—Our cricket team carried the day against West Indies.

To put the cart before the horse (to reverse the order क्रम उलट देना)—The statement of America put the cart before the horse.

A cat-and-dog life (a quarrelsome life निरन्तर कलह का जीवन)—It is not a happy thing to lead a cat-and-dog life.

To catch a glimpse of (to take a brief view एक झलक लेना)—On the way we caught a fanciful glimpse of dawn from the hill.

To catch a Tartar (बलशाली से पाला पड़ना)—He is very strong and I shall catch a Tartar if I challenge him.

To show a clean pairs of heels (to take to heels भाग खड़ा होना)—When the burglars got the air of police, they showed a clean pair of heels.

To see (one) in true colours (to see in actual form यथार्थ रूप में देखना)—One should see objects in their true colours.

To come off with flying colours (to succeed सफल होना)—His son came off with flying colours in the competition.

Fifth-columnist (traitors पंचमांगी)—Every nation has some fifth columnists.

To come to blow (हाथापाई करना, घुँसेबाजी करना)—I cannot say why the two friends came to blow.

To come to light (to come into view प्रकाश में आना)—When the day dawned, the island came to light.

In due course (काल क्रम में)—The minister assured that in due course every employee would get promotion.

Curtain lectures (rebuke by one's wife स्त्री की फटकार)—He is a drunkard. Hence he is to hear curtain lectures.

To cut a sorry figure (to produce sorry impression खेदजनक प्रभाव छोड़ना)—In lack of active steps, India has to cut a sorry figure on Kashmir problem.

To cut no ice (to produce no effect, to fall flat कोई प्रभाव न डालना)—The strong appeal by the leader could cut no ice on the mass.

To fall on evil days (to land into misfortune दुर्दिन में पड़ना)—Nowadays, Iraque has fallen on evil days.

Every dog has his day (no one is always unlucky)—After a long effort he got a good service. Really every dog has his day.

His years are numbered (he has not long to live चन्द दिनों का मेहमान)—He has crossed the nineties. Now his years are numbered.

At dead of night (in midnight अर्द्धरात्रि में)—I dreamt a pleasant dream at dead of night.

A dead letter (no longer in force लागू न रहना)—That bill has now become a dead letter.

The devil to pay (trouble ahead झंझट या बखेड़े की संभावना)—Calphurnia told Caesar that she feared he would have the devil to pay in the meeting.

To go to the devil (be ruined, भाड़ में जाओ)—The hermit turned angry and cursed him that he might go to the devil.

Down with (मुर्दाबाद)—Down with the traitor.

Drop in the ocean (समुद्र में बूँद, ऊँट के मुँह में जीरा)—The add, given to the people after the earthquake, was a drop in the ocean.

To throw dust in one's eyes (आँख में धूल झोंकना)—He is very cunning and you cannot throw dust in his eyes.

To eat the humble pie (submit to humiliation, to pocket an insult अपमान का घूँट पीना)—In the war with China, we had to eat the humble pie in 1962.

At the eleventh hour (in the nick of time, in the last moment अन्तिम क्षण में)—The physician came at the eleventh hour, consequently the patient was saved.

To end in smoke (come to nothing टाँय-टाँय फिस)—The Indian soccer always ends in smoke against a foreign team.

To face the music (not quail at moment of trial परीक्षण के समय खरा उतरना, फटकार सुनना)—He will have to face the music because he has failed to qualify in English.

By fair means and no favour (without prejudice बिना पक्षपात के उचित रूप से)—While selecting the candidates, the policy of fair means and no favour must be adopted.

To fall a prey (be a victim of शिकार होना)—If you smoke, you will fall a prey to fatal diseases.

To play fast and loose (behave dishonestly छलपूर्ण व्यवहार करना)—A man who plays fast and loose is never trusted.

At fault (at sea, confused घबड़ा जाना)—I was at fault to see him.

In fault (guilty दोषी)—Who is in fault ?

To find fault with (complain (of) दोष ढूँढ़ना)—He is a wicked man so he always finds fault with others.

To show the white feather (to show cowardice कायरता दिखाना)–Cowards always show the white feather but the brave never do so.

To play the second fiddle (take subordinate position)–Most of the prime ministers play the second fiddle in the President.

Fit as a fiddle (in good condition and spirits पूर्ण स्वस्थ)–He is going to retire from the service still he is fit as a fiddle.

To care a fig for (बिल्कुल परवाह न करना)–He cares a fig for you.

In fine (in brief संक्षेप में)–In fine the world has lost its values.

No smoke without fire (any rumour is not baseless)–Since there is no smoke without fire, the rumour is not baseless.

To set the themes on fire (कोई आश्चर्यजनक बात करना)–The bank broker Mr. Mehta's statement may set the Thames on fire.

To set on fire (आग लगाना)–The hooligans set the whole village on fire.

To pour oil on fire (to add fuel to fire or flame, to fan the fire .आग में घी डालना, आग को हवा देना)–The dispute was settled but his single sentence poured oil on fire.

To foot a bill (to bear the expenses खर्च वहन करना)–After his father's demise, his maternal uncle has to foot the bill.

To come into force (to be effective लागू होना)–The law came into force then and there.

To make a fortune (to became rich धनी होना)–By taking small contracts, he made a fortune.

To take french leave (to remain absent without information)–He was asked explanation for taking french leave.

To play to the gallery (appeal to lower taste वाहवाही पाने का प्रयास)–Some cricketers play to the gallery in the field.

To play a double game (to cheat धोखेबाजी करना)–In the dispute of Philistine, Syria plays a double game. He runs with the hares and hunts with the hounds.

Gentleman at large (man of treasure and leisure)–Everyone tries to become a gentleman at large.

To get rid of (मुक्ति पाना)–A smoker must try to get rid of smoking.

To get by heart (to learn by rote जुबानी याद करना, कंठस्थ कर जाना)–He has got the Ram Charit Manas by heart.

To get into hot water (परेशानी या झंझट में फँसना)–Due to the case, I got into hot water.

To gird up one's loins (to undertake, be ready for journey or effort बीड़ा उठाना, कमर कसना)–We should gird up our loins to control the growing population.

To give rise to (be the cause of)–His statement gave rise to many questions.

To be hand and (or in) glove with (intimate with चोली-दामन का सम्बन्ध)–U.S.A. and U.K. are hand and glove with each other.

The story goes (it is said कहा जाता है)–The story goes that there is a man on the moon.

Go-between (a broker दलाल)–He was a go-between in the settlement of the case.

Golden opportunity (सुनहरा अवसर)–This is a golden opportunity for you.

Good-for-nothing (worthless अयोग्य)–He is a man good-for-nothing.

To kill the goose that lays golden eggs (आय के श्रोत को नष्ट करना)–If you leave the job, you will kill the goose that lays golden eggs.

A snake in the grass (hidden danger, secret enemy छिपा खतरा या शत्रु)–His neighbour is like a snake in the grass for him.

To grease the palm of (to bribe, to give hush money घूँस देना–to oil the hands)–He got the job easily because he had greased the palm of the officer.

To make one's hair stand on end (with horror रोंगटे खड़े होना)–The earthquake in Maharashtra made our hair stand on end.

Hand to mouth (कमाया खाया बराबर)–He lives on hand to mouth, so he has no money for future.

Hard up (in want of money चिन्तनीय अर्थावस्था में)–I am hard up nowadays because recently I had got my two daughters married.

To harp on the same string (dwell on a single subject एक ही राग अलापना)–If you harp on the same string, the dispute cannot be decided.

To make neither head nor tail of (understand nothing कुछ भी अर्थ न समझना)–After all I made neither head nor tail of your pieces of advice.

To take heart (to encourage हिम्मत बाँधना)–Take heart even if you have lost the field.

To have one's in one's mouth (स्तम्भित हो जाना)–Seeing the hard result, we had our heart in our mouth.

In one's heart of hearts (from the inner core अन्तर मन से)–All, in their heart of hearts, were admiring the patriots.

To play hide and seek (लुका छिपी का खेल)–The moon was playing hide and seek in the cloudy sky.

To hit the nail on the head (do right thing, hit the mark ठीक निशाने पर चोट करना)–A strong enemy can be revenged by watching for the chance and then hitting the nail on the head.

To hold good (to be applicable लागू होना)–This law does not now hold good.

To pick holes (find fault with छिद्रान्वेषण करना)–Some people are such as always pick holes in others.

To take ill (to take amiss बुरा मानना)–He took it ill when I told him everything roundly.

To feel at ease (to feel relaxed आराम अनुभव करना)–After a tiresome journey I reached home and felt at ease.

Ill-will (animosity खराब मंशा)–Some countries bear ill-will against India.

To jump to the conclusion (निष्कर्ष निकालना)–The inquiry committee jumped to the conclusion after studying the situation deeply.

To keep the wolf from the door (to escape from starvation भूखमरी से बचना)–Unless you earn money, you cannot keep the wolf from the door.

To bring one to one's knees (to make one surrender घुटने टिकाना)—Prithvi Raj brought his enemy to his knees in the battle of Khanva.

In labour (प्रसव पीड़ा में)—The lady in labour was brought to maternity home.

A wolf in lamb's clothing (भेड़ की खाल में भेड़िया)—Telling his beads, he cheats others. Thus he is a wolf in lamb's clothing.

To laugh in one's sleeve (be secretly amused मुँह छिपाकर हँसना)—As soon as the teacher entered the class, the boys began to laugh in their sleeve.

To lead astray (to mislead बहकाना)—A true friend never leads his companion astray.

To turn over a new leaf (to begin a new life नया पृष्ठ खोलना)—The rise of the Marathas turned a new leaf in our history.

On its last leg (about to perish अन्तिम स्थिति में)—Polio is on its last leg in the world.

To leave one in the lurch (in difficulties विपत्ति में छोड़ देना)—It was an irony that even his relatives left him in the lurch.

To try one's level best (to leave no stone unturned शक्ति भर प्रयास करना)—Your success lies in trying your level best.

A matter of life and death (जीवन-मरण का प्रश्न)—To save the property was a matter of life and death for her.

To read between the lines (to understand the hidden meaning गुप्त भाव को समझना)—If you read between the lines of the article, you will be able to derive morality from it.

To wash dirty linen in public (to reveal personal matter in society व्यक्तिगत बात को समाज में प्रचारित करना)—It is not proper for any prudent man to wash dirty linen in public.

To look down upon (हेय दृष्टि से देखना)—The English used to look down upon us as underdogs.

To look a gift horse in the mouth (बिना प्रयास के फल की आशा)—One should not look a gift horse in the mouth without effort.

Make or mar (बनाना या नष्ट करना)—People are totally responsible to make or mar the country.

To make up one's mind (resolve इरादा करना)—He has made up his mind to spread education.

Beside the mark (irrelevant असंगत)—Your statement is not to the point. It is beside the mark.

Matter-of-fact (prosaic, dull नीरस, सौन्दर्यहीन)—(Matter of fact—What pertains to the fact).

To mind one's own business (दखलन्दाजी न करना)—Do not meddle with my affairs. Mind your business.

A miss is as good as a mile (a failure is a failure असफलता अन्ततः असफलता है)—You should not derive victory from defeat. Finally, a miss is good as a mile.

Money makes the mare go (Money is all in all पैसा ही सब कुछ है)—Everybody knows that in the world of today money makes the mare go.

To be no more (to die, all over with)–Mahatma Gandhi is no more but his ideals are still living.

To move heaven and earth (आकाश पाताल एक करना)–With a view to regain his lost wealth, he moved heaven and earth.

The naked truth (the open fact खुला तथ्य)–Hush money today is not a secret affair. It is a naked truth.

To set at naught (विफल करना)–The first attack was set at naught.

Now or never (अभी या कभी नहीं)–If you want to help me, do it now or never.

Next to nothing (Zero नहीं के तुल्य)–His help to me was next to nothing.

Even Homer sometimes nods (धियोऽपि पुंसा मलिना भवन्ति)–Even a wise man is shaken by grim misery. Really even Homer sometimes nods.

To turn up one's nose at (नाक भौं सिकोड़ना)–The child began to turn up his nose at the milk that his mother gave him to drink.

Well off (happy खुशहाल)–Due to a lot of paternal property, he was well off.

To pour water on troubled waters (pacify the dispute विवाद शान्त करना)–To patch up a quarrel)–A bad man tries to fan the fire—whereas a gentleman pours oil on troubled waters.

The order of the day (a fashion युग धर्म)–'The Salutation of Jai Shri Ram' has become the order of the day.

Out and out (completely पूर्णरूपेण)–It is reported that malaria has been eradicated out and out from the country.

To bear the palm (to be victorious विजयी होना)–In the final match Mohan Bagan bore the palm.

Palmy days (days of prosperity समृद्धि के दिन)–The Gupta's age is said to be the palmy days in our history.

To pave the way for (विपत्ति का भंडार)–(prepare the way for पथ प्रशस्त करना)–The poetic diction of Wordsworth paved the way of lucidity in writing.

To play one's cards well (make good use of opportunity अवसर से लाभ उठाना)–A wise man always plays his cards well.

To poison one's ears against (किसी के विरुद्ध कान भरना)–Manthara poisoned Kaikeyee's ears against Ram.

Every man has his price (honesty can be won over by some inducement ईमानदारी भी बेची जा सकती है। To day every man has his price for money.

To feel one's pulse (किसी का विचार जानना)–The journalist was trying to feel the pulse of the people about the coming election.

From all quarters (from all nooks and corners चारों ओर से)–In his early period Md. Sahib was criticised from all quarters.

In quest of (in search of खोज में)–He left home in quest of a better job.

In rags (in shabby clothes चिथड़ों में)–She was clad in rags.

A rainy day (in adverse days दुर्भाग्य के दिन)–A wise man saves money against a rainy day.

The rank and file (common men जन सामान्य)–Every leader promises for the welfare of the rank and file.

To reduce to ashes (to meet to dust धूल धूसरित होना/करना)–Many houses were reduced to ashes by the fire.

Riff-raff (disreputable person ऐरू गैरू)–I am also not a riff-raff. (or Tom, Dick, and Harry)

Safe and sound (quite uninjured पूर्णरूपेण सुरक्षित)–The mountaineers returned safe and sound.

To take one to task (rebuke, chide डाँटना फटकारना)–If you fail to secure first class, your father will take you to task.

To run the gauntlet (of being subjected to criticism)–He had to run the gauntlet after he made the speech.

On the spur of the moment (क्षणिक उत्तेजना में)–A decision taken on the spur of the moment is always wrong.

An ugly customer (a bad man बखेड़िया व्यक्ति)–Do not make friendship with him because he is an ugly customer.

To hold (or gain) the upper hand (पलड़ा भारी होना)–In the election the B.J.P. held the upper hand.

At the top of one's voice (very loudly ऊँचे स्वर में)–Her wealth, being robbed, she began to cry at the top of her voice.

Happy go lucky (Lucky is he who is happy) (Happy-go-lucky—haphazard, mere chance अवसरजन्य)

To talk through one's hat–to boast–His habit is to talk always through his hat.

Verbal Phrases

1. Account

Account for—give reckoning of (conduct, duty) हिसाब देना।

Account for—explain the cause of (things to person) कारण बताना।

2. Bear

Bear away—win जीतना।

Bear out—confirm पुष्टि करना।

       support समर्थन करना।

Bear up—uphold, not in despair धैर्य रखना।

Bear down—swoop उठा ले जाना, टूट पड़ना।

       treat forbearingly सहिष्णुता से बर्ताव करना।

3. Beat

   Beat down—cheapen सस्ता करना।

                back, away, off पराजित करना।

   Beat in—crust कुचलना।

   Beat up—beat black and blue खूब पीटना।

4. Blow

   Blow out, off or up—Extinguish फूँककर बुझाना, विस्फोट द्वारा उड़ाना।

   Blow over—pass off गुजर जाना।

5. Break

   Break down—fail, demolish गिरना, नष्ट होना।

   Break into (house)—सेंध लगाना।

   Break in—intrude निष्ट हेतु घुसना।

   Break out—spread (disease, war, from prison) फैलाना, कारागार से भागना।

   Break up—Dismiss depart.

   Break with—Cease relation with सम्बन्ध तोड़ना।

6. Bring

   Bring about—cause to happen, reverse (ship) घटना का कारण बनना।

   Bring down—kill, wound, cause penalty to हत्या करना, घायल करना, सजा दिलाना।

   Bring in—introduce (custom, produce as profit).

   Bring off—rescue successfully सफलतापूर्वक बचाना।

   Bring on—lead to, cause discussion of

   Bring out—express or exhibit clearly स्पष्ट रूप से व्यक्त करना।

   Bring over—convert परिवर्तित करना।

   Bring under—subdue दमित करना।

   Bring up—educate, rear शिक्षित करना, पालन-पोषण करना।

   Bring round—win over समझाकर सहमत करना, होश में लाना।

7. Call

   Call for—order, demand, need.

   Call on—invoke, appeal to, pay a short visit to पुकारना, मिलने हेतु जाना।

   Call off—cancel समाप्त करना।

   Call out—सेना को मदद हेतु बुलाना, बुलाना।

   Call up—recollect स्मरण करना।

                rouse from bed सोते से जगाना।

                imagine कल्पना करना।

                summon to talk by telephone दूरभाष पर बुलाना।

                to join the armed forces.

8. Carry

Carry away—inspire, transport, deprive of, self-control प्रोत्साहित करना, निर्यात करना, आत्म-संयम खोना, ले भागना।

Carry on—advance, continue, manage (business) go on with आगे बढ़ना, जारी रखना, प्रबन्ध करना।

Carry on with—behave strangely, have amorous intrigue आश्चर्यजनक वर्ताब करना।

Carry out—put in practice कार्यान्वित या पालन करना।

Carry through—bring safely out of difficulties, complete कठिनाई से सुरक्षित निकालना, पूरा करना।

9. Catch

Catch on—become popular प्रसिद्ध होना।

Catch up, away—snatch (used passively) झपट ले भागना, खींचना।

Catch out—dismiss.

Catch upon—छूटे कार्य को पूरा करना।

10. Come

Come about—happen.

Come across—meet with भेंट होना।

Come along—make haste.

Come at—reach, discover पहुँचना, आविष्कृत करना।

Come by—obtain प्राप्त करना।

Come down upon (on) rebuke, punish फटकारना, दंड देना।

Come into—inherit उत्तराधिकारी होना।

Come of—arise from—come of a high family.

Come off—be detached पृथक् होना।

Come out—emerge प्रादुर्भाव होना, निकलना।

Come upon—continue coming, advance.

11. Compare

Compare to—भिन्न जाति से तुलना।

Compare with—एक ही वर्ग या जाति से तुलना।

12. Deal

Deal in—व्यवसाय के सन्दर्भ में।

Deal with—treat, discuss व्यवहार करना, बातचीत करना।

13. Do

Do away with—get rid of छुटकारा पाना।

(do away with oneself आत्महत्या करना)

Do for—supervise household work, kill ruin, be defeated गृह कार्य निरीक्षण करना, हत्या करना, बर्वाद करना, पराजित होना।

Do with—finish, benefit from समाप्त करना, लाभ उठाना।

Do without—forgo के बिना कार्य करना।

14. Fall

Fall back—retreat पीछे हटना।

Fall behind—lag behind पिछड़ जाना।

Fall for—be captivated by, admire, मुग्ध होना, प्रशंसा करना।

Fall a victim of—be prey of शिकार होना।

Fall in with—meet, agree अकस्मात् मिलना, सहमत होना।

Fall off—diminish कम होना।

Fall out—disagree असहमत होना।

Fall on—attack अचानक आक्रमण करना।

15. Get

Get about—travel, spread

Get along—progress प्रगति करना, निर्वाह करना।

Get at—achieve, bribe, criticise प्राप्त करना, घूस, आलोचना करना।

Get away—run away.

Get in—enter, be returned.

Get off—alight, be acquitted उतरना, रिहा होना।

Get on—reach, progress, manage.

Get out—बाहर निकलना, निकालना।

Get over—recover from, overcome, convey facts रोग मुक्त होना, विजय करना, सम्प्रेषित करना।

Get through—reach end of, connect अन्त तक पहुँचना।

Get up—उठना, पहनना, तैयारी करना, संगठित करना।

16. Give

Give away—hand over, expose to, ridicule, distribute (prize) प्रदान करना, भेद खोलना, वितरित करना।

Give in—Cease yield.

Give out—emit, distribute, announce निकलना, बाँटना, उद्घोषण करना।

Give over—Cease from doing, abandon परित्याग करना।

Give up—छोड़ना, आत्मसमर्पण करना।

17. Go

Go out—set to work at, travel काम में लगना, यात्रा करना।

Go away—चले जाना।

Go away with—carry away उठा ले जाना।

Go after—chase पीछा करना।

Go by—pass, fallow, be guided.

Go down—sink, fall, deteriorate डूबना, गिरना, बदतर होना

Go for—to fetch, attack जाकर लाना।

Go into—enter, investigate प्रवेश करना, मामले की छानबीन करना।

Go off—let off, be senseless छोड़ना, विस्फोट करना, बेहोश होना।

Go on—continue, happen जारी रखना, घटित होना।

Go out—outside, extinguish, turn out of fashion बाहर जाना, बुझाना, बुझना, रिवाज से परे।

Go through—finish, discuss in detail undergo, read पूर्ण करना, विस्तृत विमर्श करना, से होकर गुजरना, पढ़ना।

Go up—ascend, rise आरोह।

Go with—agree सहमत होना।

Go without—के बिना काम चलना या रहना।

18. Hold

Hold by (to)—adhere to (choice, purpose) डटे रहना, चिपका रहना।

Hold back—hesitate हिचकिचाना।

Hold down—पकड़े रखना (service, situation).

Hold forth—speak publicaly.

Hold in—confine, check सीमित रहना, रोकना।

Hold off—delay विलम्ब करना।

Hold on—keep grasp on something पकड़ बनाए रखना।

Hold out—promise, offer hope, continue, last.

Hold over—postpone टाले रखना।

Hold up—support, display, stop, for a while समर्थन देना, प्रदर्शित करना, कुछ समय तक रोक रखना।

Hold with—agree सहमत होना।

19. Keep

Keep away—prevent मना करना, दूर रखना।

Keep back—conceal छिपा रखना।

Keep down—hold in subjection दबाकर रखना।

Keep in—confine, restrain सीमित रखना, नियंत्रित रखना (भावनाएँ)।

Keep off—stay at a distance दूर रहना, खड़ा होना।

Keep on—continue

Keep out—not let enter बाहर रखे रहना।

Keep up—maintain बनाए रखना।

20. Lay

Lay about—hit out on all sides.

Lay by (aside)—रख छोड़ना।

Lay down—Put on the ground, sacrifice लेटना, बलिदान करना, प्रस्तुत करना।

Lay in—store (wine), shower blows भंडारित करना, घूँसे बरसाना।

Lay on—impose (tax, penalty), connect, flatter बोझ लादना, जोड़ना, चापलूसी करना।

Lay off—discharge (temporarily for lack of work, desist.

Lay up—save money, be ill धन बचाना, बीमार पड़ना।

21. Light up—light to smoke pipe, kindle light दीप जलाना।

22. Look

Look about—examine surroundings चारों ओर देखना।

Look after—take care of, seek for देखभाल करना, ढूँढना।

Look down—with displeasure हीनता या अप्रसन्नता से।

Look for—expect, search for अपेक्षा करना।

Look into—examine, inquire (परीक्षण रूप में)

Look over—inspect, overlook or pardon निरीक्षण करना, अनदेखा करना।

Look up to—admire प्रशंसा, आदर करना।

23. Make

Make after—pursue पीछा करना।

Make against—be unfavourable to.

Make away with—get rid of, kill.

Make for—go towards, be conducive to चल पड़ना, अनुकूल होना।

Make into—change

Make off—run away.

Make out—draw up, write out, understand, represent, get together with difficulty.

Make over—transfer.

Make up—use cosmetics, recover, cement the matter प्रसाधन करना, क्षतिपूर्ति करना, कलह मिटाना, गट्ठर बाँधना।

Make up for—क्षतिपूर्ति करना।

24. Pass

Pass away—die, come to an end.

Pass by—disregard, walk उपेक्षा करना, पास या सामने से गुजरना।

Pass off—fade away, pretend to be someone.

Pass on—spread.

Pass out—faint बेहोश होना, die.

Pass over—omit, make no remark upon अनदेखा करना, हटाना, कोई टिप्पणी न करना।

25. Pick

Pick on—खोजकर निकालना।

Pick out—अन्तर करना, छाँटकर पृथक् करना।

Pick up—learn.

26. Play

Play at—engage in (game) खिलवाड़ करना।

Play down on—take mean advantage of (person) कुटिल लाभ उठाना।

Decry—महत्त्वहीन बताना।

Play into—(the hands of) act as to give advantage to opponent अनजाने में प्रतिद्वन्द्वी को लाभ दे बैठना।

Play off—oppose (person against other for advantage) स्वयं के लाभ हेतु किन्हीं दो को लड़ाना।

Play on—बाद्यवादन बजाना।

Play out—play upto the last, make use of (person's fear) अंत तक खेलना, किसी के भय का उपयोग करना।

27. Pull

Pull about—treat roughly रूखाईपूर्ण व्यवहार करना।

Pull down—demolish, lower in health, price गिराना, स्वास्थ्य या कीमत गिराना।

Pull in—enter station.

Pull off—win (prize, contest).

Pull out—row out, move out of station (train) खेना।

Pull round—रुग्णता या बुरे दिन से उबरना।

Pull through—get oneself safely through सुरक्षित रूप से निकल आना।

Pull up—stop, chide, improve रोकना, डाँटना, सुधार करना।

28. Put

Put out—cause (horse, body, vessel) to turn round.

Put across—execute successfully सफलतापूर्वक सम्पन्न करना।

Put aside (by)—set aside अलग रख छोड़ना।

Put away—divorce, lay by, consume, imprison तलाक देना (छोड़ना), उपभोग करना, कैद करना।

Put back—check the advance of आगे बढ़ने से रोकना, घड़ी की सुई पीछे करना।

Put down—supress, take away दमन करना, लिखना।

Put in—install in office, make a claim दावा करना।

Put off—postpone, take off टालना, उतारना, बुझाना (यंत्र द्वारा)।

Put on—assume, advance, add to पहनना, स्वीकारना, बढ़ना, जोड़ना।

Put out—extinguish (candle), confuse, irritate बुझाना, भ्रमित होना, झुंझलाना।

Put over—secure appreciation, impress प्रशंसा लेना, प्रभावित करना।

Put to—present, state as a fact, cause to have.

Put through—carry out (task).

Put up—lodge, display, nominate as a candidate ठहरना, प्रदर्शित करना, अभ्यर्थी का चुनाव में नामांकित करना।

Put up with—bear सहन करना।

29. Run

Run about—to and fro इधर-उधर दौड़ना।

Run across—meet संयोग से मिलना।

Run after—pursue, seek society of, give much time to पीछा करना, संसर्ग खोजना, प्रचुर समय देना।

Run away—run off, leave home, drain भागना, घर छोड़ना, बह जाना।

Run away with—प्रेम पलायन, ले भागना (किसी की सम्पति या बच्चा)।

Run down—stop, become enfeeble घड़ी बन्द होना, सम्पोषक आहार की कमी से कमजोर होना।

              discover after search, disparage ढूँढ निकालना, हतोत्साहित करना।

Run over—drive a vehicle over गाड़ी के नीचे आ जाना।

Run out (of)—came to an end (period, stock), come out of contest (cricket).

Run through—pierce with sword, draw line तलवार घुसेड़ना, रेखा खींचना।

Run up—accumulate, construct, grow rapidly, approach इकट्ठा करना, निर्माण करना, तेजी से बढ़ना, दौड़कर पहुँचना।

Run up against—encounter.

30. Set

Set about—begin (task, doing).

Set down—write, explain.

Set forth—declare, adorn, begin (journey) घोषणा करना, सजाना, यात्रा प्रारम्भ करना।

Set in—arise, get vogue उठना, प्रचलित होना।

Set off—start, enhance, begin (journey).

Set on (upon)—attack, persuade, determine, instigate (उत्तेजित करना)।

Set out—embellish, declare, begin journey आभूषित करना।

Set to—begin, fighting or arguing (esp-with plural subject).

Set up—establish, erect, raise, claim स्थिर करना, बसना, स्थापित करना, उठाना, दावा करना।

31. Sit

Sit down (under)—submit timely to बैठना

Sit on (upon)—have a place on, suppress.

Sit out—take no part (in dance) भाग न लेना, अलग बैठना।

Sit up—रात जागकर व्यतीत करना।

32. Speak

Speak for—किसी के पक्ष में बोलना, सिफारिश करना।

Speak out—address, chide सम्बोधित करना, डाँटना।

33. Stand

Stand by—support, stick to अडिग रहना।

Stand down—withdraw from contest प्रतियोगिता से बाहर होना।

Stand for—represent, advocate, tolerate.

Stand on—continue on same course.

Stand over—postpone टालना।

Stand to—adhere कथन पर अडिग रहना।

Stand up for—support.

Stand upon (upto)—face courageously साहसपूर्वक सामना करना।

Stand with—in the estimation दृष्टि में ऊँचा होना।

34. Take

Take about—carry from place to place.

Take after—resemble मिलता-जुलता।

Take away—ले भागना।

Take back—(शब्द) वापस लेना।

Take down—write down, humble, swallow, remove लिखना; नीचा दिखाना, अनिच्छा या कठिनाई से निगलना, हटाना।

Take for—समझना।

Take from—lessen, weaken कम करना, कमजोर करना।

Take in—admit (lodgers, guests etc.), digest (mentally), cheat आतिथ्य सत्कार करना, समझना, छल करना।

Take into—confide, conceive, imagine विश्वास में लेना। सोचना, कल्पना करना।

Take off—remove उतारना, छोड़ने जाना।

leave ground, deduct जमीन छोड़ना (जहाज), घटाना।

Take on—undertake बीड़ा उठाना (कार्य, जिम्मेवारी)।

Take out—cause to come out, convey out, remove (stain, partner) बाहर निकालना, पहुँचाना, दूर करना।

Take over—कार्य भार ग्रहण करना, आगे निकल जाना।

Take to—begin, fall into the habit of प्रारम्भ करना, अभ्यस्त होना।

Take up—lift up, occupy, engage, absorb, arrest, enter upon.

Take up with—संसर्ग करना।

35. Think

Think about—consider.

Think of—recollect, have an opinion about स्मरण करना, विचार बनाना।

Think out—सोचकर निकालना।

Think over—ponder over चिन्तन करना।

36. Turn

Turn about—पीछे मुड़ना, उलटना।

Turn against—become hostile to शत्रु होना।

Turn down—fold down, reduce flame of, reject बत्ती कम करना, अस्वीकार करना।

Turn in—fold inward, go to bed मोड़ना, सोने जाना।

Turn into—transform परिणत करना।

Turn off—disconnect (opp. to turn on) पृथक् करना।

Turn out—expel, inside out, muster, manufacture, dress—extinguish निकाल देना, जेब को उलटकर देखना, विस्तर से उठना, इकट्ठा होना, उत्पादन करना, पहनना, बुझाना।

Turn over—cause to fall over, do business.

Turn round—face about, adopt (new opinion or policy) घुमाना, घुमना, नई धारणा या नीति बनाना।

Turn to—begin work, apply oneself to, change into another state कार्यारम्भ करना, स्वयं को लगाना, अन्य रूप में परिवर्तित करना।

Turn up—arrive, appear, occur, find out पहुँचना, प्रगट होना, घटित होना, खोज निकालना।

Turn upon (on)—depend, attack निर्भर करना, होना।

37. Work

Work in with—co-operate सहयोग करना।

Work off—get rid of मुक्ति पाना (श्रम से, ऋण से)।

Work out—find (amount) solve (sum) by calculation, give definite result, exhaust with work, accomplish with difficulty हिसाब पाना, हल निकालना, निश्चित परिमाण देना, कार्याधिक्य से थकना, कठिनाई से पूर्ण करना।

Work up—excite, advance (gradually) उत्तेजित होना, करना, क्रमशः अग्रसर होना।

Chapter 20

Antonyms
(विलोम शब्द)

Antonyms (विपरीतार्थक शब्द) का parts of speech वही होना चाहिए जिसमें प्रस्तुत शब्द है। अंग्रेजी में प्राय: prefix (उपसर्ग) तथा suffix (प्रत्यय) के द्वारा antonyms बनाए जाते हैं। किन्तु नवीन शब्द के रूप में antonyms बेहतर कहे जाएँगे।

By negative prefix :

il-logical—illogical, illegitimate—illegal, etc.

in-accessible—inaccessible, inactive.

im-possible—impossible, etc.

ir-irregular, irresponsible, irreligion, etc.

de-defame, dethrone, decrease.

dis-displease, disability, disagree, disarmament.

mis-misbelief, misuse, misfortune, mislead.

un-unwise, untold, undo, unkind.

By suffix—यदि शब्द के अन्त में full रहे तो less और यदि less रहे तो ful जोड़कर antonym बनाया जाता है। इसका कुछ अपवाद (exception) भी संभव है।

harmful—harmless

hopeful—hopeless

careful—careless

shameful—shameless

faithful—faithless

But helpful—unhelpful ; luckless—lucky, etc.

Words	Antonyms	Words	Antonyms
above	below	acquit मुक्त करना	convict दोषी ठहराना
absence अनुपस्थिति	presence	active	passive
absurd	reasonable	admire प्रशंसा करना	criticise आलोचना करना
abundance प्रचुरता	scarcity अभाव	admit	deny
accelerate तीव्र करना	retard पीछे हटना	advance	retreat पीछे हटना
accord मेल	discord फूट	adversity कुसमय	prosperity समृद्धि
acquire प्राप्त करना	lose खोना	affection स्नेह	hatred घृणा
agree	differ	boon बरदान	bane शाप
		brave बहादुर	coward(ly) कायर
all	none	bright चमकीला, तीव्र बुद्धि का	dull धुँधला, मन्द बुद्धि का
always	never	broad विस्तृत	narrow संकीर्ण

225

Words	Antonyms	Words	Antonyms
		busy व्यस्त	idle आलसी
ample प्रचुर	meagre कम		
analysis विश्लेषण	synthesis संश्लेषण		
ancient प्राचीन	modern	care	neglect उपेक्षा करना
approval अनुमोदन	disapproval		
arrest	release, free	cheap सस्ता	dear मँहगा
arrival आगमन	departure गमन	classic	romantic
artificial कृत्रिम	natural	clear	dirty
ascend चढ़ना	descend उतरना	coarse मोटा	fine बारीक
assemble इकट्ठा होना	disperse बिखरना	compare तुलना करना	contrast विभेद द्वारा तुलना करना
attack	defend रक्षा करना	conceal छिपाना	reveal प्रगट करना
attack आक्रमण	defence	confess	deny
attract आकर्षित करना	repel विकर्षण करना	confident विश्वस्त	diffident
attractive	repulsive	conquer जीतना	surrender, submit, lose आत्मसमर्पण करना, हारना
attraction आकर्षण	repulsion विकर्षण		
bad	good	conqueror विजेता	vanquished विजित
barbarous, rude असभ्य	civil सभ्य		
barren बंजर	fertile उपजाऊ	conservative परम्परावादी, अनुदार	liberal उदार
base आधार	peak चोटी	construct	demolish नष्ट करना
beautiful	ugly कुरूप	continue	discontinue
beneficial लाभप्रद	harmful हानिकारक	cool सुखद ठंड	warm उष्ण
	injurious	create सृजन करना	destroy नष्ट करना
best	worst	credit उधार	cash नकद
		credit जमा	debit खर्च
blessing आशीर्वाद	curse श्राप	cruel निष्ठुर	kind
blunt भोथर	sharp		
bold, courageous	timid		
danger	safety	export निर्यात करना	import आयात करना
deep	shallow, light	exterior बाह्य	interior भीतरी
		ever (always)	never
defeat	victory		
defence	offence		
defendant	plaintiff	fact तथ्य	fiction गल्प
deficit	surplus		
delay विलम्ब	haste जल्दी	fail	succeed
deposit जमा करना	withdraw निकालना	failure असफलता	success
devil राक्षस	deity देवता	fall पतन	rise उत्थान
		false	true
different भिन्न	similar समान	fame प्रसिद्धि	disgrace अपयश

Words	Antonyms	Words	Antonyms
difficult कठिन	easy आसान	famous	notorious कुख्यात
diminish न्यून करना	increase बृद्धि करना	familiar परिचित	strange, unfamiliar
		fast	slow
dynamic गत्यात्मक	static स्थिर		
disclose प्रगट करना	conceal, hide छिपाना		
divide विभाजित करना	multiply, unite गुणा करना, एक करना	final	initial प्रारम्भिक
domestic घरेलू	wild जंगली	finite सीमित	infinite अनन्त
		firm अडिग, दृढ़	loose ढीला
dull नीरस	interesting	first	last
dwarf बौना	giant देव	flexible लचीला	rigid कड़ा
		follower अनुयायी	leader
		foolish	wise
eager उत्सुक	indifferent उदास	foreign विदेशी	native देशम्
early	late	frank स्पष्टवादी	reserve संकोची
easy	difficult	free	bound बँधा
economical मितव्ययी	extravagant अपव्ययी	freedom	slavery गुलामी
encourage प्रोत्साहित करना	discourage हतोत्साहित करना	frequent प्राय:	occasional आकस्मिक
efficient कुशल, दक्ष	deficient अकुशल	fresh ताजा	stale वासी
enjoy	suffer	friendship मित्रता	enmity शत्रुता
enrich धनी बनना	impoverish विपन्न होना	fruitful लाभप्रद	futile निष्फल
entrance प्रवेश	exit बहिर्गमन	full	empty रिक्त
eternal चिरन्तन	transient क्षणिक		
gain प्राप्त करना	lose खोना	individual व्यक्तिगत	collective समष्टिगत
gain (profit लाभ)	loss हानि	interested आसक्त	detached अनासक्त
general सामान्य	particular विशिष्ट	internal आन्तरिक	external बाह्य
gentle भद्र, सज्जन	rude अभद्र	intentional अभिप्रायज्जन्य	accidental अज्ञानवी
genuine असली	spurious नकली	jest मजाक	earnest गंभीर
glad	sad	join	separate
glory यश, वैभव	ignominy अपयश	keen जिज्ञासु	indifferent उदासीन
grand शानदार	commonplace सामान्य	knowledge ज्ञान	ignorance अज्ञानता
grant स्वीकारना	refuse		
great महान्	little छोटा	laborious परिश्रमी	lazy आलसी
guest मेहमान	host मेजवान	lack न्यूनता	abundance प्रचुरता
guilty अपराधी	innocent निर्दोष	lass कुमारी	lad कुमार
harm	benefit	late	early
harmony मेल	discord फूट	lead नेतृत्व करना	fallow अनुसरण करना
head	tail, foot	lend उधार देना	borrow उधार लेना
heat गर्मी	cold ठंडक	light हल्का	heavy भारी

Words	Antonyms	Words	Antonyms
healthy स्वस्थ	diseased बीमार	little	much
heredity वंशपरम्परा	environment उप्पन्त	long	short
heaven स्वर्ग	hell नरक	loose ढीला	tight कसा हुआ
height उँचाई	depth गहराई	lovely	hideous भयंकर
help	hinder बाँधा	major बड़ा	minor छोटा
Hero नायक	villain खलनायक	majority बहुमत	minority अल्पमत, अल्पसंख्यक
honour प्रतिष्ठा	disgrace कलंक	make	mar बिगाड़ना, नष्ट करना
hope	despair निराश	male	female
humble विनम्र	naughty, proud उग्र, घमंडी	masculine पुरुषज्जन्य	feminine स्त्रीज्जन्य
hurt चोट पहुँचाना	heal मरहम लगाना	material भौतिक	spiritual आध्यात्मिक
ill	well	precious बहुमूल्य	worthless व्यर्थ
improve सुधारना	deteriorate ह्रास होना	pride घमंड	humility शीलता
include सम्मिलित करना	exclude बाह्य करना	probably सम्भवत:	certainty निश्चितरूपेण
			conservative रूढ़िवादी
increase बढ़ाना	decrease घटाना	production उत्पादन	consumption खपत
maximum अधिकतम	minimum न्यूनतम	profit लाभ	loss हानि
mighty	weak	progressive प्रगतिवादी	regressive परम्परावादी
miser कृपण	spendthrift अपव्ययी	prohibit निषिद्ध करना	permit अनुमति देना
moderate नरमपंथी	extremist चरमपंथी	punish	reward
mourn शोक करना	rejoice	pure	adulterated अशुद्ध, मिश्रित
narrow संकीर्ण	broad चौड़ा	raise उठाना	lower नीचे करना
natural नैसर्गिक	artificial कृत्रिम		
near	far	rare दुर्लभ	common
noble	ignoble, mean		
normal सामान्य	abnormal असामान्य	rational मुक्तिवादी	emotional संवेगिक
nobody	everybody	real	imaginary काल्पनिक
now	then	renown कीर्ति	disgrace अपयश
Obey आज्ञा मानना	defy अवज्ञा करना	reputation ख्याति	notoriety कुख्यात
Odd विषम संख्या	even सम संख्या	ripe परिपक्व	raw कच्चा
offence आघात	defence रक्षा		
offensive आक्रामक	defensive प्रतिरक्षात्मक	round	flat चिपटा
offer	refuse	rude उदण्ड	polite विनम्र
optimism आशावाद	pessimism निराशावाद		
optimist आशावादी	pessimist	rural देहाती	urban नगरीय
optional ऐच्छिक	compulsory अनिवार्य	sacred पवित्र	profane अपवित्र
oral, verbal मौखिक	written लिखित	safe	risky, dangerous
order व्यवस्था	chaos अव्यवस्था	sale विक्रय	purchase क्रय
ordinary	unique अनुपम		
over	under	savage जंगली, असभ्य	civilized सभ्य

Words	Antonyms	Words	Antonyms
part	whole	secret रहस्य, गुप्त	open खुला
peace	war	simple सरल	complex जटिल
permanent स्थायी	temporary अस्थायी	smile मुस्कराना	frown क्रोधित होना
persuade मनाना	dissuade विरुद्ध, मंत्रणा देना	smooth	rough
praise प्रशंसा करना	criticise आलोचना करना	special	general
pleasant सुखद	painful, prosaic नीरस	strange विचित्र	familiar परिचित
plenty प्रचुर	scarcity अभाव	stranger अजनबी	acquaintance परिचित
sweet	sour खट्टा	superficial सतही	profound गहरा
sympathy सहानुभूति	antipathy	superior उत्कृष्ट	inferior निकृष्ट
tame पालक	wild जंगली		
tragedy दुखान्त	comedy सुखान्त		
transparent पारदर्शी	opaque अपारदर्शक		
trust विश्वास करना	doubt संशय करना		
truth	falsity		
union	discard फूट		
unity	diversity विभिन्नता		
use उपयोग	abuse दुरुपयोग		
vague अस्पष्ट	obvious, definite		
vertical लम्बवत्	horizontal क्षितिज		
violence हिंसा	non-violence अहिंसा		
virtue गुण	vice अवगुण		
vulgar अशिष्ट	cultured सुसंस्कृत		
weal सुख	woe दुख		
wed विवाह करना	divorce तलाक देना		
wet	dry		
wide	narrow		
win जीतना	lose खोना		
wisdom बुद्धिमानी	folly मूर्खता		

Chapter 21

Distinction Between Confusing Words

1. **Access** (n)—approach पहुँच—The access to the officer is not easy.

   Accession (n)—coming into an office सिंहासनारोहण—The accession of Shivaji opened a new page in our history.

2. **Acceptance** (n)—consent to receive स्वीकृति—The minister has not sent the letter of acceptance.

   Acceptation (n)—recognised meaning प्रचलित अर्थ—Today the acceptation of the word 'know-how' is technical expert.

3. **Accident** (n)—unexpected event दुर्घटना—Five men lost their life in the accident.

   Incident (a, n)—event, occurrence घटना—The incident of tearing posters came into light during the election.

4. **Adverse** (a)—unfortunate, going against भाग्यहीन, विपरीत—As an adverse lot, opinion, etc.

   Averse (a)—unwilling अनिच्छुक, परांमुख—Averse to smoking.

5. **Acquisition** (n)—anything acquired उपलब्धि—His reputation of teaching is his only acquisition.

   Acquirement (n)—ability योग्यता, quality गुण—You must have high acquirement if you want to secure a lucrative job.

6. **Act** (n)—deed कार्य, a law कानून, नाटक का अंक—I am much grateful to you for your act of kindness. Act of four articles. The play is limited to five acts.

   Action (n)—process of acting—Act in motion is action.

   Activity (n)—कार्यकलाप—He always watches the activity of his son.

   Actor (n) of film अभिनेता।

   Acting (n) अभिनय।

7. **Advance** (v, n)—going forward अग्रिम, बढ़ाव, payment before hand अग्रिम—The advance of the army was slow.

   A copy of the book must be supplied in advance.

   Advancement (n)—promotion of plan or person प्रगति—The advancement of science has turned our life luxurious.

8. **Admission** (n)—being admitted, acknowledgement प्रवेश, स्वीकारोक्ति—All admissions are stopped.

Admittance (n)—physical entrance सशरीर प्रवेश–His admittance into the room changed the situation.

9. Affection (n)—love स्नेह–The child was deprived of motherly affection.

Affection (n)—pretence, artificiality of manner कृत्रिमता, दिखावटी व्यवहार–Today all ceremonies are mere displays of affectation.

10. Affluence (n)—copiousness प्रचुरता–Affluence of wealth made him vain.

Influence (n)—impression प्रभाव–The influence of cinema is wide spread.

11. Alternate (n)—coming of two things by turn, बारी-बारी–The alternate explosion climbed terror in the city.

Alternative (a, n)—opt one between two विकल्प–I had no other alternative.

12. Amiable (a)—lovable रमणीय (not in a good sense)–Her look was amiable.

Amicable (a)—friendly मित्रवत्–Our relation with U.K. is amicable these days.

13. Amoral (a)—non moral धर्मशून्य–The theme of the story is amoral.

Immoral (a)—opposed to morality अनैतिक–The concerning condition of the country is due to our immoral character.

14. Artisan (n)—handicraft man हस्तशिल्पी।

Artist (n)—who practises fine arts कलाकार–The pictures of some artists were exhibited.

Artistic (a)—कलात्मक–He has given an artistic touch to his work.

Artiste (n)—professional singer, dancer etc. Hemant Kumar was a unique artiste.

Artful (a)—cunning–The politics of today has become the politics of artful policies.

Arty (a)—pretentiously artistic कृत्रिम कलात्मक।

15. Assignation (n)—appointment नियुक्ति–The assignation of the venue was changed.

Assignment (n)—allotment–The assignment of the class was against the desire of the teacher.

16. Avocation (n)—Vocation, calling आह्वान–The avocation of Minerva in the beginning of the poem was a style.

Vocation (n)—a career or occupation व्यवसाय–All vocations are overcrowded.

17. Beneficent (a)—kind दयालु–The saint is beneficent enough to help you.

Beneficial (a)—advantageous लाभदायक–Walking is beneficial to health.

18. Bliss (n)—perfect joy परमानन्द–Where ignorance is bliss, it is folly to be wise.

Blessing (n)—boon वरदान, आशीर्वाद–A pleasant climate is a blessing in disguise.

19. Break (n)—dawn ऊषाकाल–The shepherd aroused us at the break of the day.

Breakage (n)—टूट-फूट–The boys have to pay for the breakage in the laboratory.

20. Bourn (n)—a small stream छोटी नदी–It is said that after death we have to cross a bourn.

Bourne (n)—limit, goal सीमा, लक्ष्य–Our soul goes beyond the bourne of life and time.

21. Brutal (a)—savagely cruel निष्ठुर–The brutal slaughter by the terrorists shocked everyone.

Brutish (a)—stupid, beastly पाशविक–Changez Khan was known for his brutish behaviour.

22. Canvas (n) किरमिच, टाट–He bought a canvas-shoe.

Canvass (v, n)—discuss thoroughly, solicit votes शास्त्रार्थ करना, मत माँगना–The young men were canvassing for votes.

23. Ceremonial (a, n)—with or of ceremony धार्मिक विधि या रीति का–All the members of the family were busy in the ceremonial.

Ceremonious—addicted to ceremony व्यवहारिक, शिष्ट–They were too much ceremonious in their dealings.

24. Childish (a)—puerile बचकाना–Childish behaviour is improper for a grown up person.

Childlike (a)—(in a good sense) innocent like a child बच्चे जैसा निश्छल।

25. Classic (a, n)—of the first class उच्च कोटि का–The wit of Birbal was classic, a classic answer.

Classical (a)—belonging to ancient literature and writer–We must study our classical literature.

26. Concept (n)—general notion धारणा–The law of gravitation is a prevailed concept.

Conception (n)—thing conceived, idea परिकल्पना–His conception of a happy man is based on experience.

Cloth—woven or felted stuff. Clothe (v) put clothes upon. Clothed–clothed (or clad). Clothes—tailored cloth, wearing apparel.

27. Confident (a, n)—trusting विश्वासपात्र–The lecturer is said to be the confident of the principal.

Confidence (n)—firm trust दृढ़ विश्वास–He has full confidence.

28. Connective (a)—serving to connect संयोजक–The connective tissue is injured.

Connection (n)—connexion—state of being connected सम्बन्ध, संयोजन–He denied any connection with that bad person.

29. Conscientious (a)—obedient to conscience अन्तरात्मा के आदेश का पालक–A conscientious man does not believe in rumours.

Conscious (a)—award सजग, सचेत–I am fully conscious of my duty.

30. Considerable (a)—notable, worth considering, much विचारणीय, प्रचुर–The case is considerable. The valcano sent forth considerable lava.

Considerate (a)—विचारशील–Considerateness is a better part of human nature.

31. Contemptible (a)—despicable घृणित–Burning of bride is highly contemptible.

Contemptuous (a)—scornful तिरस्कारयुक्त–He took my word amiss and gazed at me with contemptuous look.

32. Continuance (n)—state of lasting long चिरस्थिरता–The continuance of chilly weather may cost many lives.

Continuation (n)—carrying सक्रमता–A brief moral story has been added in continuation of the main plot.

Continuity (n)—state of being continuous निरन्तरता—The law of continuity maintains that all changes in nature are not abrupt.

Continuous (a)—निरन्तर—The continuous rain may damage the harvest.

Continual (a)—continuing with short breaks रुक-रुक कर।

33. Definite (a)—precise उपयुक्त, निश्चित—Your labour must bring you definite result.

Definitive—decisive निर्णायक।

34. Deliverance (n)—salvation मोक्ष, मुक्ति—The Buddh paved the way of deliverance.

Delivery (n)—child birth, delivering of letters प्रसव, पत्र-वितरण—After delivery the woman with the baby is safe and sound.

The quick delivery of letters was demanded by the public.

35. Device (n)—plan, trick योजना—The police had to adopt a novel device to control the furious mob.

Devise (v, n)—give by will स्वेच्छा देना, to plan योजना बनाना—The administration devised to control anarchy.

36. Digest (n) (डाइजेस्ट)—सामान्य ज्ञान—A general knowledge digest.

(Verb) (डीजेस्ट) पचाना—Some books are to be digested.

Digestion (n)—सुपाच्यता—Taking light exercises makes digestion better.

37. Direct (a, adv)—straight सीधे—He went direct to station.

Directly (adv)—presently शीघ्र—He came directly from the station.

38. Economic (a, n) आर्थिक—The company had to bear a great economic loss due to continual curfew.

Economical (a)—thrifty मितव्ययी—You must be economical if you want to save money.

39. Educational (a)—belonging to education शैक्षिक—The candidates should write their educational qualifications in detail.

Educative (a)—didactic शिक्षाप्रद—The story is highly educative.

40. Effective (a)—having an effect प्रभावशाली—We should take effective steps against the terrorists.

Effectual (a)—producing the desired result अभीष्ट, फलदायी।

Effectuate (v)—accomplish पूर्ण करना।

41. Egoist (n)—Selfish or self-opinionated man आत्मश्लाघी—He is an egoist so he has a few friends.

Egotist (n)—self-conceited आत्माभिमानी—An egotist suffers in the final round.

42. Elemental (a, n)—of the four elements चार तत्त्वों का।

Elementary (a)—introductory प्रारम्भिक—I obtained the elementary knowledge of Sanskrit from my father.

43. Enviable (a)—calculated to excite envy स्पृहणीय—His achievements were enviable.

Envious (a)—full of envy द्वेषपूर्ण—My neighbour is envious of me.

44. Estimate (n, v)—मूल्य निरुपण—The contractor chalked out a prior estimate of expenditure.

Estimation (n)—judgement of worth योग्यता का आकलन—In my estimation, Mr. Gandhi was a man of eminent qualities.

45. Exceptionable (a)—objectionable आपत्तिजनक

Exceptional (a)—unusual अलौकिक—He cited an exceptional example.

46. Expanse (n)—wide area or extent फैलाव—The expanse of flood water was vast.

Expansion (n)—the act of expanding वृद्धि, विस्तार—In those days, the expansion of territory was the aim of British rule.

47. Exhausting (a)—wearisome थकानपूर्ण—as exhausting task.

Exhaustive (a)—comprehensive विस्तृत—A teacher must impart exhaustive knowledge to his pupils.

48. Facility (n)—सुविधा—We all have been given the facility of education.

Felicity (n)—परमानन्द—intense happiness—The poem is notable for its felicity of picturesque beauty.

49. Fatal (a)—deadly प्राणघातक—Cancer is a fatal disease.

Fatalist (n)—a believer in fate भाग्यवादी—A fatalist believes that all happenings are inevitable.

50. Forceful (a)—full of force शक्तिपूर्ण, प्रभावशाली।

Forcile (a)—done by force शक्ति से सम्पन्न।

51. Failing (n)—shortcoming कमी—Every man has his failings.

Failure (n)—ill success असफलता—One should not feel ashamed at one's failure.

52. Formality (n)—conformity to rules आचार नियम—Now our team is sure to win. Only formality is to be done.

Formalism (n)—conventional usage नियमनिष्ठता—We should make our life easy by avoiding too much formalism.

53. Graceful (a)—Charming कमनीय।

Gracious (a)—kindly दयालु—She is not only graceful but gracious also.

54. Healthy (a)—having good health स्वस्थ।

Healthful (a)—health-giving स्वास्थ्यवर्धक—He has became healthy by taking healthful tonic.

55. Historic (a)—noted in history.

Historical (a)—of history ऐतिहासिक—A history is a description of historic events and historical figures.

56. Honorary (a)—serving without pay अवैतनिक।

Honourable (a)—worthy of honour प्रतिष्ठित, श्रद्धेय।

57. Illegible (a)—not legible अपठनीय—The signature of the officer is illegible.

Ineligible (a)—not eligible अग्राह्य, अचयनीय—Any objectionable approach by the candidate will make him ineligible.

58. Imaginary (a)—having no real existence काल्पनिक–Utopia of T. More is a description of imaginary island.

Imaginative (a)—the faculty of imagination–The poem sparkles with many imaginative expressions.

59. Incomparable (a)—matchless अनुपम, अद्वितीय।

Uncomparable (a)—not capable of being compared अतुलनीय।

60. Industrial (a)—of industries औद्योगिक–The industrial revolution in Europe was a turning point in the history.

Industrious (a)—hard-working परिश्रमी, अध्यवसायी–Only the industrious hold on.

61. Inflammable (a, n)—easily set on fire ज्वलनशील–Petrol is an inflammable fuel.

Inflammatory (a)—tending to excite उत्तेजक–His inflammatory lecture turned the mob furious.

62. Ingenious (a)—clever, skilful चतुर, प्रवीण।

Ingenuous (a)—frank, innocent, artless स्पष्टवादी, निर्दोष, कलाविहीन।

63. Intelligent (a)—clever, quick of mind चतुर, बुद्धिमान।

Intelligible (a)—that can be understood सुबोध्य, समझने योग्य–His style is simple and reasoning intelligible.

64. Judicial (a)—pertaining to a judge or court of justice.

Judicious (a)—prudent न्यायोचित, बुद्धिमत्तापूर्ण–The judicial committee gave a judicious report.

65. Leave (v, n)—अवकाश–leavings (n) जूठन।

66. Limit (n, v)—bounding line सीमा–He spent money without limit.

Limitation (n)—inability, restriction–परिमितता, कमी He is a poet of great reputation but he has his limitations.

67. Literal (a)—expressed by letter(s) शाब्दिक–If you mean my statement in a literal way, I shall be mistaken.

Literate (a, n)—able to read and write शिक्षित–It is our duty to make all citizens literate.

68. Lovable (a)—deserving, amicable प्रेम करने योग्य (a bad word).

Lovely (a)—admirably beautiful मनोहर, सुन्दर।

69. Luxuriant (a)—profuse of growth अति समृद्ध–As luxuriant growth of cereal crops.

Luxurious (a)—given to luxury विलासपूर्ण–The king led a luxurious life.

70. Masterful (a)—self-willed. Masterly—very skilful अतिदक्ष।

Masterpiece—consummate piece. of workmanship विशिष्ट रचना–as a masterpiece work of art.

71. Momentary (a)—short-lived क्षणिक–Life is momentary.

Momentous (a)—important महत्त्वपूर्ण।

72. Necessaries (n)—desired things आवश्यकताएँ (वस्तु)–The poor suffer for want of necessaries of life.

Necessity (n)—imperative need आवश्यकता–Necessity is the mother of invention.

73. Neglectful (a)—उपेक्षणीय Despiteful persons are neglectful.

Negligent (a)—careless–असावधानी–He was suspended for the negligent of duty.

74. New (a, adv)—not existing before नूतन–New fashion, newcomer, etc.

Novel (a, n)—strange अनूठा, उपन्यास–Really it is a novel. She struck out a novel plan.

75. Notable (a, n)—remarkable, eminent उत्कृष्ट, विख्यात–Shelley was a notable poet of Romantic period.

Notorious (a)—कुख्यात A notorious robber.

76. Observance (n)—keeping of law, duty, custom, etc. आचरण (नियम, कर्त्तव्य, रीति, आदि का)–We should be cautious in observance of rules.

Observation (n)—noticing or being noticed निरीक्षण, निरूपण–As, a man of sharp observation.

77. Official (a, n)—person holding public office पदाधिकारी–official duty. Two officials came for inspection.

Officious (a)—intrusive, meddle some अनाधिकार हस्तक्षेपक–Officials should not be officious in personal matters.

78. Pitiable (a)—deserving pity दयनीय–Her condition was very pitiable.

Pitiful (a)—compassionate करुणामय–The scene was very pitiful.

79. Popular (a)—लोकप्रिय, प्रसिद्ध–The teacher was popular with his students.

Populous (a)—thickly inhabited सघन बसा हुआ–Uttar Pradesh is a populous province.

80. Practicable (a)—that can be done.

Practical (a)—of practice व्यवहारिक–The rules of road are practicable. In practical life we forget our ideals.

81. Provident (a)—having or showing foresight दूरदर्शी।

Providential (a)—of, by divine foresight दैविक।

82. Radiant (a, n)—emitting rays of light, splendid or dazzling as radiant light, heat, etc. चमकीला।

Rediate (v)—emit rays of light रश्मि विकीर्ण करना–Light was radiating from the centre.

83. Rapture (n)—ecstatic delight आह्लाद–The whole picturesque surroundings was humming with rapture.

Rupture (n, v)—breach of harmonious relations, break सम्बन्ध-विच्छेद।

84. Recourse (n)—resorting to a possible source of help.

Resource (n)—means साधन, उपाय–He had lost all resources.

85. Regretable (a)—worthy of regret खेद-योग्य–Your henious act is regretable.

Regretful (a)—full of regret as I am very regretful to inform you that you have not been selected.

86. Respected (a)—honoured, regarded प्रतिष्ठित।

Respectable (a)—deserving respect आदरणीय।

Respectful (a)—showing deference as respectful behaviour सम्मानजनक।

Respective (a) पूर्वनिर्धारित, क्रमानुसार—Please take your respective seats.

87. Sensible (a)—of good sense, reasonable समझदार।

Sensitive (a, n)—delicate कोमल।

Sensual (a)—indulging in carnal pleasures as—The Nawabs used to lead sensual life.

Sensuous (a)—derived from the senses ऐन्द्रिक—Keats' love of beauty was sensuous not sensual.

88. Social (a)—pertaining to society सामाजिक—Man is a social animal.

Sociable (a)—familiar, liking company मिलनसार—He was a sociable man, hence all liked him.

89. Spiritual—आध्यात्मिक।

Spirituous—मादक as, spirituous drinks.

90. Stimulant (a)—producing vitality स्फूर्तिदायक (stimulus (n)—pl.—i) that which excites प्रेरणा, उत्प्रेरक Tea and coffee are stimulant.

91. Sanguine (a, n)—hopeful, confident आशान्वित, विश्वस्त।

Sanguinary (a)—bloody, blood-thirsty रक्तपिपासु।

92. Superficial (a)—without depth, shallow छिछला as, superficial colour, knowledge, etc.

Superfluous (a)—more than enough आवश्यकता से अधिक as, superfluous use of words.

93. Suspend (v)—hang up लटकना, अटकना, debar temporarily निलम्बित करना—A piece of bone was suspended in his throat. Suspended from duty.

Sustain (v)—to bear weight of, hold up, maintain सहना, रोकना, अक्षुण रखना as, sustain the shock, the objection, etc.

Suspense (n)—State of anxious uncertainty जिज्ञासापूर्ण—The film is full of suspense.

Suspension (n)—as, suspension bridge झूला।

94. Temporal (a, n)—of this life ऐहिक oppo. to spiritual.

Temporary (a, n)—lasting for a time अस्थायी।

95. Transient (a)—passing quickly as transient days of life क्षणगामी।

Transitory (a)—not permanent क्षणभंगुर, अनित्य—Nothing is permanent in this transitory world.

96. Veracity (n)—the truth सत्यता।

Voracity (n)—greediness लोलुपता।

97. Virtual (a)—अप्रत्यक्ष—He was virtual leader of the party.

Virtuous (a)—morally good सदाचारी, धर्मपरायण—A virtuous man is honoured everywhere.

98. Wilful (a)—intentional, stubborn स्वेच्छाचारी, हठी।

Wilful disobedience, ignorance, murder, etc.

Willing (a)—not reluctant इच्छुक—Do not spur a willing horse.

Chapter 22

Homophones

The word 'Homophones' means word having same sound as another, but of different meaning or origin.

1. Absolute—perfect पूर्ण—Absolute knowledge should be the aim of education.
    Obsolete—disused अप्रयुक्त, अप्रचलित—He has used many obsolete words in his essay.

2. Accede—agree सहमत होना, स्वीकृति देना—The manager acceded to the proposals.
    Exceed—excel अधिक होना—The temperature exceeded from the normal point.

3. Accept—admit स्वीकारना—The application was accepted by the teacher.
    Except—save सिवाय—Every student except John, was making a noise.
    Expect—hope आशा करना, अपेक्षा करना—I expect gentle behaviour from him.

4. Adapt—fit, suit उपयुक्त होना, अनुकूल बनाना—He adapted himself to the situation.
    Adept—(a, n)—clever चतुर, दक्ष—He was well adept in painting.
    Adopt—take up अपनाना, गोद लेना—India has adopted the policy of secularism. The king adopted a son.

5. Affect—(v, n) move—His appeal affected the people immensely.
    Effect—(v, n)—प्रभावित होना bring about, result—The medicine brought no effect. The law was effected from July.

6. Allusion—indirect reference अप्रत्यक्ष सन्दर्भ—He has given many allusions in his ode.
    Illusion—delusion—भ्रम—life is nothing else than an illusion.

7. Altar (n)—वेदी, मंदिर—He sacrificed his life at the altar of the motherland.
    Alter (u)—change उलट देना, पलटना—By his healthy reasoning, the lawyer altered the case.

8. All together—all in a company—They jumped all together into the river.
    Altogether—totally—पूर्णरूपेण—The statement was altogether false.

9. Apposite—well put उपयुक्त—His answer was quite apposite.
    Opposite—contrary प्रतिकूल—A gust of wild wind came from the opposite direction.

10. Ascent—rise चढ़ाई, आरोहण—The ascent to the mountain was full of difficulties.
    Assent—sanction स्वीकृति—The manager did not give his assent.

11. Beacon—signal प्रतीक—The bright stars were our beacon light.
    Becon (v)—summon, call पुकारना—The sailors beconed loudly.

12. Berth—sleeping—place in ship, train, etc.—Have you got a berth reserved for me ?
    Birth—He got a lot of presents on his birth day.

238

13. Brake—apparatus for checking motion गतिनियंत्रक
    Break (v)—The servant broke the jug.

14. Cast (v)—throw फेंकना—The natural beauty cast a spell on us.
    Caste जाति, वर्ण—He was a Brahmin by caste.

15. Censor—an official examiner—The film Censor Board certifies all films.
    Censure—to blame or criticise दोष मढ़ना, आलोचना करना—The book was censured by the Government.

16. Check—restrain—All nooks and corners were checked. Check the whereabouts.
    Cheque—bank-cheque हुंडी—The bank manager issued a new cheque.

17. Coarse—common, inferior निम्न स्तरीय—This bag is made of coarse cloth.
    Course कालक्रम, पाठ्यक्रम—In the course of ; matter of course ; main course, etc.

18. Comity—courtesy शिष्टाचार—We should teach our children the common comity.
    Committee समिति—The managing committee rejected the proposal.

19. Complement—that which completes पूरक—Fill up the blank with suitable complement.
    Compliment—praise प्रशंसा, अनुकूलता—He sent a letter in compliment of his congratulations.

20. Contagious—infectious संक्रामक—A cold is a contagious disease.
    Contiguous—neighbouring पड़ोसीय—Our contiguous relation should be sympathetic.

21. Corps कोर—division of an army—My friend has joined National Cadet Corps.
    Corpse—a dead body शव—Many corpses were unearthed from the debris.
    Crop—harvest—The swarm of locusts destroyed the standing crops.

22. Council सभा, परिषद्—The bill was passed by the council.
    Counsel—advice सलाह—His counsel for the factory proved good.

23. Dairy दुग्धशाला—We buy milk from the dairy.
    Diary दैनन्दिनी—daily records of events. I keep all records of my expenditure in my diary.

24. Dear—beloved प्रिय—My village is very dear to me.
    Deer—hart हिरण—The hounds chased the deer.

25. Decease—death, die—They brought the deceased man home.
    Disease—illness—Most diseases spring from dust.

26. Desert—barren land मरुस्थल—The desert of Sahara. (verb). The army deserted many villages.
    Dessert भोजनोपरान्त का फलादि—Sweet apples as dessert were served after dinner.

27. Deprecate तिरस्कार करना।
    Depreciate—diminish value of मूल्य (महत्त्व) घटाना।

28. Die—cease to live.
    Dye—रंगना—He wore a shirt dyed in red.

29. Emigrant—one who leaves one's country to settle in another आप्रवासी।
    Immigrant—one who comes as settler. आव्रजक।

30. Eminent—distinguished विशिष्ट–He has no ability yet he has occupied an eminent post in the society.

Immanent—manifesting all सर्वव्याप्त–God is immanent.

Imminent—soon to happen आसन्न–It appears that a war between the two countries is imminent.

31. Expanse—Wide extend विस्तार।

Expense—expenditure व्यय–My uncle bore all my expenses of study.

32. Fain—glad प्रसन्न –I would be fain to see you.

Feign—pretend बहाना करना–He feigned to be mad.

33. Fair—beautiful सुन्दर, संतोषप्रद, मेला–Fair is he who does fair ; by fair means or foul.

Fare—किराया–Have you paid the fare ?

34. Feat—deed of valour पराक्रम–Maharana Pratap is known for his heroic feats.

Feet—(pl. of foot) पैर, बारह इंच का माप–Her feet were light. Ten feet long etc.

35. Gaol—jail कारागार–The patriots were sent to gaol.

Goal—destination, aim लक्ष्य–An effort without goal ends in smoke.

36. Hart—deer–Heart–A hart has a tender heart.

37. Human—manly–To err is human.

Humane—benevolent उदार–I expect humane behaviour from you.

38. Idle—lazy आलसी–An idle man is never happy.

Idol—Image मूर्ति–He hated idol-worship.

39. Impassable—That can not be traversed अगम्य, दुस्तर–The route seemed impassable by the climbers.

Impassible—Incapable of suffering कष्ट सहने में अक्षम,

Impossible—not possible असंभव–It is impossible to help you.

40. Imperial—of an empire साम्राज्ञी–Imperial power, glory, etc.

Imperious—overbearing उद्धत, ढीठ।

41. Jealous—envious द्वेषी–A jealous man never prospers.

Zealous—full of fervour उत्साही–Our zealous deeds brought freedom for us.

42. Later—Comparative degree of 'Late'. Later on, an event took place.

Latter—Latter is opp. to former. Latter denotes position.

43. Lessen—to diminish न्यून करना–His help lessened my difficulties.

Lesson—instruction शिक्षा, पाठ।

44. Lifelong—continued for a life time आजीवन–She stood by me lifelong.

Livelong—Whole length of सम्पूर्ण–The livelong day, summer etc.

45. Marshal—सैन्यप्रमुख।

Martial—of warfare सामरिक।

Morsel—mouthful ग्रास।

46. **Meter** मापक यंत्र।

Meteor—shooting star टूटता सितारा।

Metre—any form of poetic rhythm छन्द।

47. **Moral**—नैतिक–moral lesson, **Morale**—हौसला, जोश–The morale of the soldiers was high.

48. **Ordinance**—decree अध्यादेश–The Governor issued an ordinance.

Ordnance—mounted gun, canon तोपखाना–I have visited the ordnance depot in Naini.

49. **Loose** ढीला करना–Do not play fast and loose.

Lose खोना–What does it matter if we lose ?

50. **Marry**—Join in wedlock.

Merry—joyous प्रसन्न–Both the pairs were merry when they were married.

51. **Peace**—calmness शान्ति–We felt peace amidst nature.

Piece—a fragment टुकड़ा–The glass fell and broke into pieces.

52. **Peal**—loud ringing of bells घंटियों की उच्चध्वनि–The temple was filled with peals.

Peel—outer coating छिलका–The peal of the orange was thick.

Pill—tablet टिकिया–This pill is meant to cure a headache.

53. **Persecute**—harass, worry—To persecute the poor is not a human act.

Prosecute मुकदमा चलाना–Trespassers will be prosecuted.

54. **Perspective**—view, prospect दृश्य, स्वरूप–Things should be seen in their actual perspective.

Prospective—concerned with the future भविष्य जन्य–The law was held to be exclusively prospective.

55. **Physic**—medicine दवा–The art of healing as a dose of physic.

Physics भौतिकशास्त्र।

Physique—bodily structure, as a sound physique डील-डौल।

56. **Plain**—clear, simple स्वच्छ, सादा–Plain living and high thinking ; write an application on a plain paper. (मैदानी क्षेत्र)

Plane—aeroplane हवाई जहाज ; a tool of woodwork, as, went by plane ; smoothed the surface of wood with a plane.

57. **Pray**—worship वन्दना करना–She prayed that God might save her child.

Prey (v, n)—hunt शिकार करना, शिकार–The swallow became a prey of the falcon.

58. **Precede**—go before–Such duties precede all others.

Proceed—go on आगे बढ़ना–We proceeded towards the hills.

59. **Precedent**—previous case taken as example पूर्व दृष्टान्त–There is no precedent for this.

President—The head of a council, society etc. as, president of the Board of Trade.

60. **Prescribe**—lay down authoritatively—This book has been prescribed by the Board of Education.

Do not prescribe what I have to do.

Proscribe—banish, denounce, reject रोक लगाना—This book has been proscribed by the state.

61. Principal—head of some institution.

Principle सिद्धान्त, theory.

62. Polite—courteous, cultured विनम्र, शिष्ट—His polite manners pleased everyone.

Politic—Sagacious, prudent विवेकशील—The judge gave a politic decision.

63. Quiet—undisturbed शान्त—A calm and quiet life is always happy.

Quite—completely बिल्कुल—It took quite a long time ; not quite proper.

64. Rage—violent anger, speak loudly तीव्र क्रोध—The rage of wind. He raged at his wife.

Raze (rase) मिटाना erase—I have razed his name from the memory ; razed to ground.

Raise—set upright उठाना—He raised a question ; raised his voice ; raised a laugh.

65. Reign—rule शासन—The reign of Ashok was glorious.

Rein लगाम—The knight drew the rein and dismounted from the horse.

66. Rest (v, n)—Let us rest here for a while.

Wrest (v, n)—twist टेढ़ा करना।

67. Right—उपयुक्त as, right you are ; from right to left.

Rite—a religious ceremony धार्मिक संस्कार—The rites of wedding were performed.

68. Root जड़—The house was the root cause of the contention.

Rout—company of revellers or rioters. दंगाई।

Route—way रास्ता—We reached there from another route.

69. Sail (v, n)—travel on water समुद्री यात्रा करना, पतवार—We shall sail next week from London ; a fleet of twenty sails.

Sale—selling विक्री—The sales were concerning.

70. Sanatory—healing to physical or moral health स्वस्थकर।

Sanitary—of the condition that affects health—Here the sanitary condition is not sanatory.

71. Sear—withered, dried up मुर्झाया, सूखा—The green leaves are seared.

Seer—Prophet सिद्धपुरुष—India is a pilgrimage of sages and seers.

72. Sole—जूते का तलवा, अकेला।

Soul—spirit आत्मा—Our soul is immortal.

73. Spacious, roomy चौड़ा, बड़ा—My house has three spacious rooms.

Specious—of good appearance, fair as, specious argument शोभनीय।

74. Stationary—remaining to one place स्थिर—The satellite was made stationary.

Stationery—of writing materials लेखन सामग्री—His son deals in stationery articles.

75. Statue—sculptured figure मूर्ति—A statue of the leader was erected there.

Statute नियम, व्यवस्था—a written legislature as parliament runs by statutes.

76. Storey—मंजिल as, A three storeyed building.

Story—tale कथा–They all tell the same story.

77. Straight—as, A straight line.

Strait—narrow passage of water जलडमरूमध्य as, The strait of Zibralter.

78. Tale—story—Life is a tale told by an idiot.

Tail—पूँछ–The fox lost her tail.

79. Tamper—meddle with as tamper with will, authority etc.

Temper—disposition of mind मानसिक रुझान या स्वभाव–As a good temper ; a hot temper.

80. Team—दल–Our cricket team is very strong.

Teem—overflow, be prolific परिपूर्ण–The forest was teeming with beasts and birds.

81. Tenor—settled course or direction प्रचलित रीति।

Tenure—पट्टा, कार्यकाल–During his tenure of office, he was honest.

82. Umpire—निर्णायक (person) An umpire must be just and honest.

Empire—kingdom साम्राज्य as, The Moghal Empire.

83. Urban—of living or situated in a city नगरीय–Outwardly, the urban life charms many men.

Urbane—elegant in manner सभ्य।

84. Vacation—vacating, holidays रिक्त होना, अवकाश–The schools were closed for summer vacation.

Vocation—occupation पेशा।

85. Vain—useless—He tried his best but in vain व्यर्थ।

Vein—नस–Blood runs through the veins.

86. Vale—घाटी–The entire vale was filled with the song of cuckoos.

Veil—घूँघट–She drew her veil.

Wail—रोना–The world wails in its misery.

87. Waist—कमर–Her waist is thin.

Waste—lay waste, desolate—Do not waste your time in gossips ; a waste land.

88. Waive—forgo, relinquish परित्याग करना–He waived his interests aside.

Wave—लहर–a wave of enthusiasm ; a cold wave–Waves were dashing against the shore.

89. Weak—Wanting in strength, power कमजोर–So weak was he that he could not stand.

Week—period of seven days सप्ताह–What day of the week is it today ?

90. Weather—मौसम–as, a pleasant weather.

Whether—Which of the two–He asked me whether he might take my cycle.

Wither—make or become dry, deprive of freshness मुझाना, सूखना–Flowers were withered in the garden.

91. Wreak—revenge बदला (n, v) as, wreaked vengeance upon his enemy.

Wreck (v, n)—ruin विनाश, बर्बादी–The gale caused many wrecks.

Chapter 23

One-Word Substitutions

1. Adaptable—able to be made suitable उपयुक्त या अनुकूल बनाने योग्य।
2. Alien—belonging to foreign or of a different nature आप्रवासी।
3. Altruist—one who regards for others as a principle of action परोपकारी।
4. Amateur—one who cultivates a thing as a pastime अव्यवसायिक, शौकिया।
5. Ambassador—minister sent by one state on mission to another.
6. Ambidextrous—(person) able to use left hand as well as right दोनों हाथ से काम करने वाला।
7. Ambiguous—of doubtful classification संदिग्ध, अनिश्चित।
8. Ancestral—belonging to forefather पैतृक, पूर्वज का।
9. Anomaly—in a disorderly state अव्यवस्था।
10. Anonymous—of unknown source गुमनाम।
11. Antidote—medicine given to counteract poison or disease विषनाशक दवा
12. Antiseptic—counteracting putrefaction व्रण निरोधक।
13. Antonym—a word of contrary meaning to another विलोम शब्द।
14. Aristocracy—government by the best citizens or the noble शिष्टजन सत्तात्मक राज्य।
15. Armistice—cessation from hostilities युद्धविराम।
16. Ascetic—one who practises severe self-discipline or leads a retired life for this तपस्वी, वैरागी।
17. Astronaut—student or devotee of aerial navigation in space कक्षयात्री।
18. Atheist—one who has no belief in the existence of God नास्तिक।
19. Audible—perceptible to the ear श्रुत, कर्णगोचर।
20. Autobiography—writing the story of one's own life आत्मकथा।
21. Autocracy—an absolute government ruled by a king निरंकुश शासन।
22. Bellicose—inclined to fighting लड़ाकू प्रवृत्ति का।
23. Bigot—one who attacks weight to some creed or view हठधर्मी, कट्टर।
24. Biography—written life of a person जीवनवृत।
25. Blasphemy—talking impiously पाखंड, ईशनिन्दा।
26. Brittle (fragile)—apt to break टूटनीय।

27. Bureaucracy—government by officials नौकरशाही।

28. Celibacy—state of being unmarried कुमारत्व।

29. Cemetery—place for burials कब्रिस्तान।

30. Centenary—festival of the hundredth anniversary जन्मशती।

31. Circumlocution—use of many words where few would do शब्दाधिक्यता।

32. Contemporary—(person) belonging to the same time समकालीन।

33. Controversial—given to controversy विवादग्रस्त।

34. Cosmopolitan—a person free from national attachments राष्ट्रोपरि, विश्वबन्धुत्व।

35. Credible—Worthy of belief विश्वसनीय।

36. Credulous—too ready to believe सहज विश्वसनीय।

37. Crematorium—place for cremating corpses शवदाह स्थान।

38. Defensible—easily defended (war or argument) सहज रक्षणीय।

39. Democracy—government by the people प्रजातंत्र।

40. Dormant—lying inactive as in sleep निष्क्रिय।

41. Ecology—branch of biology dealing with living organisms' habits जीववैज्ञानिक संभाग।

42. Edible—fit to eat, eatable भक्षणीय।

43. Effeminate—womanish नारीतुल्य।

44. Egoist—a selfish person आत्मश्लाघी।

45. Eligible—fit to be chosen योग्य, चयनीय।

46. Emigrant—a person who settles in other country प्रवासी।

47. Empiric—based on observation and experiment परीक्षण पर आधारित।

48. Epicurean—(person) devoted to pleasure आनन्दजीवी।

49. Epilogue—concluding part of literary work उपसंहार।

50. Epitaph—words inscribed on tomb समाधिलेख।

51. Eternal—always existing शाश्वत, चिरन्तन।

52. Etymology—facts relating to formation and meaning of word शब्द-व्युत्पत्ति-सिद्धान्त।

53. Epidemic—(disease) prevalent among community at special time महामारी।

54. Expiate—pay the penalty of (sin) प्रायश्चित।

55. Expurgate—purify (book etc.) by removing matter objectionable संशोधन करना।

56. Extempore—speech without previous preparation पूर्व तैयारी बिना भाषण, लेख।

57. Fastidious—Hard to please दुस्तोषणीय।

58. Fatal—deadly, sure to kill प्राणघातक।

59. Fanatic—(person) filled with excessive and mistaken enthusiasm in religion धर्मान्ध।

60. Fatalist—one who believes in fate भाग्यवादी।

61. Flexible—that bends without breaking लचीला।

62. Frequent—often occurring प्राय: घटनीय।

63. Genocide—extermination of a race वंश निष्कासन।

64. Gregarious—living in flocks or communities समूह में रहनेवाला।

65. Gullible—able to be duped छलनीय।

66. Hereditary—transmitted from one generation to another वंशानुगत।

67. Heterogeneous—composed of diverse elements बहुतात्विक।

68. Homophone—word having same sound as another but of different origin or meaning समध्वन्यात्मक शब्द।

69. Honorary—office without pay अवैतनिक।

70. Humanitarian—one who professes humanism मानवतावादी।

71. Idolatry—worshipping of idols मूर्तिपूजा।

72. Illegible—which cannot be read अपठनीय।

73. Illiterate—person who can neither read nor write निरक्षर।

74. Immigrant—a person who comes as settler आब्रजक।

75. Immolation—to sacrifice for the welfare (esp. with fire) आत्मदाह।

76. Immutable—unchangeable अपरिवर्त्तनीय।

77. Impenetrable—that cannot be penetrated अप्रवेश्य।

78. Impervious—not affording passage अभेद्य।

79. Impracticable—impossible in practice अव्यवहारिक।

80. Inaccesible—unapproachable अगम्य।

81. Inalienable—not alienable, which ownership is not transferable.

82. Incorrigible—that cannot be corrected अशुध्य।

83. Indefatigable—that cannot be tired out अश्रान्त।

84. Indefensible—admitting of no defence अरक्षणीय।

85. Indelible—which cannot be effaced अमिट।

86. Inevitable—unavoidable, sure to happen अपरिहार्य।

87. Infallible—incapable of erring अकाट्य।

88. Infanticide—killing of an infant soon after birth शिशुहत्या।

89. Inflammable (combustible)—easily set on fire ज्वलनशील।

90. Inimitable—that cannot be imitated अनुकरण रहित।

91. Insolvent—unable to pay debts दिवालिया।

92. Insurmountable—not to be surmounted अलंघनीय।

93. Intermediary—acting between parties मध्यस्थ।

94. Intestate—not having made a will.

95. Invincible—unconquerable अजेय।

96. Invulnerable—that cannot be wounded or hurt अघात्य।

97. Irrelevant—not to the point अप्रासंगिक।

98. Irreparable—that cannot be made good अपूरणीय।

99. Irritable—quick to anger झुँझले स्वभाव का।

100. Linguist—person skilled in foreign languages बहुभाषी व्यक्ति।

101. Lactometer—instrument for ascertaining the purity of milk दुग्ध शुद्धतामापी यंत्र।

102. Maiden speech—first speech in one's life जीवन का प्रथम भाषण।

103. Manuscript—book, document written by hand पाण्डुलिपि।

104. Martyr—one who suffers for noble cause शहीद।

105. Mercenary—hired soldiers in foreign service भाड़े के सैनिक।

106. Misanthrope—hater of mankind मानव से घृणा करने वाला।

107. Mobocracy—state ruled by crowd भीड़तंत्र।

108. Monotheism—the belief that there is only one God एकेश्वरवाद, अद्वैतवाद।

109. Nephology—study of the clouds जलदशास्त्र।

110. Nepotism–undue favour to relatives (relatives) भाई भतीजावाद।

111. Notorious—one who is known for bad conduct कुख्यात।

112. Obsolete—no longer in use अप्रचलित।

113. Oligarchy—state governed by the few सीमित व्यक्तियों का शासन।

114. Omnipotent—all powerful, the Almighty God सर्वशक्तिमान।

115. Omnipresent—present everywhere, immanent सर्वत्र।

116. Omniscient—who knows all सर्वज्ञ।

117. Opaque—impenetrable to sight अपारदर्शी।

118. Optimist—one who looks at the bright side of things आशावादी।

119. Orphan—a child whose parents are dead अनाथ।

120. Orthodox—holding conventional beliefs परम्परावादी।

121. Pacifism—the doctrine that the abolition of war is both desirable and possible शान्तिवाद।

122. Panacea—universal remedy रामवाण।

123. Patricide (perricide)—murder(er) one's father पितृघात।

124. Parasite (animal, plant)—living in or upon another परजीवी।

125. Patrimony—property inherited from one's father or ancestors पैतृक सम्पत्ति।

126. Pedantic—one who overrates book-bearing पांडित्यपूर्ण।

127. Pedestrian—one who goes (going) on foot पैदलयात्री।

128. Pessimist—one who looks at the dark sides of life निराशावादी।

129. Philanderer—(of a man) one who makes love is in a trifling manner.

130. Philanthropist—a lover of mankind लोकसंग्रही।

131. Philistine—an uncultured person गँवार।
132. Plutocracy—rule of the wealthy कुलीनतंत्र।
133. Polyandry—having several husbands at one time बहुपतित्व।
134. Polygamy—having more than one mate बहुसंगी।
135. Posthumous—born after the death of father पितृशोकोपरान्त जन्म।
136. Predicament—unpleasant or dangerous situation कष्टदायी स्थिति।
137. Prologue—serving as introduction प्रस्तावना।
138. Quintessence—essence ; perfect example of quality सर्वोत्कृष्ट।
139. Reciprocate—go with alternate backward forward motion आगे पीछे गतिमान।
140. Regicide—killing of a king राजहत्या।
141. Samaritan—genuinely charitable person दयालु।
142. Sceptic—person who doubts all religious doctrines (atheist) नास्तिक।
143. Simultaneous—occurring at the same time.
144. Sinecure—office of profit without duties attached न्यून कार्य किन्तु उच्च वेतन का कार्यालय।
145. Soliloquy—talking without the presence of hearers एकान्त कथन।
146. Somnambulism—walking during sleep सुप्तावस्था में चलना।
147. Stoic—one who accounts virtue as the highest good आत्मसंयमी।
148. Suicide—the murder of one's ownself आत्महत्या।
149. Teetotaller—who totally abstains from alcoholic liquor मादक पदार्थ का सेवन न करने वाला।
150. Thermometer—instrument for measuring temperature तापमापक यंत्र।
151. Translucent—transmitting light but not transparent अर्धपारदर्शक।
152. Transmigration (of soul)–pass into a different body परकाया प्रवेश।
153. Transparent—easily seen through पारदर्शी।
154. Unanimous—of one mind or opinion सर्वसम्मत।
155. Usurer—one who lends money on high interest सूदखोर।
156. Utopian—ardent but unpractical reformer or scheme.
157. Verbose—using more words than wanted शब्दाधिक्य।
158. Veteran—a person with long experience अतिअनुभवी।
159. Vocational—one who pursues sports for money व्यवसायिक खिलाड़ी।
160. Widow—whose husband is dead विधवा।
161. Widower—whose wife is dead विधुर।
162. Zoo—place where birds, beasts are kept जैवकीय संस्थान।
163. Zoology—natural history of animals जन्तुविज्ञान।

Exercise 1

Give one word substitutes of the following :

1. Year return (or celebration) of a date.
2. A crowd of hearers.
3. A person under legal process because of insolvency.
4. Man who eats human flesh.
5. Complete list of books alphabetically written.
6. A play that ends with humour, festivity and pleasure.
7. A period of one-hundred year.
8. A person who is absolute ruler of the state.
9. That cannot be excused.
10. One who spends money lavishly.
11. That cannot be seen.
12. Science based on reasoning.
13. Class of animals having mammal for nourishment of young.
14. An eloquent public speaker.
15. A drama with unhappy ending.

Answers

1. anniversary
2. audience
3. bankrupt
4. cannibal
5. catalogue
6. comedy
7. century
8. dictator
9. inexcusable
10. extravagant
11. invisible
12. logic
13. mammals
14. orator
15. tragedy.

Chapter 24

Synonyms

The word 'Synonym' means word identical and coextensive in sense and usage with another of the same language (पर्यायवाची शब्द)

1. **Ability**—योग्यता—sufficient power (to do something) cleverness or mental faculty.
   Capacity—सामर्थ्य—holding-power, capability or legal competency.

2. **Abstain**—परहेज करना—keep oneself away (from alcohol etc.).
   Refrain अंकुश लगाना—put restraint upon (from doing something).

3. **Accept**—to agree to, to consent.
   Admit—accept as valid or true.
   Confess—दोष स्वीकारना—acknowledge (guilt, sin etc.).

4. **Accident**—दुर्घटना—unexpected event.
   Incident—घटना—an event or occurrence.

5. **Achieve**—accomplish, carryout, win.
   Acquire—gain by and for oneself (quality, fame).
   Attain—to reach, to gain.

6. **Act**—decree passed by a legislative body etc.
   Bill—draft of proposed act प्रस्तावित कानून का प्रारूप।

7. **Admire**—regard with pleased surprise or approval सराहना।
   Commend—praise प्रशंसा करना।
   Praise—commend the merits of उपलब्धि हेतु प्रशंसा करना।

8. **Affect**—have an influence on, produce an effect on प्रभावित करना।
   Consequence—result परिणाम।
   Effect—cause, produce, result in फलित होना।

9. **Aid**—help with material वस्तु-सहायता।
   Assistance—help person, process in doing कार्य में सहायता।

10. **Allow**—expresses negative action अनुमति देना (नकारात्मक)।
    Permit—denotes positive action सकारात्मक अनुमति देना।

11. **Amaze**—overwhelm with wonder विस्मित होना।
    Astonish—amazed at a trifle thing चकित होना (सामान्य बात पर)।

Surprise—astonish against expectation अद्भुत स्थिति में।

Wonder—surprise mingled with admiration, curiosity or bewilderment आश्चर्यचकित होना।

12. Amoral—unconcerned with morals नैतिकता रहित।

Immoral—opposed to morality, vicious.

Non-moral—more unorthodox than amoral नैतिकता विरुद्ध।

Unmoral—non-moral अनैतिक।

13. Amusement—pleasant diversion from serious business.

Entertainment—amusement (from public performance or show) मनोरंजन।

Pastime—recreation for getting relief, relaxation and refreshment मनोविनोद।

Recreation—agreeably occupy oneself for pastime आमोद-प्रमोद।

14. Answer—reply to a question.

Reply—make answer, respond (in word or action, conversation, correspondence).

15. Arrogant—presumptuous, haughty पूर्वाग्रही, उग्र, उच्छृंखल।

Pride—overweening opinion of one's own qualities अभिमान।

Vanity—empty pride दंभ, घमंड।

16. Avenge—take vengeance for (injury) on behalf of (person) अन्य के लिए बदला लेना।

Revenge—to satisfy the offended party's resentment, exact distribution for (offence to oneself) स्वयं हेतु।

Vengeance—to redress the balance by an offender.

17. Prize—reward given as symbol of victory or superiority etc.

Reward—return for service or merit.

18. Battle—combat between organised forces or troops लड़ाई।

War—series of attacks between nations on large scale महायुद्ध।

19. Beautiful—beauty that delights the eyes and ear (morally and intellectually impressive) मनोरम।

Charming—captivates and delights (excites love) चित्ताकर्षक।

Handsome—of fine form, figure (inviting esp. for male) सुन्दर।

Lovely—attractively or admirably beautiful (intensely amusing) रमणीय।

Pretty—(of woman, child) attractive to eye, ear (winsome, inviting) कमनीय, सलोना।

20. Brief—concise as summary, substance or central idea संक्षिप्त।

Short—brief by using a few words or giving the conclusion अतिसंक्षिप्त।

21. Begin—commence, take the first step.

Commence—begin (official use as examination, ceremony etc.).

Start—make sudden movement (of body, object etc.).

22. Bring—come with or conveying whether by carrying.

Fetch—go and bring back साथ लाना।

23. Bravery—daring, heroism वीरता।

Valour—personal courage esp. as shown in fighting ; superior to bravery शौर्य, पराक्रम।

24. Cause—what produces an effect (unconditionally followed by certain phenomenon).

Reason—(in noun clause and not in adverb clause with because) fact adduced or serving as argument, motive or justification.

25. Character—collective peculiarities, mental or moral nature चरित्र।

Conduct—mode of treatment, behaviour. वर्ताव, व्यवहार।

26. Commerce—exchange of merchandise esp. on a large scale वाणिज्य।

Trade—business carried on as means of livelihood (or profit) व्यापार।

27. Confide—trust (in private affairs) निष्ठा।

Rely—depend with confidence upon person or thing.

Trust—firm belief in the honesty, veracity, justice, strength etc. (of a person or thing) दृढ़ विश्वास।

28. Consequence—result (of something preceding) following as a result (on) परिणाम।

Result—arises as actual or follow as logical consequence (from conditions, causes etc.) फल।

29. Contentment—satisfaction with oneself, feel satisfaction (with thing, doing) तृप्ति।

Satisfaction—satisfaction in regard to desire or want or doubt संतोष।

30. Chill—excessive cold ठिठुरन पैदा करने वाला।

Cold—depressing, uninteresting, unpleasant दुखदाई ठंड।

Cool—moderately cold आनन्ददायी ठंड।

31. Cost—price to be paid for thing.

Price—money for which thing is bought or sold.

32. Crime—act punishable by law अपराध।

Sin—transgression (against divine law or morality) पाप।

Vice—evil esp. grossly immoral habit or conduct बुराई।

33. Defect—shortcoming, failing कमी।

Fault—thing wrongly done, defect (of character or structure) दोष।

34. Delight—high pleasure आह्लाद।

Joy—vivid emotion of pleasure आनन्द।

Merriment—hilarious enjoyment, fun.

35. Deny—declare untrue (charge, possibility etc.) नकारना।

Refuse—say or convey by action that one will not accept, submit or grant अस्वीकारना।

36. Discover—make known (something existed but unknown to all) खोज करना।

Invent—devise, originate (new method instrument etc.) आविष्कार करना।

37. Dreadful—awe-inspiring disagreeable डरावना।

Frightful—dreadful (shocking) भयानक।

Horrible—exciting excessive horror.

Terrible—fit to excite terror आतंकी भय।

38. Drown—suffer death by suffocation in liquid (person, animal).

Sink—to go below surface of liquid (refers to object).

39. Durable—resisting decay.

Lasting—enduring.

Permanent—intended to last indefinitely (opp. to temporary).

40. Educate—give intellectual and moral training शिक्षित करना।

Instruct—give information to.

Preach—उपदेश देना।

Teach—enable or cause (person) by instruction, give lesson at school or elsewhere.

41. Empty—containing nothing खाली।

Vacant—not filled or occupied रिक्त।

42. Enough—not less than the required number, quantity, degree.

Sufficient—adequate in amount or number to the need प्रचुर।

43. Envious—have grudge (against more fortunate person not in a good sense) डाह।

Jealous—hankering after possessing what is possessed by others ईर्ष्या।

44. Error—owing to lack of knowledge त्रुटि।

Mistake—wrong in opinion भूल।

45. Excuse—apology for lack of ceremony, interruption etc. (for trifle mistake).

Forgive—pardon (for moral offence).

Pardon—forgive (a person for his offence, fault).

46. Expect—look forward to, regard as likely अपेक्षा करना।

Hope—look with expectation and desire.

47. Fight—contend in battle or single combat.

Quarrel—violent contention.

48. Freedom—personal liberty, power of self-determination.

Liberty—right or power to do as one pleases, being free from captivity, slavery मुक्ति।

49. Genius—exalted intellectual power (superior to talent) उत्कट मेधावी।

Talent—high mental ability मेधा।

50. Good—morally excellent, having the right qualities.

Nice—agreeable, delightful, well-flavoured.

51. Guess—have a rough estimate, hazard opinion about अनुमान करना।

Suppose—take for granted, accept as probable कल्पना करना।

52. Hasten—cause (person) to make haste, be quick.

Hurry—move or act with great or undue haste in eagerness to get a thing done quickly.

53. Home—fixed residence of family गृह।

House—building for human habitation or occupation मकान।

54. Humorous—full of humour, funny हास्यपूर्ण।

Laughable—exciting laughter हास्योत्पादक।

Ridiculous—deserving to be laughed at, absurd हास्यास्पद।

55. Idle—(of action, thought, word) unoccupied, indolent बिना काम के।

Lazy—averse to labour आलसी।

56. Ill—out of health अस्वस्थ।

Sick—feeling effects of some disease रुग्ण।

57. Look—turn eyes in some direction, direct eyes at दृष्टिपात करना।

Observe—take notice of, examine and note without aid of experiment.

See—have or exercise the power of discerning objects with the eyes.

Watch—have vigilance, constant observation मनोयोग से देखना।

58. Possible—that can exist, be done or happen संभव।

Probable—that may be expected to happen होनी।

59. Pupil—one who is taught by another शिष्य।

Scholar—a learned person विद्वान्।

Student—person studying in order to qualify himself for some branch of learning विद्यार्थी।

60. Recall—bring back (revive) to memory.

Recollect—not so much remember but search in the memory (re-collect *i.e.,* collect or gather again).

Remember—retain in the memory, not forget.

61. Safety—freedom from danger or risks.

Security—thing that guards or guarantees सुरक्षा।

62. Scenery—spectacles (landscape) presented by natural features दृश्य।

Sight—thing seen, visible or worth seeing.

Chapter 25

Similar Sentences Distinguished

1.	He loves you more than I.	Loves you more than I love you.
	He loves you more than me.	So far love is concerned, he prefers you to me.
2.	Have you a scooter ?	Want to know whether you have a scooter or not.
	Do you have a scooter ?	Are you habituated of having a scooter ?
3.	Often he does not come here.	At many occasions he does not come.
	He does not come here often.	Does not come here frequently.
4.	Please, help me.	Be happy and help me.
	Help me please.	Be kind to help me.
5.	The teacher searched for the boy.	Enquired whether the boy was present.
	The teacher searched the boy.	Checked the boy thoroughly.
6.	The plane landed safe.	Descended safe and sound.
	The plane landed safely.	Without any obstacle or disturbance.
7.	He alone lifted the log.	None but he lifted.
	He lifted the log alone.	Lifted without the help of anybody else.
8.	I always helped you.	Helped you at all times.
	I helped you all ways.	Helped with all possible means.
9.	He went to prison.	Due to committing some crime.
	He went to the prison.	Not to suffer some punishment but for another purpose.
10.	I noticed the dead bird.	The bird was already dead.
	I noticed the bird dead.	When I saw I found that the bird was no more.
11.	The aid was given late.	Given after proper time.
	The aid was given lately.	Given recently, just before some time.
12.	Only Balu solved all questions.	None but Balu alone solved.
	Balu only solved all questions.	Did nothing except solving all questions.
13.	Laughing loudly, we saw him.	We were laughing.
	We saw him laughing loudly.	He was laughing when we saw him.
14.	You can ride the horse.	You have capacity or power, or technique to ride.
	You may ride the horse.	It is possible (not sure) that you may do so.
15.	We reached the hill to see the dawn.	It was our purpose to see the dawn.
	Reaching the hill, we saw the dawn.	Our purpose was not to see the dawn but by the way we saw it.

16. He naturally came to help me.   As might be expected, he came to help me.
    He came to help me naturally.   Came to help me in a natural way.
17. She got a letter written.   Caused someone to write.
    She got a written letter.   The letter was in black and white.
18. He appeared to be angry.   That time he looked so.
    He appeared to have been angry.   Appeared angry not that time but before.
19. His son deals in readymade clothes.   Does the business of readymade clothes.
    His son deals with me gently.   Behaves in a gentle way.
20. You could help me.   You had power to help me.
    You would help me.   You could help me if you wished.
21. The dog is dead.   Not alive.
    The dog has died.   Ceased to live.
22. The servant will return in no time.   Very soon, presently.
    The servant will return at no time.   Will return, in the twinkling of an eye.
23. See it.   Have a look at it.
    See to it.   Take care of it.
24. Will you provide me some room ?   Give some space to sit on.
    Will you provide me a room ?   A single room to live in.
25. I bought a gold ring.   Made of pure gold.
    I bought a golden ring.   The ring was coated with gold.
26. If the physician comes in time, the   The hope of the patient's recovery is still alive
    patient will be saved.   but it depends on the physician's arrival.
    If the physician had come in time,   It was hoped that the patient might be saved
    the patient would have been saved.   if the physician had come.
27. She consulted the doctor.   Took advice from the doctor.
    She consulted with the doctor.   Exchanged views with the doctor.
28. Do or die.   Only one alternative, either to do or die.
    Do and die.   No remedy except both to do and die.
29. I have considered about the proposal   What your friend has proposed.
    of your friend.
    I have considered about the proposal   Considered about the proposal brought by your
    of your friend's.   friend.
30. He bought a red and blue pen.   Bought a single pen. It was both red and blue.
    He bought a red and a blue pen.   Two pens—one was red and the other was blue.
31. Will you come to the pictures ?   I am going to the pictures. Will you accom-
                                                     pany me ?
    Will you go to the pictures ?   Are you alone going there ?
32. He answered the questions shortly.   Answered very soon, took no time in doing
                                                     so.
    He answered the questions in short   Answered briefly.
33. The rocket went to sky direct.   Went straight.
    The rocket went to sky directly.   Went at once.

34.	He has returned.	Has come back.
	He is returned.	Has been elected.
35.	I have advised him.	Advised him several times and still.
	I advised him.	Did so.
36.	The deer was sitting still.	Sitting peacefully and calmly.
	The deer was still sitting.	Was yet sitting.
37.	He frequented here latterly.	Latterly i.e., nowadays.
	He frequented here lately.	Lately i.e., recently.
38.	Give me the magazine.	Refers to a particular magazine.
	Give me a magazine.	Any magazine.
39.	I shall go there in a week.	May take seven days to go.
	I shall go there within a week.	May go before the end of seven days.
40.	She took it to heart.	Was much shocked by it.
	She took it by heart.	Retained in memory.
41.	He has come.	The procedure of coming is completed.
	He is come.	He has come and is here.
42.	My friend, work hard.	Here the advice to work hard is given to the friend.
	My friend works hard.	The friend labours hard.
43.	Have you ever seen a black bird ?	A bird that is black.
	Have you ever seen a black-bird ?	Black-bird i.e., a cuckoo.
44.	He came on every four hour.	Came after four hour.
	He came on every fourth hour.	On the four hour exactly.
45.	I have told you altogether.	Altogether i.e., totally, on the whole.
	I have told you all together.	All together i.e., all in company.
46.	I have to cross the river.	Cross the river before and now also.
	I am to cross the river.	From now I am to cross the river.
47.	You ought to respect him.	It was proper for you but you failed to do so.
	You must respect him.	It is your bounden duty to respect him.
48.	Show me your arm.	Arm i.e., upper limb of your body from shoulder to hand.
	Show me your arms.	Arms—i.e. weapon(s).
49.	That is a matter.	Case, question.
	What is the matter ?	What is amiss (with) you ?
50.	At present he is the principal.	At the present time.
	For the present he is the principal.	Just now, for the time being.
51.	I shall not go to play.	For the purpose of playing.
	I shall not go to the play.	Not go to see the drama.

Chapter 26

Expansion of Ideas

Expansion or amplification of ideas is meant to test one's mental power of grasping, understanding and developing the actual as well as latent meanings of the given proverb or quotation. It is a short essay. In order to explain or amplify a dictum one should keep the following suggestions in one's mind.

1. Read and try to understand the external meanings and ideas of the proverb.
2. Then think about its latent feelings and sentiments.
3. Try to know its symbolic or reflective design and purpose.
4. Your span of thought about the maxim should be deep, and broad.
5. It is notable that your reasoning pertaining to the proverb must be healthy and precise. You may also cite examples and quotations for developing and explaining the maxim.
6. You should write all that you understand or know about the quotation.
7. The style should be simple and lucid.
8. Do not mention irrelevant facts and figures rather keep your mind always centred on the subject.

1. God Helps Those Who Help Themselves

A fatalist always believes in destiny and has no confidence in his own power or deed. To him, man is nothing, destiny is everything. He thinks that man is a mere puppet in the hands of the inevitable destiny that has already decided his fate. But such concept mirrors only the dark side of life. If a man sits idly in the hope of God and thus remains inactive in life, he will spoil his future. The Sanskrit dictum 'लिखतमपि ललाटे प्रोज्झितुम् कः समर्थः ?' 'who is capable of effacing what is destined ?', is the dictum of a cowardly and timid person. Man should believe in God. He should devote himself whole heartedly to work because work is worship. Moreover we must have an unshakable faith in diligence, in labour, in our work and action and not in the result. In our earthly life, we are totally responsible for our deeds. We must think that God does not help an idle or slothful fellow. He helps those who are diligent and who believe in their work and power not in their destiny. Therefore, set the destiny aside and discharge your duty with full might. Challenge even a massive rock. God must give you the proper reward. Be sure that work in itself is success and reward. Hence 'quit ye like man'.

2. All That Glitters is not Gold

The present maxim has been reproduced from Shakespeare's comedy 'The Merchant of Venice.' Its literal meaning is that in our daily life, we notice many objects radiant and ravishing but actually they are not so valuable as gold. Similarly our society is peopled with the men who are quite different inwardly and outwardly. Things are not what they seem and appearances are often beguiling.

The world is showy and artificial. Here the reality is veiled under the garb of passing show. We should beware of the beauty, the pedantic display and the vanity of being great and glorious. We may meet such persons as are habituated of playing to the gallery. They boast of their high achievements in life. But instead of being misled by such empty claims and artificial display, we should judge precisely the merits and demerits of the things. We must be always watchful on the things and their whereabouts and should try to know the veracity of the matters and factors. It is not proper on our part to be overpowered by specious arguments and inviting appearances that are not what they outwardly appear. A man who has freed his life from rumours, flattery and false statements is a true happy man. Such a man believes in his own conscience and always does what his inner voice echoes. Moreover, we should also not be overwhelmed with the mundane attainments because they too are meaningless. In fine, we should trust in the veracity and must not be deceived by a passing show.

3. Borrowed Garments Never Fit Well

Men in their stature and size differ with one another. Some are fat, some are lean and thin, some are tall and some others are small. In this way, their clothes also differ and it is not a guarantee that the garments of one will fit another. All the same if someone wears the borrowed garments, his position will turn ridiculous. His dignity will mar and he will become a laughing stock. The reflective idea is that borrowed things like knowledge, money, manners etc. never do good to anybody. One should feel contented with one's earnings and achievements. Here is the key to real happiness. Borrowed things are like walking shadows and one must not trust such shadows because they are momentary and subject to perish away. Man should maintain self-confidence and believe in his own power. To depend on others means to repent in the final reckoning. Therefore instead of borrowing garments from others, we should weave and make our own garments so that it may suit us well. Moreover, if we want to preserve our honour and dignity, we must rely and depend upon our own means and possessions. In this situation there is no repentance after failure nor overjoy in success. In brief, to borrow means to suffer, to sigh, to sob. Imitation of others is slavery not liberty. Rightly has someone preached—Neither be a borrower nor a lender be.

4. Better to Light up a Lamp than Curse Darkness

Light follows darkness as dawn follows dusk. This is the inevitable law and nature of the universe. It is beyond the power of man to alter this rule. We should admit that the significance of light lies in the existence of darkness. If there is no light, there is no darkness.

Then the world will cease to live. Thus, both, as the complements of each other, are unavoidable. In a way darkness cannot be cursed altogether because it is also endowed with many bright aspects. It is as necessary as light. The contribution of darkness for life is incalculable. Therefore, it is not proper for one to curse darkness. Secondly, the duration of human life is short. Hence we should not wait for dawn rather light up a lamp and carry on our business. Darkness will come and go but time once passes, will never return. Therefore it is better to light up a lamp than curse darkness. Moreover we should not forget that we are entrusted with a lot of work to be done by the evening of life. If being angry with darkness, we remain idle and inactive, we shall leave the work undone and then lose the charm of life forever. We should know that darkness has nothing to do with our necessities or duties. For this we alone are responsible. Hence without worrying about darkness, we should do our duty continuously. This is life and this is light. What though the darkness prevails, all is not lost. Better to light up a lamp than curse darkness.

5. To Travel Hopefully is Better than Arrive

It is a psychological fact that in the course of journey we feel leisure and pleasure but just as we arrive at our destination all these things disappear. The reason is that there is some joy in our effort that ceases as soon as the purpose is accomplished. In lack of work and absence of aspiration our life turns dull and colourless. There is a joy, a hope, a curiosity and a taste while we are busy in some business. That time our days and dreams hum with bliss and beauty. But no sooner does our work end than we plunge into sadness and boredom. Satisfaction and success impair our interest and eagerness. Thus travelling is life, arriving is death. The joy that we feel during our efforts and endeavours vanishes when we succeed in our pursuits and gain our goal. Life is not life when it is inactive and inert. Besides these, if we ponder over the matter broadly, we shall find that the whole universe is moving. Our life too is going ahead moment by moment on the sands of time. Everything is dynamic and progressive under the sun. In such situation if we stop awhile and forget our mission, there is no meaning of life. Life hums in quest of things unsought. It is a running river and not a marshy bog. Therefore, it is better to travel hopefully than arrive.

6. Barking Dogs Seldom Bite

In our daily life we see many street dogs that bark much but never bite. It is their habit and they do so to solve their purpose by frightening the passers-by. Actually they are cowards. They themselves are afraid of men. Similarly, in our society we meet many persons who lack physical power and inner courage but always boast of their feats of bravery and adventurous deeds. They intend to occupy an eminent post in the society by wordy power and tall talk only. But so far reality is concerned, they are timid and they dare not face the approaching challenge. The present aphorism instructs that we should not be misguided by the tricks and evil designs of such persons. We must always maintain unshakable faith in our own power and ability. We should know that fear is the greatest sin that contaminates our soul. Therefore, we should not fear braggarts rather face them boldly. If once we stand against them, we will see that all the dangers are nowhere and finally the field is ours. Besides it, we should also learn that vanity and boast cannot solve our any purposes. Such a conduct is not use rather abuse of power. Hence let us be always cautious of the barking dogs.

7. A Rolling Stone Gathers no Moss

The epigram tells us that a stone that is always moving gets no taint. Similarly, anything that is always in action never loses its beauty and brightness. Even a machine gets rusted due to disuse and so is the case with our body too. If we remain lazy, slothful or inactive, we shall turn weak and may fall a victim of some fatal disease.

In brief, activity is life ; inactivity is a living death. Indolence is agony and failure ; diligence is delight and success. Besides these, the dictum also sounds that a man who is noble and upright makes the best use of life. He is never blamed or criticised from any quarter but honoured and recognised wherever he goes. Even after death he outlives because he has already occupied a permanent post in the minds of the people. Moreover, if we think a little about the propriety of the maxim in practice, we can say that he who constantly changes his place or employment does not become happy or grow rich. Since this man is always homeless and jobless, he gets nothing except sorrow and sigh ; woe and worry and finally repentance is on his part. Lastly, we may claim that a clear hearted man is always victorious. He is never vanquished.

Exercise

Expand the ideas in the following :

1. Charity begins at home.
2. Make hay while the sun shines.
3. Sweet are the uses of adversity.
4. Heard melodies are sweet but those unheard are sweeter.
5. If you wish peace, be ready for war.
6. Manner makes the man.
7. Honesty is the best policy.
8. They also serve who only stand and wait.
9. Nothing succeeds like success.
10. Reading in itself is a reward.
11. As you sow, so will you reap.
12. A live ass is better than a dead lion.
13. One swallow cannot bring a summer.
14. A bird in hand is worth two in the bush.
15. Example is better than precept.

Part II
TRANSLATION

Chapter 1

Verb To Be

TRANSLATION : AN INTRODUCTION

Translation अर्थात् 'अनुवाद'। किसी भी अभिव्यक्ति की भाषा किसी अन्य भाषा में रूपान्तरित करने की विधा को Translation अर्थात् 'अनुवाद' कहते हैं। यह एक कला है क्योंकि भाषा रूपान्तरण में पूरी तरह यह ध्यान रखना पड़ता है कि मूल भाषा (अर्थात् जिस भाषा से अनुवाद करना है) के भाव एवं अर्थ में मौलिकता होनी चाहिए अन्यथा अर्थ का अनर्थ हो सकता है।

Translation दो प्रकार से किया जाता है :

1. Literal (शब्दश:) एवं

2. Figurative (भाव के आधार पर) लाक्षणिक।

1. Literal Translation. इस तरह के अनुवाद में दिए गए वाक्य या विषय-वस्तु का शब्दश: अनुवाद दूसरी भाषा में कर दिया जाता है। जैसे—

राम खाता है—Ram eats.

वर्षा हो रही है—It is raining.

वह एक बुद्धिमान व्यक्ति है—He is a wise man.

2. Figurative Translation. इस तरह के अनुवाद में दिए गए वाक्य या विषय वस्तु के भाव या अर्थ के आधार पर अनुवाद किया जाता है। जैसे–

शिक्षा का प्रसार हो रहा है—The school master is abroad.

एक चना भाड़ नहीं फोड़ता—One swallow does not bring a summer

वह मुझसे मिलने आया—He came to me (or to see me).

Translation करते समय कुछ ध्यान देने योग्य बातें :

1. उचित शब्दों का प्रयोग

2. भाषा की सहजता एवं लयात्मकता

3. सटीक अर्थ

4. संप्रेषणीयता

5. प्रवाह

6. उचित Grammatical Pattern का प्रयोग।

अब Translation (अनुवाद) की भिन्न-भिन्न पद्धतियों को देखें :

(Am हूँ ; Is है, Are हैं, हो ; Was था, थी ; Were थे)

1. जब दिए गए हिन्दी वाक्य की क्रिया केवल हूँ, है, हैं, हो, था, थे, थी रहे तो उसका अनुवाद इस प्रकार करें–

Assertive   Subject/This/These/That/Those + to be + noun/adjective etc.

265

Negative	Not/no/never को to be के पश्चात् रखें।
Interrogative	Wh + to be + subject + not/never + noun/adjective etc.

(a) वह एक जहाज है।   That is a ship.

(b) वे पत्रिकाएँ थीं।   Those were magazines.

(c) तुम्हारी माँ नाराज नहीं थी।   Your mother was not angry.

(d) क्या वे गुलाब हैं ?   Are those roses ?

(e) क्या मैं एक अच्छा राजा नहीं हूँ ?   Am I not a good king ?

(f) कितने लोग सुखी हैं ?   How many people are happy ?

(g) वहाँ लड़के क्यों नहीं हैं ?   Why are boys not there ?

2. जब उक्त स्थिति में हिन्दी क्रिया होगा, होंगे, होगी आदि से समाप्त रहे तो उसके लिए be के पूर्व shall/will रखें।

(a) वह गरीब होगा।   He will be poor.

(b) क्या श्याम वहाँ नहीं होगा ?   Will Shyam not be there ?

3. जब प्रकृति प्रदत्त गुण, विशेषता या लक्षण का verb to be से संकेत रहे अथवा होना, रहने से क्रिया समाप्त रहे तो ऐसे वाक्यों का भी अनुवाद उपरोक्त रीति से करें। ऐसे वाक्य 'होना' क्रिया से प्रगट रहा करते हैं।

(a) कोयला काला, चमकीला तथा टूटनीय होता है।   Coal is black, bright and brittle.

(b) क्या कोयल काली नहीं होती है ?   Is a Cuckoo not black ?

(c) आकाश क्यों नीला होता है ?   Why is the sky blue ?

(d) सभी आम मीठे नहीं होते।   All mangoes are not sweet.

(e) वहाँ मौसम हमेशा ठंडा रहता है।   There the weather is always cold.

4. उम्र बताने के लिए या तो केवल संख्या रखें या उसके साथ months/years old अथवा noun के पूर्व संख्या तथा समय के बीच Hyphen (-) दें–

He is nine or nine years old. He is a three-year old child.

Exercise 1

Translate into English :

1. वहाँ एक आदमी है।
2. वे लोमड़ियाँ हैं।
3. रमेश एक वकील है।
4. वह जुलाहा नहीं था।
5. हम सभी भारतीय हैं।
6. मैं एक छात्र हूँ।
7. वे लोग मूर्ख नहीं थे।
8. वह एक अच्छा कलाकार नहीं है।
9. वे लोग सुखी हैं।
10. यह एक सुन्दर चित्र है।
11. वे गोरे नहीं थे।

12. यूरेनियम भारी होता है।
13. जीवन एक शवयात्रा है।
14. संसार कुरूप नहीं है।
15. मैं बीमार नहीं था।
16. रंजना स्वस्थ है।
17. यहाँ एक आदमी था।
18. सम्पूर्ण वातावरण नीरस था।
19. शिवाजी की माँ बड़ी बुद्धिमान थीं।
20. वे कमीजें नीली थीं।
21. सूर्य चमकीला है।
22. फ्रीज में वस्तुएँ ताजी एवं ठंडी रहती हैं।

23. सन्ध्या शान्त है।
24. उसका चेहरा आकर्षक नहीं है।
25. हब्शी काले होते हैं।
26. अध्यापक का कार्य-कठिन होता है।
27. सभी अंगुलियाँ बराबर नहीं होतीं।
28. यह पेड़ अस्सी वर्ष का है।

29. मेरा भाई बीस वर्ष का है।
30. तुम्हारी उम्र क्या है ?
31. वे किसान नहीं थे।
32. मि० जैक्सन राजदूत हैं।
33. बलिया की सड़कें चौड़ी नहीं थीं।

Hints—वकील–lawyer, जुलाहा–weaver, गोरा–white, यूरेनियम–uranium, भारी–heavy, शवयात्रा–funeral march, कुरूप–ugly, स्वस्थ–healthy, किसान–farmer, राजदूत–ambassador, चौड़ी–wide, सम्पूर्ण–whole, वातावरण–atmosphere, नीरस–dull, बुद्धिमान–wise, चमकीला–bright, फ्रीज–freeze, ताजी–fresh, शान्त–calm, आकर्षक–attractive, inviting, कठिन–hard, बराबर–equal, तुम्हारी उम्र क्या है ?–How old are you ? What is your age ? हब्शी–Negroes.

Exercise 2

Translate into English :

1. क्या वहाँ पानी नहीं है ?
2. क्या डाक्टर अनुपस्थित था ?
3. क्या आकाश स्वच्छ नहीं है ?
4. क्या वे लोग कमजोर हैं ?
5. क्या तुम चिन्ता में हो ?
6. क्या वह आंग्ल भारतीय नहीं था ?
7. क्या यह पुस्तक उपदेशात्मक नहीं है ?
8. तुम कौन हो ?
9. तुम्हारी घड़ी कहाँ है ?
10. अब वह कैसा है ?

11. तुम क्यों क्रोधित थे ?
12. यह वैसा क्यों है ?
13. संसार रंगहीन नहीं है।
14. आज आकाश चुप है।
15. कितने लड़के गरीब थे ?
16. किसका घोड़ा बहुत तेज है ?
17. वह अब तक कहाँ था ?
18. सोना तथा चाँदी में कौन अधिक चमकीला है ?
19. वह कब सज्जन था ?
20. शिक्षा का प्रसार हो रहा है।

Hints—अनुपस्थित–absent, out, स्वच्छ–clear, चिन्ता में–in worry, आंग्ल भारतीय–Anglo-Indian, उपदेशात्मक–didactic, वैसा–so, रंगहीन–colourless, चुप–silent, तेज–swift, अब तक–by now, till now, अधिक चमकीला–brighter, सज्जन–gentle, शिक्षा .... है–The school master is abroad.

Exercise 3

Fill up the blanks with verb to be or wh words :

1. ...... the ocean deep ?
2. ...... the plants dry ?
3. Why ...... the mountain hot ?
4. ...... are you, my friend ?
5. ...... is life ?
6. ...... he a mere child ?
7. ...... are we, and ...... are we ?

8. ...... we all actors or spectators of the drama ?
9. ...... the book valuable ?
10. ...... you sure ?
11. Children dear ! ...... it yesterday when she parted ?
12. ...... are our old customs ?
13. Flattery ...... my abhorrence.

Exercise 4

Correct or justify the following sentences :

1. There was a king.
2. Are not the east red ?
3. Was they brave ?
4. Are not life a sorry business ?
5. Was you sick of the whole business ?
6. Is there Arabian horses ?
7. Were he shy ?
8. What there was ?
9. What popularity is a bad measure of merit ?
10. What is he an intelligent boy ?
11. What your father is ?
12. Where the Roman Empire is now ?
13. Where is light ?
14. Are you whom loyal to ?
15. How much is milk there in the cup ?
16. What your name is ?

Exercise 5

Translate into English :

1. विवेकानन्द कहाँ पैदा हुए थे ?
2. गाँधी जी की मुख्य शिक्षा क्या थी ?
3. क्या वह तुम्हारा स्कूटर नहीं है ?
4. कितने लड़के साफ सुथरे थे ?
5. यह किसका छाता है ?
6. कमरे में प्रकाश क्यों नहीं है ?
7. वहाँ किसका लड़का है ?
8. यह किसकी चिल्लाहट है ?
9. तुम्हारी किताब कौन सी है ?
10. यह एक बुद्धिमत्तापूर्ण निर्णय क्यों नहीं है ?

Hints—पैदा हुए थे—was born, मुख्य शिक्षा—main teaching, स्कूटर—scooter, साफ सुथरे—neat and clean, चिल्लाहट—cry, बुद्धिमत्तापूर्ण निर्णय—a wise decision.

Chapter 2

Has, Have, Had

1. जब किसी व्यक्ति या वस्तु के गुण/अवगुण के होने या न होने का भाव व्यक्त रहे अथवा अधिकार, धारण करने/न करने, स्वामित्व या सम्बन्ध का संकेत रहे तो उसे Has, have या had से प्रगट करते हैं। इस प्रसंग में ये finite verbs (मुख्य क्रिया) का काम करते हैं, auxiliary verbs (सहायक क्रिया) का नहीं। ऐसे वाक्यों की हिन्दी-क्रिया प्रायः होता, होते, होती, रखना, पास होना आदि जैसी समाप्त रहती है। Has एकवचन (singular number) है और have बहुवचन (plural number)। Had इन दोनों का भूतकाल (past tense) है, अर्थात् रखा, रखे थे, रखता था, पास था, थे, थी इत्यादि। ध्यान रखें कि किसी भी वाक्य का verb उसके subject के number तथा person के अनुसार निश्चित की जाती है। संक्षेप में singular subject के साथ (यहाँ I अपवाद है) singular verb तथा plural subject के साथ plural verb रखें। ऐसे वाक्यों का अंग्रेजी अनुवाद निम्न रीति से करें–

Assertive	Subject + has, have or had + noun etc. Has, have, had के साथ got भी रखा जा सकता है।
Negative	Subject +has, have or had + not/no/never + noun etc.
Interrogative	Wh +has, have or had + subject + not/no etc. + noun etc.

(i) हमारे पास (हमको) दो हाथ हैं।	We have two hands.
	Or We have got two hands.
(ii) परियों के पंख होते हैं।	Fairies have wings.
(iii) उस कुत्ते को दुम नहीं है।	That dog has no tail.
(iv) उसके पास एक जादू का घोड़ा था।	He had a magic horse.
(v) क्या तुम्हारे पास एक अच्छी कलम है ?	Have you a good pen ?
(vi) हरि के पास कोई किताब नहीं थी।	Hari had not any books.
	Or had no books.
(vii) त्रिभुज की तीन भुजाएँ होती हैं।	A triangle has three sides.
(viii) तुम्हारे पास एक बाइसिकल क्यों नहीं थी ?	Why had you not a bicycle ?
(ix) कौन एक चाकू रखा था ?	Who had a knife ?
(x) उसको कोई मित्र नहीं है।	He has no friends
	Or (...... has no any friends)
	Or He is friendless.

Note. जब वाक्य negative या interrogative रहे तो any के पश्चात् वाला noun plural रहता है। जैसे–

(i) क्या तुम्हारे पास कोई प्रमाण है ?	Have you any proofs ?
(ii) नहीं, मेरे पास कोई प्रमाण नहीं है ?	No, I have not any proofs.

इस सम्बन्ध में Fowler के विचार देखें :

'This use of any (some) is idiomatic only in negative or interrogative statements expressed or implied. Have you any bananas ? No, I haven't any bananas.' But 'yes, we have some bananas'. (Modern English usage.)

American English में इस सन्दर्भ में do, does, did से ऐसे वाक्य बनाने की एक शैली प्रचलित है। जैसे–

क्या तुम्हारे पास गाय है ?

Have you a cow ? (English English)

but–Do you have a cow ? (American English)

किन्तु Do you have a cow ? जैसी बनावट आदतजन्य है, सामान्य कथन नहीं और इसका तात्पर्य होगा–क्या तुम गाय रखा करते हो ?

He does not have a cow–वह गाय नहीं रखा करता है।

'...... in U.S. 'Do you have a match ?' 'I do not have a match' are idiomatic where our own idiom requires 'Have you (got) a match ?' 'I have not got a match ......' 'Do you have coffee ?' means for us is it your habit to drink it ? .... 'People under 21 do not have the vote. (*i.e.*, it is not our custom to give them one.' (Fowler's M.E.U.)

2. सम्बन्ध, अधिकार या स्वामित्व (possessive case) के लिए निम्नस्थ तालिका का अध्ययन करें–

Pronoun	Possessive Adjective	Possessive Pronoun
I	my	mine
We	our	ours
You	your	yours
He	his	his
She	her	hers
They	their	theirs
It	its	its

'अपना' के भाव में उपर्युक्त subject के अनुसार possessive adjective का प्रयोग किया जाता है। यदि उस पर बल दिया गया हो तो उसके साथ own का प्रयोग भी हो सकेगा।

(*i*) वह मेरी अपनी बहन है।	She is my own sister.
(*ii*) वह उसका अपना मकान था।	That was his own house.
(*iii*) अपनी कलम दो।	Give your pen.
(*iv*) उन लोगों ने अपना कर्त्तव्य पूरा किया।	They discharged their duty.
(*v*) क्या वे तुम्हारे अपने चाचा हैं ?	Is he your own uncle ?
(*vi*) मेरे पास कोई चारा नहीं था।	I had no other alternative.

3. Possessive pronoun–का, के, की, रा, रे, री से प्रगटित अधिकार या सम्बन्ध हेतु सामान्यतया of का प्रयोग किया जाता है। Apostrophe ('s) अथवा possessive pronoun या of + possessive pronoun द्वारा भी उक्त भाव प्रगट किया जाता है। इसे belong to से भी व्यक्त किया जा सकेगा।

(*i*) वह गोविन्द का बाग है।	That is Govind's garden.
	Or That is the garden of Govind.
	Or That garden belongs to Govind.
	Or That garden is of Govind.
(*ii*) वह बालू का मित्र था।	He was a friend of Balu.

(*iii*) यह तुम्हारा छाता है। This is your umbrella
Or This umbrella is yours
Or This umbrella belongs to you.

(*iv*) मेरा एक भाई वहाँ था। A brother of mine was there.

Possessive pronoun का प्रयोग प्राय: predicative हुआ करता है।

Exercise 1

Translate into English :

1. उसके दो लड़के हैं।
2. पुरुष को मूँछें होती हैं।
3. कुत्ते के चार पैर होते हैं।
4. उसका कोई चचेरा भाई नहीं है।
5. मुझे एक आवश्यक काम है।
6. तुम्हारी बराबरी का कोई नहीं है।
7. जून तीस दिन का होता है।
8. पेड़ों में पत्तियाँ होती हैं।
9. उसका स्वयं का व्यापार है।
10. मुझे अँधेरे में कोई भय नहीं होता।
11. मुझे इसमें कोई संदेह नहीं।
12. उसके सिर में दर्द है।
13. क्या तुम्हारे पास कोई समाचार है ?
14. गोविन्द के पास कितनी कुर्सियाँ थीं ?
15. राम के पास एक काला घोड़ा था।
16. घोड़े की पूँछ लम्बी थी।
17. मेरी एक अच्छी आदत है।
18. उसके पास कब एक लम्बा कोट था ?
19. किस लड़के के पास एक पुरानी किताब है ?
20. लकड़हारे के पास कोई कुल्हाड़ी नहीं थी।
21. यह मोहन की बस है।
22. वह मेरी रूमाल नहीं थी।
23. कुत्ते के चार पैर होते हैं।
24. उसकी कोई स्पष्ट नीति नहीं है।
25. किसके पास एक सादा कागज है।
26. तुम्हारी जेब में क्या है ?
27. उसके पास दो रेडियो नहीं थे।
28. गाय की दो सींगें होती हैं।
29. उसके पास एक अनूठी चाल थी।
30. मुझको एक हवादार अध्ययन-कक्ष है।
31. यह मेरा विद्यालय है।
32. वह कार गोविन्द की है।
33. वह अभ्यास-पुस्तिका तुम्हारी थी।
34. यह फ्राक ऊषा का है।
35. चिड़ियों को सींग नहीं होती।

Hints—मूँछ—moustache, चचेरा भाई—cousin, एक आवश्यक काम—an urgent piece of work, कोई बराबरी नहीं—no equals (or match); पत्तियाँ—leaves, व्यापार—business, भय—fear, सन्देह—doubt, सिरदर्द—a headache, आदत—habit, लकड़हारा—woodcutter, कुल्हाड़ी—axe, hatchet, रूमाल—handkerchief (हैन्करचीफ), स्पष्टनीति—clear policy, सादा कागज—blank paper, सींग—Horn, अनूठी चाल—novel trick, हवादार अध्ययन-कक्ष—airy study room, अभ्यास पुस्तिका—exercise book.

Chapter 3

There and It

A. There—(*a*) जब वाक्य का verb मात्र be होना (is, am, are, was, were) हो ;

(*b*) अस्तित्व या स्थिति (existence or position) का संकेत हो ;

(*c*) Subject कोई indefinite noun या pronoun हो ;

(*d*) उक्त noun/pronoun के पश्चात्—में, बीच, पर, वहाँ निकट, सामने, नीचे, चारों ओर आदि रहे तो इनका अनुवाद 'There' से करेंगे।

There तथा It दोनों ही Introductory or Provisional (भूमिका/अस्थायी) subjects कहे जाते हैं। इनका अनुवाद निम्नस्थ रीति से करें—

Assertive   There/It + verb + noun + extension.

Negative   Not, no, never, not any को is, are, was आदि के पश्चात् रखें।

Interrogative   Wh + is, are, was etc. + There/it + not, no etc. + noun + extension.

It के प्रसंग में भी वाक्य को उक्त स्थिति में रखें।

1.	एक राजा था।	There was a king.
2.	कमरे में पाँच आदमी हैं।	There are five men in the room.
3.	किसी गाँव में एक शूद्र स्त्री रहती थी।	There lived a woman of low caste in a certain village.
4.	एक रुपये में सोलह आने होते थे।	There were sixteen annas in a rupee.
5.	वहाँ पानी ही पानी था।	There was nothing but water.
6.	वहाँ एक हवाचक्की है।	There is a windmill.
7.	हाल में कोई नहीं है।	There is none in the hall.
8.	अग्नि के बिना धुँआ नहीं होता।	There is no smoke without fire.
9.	वहाँ पग-पग पर बाधाएँ थीं।	There were obstacles on each and every step.
10.	कण-कण में भगवान हैं।	There is God in each and every particle.
11.	एक सप्ताह में कितने दिन होते हैं ?	How many days are there in a week ?
12.	चारों ओर एक अफवाह फैली है।	There is a rumour abroad.

B. 'It' का प्रयोग

(*a*) जब subject समय या समय के अनुभाग का संकेत दे।

(*b*) वह प्रकृति या मौसम के परिवर्तन या स्थिति को व्यक्त करे तो उन्हें 'It' से प्रगट करेंगे।

(*i*) आज सोमवार है।   It is Monday today.

(ii) पाँच बजे हैं।	It is five o'clock (o'—of)
(iii) जाड़े का समय था।	It was winter.
(iv) कल बड़ी गर्मी थी।	It was very hot yesterday.
(v) सन्ध्या मनोरम, शांत एवं निर्बाध है।	It is a beauteous evening calm and free.
(vi) मूसलाधार पानी बरस रहा था।	It was raining (pouring) heavily.

Note. समय-संकेत में कम बजने के लिए to और अधिक के लिए past का प्रयोग करें। Past—after

(i) ठीक तीन बजा है।	It is just three.
(ii) तीन बजने में आठ मिनट बाकी है।	It is eight minutes to three.
(iii) चार बजकर पन्द्रह मिनट हुए हैं।	It is a quarter past four.

(c) अस्थायी कर्त्ता के रूप में 'it' का प्रयोग करें–

(i) वैसा कहना व्यर्थ है।	It is useless to say so.
(ii) यह निश्चित है कि वह आएगी।	It is definite that she will come.
(iii) अब स्पष्ट है कि मेरा कथन सत्य है।	Now, it is obvious that my statement is true.
(iv) कहा जाता है कि मछलियाँ हवा में तैरती हैं।	It is said that fish swim into the air.

(d) Noun/Pronoun पर बल देने के लिए–

(i) तुम्हीं ने मेरी घड़ी चुराई है।	It is you who have stolen my watch.
(ii) मैंने ही उसे बचा लिया।	It was I who rescued him.
(iii) जहाँ अज्ञानता में परमानन्द है	Where ignorance is bliss,
वहाँ बुद्धिमान बनना अविवेक है।	it is folly to be wise.

It is excellent to have a giants' strength, but it is tyrannous to use it like a giant.

(Shakespeare)

(e) निर्जीव वस्तु के लिए, जानवरों एवं छोटे बच्चों के लिए 'It' का प्रयोग होता है।

(i) जब मैंने बच्चे को देखा तो वह गाढ़ी नींद में सो रहा था।

When I saw the child, it was sleeping soundly.

(ii) यह मेरी मेज है। यह अच्छी लकड़ी की बनी है।

This is my table. It is made of fine wood.

(iii) यह व्यंग का व्यंग है और उपदेश का उपदेश!

It is both a satire and a preaching.

(iv) यह रूचिकर का रूचिकर है तथा उपदेशात्मक भी।

It is both interesting and didactic.

Exercise 1

Translate into English (There से) :

1. वहाँ एक लोमड़ी है।
2. बहुत पूर्व नालन्दा में एक प्रसिद्ध विश्वविद्यालय था।
3. इस पुस्तक में हास्य के अनेक स्थल हैं।
4. खेत में कोई किसान नहीं था।
5. उस गुफा में संयासी था।
6. इस लेख में व्याकरण की अनेक त्रुटियाँ हैं।
7. कहते हैं कि चन्द्रमा पर एक आदमी रहता था।
8. उसके समान अनेक मन्द बुद्धि बालक हैं।

9. इसे सिद्ध करने के लिए अनेक उदाहरण हैं।

10. एक समय इंग्लैंड में भीषण आग लगी।

11. एक रुपये में कितने आने होते हैं ?

12. एक वर्ष में 12 माह होते हैं।

13. बर्तन में कितना दूध है ?

14. वहाँ बड़ी भीड़ थी।

15. बल्ब के अन्दर हवा नहीं होती।

16. प्याले में थोड़ी चीनी है।

17. वहाँ कुछ खाली कुर्सियाँ थीं।

18. वहाँ सुख कब था ?

19. लोगों द्वारा विरोध क्यों नहीं हुआ ?

20. उस पेड़ के नीचे क्या था ?

21. उस कमरे में कितनी खिड़कियाँ हैं ?

22. क्या कमरे में प्रकाश नहीं था ?

23. घर-घर में कलह है।

24. शत्रुता का कोई कारण नहीं था।

25. वहाँ मलवा ही मलवा था।

26. वहाँ निराशा ही निराशा थी।

27. गाँठ-गाँठ में दर्द है।

28. वहाँ कुछ नहीं था।

29. रात्रि के भोजन में क्या-क्या है ?

30. समाज-समाज में फूट है।

31. यहाँ पग-पग पर बाधा है।

32. हाथ-हाथ को रोजगार दिया जाएगा।

33. वहाँ पल-पल में जीवन को खतरा था।

Exercise 2

Translate into English ('It' से) :

1. ज्ञात होता है कि वह गल्ती पर है।

2. प्रतीक्षा करना बेहतर है।

3. आप ही ने तो कहा था।

4. दिन में सोना बड़ा हानिकारक है।

5. इस कठिन समय में जीना कठिन है।

6. बिजली चमकती है।

7. सुबह के चार बजे थे।

8. आज बहुत ठंडा है।

9. आश्चर्य है कि वह अनुत्तीर्ण हो गया।

10. आज कौन दिन है ?

11. आज रविवार है।

12. दस बजने में पाँच मिनट कम है।

13. पाँच बजकर पन्द्रह मिनट हुए हैं।

14. हवा जोर से बह रही थी।

15. यह मूर्खतापूर्ण है।

16. आधी रात का समय था।

17. क्या यह तुम्हारी पुस्तक है ?

18. यह मेरी मंशा नहीं थी।

19. क्या यही उसकी रीति है ?

20. कल अवकाश रहेगा।

21. क्या बजा था ?

22. अब बहुत विलम्ब हो गया है।

23. उसकी सहायता करना मेरे लिए कठिन है।

24. बर्फ गिर रही थी।

25. आजकल कौन सी ऋतु है ?

26. आज दशहरा है।

27. तुम्हारे लिए वह अच्छा नहीं था।

28. सन् 1994 का समय था।

29. यह हरी अथवा राम है।

30. यह सत्य क्यों नहीं था ?

31. यह एक मनगढ़न्त कथन है।

32. यह व्यर्थ था।

33. यह अविश्वसनीय है।

34. यह तुम्हारा कर्त्तव्य था।

35. तुमने ही तो ऐसी सलाह दी थी।

36. भारत ने ही सर्वप्रथम शान्ति की पहल की।

37. यह दवा की दवा और टॉनिक का टॉनिक है।

Exercise 1

Hints—बहुत पूर्व–long ago, एक प्रसिद्ध विश्वविद्यालय–a famous university, हास्य–humour, स्थल–rooms, गुफा–cave, संन्यासी–hermit, लेख–essay, व्याकरण की त्रुटियाँ–grammatical errors, कहते हैं–it is said, it goes, it is believed, मन्दबुद्धि–dull, सिद्ध करना–to prove, भीषण आग–conflagration, आने–annas, भीड़–crowd, खाली–vacant, सुख–happiness, विरोध–protest, कलह–quarrel, contention, शत्रुता–enmity, मलवा–debris, निराशा–dismay, disappointment, गाँठ–joint, दर्द–ache, रात्रि का भोजन–supper, समाज–society, फूट–discord, रोजगार–employment, पल-पल–moment.

Exercise 2

Hints—ज्ञात होता है–it seems or appears, गल्ती पर–in fault, बेहतर–better, हानिकारक–harmful, कठिन समय–critical time, कठिन–hard, difficult, बिजली चमकना–to thunder, आश्चर्य–surprising, आधी रात–midnight, मन्शा–intention, रीति–manner, way, मनगढ़न्त कथन–fabricated statement, व्यर्थ में–in vain, of no (or without) avail, अविश्वसनीय–incredible, शान्ति–peace, पहल करना–to take initiative.

Exercise 3

Make questions of the following answers :

1. He is Govind.
2. It is Friday today.
3. There are twenty rooms in my school.
4. It is six miles far from Ballia.
5. It is a dirty business.
6. It was the purse that she dropped.
7. It is ten o'clock.
8. There is fate in my hand.
9. It is the miller's baby.
10. It is an absurd talk.
11. It is a bad manner.
12. It was in North U.P.
13. There is no precedent for this.
14. There was nothing here.
15. There are cakes for dinner.
16. There are twenty four hours in a day.

Chapter 4

Can, Could, May, Might

A. May तथा can दोनों का अर्थ होता है 'सकना'। May का past tense 'might' (सका, सकता था) और can का past tense 'could' (सका, सकता था) होता है।

May का प्रयोग निम्नस्थ स्थितियों में करें–

1. वह आ सकती है। — She may come. (Possibility संभावना)
2. यह सत्य हो सकता है। — It may be true. (Possibility संभावना)
3. तुम बहुत दिनों जीओ। — May you live long ! (Wish आकांक्षा)
4. इसका पश्चाताप करने के लिए जीओ। — May you live to repent it. (Wish)
5. जो चाहो कर सकते हो। — You may do what you wish. (Order/Permission)
6. तुम भाड़ को जाओ। — May you go to the dogs. (Curse श्राप)
7. वह अत्यधिक कोशिश करता है ताकि वह सफल हो सके। — He tries his utmost so that he may succeed. (Purpose)
8. मुझे डर था कि वह बाजी हार सकता था। — I feared if he might lose the game (or field).
9. वह तुम्हें नीचा दिखा सकता था किन्तु उसने ऐसा नहीं किया। — He might abase you but he did not do so.

ऐसे वाक्यों की बनावट निम्नस्थ सूत्रों से करें–

Assertive	Subject + may/might/can/could + verb¹ + object etc.
Negative	Not/never - may/can आदि के पश्चात् रखें।
Interrogative	Wh +/may/can etc. + subject + not/never + verb¹ + object etc.

B. May तथा can में अन्तर यह है कि may अनुमति, संभावना, असंभावना, इच्छा बताता है जबकि can सामर्थ्य, अनुमति का संकेत देता है।

1. क्या मैं अन्दर आ सकता हूँ ? — May I come in ?
2. हाँ, तुम अन्दर आ सकते हो। — Yes, you may (come in).
3. वह सभी प्रतियोगियों से आगे निकल सकता है। — He can outdo all competitors.
4. मैं इस सन्दूक को उठा सकता हूँ ? — I can lift this box.
5. क्या मैं आपकी कोई सेवा कर सकता हूँ ? — Can I be of any services to you ?
6. क्या तुम इंगलिश चैनल पार कर सकते हो ? — Can you cross the English channel ?
7. हमारी सेना लाहौर पर घेरा डाल सकती थी। — Our army could siege Lahore.
8. तुम अपने शत्रुओं को हरा सकते थे। — You could defeat your enemies.
9. अनुमति के पश्चात् हम अन्दर जा सके। — We could go in after (getting) permission.

276

C. सामर्थ्य/असामर्थ्य का भाव able to/not able to/unable to से भी व्यक्त किया जाता है। Capable/incapable (of) शारीरिक/क्षमता/अक्षमता का संकेत देते हैं–

1. मुझसे बोला नहीं जाता।	I am not able to speak.
2. क्या उससे वह पत्र नहीं पढ़ा जाता ?	Is she not able to read the letter ?
3. वह प्रथम आ सकेगा।	He will be able to stand first.
4. वह इसे करने में असमर्थ थी।	She was unable to do it.
5. तुम उसकी उचित सेवा नहीं कर पाए थे।	You were not able to serve him properly.

D. संभावना/असंभावना के भाव वाले वाक्य को possible, likely, probably आदि से व्यक्त कर सकते हैं अथवा may be/might be से भी इसे प्रगट किया जा सकता है।

1. वह आज यहाँ पहुँच सकता है।	He is likely to arrive here today.
	Or He may probably arrive here today.
	(*i.e.*, less possibility बताता है)
	Or Perhaps he may arrive here today.
2. वह विख्यात हो सकता था।	He might be famous.
3. सन्ध्या में बर्फ गिर सकती है।	Snow may fall in the evening.
	Or It may snow in the evening.
4. क्या वह तुम्हें धोखा नहीं दे सकता था ?	Might he not deceive you ?

E. यदि अत्यधिक संभावना अथवा विश्वासपूर्वक अनुमान रहे तो must be + noun/adjective or must have + verb³ आदि जैसा वाक्य बनाएँ।

1. वह अवश्य ही पागल होगा।	He must be mad.
2. तुमने शिवाजी का नाम अवश्य सुना होगा।	You must have heard the name of Shivaji.
3. क्या तुमने कभी गंधर्वों का नाम सुना है ?	Have you ever heard the name of the Gandharvas ?

F. अत्यधिक संभावना को would be से भी प्रगट कर सकते हैं–

1. वह करीब (लगभग) पचास वर्ष का होगा।	He would be about fifty.
2. यह मोहन का बाग होगा।	It would be Mohan's garden.
3. पहाड़ पर वर्षा हो रही होगी।	It would be raining on the mountain.
4. उसकी इच्छा है कि उसका लड़का प्रतियोगिता में सफल हो जाय।	His desire is that his son may (or might) compete.

Exercise 1

Translate into English

1. यह भवन गिर सकता है।
2. तुम समय पर नहीं लौट सकते।
3. क्या तुम कभी धनी बन सकते हो ?
4. घोड़ा सवार को फेंक सकता है।
5. मैं अँधेरे में दौड़ सकता हूँ।

6. तुम इस प्रश्न को क्यों नहीं हल कर सकते थे ?

7. वह यहाँ कब आ सकता है ?

8. वह इस कार्य को सफलतापूर्वक कर सकता है।

9. तुम कभी अभियन्ता नहीं बन सकते।

10. यह अवश्य झूठ होगा।

11. उसने तुम्हारी मदद की होगी।

12. वह कहीं गया होगा।

13. गाड़ी प्लेटफार्म पर नहीं आई होगी।

14. क्या उनका छोटा बच्चा अब सुगमता से चल सकता है ?

15. क्या मैं आपकी यह पत्रिका ले सकता हूँ ?

16. मैं कल जा सकता हूँ।

17. क्या वह अंग्रेजी नहीं पढ़ लिख सकती ?

18. वह वृद्ध एक मील टहल सकता है।

19. तुम अपना रास्ता भूल सकते हो।

20. मैं गलती पर हो सकता हूँ।

21. क्या तुम खतरे को नहीं टाल सकते थे ?

22. तुम जा सकते हो।

23. हमारी टीम जीत सकती है।

24. आज वर्षा हो सकती है।

25. क्या वे लोग इसे पढ़ सकते हैं ?

26. सरला अच्छी तरह गा सकती है।

27. ऊँचे मनोबल के कारण कोलम्बस नई दुनिया का पता लगा सका।

28. हम लोगों ने अपना रास्ता बदल दिया ताकि हम शीघ्र पहुँच सकें।

29. क्या तुम उन्हें रोक सकते थे ?

30. महात्मा गांधी सुगमतापूर्वक भीड़ में भी पढ़ सकते थे।

31. उससे खाया नहीं जाता।

32. वह निवेदन स्वीकृत करने में असमर्थ था।

33. रात में मुझसे पढ़ा नहीं जाता।

34. वह वहाँ उपस्थित होगा।

35. चन्द्रशेखर आजाद का नाम तुमने अवश्य सुना होगा।

36. व्यापारी अपनी दुकान बन्द कर दिया होगा।

37. वह अवश्य बुद्धिमान होगा।

38. इस बारे में कोई भी टिप्पणी करने में मैं असमर्थ हूँ।

39. आकाश में बादल होंगे।

40. मुझसे तैरा नहीं जाता।

Hints—भवन–building, गिरना–to raze (rase), turn down, समय पर–in time, धनी–wealthy, rich, सवार–rider, हल करना–to solve, सफलतापूर्वक–successfully, अभियन्ता–engineer, झूठ–false, कहीं–somewhere, सुगमतापूर्वक–easily, पत्रिका–magazine, भूलना–lose, गल्ती पर–in fault, खतरा–danger, टालना–ward off or keep off, जीतना–to win, अच्छी तरह से–well, ऊँचा मनोबल–high morale, पता लगाना–to discover, ताकि–so that, that, शीघ्र–soon, रोकना–to forbid, व्यापारी–merchant, बुद्धिमान–wise, टिप्पणी करना–to give remark, बादल–cloud.

Exercise 2

Fill can, could, may or might in the blanks appropriately :

1. I ...... break the ice.
2. He ...... do well.
3. ...... I take your pen ?
4. You ...... top the list of the successful candidates.
5. The sky ...... rain today.
6. The boy ...... be Kanak.
7. I am sorry, I ...... not stand by you.
8. ...... you cross the river ?
9. He ...... arrive today.
10. She ...... win.

Chapter 5

Should, Must, Ought to, Would

A. (a) Should and would—Should (चाहिए) shall का past tense है और would, will का। सामान्यत: जिसके साथ shall प्रयुक्त होता है उसके साथ should तथा जिसके साथ will लगता है उसके साथ would का प्रयोग करते हैं। Like, prefer, care, be glad, be inclined आदि के प्रसंग में would का प्रयोग first person के साथ भी समान रूप से किया जाता है। इसे Norman Lewis ने भी अपनी पुस्तक 'Word Power' में उचित ठहराया है। इस प्रसंग में Modern English Usage में श्री Fowler का विचार अन्यथा रूप में देखें—

'If anything it (I would like) makes the matter worse ; would is properly used without 'like' because it contains the idea of volition ; to use it with 'like' is equivalent to saying I should like to like. I would like is no better than any of the wills and woulds that are well recognized as Scottish, Irish, American and other kinds of English but not English English.

1. मैं तुमसे कहना चाहूँगा।

   I would like to tell you. (not logical)

   I should like to tell you. (logical)

2. तुमसे मिलकर वह प्रसन्न होगा।

   He would be glad to see you. (admissible)

   He would be glad to receive you.

किन्तु आधुनिक अंग्रेजी में would like अधिक प्रयुक्त होने लगा है।

(b) यदि main clause, shall या will से रहे तो should या would का उसके subordinate में प्रयोग नहीं होगा।

You will feel at ease if he would go. (Incorrect)

You will feel at ease if he goes. (Correct)

(c) कर्त्तव्य (Duty) प्रगट करने के लिए should का प्रयोग तीनों persons में होता है।

1. आयोग को सबसे निष्पक्ष तथा समान अवसर की नीति पर चलना चाहिए।

   The commissions should follow the policy of fair field and no favour.

2. सम्पादक के रूप में आपका कथन निष्पक्ष होना चाहिए।

   Being an editor, your statement should be impartial.

3. हमें नि:स्वार्थी होना चाहिए।

   We should be selfless.

(d) जब main clause, past tense में रहें तो उसके subordinate में प्रयुक्त shall को should तथा will को would करेंगे।

She wrote that she would come. (not will)

I told him roundly that I should not give him any vents. (not shall)

(e) Supposition के भाव में should का प्रयोग करें। इसके अतिरिक्त lest (अन्यथा, कहीं ऐसा न हो) के साथ भी should का प्रयोग करें।

1. यदि तुम चाहोगे तो मैं तुमसे वहाँ मिलूँगा।

Should you want, I will see you there.

2. यदि मैं खूब मेहनत करूँ तो मैं उत्तीर्ण हो सकता हूँ।

Should I work hard, I can pass.

3. हम लोग भाग गए ताकि कहीं ऐसा न हो कि हम मार दिए जायँ।

We fled away lest we should be killed.

4. वह तेज दौड़ा ताकि कहीं वह गाड़ी न छोड़ दे।

He ran fast lest he should miss the train.

(f) Would का प्रयोग आदत (Habit) के लिए भी किया जाता है–

1. भिखारी प्रायः प्रत्येक दिन आया करता था।

The beggar would often come everyday.

2. यदि वह कठिन परिश्रम किया होता तो वह सफल हो गया होता।

Had he worked hard, he would have succeeded.

B. Must (चाहिए, गा, गे, गी)–जब कर्त्तव्य/बाध्यता अथवा कथन पर बल (emphasis) दिया गया हो अर्थात् 'अवश्य चाहिए' जैसा कथन हो तो must का प्रयोग वांछनीय होगा और जैसा कि पूर्व के अध्याय में प्रकाश डाला गया है must संभावना, असंभावना तथा अनुमान भी बताता है।

1. न्यायाधीश को ईमानदार होना चाहिए।

A judge must be honest.

2. क्या तुम्हें वहाँ अवश्य नहीं जाना चाहिए ?

Must you not go there ?   *Or*   Mustn't you go there ?

3. तुम्हें अवश्य ही ऐसी किताबें नहीं पढ़नी चाहिए।

You must not (mustn't) read such books.

4. हम सबको स्वदेश से अवश्य प्रेम करना चाहिए।

We all must love our country.

5. भिक्षुकों को चयनकर्त्ता नहीं होना चाहिए।

Beggars must not be choosers.

C. Ought (to) (चाहिए, चाहिए था)–यह owe का पुराना past form है। Ought to का प्रयोग कर्त्तव्य, औचित्य, दोष, अनुमोदन, दृढ़ संभावना तथा नैतिकता (Rightness, shortcoming, advisability and strong probability) के अर्थ में करना चाहिए।

1. हमें अपने पड़ोसियों से प्रेम रखना चाहिए।

We ought to love our neighbours.

2. इसकी अनुमति नहीं दी जानी चाहिए।

It ought not to be allowed.

3. तुम्हें बेहतर जानना चाहिए था।

You ought to know better.

4. तुम्हें मातृभूमि के लिए मर जाना चाहिए था।

You ought to die for the motherland.

5. उसे जीत जाना चाहिए। (अनुमान)

She ought to win.

6. इसे बहुत पहले शीघ्र कर लेना चाहिए था।

It ought to be done at once long ago.

7. हमें विचारशील होना चाहिए।

We ought to be considerate.

निष्कर्ष (conclusion)—कर्त्तव्यबोध तथा सामान्य 'चाहिए' के भाव में should ; 'अवश्य चाहिए' का संकेत रहने पर must और 'चाहिए' या 'चाहिए था' अर्थात् नैतिकता हेतु ought to का प्रयोग करें। Should, would, must, ought to के सन्दर्भ में अनुवाद निम्नस्थ रीति से करें—

Assertive—Subject + should, must etc. + verb[1] + object etc.

Negative—Not, never को should, must etc. के पश्चात् रखें।

Interrogative—Wh + should must etc. + subject + not/never + verb[1] + object etc.

D. जब भूतकाल में सम्पन्न किसी कार्य के मूल्यांकन का औचित्य/अनौचित्य संकेतित हो, जैसे—तुम्हें उसका आदर करना चाहिए था। अर्थात् तुम उसका आदर करने में उस समय असफल रहे, तो ऐसे वाक्यों को इस रीति से अनुवाद करें—

Subject + should have (been)/ought to have (been) + verb, adjective etc.

1. तुम्हें उसका आदर करना चाहिए था।

You should have been respected him.

Or You ought to have respected him.

2. उसे थोड़ा सावधान रहना चाहिए था।

He should have been a little cautious.

Or He ought to have been a little cautious.

Exercise 1

Translate into English :

1. हमें खूब तड़के टहलना चाहिए।

2. तुम्हारे मित्र को इस प्रकार से बात नहीं करनी चाहिए।

3. क्या हम सबको सत्यवादी नहीं होना चाहिए ?

4. तुम्हें ईमानदारी से अपने कर्त्तव्य का पालन अवश्य करना चाहिए।

5. क्या विद्यार्थियों को अवश्य विद्यालय नहीं जाना चाहिए ?

6. चाय की अपेक्षा मैं दूध को प्राथमिकता देना चाहूँगा।

7. उसे घर लौट जाना चाहिए था।

8. तुम्हें अपने भाई की मदद करनी चाहिए थी।

9. क्या रेलगाड़ी को समय पर नहीं आना चाहिए था ?

10. डाक्टर को परोपकारी होना चाहिए।

11. नेताओं को अवश्य आदर्शवादी होना चाहिए।

12. तुम्हें उसकी सम्पत्ति लौटा देनी चाहिए थी।

13. हमें कब खेलना चाहिए ?

14. किसी को भी धूम्रपान नहीं करना चाहिए।

15. हमें वहाँ क्यों नहीं जाना चाहिए था ?

16. हमें उसकी बहन के विवाह में अवश्य जाना चाहिए।

17. हम सबको ईश्वर की पूजा करनी चाहिए।

18. तुम्हें उससे उग्र बहस नहीं करनी चाहिए थी।

19. अपने घरों को स्वच्छ रखना चाहिए।

20. हमें कब सोना चाहिए ?

21. अब मुझे अवश्य बोलना चाहिए।

22. क्या तुम्हें उस अवसर पर चुप्पी साध लेनी चाहिए थी ?

23. क्या स्वास्थ्य के लिए हमें संतुलित आहार नहीं लेना चाहिए ?

24. अब हमें आराम करना चाहिए।

25. उसे प्रतियोगी परीक्षाओं में बैठना चाहिए था।

26. तुम्हें किसलिए झूठ बोलना चाहिए था ?

27. उन लोगों को सवाल क्यों नहीं सुगमता से हल कर लेना चाहिए ?

28. तुम्हें अपने पिता से अवश्य समझौता कर लेना चाहिए था।

29. हमें सभी जीवों से प्रेम करना चाहिए।

30. कितने आदमियों को नाटक में अवश्य भाग लेना चाहिए ?

Hints—खूब तड़के–early in the morning, इस प्रकार से–in this way, thus, सत्यवादी–truthful, कर्त्तव्य पालन करना–to discharge one's duty, प्राथमिकता देना चाहूँगा–would prefer, परोपकारी–altruist, आदर्शवादी–ideal, सम्पत्ति–property, किसी को–one, (किसी को नहीं–none), धूम्रपान–smoking, पूजा करना–to worship, उग्र बहस करना–to exchange hot dialogues, स्वच्छ–neat and clean, अवसर–occasion, चुप्पी साधना–to keep mum, संतुलित आहार–balanced diet, प्रतियोगी परीक्षा–competitive examination, बैठना–to appear at, सुगमता से हल करना–to solve (to work out) easily, सवाल–sum, समझौता करना–to compromise, जीवों–creatures, भाग लेना–to take part.

Chapter 6

Degree of Comparison

व्यक्ति/वस्तु के गुण/अवगुण ; कमी/आधिक्य, परस्पर तुलना, समता आदि को दृष्टिगत करते हुए विशेषण, क्रिया विशेषण को तीन स्तरों में विभाजित किया गया है जिन्हें Degree of comparison कहा जाता है। (a) Positive degree—जो सामान्य विशेषता के लिए है। (b) Comparative degree—जिसे दो व्यक्तियों/वस्तुओं (या अधिक) की तुलना/समता के लिए प्रयोग किया जाता है, तथा (c) Superlative degree—जो सर्वाधिक गुण/दोष बताता है। प्राय: positive में -er जोड़कर comparative तथा -est जोड़कर Superlative बनाया जाता है। कुछ एक के पूर्व क्रमश: more तथा most (जैसे–more difficult, most difficult) जैसा बनाया जाता है।

A. Positive degree—सामान्यतया इसे qualified word के पूर्व रखा जाता है किन्तु यदि adjectives अनेक हों तो उक्त word के पूर्व या पश्चात् कहीं भी रखा जा सकता है। ध्यान रहे कि पहले कम अक्षर वाला तथा पश्चात् क्रमश: अधिक अक्षर वाला रखें।

1. वह एक तेज विद्यार्थी है। — He is a brilliant student.

2. क्या वह लड़की लम्बी नहीं है ? — Is that girl not tall ?

3. ईमानदार, सच्चा तथा विचारवान व्यक्ति चारों ओर आदर पाता है।

An honest, truthful and considerate man gets respect everywhere.

4. वह आदर्शवादी, कुलीन तथा गम्भीर व्यक्ति है।

He is a man ideal, noble and serious.

B. जब तुलना -er से समाप्त रहे तो than + nominative case रखें और यदि -or (जैसे–senior, junior etc.) से समाप्त रहे तो उसके पश्चात् to + objective case रखें। Elder, prefer के साथ भी to रहेगा। उन 'दोनों से' जैसा रहने पर of the two करेंगे।

1. राम मोहन से छोटा है। — Ram is smaller than Mohan.

2. तुम उससे अधिक चतुर हो। — You are cleverer than he.

3. वह मुझसे ज्येष्ठतर नहीं था। — He was not senior to me.

4. क्या कानपुर वाराणसी से अधिक बड़ा नहीं है ? — Is Kanpur not bigger than Varanasi ?

5. यह लोहा उन दोनों से भारी है। — This iron is heavier of the two.

6. यह लड़का उन दोनों से पढ़ने में तेज है। — This boy is more intelligent of the two.

C. तुलना (comparison)–किन्हीं दो में होती है। सर्वाधिक गुण हेतु superlative degree दो से अधिक में प्रयुक्त होती है। यदि तुलना दो से अधिक में रहे तो any other/all other/any one else का प्रयोग करें अथवा than that of/than those of का प्रयोग करें।

1. मेरा मकान गाँव के सभी मकानों की अपेक्षा अधिक ऊँचा है।

My house is higher than all other houses of the village.

2. इलाहाबाद की सड़क वाराणसी की सड़क की अपेक्षा अधिक चौड़ी है।

The road of Allahabad is wider than that of Varanasi. (Singular में)

The roads of Allahabad are wider than those of Varanasi. (Plural में)

3. ऊषा किसी से भी अधिक विनम्र है।

Usha is humbler than anyone else.

4. यह प्रश्न उस प्रश्न की अपेक्षा कम आसान है।

This question is less easy than that.

5. यह कमीज उस कमीज से कम लाल है।

This shirt is less red than that.

D. जब एक ही व्यक्ति/वस्तु के दो विशेषताओं की परस्पर तुलना हो तो more का प्रयोग इस प्रकार करें—

1. पोरस बहादुर की अपेक्षा बुद्धिमान अधिक था।

Porus was more wise than brave.

2. धन स्वास्थ्यकारक की अपेक्षा सहायक अधिक है।

Wealth is more helpful than healthful.

3. यह आम महँगा से मधुर अधिक है।

This mango is more sweet than dear.

E. ज्यों ज्यों ...... त्यों त्यों ; जितना ही ...... उतना ही के लिए Comparative degrees के पूर्व the लगाएँ—

1. जितना ही अधिक उतना ही बेहतर।

The more, the better.

2. वह जितना ही कमाता है उतना ही उदास रहता है।

The more he earns, the more is he sad.

3. जितना ही धनी, उतना ही सुखी।

The richer, the merrier.

4. दिन जितना बेहतर, उतना ही बेहतर कार्य।

The better the day, the better the deed.

F. एक समान, एक जैसा के लिए like, just like, alike, just the same का प्रयोग करें।

1. दोनों एक जैसे हैं।

Both are alike.

2. वह निपट डाइन जैसी लग रही थी।

She was appearing like a sheer witch.

3. हम दोनों एक जैसा सोचते हैं।

We both think alike.

4. वे सभी एक जैसे हैं।

All are just the same.

G. इतना, उतना, जितना के भाव में as, (so) + positive + as जैसी बनावट करें।

1. यमुना इतनी चौड़ी नहीं, जितनी गंगा।

The Yamuna is not so wide as the Ganga.

2. श्याम जितना साहसी है उतना ही सतीश भी।

Satish is as courageous as Shyam.

3. वह कोयले जैसा काला है।

He is as black as coal   *Or*   He is black like coal.

4. घोड़ा उतना लाभदायक नहीं जितनी गाय।

A horse is not so useful as a cow.

5. रामदीन जैसा इस गाँव में कोई सुखी नहीं था।

None in this village was so happy as Ramdin.

6. पन्त हिन्दी के सबसे महान कवियों में से एक थे।

Pant was one of the greatest Hindi poets.

7. बालू विद्यालय का सबसे लम्बा लड़का नहीं है।

Balu is not the tallest boy (of) in the school.

H. संख्या में अधिक/कम से तुलना का संकेत रहने पर **more + noun + than + noun** जैसी बनावट करें।

1. वहाँ लड़कों से लड़कियाँ अधिक थीं।

There were more girls than boys.

2. यहाँ गरीबी की अपेक्षा अशिक्षा अधिक है।

There is more illiteracy than poverty here.

I. Subject + verb + numeral adjective + times + as + positive + as ....

1. यह प्रश्न उस प्रश्न से कई गुना कठिन है।

This question is several times as difficult as that.

2. वह तुमसे दुगुना लम्बा था।

He was two times as tall as you.

3. हरी गोविन्द से तीन गुना मोटा है।

Hari is three times as fat as Govind.

J. सर्वाधिक गुण हेतु **superlative degree** का प्रयोग करें। जिसके पूर्व **the** लगाएँ। इसका प्रयोग दो से अधिक में किया जाता है।

1. दूध सबसे उजला द्रव है।

Milk is the whitest liquid.

2. यह सबसे खराब निर्णय है।

This is the worst decision.

3. मेरे जीवन में वह सबसे काली रात थी।

That was the darkest night in my life.

Or That night was the darkest night in my life.

4. वह लड़का सबसे लम्बा नहीं, तो कम से कम उनमें से एक तो है ही।

That boy is one of the tallest if not the tallest.

Exercise 1

1. अशोक एक महान राजा था।
2. गीदड़ मूर्ख नहीं था।
3. तुम्हारा काम कब दुखदायी था ?
4. यह पेन्सिल उन दोनो से काली है।
5. इस बूशर्ट से वह बूशर्ट गन्दा नहीं है।
6. धोन्धू फटिक से अधिक बलवान नहीं है।
7. तुम्हारी गाय गाँव की अन्य गायों से अधिक स्वस्थ है।
8. तुम मुझसे कनिष्ठतर हो।
9. क्या तुम्हारी बहन तुमसे बड़ी है ?
10. वे दिन आजकल से बेहतर थे।
11. कौन सा कपड़ा अन्य कपड़ों से अधिक पतला है ?
12. वह तुमसे अधिक योग्य थी।
13. शिवाजी सबसे अधिक साहसी थे।
14. कितने लड़के तुमसे छोटे हैं ?
15. हरीश अन्य अध्यापकों से अधिक विद्वान थे।
16. तुम्हारी साइकिल मोहन से अधिक नई है।
17. नौकरी उतनी अच्छी नहीं जितना व्यापार।
18. धन उतना महत्त्वपूर्ण नहीं जितना स्वास्थ्य।
19. वह तुमसे दस गुना धनी था।
20. क्या भवतोष राक्षस जैसा नहीं लगता ?
21. कौन सा लट्ठा सबसे भारी है ?
22. वह अपने पुत्र से अधिक मुझे पसन्द करते थे।
23. नगर का सौन्दर्य गाँव से अधिक आकर्षक हो गया है।
24. दीपक सबसे गरीब विद्यार्थी है।
25. गंगा जितनी पवित्र है उतनी अन्य नदियाँ नहीं।
26. यह हलवाई उससे अधिक ईमानदार है।
27. मैं तुमसे दुगुना रुपया रखता हूँ।
28. वह सुन्दर से अधिक सत्यवादी है।
29. मंसूरी हरिद्वार से अधिक ठंडा है।
30. यह दवा उससे अधिक कड़वी है।
31. एवरेस्ट सबसे ऊँची चोटी है।
32. वह जैसा कुरूप है वैसा ही धूर्त भी।
33. चाँदी सोने से अधिक चमकीली है।
34. तुम उतने ही मूर्ख हो जितना गधा।
35. क्या तुम्हारे केश उसके ही जैसे मुलायम हैं ?
36. श्याम को उतने ही बच्चे हैं जितने सुदेश के।
37. दोनों एक जैसा बर्ताव करते थे।
38. क्या वह बच्चा जैसा नहीं लगता ?
39. यह फूल उन दोनों से सुन्दर है।
40. इस बाग में पेड़ों की अपेक्षा झाड़ियाँ अधिक हैं।
41. तुम्हारी बहन तुमसे कम चालाक है।
42. यह सबसे अधिक रुचिकर उपन्यासों में से एक है।

Hints—गीदड़—jackal, दुखदायी—troublesome, गन्दा—dirty, कनिष्ठतर—junior, बेहतर—better, योग्य—able, साहसी—bold, courageous, विद्वान—learned, महत्त्वपूर्ण—important, राक्षस—demon, लट्ठा—log, भारी—heavy, सौन्दर्य—charm, आकर्षक—attractive, पवित्र—holy, sacred, हलवाई—confectioner, सज्जन—gentle, सत्यवादी—truthful, कड़वी—bitter, चोटी—peak, कुरूप—ugly, धूर्त—cunning, मुलायम—soft, बर्ताव करना—to behave, बच्चा जैसा—childlike, झाड़ियाँ—bushes, रुचिकर—interesting, उपन्यास—novel, हो गया है—has turned or become.

Exercise 2

Correct the following sentences :

1. Ashok was more greater than Akbar.
2. That was the most boldest actor.
3. The red fort is an elder fort.
4. Humayun was an unsuccessful and the most unfortunate king.
5. This incident is more former than that.
6. Raghu has got more minor injury than Ramlal.

7.   Rajan is superior than Sunil.
8.   Do you prefer the reign of hell than the service of heaven ?
9.   This work of art seems to be more perfect than yours.
10. He is junior than I.

Exercise 3

Translate into English :

1.   वह एक सज्जन व्यक्ति है।
2.   रेखा एक विनम्र लड़की है।
3.   वह एक अच्छी क्षमा थी।
4.   मेरा एक ठीक चित्र खींचो।
5.   जंगल सुन्दर चित्रमय और अँधेरा था।
6.   अरुण ओमप्रकाश से छोटा है।
7.   तुम मुझसे मोटे हो।
8.   सिकन्दर बहादुर की अपेक्षा बुद्धिमान अधिक था।
9.   राम का घोड़ा अर्जुन के घोड़े से तेज है।
10. तैमूर दुष्ट की अपेक्षा निष्ठुर अधिक था।
11. लखनऊ की जनसंख्या इलाहाबाद से अधिक है।
12. वह कविता किसी भी कविता से अधिक प्रभावोत्पादक है।
13. कलम तलवार से शक्तिशाली है।
14. कक्षा में सबसे अच्छा लड़का कौन है ?
15. गौल और मंगोलों में से कौन अधिक बहादुर थे ?

Hints—विनम्र—modest, humble, अच्छी क्षमा—a nice excuse, ठीक—apposite, चित्रमय—picturesque, सिकन्दर—Alexander, तेज—swift, दुष्ट—wicked, निष्ठुर—cruel, जनसंख्या—population, प्रभावोत्पादक—impressive.

Chapter 7

Interrogative Sentence
(प्रश्नवाचक वाक्य)

1. What (क्या)–(a) जब 'क्या' शब्द दिए गए हिन्दी वाक्य के प्रारम्भ में रहे (जिसका उत्तर yes/no में संभव हो) तो helping verb + subject + verb/noun/adjective etc. जैसी उसकी बनावट करें। Helping verb से तात्पर्य verb to be (is, am, are, was, were) तथा shall, will, can, do, has, may etc. आदि से है। जैसे–

(a) क्या तुम बीमार हो ?   Are you ill ?

(b) क्या वह रोज विद्यालय जाता है ?   Does he go to school daily ?

(c) क्या वह तुम्हारा मित्र था ?   Was he your friend ?

(b) जब 'क्या' शब्द वाक्य के मध्य में हो (जिसका उत्तर yes/no में न होकर किसी पूरे वाक्य में संभव हो) तो उसकी बनावट इस प्रकार करें।

What + helping verb + subject + verb/noun etc.

(a) नेताजी के बारे में तुम क्या जानते हो ?   What do you know about the Netaji ?

(b) यूरेनियम क्या होता है ?   What is uranium ?

(c) जब what किसी noun को govern करे (अर्थात् जब इसके साथ सम्बन्धित noun रहे) तो what + noun + helping verb + subject + verb etc. जैसा उसे बनाएँ।

(a) क्या बजा है ?   What o'clock is it ?

(b) तुम्हारा उससे क्या सम्बन्ध है ?   What relation is he to you ?

(d) जब what स्वयं subject रहे तो what + verb + object जैसी बनावट करें। जैसे–
What brought you here ? What causes the fire ?

2. Who (कौन, किसने)–इसे केवल person के लिए प्रयोग किया जाता है। जब वाक्य negative रहे तो who + does/did + not + verb[1] जैसी बनावट indefinite tense में करेंगे और यदि negative न रहे (who स्वयं subject रहे) तो who + verb जैसा प्रयोग करेंगे।

(a) तुम्हें कौन जानता है ?   Who knows you ?

(b) तुम्हें कौन नहीं जानता ?   Who does not know you ?

(c) इसे किसने किया है ?   Who has done this ?

(d) इस दुखान्त के लिए आप किसे उत्तरदायी मानते हैं ?   Who do you think is accountable for this tragedy ?

3. Which (कौन, कौन सा)–Which चयन (selection or choice) बताता है। सामान्यतया which के पश्चात् helping verb रखते हैं। जैसे–

(a) कौन से तुम्हारे पिता हैं ?   Which is your father ?

289

(b) कलम तथा तलवार में कौन अधिक शक्तिशाली है ? Which is mightier-pen or sword ?

यदि which किसी noun को govern करे (सम्बन्धित noun रहे) तो which + noun + helping verb + subject + verb etc. जैसी उसकी बनावट करें। जैसे–

(a) तुम कौन सी पुस्तक अधिक पसन्द करते हो ?   Which book do you like most ?

(b) किस लड़के ने शोर मचाया था ?   Which boy had made a noise ?

4. How (कैसे), when (कब), whence (कहाँ से), where (कहाँ), whom (किसे, किसको), why (क्यों) आदि के प्रसंग में बनावट कुछ इस प्रकार करें–

wh + helping verb + subject + verb etc.

wh अर्थात् प्रश्नवाचक शब्द जो w या h से प्रारम्भ रहते हैं।

(a) तुमने इस सवाल को कैसे हल किया है ?   How have you worked out this sum ?

(b) वह इतनी उदास क्यों थी ?   Why was she so sad ?

(c) नौकर ने छाता कहाँ खो दिया है ?   Where has the servant lost the umbrella ?

5. How many (कितना, कितने, कितनी-संख्या बताता है) ; How much (कितना, कितने, कितनी-माप, तौल बताता है) ; whose (किसका, किसकी, किसके)-इन सबके शीघ्र पश्चात् (तथा कभी-कभी what तथा which के साथ भी जैसा कि पहले बताया जा चुका है) इनसे सम्बन्धित noun (यदि वाक्य में रहे) रखें। पश्चात् helping verb + subject + verb etc. रखें।

(a) तुम कितना दूध पीते हो ?   How much milk do you drink ?

(b) कितने लड़के किताब लाए हैं ?   How many boys have brought the book ?

(c) बाजार में इसकी कितनी लागत होती है ?   How much does it cost in the market ?

(d) तुमने किसकी छड़ी ले रखी है ?   Whose stick have you taken ?

Note. दिए गए हिन्दी वाक्य में कितना, कितने, किसका आदि के शीघ्र पश्चात् जो noun आता है उसे सम्बन्धित noun (governing noun) कहा जाता है। How many, How much के साथ यदि उक्त noun न रहे तो उसके बाद helping verb रखें–How much do I owe to you ? How many are there ? How many (of them) can I have ? (Concise Oxford Dictionary–C.O.D.)

Exercise 1

Frame questions to get the following answers. Begin each question with the wh words in the bracket :

1.	It is Monday today.	(What/Which)
2.	Owing to poverty, he committed suicide.	(Why)
3.	He worked out the sum very cleverly.	(How)
4.	I saw him in the last month.	(When)
5.	The tall man among them is my father.	(Which)
6.	An accident occurred there.	(What)
7.	Ten persons were sitting on the front chairs.	(How many)
8.	The old man drank one litre milk.	(How much)
9.	Ram's son topped the list of successful candidates.	(Whose)
10.	The child was weeping for the moon.	(For what)
11.	People liked him due to his inviting personality.	(Why)
12.	They were talking with their friends.	(With/To whom)

13. Cotton is grown in India.   (Where)
14. His father is Inspector of Schools.   (What)
15. Even Homer sometimes nods.   (Who)

Exercise 2

Correct (if necessary) the following sentences :

1. Who did call you a philosopher ?
2. Why is water not there ?
3. Whom they account wise ?
4. What brought you here ?
5. I forget where have I seen him ?
6. Which idea moves you ?
7. Who did spoke first ?
8. I cannot say what will he do ?
9. I am not sure where does he live ?
10. What happened of him ?

Chapter 8

Imperative, Optative and Exclamatory Sentences (आज्ञासूचक, अभिलाषाबोधक एवं विस्मयादिबोधक वाक्य)

1. Imperative Sentence (आज्ञासूचक वाक्य)

1. इसके अन्तर्गत वे सभी वाक्य आयेंगे जिनसे आज्ञा (order, command) ; निवेदन (request, entreaty) ; सलाह (advice) आदि का बोध होता हो। इसमें subject छिपा रहता है। जैसे–

Sit down. (You छिपा है)

Thank you (I छिपा है)

सामान्यतया Imperative sentences को subject के बिना verb[1] से प्रारम्भ किया जाता है। होना, बनना के लिए be का प्रयोग करें।

1. यहाँ आओ।	Come here.
2. तुम बाजार जाओ।	Go to market.
3. एक ग्लास लाओ।	Bring a glass.
4. एक डाक्टर जाकर लाओ।	Fetch a doctor.
5. हमेशा सत्य बोलो।	Always speak the truth.
6. खिड़की खोल दो।	Open the window.
7. सज्जन बनो।	Be gentle.

2. Negative—Imperative sentence का नकारात्मक भाव do not/never + verb[1] से प्रगट करते हैं–

1. यहाँ इश्तहार मत चिपकाओ।	Stick no bills here.
2. यहाँ गाड़ी मत खड़ी करो।	No parking here.
3. कुत्ते को मत पीटो।	Do not beat the dog.
4. समय व्यर्थ मत गँवाओ।	Do not waste time.
5. कभी झूठ मत बोलो।	Never tell a lie.
6. कभी धूम्रपान मत करो।	Never smoke.
7. कोई निवेदन मत करो।	No request.
8. सुधारों के खिलाफ मत होओ।	Do not be against reforms.

3. यदि निवेदन रहे तो उसमें please/kindly का प्रयोग करें। अनुमति के भाव में may be allowed/permitted जैसा प्रयोग करें।

1. कृपया अपनी कलम दीजिए।	Please, give your pen.
2. मॉड् मेरे साथ उपवन में आओ।	Come with me in the garden, Maud.
3. कृपया इसे अभी कीजिए।	Please do it just now.

4. कृपया ऐसा न कहें।	Kindly do not say so.
5. कृपया आवाज नहीं।	No murmuring, please.
6. इस दुखदाई संसार में कृपया मुझे न छोड़ें।	Please do not leave me in this woeful world.

4. जब आज्ञा, निवेदन पर अधिक बल दिया गया हो तो you का प्रयोग किया जा सकता है अथवा Do + verb[1] जैसा रूप दिया जा सकता है। इस प्रसंग में must से भी बल का भाव व्यक्त किया जा सकता है।

1. कृपया शान्त हो जाइए।	Do be quiet, please.
2. सोमवार को (अवश्य) आएँ।	Do come on Monday.
3. तुम बाहर निकलो।	You go out or go out, you.
4. कृपया मुझे पुन: सूचित करें।	Please, do inform me again.
5. तुम समाचार-पत्र अवश्य पढ़ो।	You must read newspaper.

Note. Shall, will, can, may आदि से भी प्रश्नवाचक वाक्य द्वारा निवेदन का भाव प्रगट किया जाता है। जैसे—

1. मेरे अन्दर आने का बुरा तो न मानिएगा ?

   Will (or would) you please mind my coming in ?

2. श्रीमान्, क्या मैं अन्दर आ सकता हूँ ?

   May, I come in Sir ?

(उत्तर में–yes, you may or No, you may not.)

3. क्या मेरा टिकट भी कृपया खरीद सकेंगे ?

   Could you please buy my ticket also ?

4. क्या कृपया आप स्टेशन तक मेरा साथ देंगे ?

   Would you please accompany me to the station ?

5. क्या आप मेरे साथ नाचेंगी ?

   Will you please dance with me ?

5. यदि हिन्दी की क्रिया ना, ने, नी से समाप्त रहे और उसके बाद 'दो' रहे तो Let + objective case + verb[1] जैसी बनावट करें।

1. मुझे जाने दो।	Let me go.
2. उसे रोने दो।	Let him weep.
3. जो वे कहते हैं, कहने दो।	Let them say what they say.
4. हम असहमत होने हेतु सहमत हो जायँ।	Let us agree to disagree.
5. वह मुझसे कल मिले।	Let him see me tomorrow.
6. अब हम चलें।	Let us go now.

2. Optative Sentences (अभिलाषाबोधक वाक्य)

1. इससे अभिलाषा, लालसा, इच्छा (wish, desire, longing etc.) ; आशीर्वाद (blessing) ; श्राप (curse) ; नमस्कार (good morning, goodbye etc.) प्रगट किया जाता है। ऐसे वाक्यों को बहुधा May से प्रारम्भ किया जाता है जिसके अन्त में सम्बोधन (!) का चिह रहता है।

1. उसका वंश चिर दिनों जीए।	May his race live long !
2. ईश्वर तुम्हें आशीर्वाद दें।	May God bless you !
3. हमारे राष्ट्रपति चिरंजीवी हों।	Long live our President !

4. तुम्हारी यात्रा सुखद हो।

May you have a pleasant journey !
Or May your journey be ...... !

5. नववर्ष मंगलमय हो।

May you have a happy new year !
Or Happy new year !

6. तुम भाड़ में जाओ।

May you go to the dogs !

7. तुम नरक को जाओ।

May you go to hell !
Or Hell to you !

8. उसकी आत्मा को शांति मिलें।

Peace to his soul !
Or Ashes !

इसी तरह—goodbye, to meet again, Adieu friends ! now we are parting.

2. अगर/यदि के द्वारा भविष्य की लालसा/इच्छा के लिए I wish/if only/would that/o (or oh) that + clause जिसमें प्रायः सभी प्रकार के subjects के साथ were का प्रयोग होता है। एक उदाहरण—

1. यदि मैं करोड़पति होता !

I wish I were a millionaire !
Or If only I were a millionaire !
Or Would that I were a millionaire !
Or O/Oh that I were a millionaire !

3. Exclamatory Sentences (*विस्मयादिबोधक वाक्य*)

1. जिससे मानसिक भाव (feeling) प्रगट होता हो। जैसे—दुख (sorrow, grief) ; क्रोध (anger) ; आनन्द (delight, joy) ; आश्चर्य (surprise) आदि। दुख, खेद हेतु alas, ah, oh, how, what, regret ; आश्चर्य के लिए how, what ; खुशी के लिए ah, oh, hurrah ; शाबास आदि के लिए bravo ; घृणा, तिरस्कार हेतु fie ; असंतोष के लिए tut-tut ; उपहास हेतु pooh ; स्वागत, ध्यानाकर्षण के लिए hark, lo, hush, hello, hi का प्रयोग किया जाता है। सूत्र होगा—

How/what + adjective/noun/adverb etc. + subject + verb.......

1. कितना अच्छा !

How good ! *Or* nice !

2. कितना चित्ताकर्षक !

How persuasive !

3. क्या ही विचार (है) !

What an idea !

4. तुम कैसा मूर्ख हो !

What a fool you are !

5. क्या ही सुन्दर प्रभात है !

What a fine morning it is !

6. रात कितनी अँधेरी है !

How dark the night is !
Or What a dark night it is !

7. कितना सुन्दर वह दिखाई देती है !

How lovely she looks !

8. कितनी लज्जा की बात है कि तुम मैदान से भाग गए !

What a shame that you fled from the field !

2. How + noun/adjective etc. + of + object + Infinitive etc.

1. कितनी चतुराई से उसने मुझसे बात किया !

How clever of him to talk with me !

2. कितने साहस से उसने अपनी कठिनाइयों पर काबू पाया !

How courage of him to overcome his difficulties !

3. इतनी काली और मेरी पत्नी।   Such black and my wife !

4. इतना शरारती और मेरा लड़का।   Such naughty and my son !

5. हाय ! मैं बर्बाद हो गया।   Alas ! I am undone.

6. हाय ! मैं मर गया।   Ah ! I die.

7. वाह ! हम लोग मैच जीत गए।   Hurrah ! we won the match.

8. शाबाश ! खूब लड़ा।   Bravo ! well fought.

Exercise 1

Imperative Sentences

Translate into English :

1. शान्तिपूर्वक चलो।
2. जोर से बोलो।
3. तेज दौड़ो।
4. एक प्याला काफी लाओ।
5. तुम कक्षा से बाहर जाओ।
6. एक कथा कहो।
7. कृपाकर मेरी मदद कीजिए।
8. स्वयं को पहचानो।
9. शीघ्रता करो।
10. केवल पाँच प्रश्नों का उत्तर दो।
11. निम्नलिखित की व्याख्या करो।
12. हिन्दी में अनुवाद करो।
13. ईमानदार बनो।
14. उसे अन्दर आने दो।
15. मुझे जाने दो।
16. बच्चों को खेलने दो।
17. कल्पना करो कि अ ब स एक त्रिभुज है।
18. गड़े मुर्दे मत उखाड़ो।
19. उन्हें बर्बरता से ऊपर उठाओ और अच्छे ढंग सिखाओ।
20. क्षमा करो और भूल जाओ।
21. पहले योग्य बनो तब इच्छा करो।
22. अपनी छाया से मत डरो।
23. कभी लालची मत बनो।
24. अपना जीवन बर्बाद मत करो।
25. गप मत मारो।

26. आग में घी मत डालो।
27. दूसरों पर कीचड़ मत उछालो।
28. तुम देर रात तक काम मत करो।
29. कभी साहस मत खोओ।
30. मुझे जीने दो।
31. उन्हें बढ़-बढ़ कर बोलने दो।
32. जो बीत गई उसे बीत जाने दो।
33. मुगल साम्राज्य के पतन के कारण बताओ।
34. कृपया मुझे वोट दें।
35. कृपया दरवाजा खोल दें।
36. क्या मेरे यहाँ आने की कृपा करेंगे ?
37. क्या मुझे एक अवसर देने की कृपा करेंगे ?
38. हल्का भोजन लें।
39. तुम प्रातःकाल अवश्य टहलो।
40. तुम उनके यहाँ अवश्य जाओ।
41. हम लोग खूब तड़के चल दें।
42. मुझे अपना कार्य समाप्त करने दो।
43. यह किताब ले लूँ ?
44. बत्ती बुझा दूँ ?
45. मुझे घर जाने की अनुमति दी जाय।
46. मेरा निवेदन स्वीकार करने की कृपा की जाय।
47. मुझे वचन दो।
48. गन्दे कपड़े मत पहनो।
49. अपने को दीन मत दिखाओ।
50. क्या आप मेरी एक सेवा करेंगे ?

Hints—शान्तिपूर्वक–quietly, जोर से–loudly, कॉफी–coffee, पहचानना–to know, शीघ्रता करो–make haste, hurry up, व्याख्या करना–to explain, कल्पना करना–to suppose, त्रिभुज–triangle, गड़े मुर्दे उखाड़ना–to dig the dead from the grave, बर्बरता से ऊपर उठाना–to raise up from barbarity, अच्छे ढंग–good manners, सिखाना–to teach, क्षमा करना–to forgive, भूलना–to forget, योग्य बनना–to deserve, इच्छा करना–to desire, छाया–shadow, लालची–greedy, बर्बाद करना–to spoil, गप मारना–to gossip, आग में घी डालना–to add fuel to fire, to fan the fire (or flame), to pour oil on the fire, कीचड़ उछालना–to fling mud at, देर रात तक काम करना–to burn the mid-night oil, साहस खोना–to break the heart, बढ़-बढ़ कर बोलना–to brag (flaunt), to play to the gallery, जो बीत गई ......—Let bygones be bygones, कारण बताना–to account for, अवसर देना–to give (or provide) a chance, हल्का भोजन–light diet, चल दें–to set out, बुझाना–to put out (off), to blow out—फूँककर, to switch off, to extinguish, वचन देना–to give word, to promise, पहनना–to wear, to put on, दिखाना–to show, दीन–poor, inferior.

Exercise 2
Optative Sentences

Translate into English :

1. हमारा लोकतंत्र चिर दिनों रहे।
2. तुम्हें एक पुत्र का आशीर्वाद मिले।
3. ईश्वर तुम्हें सफलता दे।
4. नमस्ते रमेश ! तुम कैसे हो ?
5. नमस्कार मित्र ! मैं ठीक हूँ।
6. तुम्हारा नाश हो जाय।
7. ईश्वर तुम्हें भाग्यशाली बनाएँ।
8. तुम सुखी रहो।
9. विदा बन्धुओं ! अब हम जा रहे हैं।
10. शैतान तुम्हारा ख्याल करे।
11. तुम्हारा राज्य धनी हो।
12. तुम्हारा लड़का अधिकारी बने।
13. तुम परीक्षा में अच्छा करो।
14. मृत्यु तुम्हें ले जाय।
15. तुम ख्याति पाओ।

Hints—लोकतंत्र–democracy, आशीर्वाद मिलना–to be blessed (with), सफलता–success, नाश होना–to meet (or reduce) to dust, भाग्यशाली–fortunate, सुखी–happy, शैतान–satan, ख्याल करना–to take care of, राज्य–state, अधिकारी–officer, अच्छा करना–to do well, ले जाना–to take away, to snatch away, ख्याति–name and fame, धनी–rich (prosperous).

Exercise 3
Exclamatory Sentences

Translate into English :

1. तुम कितना सुन्दर लिखते हो !
2. वह कितना सुन्दर पढ़ाते हैं !
3. क्या ही सुन्दर तुम्हारी मुस्कान है !
4. कितना प्यारा बच्चा है !
5. कैसी सुन्दर वर्षा है !
6. कितना आरामदायक स्थान है !
7. कैसी महिला !
8. कैसी बातचीत !
9. कितना मुलायम !
10. कितनी मूर्खता से उसने व्यवहार किया !
11. उस गरीब की सेवा करने में वह कितना दयालु है !
12. तुम और मेरा मित्र !
13. इतना बेईमान और मेरा भाई !
14. हाय ! मेरा कुत्ता अब न रहा।

15. शाबाश ! मैं प्रथम आ गया।
16. आह ! मैंने अपनी प्रतिष्ठा की हत्या कर दी।
17. हाय मेरी प्रिय पुत्री ! कैसे जीवित रहूँगी ?
18. क्या ही अच्छा होता कि मैं एकान्त में रहता !
19. यह चाँदनी कितनी सुन्दर है !
20. शाबाश ! एक अच्छी छलांग।

21. वाह ! हम लोग विजयी हुए।
22. वह कम्पनी का प्रबन्ध कितना खराब करता है !
23. ये आम कितने स्वादिष्ट हैं !
24. आह ! एक बूँद पानी के लिए !
25. पिता अब्राहम ! ये ईसाई भी कितने शंकालु होते हैं !

Hints—मुस्कान—smile, प्यारा—lovely, pretty, आरामदायक—comfortable, मूर्खता से—foolishly, व्यवहार करना—to behave, बेईमान—dishonest, न रहा (मर गया)—no more, प्रथम आना—to stand (or secure) first, प्रतिष्ठा—honour, dignity, एकान्त—solitude, चाँदनी—moonlight, छलांग—jump, विजयी—victorious, प्रबन्ध करना—to manage, स्वादिष्ट—tasteful, बूँद—drop, पिता अब्राहम—father Abraham, ईसाई—christians, शंकालु—suspicious.

Chapter 9

Tenses (Active Voice कर्त्तृवाच्य)

1. Present Tense (वर्तमान काल)

1. Present Indefinite—इसकी हिन्दी–क्रिया ता हूँ, ते हैं, ते हो, ता है, तो है से समाप्त रहती है। यह (a) वर्तमान में घटित होने वाले कार्य का संकेत देता है। (b) शाश्वत सत्य, प्राकृतिक स्वभाव बताता है, तथा (c) आदत प्रगट करता है। जब subject first person, second person अथवा plural number में रहे तो–

Assertive—Subject + verb¹ object ......

Negative—Subject + do not/never + verb¹ + object ......

Interrogative—Wh + do + sub. + not/never + verb¹ + object ......

1. हम व्याकरण पढ़ते हैं।	We read grammar.
2. तुम चाय नहीं पीते हो।	You do not take tea.
3. मैं उससे कभी बात नहीं करता।	I never talk to him.
4. क्या घोड़े मैदान में नहीं दौड़ते हैं ?	Do the horses not run in the field ?
5. तुम प्रातःकाल कब उठते हो ?	When do you get up in the morning ?
6. तुम कितना दूध पीते हो ?	How much milk do you drink ?
7. चिड़ियाँ सुबह में चहचहाती है।	Birds twitter in the morning.

जब subject, third person तथा singular number में रहे तो–

Assertive—Subject + verb¹ में s या es + object ......

Negative—Subject + does not + verb¹ + object ......

Never रहने पर–sub. + never + verb में -s या -es ......

Interrogative—Wh + does + sub. + not/never + verb¹ + object ......

प्रकृति प्रदत्त गुण के संकेत रहने पर यदि क्रिया होता है, होती है रहे तो is और होते हैं रहने पर उसे are से प्रगट करें। (see Chapter 1, Rule 3 verb to be)

1. वह अपनी कार चलाती है।	She drives her car.
2. हवा जोर से नहीं बहती है।	The wind does not blow violently.
	Or It does not blow hard.
3. पोस्टमैन यहाँ कभी नहीं आता।	The postman never comes here.
4. कौन जोर से चिल्लाता है ?	Who cries loudly ?
5. वह यहाँ क्यों नहीं आता है ?	Why does he not come here ?
6. तुम्हारा मित्र कहाँ रहता है ?	Where does your friend live ?
7. धन की लालसा कौन नहीं करता ?	Who does not long for money ?

8. कौन लड़का विलम्ब से आया करता है ?   Which boy does come late ?

9. आकाश नीला होता है।   The sky is blue.

10. आशा प्राय: निराशा से पैदा होती है ?   Hope often springs from dismay.

2. Present Continuous—इसकी हिन्दी–क्रिया रहा हूँ, रहे हैं, रहे हो, रहा है, रही है जैसी समाप्त रहती है। इस tense द्वारा कार्य की गतिशीलता, निरन्तरता आदि का बोध होता है। अत: इसमें stative verbs (स्थिर, गतिहीन क्रियाओं) के प्रयोग से बचना चाहिए। Stative verbs वे हैं जो अन्तरबोध, बाह्यदर्शन, संवेग, अनुभव या स्वामित्व से सम्बन्धित हों जिनसे किसी गतिशीलता, क्रियाशीलता का बोध न हो बल्कि जो चेतना, भावना तथा अनुभवजन्य हो। जैसे–know, hope, seem, see, want, agree, have etc. इसके विपरीत इस tense में progressive verbs (गत्यात्मक क्रियाएँ) का प्रयोग स्वीकार्य है अर्थात् उन dynamic verbs का जिनसे activity, progress या movement का बोध होता हो। जैसे–jump, run, laugh etc.

Assertive—subject + to be (is, am, are) + verb में ing + object ......

Negative—not/never को to be के पश्चात् रखें।

Interrogative—Wh + to be + sub. + not/never + verb में ing + object ......

1. जोर से वर्षा हो रही है।   It is raining heavily. *Or*   It is pouring.

2. वह मुझसे नहीं बोल रहा है।   He is not speaking to me.

                                              Or   He is not on speaking terms with me.

3. क्या वे अंगूरों को इकट्ठे कर रहे हैं ?   Are they gathering the grapes ?

4. तुम वहाँ क्या कर रहे हो ?   What are you doing there ?

5. तुम किससे बातें कर रहे हो ?   Whom are you talking with ?

                                              Or   With whom ......

3. Present Perfect—इस tense से ऐसा ज्ञात होता है कि कार्य पूर्व में समाप्त हो गया किन्तु वर्तमान से उसका सम्बन्ध है। चुका है, चुके हैं, चुकी है आदि से इसकी क्रिया समाप्त रहती है।

Assertive—Sub. + has/have + verb^3 + obj ......

Negative—Not/never को has/have के पश्चात् रखें।

Interrogative—Wh + has/have + sub. + not/never + verb^3

Note. इसमें ऐसा काल-संकेत न दें जिससे कार्य भूतकाल में समाप्त हो गया बताए। जैसे–

He has passed the examination last year. (incorrect)

He passed the examination (or had passed ....) last year. (Correct)

1. उसके सभी प्रयास निष्फल हो चुके हैं।

   All his efforts have ended in smoke. (or .... have come to nought.)

2. तूफान पीड़ित लोगों की अभी तक प्रशासन ने सहायता नहीं की है।

   The administration has not yet provided relief-work to the storm-stricken people.

3. क्या तुमने अपने बाग में गुलाब के फूल नहीं लगाए हैं ?

   Have you not planted roses in your garden ?

4. तुम यहाँ किसका छाता लाए हो ?

   Whose umbrella have you brought here ?

5. किस चीज ने तुम्हें दुखी किया है ?

   What (or which thing) has distressed you ?

4. Present Perfect Continuous—Continuous जैसी ही इसकी भी क्रिया रहा है, रहे हैं, रही है आदि जैसी समाप्त रहती है किन्तु इसमें समय का संकेत रहता है जिसके लिए since/for का प्रयोग किया जाता है। इस प्रसंग में since/for + time का प्रयोग indefinite तथा continuous tense में नहीं करना चाहिए।

Assertive—Sub. + has/have + been + verb में ing + since/for + time.

Negative—Has/have के पश्चात् not/never को रखें।

Interrogative—Wh + has/have + sub. + not/never + been + verb में ing since/for + time.

1. रघू तीन दिनों से काम पर आ रहा है।

Raghu has been coming on duty for three days.

2. हम लोग जुलाई से लखनऊ में नहीं रह रहे हैं।

We have not been living in Lucknow since July.

3. कितने विद्यार्थी एक माह से बिना टिकट यात्रा कर रहे हैं।

How many students have been travelling without ticket for one month ?

4. किस सड़क को मजदूर सोमवार से बना रहे हैं ?

Which road have the labourers been constructing since Monday ?

5. कितने तीर्थयात्री सुबह से संगम में स्नान कर रहे हैं ?

How many pilgrims have been bathing in the confluence since morning ?

Exercise 1
(Present Indefinite)

Translate into English :

1. वह यहाँ रहता है।
2. मैं धूम्रपान नहीं करता हूँ।
3. वे लोग चित्र बनाते हैं।
4. बन्दर वृक्ष पर चढ़ते हैं।
5. हवा बहती है।
6. सूर्य पश्चिम में डूबता है।
7. बच्चा ठंड से काँपता है।
8. वह कुर्सी पर बैठती है।
9. मेरी माता मुझे प्यार करती हैं।
10. मनुष्य इच्छा करता है।
11. ईश्वर अन्यथा सोचता है।
12. इस पर राजा आर्थर (Arthur) आज्ञा देता है और पर्दा गिरता है।
13. हमें दो हाथ हैं।
14. अच्छे दिन हवा के सदृश चले जाते हैं।
15. नदी तेज बहती है।
16. उस वन में एक साधू रहते हैं।
17. मेरा नौकर झपकी लिया करता है।
18. दो दो मिलकर चार होते हैं।
19. उधार लिए कपड़े उपयुक्त नहीं बैठते।
20. धुँआ आग से निकलता है।

Hints—धूम्रपान करना—to smoke, चढ़ना—to climb, डूबना—to set, काँपना—to shiver, इच्छा करना—to desire, to wish, अन्यथा—otherwise, पर्दा—curtain, गिरना—to fall, हवा के सदृश—like (or as) wind, तेज—rapidly, साधु—saint, sage, झपकी लेना—to doze or to take nap, उधार लिए कपड़े—borrowed garments, उपयुक्त बैठना—to fit well, निकलना—to come out, to emanate.

1. क्या तुम्हारे पिता कलकत्ता जाते हैं ?
2. क्या वे लोग घोड़े पर चढ़ते हैं ?
3. गोविन्द क्यों रोता है ?
4. तुम सिनेमा क्यों नहीं जाते हो ?
5. बच्चे कक्षा में शोर क्यों मचाते हैं ?
6. तुम उसे सलाह क्यों नहीं देते हो ?
7. मैं कभी झूठ नहीं बोलता।
8. संसार इस बारे में कुछ नहीं जानता।
9. शिवाजी को कौन नहीं जानता ?
10. क्या तुम मेरे मित्र को पहचानते हो ?
11. यहूदी कहाँ रहते हैं ?
12. वह पढ़ाने में रुचि नहीं लेता।
13. क्या बच्चे घरौंदा बनाते हैं ?
14. तुम कब सोने जाते हो ?
15. इस जंगल में कितने शेर रहते हैं ?
16. गरीबों के जीवन में बसन्त कभी नहीं आता।
17. क्या तुम मेरा घर जानते हो ?
18. तुम समाचार-पत्र क्यों नहीं पढ़ते ?
19. ग्रीष्म में तुम कितनी बार नहाते हो ?
20. वह किसे झूठा कहता है ?

Hints—चढ़ना (घोड़े पर)–to ride, शोर मचाना–to make a noise, सलाह देना–to advise, इस बारे में–about this, पहचानना–to recognise, यहूदी–Jews, रुचि लेना–to take interest, पढ़ाने में–in teaching, घरौंदा–mud castle, सोने जाना–to go to bed, बसन्त–spring, गरीबों के जीवन में–in the life of the poor, झूठा–liar, कहना–to call.

Exercise 2
(Present Continuous)

Translate into English :

1. मैं बलिया जा रहा हूँ।
2. वह एक सेब खा रहा है।
3. राधा बाँसुरी बजा रही है।
4. गोपी नाच रहा है।
5. हम लोग मैच देखने जा रहे हैं।
6. सियार हुँआ-हुँआ कर रहे हैं।
7. सूखे पत्ते पेड़ से गिर रहे हैं।
8. कुछ लोग वहाँ मछली मार रहे हैं।
9. किसान खेत जोत रहे हैं।
10. मजदूर पत्थर तोड़ रहे हैं।
11. अँधेरा हो रहा है।
12. कुत्ते भौंक रहे हैं।
13. वह तुम्हारा स्कूटर इधर-उधर चला रहा है।
14. अध्यापक एक कहानी नहीं लिख रहे हैं।
15. वह दीपक जला रही है।
16. नौकरानी कभी नहीं आ रही है।
17. बहुत लोग इस पवित्र अवसर पर गंगा में स्नान कर रहे हैं।
18. हरी पत्तियाँ टहनियों से निकल रही हैं।
19. तुम कभी विद्यालय नहीं जा रहे हो।
20. विमान धीरे-धीरे नीचे आ रहा है।

Hints—बाँसुरी बजाना–to play the flute, हुँआ-हुँआ करना–to howl, सूखे पत्ते–dry leaves, मछली मारना–to fish, जोतना–to plaugh, to till, अँधेरा हो रहा है–is getting dark, भौंकना–to bark, इधर-उधर–to and fro, चलाना–to drive, जलाना–to light (up), to kindle, इस पवित्र अवसर पर–on (at) this holy occasion, टहनियाँ–twigs, निकलना–to sprout, धीरे-धीरे–slowly, विमान–plane, aeroplane, देखना–to see.

1. क्या बिल्ली कुत्ते पर नहीं झपट रही है ?
2. क्या वह अन्तिम साँस ले रहा है ?
3. क्या बुड्ढा नहीं कराह रहा है ?
4. वे लोग क्यों मेरा अपमान कर रहे हैं ?
5. आजकल तुम कहाँ रह रहे हो ?
6. क्या लोग पूजा की तैयारी नहीं कर रहे हैं ?

7. हवा नहीं बह रही है।

8. ये झरने क्या कह रहे हैं ?

9. क्या फसल कटने का समय आ रहा है ?

10. पानी नहीं बरस रहा है।

11. तुम कैसे लिख रहे हो ?

12. आज माँ कहानी क्यों नहीं सुना रही है ?

13. वे लोग झटपट कहाँ जा रहे हैं ?

14. हरी मेरे बारे में क्या कह रहा है ?

15. दरवाजा कौन खटखटा रहा है ?

16. कौन दूसरे कमरे में हँस रहा है ?

17. तुम किसकी किताब पढ़ रहे हो ?

18. कितने लोग मलेरिया से पीड़ित हो रहे हैं ?

19. लड़के प्रयोगशाला में क्या कर रहे हैं ?

20. आकाश से क्या गिर रहा है ?

Hints—झपटना—to jump upon, to pounce upon, अन्तिम साँस लेना—to breath one's last, कराहना—to moan, अपमान करना—to insult (or to affront), तैयारी करना—to prepare, झरने—springs, फसल—harvest, झटपट—hurriedly, खटखटाना—to knock at, मलेरिया—malaria, पीड़ित होना—to suffer, प्रयोगशाला—laboratory.

Exercise 3
(Present Perfect)

Translate into English :

1. मैंने शाकुन्तलम् पढ़ा है।

2. वह स्नान कर चुका है।

3. वे दिन हवा के साथ जा चुके हैं।

4. अतिथि आ चुके हैं।

5. बादल पहाड़ पर इकट्ठे हो गए हैं।

6. नेताजी ने भाषण दिया है।

7. भारत ने अपना सम्बन्ध उस राष्ट्र से तोड़ लिया है।

8. जहाजों ने शरण ले लिया है।

9. शत्रु तलवार खींच चुका है।

10. सितारे डूब चुके हैं।

11. मैंने बेहतर दिन देखे हैं।

12. हम लोग इन्द्रधनुष देखें हैं।

13. पुलिस ने चोर को पकड़ लिया है।

14. हमारी टीम ने मैच जीत लिया है।

15. शत्रुओं ने हथियार डाल दिया है।

16. उसने सभी प्रश्न हल नहीं किया है।

17. मैंने कश्मीर भ्रमण नहीं किया है।

18. मैंने उसे कभी नहीं बुलाया है।

19. कम्पनी ने उसे नियुक्त नहीं किया है।

20. अध्यापक ने उसका आवेदन अस्वीकार कर दिया है।

Hints—पढ़ा है—have read (or gone through), हवा के साथ—with the wind, अतिथि—guests, बादल—clouds, इकट्ठा होना—to muster, भाषण देना—to make a speech, to deliver a lecture, सम्बन्ध तोड़ना—to severe the relation, शरण लेना—to take shelter, शत्रु—enemy, तलवार—sword, खींचना—to draw, डूबना—to sink (or to set), इन्द्रधनुष—rainbow, पकड़ना—to catch (or to arrest), जीतना—to win, हथियार डालना—to lay down arms, हथियार उठा लेना—to take up arms, हल करना—to solve (or to work out), भ्रमण करना—to visit, नियुक्त करना—to appoint, आवेदन—application, अस्वीकार करना—to reject.

1. क्या कभी तुमने यह सोचा है ?

2. क्या हमारे सैनिकों ने दुश्मन को पीछे ढकेल दिया है ?

3. क्या उसने उच्च शिक्षा प्राप्त नहीं किया है ?

4. तुमने कालेज क्यों छोड़ दिया है ?

5. वह अपना छाता कहं खो दी है ?

6. गाड़ी अभी तक क्यों नहीं आई है ?

7. तुम लोगों ने निबन्ध कैसे लिखा है ?

8. क्या आज बर्फ गिर रही है ?

9. क्या उसके अभिनन्दन में परियाँ गीत नहीं गाई हैं ?

10. काव्यात्मक शैली पर किसने प्रचुर प्रकाश डाला है ?

11. तुमने उसे सूचित नहीं किया है ?
12. बिल्ली कितना दूध पी चुकी है ?
13. तुम्हें किसने प्रेरित किया है ?
14. तुमने यह कलम कहाँ पाई है ?
15. क्या यह रीति अब असामयिक नहीं हो गई है ?

16. तुम्हारे पिताजी ने नौकर को कहाँ भेजा है ?
17. मैंने तुम्हारी सहायता कब नहीं की है ?
18. डाक्टर ने रोगियों को अभी तक क्यों नहीं देखा है ?
19. शायद तुमने वह ऊषाकाल नहीं देखा है ?
20. किस आधार पर न्यायाधीश ने उसे दोषी पाया है ?

Hints—कभी–ever, सैनिक–soldier, पीछे ढकेल देना–to thrust back, उच्च शिक्षा प्राप्त करना–to obtain high education, छोड़ना–to leave, खोना–to lose, आना–to arrive, अभिनन्दन–reception (or welcome), परियाँ–fairies, काव्यात्मक शैली–poetic diction (or style), प्रचुर प्रकाश डालना–to throw ample light on, सूचित करना–to inform, प्रेरित करना–to inspire (or to motivate), रीति–custom, असामयिक होना–to turn out-dated (or become out-dated or obsolete), रोगी–patient, अभी तक–by now, till now, yet, शायद–perhaps, ऊषाकाल–dawn, किस आधार पर–on which (or what) ground, न्यायाधीश–judge, दोषी पाना–to find guilty.

Exercise 4
(Present Perfect Continuous)

Translate into English :

1. भोला चार वर्षों से इस विद्यालय में काम कर रहा है।
2. बच्चा डेढ़ घंटे से रो रहा है।
3. पिछले बुधवार से वर्षा हो रही है।
4. विद्यालय पूर्वाह्न के दस बजे से आरम्भ हो रहा है।
5. दुश्मन बहुत दिनों से सैन्य संगठन कर रहा है।
6. हम लोग बलिया में 1970 से रह रहे हैं।
7. ये राजमिस्त्री छ: माह से यह भवन बना रहे हैं।
8. दुर्भाग्य मार्च से ही मुझ पर काली छाया डाल रहा है।
9. लड़के सन्ध्या से अपने कमरे में पढ़ रहे हैं।
10. वह महिला अपने बच्चे को पाँच मिनट से खिला रही है।

11. वे डेढ़ घंटे से वहाँ जमीन खोद रहे हैं।
12. किसान प्रात:काल से खेत जोत रहे हैं।
13. अध्यापक जुलाई से अंग्रेजी पढ़ा रहे हैं।
14. मैं आधे घंटे से उस समस्या पर सिर खुजला रहा हूँ।
15. लड़के दोपहर से पतंग नहीं उड़ा रहे हैं।
16. उसकी बहन उसे दस मिनट से डाँट रही है।
17. वह आधे घंटे से घुमा फिराकर बातें कर रहा है।
18. वह सुबह से कभी प्यानों नहीं बजा रही है।
19. अध्यापक आठ माह से वह किताब लिख रहे हैं।
20. वह दस वर्षों से विपत्ति का सामना कर रही है।

Hints—काम करना–to serve, डेढ़ घंटा–an hour and a half, पूर्वाह्न–A.M. (or a.m. Ante meridiem), उत्तराह्न–P.M. (or p.m. post meridiem), सैन्य संगठन करना–to mobilize, राजमिस्त्री–mason, बनाना, निर्माण करना–to construct (or to erect), भवन–building, दुर्भाग्य–misfortune, काली छाया डालना–to cast gloomy shadow on, खिलाना–to feed, खोदना–to dig, to turn up, समस्या–problem, सिर खुजलाना–to cudgel one's brains for, डाँटना–to chide, to scold, घुमा फिराकर बात करना–to beat about the bush, प्यानो बजाना–to play the piano, विपत्ति–calamity, misery, सामना करना–to face.

1. क्या आप लोग आगामी शुक्रवार से मुम्बई नहीं जा रहे हैं ?
2. वे लोग दोपहर से आपस में क्यों झगड़ रहे हैं ?
3. क्या फटिक पाँच वर्षों से नौकरी नहीं ढूँढ़ रहा है ?
4. क्या संसद-सत्र एक माह से चल रहा है ?
5. पिछले कुछ दिनों से वह क्यों विद्यालय से भाग रहा है ?
6. क्या हम उनको जुलाई से ही पत्र नहीं लिख रहे हैं ?

7. तुम किस तस्वीर को तीन दिनों से खींच रहे हो ?

8. क्या सीमा रविवार से ज्वर से पीड़ित हो रही है ?

9. तुम बहुत दिनों से दवा क्यों नहीं ले रहे हो ?

10. क्या मई से ही बादल आकाश में घिर रहे हैं ?

11. छ: माह से तुम क्या कर रहे हो ?

12. अध्यापक तीन घंटों से क्यों पढ़ा रहे हैं ?

13. वह कितने दिनों से यहाँ नहीं आ रहा है ?

14. यांत्रिक एक घंटे से कार की मरम्मत नहीं कर रहा है।

15. तुम लोग किसके बारे में दो बजे से बात कर रहे हो ?

16. चिड़ियाँ आधे घंटे से वहाँ क्यों इकट्ठी हो रही हैं ?

17. गिद्ध प्रातःकाल से आकाश में नहीं उड़ रहे हैं।

18. मैं वहाँ दो दिनों से कभी नहीं जा रहा हूँ।

19. कितने सैनिक आधी रात से गोली नहीं चला रहे हैं ?

20. आधे घंटे से तुम अकेले में किससे बातें कर रहे हो ?

Hints—आगामी–coming, आपस में–among, संसद्-सत्र–the session of the parliament, चलना–to go on, भागना (विद्यालय से)–to play truant, ज्वर से पीड़ित होना–to suffer from fever, यांत्रिक–mechanic, मरम्मत करना–to repair, इकट्ठा होना–to flock (to swarm), गोली चलाना–to fire, आधी रात–midnight, अकेले में–lonely, गिद्ध–vulture.

Exercise 5

Correct the following sentences :

1. Where you goes ?

2. Have he finish his work ?

3. They are reading here for last Monday ?

4. Jackals howls in the woods.

5. Have the trees dancing in the wind ?

6. I have tell you yesterday.

7. Are you knowing him ?

8. Have not you performed the duty ?

9. Have the Inspector reported against you yesterday ?

10. Do not I request you for two months ?

11. The elephants does not drink water in the river.

12. Have the physician not treating him since twenty days ?

13. We have lodged a protest long before.

14. Death quitted all scores.

15. A live ass was better than a dead lion.

16. Do alcohol not act on brains ?

Exercise 6

Fill up the appropriate forms of Present tense in the following sentences :

1. The peasants ...... threshing ...... ten days.

2. ...... we not ...... complaining of food shortage ...... last April ?

3. His manners ...... revealed his vulgarity.

4. Authority ...... a dying king. (forget).

5. ...... you done, my friend ?

6. I ...... tea daily in the morning. (take)

7. One swallow ...... not bring a summer. (can)

8. Of course, you ...... a yeoman's service. (do)

9. Who ...... his heart's desire ? (find)

10. We ...... here a miracle. (see)

Exercise 7

Translate into English :

1. डाकिया तुम्हारे यहाँ कब आता है ?

2. परियाँ कब तुमसे कहानी कहती हैं ?

3. तुम लोग उसकी देख-रेख क्यों नहीं करते हो ?

4. तुम कौन से सर्ग को सबसे अधिक पसन्द करते हो ?

5. वह किस रास्ते से जाता है ?

6. किसका लड़का कक्षा में प्रथम आता है ?

7. वे किससे घृणा करते हैं ?

8. तुम वास्तव में इसका क्या अर्थ लगाते हो ?

9. तुम्हारा क्या हाल है ?	16. वह किस चीज के लिए चिल्ला रहा है ?
10. चन्द्रमा देखने में कैसा लगता है ? ·	17. हम लोग कितनी दूर चले हैं ?
11. विवेकानन्द के जीवन से तुम क्या सीखते हो ?	18. अपनी प्रशंसा किसने पसन्द नहीं की है ?
12. बलिया से वाराणसी कितनी दूर है ?	19. ये फूल किसके लिए खिल रहे हैं ?
13. तुम्हारे पास कितनी कुर्सियाँ हैं ?	20. कितने लड़के सोमवार से अनुपस्थित हो रहे हैं ?
14. क्या पृथ्वी सूर्य के चारों ओर नहीं घूमती ?	21. इस कहानी से तुमने क्या सीखा है ?
15. वह किसके लिए फूट-फूट कर रो रही है ?	

Hints—डाकिया–postman, खजाना–treasure, देख-रेख करना–to look after, सर्ग–chapter, सबसे अधिक–most, घृणा करना–to hate, वास्तव में–really, अर्थ लगाना–to mean, देखने में लगता है–to look like, सीखना–to learn, घूमना–to move, फूट-फूट कर रोना–to weep bitterly, किस चीज के लिए–for what, प्रशंसा–praise, खिलना–to bloom, अनुपस्थित रहना–to remain absent.

2. Past Tense (भूतकाल)

1. Past Indefinite—इसे simple past भी कहा जाता है। ता था, ते थे, ती थी आदि अथवा पढ़ा, दौड़ा आदि जैसी इसकी क्रिया समाप्त रहती है। इससे आदत का भाव भी व्यक्त होता है।

Assertive—Subject + verb^2 object ......

Negative—Subject + did not + verb^1 + object ......

      Subject + never + verb^2 + object

Interrogative—Wh + did + sub. + not/never + verb^1 + object ......

1. राजपूत बहादुरी से लड़े।	The Rajputs fought bravely.
2. तुमने खूब प्रयास नहीं किया।	You did not try your best.
3. मैंने वैसी कभी टिप्पणी नहीं की।	I never remarked so.
4. क्या कभी तुमने वैसा सोचा ?	Did you ever think so ?
5. क्या तुमने उसकी असफलता के बारे में नहीं सुना ?	Did you not hear of his failure ?
6. विमान कब दुर्घटनाग्रस्त हुआ ?	When did the plane crash ?
7. तुम लोग मुँह छिपाकर क्यों हँसे ?	Why did you laugh in your sleeve ?
8. वह हमेशा नई पुस्तकें खरीदा करता था।	He always bought new books.

2. Past Continuous—यह भूतकाल में निरन्तरता से घटित क्रिया को रहा था, रहे थे, रही थी आदि से प्रगट करता है।

Assertive—Subject + to be (was, were) + verb में ing + object ......

Negative—not/never को to be के बाद रखें।

Interrogative—Wh + to be + sub. + not/never + verb में ing + object ......

1. सितारे आकाश में टिमटिमा रहे थे।	Stars were twinkling in the sky.
2. हवा नहीं बह रही थी।	The wind was not blowing. *Or* It was not blowing.
3. क्या लोग मतदान करने नहीं जा रहे थे ?	Were the people not going to vote ?
4. तुम लोग भोजन कैसे पका रहे थे ?	How were you cooking ?

5. कितने लोग विषाक्त भोजन से पीड़ित हो रहे थे ? How many men were suffering from the poisonous (or contaminated) food ?

3. Past Perfect—यहाँ हिन्दी की क्रिया प्रायः चुका था, चुके थे, चुकी थी आदि से समाप्त रहती है। Simple past की अपेक्षा यह सुदूर का भूतकाल बताता है। इसमें प्रायः दो कार्यों का संकेत रहा करता है—एक पूर्व में घटित तथा अन्य उसके पश्चात्। जो कार्य पहले हो चुका था उसे past perfect (had + verb³) तथा जो बाद में हुआ उसे simple past में रखा जाता है। इस हेतु before/after का प्रयोग किया जाता है।

Assertive—Subject + had + verb³ + object + before/after + sub. + verb² ......

Negative—not/never को had के पश्चात् रखें।

Interrogative—Wh + had + sub. + not/never + verb³ + object + before/after + sub. + verb² ......

1. पुलिस के आने से पूर्व डाकू भाग गए थे।

The robbers had escaped before the police arrived.

2. डाक्टर के आने के पश्चात् रोगी नहीं मरा था।

The patient did not die after the doctor had come.

3. क्या परीक्षा निकट आने से पूर्व तुमने अच्छी तैयारी नहीं की थी ?

Had you not prepared well before the examination came near ?

4. नेता के बोलने के पश्चात् श्रोता क्यों नहीं शान्त हो चुके थे ?

Why did the audience not become quiet after the leader had spoken ?

5. स्वामी के आज्ञा देने से पूर्व नौकर ने क्या किया था ?

What had the servant done before the master ordered ?

6. तुमने किस स्थान को प्राथमिकता दिया था ?

Which place had you preferred ?

4. Past Perfect Continuous—इसकी क्रिया continuous tense जैसी हुआ करती है किन्तु इसके साथ समय-संकेत रहा करता है।

Assertive—Subject + had been + verb में ing + object + since/for + time ......

Negative—not/never को had के पश्चात् रखा जाता है।

Interrogative—Wh + had + sub. + not/never + been + verb में ing + object + since/for + time ......

1. ग्रामीण दो दिनों से पानी का बहाव रोक रहे थे।

The villagers had been stopping the flow of water for two days.

2. जून से ही वर्षा नहीं हो रही थी।

It had not been raining since June.

3. क्या कीमतें चार माह से नहीं बढ़ रही थीं ?

Had the prices not been rising for four months ?

4. तुम्हारे साथ कौन एक वर्ष से सौदेबाजी कर रहा था ?

Who had been making a bargain with you for one year ? (... or been bargaining with ?)

5. वे लोग जुलाई से कहाँ रह रहे थे ?

Where had they been living since July ?

Exercise 1
(Past Indefinite)

Translate into English :

1. चपरासी ने घंटा बजाया।
2. उसके मन में एक अनुपम विचार आया।
3. वह तड़के उठता और एक मील टहलता।
4. भूत आया और मेरे सामने खड़ा हो गया।
5. नौका नदी में डूब गई।
6. श्री मारकोनी ने बेतार के तार का आविष्कार किया।
7. दुर्घटना में 25 आदमी अपने जान गँवाए।
8. मगध में एक राजा रहता था।

9. उन्होंने अपने युग के कवियों की आलोचना की।
10. कुछ लोगों ने उसकी हत्या का प्रयास किया।
11. मैं आया, मैंने देखा, मैंने जीत लिया।
12. उसने एक मोटर साइकिल खरीदा।
13. चोर नौ दो ग्यारह हो गए।
14. उसने कर्ज से छुटकारा पा लिया।
15. शिकारी कुत्तों ने नदी पार कर ली।
16. उसने अपना सबकुछ खो दिया।

Hints—चपरासी—peon, बजाना—to ring, मन में—in mind, एक अनुपम विचार—a unique idea, आया—dawned on, भूत—ghost, सामने—in front of, डूबना—to sink, बेतार का तार—wireless telegraphy, आविष्कार करना—to invent, दुर्घटना—accident, जान गँवाना—to lose one's life, युग—age, आलोचना करना—to criticise, हत्या का प्रयास करना—to attempt one's life, जीतना—to conquer, नौ दो ग्यारह होना—to take to one's heels, कर्ज—debt, छुटकारा पाना—to get rid of, शिकारी कुत्ते—hounds, पार करना—to cross, सब कुछ खो दिया—lost all.

1. उसने अपना साहस नहीं खोया।
2. बुद्ध ने अपना राजमहल क्यों छोड़ा ?
3. क्या मोहन ने परीक्षा नहीं दी ?
4. राम आज काम पर क्यों नहीं आया ?
5. उनका कोई स्पष्ट जीवन दर्शन नहीं था।
6. क्या मैंने तुम्हें हृदय से नहीं चाहा ?
7. वे लोग कैसे निर्णय लिया करते थे ?
8. तुम लोगों ने जल्दबाजी में क्यों कदम उठाया ?

9. छात्रों ने अपना पाठ याद नहीं किया।
10. क्या शंकराचार्य ने हिन्दुओं में नवजीवन का संचार नहीं किया ?
11. आपके बारे में क्या हुआ ?
12. तुम किसलिए यहाँ आए ?
13. क्या उसे एक अनूठी उपाय सूझी ?
14. उस अवसर पर तुमने कायरता क्यों दिखाई ?
15. यह कहकर उसने अनाधिकार हस्तक्षेप क्यों किया ?

Hints—साहस खोना—to break one's heart, राजमहल—palace, छोड़ना—to renounce, परीक्षा देना—to take the examination, स्पष्ट जीवन दर्शन—a clear philosophy of life, हृदय से—from one's heart (wholeheartedly), निर्णय लेना—to take decision, कदम उठाना—to take step, नवजीवन का संचार करना—to charge a new life into, तुम्हारे बारे में क्या हुआ ?—what about you ?, किसलिए—why, for what, what brought you here ?, अनूठी उपाय सूझना—to strike out a novel (or strange) trick (or plan), अवसर—occasion, कायरता दिखाना—to show the white feather, to act cowardly, यह कहकर—saying this, अनाधिकार हस्तक्षेप करना—to meddle with (or to interfere in or be officious to).

Exercise 2
(Past Continuous)

Translate into English :

1. बर्फ गिर रही थी।
2. नदी बह रही थी।
3. चन्द्रमा आकाश में चमक रहा था।
4. चिड़ियाँ गा रही थीं।
5. वह फूट-फूट कर रो रही थी।
6. वह एक महाकाव्य लिख रहे थे।
7. जुलूस कचहरी की ओर बढ़ रहा था।
8. पुलिस लोगों पर लाठी चार्ज कर रही थी।
9. वे पृष्ठ कल्पनाओं से चमक रहे थे।
10. बच्चा ठंड के कारण सिर से पैर तक काँप रहा था।
11. उसकी असहायता का अनुचित लाभ वे लोग उठा रहे थे।
12. लड़के मुँह बना रहे थे ?
13. वह स्वयं को बेवकूफ बना रहा था।
14. लोग चोर की खूब हजामत बना रहे थे।
15. वह अपने भाई की बदनामी कर रहा था।

Hints—चमकना–to shine, महाकाव्य–epic, जुलूस–procession (rally), बढ़ना–to advance, लाठी चार्ज करना–to lathi charge, कल्पना–imagination, चमकना–to sparkle with, ठंड के कारण–due to cold, सिर से पैर तक–from head to foot, असहायता–helplessness, अनुचित लाभ उठाना–to take undue advantage (of), मुँह बनाना–to make faces, स्वयं को बेवकूफ बनाना–to make an ass of oneself, खूब हजामत बनाना–to beat black and blue. बदनामी करना–to blackmail.

1. क्या हरी तुम्हारी सहायता नहीं कर रहा था ?
2. क्या उस समय तुम लोग सो रहे थे ?
3. वे लोग पूजा नहीं कर रहे थे।
4. तुम उसे क्यों पीट रहे थे ?
5. रमेश किसे बुला रहा था ?
6. कितने सदस्य बिल (bill) का विरोध कर रहे थे ?
7. मैं तुम्हें गाली नहीं दे रहा था।
8. तब वे लोग क्या कर रहे थे ?
9. राहुल प्रतियोगिता परीक्षा में नहीं बैठ रहा था।
10. तुम अपना ही राग क्यों अलाप रहे थे ?
11. क्या पानी की कमी से लोग वहाँ नहीं मर रहे थे ?
12. तुम कहाँ से आ रहे थे ?
13. कौन लड़का उसे धमकी दे रहा था ?
14. अध्यापक तुम्हें क्यों पीट रहे थे ?
15. पिताजी किसे उपदेश दे रहे थे ?

Hints—पूजा करना–to worship, विरोध करना–to oppose, प्रतियोगी परीक्षा–competitive examination, अपना राग अलापना–to blow one's own trumpet, पानी की कमी से–in lack of (for want of) water, धमकी देना–to threaten, उपदेश देना–to preach.

Exercise 3
(Past Perfect)

Translate into English :

1. मेरे स्टेशन पहुँचने से पहले गाड़ी खुल चुकी थी।
2. शिक्षक के आने से पहले लड़के पाठ याद कर चुके थे।
3. तुम्हारे आने से पहले मैं जा चुका था।
4. वर्षा होने के पूर्व किसान भूसा उड़ा चुका था।
5. उसकी मृत्यु के बाद उसकी ख्याति समाप्त हो गई थी।
6. कुमुक आने से पहले ही सैनिकों ने हथियार डाल दिए थे।
7. मेरी चिट्ठी पहुँचने से पूर्व ही वह चल दिया था।

8. पेड़ गिरने के पूर्व मेरी कार गुजर चुकी थी।
9. खेल शुरू होने से पूर्व भीड़ जमा हो चुकी थी।
10. सूर्यास्त से पूर्व अँधेरा हो चुका था।
11. मेरे वहाँ पहुँचने से पहले दोनों हाथापाई कर चुके थे।
12. दोनों देश पुरानी शत्रुता मिटा चुके थे।

13. मेरे आने के पश्चात् उसने मुझसे बात नहीं किया था।
14. हम लोगों के पहुँचने के बाद सिनेमा शुरू हो चुका था।
15. उसके सलाह देने से पहले ही मैं स्थान छोड़ने का निश्चय कर चुका था।

Hints—खुलना–to depart, भूसा उड़ाना–to winnow the chaff, ख्याति–popularity, समाप्त होना–to sink, कुमुक–convoy, गुजरना–to pass on, भीड़–crowd, जमा होना–to assemble, हाथापाई करना–to come to blow, शत्रुता मिटाना–to bury the hatchet, निश्चय करना–to determine, make up one's mind.

1. बालू के रोने से पहले तुम मिठाई नहीं लाए थे।
2. खेल शुरू होने से पहले वह कहाँ चला गया था ?
3. सूर्य निकलने से पहले हम लोग नहीं जगे थे।
4. शिक्षक के आने से पहले किसने कक्षा में शोर मचाया था ?
5. क्या नौकरी मिलने से पूर्व आपने उसकी सहायता नहीं की थी ?
6. क्या वहाँ जाने के बाद मैंने तुम्हें चेतावनी नहीं दी थी ?
7. भाषण शुरू होने से पूर्व कितने लोग वहाँ जा चुके थे ?
8. उनके बोलने से पहले तुम क्यों बिगड़ गए थे ?

9. मेरे आने से पहले किसने दरवाजा खटखटाया था ?
10. क्या सबेरा होने से पहले ही चीनी सैनिक हार चुके थे ?
11. तुम्हें किसने बहकाया था ?
12. क्या पिता की मृत्यु के पूर्व ही वह अपने पैर पर खड़ा हो चुका था ?
13. क्या उस घटना ने लोगों की आँख नहीं खोल दी थी ?
14. सुबह होने के पश्चात् तुम लोग कितनी दूर जा चुके थे ?
15. अध्यापक द्वारा प्रकाश डालने से पहले तुमने इस प्रश्न को कैसे हल कर लिया था ?

Hints—मिठाई–sweets, जगना–to get up, to wake, चेतावनी देना–to warn, बिगड़ जाना–to become angry, to lose the temper, हारना–to lose the field, बहकाना–to lead astray to mislead, to misguide, पैर पर खड़े होना–to stand on one's own leg, घटना–incident, आँख खोलना–to open the eyes of, प्रकाश डालना–to throw light (on).

Exercise 4
(Past Perfect Continuous)

Translate into English :

1. हम लोग तीन बजे सुबह से ही पढ़ रहे थे।
2. दुश्मन बहुत दिनों से आक्रमण की तैयारी कर रहा था।
3. डा० प्रसाद पाँच वर्षों से मराठों का इतिहास लिख रहे थे।
4. वे लोग दोपहर से नदी में मछली मार रहे थे।
5. घड़ा मंगलवार से ही चू रहा था।
6. पिछली जुलाई से ही तुम मुझसे वादा कर रहे थे।
7. वे लोग दो घंटे से मेरी प्रतीक्षा कर रहे थे।
8. हम लोग परीक्षा की बहुत दिनों से तैयारी कर रहे थे।

9. किसान बीस दिनों से फसल काट रहे थे।
10. तुम दो घंटे से कहानी लिख रहे थे।
11. आचार्य बुधवार से पढ़ा रहे थे।
12. वह एक माह से नशीला पदार्थ ले रहा था।
13. अतिथि आधे घंटे से कुप्रबन्ध पर नाक भौं सिकोड़ रहे थे।
14. पुलिस बीस दिनों से अपहृत लड़की की तलाश कर रही थी।
15. उसका भतीजा बारह बजे से स्कूटर का दुरुपयोग कर रहा था।

Hints—आक्रमण–attack, मराठों का इतिहास–the History of the Marathas, चूना–to leak, to ooze, घड़ा–pitcher, वादा करना–to give word, to promise, काटना–to reap, फसल–crop, नशीला पदार्थ लेना–to take drugs, कुप्रबन्ध–poor (bad) arrangement, नाक भौं सिकोड़ना–to turn up one's nose at, अपहृत–abducted, तलाश करना–to search for, भतीजा–nephew, दुरुपयोग करना–to misuse.

1. क्या रसोइया एक घंटे से नाश्ता तैयार कर रहा था ?
2. वह तीन दिनों से विद्यालय क्यों नहीं आ रहा था ?
3. सुबह से ही बाग में कौन गा रहा था ?
4. कितने अभ्यर्थी अक्तूबर से आवेदन कर रहे थे ?
5. तुम क्यों नहीं जुलाई से ही मेहनत कर रहे थे ?
6. कृष्ण चार वर्षों से इस संस्था में काम नहीं कर रहा था।
7. दोपहर से तुम कहाँ घूम रहे थे ?
8. क्या वह एक घंटे से समाचार-पत्र पढ़ रहा था ?
9. वे लोग इतने दिनों से लोगों का शोषण क्यों कर रहे थे ?
10. क्या वर्षा कल से नहीं हो रही थी ?
11. कितने आतंकवादी बहुत दिनों से षड्यंत्र की योजना बना रहे थे ?
12. तुम किसलिए दोपहर से मुझे तंग कर रहे थे ?
13. वह भिखारी पन्द्रह मिनट से किस बारे में बड़बड़ा रहा था ?
14. कितने लड़के उस छात्रावास में चार वर्षों से रह रहे थे ?
15. कौन लड़का कल से दीवार पर लिख रहा था ?

Hints—रसोईया–cook, नाश्ता तैयार करना–to prepare breakfast, अभ्यर्थी–candidate, आवेदन करना–to apply, संस्था–institution, घूमना–to wander, शोषण करना–to exploit, आतंकवादी–terrorist, योजना बनाना–to contrive, षड्यंत्र–conspiracy, तंग करना–to tease, बड़बड़ाना–to grumble.

Exercise 5

Correct the following sentences :

1. You did reach in time ?
2. They not perform their duty.
3. By hatred the emperor had been ruled over the country for forty years.
4. Danger had hanged over his head.
5. He were fighting for a noble cause.
6. Had the poor woman not seeking asylum ?
7. Why not his poems were participating with the society ?
8. When their glory faded ?
9. Idealism did breathed in his pages.
10. Tomorrow I got rid of my debt.
11. All that glittered is not gold.
12. She had been hoping for better days for five years.

Exercise 6

Translate into English :

1. राम ने कितने रन बनाये ?
2. बाबर ने राणासांगा को कब हराया ?
3. तुम कितने घंटे पिछली रात पढ़े ?
4. ग्रीष्म की छुट्टियों में वह क्या करता था ?
5. तुमने कितने बोझे बाँधे ?
6. किस आदमी ने दरोगा को घूस दिया ?
7. नेताजी जेल में क्या कर रहे थे ?
8. उसने तुम्हें कुछ नहीं समझा।
9. तुम कहाँ भागे जा रहे थे ?
10. चोर कितना धन चुरा ले गए थे ?
11. मैंने पहले भी तुमसे कई बार कहा था।
14. हम लोग किस रास्ते से एक घंटे से चल रहे थे ?

Hints—बनाना (रन)–to score, हराना–to defeat, ग्रीष्म की छुट्टी–summer vacation, बोझा–sheaf (sheaves), बाँधना–to bind, घूस देना–to grease the palm of, to bribe, to oil the hand of, कुछ नहीं समझना–to count a fig for, भागे जाना–to head, किस रास्ते से–through which way.

3. Future Tense (भविष्यत् काल)

(a) **Future Indefinite**—सामान्यत: इसकी क्रिया गा, गे, गी से समाप्त होती है। First person (I and we) के साथ shall तथा शेष persons के subjects के साथ will का प्रयोग होता है। यदि कथन पर बल दिया गया हो तो प्रक्रिया विपरीत हो जाती है, अर्थात् I, we के साथ will तथा शेष के साथ shall। इस स्थिति में shall/will के स्थान पर must का भी प्रयोग हो सकेगा।

Assertive—Subject + shall/will + verb[1] object ......

Negative—Shall/will के पश्चात् not/never + verb[1] + object ......

Interrogative—Wh + shall/will + sub. + not/never + verb[1] + object ......

1. मैं तुम्हें एक गोपनीय बात बताऊँगा।	I shall tell you a secret.
2. वह तुम्हें कभी पत्र नहीं लिखेगा।	He will never write you a letter.
3. क्या लोमड़ी हिरन को धोखा नहीं देगी ?	Will the fox not deceive the deer ?
4. गाड़ी कब प्लेटफार्म पर आएगी ?	When will the train arrive at the platform ?
5. बैठक में कितने सदस्य भाग लेंगे ?	How many members will take part in the meeting ?
6. वह अवश्य लौटेगी।	She shall return (or she must return). Give me the robe, I will go. (Caesar)

(b) **Future Continuous**—इसमें क्रिया रहेगा, रहेंगे, रहेगी आदि से समाप्त होती है।

Assertive—Subject + shall/will + be + verb में ing + object ......

Negative—Not/never को shall/will के पश्चात् रखें।

Interrogative—Wh + shall/will + sub. + not/never + be + verb में ing + object ......

1. बाग में आम गिर रहे होंगे।	Mangoes will be falling in the garden.
2. कर्मचारी काम पर नहीं जा रहे होंगे।	Employees will not be going on duty.
3. क्या स्वर्णकार अंगूठी नहीं बना रहा होगा ?	Will the goldsmith not be making the ring ?
4. वे लोग कहाँ जा रहे होंगे ?	Where will they be going ?
5. कितने राजमिस्त्री भवन बना रहे होंगे ?	How many masons will be constructing the building ?

(c) **Future Perfect**—इसमें चुका होगा, चुकी होगी, चुके होंगे आदि जैसी क्रिया अन्त में रहती है। Past perfect की भाँति इस tense में भी प्राय: दो कार्य पूर्व पर सम्पन्न रहा करते हैं जिनका आधार भविष्यगत अनुमान, विश्वास आदि होता है। जो कार्य बाद में रहेगा उसे Present indefinite में रखेंगे क्योंकि एक ही वाक्य में दो future tenses नहीं होते।

Assertive—Subject + shall/will + have + verb[3] + object + before/after + sub. + pre. Ind.......

Negative—Not/never को shall/will के पश्चात् रखें।

Interrogative—Wh + shall/will + sub. +not/never + have + verb[3] +obj. + before/after + sub. + pre. Ind. ......

1. मेरे कार्यालय पहुँचने से पहले लिपिक पत्र-प्रारूप तैयार कर चुकेगा।

The clerk will have made the draft before I reach office.

2. रोगी के सोने के बाद डाक्टर बाहर नहीं जा चुकेगा।

The doctor does not go out after the patient will have slept.

3. क्या दस बजने से पूर्व गाड़ी नहीं पहुँच चुकेगी ?

Will the train not have arrived before it strikes ten ?

4. मैच शुरु होने से पहले कितने लोग वहाँ आ चुकेंगे ?

How many people will have come there before the match starts ?

5. मेरे पढ़ाने से पहले तुम उस प्रश्न को कैसे हल कर चुकोगे ?

How will you have solved the question before I teach you ?

(*d*) **Future Perfect Continuous**—Continuous tense में समय-संकेत इस tense की पहचान है, अर्थात् रहेगा, रहूँगा, रहेगी आदि के साथ समयावधि। इस tense में समय के लिए since का प्रयोग प्रचलित तो है किन्तु व्याकरणाचार्यों के अनुसार since के स्थान पर from का प्रयोग उचित होगा।

Assertive—Subject + shall/will + have been + verb में ing + obj. + from/for + time ......

Negative—Not/never को shall/will के बाद रखें।

Interrogative—Wh + shall/will + sub. + not/never + have been + verb में ing + object + from/for + time ......

1. गड़ेरिए पौ फटने से ही भेड़ों को हाँक रहे होंगे।

The shepherds will have been driving the (heads of) sheep from the break of the day.

2. मजदूर एक माह से फसल नहीं काट रहे होंगे।

The workers will not have been reaping the crop for one month.

3. क्या वे लोग पन्द्रह दिनों से विवाह की तैयारी नहीं कर रहे होंगे ?

Will they not have been preparing for the marriage for fifteen days ?

4. तुम लोग खजाने की खोज में रविवार से ही कहाँ घूम रहे होंगे ?

Where will you have been roaming in quest of the treasure from Sunday ?

5. मेरे प्रस्थान करने के समय से ही अब वे लोग क्यों सिर धुन कर पश्चाताप कर रहे होंगे ?

Why will they have been now repenting sorely from my departure ?

Exercise 1
(Future Indefinite)

Translate into English :

1. हम लोग मंसूरी जाएँगे।
2. लड़कियाँ गीत गाएँगी।
3. डाक्टर आज आएगा।
4. जिलाधिकारी इनाम बाँटेंगे।
5. मैं अपनी कक्षा प्रारम्भ करूँगा।
6. कल मैं उनको एक पत्र लिखूँगा।
7. ईश्वर तुम्हें आशीर्वाद देंगे।
8. आप मेरी प्रार्थना स्वीकार करेंगे।
9. प्रकाशक मुझे शीघ्र जवाब देगा।
10. तुम्हारे दुर्दिन शीघ्र दूर होंगे।
11. तुम वहाँ अवश्य जाओगे।
12. वह परीक्षा में बेहतर करेगा।
13. इस पर मैं अधिक समय तक नहीं टिकूँगा।
14. यह चीज उसके स्वभाव के उपयुक्त नहीं होगी।
15. उसका महत्त्वाकांक्षी प्रयास उसे हतोत्साहित करेगा।

Hints—जिलाधिकारी–collector (or District Magistrate), इनाम बाँटना–to give away the prize, आशीर्वाद देना–to bless, प्रार्थना–request, प्रकाशक–publisher, जवाब देना–to reply, शीघ्र–presently, दुर्दिन–broken (or adverse days), शीघ्र दूर होंगे–to be soon no more, to be over presently, इस पर–at this, अधिक समय तक नहीं–no longer, टिकना–to stand by, स्वभाव–nature, उपयुक्त होना–to suit, महत्त्वाकांक्षी प्रयास–ambitious attempt, हतोत्साहित करना–to discourage.

1. क्या तुम उसे सूचित करोगे ?
2. बादल शीघ्र नहीं छँटेंगे।
3. क्या तुम्हारी दादी कहानी सुनाएगी ?
4. क्या समाज इस घटना से शिक्षा लेगा ?
5. माखन परीक्षा में क्यों नहीं बैठेगा ?
6. क्या राष्ट्रपति आज आएँगे ?
7. महासभा में कितने लोग भाग लेंगे ?
8. वे लोग इसे कभी नहीं स्वीकार करेंगे।
9. क्या आप कृपया मुझे तथ्यों से अवगत कराएँगे ?
10. मैं तुम्हें कभी गलत दिशा नहीं दूँगा।
11. ऐसे बर्ताव के पश्चात् तुम्हारे साथ कौन रहेगा ?
12. तुम वहाँ कैसे रहोगे ?
13. फूल किसके लिए खिलेंगे ?
14. अब तुम कहाँ जाओगे ?
15. कौन सा लड़का सही उत्तर बताएगा ?

Hints—सूचित करना–to inform, छँटना–to disperse, समाज–society, शिक्षा लेना–to take lesson, महासभा–conference, तथ्यों से अवगत कराना–to make oneself acquaint of the facts, गलत दिशा देना–to lead astray (to misguide or to mislead), ऐसे बर्ताव के पश्चात्–after such behaviour.

Exercise 2
(Future Continuous)

Translate into English :

1. पहाड़ पर बादल इकट्ठे हो रहे होंगे।
2. डाक्टर उपचार लिख रहा होगा।
3. आश्रम में कथा चल रही होगी।
4. कलाकार चित्र खींच रहा होगा।
5. बहेलिया आ रहा होगा।
6. मछुआरे जाल डाल रहे होंगे।
7. वे अपने शिविर में खुशी मना रहे होंगे।
8. चन्द्रमा पहाड़ियों के पीछे ढल रहा होगा।
9. क्या पेड़ से सूखे पत्ते गिर रहे होंगे ?
10. वस्तुएँ अपनी कहानी नहीं कह रही होंगी।
11. वह किससे बातें कर रहा होगा ?
12. वह मूर्खता से क्यों व्यवहार कर रहा होगा ?
13. कितने नवयुवक रोजगार बिना समय गँवा रहे होंगे ?
14. वहाँ क्या हो रहा होगा ?
15. वे लोग किस चीज के लिए शोर मचा रहे होंगे ?

Hints—उपचार–prescription, चलना–to go on, बहेलिया–fowler, मछुआरे–fishermen, जाल डालना–to cast net, खुशी मनाना–to rejoice, पहाड़ियों के पीछे–behind the hills, सूखे पत्ते–dry leaves, मूर्खता से–foolishly, रोजगार बिना–without (for want of) employment, समय गँवाना–to waste (or to kill) time, होना–to happen, शिविर–camp.

1. कुहरा गिर रहा होगा।
2. पश्चिमी हवा पहाड़ियों के उस पार बह रही होगी।
3. वह इस बारे में सोच रहा होगा।
4. बच्चा माँ की अनुपस्थिति में रो रहा होगा।
5. लोग आलोचना कर रहे होंगे।
6. खेत सूख रहे होंगे।
7. लड़के परीक्षा दे रहे होंगे।
8. क्या बच्चे खेल रहे होंगे ?

9. बढ़ई कुर्सी नहीं बना रहा होगा।

10. कितने लड़के लगातार विद्यालय आ रहे होंगे ?

11. क्या वह आवाज समाप्त हो रही होगी ?

12. क्या तुम अपना घर नहीं सजा रहे होगे ?

13. मनुष्य कब बृहस्पति पर पदार्पण कर रहा होगा ?

14. आँधी जोर से नहीं चल रही होगी।

15. परीक्षा क्यों नहीं आरम्भ हो रही होगी ?

Hints—कुहरा–fog, उस पार–across, अनुपस्थिति में–in absence of, आलोचना करना–to criticise, सूखना–to dry up, बढ़ई–carpenter, लगातार–regularly, समाप्त होना–to sink, सजाना–to decorate, बृहस्पति–Jupiter, आँधी–storm, जोर से–violently, प्रारम्भ होना–to commence.

Exercise 3
(Future Perfect)

Translate into English :

1. मुझे कोई नुकसान पहुँचाने से पूर्व वे घुटने टेक चुकेंगे।

2. उनके आने से पहले हम लोग धूल में मिल चुकेंगे।

3. ईश्वर के मुस्कराने से पहले संसार वीरान हो चुकेगा।

4. हमारे यहाँ से चलने से पहले ही उसे पत्र मिल चुकेगा।

5. पुलिस के आने के बाद डाकू भाग चुकेंगे।

6. तुम्हारे सोचने से पूर्व मैं सोच चुकूँगा।

7. मजदूरों के आवाज उठाने के पश्चात् वह माँगें स्वीकार कर चुकेगा।

8. वर्षा होने से पहले राजमिस्त्री कार्य बन्द कर चुकेगा।

9. मेरे विद्यालय पहुँचने से पहले ही घंटी बज चुकेगी।

10. इस समय तक वह नदी पार कर चुकेगा।

11. वहाँ नाविकों से नदी सजीव हो उठी होगी।

12. बस अब तक जा चुकेगी।

13. हम लोगों के वहाँ पहुँचने से पहले वर्षा हो चुकेगी।

14. मेरे मना करने से पूर्व वे लोग उसे पीट चुकेंगे।

15. धोबी कल तक कपड़ा धो चुकेगा।

Hints—कोई नुकसान पहुँचाना–to inflict any harm, घुटने टेकना–to bow down upon one's knees, to surrender, धूल में मिलना–to reduce (or to meet) to dust, वीरान होना–to turn deserted, आवाज उठाना–to raise voice, माँग स्वीकार करना–to concede the demand, बज चुकी होगी–will have gone (or rung), इस समय तक–by this time (or by, till now), नाविक–sailors, सजीव हो उठना–to hum with life, मना करना–to forbid.

1. क्या समय आने से पहले वह अपने वचन से पीछे हट चुकेगा ?

2. क्या मेरे भोजन करने से पहले तुम्हारा नौकर आ चुकेगा ?

3. हमारे वहाँ पहुँचने से पहले पिताजी कहाँ जा चुकेंगे ?

4. छात्रावास-अधिकारी के जगने से पहले विद्यार्थी दीपक नहीं जला चुकेंगे।

5. सबेरा होने से पहले हम लोग दस मील क्यों नहीं चल चुकेंगे ?

6. दशहरा आने से पूर्व तुम रामायण के कितने पृष्ठ समाप्त कर चुकोगे ?

7. परिस्थिति खराब होने से पूर्व पुलिस नहीं आ चुकेगी।

8. तुम्हारे टिकट लेने से पहले कितने लोग सिनेमा भवन में प्रवेश कर चुकेंगे ?

9. वकील के बहस करने से पूर्व न्यायाधीश अपना फैसला नहीं सुना चुकेगा।

10. अवसर उसके प्रतिकूल क्यों हो चुकेगा ?

11. क्या अतिथियों के आने से पहले नौकर मेज से भोजन साफ कर चुका होगा ?

12. कितने दुकानदार सन्ध्या होने से पहले अपनी दुकानें बन्द कर चुकेंगे ?

13. क्या खाने से पूर्व वह सो चुकेगा ?

14. वक्ता के आने से पहले कितने लोग वहाँ एकत्रित हो चुकेंगे ?

15. सूर्यास्त होने से पूर्व तीर्थयात्री कितनी दूर जा चुकेंगे ?

Hints—वचन से पीछे हटना–to go back (or behind) from one's word, छात्रावास-अधिकारी–hostel warden, दीपक जलाना–to kindle (or to light up) the lamp, सबेरा होना–day break, परिस्थिति–situation, खराब होना–to worsen, वकील–lawyer (advocate), बहस करना–to plead, फैसला सुनाना–to give one's verdict, प्रतिकूल होना–to go against, मेज से भोजन साफ करना–to clear away the table, दुकानदार–shopkeeper, बन्द करना–to shut, वक्ता–speaker, एकत्रित होना–to assemble, तीर्थयात्री–pilgrim.

Exercise 4
(Future Perfect Continuous)

Translate into English :

1. माली सन्ध्या से बाग सींच रहा होगा।

2. गेहूँ चार माह से सड़ रहा होगा।

3. वे फरवरी से कार्य कर रहे होंगे।

4. नदी पन्द्रह दिनों से बढ़ रही होगी।

5. भारतीय लोकतंत्र शताब्दियों तक फलता फूलता रहेगा।

6. सर्जन उसकी गिल्टी का चीर फाड़ करता रहेगा।

7. वह तीन घंटे से फ्राक सी रही होगी।

8. संगम में सुबह से ही लोग डुबकी लगा रहे होंगे।

9. उनके मन में तीन दिनों से कल्पना घूम रही होगी।

10. यात्रीगण आधी रात से ही गाड़ी की प्रतिक्षा कर रहे होंगे।

11. मेरा मित्र बहुत देर तक फाटक पर क्रोधित भीड़ का सामना करता रहेगा।

12. खोंचे वाला एक हफ्ते से सड़े सन्तरे बेच रहा होगा।

13. आलू आधे घंटे से ऊबल रहा होगा।

14. वे लोग दो माह से विवाह तय कर रहे होंगे।

15. सन्ध्या से ही वे लोग नवागन्तुक का स्वागत कर रहे होंगे।

Hints—माली–gardener, सींचना–to water, सड़ना–to rot, बढ़ना–to deluge, to inundate, लोकतंत्र–democracy, शताब्दियों–centuries, फलना फूलना–to prosper, to flourish, गिल्टी–tumour, चीर फाड़ करना–to operate, सीना–to sew, to tailor, संगम–confluence, डुबकी लगाना–to dip, कल्पना–imagination,

घूमना—to hover, क्रोधित भीड़—angry mob, सामना करना—to face, खोंचे वाला—hawker, सड़े सन्तरे—rotted oranges, उबलना—to boil, नवागन्तुक—newcomer.

1. क्या रमेश प्रतियोगिता के लिए तीन माह से तैयारी नहीं कर रहा होगा ?

2. माँ दिनेश को पन्द्रह मिनट से नहीं डाँट रही होगी।

3. वे लोग तीन बजे से कहाँ मैच खेल रहे होंगे ?

4. ऊषा किस चित्र को दस दिनों से खींच रही होगी ?

5. कितने मजदूर दो दिनों से दँवाई कर रहे होंगे ?

6. वे लोग एक हफ़्ते से मजदूरी क्यों नहीं दे रहे होंगे ?

7. हम लोग इस कमरे में तीन वर्षों तक नहीं रहते रहेंगे ?

8. सन्ध्या से ही तुम किस चिन्ता में डूब रहे होंगे ?

9. क्या सूर्यग्रहण दो बजे से लग रहा होगा ?

10. पाँच मिनट से कौन दरवाजा खटखटा रहा होगा ?

11. ग्वाला एक घंटे से कहाँ दूध दूह रहा होगा ?

12. नृत्य की किस शैली का वह सन्ध्या से अभ्यास कर रही होगी ?

13. किसकी उत्तर पुस्तिका से तुम दस मिनट से नकल कर रहे होंगे ?

14. जुलाई से तुम्हारे साथ कौन आ रहा होगा ?

15. क्या सत्रारम्भ से ही वह खूब मेहनत नहीं कर रहा होगा ?

Hints—दँवाई करना—to thresh, मजदूरी—wages, चिन्ता—worry, anxiety, डूबना—to plunge (into), सूर्यग्रहण—solar eclipse, चन्द्रग्रहण—lunar eclipse, लगना—to commence, दूध दूहना—to milk, शैली—style, अभ्यास करना—to practise (to exercise), उत्तर पुस्तिका—answer book, नकल करना—to copy, सत्र—session.

Exercise 5
(Begin with Wh Words)

Make questions of the following answers :

1. My name is Shyam.

2. My father is a V.I.P.

3. I am working out a sum here.

4. This road will lead to eternity.

5. There were sixteen annas in a rupee.

6. They have saved fifteen men from drowning.

7. It was really a very pitiable sight.

8. He will have retired in June.

9. He is no relation to me.

10. It is Sunday today.

11. The giraffe has a long neck.

12. I have received the appointment.

Exercise 6

Translate into English :

1. किस विद्यालय के छात्र पाँच बजे से झगड़ा कर रहे होंगे ?
2. उनसे क्यों बातें करें ?
3. इससे क्या जो हम गरीब हैं ?
4. वह कहाँ से आता है ?
5. तुम्हें मूर्ख किसने कहा ?
6. वर्षा कब से हो रही है ?
7. वे किसलिए उसका अपमान कर रहे होंगे ?
8. मेरे दौड़ने से पहले तुम वहाँ कैसे पहुँच चुके थे ?
9. वे लोग क्यों नहीं अब तक समस्या हल कर चुके हैं ?
10. किस कारण तुम्हारे चाचा तुम्हारी सहायता नहीं कर रहे हैं ?
11. माँ के आने से पूर्व तुम किसका उपन्यास पढ़ चुकोगे ?
12. मन्दिर में कौन पूजा कर रहा था ?
13. सन्ध्या से किसके लिए सितारे जगमगा रहे थे ?
14. वह क्या कह रहा है ?
15. शिवाजी ने कौन सी नीति स्वीकार की ?

Hints—अपमान करना–to insult, समस्या–problem, उपन्यास–novel, जगमगाता–to shine (to twinkle), नीति–policy.

Exercise 7

Fill up the blanks and complete the following sentences according to the rules of future tense :

1. ...... you please ...... me for shameful behaviour ?
2. I shall have blazed the news abroad ......
3. ...... be taking part in the procession ?
4. The French army ...... seizing the castle ...... three o'clock in the morning.
5. But ...... bell the cat ?
6. I ...... attach no importance to your words.
7. The ultimate victory ...... ours.
8. O, God ! when ...... this earth ...... ready to receive thy saints ?
9. Let us meet to dust ...... but we ...... not stand to beggary.
10. 'Literature ...... take care of itself ', answered Mr. Pitt.
11. To it Mr. Southey added, 'yes, and it ...... take care of you too.'
12. They ...... killed the goose before it ...... the golden egg.
13. ...... we ...... making hay ...... the break of the day ?
14. ...... you please ...... me the hospitality of your column ?
15. ...... that road not lead you to destruction ?
16. The principal ...... responsible for the internal management.

Chapter 10

Tenses (Passive Voice कर्मवाच्य)

1. Present Tense

Passive voice (कर्म वाच्य) Transitive verb (सकर्मक क्रिया) का होता है, Intransitive verb (अकर्मक क्रिया) का नहीं। यदि वाक्य में Double objects हो तो दो रूपों में उसका passive voice बनाया जा सकता है। यदि object कोई Reflexive Pronoun (-self or selves *viz*. himself, yourselves etc.) या Reciprocal pronouns (each other, one another) रहेगा तो उसका passive form संभव नहीं है। पुन: यदि वाक्य का verb have, hold, contain, suit, fit, resemble या lack रहेगा तो उस स्थिति में भी वाक्य का passive form अतार्किक होगा। Passive voice में active का object, subject होता है और subject को agent माना जाता है जिसे प्राय: by के द्वारा प्रगट करते हैं। वाक्यों के लक्षण वही होते हैं जिन्हें पिछले अध्यायों में बताया गया है। Passive voice की verb हमेशा third form में रहती है। Active के who से प्रारम्भ होने वाले प्रश्नवाचक वाक्य को By whom से प्रारम्भ करें।

(a) Present Indefinite

Assertive—Object (nominative case में) + to be (is, am, are) + verb^3 + by subject (Active के subject को objective case) में रखें।

Negative—Obj. + to be + not/never + verb^3 + by ......

Interrogative—wh + to be + not/never + verb^3 + by ......

Helping verb do तथा does का passive में लोप हो जाता है।

1. वह शृंगारिक वस्तुएँ बेचता है।
He sells cosmetic items. (Active)
Cosmetic items are sold by him. (Passive)

2. पत्र उसके द्वारा नहीं लिखा जाता है।
The letter is not written by him.

3. क्या अंग्रेजी तुम्हारे अध्यापक द्वारा नहीं पढ़ाई जाती है ?
Is English not taught by your teacher ?

4. किताबें कहाँ छापी जाती हैं ?
Where are books printed ?

5. डकैतों द्वारा बैंक कब लूटा जाता है ?
When is the bank robbed by the dacoits ?

(b) Present Continuous

Assertive—Object + to be + being + verb^3 + by ......

Negative—Not/never को to be के बाद रखें।

Interrogative—wh + to be + obj. + not/never + being + verb^3 + by ......

1. खेत सींचे जा रहे हैं।
Fields are being irrigated.

2. उसके द्वारा एक फ्राक नहीं खरीदा जा रहा है।
A frock is not being bought by her.

3. क्या उन लोगों द्वारा प्रश्नों के उत्तर नहीं दिए जा रहे हैं ?
Are the answers of the questions not being given by them ?

4. किसके द्वारा गुड़िया रंगी जा रही है ?   By whom is the doll being painted ?

5. किसका लड़का अध्यापक द्वारा पीटा जा रहा है ?   Whose son is being beaten by the teacher ?

(c) Present Perfect

Assertive—Object + has/have + been + verb³ + by ......

Negative—Not/never को has/have के पश्चात् रखें।

Interrogative—wh + has/have + obj. + not/never + been verb³ + by ......

1. मेरे द्वारा एक लेख लिखा जा चुका है।   An essay has been written by me.

2. नौकर द्वारा पत्र नहीं छोड़ा गया है।   The letter has not been posted by the servant.

3. क्या अभियन्ताओं द्वारा पुल तैयार नहीं किया जा चुका है ?   Has the bridge not been completed by the engineers ?

4. जवाब क्यों नहीं भेजा जा चुका है ?   Why has the reply not been sent ?

5. बिल्ली द्वारा कितना दूध पीया जा चुका है ?   How much milk has been drunk by the cat ?

Exercise 1
(Present Indefinite)

Translate into English :

1. गेंद बच्चों द्वारा मारी जाती है।
2. खेत जोते जाते हैं।
3. रामलीला लोगों द्वारा देखी जाती है।
4. पुलिस द्वारा रिपोर्ट दी जाती है।
5. फल तोड़े जाते हैं।
6. पत्र छोड़े जाते हैं।
7. लड़के अध्यापक द्वारा दण्डित किए जाते हैं।
8. क्या सद्गुण पढ़ाया जाता है ?
9. तुम किसके द्वारा दुखी किए जाते हो ?
10. अच्छे मनुष्य कहाँ नहीं पाए जाते ?
11. क्या वीरता के गीत गाए जाते हैं ?
12. राजमिस्त्री द्वारा ईंट क्यों नहीं जोड़ी जाती है ?
13. कोयला की खानें अधिकतर कहाँ पायी जाती हैं ?
14. शिक्षक द्वारा व्याकरण कब पढ़ाया जाता है ?
15. कितने घोड़ों को खिलाया जाता है ?

Hints—मारना—to kick, जोतना—to plough, to till, तोड़ना—to pluck, छोड़ना—to post, दंडित करना—to punish, सद्गुण—virtue, किसके द्वारा—by whom, दुखी करना—to trouble, to vex, वीरता के गीत—songs of bravery, ईंट—brick, जोड़ना—to lay, कोयला की खानें—coal-mines, अधिकतर—mostly, खिलाना—to feed.

Exercise 2
(Present Continuous)

Translate into English :

1. फसल काटी जा रही है।
2. सैनिक भर्ती किए जा रहे हैं।
3. कानून तोड़े जा रहे हैं।
4. चित्र बनाए जा रहे हैं।
5. पुस्तकें लिखी जा रही हैं।
6. कार्य किए जा रहे हैं।
7. बीज किसानों में बाँटा जा रहा है।
8. परीक्षार्थियों द्वारा प्रपत्र भरे जा रहे हैं।

9. क्या भक्तों द्वारा ईश्वर की पूजा की जा रही है ?

10. उन लोगों द्वारा प्रयोगात्मक अभ्यास पुस्तिका नहीं लाई जा रही है।

11. किसके द्वारा उनका विश्वास विचलित किया जा रहा है ?

12. कितने घर निर्मित किए जा रहे हैं ?

13. क्या देशभक्त गिरफ्तार किए जा रहे हैं ?

14. क्या अकाल पीड़ित लोगों की सहायता की जा रही है ?

15. कच्चे माल विदेशों से क्यों नहीं मँगाए जा रहे हैं ?

Hints—काटना–to reap, सैनिक–soldier, भर्ती करना–to recruit, to enlist, बीज–seed, बाँटना–to distribute, परीक्षार्थी–examinee, प्रपत्र–form, भरना–to fill up, भक्त–devotee, पूजा करना–to worship, प्रयोगात्मक अभ्यास पुस्तिका–practical exercise book, विश्वास–faith, विचलित करना–to shake, देशभक्त–patriot, गिरफ्तार करना–to arrest, to take into custody, अकाल पीड़ित–famine sricken, कच्चा माल–raw material, विदेश–foreign, मँगाना–to import, निर्यात करना–to export).

Exercise 3
(Present Perfect)

Translate into English :

1. चपरासी द्वारा फाटक खोला जा चुका है।
2. तीन बसें बदमाशों द्वारा जलाई गई हैं।
3. छाया द्वारा बच्चे डराये जा चुके हैं।
4. पन्द्रह यात्री चलती गाड़ी में लूटे गए हैं।
5. मेरे द्वारा सम्पूर्ण दूध पीया गया है।
6. उन लोगों द्वारा धोंधू को घूँसा मारा गया है।
7. तूफान द्वारा जहाज नष्ट कर दी गई है।
8. व्याकरण की एक किताब मेरे शिक्षक द्वारा लिखी गई है।

9. क्या डकैत को दोषी नहीं पाया गया है ?
10. फसल नहीं काटी जा चुकी है।
11. क्या मलबे से पचास आदमियों को नहीं निकाला जा चुका है ?
12. कितने कलाकारों को पुरस्कृत किया गया है ?
13. चपरासी द्वारा कब घंटी बजाई जा चुकी है ?
14. क्या चुनाव में निष्पक्ष नीति अपनाई गई है ?
15. प्रस्ताव किसी के द्वारा स्वीकार नहीं किया गया है।

Hints—बदमाश–miscreant, छाया–shadow, डराना–to frighten, चलती गाड़ी–running train, घूँसा मारना–to box, तूफान–tempest, नष्ट करना–to wreck, दोषी पाना–to find guilty, मलवा–debris, निकालना–to discover, to unearth, पुरस्कृत करना–to reward, निष्पक्ष नीति–the policy of fair field and no favour, the impartial policy, अपनाना–to adopt, to observe, प्रस्ताव–proposal.

2. Past Tense
(a) Past Indefinite
Assertive—Object + to be (was, were) + verb[3] + by ......
Negative—Not/never को to be के पश्चात् रखें।
Interrogative—wh + to be + obj. + not/never + verb[3] + by ......
Helping verb did का passive में प्रयोग नहीं होता है।

1. उनके द्वारा एक सॉनेट लिखा गया।   A sonnet was written by him.
2. तुम्हारे द्वारा मुझे सलाह नहीं दी गई।   I was not advised by you.
3. क्या तुम्हारे द्वारा खिड़की नहीं बन्द की गई ?   Was the window not shut by you ?

4. किसके द्वारा टिकट खरीदा गया ?	By whom was the ticket bought ?
5. उसका छाता कब बस में चुरा लिया गया ?	When was his umbrella stolen in the bus ?

(b) Past Continuous

Assertive—Object + to be + being + verb^3 + by ......

Negative—Not/never को to be के बाद रखें।

Interrogative—wh + to be + obj + not/never + being + verb^3 + by ......

1. नौकर द्वारा कमरा साफ किया जा रहा था।	The room was being cleaned by the servant.
2. उसके द्वारा गाना नहीं गाया जा रहा था।	A song was not being sung by her.
3. क्या एक कहानी उसके द्वारा नहीं कही जा रही थी ?	Was a tale not being told by him ?
4. लड़के कैसे पढ़ाये जा रहे थे ?	How were the boys being taught ?
5. कौन सा लड़का पीटा जा रहा था ?	Which boy was being beaten ?

(c) Past Perfect

Assertive—Object + had been + verb^3 + by ......

Negative—Had के पश्चात् not/never को रखें।

Interrogative—wh + had +obj. + not/never + been + verb^3 + by ......

1. वह कार्य हरी द्वारा किया गया था।	That work had been done by Hari.
2. कुर्सी लड़कों द्वारा नहीं तोड़ी गई थी।	The chair had not been broken by the boys.
3. क्या रिक्त पदों को नई नियुक्ति द्वारा नहीं भरा गया था ?	Had the vacant posts not been filled with the new appointments ?
4. दुर्घटना के स्थान को क्यों नहीं दिखाया गया था ?	Why had the place of accident not been showed ?
5. उषा द्वारा पत्र कहाँ छुपाया जा चुका था ?	Where had the letter been hidden by Usha ?

Exercise 1
(Past Indefinite)

Translate into English :

1. बालू द्वारा एक गाय खरीदी गई।
2. सीमा द्वारा एक मूर्ति बनाई गई।
3. प्रशासन द्वारा क्रान्ति कुचल डाली गई।
4. इस संस्था द्वारा तकनीकी शिक्षा दी जाती थी।
5. मेरे द्वारा घड़ी में चाबी दी गई।
6. हरीश को उसके पिता द्वारा थप्पड़ मारा गया।
7. गरीब आदमी द्वारा धन उधार लिया गया।
8. उन लोगों द्वारा समस्या का हल नहीं किया गया।
9. क्या कक्षा का कार्य बालकों द्वारा नहीं किया गया ?
10. रामायण किसके द्वारा लिखा गया ?
11. क्या कार तुम्हारे द्वारा नहीं चलाई गई ?
12. चोर कहाँ पकड़ा गया ?
13. क्या धोबी द्वारा कपड़े धोए गए ?
14. आप लोगों द्वारा प्रथम शुरुआत क्यों नहीं की गई ?
15. चोरों द्वारा सम्पूर्ण धन कब चुराया गया ?

Hints—प्रशासन–administration, क्रान्ति–revolution, कुचलना–to crush, संस्था–institution, तकनीकी शिक्षा–technical education, देना–to impart, चाबी देना–to wind up (wind-wound-wound), थप्पड़ मारना–to slap, उधार लेना–to borrow, प्रथम शुरुआत–initiative, करना–to take.

Exercise 2
(Past Continuous)

Translate into English :

1. गरीबों पर उचित ध्यान नहीं दिया जा रहा था।
2. सरकार द्वारा रोजगार दिया जा रहा था।
3. वे लोग डाँटे जा रहे थे।
4. स्वतंत्रता के गीत गाए जा रहे थे।
5. असंख्य सैनिक युद्ध में मारे जा रहे थे।
6. इतिहास विद्यार्थियों द्वारा नहीं पढ़ा जा रहा था।
7. नगाड़े बजाए जा रहे थे।
8. क्या छात्रों द्वारा गद्यखंड की व्याख्या की जा रही थी ?

9. क्या दिन दहाड़े बाजार नहीं लूटा जा रहा था ?
10. रसोइया द्वारा चावल नहीं पकाया जा रहा था।
11. कितने विद्यार्थी विद्यालय से निष्कासित किए जा रहे थे ?
12. क्या तुम्हारे द्वारा पत्र लिखा जा रहा था ?
13. मलहम क्यों नहीं लगाया जा रहा था ?
14. किसके द्वारा सामान बाँधा जा रहा था ?
15. पहाड़ियाँ कैसे कुहरे से ढँकी जा रही थीं ?

Hints—उचित ध्यान–proper attention, डाँटना–to chide, to scold, स्वतन्त्रता के गीत–songs of freedom, असंख्य–countless, नगाड़े–drums, बजाना–to beat, to blow, गद्यखंड–passage, व्याख्या करना–to explain, दिन दहाड़े–broad daylight, निष्कासित करना–to expel, to rusticate, मलहम–ointment, लगाना–to apply, सामान–luggage, बाँधना–to pack, to fold, कुहरा–fog, ढँकना–to cover.

Exercise 3
(Past Perfect)

Translate into English :

1. मुट्ठीभर सिक्का कलाकार को दिया गया था।
2. पानी पीने से पहले हिरण शिकारी कुत्तों द्वारा पीछा किए गए थे।
3. वर्षा शुरू होने से पहले वस्त्र नहीं सुखाए जा चुके थे।
4. क्या उस लड़की द्वारा एक सवाल नहीं पूछा गया था ?
5. शत्रु की गतिविधियों को अच्छी तरह देखा जा चुका था।
6. खबर आकाशवाणी से प्रसारित की जा चुकी थी।
7. मेरे द्वारा टी०वी० नहीं खोली गई थी।
8. क्या मोहन के खड़ा होने से पूर्व तुम्हारे द्वारा भाषण दिया जा चुका था ?

9. वर्षा ऋतु के पश्चात् मकान की सफेदी नहीं की गई थी।
10. दाल को क्यों नहीं बघारा गया था ?
11. उसे पहले ही धन्यवाद कैसे दिया जा चुका था ?
12. क्या अपराधी द्वारा पहले ही दोष अस्वीकार किया जा चुका था ?
13. तुम्हें सूचित करने से पूर्व तुम्हारी कार क्यों बेच दी गई थी ?
14. कितने लोगों द्वारा उसे प्रशंसित किया गया था ?
15. पिताजी के आने से पहले क्या किया गया था ?

Hints—मुट्ठीभर सिक्का–a handful of coins, शिकारी कुत्ते–hounds, पीछा करना–to chase, गतिविधियाँ–whereabouts, movements, अच्छी तरह से देखना–to watch well, प्रसारित करना–to broadcast, खोलना–to switch on, सफेदी करना–to whitewash, दाल–pulse, बघारना–to fry, अपराधी–criminal, guilty man, अस्वीकार करना–to deny, प्रशंसा करना–to praise, to admire.

3. Future Tense

(a) Future Indefinite

Assertive—Object + shall/will + be + verb³ + by ......

Negative—Not/never को shall/will के बाद रखें।

Interrogative—wh + shall/will + obj. + not/never + be + verb³ + by ......

1. नेताजी का कल स्वागत किया जाएगा।   The Netaji will be welcomed tomorrow.

2. कल मैच नहीं खेला जाएगा।   The match will not be played tomorrow.

3. क्या तुम्हारे मामा द्वारा उसकी देखभाल की जाएगी ?   Will he be looked after by your maternal uncle ?

4. तुम क्यों विश्वास किए जाओगे ?   Why will you be trusted ?

5. क्या लोगों द्वारा हमलोग संतुष्ट नहीं किए जाएँगे ?   Shall we not be satisfied ?

(b) Future Perfect

Assertive—Object + shall/will + have been + verb³ + by ......

Negative—Not/never को shall/will के बाद रखें।

Interrogative—Wh + shall/will + obj. + not/never + have been + verb³ + by ......

1. क्रोधित होने से पहले उसे प्रसन कर दिया जाएगा।

He will have been pleased before he becomes angry.

2. वर्षा ऋतु आने से पहले पेड़ों को नहीं लगाया जा चुकेगा ?

Trees will not have been planted before the rainy season comes.

3. क्या लड़कों द्वारा तुम खिल्ली नहीं उड़ाए जा चुकोगे ?

Will you not have been laughed at by the boys ?

4. बढ़ई द्वारा कब कुर्सियों की मरम्मत की जा चुकेगी ?

When will the chairs have been repaired by the carpenter ?

5. किसके द्वारा फूल चुने जा चुकेंगे ?

By whom will the flowers have been picked up ?

(c) जब can, could, should, would, may, might, ought to आदि helping verbs (सहायक क्रियाएँ) रहे तो passive के लिए—

Object + helping verb + be + verb³ जैसी बनावट करें अथवा

Object + helping verb + have been + verb³ जैसा करें।

उदाहरण एवं अन्तर देखें—

1. गरीबों की सहायता की जानी चाहिए (या सहायता की जाय)

The poor should (or ought to) be helped.

(In Interrogative and Negative)

Should the poor not be helped ?   Or   Ought the poor not to be helped ?

2. उनका आदर किया जाना चाहिए था।

He ought to (should) have been respected.

3. छोटी कक्षा के लड़कों को शिक्षित किया जाना चाहिए था।

Boys of lower classes should be educated ?

4. तुम्हारे द्वारा किताबें खरीदी जानी चाहिए थीं।

Books should (ought to) have been bought by you.

Exercise 1
(Future Indefinite)

Translate into English :

1. महात्मा गाँधी का जन्मदिन कल मनाया जाएगा।
2. सूखी हड्डियों में जीवन डाला जाएगा।
3. बल का जवाब बल से दिया जाएगा।
4. पूरी शक्ति से देश की रक्षा की जाएगी।
5. निकृष्ट धातुओं को सोने में बदला जाएगा।
6. भाषा को उन्नत किया जाएगा।
7. हम लोगों का अर्थदण्ड माफ नहीं किया जाएगा।
8. हवाई जहाज नीचे गिराया जाएगा।
9. भविष्य द्वारा उसे क्षमा नहीं किया जाएगा।
10. शरणार्थियों को कहाँ बसाया जाएगा ?
11. क्या तुम अनुमति नहीं दिए जाओगे ?
12. कितने सदस्यों द्वारा देश का प्रतिनिधित्व किया जाएगा ?
13. दीक्षान्त समारोह कब मनाया जाएगा ?
14. लोगों द्वारा वह कब याद किया जाएगा ?
15. टेलीग्राम क्यों नहीं किया जाएगा ?

Hints—मनाना–to celebrate, सूखी हड्डियाँ–dry (parched) bones, जीवन डालना–to charge life, to animate, बल–force, जवाब देना–to meet, पूरी शक्ति से–with full might, रक्षा करना–to defend, निकृष्ट धातु–baser metal, बदलना–to transmute (into), भाषा–language, उन्नत करना–to enrich, अर्थदण्ड–fine, माफ करना–to exempt, नीचे गिराना–to down, क्षमा करना–to forgive, शरणार्थी–refugee, बसाना–to settle, प्रतिनिधित्व करना–to represent, दीक्षान्त समारोह–convocation, (टेलीग्राम) करना–to wire, to tick.

Exercise 2
(Future Perfect)

Translate into English :

1. वह मदद किया जा चुकेगा।
2. तलवार सरदार द्वारा म्यान में रखी जा चुकेगी।
3. आग बुझायी जानी चाहिए थी।
4. पिताजी के आने से पूर्व पत्र छोड़ा जा चुकेगा।
5. फिसलने से पहले उसे चेतावनी नहीं दी जा चुकेगी।
6. खेल शीघ्र समाप्त किया जाना चाहिए।
7. तुम्हारा आवेदन-पत्र क्या बिना विचार किए रद्दी की टोकरी में फेंक दिया जाएगा ?
8. क्या उसके केश अच्छी तरह से सँवारे जा चुकेंगे ?
9. क्या तुम्हारे आने से पूर्व भाषण समाप्त किया जा चुकेगा ?
10. घोड़े कब कसे जा चुकेंगे ?
11. परीक्षा आने से पूर्व क्या तुम्हारे द्वारा तैयारियाँ की जा चुकेंगी ?
12. तुम्हारे द्वारा कौन सा उपन्यास पढ़ा जा चुकेगा ?
13. दोपहर तक आधा खेत क्यों नहीं जोता जा चुकेगा ?
14. क्या मध्यकालीन इतिहास तुम्हारे द्वारा लिखा जा चुकेगा ?
15. कितनी पतंगें लड़कों द्वारा उड़ाई जा चुकेंगी ?

Hints—तलवार–sword, सरदार–knight, म्यान–sheath, बुझाना–to extinguish, फिसलना–to slip, चेतावनी देना–to warn, बिना विचार किए–without consideration, रद्दी की टोकरी–waste paper basket, अच्छी तरह से सँवाँरना–to trim (or to groom) well, कसना (घोड़ा)–to saddle, तैयारियाँ–preparations, मध्यकालीन इतिहास–the mediaeval (medieval) history.

The Table of Tenses

Tense		Indefinite	Continuous	Perfect	Perfect Continuous
Present	Active	She praises	She is praising	She has praised	She has been praising
	Passive	She is praised	She is being praised	She has been praised	×
Past	Active	She praised	She was praising	She had praised	She had been praising
	Passive	She was praised	She was being praised	She had been praised	×
Future	Active	She will praise	She will be praising	She will have praised	She will have been praising
	Passive	She will be praised	×	She will have been praised	×

Imperative Sentences (Passive Voice)

1. सामान्य आज्ञासूचक वाक्य–Let + obj. + be + verb³

Active	Passive
1. Bring the glass.	Let the glass be brought.
2. Obey your parents	Let your parents be obeyed.
	Or You are advised to obey your parents.
3. Do it.	Let it be done.

2. यदि वाक्य Do not से प्रारम्भ रहे तो do को हटा दें तथा Let + obj. + not/never + be + verb³ जैसी बनावट से passive voice बनाएँ।

1. Do not kill the bird.	Let the bird not be killed.
2. Never look a gift horse ...	Let a gift horse never be looked.
	Or You are forbidden to look a gift horse ...
3. Do not break your heart.	Let your heart not be broken.

3. यदि please/kindly रहे तो उन्हे हटाकर you are requested + infinitive जैसा परिवर्तन करें।

1. Please help me.	You are requested to help me.
2. Kindly make some room.	You are requested to make some room.

Exercise 1

Turn the voices in the following sentences :

1. They fanned the flame.
2. Write a letter.
3. The country was liberated by the Salvation Army.
4. The tragedy has been written in poetic prose.
5. Our college will play a match.
6. Do not cheat me.

7. The mouse was not being killed by the cat.

8. Has he abandoned the scheme ?

9. The Romans defended their empire with prudence.

10. The sin had not been confessed by the sinner.

11. God has created all of us.

12. Did the peasants thresh the harvest ?

13. Please give a chance.

14. How many votes did he get ?

15. Have they struck out a novel plan ?

16. Let your friend not be brought here.

17. You are requested to review the matter.

18. Who has done it ?

19. Why do the critics remark Robert Bridges 'A poet of nine o'clock' ?

20. Who will resist death ?

21. Who has written 'Laughter in the Next Room' ?

22. Let morality be derived from fear.

23. Do not long for future.

24. Focus your attention.

25. Melancholy settles on his face.

26. Never look at the dark side.

27. They exchanged hot dialogues.

28. Do not make a virtue of necessity.

29. My pocket has been picked.

30. Please, do not account him a fool.

Exercise 2

Translate into English :

1. उसने मुझे एक रहस्य बताया।

2. नागरिकों को एक अवसर दिया गया।

3. अन्त में आचार्य ने अतिथि को धन्यवाद दिया।

4. क्या निष्पक्ष सुनवाई के लिए आप मुझसे प्रतिज्ञा करते हैं ?

5. घुड़सवार ने लगाम को एक झटका दिया।

6. उसने मुझे एक नमूना दिखाया।

7. क्या अभाग्य ने उसे भिक्षाटन नहीं सिखा दिया ?

8. इतिहासकारों ने उसे बहादुर नहीं माना।

9. उसने मुझे एक सीख दी।

10. कम्पनी ने बोनस अस्वीकार नहीं किया।

11. मेरे चाचा ने मेरे लिए एक साइकिल खरीदा।

12. क्या जवानों को नए उपहार दिए गए ?

13. राज्य की ओर से उन लोगों को अधिकार दिया गया।

14. क्या तपन को कप्तान चुना गया ?

15. भरत लोगों द्वारा राजा घोषित किए गए ?

16. जानसन ने साहित्य को एक मोड़ दिया।

17. मैंने उनसे क्षमा माँगी।

18. आप लोगों ने मुझे खून दिया।

19. मैंने आपको आजादी दी।

20. मुझे अनिच्छुक सहायता मत दो।

21. सड़क की मरम्मत की जानी चाहिए।

22. लोगों में राशन बँटवाना चाहिए।

23. पाठ पढ़ाया जाना चाहिए था।

24. क्या उसका अपमान किया जाना चाहिए था ?

25. किस आधार पर आप वैसी टिप्पणी करते हैं ?

Hints—बताना–to unfold, to unveil, नागरिक–citizen, देना–to provide, अन्त में–at last, निष्पक्ष सुनवाई–impartial hearing, घुड़सवार–rider, लगाम–rein, झटका देना–to give a shake, नमूना–model, specimen, अभाग्य–misfortune, भिक्षाटन–beggary, मानना–to account, सीख–lesson, बोनस–bonus, उपहार–gift, अधिकार–right, चुनना–to choose, साहित्य–literature, मोड़ देना–to give a twist and orientation, अनिच्छुक सहायता–reluctant assistance, मरम्मत करना–to repair, राशन–ration, बाँटना–to distribute, अपमान करना–to insult, आधार–ground.

Sentences Expressing Habits

यहाँ वैसे वाक्यों की चर्चा की जायेगी जिनसे आदत, शाश्वत सत्य अथवा पुनरावृत्ति का बोध होता है।

1. Present and Future Tenses—आदत, पुनरावृत्ति, चिरन्तन सत्य तथा वैसे Idioms and phrases जो व्यवहारिक तथा सर्वकालिक सत्य को व्यक्त करें–Present Indefinite तथा Future Indefinite से प्रगट किए जाते हैं।

1.	सितारे टिमटिमाते हैं।	Stars twinkle.
2.	वहाँ एक जादूगर रहा करता है।	There lives a magician (or a magician lives there).
3.	वह बाएँ हाथ से लिखता है।	He writes with the left hand.
4.	ग्वाला रोज आया करेगा।	The milkman will come daily.
5.	क्या तुम्हारा भाई तुम्हारी सहायता नहीं किया करता है ?	Does your brother not help you ?
6.	उधार लिए कपड़े कभी उपयुक्त नहीं होते।	Borrowed garments never fit well.
7.	मशीन की आवाज बार-बार पड़ोसियों को बाधा डाला करती है।	The noise of the machine frequently disturbs the neighbours.
8.	वह रह-रह कर तुम्हें क्यों तंग किया करता है ?	Why does he tease you every now and then ?

2. Past tense—(*a*) Past Indefinite के द्वारा–

1.	भिखारी रोज आया करता था।	The beggar came every day.
2.	लोग उसकी बुराई किया करते थे।	People talked ill of him.
3.	मेरे दादा कभी चाय नहीं पीया करते थे।	My grandfather never took tea.
4.	क्या वह साधु सामान्यतया जमीन पर नहीं सोया करता था ?	Did that saint not usually sleep on the ground ?
5.	मैं तुम्हें हमेशा चेतावनी दिया करता था।	I always warned you.

(*b*) Used to + verb[1] (*i.e.*, used + infinitive) के द्वारा–इस प्रसंग में Concise Oxford Dictionary के विचार को देखें–

'Used—now only in past usually pronounced 'use' especially when followed immediately by 'to', means be accustomed or frequent practice, as I used to take the bus'.

'Use is now confined to the past tense. We may say, 'He used to live in London', but not as we might once have done', He uses to live in London'. The proper negative form is therefore 'He used not to' ; but 'He did not use to' should be regarded rather as an archaism. (Fowler's Modern English Usage)

निष्कर्ष यह कि used to का प्रयोग केवल Past tense तक सीमित है। He did not use to जैसा Negative न लिखकर used not to जैसा व्यक्त करना चाहिए। प्रश्नवाचक में used he go by bus ? जैसी बनावट स्वीकार्य है। कुछ और उदाहरण–

1.	साँप कबूतर के अंडों को खा जाया करता था।	The snake used to eat the eggs of the pigeon.
2.	वह टोपी पहना करता था।	He used to wear a cap.

3. गाड़ी समय पर नहीं आया करती थी।   The train used not to arrive in time.

4. नौकर देर से भोजन बनाया करता था।   The servant used to cook late.

5. क्या तुम्हारा भाई पैदल जाया करता था ?   Used your brother go on foot ?

He did not use to speak loudly or Did he not (Did he use to go there) use to go there ? आदि प्रयोग भी दर्शनीय हो सकेंगे किन्तु ये केवल बोलचाल तक ही सीमित हैं ; साहित्यिक अभिव्यक्ति में नहीं।

(c) Would + verb¹ के द्वारा–विशेषत: जब वाक्य में बहुधा, प्राय:, कभी-कभी आदि रहे तो इसका प्रयोग उचित होगा।

1. आपका लड़का विद्यालय से प्राय: भाग जाया करता था।   Your son would often play truant.

2. कभी-कभी वह क्लब जाया करती थी।   She would sometimes go to club.

3. वे लोग वैसा कभी नहीं कहा करते थे।   They would never say so.

4. सफलता बहुधा समय पर निर्भर रहा करती है।   Success often depends upon time.

5. वह कभी-कभी चिन्ता में डूब जाता था।   He would sometimes plunge into worry.

3. जब 'आदत' शब्द का वाक्य में प्रयोग रहे तो उसे in the habit of या accustomed to + noun, gerund etc. से प्रगट किया जाता है। आदत को has/have/had से भी प्रगट कर सकते हैं।

Accustom—commonly used in passive. (Fowler C.O.D.)

1. उसे सिगरेट पीने की आदत है।   He is accustomed to smoking cigarette.

2. कहानियाँ पढ़ना उसकी आदत है।   He is in the habit of reading stories.

3. मैं सुबह में टहला करता हूँ।   I have my walk in the morning.

4. वह दोपहर में भोजन किया करता था।   He had his dinner in the noon.

4. जब 'आदत' में ही रहे, जैसे–बच्चा रोता ही रहता है। ऐसे वाक्यों का अनुवाद ...... helping verb + nothing + but + verb¹ आदि जैसा करें।

1. बच्चा रोता ही रहता है।   The child does nothing but weep.

2. तुम हँसते ही रहते हो।   You do nothing but laugh.

Exercise 1

Translate into English :

1. हम खूब तड़के उठा करते और एक मील टहला करते थे।

2. शिक्षक कक्षा में प्राय: झपकी लिया करते थे।

3. डाकिया यहाँ रोज नहीं आया करता है।

4. मेरा नौकर हकलाकर बोला करता है।

5. वह वृद्ध जम्हाई लिया करता था।

6. वह समाचार-पत्र बहुत दूर-दूर तक प्रसारित होता था।

7. प्रकृति जनसंख्या रोका करती है।

8. वह हमेशा व्यर्थ की बहस किया करता है।

9. उसके पृष्ठ प्राय: हास्य से मुखरित हुआ करते थे।

10. क्या वह हमेशा फूट-फूट कर रोया करती थी ?

11. अध्यापक बच्चों को हँसाते-हँसाते लोट-पोट कर देते थे।

12. मेरी घड़ी धीमी चला करती है।

13. वह बहुधा पेड़ के नीचे बैठा रहता और भक्तिगीत गाता था।

14. वह वहाँ रोज नहीं जाया करता था।

15. सिद्धार्थ जीवन और मृत्यु के बारे में सोचा करते।

16. आग धुआँ पैदा किया करती है।

17. आशा प्रायः निराशा से पैदा होती है।

18. आज मनुष्य पर खतरा हमेशा बना रहता है।

19. उस समय दुर्घटनाएँ नहीं हुआ करती थीं।

20. क्या तुम रोज मक्खन लिया करते थे ?

21. उसे सभी का विरोध करने की आदत थी।

22. घर में वह अंग्रेजी नहीं बोला करता था।

23. क्या उसे शराब पीने की आदत थी ?

24. तुम दिन में क्यों सोया करते हो ?

25. वह अपने पुत्र के बारे में सोचती ही रहती थी।

26. तुम्हारा नौकर पैसा माँगता ही रहता था।

27. सम्बन्धी यहाँ रोज आया ही करते हैं।

28. बादल आया करेंगे, जाया करेंगे किन्तु पृथ्वी जीवित रहेगी।

29. कुत्ते रात में भौंका करते हैं।

30. बहुत लोग आलस्य में पड़े रहते हैं।

Hints—झपकी लेना—to take a nap, to doze, हकलाना—to stammer, जम्हाई लेना—to yawn, दूर-दूर तक प्रसारित होना—to circulate widely, जनसंख्या—population, रोकना—to check, व्यर्थ बहस करना—to argue a weak case, हास्य से मुखरित होना—to sparkle (or to hum) with humour, हँसाते-हँसाते लोट-पोट करना—to set the table laughing (or in a roar), to move one's into peals of laughter, भक्ति गीत—devotional song, hymn, पैदा करना—to produce, to generate, (खतरा) बना रहना—to hang over one's head, मक्खन—butter, विरोध करना—to oppose, माँगना—to demand, सम्बन्धी—relatives, जीवित रहना—to exist, आलस्य में—idly.

Causative Verbs
(प्रेरणार्थक क्रियाएँ)

1. Get या have से—जब कर्त्ता किसी कार्य को स्वयं न करके किसी अन्य को करने के लिए प्रेरित करता है तो वैसे वाक्य की क्रिया प्रेरणार्थक क्रिया (causative verb) कहलाती है। कर्त्ता कार्य के सम्पादन हेतु प्रेरक होता है। इसमें प्रत्येक प्रकार के वाक्य की बनावट का आधार get/have होता है जिसे main verb मानकर tenses आदि का परिवर्तन किया जाता है। लेकिन कार्य की प्रेरक क्रिया third form की होती है। इनका प्रयोग (कर्म वाच्य) passive verb की क्रिया के साथ होगा। निम्नस्थ उदाहरणों को देखें—

(a) Get के द्वारा

1.	महिला मुझसे एक पत्र लिखवाती है।	The woman gets a letter written by me. (Pre. Ind.)
2.	महिला ने मुझसे पत्र लिखवाया है।	The woman has got a letter written by me. (Pre. Perf.)
3.	क्या महिला मुझसे पत्र नहीं लिखवाई थी ?	Had the woman not got a letter written by me? (Past Perf.)
4.	महिला मुझसे पत्र क्यों लिखवाई ?	Why did the woman get a letter written by me? (Past. Ind.)
5.	मैं वह कार्य हरी से करवाऊँगा।	I shall get that work done by Hari. (Fut. Ind.)
6.	हरी से वह कार्य करवाओ।	Get that work done by Hari. (Imperative sent.)

(b) Have के द्वारा

1.	तुमने धोंधू से मेज बनवाया है।	You have had the table made by Dhondhu. (Pre. Perf.)
2.	तुम धोंधू से मेज बनवाए थे।	You had had the table made by Dhondhu. (Past Perf.)
3.	तुम धोंधू से मेज बनवाओगे।	You will have the table made by Dhondhu. (Fut. Ind.)
4.	क्या तुम धोंधू से मेज बनवाए ?	Did you have the table made by Dhondhu? (Past. Ind.)
5.	पिताजी से पुस्तक खरीदवाओ।	Have the book bought by the father. (Imperative sent.)
6.	हरी से अपने प्रश्न हल मत करवाओ।	Do not have (or get) your question solved by Hari? (Imp. sent.)

2. Cause या Make से—Get/have जैसा ही किसी भी वाक्य की बनावट cause/make को main verb मानकर की जाएगी। अन्तर यह है कि प्रेरित क्रिया infinitive होगी अर्थात् cause के प्रसंग में to + verb[1] परन्तु make की स्थिति में to हट जाएगा।

1.	वह लड़कों को हँसाता है।	He makes the boys laugh. Or He causes the boys to laugh. (Pre. Ind.)
2.	घोड़े को तेज दौड़ाओ।	Make the horse run fast. Or cause the horse to run fast. (Imp. sent.)
3.	क्या वह घोड़े को तेज दौड़ाएगा ?	Will he make the horse run fast? Or Will he cause the horse to run fast? (Fut. Ind. Interrog.)

Note. Get/have तथा cause/make के प्रयोग में अन्तर यह है कि get/have–passive voice वाले वाक्य में प्रयुक्त होते हैं। जैसे—

1.	वह फटिक से लड़कों को रूलवाता है।	He gets the boys wept by Phatik. (Passive voice)
2.	वह लड़कों को रूलाता है।	He makes the boys weep. (Active voice)

3. यदि 'जाना' से वाक्य की क्रिया passive voice में हो तो make के साथ to लगेगा।

1.	पौधे सिंचवाए जाते हैं।	Plants are made to water.
2.	गोविन्द को पिटवाया गया।	Govind was made to beat.
3.	क्या लड़के दौड़वाए जायेंगे ?	Will boys be made to run ?

Note. जैसा कि नियम 1 में उदाहरण है, इसके Imperative Sentence को get/have or make/cause को सर्वप्रथम रखकर बनाएँगे–Get your shoes mended by the cobbler. Make the horse run fast.

Exercise 1

Translate into English :

1. उसने मुझसे एक घड़ी खरीदवाई है।
2. उन लोगों ने अपना उपनिवेश शत्रुओं से खाली करवाया।
3. तुमने उसे नहीं दौड़वाया।
4. खराब मौसम ने सैनिकों से हथियार डलवाया।
5. उसने अपने चाचा को षड्यन्त्र से मरवाया।
6. पुलिस अपराधी से अपराध स्वीकार कराएगी।
7. नाविकों ने तीर्थयात्रियों से डाँड़ चलवाया।
8. शिक्षक बच्चों को लिखना सिखाते हैं।
9. अधिकारी काले धनखोरों को कोड़े लगवाएगा।
10. क्या तुमने अपना स्वेटर नए रंग में रंगवाया है ?
11. अनपढ़ लड़की ने मुझसे एक पत्र लिखवाया।
12. अपना चित्र खिंचवाओ।
13. क्या वे अपने घर की सफेदी करवायेंगे ?
14. अपना केश नाई से छोटा करवाओ।
15. अपने पुत्रों को अच्छे ढंग सिखवाओ।
16. लोगों द्वारा प्रतिनिधि चुनवाए गए।
17. अध्यापक चपरासी से घंटी क्यों नहीं बजवा रहे हैं ?
18. तुम्हारे द्वारा उसका विश्वास कब विचलित कराया जाता है ?
19. वह नौकर से जानवरों को खिलवा रहा है।
20. कितने लड़कों को इनाम दिलवाया जाएगा ?

Hints—उपनिवेश–colony, खाली करना–to vacate, खराब मौसम–wretched weather, हथियार डालना–to lay down arms, षड्यंत्र से–in a plot, अपराधी–criminal, स्वीकार करना–to confess, नाविक–sailor, डाँड़ चलाना–to row, to oar, काले धनखोर–black money hoarder, कोड़े लगाना–to whip, स्वेटर–sweater, रँगना–to dye, अनपढ़–illiterate, सफेदी करना–to whitewash, नाई–barber, छोटा करना–to shingle, अच्छे ढंग–good manners, प्रतिनिधि–representative, विश्वास–faith, विचलित करना–to shake, खिलाना–to feed.

Exercise 2

Correct the following sentences :

1. I shall make my furniture to repair.
2. I got the portrait hang on the cross-road.
3. The horrid drought caused teeming persons starve.
4. I have my work to do by the labourers as early as possible.
5. The wings cause the birds fly.
6. A vulture got the plane to change its route.
7. Have your clothes tailor well ?
8. Cause them read loudly.
9. Make the druggist to fill this bottle with old wine.
10. Do you get him appoint ?

Chapter 11

Non-Finites

A. Infinitive (क्रियात्मक संज्ञा एवं विशेषण)

1. जब हिन्दी की क्रिया ना, ने, नी से समाप्त रहे अथवा इनके साथ में, के लिए, को रहे तो उसे Infinitive (to + verb[1]) से प्रगट करेंगे। इस तरह noun के अतिरिक्त Infinitive किसी Verb, Noun, Adjective या पूरे वाक्य को Qualify करता है।

1.	दूसरों में गलती *निकालना* आसान है।	*To find* fault with others is easy.
		Or It is easy to find fault with others.
2.	*कहना* आसान है। लेकिन *करना* कठिन।	*To say* is easy but *to do* is difficult.
		Or It is easier *to say* than *do*.
3.	गलती *करना* मनुष्य का काम है ; क्षमा *करना* ईश्वर का काम है।	*To err* is human ; *to forgive* is divine.
4.	वह *पढ़ने के लिए* आया।	He came *to read*.
5.	मैं किताब *खरीदने के लिए* बाजार गया।	I went to market *to buy* a book.
6.	ये कपड़े *पहनने के लिए (को)* हैं।	These clothes are *to wear*.
7.	दुख *भोगना* कौन पसन्द करता है ?	Who likes *to suffer* ?
8.	यह प्रश्न *समझने में* कठिन है।	This question is difficult *to understand*.

2. (a) जब उक्त प्रकार की क्रिया के साथ वाला, वाले, वाली रहे तो उन्हें इस रूप में अनुवाद करें–

Subject + to be + Infinitive etc.

1.	वह *जाने वाला* है।	He is to go.
2.	मैं एक कार *खरीदने वाला* था।	I was to buy a car.
3.	तुम किसे *पढ़ाने वाले* थे ?	Whom were you to teach ?
4.	हम लोग एक धंधा *शुरू करने वाले* हैं।	We are to open a business.
5.	मैं एक पत्र *लिखने वाला (को)* हूँ।	I am to write a letter.

(b) Have/has/had + Infinitive के द्वारा। इसमें पड़ना, पड़ने, पड़नी जैसे शब्द प्राय: रहा करते हैं। जैसे–

1.	उसे नदी *पार करनी पड़ती* थी।	He had to cross the river.
2.	बच्चों को विशेष वस्त्र *पहनना पड़ता* है।	Children have to wear uniforms.
3.	मुझे कठिनाईयों का *सामना करना पड़ेगा।*	I will have to face the difficulties.
4.	तुम्हें गोली *चलानी ही पड़ेगी।*	You shall (or must) have to fire.
5.	ऐसी हालत में उसे मेरी *मदद करनी पड़ी।*	In such condition, he had to help me.

333

(c) About + Infinitive के द्वारा—

1. वृद्ध मरने ही वाला था।   The old man was about to die.
2. चन्द्रमा पश्चिम में गिरने ही वाला है।   The moon is about to fall in the west.
3. क्या पानी बरसने ही वाला नहीं है ?   Is it not about to rain ?
4. गाड़ी प्लेटफार्म पर आने ही वाली है।   The train is about to arrive at the platform.
5. वह होश में आने ही वाली है।   She is about to come into senses.

Note. नियम 2 के तीनों उपनियमों में अन्तर यह है कि जहाँ (a) को सामान्य स्थिति में प्रयोग किया जाता है ; (b) को अधिक बाध्यता, बल या अटल कर्तव्य के भाव में प्रयोग किया जाता है ; जबकि (c) को अन्तिम क्षण में घटित होने वाले कार्य के लिए प्रयोग करेंगे। Infinitive के प्रयोग में ध्यान देने योग्य तथ्य यह है कि वाक्य नियमों (जैसा कि tenses आदि के प्रसंग में निर्दिष्ट हैं) के अनुसार ही बनेंगे। जहाँ Infinitive का position होगा उसका प्रयोग वहीं होगा। इस तरह Infinitive एक Noun जैसा subject, object, complement आदि अनेक प्रकार से कार्य करेगा तथा Adjective के रूप में qualify भी करेगा।

3. Infinitive का Passive voice—to be + verb³ तथा perfect में to have + been + verb³ जैसा बनाएँगे।

1. लड़कों को पढ़ाया जाना है। (या पढ़ाये जाने को हैं।) Boys are to be taught.
2. कार्य मजदूरों से पूरा करवाना पड़ेगा।   The work will have to be completed by the labourers.
3. किताब को पुन: छपाया जाना पड़ा है।   The book has (got) to be reprinted.
4. लड़के पढ़ाए जा सकते थे।   Boys could have been taught.
5. लड़कों को पढ़ाया जाय।   Boys should be taught.
   ...... पढ़ाया जाना चाहिए था।   ...... should have been taught.

4. ऐसे वाक्यों का अनुवाद जैसे 'सीखने को उत्सुक' ; 'मिलने को (के लिए) व्याकुल'—to be + adj. + infinitive जैसा करें।

1. वह सीखने को उत्सुक है।   He is eager to learn.
2. क्या तुम जानने को उत्सुक हो ?   Are you curious to know ?
3. मैं उससे मिलने को व्याकुल हूँ।   I am anxious to see him.
4. वह चलने में कमजोर है।   He is weak to walk.

5. इतना/उतना ...... कि—जैसा कथन जिसमें Negative sense छिपा हो, का अनुवाद .... too + adj./adverb + infinitive से करें।

1. वह इतना मोटा है कि आसानी से नहीं दौड़ सकता।

   He is too fat to run easily.

2. अन्धकार इतना घना था कि कोई आगे नहीं बढ़ सकता था।

   The darkness was too dense for one to advance.

3. यह सवाल इतना कठिन है कि मैं हल नहीं कर सकता।

   This sum is too hard for me to solve.

6. ऐसे वाक्य जैसे—माँगने से मरना भला (या अच्छा)—का अनुवाद better than, would rather, rather than आदि से करते है।

1. **Better to die than beg.** Or It would be better to die than beg.
2. स्वर्ग में **गुलामी करने की** अपेक्षा नरक पर शासन करना कहीं बेहतर है।

   Better to reign in hell than serve in heaven. (or It is better...... etc.)

3. (गन्तव्य तक) पहुँचने से यात्रा जारी रखना बेहतर है।

To travel is better than arrive.

4. उससे बात करने की अपेक्षा मैं किसी राक्षस से बात कर लूँगा।

I would rather talk to a devil than speak to him.

7. 'गैर तो गैर/गैरों को कौन कहे/क्या कहना/गैर तो दूर मेरे परम भित्रों ने भी मेरी सहायता न की।'–ऐसे वाक्यों का अनुवाद Not to speak of + pronoun/noun/gerund etc. से करें। इसमें even का भी प्रयोग वांछित है।

1. Not to speak of others, even my dearest friends did not help me.

2. तुम क्या तुम्हारे पिताजी भी मुझे चुनौती नहीं दे सकते।

Not to speak of you, even your father cannot challenge me.

3. आपका क्या कहना, आपका वंश भी कभी बन्दूक नहीं पकड़ा है।

Not to speak of you, even your race has never handled a gun.

4. यहाँ आने की कौन कहे, उसने तो एक पत्र भी नहीं भेजा।

Not to speak of coming here, he did not send even a letter.

8. जब Infinitive किसी noun को govern करे तो उसके साथ उसका preposition भी रखें।

1. बैठने के लिए एक कुर्सी लाओ।	Bring a chair to sit in (or on).
2. मुझे लिखने के लिए एक कलम दो।	Give me a pen to write with.
3. भोगने के लिए उसे अनेक कठिनाईयाँ हैं।	She has many troubles to suffer from.
4. वह बात करने के लिए किसी के फेर में है।	He is after someone to talk with.

9. Split Infinitive—सामान्यतया Infinitive को उसके to से पृथक् न करें–

Incorrect	Correct
1. I request you to kindly give me a chance.	I request you kindly to give me a chance.
2. It is our duty to considerably improve the situation.	It is our duty to improve the situation considerably.

10. जब किसी कला/गुण आदि के जानने या न जानने का भाव रहे तो उसे प्रायः ...... how + infinitive से प्रगट किया जाता है। इस नियम के अनेक अपवाद भी हैं।

1. वह नाचना जानती है।	She knows how to dance.
	(She knows to dance नहीं)
2. क्या तुम तैरना नहीं जानते ?	Do you not know how to swim ?
3. वह गाड़ी की मरम्मत करना जानता था।	He knew how to repair a car.

4. Teach him to swim. He will teach you to speak the truth.
(Concise Oxford Dictionary)

Note. यदि एक ही वाक्य में अनेक infinitives क्रमवार रहें तो बाद वाले के साथ to नहीं रहेगा। मैं तुम्हें धोखा देना या नीचा दिखाना नहीं चाहता–I do not intend to deceive or abase you. A true warrior knows how to advance and when retreat. When, where, what, which आदि के साथ भी Infinitive का प्रयोग उक्त भाव में इस प्रकार कर सकेंगे–मैं नहीं समझ सका कि मैं क्या करूँ और कहाँ जाऊँ–I could not understand what to do and where to go.

11. जब ना, ने, नी से समाप्त क्रिया के साथ लगा, लगे, लगी रहे तो उसे ...... begin + infinitive से प्रगट करें–

1. वह मुस्कराने लगा।	He began to smile.
2. तुम उसे गाली क्यों देने लगे ?	Why did you begin to abuse him ?
3. सभी लोग वहाँ से भागने लगे।	All men began to run away from there.

12. 'मैं बैंक में खाता खोलने जा रहा हूँ'–ऐसे वाक्यों को verb to be + going (or intending) + infinitive के आधार पर बनाना चाहिए।

1. I am going to open an account in bank.

2. वह एक रंगीन टी०वी० खरीदने जा रहा है।   He is going to buy a colour T.V.

3. क्या तुम इस वर्ष परीक्षा में बैठने जा रहे हो ?   Are you going to appear at the examination this year ?

4. हरी एक मकान बनाने जा रहा था।   Hari was going to build a house.

13. मालूम पड़ना/प्रतीत होना/दिखाई पड़ना/ज्ञात होना–इनके साथ यदि कोई noun/adjective आदि हो तो to be या to have been से उसे इस प्रकार बनाएँ। इस स्थिति में to be वर्तमान का संकेत देता है जबकि to have been उससे पूर्व होने का संकेत देता है।

1. वह एक सज्जन आदमी लगता है।   He seems to be a gentle man.

2. तुम बीमार हुए लगते हो।   You appear to have been ill.

14. It + to take + objective case + time + Infinitive

1. परीक्षा उत्तीर्ण करने में उसे चार वर्ष लगे।

It took him four years to pass the examination.

2. निर्णय लेने में मुझे कई घंटे लग गए।

It took me several hours to take the decision.

Exercise 1

Translate into English :

1. मैं कठिनाईयों का सामना करना जानता हूँ।
2. मेरा नौकर घड़ी में चाबी देना भूल गया।
3. दिन में सोना हानिकारक है।
4. उन्होंने मुझे हँसना सिखाया।
5. कहने से करना अच्छा होता है।
6. क्या तुम घुड़सवारी करना जानते हो ?
7. लेने से देना बेहतर है।
8. कौन यहाँ जीने के लिए आया है ?
9. वे खजाने की खोज करने चल पड़े।
10. उन दिनों आकाश में उड़ना कल्पना मात्र था।
11. सिद्धार्थ ने दुखों का कारण जानने के लिए महल त्याग दिया।
12. ये आम खाने के लिए है।
13. जीवन आनन्द लेने के लिए है।
14. कुछ चोर दुकान लूटने के लिए आए।
15. चिन्ताओं से ग्रस्त रहने की अपेक्षा बल्कि वह त्याग-पत्र दे देगा।
16. लड़के पदकन्दुक खेलने के लिए इकट्ठे हुए हैं।
17. क्या वह दवा खाने में कड़वी नहीं है ?
18. बच्चे अन्धकार में जाने से डरते हैं।
19. वह मेमना स्पर्श करने में मुलायम था।
20. ये प्रश्न पूछे जाने के लिए हैं।

Hints—कठिनाईयाँ–difficulties, सामना करना–to face, चाबी देना–to wind up (wind-wound-wound), खजाना–treasure, चल पड़ना–to set out, to go out, एक कल्पना मात्र–a mere fairy tale (or day-dream), त्यागना–to renounce, चिन्ता–worry, ग्रस्त रहना–to weigh down with, त्याग-पत्र देना–to resign, कड़वी–bitter, मेमना–lamb.

Exercise 2

Translate into English :

1. वह बोलने ही वाली थी।
2. राष्ट्रपति कल यहाँ आने वाले हैं।
3. हमें यह स्थान छोड़ना ही पड़ेगा।
4. खेत सींचे जाने वाले थे।
5. मुझे आप लोगों से दो शब्द कहना है।
6. गुलाम होने से मर जाना कहीं बेहतर है।
7. गणित तो गणित वह इतिहास भी नहीं जानता।
8. कक्षा में आने को क्या कहना तुम तो विद्यालय भी नहीं आते।
9. धोंधू इतना मोटा है कि आसानी से चल फिर नहीं सकता।
10. आपका लड़का अंग्रेजी में इतना कमजोर है कि उत्तीर्णांक नहीं प्राप्त कर सकता।

11. क्या तुम नदी में स्नान करने और तैरने जाओगे ?
12. भाइयों में गरीब बनकर रहने से जंगल में रहना बेहतर है।
13. उन्हें मातृभूमि के लिए न्यौछावर हो जाना चाहिए था।
14. क्या वह एक स्कूटर खरीदने जा रहा है ?
15. जले पर नमक छिड़कना आपत्तिजनक है।
16. नाचना उसका शौक है।
17. बच्चा रोने ही वाला था।
18. कभी-कभी मुझे दिन भर खड़ा रहना पड़ता था।
19. फोटो को साफ किया जाना है।
20. तस्वीर इतनी धुँधली थी कि कोई उसे स्पष्ट नहीं देख सकता था।

Hints—गुलाम–slave, उत्तीर्णांक पाना–to get a pass, मातृभूमि–motherland, homeland, न्यौछावर करना–to sacrifice, स्कूटर–scooter, जले पर नमक छिड़कना–to add insult to injury, आपत्तिजनक–objectionable, शौक–hobby, दिन भर–all day long, साफ करना–to wash, धुँधली–dim.

(b) Gerund (क्रियात्मक संज्ञा)

1. Gerund (verb + ing) भी हिन्दी के उन्हीं प्रयोगों के लिए है जो Infinitive के प्रयोग के लिए हैं। Infinitive की तरह gerund भी एक Noun की भाँति subject, object आदि जैसा कार्य करता है। इसे verb में -ing लगाकर बनाया जाता है।

1. टहलना एक अच्छा व्यायाम है।
   Walking is a good exercise.
2. लिखना बन्द करो।
   Stop *writing*.
3. देखना ही विश्वास करना है।
   Seeing is *believing*.
4. उपन्यास पढ़ना उसका प्रिय मनोरंजन था।
   Reading novel was his favourite pastime.
5. उसका यह करना सन्देहास्पद है।
   His *doing* this is doubtful.

2. जब Noun/Pronoun किसी gerund को govern करे तो वह possessive case में रहता है। Transitive verb के gerund के कई रूप होते हैं—

Placing before	(Present-active)
Having placed before	(Perfect-active)
Being placed before	(Present-passive)
Having been placed before	(Perfect-passive)

1. मैंने स्पष्ट रूप से उसका परीक्षा उत्तीर्ण किया सुना।
   I distinctly heard of his having passed the examination.
2. विलम्ब के लिए कृपया मुझे क्षमा करें।
   Please excuse my being late. (not me being ......)

3. मुझे विश्वास है कि यहाँ मेरे बैठने का आप बुरा न मानेंगे।

I believe that you will not mind my (not me) sitting here.

3. Gerund के पहले जब the और बाद में of रहेगा तो उसे Verbal Noun कहा जाएगा।

1. मैं धूम्रपान से घृणा करता हूँ।   I hate smoking (Gerund).

2. सिगरेट पीना बहुत हानिप्रद है।   The smoking of cigarette is very harmful. (verbal noun)

3. इतिहास पढ़ना हमारे ज्ञान को विस्तृत करता है।   The reading of history enhances (or expands) our knowledge.

4. Infinitive तथा gerund में प्रयोगान्तर—preposition के पश्चात् gerund का प्रयोग होता है अन्यथा दोनों में से किसी का भी प्रयोग किया जा सकता है।

1. मैं बहुधा वहाँ जाने को सोचता हूँ।   I often think of going there (not think to go. ......)

2. वे अपने उद्देश्य को प्राप्त करने के लिए प्रयत्न करते हैं।   They strive after attaining their goal. (not strive to attain)

3. तुम हमेशा श्रेष्ठतर बनने का उद्देश्य रखते हो।   You always aim at being superior.

4. वह ताश खेलने का शौकीन है।   He is fond of playing cards. (not to play)

5. देखना ही विश्वास करना है।   Seeing is believing.   *Or*   To see is to believe.

5. निम्नस्थ verb के साथ gerund आना चाहिए Infinitive नहीं—

Despair, hinder, persist, prevent, prohibit, succeed, think etc.

1. हम लोग वहाँ जाने से रोके गए।   We were prevented from going there. (not prevented to go).

2. वह प्रथम श्रेणी लाने में सफल हो गया।   He succeeded in securing first class. (not succeeded to secure).

Exercise 1

Translate into English :

1. मेरा मित्र जासूसी उपन्यास पढ़ने का शौकीन है।
2. देर रात जागते रहने से मेरी दृष्टि कमजोर हो गई है।
3. व्याकरण पढ़ाना एक कठिन काम है।
4. वहाँ शिकार करना एक साहसिक कार्य था।
5. दूसरों पर कीचड़ उछालना अच्छी आदत नहीं।
6. अधिक चिन्तन करना लाभदायक नहीं होता।
7. तुम उससे बात करने से क्यों डरते हो ?
8. यहाँ इश्तहार चिपकाना मना है।
9. कृपया अपने यहाँ आने का उद्देश्य कहें।
10. प्रश्न पूछने से उत्तर देना कठिन है।
11. आदर करने की कौन कहे उसने तो मुझसे बात भी नहीं किया।
12. कैकेयी के सोचने का क्षेत्र संकुचित था।

13. मकान की कौन कहे, उसके नाम पर एक झोंपड़ी भी नहीं है।

14. यहाँ आना बुरा नहीं है, किन्तु शोर मचाना आपत्तिजनक है।

15. धन इकट्ठा करना स्वास्थ्य खराब करना है।

Hints—जासूसी उपन्यास—detective novel, शौकीन—fond of, देर रात तक जगना—to burn the midnight oil, दृष्टि—eyesight, शिकार करना—to hunt, एक साहसिक कार्य—an adventurous deed, दूसरों पर कीचड़ उछालना—to throw (or fling) mud at others, लाभदायक—useful, beneficial, इश्तहार चिपकाना—to stick bills, क्षेत्र—span, संकुचित—narrow, नाम पर—after his name, आपत्तिजनक—objectionable, धन—wealth, इकट्ठा करना—to amass, to hoard, खराब करना—to ruin.

Exercise 2

Correct these sentences :

1. The messenger could to reach early.
2. Let me to sleep.
3. You need not to worry.
4. They ought die for the motherland.
5. This is the thing to aim.
6. Is there any morality to draw ?
7. My father taught me to hopefully go on the business.
8. The Buddha was possessed with the idea to liberate mankind.
9. He left no stone unturned to narrowly escape from the danger.
10. Please, excuse me being late.

(c) Participle (क्रियात्मक विशेषण)

Participle क्रिया के उस रूप को कहा जाता है जो verb से बनता है लेकिन कार्य विशेषण का करता है। जैसे—न्यूटन ने एक गिरते हुए सेव को देखा—Newton noticed a falling apple. यहाँ falling—apple की विशेषता बताता है। Participle के तीन भेद हैं—

1. Present Participle—verb + ing—जब क्रिया की निरन्तरता हुआ, हुए, हुई से प्रगट हो या पूर्वकालिक क्रिया हो, अर्थात् एक क्रिया पूर्व में समाप्त हो गई हो जो प्राय: कर, करके से प्रगट रहती है, तो उसे Present Participle से प्रगट करते हैं। प्राय: प्रथम सम्पन्न कार्य वाक्य में पहले रखा जाता है।

1. लुढ़कते (हुए) पत्थर को काई नहीं लगती।	A *rolling* stone gathers no moss.
2. राजसत्ता मरते हुए राजा को भूल जाती है।	Authority forgets a *dying* king.
3. जीवन एक चलती फिरती छाया है।	Life is a *walking* shadow.
4. तलवार निकालकर उसने शेर को मार डाला।	*Drawing* the sword, he killed the lion.
5. शोर सुनकर हमलोग वहाँ पहुँचे।	*Hearing* the noise, we reached there.

2. Past Participle—जब हिन्दी की क्रिया भूतकाल में रहे ; उसके साथ हुआ, हुए, हुई, रहे तो उसे Past Participle से प्रगट करेंगे। प्राय: इसे (verb³ को) qualified word के निकट रखा जाता है।

1. एक जला हुआ बच्चा आग से डरता है।	A burnt child dreads the fire.
2. हम लोगों ने आम से लदे हुए पेड़ को देखा।	We saw the tree laden with mangoes.
3. वह फटे (हुए) कपड़े पहनी है।	She was dressed in worn-out clothes.
4. ऊजड़े हुए गाँव अपनी कहानी कह रहे थे।	The deserted villages were telling their tales.

5. मुझे भूली (हुई) कहानी को याद मत दिलाओ।   Do not remind me of the forgotten story.

Home they brought her warrior dead. (Tennyson)

Borrowed garments never fit well.

3. Perfect Participle—having + verb³–यह भी पूर्वकालिक क्रिया (present participle) के भाव को व्यक्त करता है।

1. सभी तथ्य जानकर उन लोगों ने उस स्थान को छोड़ने का निश्चय किया।

Having known all the facts, they decided to leave the place.

2. पत्र लिखकर मैं उसे छोड़ने गया।

Having written the letter, I went to post it.

3. यात्री को ठगकर दलाल गायब हो गया।

Having swindled the traveller, the broker disappeared.

4. अपना काम समाप्त कर, वह घर लौट आया।

Having finished his work, he returned home.

5. चोटी पर पहुँचकर, पर्वतारोहियों ने झंडा फहराया।

Having reached the peak, the mountaineers hoisted the flag.

4. Being के साथ adjective/verb³ आदि रखकर भी उक्त आशय को प्रगट किया जाता है जिसे Absolute Phrase कहा जाता है। इसे having + verb³ से भी प्रगट किया जा सकेगा।

1. मौसम सुन्दर होने पर हम लोग पुन: चल पड़े।

The weather being fine, we again set out.

2. सूर्य डूबने पर चिड़ियाँ अपने घोंसलों में शरण लीं।

The sun having set, the birds took shelter in their nests.

3. बोझ भारी होने पर बैल मर गया।

The load being heavy, the bullock died.

4. प्यास से व्याकुल होकर हम लोग एक झरने के पास गए।

Being driven by thirst, we went near a spring.

5. जैसा कि ऊपर संकेत है, Participle–Active तथा Passive दोनों voices में बनता है। Passive में being + verb³ या Having been + verb³ जैसी बनावटें होंगी।

1. निराश किये जाने पर वह घर से भाग गया।

Having been disappointed, he went away from home.

2. शिक्षक द्वारा दंडित होने पर, लड़के ने विद्यालय छोड़ दिया।

Having been punished by the teacher, the boy left the school.

3. छड़ी तोड़ दिए जाने पर बेकार हो गई।

The stick having been broken, became useless.

4. पुस्तक को संक्षिप्त करके आपके सामने प्रस्तुत की गई।

The book being abridged, is presented before you.

ऐसे ही भावों को तोड़कर भी रखा जा सकता है—

1. वह दौड़कर अपने पिता के पास गई।   She ran and went near her father.

2. बेन्च पर खड़ा होकर, वह बोला।   He stood on the bench and spoke.

3. निकट आकर, उसने मुझे एक रहस्य बताया।   He approached to me and unfolded a secret (or told me a secret).

6. Unattached Participle (असम्बद्ध क्रियात्मक विशेषण) ध्यान देने की आवश्यकता है कि participle का कोई noun absolute या उसका स्पष्ट निर्देश होना चाहिए अन्यथा आशय भ्रमास्पद हो सकता है।

(a) Entering the room, the light was quite dazzling.

(b) Sitting on the gate, a scorpion stung him. (Wren)

यहाँ entering तथा sitting दोनों के कर्त्ता अस्पष्ट हैं। इन्हें when, while या निम्नस्थ रीति से स्पष्ट करें—

(a) Entering the room, I found the light quite dazzling.

(b) Sitting on the gate, he was stung by a scorpion or while he was sitting on the gate, a scorpion stung him.

किन्तु Regarding, concerning, considering, taking, speaking, touching, owing to etc. को बिना सन्दर्भ या nominative absolute के भी प्रयोग किया जा सकता है।

1. इस बिल से सम्बन्धित कोई भी विरोध नहीं उठाया गया।

Regarding this bill, no objection was raised.   *Or*   No objection was raised regarding this bill.

2. स्पष्ट रूप से कहा जाय तो दोष तुम्हारा है।

Speaking frankly, the fault is yours.

7. कर, करके जैसी पूर्वकालिक क्रिया का अनुवाद Preposition या Prepositional Phrase को gerund के पूर्व रखकर भी किया जा सकता है।

1. अपने पति की मृत्यु का समाचार सुनकर, वह मुर्छित हो गई।

On hearing the news of her husband's death, she fainted.

2. दिन भर गोलीबारी करने के पश्चात् दुश्मन के तोप रात भर ठंडे रहे।

After celling all day, the tanks of the enemy remained silent throughout the night.

3. विलम्ब की क्षतिपूर्ति करके गाड़ी ठीक समय पर स्टेशन पहुँची।

By making up late running, the train reached the station in time.

8. कर, करके जैसी पूर्वकालिक क्रियाओं का अनुवाद Infinitive से भी किया जा सकता है किन्तु ऐसी क्रियाएँ सीमित हैं। उनमें से कुछ प्रमुख हैं—to see, to know, to meet, to hear, to find, to do etc.

1. यह सब सुनकर मुझे दुख हुआ।   I was sorry to hear all this.

2. वह मुझे देखकर सुखी होगी।   She will be happy to see me.

3. यह जानकर तुम क्या करोगे ?   What will you do to know this ?

9. हुआ, हुए, हुई से कार्य की निरन्तरता का भाव रहने पर उसे निम्नस्थ verbs के साथ Infinitive द्वारा भी उसका to हटाकर प्रगट किया जाता है—

> bid, feel, hear, help, let, make, notice, observe, watch, listen etc.

1. मैंने उसे कहते हुए सुना ।   I heard him say.

I felt him move. She bade me go. We helped him lift the log.

Exercise 1

Translate into English :

1. डूबते सूर्य की कौन पूजा करता है ?

2. वह अब एक कालातीत कवि है ।

3. एक चम्मचभर चीनी ऊबलते जल में डाल दो ।

4. दुखों से हारकर उसने आत्महत्या कर ली ।

5. मुझे ध्वनि-संकलित संगीत अच्छा लगता है ।

6. वह मुझाया हुआ फूल तुम्हें क्या शिक्षा देता है ?

7. तेज दौड़ता हुआ धावक जमीन पर गिर पड़ा ।

8. घर पहुँचने पर वह अपने बच्चे को सोते हुए पाई ।

9. प्रसन्न होकर उसने अजनवी की मदद की ।

10. ऊगता हुआ सूर्य उत्थान का प्रतीक है ।

11. घूमती हुई आँखें कुछ कह रही थीं ।

12. तुम हमारे समाज के सबसे आलोच्य व्यक्ति हो ।

13. भरत तूफान से आहत पक्षी के समान दिखाई देते थे ।

14. अचानक एक महिला जलती झोंपड़ी में घुस गई ।

15. यह एक निर्णीत तथ्य है ।

16. अवकाश प्राप्त कप्तान की पेंशन स्वीकृत की गई ।

17. तीर चलाकर राजा दशरथ नदी के किनारे पहुँचे ।

18. पश्चिम की अंधी नकल करके हम अपनी संस्कृति की खिल्ली उड़ा रहे हैं ।

19. यह सोचकर मुझे बार-बार क्रोध आता है ।

20. उनका नाम इतिहास के चमकते पृष्ठों पर देखा जा सकेगा ।

21. अन्त में थककर हम लोग एक छायादार पेड़ के नीचे बैठ गए ।

22. एक बार खोया समय कभी नहीं लौटता ।

23. सड़क पर एक मरा हुआ कुत्ता था ।

24. मेरी खरीदी हुई कलम कहाँ है ?

25. हम लोगों ने आते हुए तूफान को देखा ।

Hints—कालातीत—out dated, outmoded, एक चम्मचभर—a spoonful, ऊबलना—to boil, डालना—to mix, हारना—to be overpowered or to be submitted, आत्महत्या करना—to commit suicide, मुझलना—to fade, धावक—athlete, अजनवी—stranger, उत्थान—progress, प्रतीक—symbol, sign, token, घूमना—to move, आलोच्य—criticised, तूफान—storm, आहत—stricken, दिखाई देना—to look, to appear, अचानक—suddenly, निर्णीत तथ्य—decided fact, पेंशन—pension, स्वीकृत करना—to grant, तीर—arrow, चलाना—to shoot, अंधी नकल करना—to imitate blindly, संस्कृति—culture, खिल्ली उड़ाना—to mock (at) to ridicule, बार-बार—again and again, चमकना—to sparkle, छायादार—shady, छुपाना—to hide, आना—approach, ध्वनि-संकलित—recorded.

Exercise 2

Make participles from these words and use them in your own sentences :

Burn, bereave, fling, encourage, weary, dissatisfy, flee, angry, approach, determine, people, find, found, scotch, make, turn, take, throb.

Sequence of Tenses

(कालों का अनुक्रम)

Sequence of Tenses से तात्पर्य है subordinate clause के verb को Principal clause (p.c) के verb के अनुसार रखना। "...... accommodation of subordinate verb in tense or mood according to certain rules to tense or mood of principal verb." (C.O.D.)

1. जब Main clause, Past Tense में हो तो उसका subordinate clause भी Past Tense में होगा।

1. श्री लालबहादुर ने कहा कि पाकिस्तान ने सबसे पहले आक्रमण किया है।
   Shri Lal Bahadur Shashtri said that Pakistan had attacked first.

2. उसने सोचा कि शीघ्र कमरा छोड़ देना उचित है।
   He thought that it was proper to leave the room at once.

3. उसने धमकी दी कि वह कभी घर नहीं लौटेगा।
   He threatened that he would never return home.

4. उसने प्रयास किया ताकि उसे भी एक अवसर मिले।
   He tried so that he too might get a chance.

2. उक्त नियम के दो अपवाद (exceptions) हैं—

(a) जब Main Clause—past tense में रहे और subordinate में कोई सर्वकालिक सत्य, प्राकृतिक स्वभाव या व्यावहारिक सत्य का भाव रहे तो उसे Present tense में ही रखेंगे।

(b) यदि subordinate clause में than से तुलना/समता रहे तो उसे present tense में रख सकते हैं।

1. जे॰सी॰ बोस ने माना कि पौधों में भी जीवन है।
   J.C. Bose maintained that there is life in plants also.

2. माँ ने अपने बच्चों से कहा कि पृथ्वी गोल है।
   The mother told her children that the earth is round.

3. अध्यापक ने कहा कि त्रिभुज की दो भुजाएँ तीसरी से बड़ी होती हैं।
   The teacher said that the two sides of a triangle are bigger than the third one.

4. सावित्री ने कहा कि संसार में कोई भी अपने हृदय की लालसा को नहीं पाया है।

Savitri said that none in the world has got his heart's desire.

3. जब Main clause–Present या future tense में रहे तो उसका subordinate clause भावानुसार किसी भी tense में हो सकता है।

1. वह सोचता है कि वह अभागा है। (अभागा था/अभागा होगा)

He thinks that he is unlucky. (...... was or will be unlucky)

2. जो कुछ मैं चाहता हूँ, मैं करूँगा, (या मैंने किया)।

I will do what I like or (...... what I liked).

Exercise

Insert the correct tense of the verb in the following according to the rules of the sequence of tenses :

1. My friend said that a bird in the hand ...... worth two in the bush.   (to be)
2. She cried that someone ...... away her purse.   (to take)
3. I think that I ...... go there.   (shall)
4. People believed that the war ...... end presently.   (will)
5. He laboured hard that he ...... pass.   (may)
6. As soon as I ...... the letter, I wrote to you.   (to get)
7. Whenever you ...... there you will not feel at ease.   (to go)
8. Although the bill ...... strongly, it was passed ultimately.   (to oppose)
9. Who said that the city on the hill ...... seen by all ?   (to be)
10. Just as the bell ......, the boys entered the room.   (to ring)
11. So long as he ...... from his own conscience, he can be believed.   (to speak)
12. The police ...... of me if I had seen any stranger.   (to enquire)
13. The teacher maintained that mathematics ...... the science of pure quantity. (to be)
14. My mother told me that all that ...... not gold.   (to shine–to be)
15. Whenever I ...... the questions, he answered them.   (to ask)
16. You might try if I ....   (to request)
17. He held that the laws of science ...... universal in their application.   (to be)
18. I liked that film more than you ...... it.   (to like)
19. I burnt the midnight oil in order that I ...... get success.   (may)
20. My father said that popularity ...... a bad measure of merit.   (to be)

Chapter 12

Conditional Sentences
(शर्त वाले वाक्य)

1. Present तथा Future Tenses—जब दिए गए वाक्य की क्रिया गा, गे, गी से समाप्त रहे या वर्तमान काल में रहे तो If + sub. + present indefinite etc. पश्चात् sub. + future indefinite etc. जैसी वाक्य की बनावट करेंगे। If, when, while, until, till, unless आदि के साथ shall/will न रखें और नहीं _तो_ या _तब_ के लिए Then का प्रयोग करें ; वहाँ comma दें। इस नियम के उल्लंघन का एक उदाहरण लें—

If the public is fascinated by a politician only then is he a seller. (from Editorial - June - India Today)

यद्यपि कि यह भी सही है कि आधुनिक बोलचाल की अंग्रेजी में इस प्रसंग में then का प्रयोग एक सामान्य बात हो गई है।

1.   यदि वर्षा होगी तो मैं विद्यालय नहीं जाऊँगा।

     If it rains, I shall not go to school.

2.   यदि भाव बढ़ते हैं तो हम क्या करेंगे ?

     What shall we do if prices rise ?

3.   यदि तुम्हारा साधन अच्छा है तो परिणाम भी अच्छा होगा।

     If your means is good, the result will also be good.

2. Past Tense—(a) जब हिन्दी की क्रिया भूतकाल की रहे तथा उसके साथ होता, होते, होती रहे तो उसे इस आधार पर अनुवाद करें—

If + sub. + past perfect etc. पश्चात् sub. + should/would/could/might + have + verb³ etc. or
Had + sub. verb³ etc ......

1.   यदि वह खूब मेहनत किया होता तो प्रथम आ गया होता।

     If he had worked hard, he would have stood first.

     _Or_ Had he worked hard, he ......

2.   अगर तुम पहले मिल गए होते तो मैं गाड़ी छोड़ दिया होता।

     If you had met before, I should have left the train.

(b) जब किसी noun/adjective/infinitive etc. के साथ होता, होते, होती रहे, तो उसे निम्नस्थ रीति से बनाएँ—

If + sub. + were/past indef. etc. + adj./noun etc. पश्चात्

sub. + should/could/might + verb¹ etc. or

were + sub. noun/adj. etc. ......

1.   यदि मैं राजा होता तो तुम्हें अपना मंत्री बनाता।

     If I were a king, I should appoint you my minister. _Or_

     Were I a king, I should ......

345

2. यदि मैं चिड़िया होता तो स्वच्छन्दता से आकाश में उड़ता।

    If I were a bird, I should fly in the sky at large.

3. अगर वह यहाँ आए तो मैं उसकी सहायता करूँ।

    If he came here, I should help him.

3. Conditional Sentence (Imperative)—आदेश आदि की स्थिति में पहले Imperative sentence रखें, पुन: comma दें जिसके बाद and से शेष वाक्य बनाएँ। If से वाक्य प्रारम्भ करके बाद में भी Imperative sentence रखा जा सकता है।

1. एक बार और धक्का दो तो दीवार गिर जाएगी।

    Push once more, and the wall will fall flat (or will turn to ground).

2. एक बार देख लो तो भूखे मनुष्यों की जान में जान आ जाएगी।

    Have a look and the starving men will feel relief.

3. यदि तुम मेरे लड़के से मिल जाओ तो उसे मेरी सदिच्छा दे देना।

    If you should meet my son, give him my best wishes.

4. अगर डाकघर से होकर जाओ तो कृपया मेरे लिए कुछ टिकट ला देना।

    If you should pass by the post office, please bring some stamps for me.

4. Negative भाव में unless/until (जब तक कि ...... नहीं) से conditional sentences बनाए जाते हैं। इनके साथ no/not/never न रखें क्योंकि ये स्वयं में negative sense रखते हैं। इनके बाद के हिस्से में no/not आदि रखा जा सकता है।

1. जब तक तुम अपनी गलती स्वीकार नहीं करोगे, मैं पुस्तक नहीं दूँगा।

    Unless you confess your fault, I will not give the book.

2. जब तक तुम प्रयास नहीं करोगे तो सफल नहीं होगे।

    Unless you try, you will not succeed.

5. In case, supposing, provided, but for तथा one more के द्वारा—

1. अगर विख्यात नेता आएँ तो वह चुनाव जीत सकता है।

    In case famous leaders come, he may win the election.   *Or*

    Supposing that famous leaders come, he may ......

2. यदि तुम खेद प्रगट करो तो मैं तुम्हें क्षमा कर दूँगा।

    I shall forgive you provided you express regret.

3. एक बार और प्रयास करो तो सफल हो जाओगे।

    One more attempt and you will succeed.

4. तुम्हारी सहायता बिना मैं बर्बाद हो गया होता।

    But for your help, I should have been ruined.

5. अगर अविश्वास प्रस्ताव गिर पड़ता है तो हम लोग संसद से बहिर्गमन करेंगे।

    In case no confidence motion drops, we shall walk out from the parliament.

6. अगर इस कमरे में भूत आ जाय तो सभी भाग खड़े होंगे।

    If a ghost appeared in this room, all would flee away.

Exercise

Translate into English :

1. अगर मैं तुम्हारी जगह पर होता तो मैं कभी वैसा नहीं सोचता।
2. यदि तुम प्रयाग जाओगे तो इतिहास प्रसिद्ध किला देखोगे।
3. अगर वह मुझसे पहले कहा होता तो मैं उसे अनुमति दे दिया होता।
4. यदि मैं देवदूत होता तो परियों के बच्चों को जगाता।
5. ऐसी स्थिति में जबकि वर्षा होती है तो मैं सिनेमा नहीं जाऊँगा।
6. वह प्रथम श्रेणी ला सकती है यदि वह कठिन परिश्रम करे।
7. तुम आओगे तो मैं तुम्हें सब कुछ बताऊँगा।
8. यदि राम को चुनाव टिकट मिलेगा तो वे जीत जाएँगे।
9. मुझे गाली दो तो मैं तुम्हें खूब पीटूँगा।
10. कहो कि तुम्हें खेद है तो मैं तुम्हें क्षमा कर दूँगा।
11. अगर कृष्ण पांडवों का पक्ष न लेते तो क्या होता ?
12. यदि तुम्हें यही करना था तो यहाँ क्यों आए ?
13. मैं सब कुछ मान सकता हूँ यदि वह केवल मेरे यहाँ चला आए।
14. यदि परीक्षाफल बीस प्रतिशत से कम होने लगे तो तुरंत तार करो।
15. अगर आप कहे होते तो मैं आपको धन्यवाद दिया होता।
16. अगर तुम मेरी जगह होते तो हताश हो जाते।
17. इस साल अच्छी फसल संभव है यदि वर्षा समय पर हो।
18. माना कि अ ब स एक त्रिभुज है तो इसमें एक वर्ग कैसे बनाओगे ?
19. एक बार झूठ बोले तो सभी तुम पर अविश्वास करेंगे।
20. अगर तुमको चापलूसी का गुण है तो समाज में तुम अपना स्थान पा सकते हो।
21. यदि आप दवा नहीं लेंगे तो कैसे अच्छे होंगे ?
22. मैं तुम्हें उधार दे सकता हूँ, यदि तुम उसे एक माह में लौटा दो।
23. यदि तुम्हें साहस हो तो उससे लड़ो।
24. तुम्हें मोती मिल सकता है यदि तुम्हें समुद्र में कूदने की हिम्मत हो।
25. यदि वह मोटरसाइकिल से गया होता तो जल्दी आ गया होता।
26. यदि तुम्हारा कोई साथ न दे तो अकेला चलो।
27. यदि तुम शान्ति चाहते हो तो युद्ध के लिए तैयार हो जाओ।

Hints—तुम्हारी जगह पर होता—to be at your place, वैसा—so, किला—fort, देवदूत—angel, परियाँ—fairies, जगाना—to arouse, to awake, लाना—to secure, पक्ष लेना—to take the side of, to favour, to support, मानना—to accept, तार करना—to wire, हताश होना—to be disheartened, संभव—possible, माना—suppose, वर्ग—square, अविश्वास करना—to distrust, to disbelieve, चापलूसी—flattery, गुण—skill, technique, स्थान पाना—to occupy a place or post, अच्छा होना—to recover, उधार देना—to lend, साहस होना—to dare, to have courage, मोती—pearl, gem, कूदना—to jump into, to plunge, साथ देना—to accompany, तैयार हो जाना—to be ready, शान्ति—peace, खूब पीटना—to beat black and blue.

Chapter 13

Complex Sentences
(मिश्रित वाक्य)

Complex sentences में एक principal clause (main clause—मुख्य उपवाक्य) होता है और एक या एक से अधिक subordinate clauses (आश्रित उपवाक्य) हुआ करते हैं। ये subordinate clauses तीन प्रकार के होते हैं—

(a) Noun clause (संज्ञा उपवाक्य) ; (b) Adjective clause (विशेषण उपवाक्य) तथा (c) Adverb clause (क्रिया विशेषण उपवाक्य)

1. Noun Clause (संज्ञा उपवाक्य)

संज्ञा उपवाक्य मुख्यत: 'कि' से प्रारम्भ रहा करता है जिसे that से प्रगट किया जाता है। इसे wh words से भी प्रारम्भ किया जाता है जब उनका उच्चारण 'क' अक्षर से प्रारम्भ रहे। ध्यान रहे कि इस प्रकार wh से प्रारम्भ subordinate N.C. साधारण वाक्य हुआ करते हैं, प्रश्नवाचक नहीं। अत: वाक्य में इनका स्वरूप होगा–Wh + sub. + verb .... Noun की तरह यह पाँच प्रकार से काम करेगा।

(a) Subject of a verb (p.c. के verb के कर्त्ता के रूप में)–

1. कि वह मेरी मदद नहीं करेगा (यह) एक खुला तथ्य है।

That he will not help me is an open fact.

2. मैं कैसे वहाँ पहुँचा (यह) एक रहस्य है।

How I reached there is a mystery.

3. यह कल्पनातीत है कि वह क्या सोचती है (जो कुछ वह सोचती है कल्पनातीत है)।

What she thinks is beyond imagination.

4. यह एकदम अज्ञात है कि वे क्यों झगड़ते हैं।

Why they quarrel is quite unknown.

प्रथम उदाहरण में p.c. के verb 'is' का that he .... me–subject है।

(b) Object of a transitive verb (सकर्मक क्रिया के कार्य के रूप में)–

1. कोई नहीं जानता कि कल क्या होगा।

No one knows what will happen tomorrow.

यहाँ p.c. के verb 'knows' का what .... tomorrow–object है।

2. उसने मुझे विश्वास दिलाया कि वह निर्दोष है।

He assured me that he was innocent.

3. उन्हें सिखाओ कि कैसे मानव मस्तिष्क पृथ्वी से सुन्दरतर होता है।

Teach them how the mind of man becomes more beautiful than the earth.

4. जो मेरा उचित हिस्सा है, मुझे दो।

Give me what my due is ?

5. मैं नहीं जानता कि वह कब आएगा।

I do not know when he will come.

(c) Object of a preposition–

1. जो कुछ मैं कहता हूँ, सुनो।

Listen to what I say.

2. जो कुछ तुम कहते हो उस पर मैं विश्वास नहीं करता।

I do not believe in what you say.

(d) Apposition to a Noun–Subject का उसके शीघ्र पश्चात् वर्णन या परिचय देना apposition कहलाता है। इस तरह वाक्य में उसकी स्थिति होगी–p.c. का sub. + apposition + p.c. के sub. से सम्बद्ध शेष भाग।

Wellington, the great conqueror, invaded Britain–यहाँ the great conqueror–p.c के subject–Wellington का परिचय स्वरूप प्रयुक्त है, अत: वह Apposition है। Apposition means placing side by side.

1. उसका स्पष्ट उत्तर कि वह मदद नहीं कर सकता, मुझे निराश कर दिया।

His flat reply that he could not help, disappointed me.

2. तुम्हारी आकांक्षा कि तुम एक विख्यात नेता बन जाओ व्यर्थ है।

Your aspiration that you may become a famous leader is empty.

3. तुम्हारा विचार कि मात्र तुम्हारा ही धर्म अर्थपूर्ण है पक्षपात पर आधारित है।

Your view that your creed alone is meaningful is based on partiality.

(e) Complement of a verb (क्रिया का पूरक)–

1. उसकी आशा है कि वह परीक्षा उत्तीर्ण कर लेगा।

His hope is that he will pass the examination.

...... that he will ...... examination—p.c. के verb–is का complement है।

2. सत्य तो यह है कि यहाँ प्रत्येक पार्टी पराजित है।

The truth is that every party here is a loser.

(f) विशेष–

1. मैं नहीं कह सकता कि वह कहाँ रहता है।

I cannot say where he lives. (कि कहाँ–स्थान हेतु)।

2. मैं नहीं जानता कि गाड़ी कब आएगी।

I do not know when the train will arrive. (कि कब–समय हेतु)।

3. तुम सफल होगे कि नहीं मुझे संदेह है।

I doubt if (or whether) you will succeed or not.

4. क्या तुम जानते हो कि सद्गुण क्या है और दुर्गुण क्या है ?

Do you know what virtue is and what vice is ?

5. उसने इसे कैसे किया यह एक रहस्य है।

How he did it is a secret. (कि कैसे या किस प्रकार i.e., manner)

6. जो कुछ भी हम देखते हैं क्षणिक है।

   Whatsoever we see is momentary.

7. वह जानता है कि वह क्या कहता है।

   He knows what he says. (कि क्या—जो कुछ)।

Exercise 1

Translate into English :

1. अनुमान है कि लगभग 50 आदमी भूकम्प में अपनी जान गँवाए।

2. आश्चर्य है कि उसने मेरा क्यों विरोध किया।

3. कोलम्बस ने अपने मित्रों से कहा कि लक्ष्य बहुत दूर है।

4. मैंने सोचा कि तुम वहाँ हो।

5. यह आशा नहीं थी कि खानवा का युद्ध बाबर जीत लेगा।

6. युद्ध से शान्ति आती है। यह एक अप्रासंगिक सिद्धान्त है।

7. आश्चर्य है कि वह अनुत्तीर्ण हो गया।

8. यह सन्देह है कि रमेश प्रथम आएगा।

9. यह विचार कि मृत्यु के बाद जीवन है आस्था पर निर्भर करता है।

10. क्या तुम जानते हो कि मौसम कैसे बदलते हैं ?

11. तुम्हारा कथन कि वस्तुतः तुमने बुरे मौके पर साथ दिया, एक आत्मछल है।

12. भाव यह है कि यह संसार हमारा वास्तविक घर नहीं है।

13. कोई नहीं जानता कि युद्ध कब फूट पड़ेगा ?

14. हम लोगों ने देखा कि एक साँप बच्चे के साथ खेल रहा है।

15. मैं जानना चाहता हूँ कि तुम विलम्ब से क्यों आए।

Hints—अनुमान है–it is supposed (or thought), लगभग–nearly, भूचाल–earthquake, अपनी जान गँवाए–lost their life, बहुत दूर–afar, अप्रासंगिक सिद्धान्त–irrelevant principle, आस्था पर निर्भर करना–to depend (or rest) on faith, मौसम–weather, कथन–statement, वस्तुतः–really, of course, indeed, बुरे मौके पर साथ देना–to do yeoman's service, आत्मछल–self-deceit, भाव यह है कि–the idea is that, फूट पड़ना–to break out.

Exercise 2

Complete the following sentences by adding suitable noun clause :

1. ...... is an outmoded belief.
2. I see ......
3. Do not think ....
4. It is uncertain ......
5. Do you know ...... ?
6. ...... was correct.
7. The truth is ......
8. My hope ......
9. He sought for ......
10. The idea is ....

Exercise 3

Translate into English :

1. क्या मैं समझता था कि तुम क्या कर रहे थे ?

2. प्रकृति जनसंख्या नियंत्रित करती है यह अब असत्य हो चुका है।

3. कुछ ऐसा हुआ कि सिन्दबाद एक निर्जन वन में पहुँचा।

4. यह सुनने में आता है कि सरकार सभी पद पिछड़े वर्गों के लिए सुरक्षित करने जा रही है।

5. जो मैं चाहता था यही है।

6. आवश्यक नहीं कि प्रत्येक एक साथ ही जायँ।

7. मेरी इच्छा है कि तुम एक डाक्टर बनो।

8. जो कुछ है, ठीक है।

9. ऐसा प्रतीत होता है कि वह नहीं लौटेगा।

10. सत्य यह है कि इस बारे में तुम कुछ भी नहीं जानते।

11. क्या तुम बता सकते हो कि वहाँ लोग क्यों इकट्ठे हुए हैं ?

12. तुम जो कुछ करते हो उसी से हम लोग तुम्हारा मूल्यांकन करेंगे।

13. यह दुख की बात है कि उसकी नौकरी छूट गई है।

14. यह सुनकर कि वह कठिनाई में है मैं उसकी मदद के लिए गया।

15. मैंने उसे सूचित किया कि मैं इसके बाद उसकी सहायता नहीं करुँगा।

Hints—जनसंख्या–population, नियंत्रित करना–to check, कुछ ऐसा हुआ–it so happened (or ocurred), निर्जन–desolate, सुनने में आता है–it is heard (or learnt), पिछड़े वर्ग–backward classes, सुरक्षित करना–to reserve, एक साथ–all together, प्रतीत होना–to seem, to appear, दुख की बात है–it is a pity, it is a matter of regret (or sorrow), छूट गई है–is dismissed from.

2. Adjective Clause (*विशेषण उपवाक्य*)

हिन्दी के जो, जिसने, जिसको, जिसका, जब, जहाँ आदि से प्रारम्भ वाक्य को अंग्रेजी में who, which, that, whom, when, where etc. से प्रगट किया जाता है। इन Relative Pronouns पर पृथक्-पृथक् विचार करना आवश्यक है।

1. Who (जो, जिसने)–केवल व्यक्ति के लिए प्रयोग किया जाता है, वस्तु के लिए नहीं।

1. मैं एक आदमी से मिला जिसने मुझे एक रहस्य बताया।

   I met a man who unfolded me a secret.

2. जो साहस करता है वह पराजय नहीं जानता।

   He who dares knows no fall.

3. वह आदमी जो फटे पुराने कपड़े पहना है एक विख्यात दार्शनिक है।

   The man who has worn shabby clothes is a celebrated philosopher.

2. Whose (जिसका, जिसकी, जिसके)–इसका प्रयोग व्यक्ति तथा वस्तु दोनों के लिए किया जाता है।

(a) जेम्स जिसका चेहरा अज्ञात है एक कुख्यात समुद्री लुटेरा है।

   James whose face is unknown is a notorious pirate.

(b) वह ग्रन्थ जिसके पृष्ठ उदात्त माने गए हैं मिल्टन का पैराडाइज़ लॉस्ट है।

   The book whose pages are marked with sublimity is Milton's Paradise Lost. (which)

(c) जिस छाते की मुट्ठी टूटी है वह मेरी है।

   The umbrella whose handle is broken is mine. (or which)

3. Whom (जिसे, जिसको)—इसे केवल व्यक्ति के लिए प्रयोग करें—

(*a*) वह लड़का जिसे तुमने कल बाजार में देखा मेरा भाई है।

 The boy whom you saw in the market yesterday is my brother.

(*b*) यही वह व्यक्ति है जिसे हम सभी पूजते हैं।

 This is the man whom we all adore.

(*c*) वह बुड्ढा जिसकी तुमने सहायता की एक धनी व्यक्ति है।

 The old man whom you helped is a rich man.

4. Which (जो, जिसने, जिसको आदि)—इसे केवल वस्तुओं के लिए nominative तथा objective case में प्रयोग किया जाता है।

(*a*) जो सुराही हम कल खरीदे वह गिर पड़ी और चूर-चूर हो गई।

 The jug which we bought yesterday fell and broke into pieces.

(*b*) जो कुर्सी कोने में है उसे लाओ।

 Bring the chair which is in the corner.

(*c*) वह कलम जिसे तुमने खोया था, यहाँ है।

 Here is the pen which you had lost.

5. That (जिसने, जिसको आदि)—व्यक्ति और वस्तु दोनों के लिए who/which के स्थान पर इसे प्रयोग किया जाता है। बहुधा विचारों, भावनाओं के लिए इसका प्रयोग दर्शनीय होता है। Superlative degree, all, same, any, none, nothing (the) only, who तथा what के पश्चात् इसका प्रयोग होता है। जानवरों के लिए भी इसका प्रयोग स्वीकार्य है।

(*a*) जिस सिर पर मुकुट होता है वह परेशान रहता है।

 Uneasy lies the head that wears a crown.

(*b*) जो बादल पहाड़ पर इकट्ठे थे वे हवा के झोंके से तितर बितर हो गए।

 The clouds that were mustered on the hill were dispersed with the gusts of wind.

(*c*) यह सबसे अच्छा है जिसे हम लोग कर सकते हैं।

 This is the best that we can do.

(*d*) वह शहर जो दिन में भीड़ से भरा था अब स्वप्नों की बाँहों में हैं।

 The town that was thronged in day is now in the arms of orpheus.

(*e*) जो रेडियो तुमने खरीदा वह अब ठीक हालत में नहीं है।

 The radio that you bought is now out of order.

(*f*) सभी जो चमकते हैं सोना नहीं होते।

 All that glitters is not gold.

(*g*) केवल मनुष्य ही ऐसा जानवर है जिसे सौन्दर्यबोध है।

 Man is the only animal that has aesthetic sense.

(*h*) यह क्या है जो तुम्हें इतना अधिक कष्ट देता है।

 What is it that troubles you so much ?

(i) जिसका कोई इलाज न हो उसे सहन करना पड़ेगा।

What cannot be cured must be endured.

6. When (जब) और Where (जहाँ)–क्रमश: समय (time) तथा स्थान (place) बताते हैं। Why (जिससे, जिस कारण से) कारण (Reason) बताता है।

(a) क्या तुम वह समय जानते हो जब वह आएगा ?

Do you know the time when he will arrive ?

(b) यही वह जगह है जहाँ दुर्घटना हुई थी।

This is the place where the accident had occurred.

(c) जहाँ वह मरा वह घर भूतों का डेरा है।

The house where he died is a haunt of ghosts.

(d) जिस कारण से वह अनुत्तीर्ण हुआ वह स्पष्ट है।

The reason why he failed is obvious.

7. यही, वही (same) तथा ऐसा (such)–के पश्चात् as या that से adjective clause बनाए जाते हैं। Who/which आदि से नहीं। Same के साथ that और such के साथ as का प्रयोग अधिक तर्कसंगत है।

(a) तुम्हारे व्यवहार ऐसे हैं जिन्हें सभ्य नहीं माना जा सकता।

Your behaviours are such as cannot be accounted civil.

(b) हम ऐसे तत्त्व से बने हैं जिसे धूल कहा जा सकता है।

We are made of such a stuff as can be called dust.

(c) बहुत से लोग ऐसे हैं जो अज्ञात मर जाते हैं।

Lots of men are such as die unknown.

(d) यह वही चीज है जिसे मैं चाहता था।

This is the same thing that I wanted.

Note. Relative Pronouns से प्रगट किए जाने वाले adjective clauses को उसके antecedent (पूर्ववर्ती या मूल कर्त्ता) के सन्निकट से शुरू करना चाहिए अन्यथा वाक्यार्थ भ्रमास्पद हो सकता है।

Incorrect	Correct
The world is highly impressed with Mahatma Gandhi's ideals who was the beacon light of the century.	The world is highly impressed with the ideals of Mahatma Gandhi who was the beacon light of the century.

ऐसे कथन भी देखें–

(a) जो कुछ उसने किया वह आशा से परे है।

What he did is beyond expectation.

(b) जो कुछ भी कहा उसे गारन्टी नहीं समझनी चाहिए।

Whatsoever is said should not be taken as a guarantee.

(c) जो एक के लिए दवा है दूसरों के लिए विष हो सकता है।

What is a remedy for one may be poison for others.

8. कभी-कभी Relative Pronouns को छिपा दिया जाता है—

(*a*) जो आम हम खाये वे खट्टे थे।

The mangoes we tasted were sour.

(*b*) जो किताब मैंने खरीदी वह बड़ी रुचिकर है।

The book I bought is very interesting.

9. कभी-कभी जो, जिसने से हिन्दी वाक्य प्रारम्भ रहा करता है जबकि Antecedent (पूर्ववर्ती कर्ता) का पता नहीं चलता। ऐसी स्थिति में He (singular हेतु) तथा Those (plural हेतु) परिकल्पित करके उसके बाद Adjective clause शुरू करें।

(*a*) जो बहुत हँसता है वह अवश्य रोता है।

He who laughs much must weep.

(*b*) जो ऊँचे चढ़ते हैं वे अवश्य नीचे गिरते हैं।

Those who climb high are sure to fall.

(*c*) जो बोएगा वह काटेगा।

He who sows will reap. (Who sows will reap.)

(*d*) जिसने चोरी किया है उसे अवश्य सजा दिया जाना चाहिए।

He who has committed the theft must be punished.

(Who has committed the theft must be punished.)

(*e*) जिसे देवता प्यार करते हैं वह कम उम्र में मर जाता है।

He whom gods love dies young. (Whom gods love die young.)

10. Negative sense में none but द्वारा भी Adjective clause प्रगट किया जाता है।

वहाँ कोई नहीं था जो मेरा समर्थन नहीं करना चाहता था।

There was none but wished to support me.

इसी तरह—There was none but wept to hear the pitiable tale of the widow.

There is none but agree with me.

(but will agree—who will not agree)

Note. Relative Pronoun से प्रारम्भ Adjective clause का verb उसके antecedent के number तथा person के अनुसार होना चाहिए।

(*a*) मैं जो तुम्हारा मित्र हूँ तुम्हारी सहायता करुँगा।

I who am your friend must help you.

(*b*) जो लड़के यात्रा पर थे वे लौट आए हैं।

The boys who were on tour have returned.

11. एक ही noun या pronoun के लिए बहुधा एक से अधिक Relative Pronouns रखने की आवश्यकता पड़ती है, किन्तु ध्यान रहे प्रत्येक clause स्वयं में व्याकरण के नियमों का कहीं उल्लंघन न कर दे। उदाहरणार्थ—

Mr. Roche is practising a definite system which he is able to describe and could be studied by others. (Incorrect—Fowler's Modern English Usage.)

यहाँ भ्रम यह है कि दूसरे clause का subject है he जो system का 'वर्णन करने में समर्थ है' किन्तु अन्तिम clause जो (system) 'दूसरों के द्वारा अध्ययन किया जा सकता था' विचारणीय है। संक्षेप में प्रथम clause का which, objective case (कर्म कारक) है किन्तु अन्तिम में nominative (कर्त्ता) रूप में प्रयुक्त है। अच्छा हो कि इसे ऐसे लिखा जाय—

(a) Mr. Roche is practising a definite system which he is able to describe and which could be studied by others.   *Or*

(b) Mr. Roche is practising a definite system which is described by him and could be studied by others.

Exercise 1

Translate into English :

1. जो जन्म लेता है अवश्य मरता है।
2. जो सन्दूक मैंने कल खरीदी थी वह घटिया लोहे की बनी है।
3. वह आदमी जिसे तुमने एक भद्र पुरुष समझा था वह एक डाकू है।
4. वह लड़का जिसका बायाँ पैर टूट गया था मोहन का भाई है।
5. वह सौन्दर्य जो प्रत्येक वस्तु में प्रगट है, ईश्वरीय है।
6. जिन विचारों ने संसार को प्रभावित किया वे कभी नहीं मरेंगे।
7. जहाँ देवता भी नहीं जा सकते वहाँ मूर्ख जाते हैं।
8. जो कला युग की चेतना प्रगट करती है वह अमर है।
9. हमारा जीवन जिसे हम जीते हैं हमारे धर्म पर व्यंग्य है।
10. उस सूचना ने जिसे उसने कल सुना उसे उदास कर दिया।
11. मैं उस आदमी से मिला जिसके केश सुनहरे थे।
12. यह एक ऐसी खराब हवा है जो किसी के लिए अच्छी नहीं होती।
13. जो मैं आज सोचता हूँ उसे तुम कल सोचोगे।
14. जहाँ सत्य है वहाँ शान्ति है।
15. जो जीएगा वह उपभोग करेगा।

Hints—घटिया लोहा–baser steel, भद्र–gentle, समझना–to account, डाकू–robber, decoit, highwayman, टूटना–to fracture, प्रत्येक वस्तु में प्रगट है–is pervading all objects, is immanent, ईश्वरीय–godly, divine, प्रभावित करना–to influence, to move, जाना–to tread, युग की चेतना प्रगट करना–to reveal the temper of the age, अमर–immortal, व्यंग्य–satire, irony, उदास करना–to sadden, उपभोग करना–to enjoy.

Exercise 2

Complete the following sentences by the use of adjective clauses :

1. I am not among those ......
2. Those ...... never fail.
3. Blessed are they ......
4. He ...... gets the gems.
5. The book ...... is lost.
6. The statement ...... is false.
7. The horse ...... is troublesome (to stumble).
8. He ...... never succeeds.
9. Put out the candle ......
10. Where is the man ...... ?
11. ...... is an old wive's tale.
12. Why did you keep the word ...... ?
13. There was not a corner ...... peeped carefully.
14. These mangoes are such ....
15. This is the same model ....

Exercise 3

Correct if necessary, the following sentences :

1. I have read the 'Essays of Elia' by lamb who are interesting.
2. The man which you chid yesterday is Hari's uncle.
3. The lady that eyes are blue is a spy.
4. The peace who is inherent is argued on the political platform
5. The boy of your class who stood first is my nephew.
6. The theory that he expounded has been marked as shallow.
7. The mundane beauty is such which cannot keep its lustre beyond tomorrow.
8. This is the same case that has been discussed.
9. The table whom you bought is broken.
10. The matter I concern is alien to your remark.
11. They never fail who die in a great cause.
12. They also serve who only stand and wait.
13. This is the best book which is published lately.
14. I see both the master and the dog who are in the mid-field.
15. The only question which was easy was also left unanswered.

Exercise 4

Translate into English :

1. जो सोता है वह सब खोता है।
2. जिन आदर्शों का उन्होंने उपदेश किया वे विश्व को शान्ति दे सकते हैं।
3. क्या तुमने उस छाता को खो दिया है जिसे मैंने तुम्हें दिया था ?
4. जो जीवन साहसिक नहीं है वह जीवन नहीं है।
5. जो ईश्वर के अस्तित्व को नहीं स्वीकारता वह नास्तिक है।
6. यह नीति उनमें से एक है जो धर्म सुधार के विरुद्ध थी।
7. प्रक्षेपास्त्र ने जिसका लक्ष्य उपमहाद्वीप का दूसरा छोर था, दुश्मनों की भारी क्षति की।
8. जिन्हें तुम अपना मित्र समझते हो वे वास्तव में तुम्हारे शत्रु हैं।
9. यह ऐसा साबुन है जो बहुत स्वास्थ्यवर्धक है।
10. वह भवन जो कल ऊँचा खड़ा था आज विनष्ट हो गया।
11. उस अपराधी ने जिसे न्यायालय ने छोड़ दिया था पुनः एक व्यक्ति की हत्या की।
12. उन कारणों को बताओ जो तुगलक वंश को पतन की ओर ले गए।
13. वह भवन जो पहाड़ी पर है सभी द्वारा देखा जाता है।
14. वह स्थान जहाँ राष्ट्रपति भाषण देंगे निकट है।
15. जो धन इकट्ठा करता है स्वास्थ्य खराब कर लेता है।

Hints—खोना–to lose, आदर्श–ideal, उपदेश करना–to preach, देना–to afford, साहसिक–adventurous, अस्तित्व–existence, नास्तिक–atheist, धर्मसुधार–reformation, प्रक्षेपास्त्र–missile, लक्ष्य उपमहाद्वीप का दूसरा छोर था–aimed across the sub-continent, भारी क्षति की–caused a heavy loss, स्वास्थ्यवर्धक–hygienic, ऊँचा खड़ा था–had raised its head high (or aloft), विनष्ट होना–to rage to ground, to tumble down, छोड़ना–to acquit, हत्या करना–to murder, कारण बताना–to account for, तुगलक वंश–the Tuglaque dynasty, पतन–downfall, decline, भाषण देना–to address, धन–wealth, इकट्ठा करना–to amass.

COMPLEX SENTENCES

3. Adverb Clause (क्रिया विशेषण उपवाक्य)

हिन्दी के क्रिया विशेषण उपवाक्यों का निम्नांकित नियमों के आधार पर अंग्रेजी में अनुवाद किया जाता है।

1. Adverb clause of time—When, whenever (जब कभी भी) after, before, since, as, till (जब तक) so long as (जहाँ तक, जब तक) as soon as (ज्यों ही, जैसे ही)—समय-संकेत रहने पर क्रिया विशेषण उपवाक्य को उक्त conjunctions द्वारा main clause से जोड़ा जाता है।

Note. Since जब conjunction रूप में दो clauses को जोड़े तो उसके पूर्व present verb तथा पश्चात् में Past Indefinite का प्रयोग किया जाता है। इसी प्रकार so long as तथा until, period of time बताते हैं और till-point of time बताता है। Till तथा until के अन्तर को स्पष्ट करते हुए कहा गया है—When the clause or phrase precedes the main sentence, until is perhaps actually the commoner-until his accession he had been popular. (Fowler-M.E.U.) संक्षेप में जब main clause बाद में हो तो until का प्रयोग उसके पूर्व होगा और यदि main clause पहले होगा तो बाद में till का प्रयोग करेंगे।

(a) जब मैं चारों ओर देखता हूँ तो अपने को मित्रहीन पाता हूँ।

When I look around, I find myself friendless.

(b) जब कभी (जब-जब) बर्फ गिरती है, ठंडक अधिक बढ़ जाती है।

Whenever snow falls, cold grows more.

(c) जब तक साँस तब तक आस।

While there is life there is hope.

(d) जब तक अवसर रहे तब तक लाभ उठा लो।

Make hay while the sun shines.

(e) जब वे निकट से गुजरें कास्का को बाँह से खींच लो!

As they pass by, pluck Casca by the sleeve.

(f) जब अर्धरात्रि बीत चुकी थी तब वह आया।

He came after the mid-night had passed (or fallen).

(g) सैकड़ों वर्ष बीत गए जब शिवाजी मरे।

Hundreds of years have passed since Shivaji died.

(h) जब तक मैं आता हूँ यहीं प्रतीक्षा करो।

Wait here till I come.

(i) जब तक वह नहीं आता तब तक एक गीत गाओ।

Until he comes, sing a song.

Bible—'Thou shalt wander on the earth till I return.'

(j) जब तक वर्षा होती रहेगी मैं घर पर ही रहूँगा।

So long as the rain continues I shall remain at home.

(k) ज्योंही (जैसे ही) मैंने कमरे में प्रवेश किया दीपक गिर पड़ा।

As soon as (or just as) I entered the room the lamp fell.   *Or*

No sooner did I enter the room than the lamp fell.

(l) जब मैं आया तब वह गया।

When I came he went.   *Or*   He went when I came.

Note. Since तथा ago के अन्तर को दर्शाते हुए Fowler ने लिखा है—If 'ago' is used and the event to be dated is given by a clause, it must be by one beginning with 'that' and not 'since'. The right forms are : He died

20 years ago (No clause). It is twenty years since he died (not ago) It was twenty years ago that he died.
No sooner के लिए वाक्य का सूत्र इस प्रकार होगा—

No sooner + helping verb/verb to be + sub. + verb etc. + than ......

2. Adverb clause of place—Where, wherever (जहाँ कहीं भी), whence (जहाँ से), whither etc.

(a) जहाँ चाह है वहाँ राह है।

Where there is a will, there is a way.

(b) जहाँ जहाँ धुँआ है, वहाँ वहाँ आग है।

Where there is smoke, there is fire.

(c) तैमूर जहाँ कहीं भी गया सर्वनाश आया।

Wherever Taimur went, destruction awaited (there).

(d) 'Around me I behold,

Wherever these casual eyes are cast

The mighty minds of old.' (Southey)

(e) जहाँ से आए हो (वहाँ) शीघ्र चले जाओ।

Go quickly whence you came.

(f) जहाँ अज्ञानता ही परमानन्द है वहाँ बुद्धिमान बनना मूर्खता है।

Where ignorance is bliss, it is folly to be wise.

3. Adverb clause of purpose—उद्देश्य, मन्शा, तात्पर्य प्रगट करने के लिए that (ताकि, जिससे कि), lest (अन्यथा, कहीं ऐसा न हो), so as to से सहायता ली जाती है। Lest के बाद verb के साथ should का प्रयोग करें। साथ ही not जैसे निषेधात्मक शब्दों का प्रयोग न करें।

(a) छाता ले लो कहीं ऐसा न हो कि इसे हम भूल जायँ।

Take the umbrella lest we should forget it.

(b) हम खाते हैं ताकि हम जी सकें।

We eat that we may live.

(c) हम पीछे हट गए जिससे कि शान्ति स्थापित हो सके।

We withdrew that (*i.e.*, so that, in order that) peace might be restored.

(d) मैंने अपना शोध प्रबन्ध प्रकाशित कर दिया ताकि मेरी मृत्यु के पश्चात् संसार अंधकार में न रह जाय।

I published my research work lest the world should remain in the dark after my death.

God fulfils himself in many ways.

Lest one good custom should corrupt the world. (Tennyson)

(e) मैं मरता हूँ ताकि मेरा देश जी सके।

I die that my country may live.

4. Adverb clause of cause or Reason—क्योंकि, कारण से, चूँकि के भाव में because, as since आदि का प्रयोग होता है। ऐसे वाक्यों में एक से कारण तथा अन्य से परिणाम का भाव व्यक्त रहता है। 'कारण से' प्रगट करने के लिए कई phrases हैं—due to, owing to, by this reason, because of, why or because or reason (this is why, it was the reason etc.) on account of आदि। इसमें इसलिए, अत: हेतु so का प्रयोग न करें।

(a) चूँकि तुम तैयार नहीं हो अत: हमें अवश्य जाना चाहिए।

As you are not ready, we must go.

(b) क्योंकि वह बीमार था इसलिए वह परीक्षा नहीं दे सका।

Because he was ill, he could not take the examination.

(c) चूँकि तुम बहुत बुद्धिमान हो तुम उचित उपाय निकाल सकते हो।

Since you are very wise, you may find out a proper solution.

(d) लोगों ने उसे अस्वीकार कर दिया क्योंकि वह योग्य नहीं था।

People refused him because he was not worthy.

(e) चूँकि कोई सवारी नहीं थी अत: मैं नहीं आ सका।

Since there was no convenience, I could not come.

अब उपरोक्त phrases से बनने वाले कुछ सामान्य वाक्यों को देखें–

(a) अत्यन्त निर्धनता के कारण मैंने अपनी पढ़ाई छोड़ दी।

Owing to utter poverty, I left my study.

Note. Due to का प्रयोग तब करना चाहिए जब इसके पूर्व पश्चात् कोई noun या pronoun हो। इस प्रसंग में owing to अधिक उचित होता है।

(b) फूट के कारण मराठे मैदान हार गए।

The Marathas lost the field due to discord.

(c) दुर्घटना लापरवाही से हुई है।

The accident has occurred due to slackness.

(d) कठिनाई हमारी अज्ञानता के कारण है।

The difficulty is due to our ignorance.

'...... it seems clear that idiom (due to) though still resisting stoutly, is fighting a losing battle. The offending usage has indeed become literally part of the Queen's English.' (Fowler)

5. Adverb clause of Condition—(Chapter 12 देखें)

6. Adverb clause of Result—जब कार्य और उसके परिणाम का बोध हो तो उसे so ... that या such ... as (इतना ...... कि, उतना ...... कि, ऐसा कि) से प्रगट करते हैं।

(a) वह इतना असभ्य है कि कोई भी उसका साथ नहीं देता।

So uncivil is he that no one favours him.

(b) वह इतने जोरों से हँसा कि मेरी निद्रा में बाधा पड़ी।

So loudly did he laugh that my slumber was interrupted.

(c) उसने रोहन को ऐसा घूँसा मारा कि वह मूर्छित हो गया।

He boxed Sohan in such a way as he fainted.

(d) पिताजी इतने नाराज थे कि उन्होंने मुझसे बात नहीं की।

The father was so angry that he did not talk to me.

(e) वे इतनी बहादुरी से लड़े कि शत्रु भाग गए।

So bravely did they fight that the enemy ran away.

7. Adverb clause of comparison and manner–(Chapter 6 देखें)

8. Adverb clause of supposition or concession— हिन्दी के 'यद्यपि कि' (हालांकि), 'भले ही' आदि से बने वाक्यों का अनुवाद though, although, even if या even though आदि द्वारा किया जाता है। As if, as though (मानो) के पश्चात् Past Verb रखें। वैसे प्रचलन <u>were</u> के प्रयोग का है।

(a) यद्यपि कि मूसलाधार वर्षा हो वह छाता नहीं लेगा।

He would not take an umbrella though it should rain cats and dogs.

(b) यद्यपि कि उसने सबसे अधिक अंक पाया वह द्वितीय श्रेणी की योग्यता का था।

Although he obtained the highest marks, he was of mediocre ability.

(c) यद्यपि कि मैंने बहुत प्रयास किया किन्तु सफल न हो सका।

Although I tried my best I could not succeed.

(d) यद्यपि कि दिन खुला था किन्तु कुछ भी दिखाई नहीं दिया।

Nothing was visible though it was broad day light.

(e) तुम भले ही रोओ किन्तु मैं तुम्हें कुछ भी नहीं दे सकता।

Even if you weep I cannot give you anything.

(f) भले ही वह झूठ बोलता है वह ईमानदार है।

Even if he tells a lie he is honest.

(g) यद्यपि वह धनी है वह बहुत विनम्र है।

Although he is wealthy he is very humble.

(h) यद्यपि वह कमजोर है फिर भी वह साहसी है।

Weak as he is, he is bold.

(i) वह ऐसी बातें करता है मानो वह मेरा अधिकारी हो।

He talks as if he were my officer.

Exercise 1

Translate into English :

1. जब भी जरूरत हो मुझे बुला लेना।
2. जब बिल्ली बाहर रहेगी तब चूहे खेलेंगे।
3. जब तक कुन्दन जीएगा पड़ोसी शान्तिपूर्वक नहीं रह सकते।
4. जहाँ तुम गरीबों को सताते हो, मैं उनकी सहायता करता हूँ।
5. जब-जब वह यहाँ आया उसने तुम्हारी सहायता की।
6. जब तक सत्य नहीं बोलोगे तुम्हें पुलिस नहीं छोड़ेगी।
7. जब तक तुम आओगे तब तक हमारा सर्वनाश हो जाएगा।
8. जब तक ईमानदार नहीं बनोगे तुम ख्याति नहीं पा सकते।
9. हम लोग वहाँ गए जहाँ वह रहता है।
10. जहाँ-जहाँ हम जाते हैं हमारी छाया पीछा करती है।
11. जब तक खेलते हो खेलो, जब तक काम करना है काम करो।
12. पहले की अपेक्षा वह आज बेहतर दिखाई देता है।

13. प्रश्न इतना कठिन था कि कोई हल नहीं कर सका।

14. जैसा तुम बोओगे वैसा काटोगे।

15. उसने ऐसा बर्ताव किया मानो वह पागल हो।

Hints—जरूरत हो–it needs, पड़ोसी–neighbour, सताना–to tease, सर्वनाश होना–to ruin, to undo, पीछा करना–to follow, बोना–to sow, काटना–to reap, बर्ताव करना–to behave.

Exercise 2

Correct the following sentences :

1. Till you account him a noble man, you will be deceived.
2. Wait until it rains.
3. Unless we do not make ourselves strong and powerful our mission will be ridiculed.
4. Five years had passed since he came.
5. Though my purse is empty but my patience is ample.
6. Although she shed copious tears yet nobody took pity on her.
7. Ages went into the wombs of oblivion since his letter came.
8. Unless you do not stick to your gun none will believe you.
9. Watch lest you will fall the victim of temptation.
10. So loudly he spoke as the child woke up.

Exercise 3

Translate into English :

1. हम जहाँ कहीं भी गए सभी को चोर पाए।
2. मैंने एक कलम तथा कागज लिया ताकि मैं एक कविता लिख सकूँ।
3. कुछ लोग जीते हैं ताकि खा सकें।
4. तुमने इसे किया क्योंकि तुम इसे करना चाहते थे।
5. सिद्धार्थ ने महल छोड़ दिया क्योंकि संसार उन्हें दुखी दिखाई दिया।
6. हम दुख भोगते हैं क्योंकि हमारा हृदय शुद्ध नहीं।
7. नैपोलियन इतनी बहादुरी से लड़ा कि आंग्ल फौज पीछे हट गई।
8. उसने ऐसा बर्ताव किया कि सभी सन्तुष्ट हो गए।
9. भले ही तुम सत्य बोलो किन्तु कोई भी तुम पर विश्वास नहीं करेगा।
10. यद्यपि कि वे लोग बहादुर थे फिर भी वे हार गए।
11. जहाँ प्रकाश है वहाँ जीवन है।
12. यद्यपि मैंने अपना सब कुछ दाँव पर लगा दिया फिर भी मुझे कुछ भी लाभ नहीं हुआ।
13. चूँकि तुमने गलत उत्तर दिया अतः तुम्हें अंक नहीं मिलेंगे।
14. जैसे ही वह बोलने वाला था कि लोग शोर मचाने लगे।
15. हरी ने इतना परिश्रम किया कि वह प्रथम आ गया।

Hints—लेना–to take, to wield, महल–palace, दुखी–miserable, भोगना (दुख)–to suffer, शुद्ध–pure, clear, पीछे हटना–to retreat, to subvert, दाँव पर लगाना–to stake, लाभ–profit, fruits, गलत–wrongly, प्रथम आना–to stand first.

Chapter 14

Compound Sentences
(यौगिक वाक्य)

1. Cumulative Conjunction (समानार्थी संयोजक)—अर्थात् And, as well as, both ...... and, not only ...... but also (यही नहीं बल्कि वह भी), besides आदि से दो (या अधिक) स्वतंत्र एवं समानार्थी वाक्यों को या जब यह संकेत रहे कि एक के पश्चात् दूसरा काम हुआ है तो ऐसे वाक्यों को उक्त Co-ordinative Conjunctions से जोड़ा जाता है।

(a) कला विस्तृत है और जीवन छोटा। **Art is long and life is short.**

(b) आवश्यकता नियम नहीं जानती और समय किसी की प्रतीक्षा नहीं करता।
Necessity knows no law and time waits for none.

(c) वह अभागा है और गरीब भी।
He is unfortunate as well as poor.
Or **He is both unfortunate and poor.**
Or **He is unfortunate and poor.**
Or **He is not only unfortunate but poor also.**

(d) उसे केवल अर्थदंड ही नहीं हुआ बल्कि वह विद्यालय से भी निकाल दिया गया।
He was not only fined but was expelled from school also.

(e) मुहम्मद गोरी ने भारत पर आक्रमण किया और गुलाम वंश की नींव डाली।
Md. Ghori invaded India and founded the Slave Dynasty.

(f) मौसम सुन्दर था और चित्ताकर्षक भी। (केवल सुन्दर ही नहीं था बल्कि चित्ताकर्षक भी)।
The weather was not only fine but also persuasive. *Or*
The weather was both fine and fascinating.

Note. Not only ...... but also, either ...... or, neither ...... nor—वाक्य में इनका प्रयोग उन्हीं दोनों व्यक्तियों/वस्तुओं/कार्यों आदि के यथासंभव निकट करना चाहिए जिनसे ये सम्बद्ध हों।

Incorrect	**Correct**
(a) Not only he is gentle but also intelligent.	He is not only gentle but also intelligent.
(b) Either they will accept or reject the proposal.	They will either accept or reject the proposal. (कथन पर बल हेतु Either will they accept *Or* .....)

2. Alternative Conjunctions (विकल्पबोधक संयोजक)—Either ..... (या तो) or, neither ...... nor (न ...... तो), or nor, otherwise (अन्यथा), else द्वारा उन वाक्यों/शब्दों आदि को जोड़ा जाता है जिनसे विकल्प या चुनाव (choice or selection) का बोध हो।

(a) कायरता पराजय को न तो सुनिश्चित करती है और न ही साहस उसे रोकता है।

Neither does cowardice ensure nor courage preclude defeat.

(b) न तो मैं जानता हूँ और न ही अनुमान कर सकता हूँ।

I neither know nor can guess. (Neither do I know nor ......)

(c) या तो अन्दर आओ या चले जाओ।

Either come in or go out.

(d) भागो नहीं तो मार दिए जाओगे।

Be off, otherwise you will be killed.

(e) या तो क्षमा माँगो या सजा के लिए तैयार हो जाओ।

Either ask pardon or be ready for punishment.

3. Adversative Conjunctions (विरोधाभास)—But, however, nonetheless (फिर भी) only, still, yet (तो भी, फिर भी), whereas (जबकि)—इनका प्रयोग दो परस्पर विरोधी तथ्यों, विचारों आदि को जोड़ने के लिए किया जाता है।

(a) वह सहमत नहीं हो सकता किन्तु मैं अवश्य आऊँगा।

He cannot agree, but I must come.

(b) बहुत लोग धनी हैं परन्तु वे सुखी नहीं हैं।

Many men are rich, but they are not happy.

(c) तुम चाहे जितनी भी कोशिश करो परन्तु सफल नहीं हो सकते।

You cannot succeed, however best you may try.

(d) गुलाम मर गया फिर भी उसकी आत्मा स्वतन्त्र हो गई।

The slave died, nonetheless his soul became free.

(e) वह उपदेश अच्छा दे लेता है केवल उस पर अमल नहीं करता।

He preaches well, only he does not keep to it.

(f) मैं कमजोर तो अवश्य हूँ, फिर भी सत्य से विमुख नहीं हो सकता।

Weak as I am I cannot deviate from the truth.

(g) तुम धनी हो फिर भी परोपकारी हो।

You are rich, yet you are altruistic.

(h) ज्ञान परीक्षणीय है जबकि विवेक स्थायी।

Knowledge is tentative, whereas wisdom is permanent.

Science knows but art does.

4. Illative Conjunctions (परिणामबोधक संयोजक)—जब कारण, परिणाम, निष्कर्ष (cause and effect) का संकेत रहे तो ऐसे वाक्यों के लिए निम्नस्थ परिणामबोधक संयोजक का प्रयोग किया जाता है–So, therefore, hence (अत:, इसलिए), for (क्योंकि)–

(a) उत्तरी साइबेरिया हमेशा बर्फ से ढँका रहता है इसलिए वह निर्जन है।

The North Siberia is always covered with snow, therefore it is desolate.

(b) आज तुम्हारा जन्मदिन है अत: मैं बहुत प्रसन्न हूँ।

It is your birthday today, so I am very happy.

(c) तुमने निश्चित रूप से नहीं कहा था अत: मैं नहीं आ सका।

You did not tell me definitely, hence I could not come.

(d) उससे बात मत करो क्योंकि वह पागल है।

Do not have a dialogue with him, for he is mad.

(e) उसकी हालत अच्छी नहीं है क्योंकि वह दवा नहीं लेता।

His condition is not good, for he does not take medicine. *Or*
He does not take medicine, so his condition is not good.

5. Relative Pronouns or Adverbs—Where (*i.e.*, and there) ; who, when आदि से भी compound sentences बनाए जा सकेंगे जब कार्य की निरन्तरता (continuity) का बोध हो। ऐसे वाक्य एक ही क्रम या सिलसिले में दोनों कार्यों के होने या न होने का संकेत देते हैं।

(a) मैं अपने अध्यापक से मिला जिन्होंने मुझे तत्काल पहचान लिया।

I met my teacher, who recognized me at once (who—and he)

(b) वह आगरा गया जहाँ उसने अपने मित्र से बात की।

He went to Agra, where he talked to his friend. (where—and there)

Semi-colon के द्वारा (;)–I came ; I saw ; I conquered.

Exercise 1

Translate into English :

1. मुहम्मद तुगलक भावुक था किन्तु दूरदर्शी भी।
2. आकाश साफ था और मौसम भी समरस था।
3. एक मन्थर किन्तु सुस्थिर चित्त व्यक्ति मैदान मार लेता है।
4. सूर्य उगा और कुहरा फट गया।
5. उसने केवल गाली ही नहीं दिया बल्कि मुझे मारा भी।
6. श्री नेहरू केवल राजनीतिज्ञ ही नहीं थे बल्कि शान्ति के पुजारी भी थे।
7. बालू निष्ठुर है और धूर्त भी।
8. राजेन्द्र अच्छा बोलता है केवल शुरू में वह हताश हो जाता है।
9. न तो मैंने तुम्हारे बारे में कुछ कहा और नहीं तुमसे बात किया।
10. या तो तुमने या तुम्हारे भाईयों ने गलती किया है।
11. मुझे आशीर्वाद दो या अपयश लो।
12. न तो तुमसे वह कभी मिला और न ही लिखित रूप में कुछ दिया।
13. मुझ पर विश्वास करो या भार अपने कन्धों पर लो।
14. करो या मरो।
15. चुप रहो अन्यथा तुम बाहर कर दिए जाओगे।

Hints—भावुक–sentimental, दूरदर्शी–farsighted, समरस–mild, मन्थर–slow, स्थिर चित्त–steadfast, मैदान मारना–to reap the field, कुहरा–fog, फटना–to disperse, राजनीतिज्ञ–politician, statesman,

पुजारी–worshipper, priest, निष्ठुर–cruel, धूर्त्त–cunning, हताश होना–to become nervous, आशीर्वाद देना–to bless, अपयश–disgrace, लिखित रूप में–in black and white, भार लेना–to bear the yoke, बाहर करना–to oust.

Exercise 2

Translate into English :

1. मैंने बहुत कोशिश की किन्तु सब व्यर्थ।
2. विज्ञान जानता है जबकि कला करती (सृजन) है।
3. दूत ने सभी बातें स्पष्ट रूप से कह दिया फिर भी राजा को विश्वास नहीं हुआ।
4. खाद्य पदार्थों की वास्तव में कमी नहीं है फिर भी दाम बढ़ रहे हैं।
5. चाहे कितना भी सिर मारो किन्तु भागने का कोई रास्ता नहीं है।
6. हम लोग नरक में ढकेल दिए गए हैं, फिर भी सब कुछ समाप्त नहीं हुआ है।
7. हम दुख भोगते हैं क्योंकि हम भोगने योग्य हैं।
8. अफ्रीका का एक बहुत बड़ा भाग भूमध्य रेखा पर है इसलिए वहाँ के निवासी काले होते हैं।
9. मैं देर से पहुँचा अतः अनुपस्थित कर दिया गया।
10. तुम्हारा हृदय अपवित्र है इसलिए तुम हमेशा अस्वस्थ रहते हो।
11. मैं हरि से मिला जिसने मुझे सबकुछ बताया।
12. हमारे विद्यालय का पर्यटक दल काँची गया जहाँ उसने मीनाक्षी का मंदिर देखा।
13. आज की भरी पूरी सभ्यता एक दिन अवश्य विनष्ट होगी क्योंकि प्रकृति का यही नियम है।
14. हम इच्छा करते हैं अतः हमें शान्ति नहीं है।
15. अपने रास्ते सुधारो अन्यथा तुम दुख भोगोगे।

Hints—सब व्यर्थ–all was in vain, of no avail, but in vain, दूत–envoy, messenger, स्पष्ट रूप से–categorically, clearly, सिर मारना–to beat one's brains, भागना–to escape, नरक–hell, ढकेलना–to hurl, to thrust, योग्य–liable, भूमध्य रेखा–equator, अनुपस्थित करना–to mark absent, पर्यटक दल–touring party, भरी पूरी–flourished, विनष्ट होना–to reduce (or meet) to dust, नियम–law, सुधारना–to mend.

Chapter 15

Miscellaneous Sentences

1. 'कुछ तो बीमारी के कारण और कुछ अच्छी तैयारी न करने के कारण वह उत्तीर्ण न हो सका।'–ऐसे वाक्यों का अनुवाद Partly because of, partly due to, owing to आदि से करेंगे।

1. कुछ तो बीमारी के कारण और कुछ अच्छी तैयारी न करने के कारण वह उत्तीर्ण न हो सका।

   Partly because of illness and partly because of not preparing well, he could not pass.

2. कुछ तो अनिच्छा और कुछ असावधानी के कारण उसने नौकरी छोड़ दी।

   Partly because of reluctance and partly because of carelessness, he left the service.

3. कुछ तो धन की कमी से और कुछ साधनहीनता के कारण वह मकान न बना सका।

   Partly owing to lack of money and partly owing to want of means, he could not build a house.

2. 'उसके यहाँ क्यों जायँ ?' या 'हारता हुआ युद्ध क्यों लड़ा जाय ?' आदि जैसे वाक्यों में बिना to के Infinitive का प्रयोग होता है। इसका आशय होता है–It is useless ....

1. उसके यहाँ क्यों जायँ ?   Why go to him ?

2. हारता हुआ युद्ध क्यों लड़ा जाय ?   Why fight a losing battle ?

3. 'मुश्किल से' इससे बने वाक्य को hardly/scarcely से प्रगट करें। Hardly/scarcely + to be or helping verb + sub. पश्चात् when या before से वाक्य बनाएँ।

1. मुश्किल से वह दो कदम चला होगा कि गिर पड़ा।

   Hardly did he walk a step or two when he fell down.

2. मुश्किल से तुम एक दो वाक्य बोले थे कि लड़के शोर करने लगे।

   Scarcely had you spoken a sentence or two when the boys began to make a noise.

4. 'धनी तो वह था ही, भाग्य ने भी उसका साथ दिया'।–

ऐसे वाक्य को Adjective/noun + as + sub. +verb...... जैसा बनाएँ।

1. धनी तो वह था ही, भाग्य ने भी उसका साथ दिया।

   Rich as he was, fortune also favoured him.

2. ईमानदार तो तुम हो ही, तुम्हारा विचार भी उत्तम है।

   Honest as you are, your idea is also noble.

3. 'Dust as we are, the inscrutable things grow in us like harmony in music.' (Wordsworth)

5. 'तुम आओ या न आओ, मैं तुम्हे निमंत्रित करूँगा।'–ऐसे वाक्य का अनुवाद whether ...... or not + main clause ......

1. तुम आओ या न आओ, मैं तुम्हें निमंत्रित करुँगा।

Whether you come or not, I will invite you.

2. तुम मेरे साथ रहना पसन्द करो या न करो, मैं तुम्हें नहीं छोड़ूँगा।

Whether you like to live with me or not, I will not forsake you.

3. पानी बरसे या न बरसे, किसान खेत बोएँगे।

Whether it rains or not, the farmers will sow the field.

6. 'गाँव का गाँव अकाल का शिकार हो गया'।—ऐसे वाक्य को Noun (singular) + after + noun जैसा प्रारम्भ करें। इसका verb भी singular होगा।

1. गाँव का गाँव अकाल का शिकार हो गया।

Village after village was fallen the victim of famine.

7. 'तुमने काम पूरा कर लिया है, न' ? 'तुमने उसे गाली नहीं दिया, न ?'—ऐसे वाक्यों का अनुवाद पहले सामान्य वाक्य (Tense के आधार पर) जैसा करेंगे और अन्त में उस Tense का helping verb + sub. + not...... रखेंगे। यदि पूर्व के भाग में not रहेगा तो अन्त में इसे न रखें और यदि नहीं रहेगा तो अन्त में not जोड़ें। प्रश्नवाचक चिह्न भी रखें। ऐसे वाक्य Question-Tag कहे जाते हैं।

1. तुमने काम पूरा कर लिया है, न ?

You have completed the work, haven't you ?

2. तुमने उसे गाली नहीं दिया, न ?

You did not abuse him, did you ?

Exercise

Translate into English :

1. उनसे क्यों बात करें ?
2. व्यर्थ में क्यों पैसा लगाया जाय ?
3. इतनी महँगी पुस्तकें क्यों खरीदी जाय ?
4. उससे सम्बन्ध तोड़ देना कैसा रहेगा ?
5. चिन्ता क्यों की जाय ?
6. आपके पास रहना कैसा रहेगा ?
7. एक नई कमीज क्यों खरीदें ?
8. यह टॉनिक कैसा रहेगा ?
9. तुम मेरी मदद करो या न करो परन्तु मैं तुम्हारे सम्मुख नहीं झुकूँगा।
10. उसे यह अच्छा लगे या न लगे मैं दो टूक कह दूँगा।
11. कभी वर्षा हो जाती है, कभी सूखा हो जाता है।
12. तुम खुश रहो या न रहो वह अपने मन की ही करेगा।
13. अभी वह खुश होती है, अभी क्रोधित हो जाती है।
14. मुश्किल से मैंने दो पृष्ठ पढ़ा था कि उसने पत्रिका ले ली।
15. जब भी तुम्हें बुलाया जाता है, शायद ही तुम आते हो।

16. जंगल के जंगल जलकर राख हो गए।

17. वह अपने परिवार को शायद ही कभी याद करता था।

18. छात्र के छात्र परीक्षा में अनुचित साधन प्रयोग के कारण पकड़े गए।

19. मुश्किल से मैं दस कदम गया था कि उसने मुझे बुलाया।

20. भीड़ की भीड़ मेले में आ रही थी।

21. तुम विद्यालय गए थे न ?

22. वह मेरी पुस्तक नहीं लाया है, न ?

23. कुछ मेरी अन्यमनस्कता और कुछ आलस्य के कारण मैं वहाँ नहीं जा सका।

24. उसी डाक्टर ने उपचार किया था, न ?

25. वह जवाब भेजे या न भेजे, मैं अवश्य पत्र दूंगा।

26. कमजोर तो वह था ही बीमारी ने भी उसे धर दबोचा।

27. कुछ तो अज्ञानता और कुछ अनुभवहीनता से उसे असफलता मिली।

Hints—महँगी–costly, व्यर्थ में–for nothing, लगाना–to invest, चिन्ता–worry, टॉनिक–tonic, झुकना–to submit, दो टूक कहना–to tell roundly, to call a spade a spade, सूखा–drought, अपने मन की करना–to do as one's conscience allows, जलकर राख होना–to burn to ashes, अनुचित साधन प्रयोग करना–to use unfair means, भीड़–crowd, आना–to influx, बीमारी–disease, धर दबोचना–to make one's victim of, अन्यमनस्कता–indifference, आलस्य–idleness, अज्ञानता–ignorance, अनुभवहीनता--inexperience.

Chapter 16

Passages for Practice (Solved and Unsolved)

SOLVED EXERCISES

Exercise 1

गंगा हिमालय से निकलती है। यह आमतौर से दक्षिण-पूर्व दिशा की ओर बहती है। लम्बी दूरी तय करके यह बंगाल की खाड़ी में जा गिरती है। ऋषिकेश तक गंगा पहाड़ों में बहती है किन्तु इसके बाद यह मैदानों में आ जाती है। इलाहाबाद में इसकी मुख्य सहायक नदी यमुना इससे मिल जाती है। सर्दी में गंगा पानी की एक संकरी धारा बन जाती है। किन्तु बरसात में यह अपने किनारों से बहने लगती है। अन्य कई नदियाँ भी हिमालय से निकलती हैं। किन्तु लोग सबसे अधिक महत्त्व गंगा को ही देते हैं। हिन्दु लोग इसकी पूजा करते हैं। गंगा के पश्चिम में यमुना भी हिमालय से निकलती है। किन्तु यह दूसरा समानान्तर पथ धारण करती है। यमुना हरिद्वार और ऋषिकेश से होकर नहीं बहती। यह दिल्ली और आगरा से होकर निकलती है।

The Ganga emerges from the Himalayas. Generally it flows down towards the South-east. Having recovered a long distance, it falls down into the Bay of Bengal. The Ganga glides along the mountains upto Rishikesh but after this it comes down into the field. Its main tributary Yamuna merges in it at Allahabad. In winter, the Ganga turns to be a narrow stream. But in rainy season, it overflows its banks. Several other rivers also flow from the Himalayas. But the people attach more importance to the Ganga only. The Hindus adore it. In the west of the Ganga, the Yamuna also rises from the Himalayas. But it takes another parallel course. The Yamuna does not flow through Haridwar and Rishikesh. It courses through Delhi and Agra.

Exercise 2

जब रात्रि में मैं ऊपर के कमरे में सोया हुआ था तो टेलीफोन की घंटी बजी। मैं जाग गया। जैसे ही मैं नीचे टेलीफोन सुनने के लिए जा रहा था तो मैंने दरवाजे के बाहर कुछ अजीब सा शोर सुना। ऐसा लगा जैसे कि कोई महिला रो रही हो और लोग उसकी समस्या जानने की कोशिश कर रहे हों। मैं तुरन्त दरवाजे की ओर गया और दरवाजा खोला। जब मैं भीड़ की ओर बढ़ रहा था तो पुलिस की एक गाड़ी वहाँ आकर रूकी। शोर कुछ कम हुआ और लोग तितर बितर होने लगे। वह महिला अब भी जोर जोर से चिल्ला रही थी। पूछने पर उसने अपनी दुखभरी कहानी सुनाई। पुलिस कर्मी उस महिला को अपने साथ ले गए और मैं भी दुखी मन और भारी कदमों के साथ घर लौटा।

When I was sleeping in the attic at night, the telephone rang. I got up. Just as I was coming down to attend the telephone, I heard some strange noise outside the door. It appeared as if a certain woman was weeping and the men were trying to know her problem. I at once hurried towards the door and opened it. When I was proceeding towards the crowd, a police van approached and stopped there. The noise subsided a little and the mob began to disperse. That woman was still crying loudly. On enquiry, she narrated her woeful tale. The police took the woman with them and I too returned home with a sad heart and heavy footsteps.

Exercise 3

जब भारत स्वतन्त्र हुआ तब यहाँ अनेक रियासतें थीं। सरदार पटेल जब तक उन्हें भारतीय गणराज्य में सम्मिलित नहीं कर लिया चैन से नहीं बैठे। जब तक वे जीवित रहे, देश के एकीकरण में लगे रहे। उनके मरने से पूर्व ही हैदराबाद जैसी रियासतें भी विशाल भारत का अंग बन चुकी थीं। हाँ, गोवा का पुर्तगाली राज्य ही ऐसा था जो सरदार पटेल की मृत्यु के बाद भारत में सम्मिलित हुआ। जब तक गंगा में जल प्रवाहित रहेगा, सरदार पटेल का नाम अमर रहेगा। ज्योंही उनका ध्यान आता है, एक लौह पुरुष का चित्र सामने आता है। क्योंकि आज वे हमारे बीच में नहीं हैं, हमें उनकी स्मृति का सम्मान करना चाहिए। हमें प्रतिज्ञा करनी चाहिए कि जब तक हमारी जान में जान है, हम सरदार पहले के पदचिह्नों पर चलते रहेंगे। जहाँ महापुरुष जन्म लेते रहते हैं, वहाँ सदैव शान्ति का साम्राज्य रहता है। हमें उनका अनुसरण करना चाहिए जिससे कि हम उनके स्वप्नों के भारत का निर्माण कर सकें। हमें शान्तिपूर्वक रहना चाहिए, ऐसा न हो कि हमारी एकता संकट में पड़ जाय।

When India became free, there were many dominion states here. Sardar Patel did not feel at home till he annexed them with Indian Republic. He went on unifying the country so long as he breathed. Before his death, the large states like Hyderabad had become part and parcel of greater India. Yes, Goa was only such a Portuguese state as was annexed with India after the death of Patel. As long as the water flows in the Ganga, the name of Sardar Patel shall remain immortal. Just as we recall him, a picture of an iron man flashes before us. Since he is not amidst us, we should esteem his memory. We should swear that till our breath, we will follow the footprints of the Sardar Patel. Where great sages and seers incarnate oftener, there always prevails a realm of peace. We should follow him so that we may build India of his dream and desire. We should live peacefully lest our unity should fall into peril.

Exercise 4

सन् 1928 की घटना है। लाहौर में अंग्रेजी सरकार की नीतियों के विरोध में लाला लाजपत राय के नेतृत्व में एक जुलूस निकाला जा रहा था। जुलूस पूर्ण रूप से अनुशासित होकर चल रहा था। तभी एक अंग्रेज पुलिस अधिकारी ने जिसका नाम सांडर्स था, जुलूस पर लाठी चार्ज करा दिया। इस लाठी चार्ज में लाला लाजपत राय को बहुत गंभीर चोटें आईं जिनके कारण बाद में उनकी मृत्यु हो गई। समस्त देशवासियों को लालाजी की मृत्यु से गहरा आघात पहुँचा। क्रान्तिकारी चन्द्रशेखर आजाद, भगत सिंह व शिवराम राजगुरु ने लालाजी की मृत्यु का बदला सांडर्स को मारकर लिया। देश को आजाद कराने के लिए क्रान्तिकारी अपने जान की परवाह नहीं करते थे। भगत सिंह तो हँसते हँसते फाँसी पर चढ़ गये और चन्द्रशेखर आजाद पुलिस से लड़ते हुए शहीद हुए। इन महान शहीदों का नाम भारत के इतिहास में सदा के लिए सुनहरे अक्षरों में लिखा रहेगा।

It was the event of 1928. A procession under the leadership of Lala Lajpat Ray was going to be organised in Lahore against the policies of British rule. The procession was going on well disciplined. Meanwhile an English police officer named Saunders ordered lathi charge upon the procession. In this charge, Lala Lajpat Ray was badly injured in consequence of which he died afterward. All the countrymen were deeply shocked by the death of Lala Lajpat Ray. Revolutionaries like Chandra Shekhar Azad, Bhagat Singh and Shiv Ram Rajguru avenged on Saunders for the Lalajee by shooting him down. The revolutionaries never cared for their lives to make the country free. Bhagat Singh did go to gallow laughingly and Chandra Shekhar Azad became a martyr fighting with the police. The names of these great martyrs will ever remain inserted in the golden letters in The History of India.

Exercise 5

सही शिक्षा का वास्तविक ध्येय हमारे बौद्धिक स्तर को उठाना है। बौद्धिक स्तर को उठाने का अर्थ शिक्षार्थी के मस्तिष्क में दुनियाँभर के तथ्य और आंकड़े भरना नहीं है, बल्कि उसे इस योग्य बनाना है कि वह दूसरे के दृष्टिकोण को ठीक प्रकार समझ सके। साथ ही शिक्षा का ध्येय उसमें मौलिक चिन्तन की क्षमता विकसित करना है। सच्ची शिक्षा हमें यह सिखाती है कि हम किस प्रकार दूसरे के दृष्टिकोण से समझौता करें और किस प्रकार अपने विचारों को दूसरों के सम्मुख प्रस्तुत

करें। इसके अतिरिक्त सही अर्थों में विद्यार्थी वह है जो सदैव सीखने को तत्पर हो और जो दूसरों के विचारों की कदर कर सके। वह यह जानता है कि जब उसके पास कहने योग्य कुछ नहीं है तो वह चुप रहे और यह भी समझता है कि वह कितना बोले और कब बोले। अर्थात् सही शिक्षा का प्रयोजन विद्यार्थी के मस्तिष्क को सही प्रकार से अनुशासित करना है।

The real aim of real education is to uplift our intellectual standard. The uplift of intellectual standard does not mean to stuff the students' mind with a host of facts and figures rather they are to be enabled in such a way as they may understand precisely the attitudes of other men. Besides it, the aim of education is to cultivate in them the ability of original thinking. A true education teaches us how we may adopt ourselves to the ideas of others. Besides this, a true student is he who is always eager to learn and who can appreciate the ideas of others. He knows fully that he should keep mum when he has nothing to say and he also knows how much and when he should speak. The sum and substance is that the aim of true education is to discipline properly the mind of the student.

Exercise 6

किसी ने खूब कहा है कि व्यक्ति का भाग्य काफी हद तक उसके परिश्रम और चरित्र पर निर्भर करता है। यह बात तो सत्य है कि कोई भी व्यक्ति महान नहीं बन सकता यदि वह परिश्रम से जी चुराता है और यदि उसमें चरित्र की कमी है। इसी प्रकार कोई भी राष्ट्र महान नहीं बन सकता यदि उसके निवासी आलसी हैं अथवा उनका चरित्र उत्कृष्ट नहीं है। परिश्रम और चरित्र एक नींव के समान हैं जिस पर सफलता और महानता के भवन का निर्माण होता है। यदि नींव कमजोर है तो क्या कोई मजबूत और टिकाऊ भवन उसपर बनाया जा सकता है ? क्या हमारा पर्वत पर चढ़ना संभव है यदि हमारे पैरों के नीचे की धरती खिसक रही हो ?

Rightly has someone remarked that man's destiny depends to a considerable extent upon his labour and character. It is indeed true that anyone cannot become great if he grudges labour and if he is lacking in character. Similarly any nation cannot become great if its natives are idle or their character is not noble. Labour and character are like a foundation on which the building of success and greatness is erected. Can any strong and durable buildings be built if its foundation is weak ? Is it possible for us to climb upon a mountain if the ground under our feet is slipping ?

Exercise 7

हमारा एक महान देश है। शताब्दियों तक हमारा इतिहास बहुत शानदार रहा है। न कि केवल पूर्व के देश बल्कि समस्त पश्चिम के देश हमारी प्राचीन संस्कृति की छाप लिए हुए हैं। हमारे दर्शन एवं कलाओं ने पाश्चात्य विचार और जीवन को काफी प्रभावित किया है। अब जब हमारा देश आगे बढ़ने की चेष्टा कर रहा है तो सभी भारतवासियों का कर्त्तव्य है कि देश की सेवा में जुटे रहें। जो कार्य समाज ने हमें दिया है उसे निष्ठापूर्वक सम्पन्न करने में कोई कमी न छोड़ें। विद्यार्थियों का उत्तरदायित्व और बड़ा है। कल का भारत क्या होगा यह आज के विद्यार्थियों के परिश्रम और चरित्र पर ही निर्भर है। देश विद्यार्थियों से अपेक्षा करता है कि उनके जीवन स्वच्छ एवं उत्कृष्ट हों और देश की निःस्वार्थ सेवा के लिए समर्पित हों। तभी हमारा देश आने वाले समय में अपने गौरव को प्राप्त कर सकेगा।

Ours is a great country. For centuries our history has been immensely splendid. Not only oriental countries but also all western countries bear the stamp of our ancient culture. Our philosophy and arts have considerably cast an impact on Western thought and life. Today when our country is endeavouring to go ahead, it is the duty of all Indians that they should keep themselves devoted to the service of the country. We should leave no stone unturned to accomplish faithfully the duty that society has entrusted to us. The responsibility of students is greater. What shape India will take in the time to come, depends only on the diligence and character of the students of today. The country expects from the students that their life may become clean and noble and they may dedicate themselves selflessly for the service of the country. In that condition only our country will achieve its ancient glory in the time to come.

Exercise 8

भारत के इतिहास पर एक सरसरी नजर डालने से हमें यह पता चलेगा कि अपने इतिहास के महानतम कालों में हमारे लोग एक दूसरे के धर्मों व मतों के प्रति कितने सहिष्णु थे। यद्यपि अशोक ने दूर देशों में भी अपने धर्मप्रचारक भेजे थे, वे समन्वय के सिद्धान्त को प्राथमिकता देते थे। गुप्तकाल में एक चीनी यात्री भारतवर्ष आया था। उसका नाम था फाहियान। दस वर्ष तक यहाँ रहकर उसने हमारे जीवन के पहलुओं का गहराई से अध्ययन किया। हमारे देशवासियों की धार्मिक सहिष्णुता व उनके आपसी सद्भाव से प्रभावित होकर उसने हमारे धार्मिक दृष्टिकोण की खुले दिल से प्रशंसा की। अकबर महान ने तो अपने प्रशासन व व्यक्तिगत जीवन में सब धर्मों को बराबर सम्मान दिया और यह तो किसी से छिपा नहीं है कि इन कालों में हमारा देश बहुत शक्तिशाली व सम्पन्न था।

If we cast a bird's eye view on the History of India, we shall come to know how our people were tolerant to the creeds and faiths of one another in the greatest ages of the history. Although Ashok sent his missionaries to the countries abroad also, they preferred the ideal of concord. A Chinese traveller arrived in India during the reign of the Guptas. His name was Fa-Hein. Living here for ten years, he deeply studied the various aspects of our life. Being impressed with the religious tolerance and common goodwill of our nation, he admired our religious outlooks open-heartedly. In his administration and individual life, Akbar the great, esteemed all the religions equally and this fact is not concealed from anybody that during these periods our country was very powerful and prosperous.

Exercise 9

यह सर्वविदित है कि जब-जब हमारे लोगों अथवा शासकों ने सहिष्णुता के स्थान पर धर्मान्धता का मार्ग चुना तो जीवन के प्रत्येक क्षेत्र में हमारा पतन हुआ। अब भी हमें अपने इतिहास से सबक लेना चाहिए। यह जानते हुए कि परस्पर मतभेद से हम कमजोर होते हैं, हमें कोई काम ऐसा नहीं करना चाहिए जिससे हमारे लोगों में दुर्भावना उत्पन्न हो। भले ही हमारे देश में विभिन्न बोलियाँ बोली जाती हैं व विभिन्न धर्म व रीति-रिवाज पाए जाते हों, हमारे समूचे देश की जीवन-चर्या में काफी समानता है। विविधता के बावजूद हमारे देश में एक गहन एकता अन्तर्निहित है। हमें अपने विचारों व कार्यों द्वारा इसी एकता की भावना को पुष्ट करने की चेष्टा करनी है।

It is known to all that whenever our people or rulers chose the path of fanaticism in lieu of tolerance, we faced decline in every walk of life. Even now we should derive lesson from our history. Knowing that we turn weak by common dissensions, we should not do such work as ill-will may sprout in our people. Even if various dialects are spoken in our country and many creeds and customs are found, there is a considerable similarity in the life routine of the whole country. In spite of diversity, a deep unity is latent in our country. We have to try to strengthen this feeling of unity by our thoughts and deeds.

Unsolved Exercises

Exercise 1

गोस्वामी तुलसीदास का नाम आपने अवश्य सुना होगा। उनका जन्म संवत् 1554 में बाँदा जिले में हुआ था। वे एक उच्च ब्राह्मण वंश के थे। उनकी बाल्यावस्था में ही उनके माता-पिता का देहान्त हो गया। कुछ दिनों तक उनका जीवन बड़ा कष्टमय रहा। सौभाग्य से वे बाबा नरहरि दास के सम्पर्क में आए। उनके साथ रहकर उन्होंने विद्याध्ययन किया एवं तीर्थों का भ्रमण किया। उन्होंने संस्कृत की उच्च शिक्षा काशी में प्राप्त की। उसके बाद वे अपने गाँव लौट आए जहाँ उनका विवाह

रत्नावली से हुआ। अचानक उनके वैवाहिक जीवन में एक घटना घटी जिसने उनके जीवन की दिशा मोड़ दी। अन्धकार दूर हो गया एवं उनमें प्रकाश फैला। उन्होंने घर का परित्याग कर दिया और सन्यासी हो गए। तत्पश्चात् काशी में आकर रामभक्ति में उन्होंने अनेक साहित्यिक कृतियाँ प्रस्तुत कीं। उनमें 'रामचरितमानस' सर्वाधिक प्रसिद्ध महाकाव्य है। सम्वत् 1680 में काशी में उनका देहान्त हो गया।

Hints : उच्च ब्राह्मण वंश, a high Brahmin line (or race). बड़ा कष्टमय रहा, was full of grim hardship. सौभाग्यवश, fortunately. सम्पर्क में आए, came into contact with. विद्याध्ययन किया, studied. तीर्थों, pilgrimages. प्राप्त की, obtained. वैवाहिक जीवन, conjugal life. घटना, incident. घटी, happened, occurred. दूर हो गया, dissipated, dispersed. प्रकाश फैला, light flashed. परित्याग कर दिया, renounced. सन्यासी हो गए, became a saint. रामभक्ति में, in the devotion of Ram. साहित्यिक कृतियाँ, literary works. महाकाव्य, epic. सर्वाधिक प्रसिद्ध, most celebrated.

Exercise 2

कन्नौज का राजा बहुत बुद्धिमान था। उसे एक पुत्र था। राजकुमार बहुत छोटा था और राजा बहुत बूढ़ा था। इसलिए राजा अपने पुत्र के लिए एक ईमानदार सलाहकार चाहता था। एक दिन उसने अपने सभी दरबारियों को बुलाया। उसने कहा, 'क्या मैं एक अच्छा राजा हूँ ?' कुछ दरबारियों ने कहा, 'श्रीमान, आप संसार के सबसे अच्छे राजा हैं।' यह सुनकर राजा बहुत प्रसन्न हुआ। उसने प्रत्येक दरबारी को एक-एक हीरा दिया। एक दरबारी चुप बैठा था। राजा ने उससे भी वही प्रश्न किया। उसने कहा, 'महानुभाव, आप वास्तव में अच्छे राजा हैं किन्तु संसार में आपसे भी अच्छे राजा हैं।' इस उत्तर से राजा बहुत संतुष्ट हुआ। उसने उस दरबारी को अपने पुत्र का संरक्षक बना दिया।

Hints : एक ईमानदार सलाहकार, an honest counsellor (adviser). दरबारी, courtier. हीरा, diamond. चुप, quietly. वही प्रश्न, the same question. वास्तव में, indeed, of course. संरक्षक, guardian. बना दिया, appointed.

Exercise 3

गौतम बुद्ध निकट के शहर में भोजन माँगने जाया करते थे। एक दिन वे एक घर पर गए। घर का मालिक बाहर आया और उन्हें गाली देने लगा। बुद्ध बिना एक शब्द बोले शान्तिपूर्वक गाली सुनते रहे। किन्तु जब मकान मालिक ने गाली देना बन्द कर दिया तब उन्होंने कहा, 'मित्र, जब तुम कोई वस्तु किसी को देते हो और वह उसे स्वीकार नहीं करता तो वह वस्तु कहाँ जाती है ?' 'क्यों ? यह देने वाले के यहाँ लौट जाती है', मकान मालिक ने जबाब दिया। इस पर बुद्ध ने कहा, 'अच्छा, मैं भी तुम्हारी दी गई वस्तु स्वीकार करने नहीं जा रहा हूँ।' बुद्धिमानी के ये शब्द सुनकर मकान मालिक लज्जित हुआ। वह बुद्ध के चरणों पर गिर गया और क्षमा याचना करने लगा।

Hints : निकट के शहर में, in a neighbouring city. बिना एक शब्द बोले, without uttering a single word. शान्तिपूर्वक, quietly, calmly. मकान मालिक, master of the house. बन्द कर दिया, ceased. देने वाले के यहाँ, to the giver. अच्छा, well, all right. दी गई वस्तु, given thing (offered thing). लज्जित हुआ, was (or felt) ashamed.

Exercise 4

प्राचीन काल में भारत में अनेक ज्ञानी थे। वे ऋषि कहे जाते थे। सामान्यतः वे वनों में रहते थे और ईश्वर भक्ति में अपना समय लगाया करते थे। उनका जीवन बड़ा सादा था। वे लम्बे केश रखते, पेड़ की छाल पहनते और फल खाते थे। वे ऋषि महान आत्मिक शक्ति के मनुष्य थे और अनेक आश्चर्यपूर्ण कार्य करते थे। उनमें से एक का नाम अगस्त्य था। अगस्त्य छोटे डील के थे। उनकी दाढ़ी लम्बी और श्वेत थी। वे अपनी बुद्धि तथा ज्ञान के लिए प्रसिद्ध थे। एक दीर्घ समय तक उन्होंने विवाह नहीं किया। एक रात उनके पूर्वज स्वप्न में उनके समक्ष प्रगट हुए। उन्होंने उनसे कहा, 'ओ अगस्त्य ! विवाह न करना तुम्हारे लिए उचित नहीं है। विवाह शीघ्र करो।' अगस्त्य ने उनकी आज्ञा का पालन किया।

Hints : ज्ञानी, scholars, learned men. ईश्वर भक्ति में, in the devotion of God. छाल, bark. आत्मिक शक्ति, spiritual power. राजागण तक, even kings. छोटे डील का, of small stature. बुद्धि और ज्ञान, wisdom and learning. प्रगट हुए, appeared. उचित, proper. दाढ़ी, beard. पूर्वज, forefather, ancestor.

Exercise 5

शीतल एक चारण था। वह मेवाड़ में रहता था और एक बुद्धिमान व्यक्ति था। एक दिन वह अकबर बादशाह के दरबार में गया। बादशाह को सलाम करने से पहले उसने अपनी पगड़ी उतार ली। यह देखकर बादशाह को बहुत आश्चर्य हुआ। उसने शीतल से पगड़ी उतारने का कारण पूछा। उसने बादशाह को उत्तर दिया, 'श्रीमान् ! यह पगड़ी राणा प्रताप की है जिन्होंने कभी किसी के सामने अपना सिर नहीं झुकाया। यही कारण है कि मैंने इसे उतार दिया है। अपने कार्य से मैं राणा प्रताप का अपमान नहीं कर सकता।' बादशाह इस उत्तर से अत्यन्त प्रसन्न हुआ। उसने महाराणा प्रताप की वीरता की प्रशंसा की और शीतल को पुरस्कार दिया। मातृभूमि के सम्मान की रक्षा करना सबका परम कर्त्तव्य है।

Hints : चारण, bard. सलाम करना, to salute. पगड़ी, turban. उतारना, to take off. बहुत आश्चर्य हुआ, was much surprised. अपना सिर कभी नहीं झुकाया, never bowed his head. कार्य, deed. अपमान करना, to insult. वीरता, bravery. प्रशंसा की, admired. पुरस्कार, reward. मातृभूमि, motherland. सम्मान, dignity. रक्षा करना, to defend, to protect. परम कर्त्तव्य, bounden duty.

Exercise 6

जाड़े का समय था। पहाड़ियाँ, मैदान, पेड़, घर और सड़कें सभी बर्फ से ढके थे। हवा इतनी ठंडी थी कि घर से बाहर निकलना कठिन था। किसी ने दरवाजा खटखटाया और एक वृद्ध मनुष्य कमरे में प्रवेश किया। ठंड के कारण वह सिर से पैर तक काँप रहा था। दीन विधवा माता ने अपने बीमार बच्चे को चारपाई पर लिटा दिया और अतिथि के लिए चाय बनाने को उठी। उसने केतली को आग पर रखा और बच्चे के निकट आकर बैठ गई। उसने बच्चे को कई बार चूमा और तब वृद्ध मनुष्य की ओर घूम कर कहा, 'बाबा, क्या अपने प्रिय बच्चे को मैं मृत्यु के क्रूर हाथों से नहीं बचा पाऊँगी ? कृपया उसको आशीर्वाद दीजिए ताकि वह बच जाय।' वृद्ध मनुष्य ने अपने सिर को इस प्रकार हिलाया कि दीन माता को ठेस लगी। वह तीन दिन, तीन रात से निरन्तर जागती रही थी। वह चक्कर खाकर गिर पड़ी और बहुत देर तक वहीं पड़ी रही। जब वह चेतना में आई तो वह वृद्ध पुरुष अदृश्य हो चुका था। किन्तु बच्चा मुस्करा और खेल रहा था।

Hints : बर्फ से ढंके थे—were covered with snow, इतनी ठंडी थी—was so chilly, खटखटाया—knocked at, सिर से पैर ...... रहा था—was shivering from head to foot, दीन विधवा माता—the poor widow mother, चारपाई पर—in bed, लिटा दिया—lay, अतिथि—guest, केतली—kettle, मृत्यु के क्रूर हाथों से—from the cruel hands of death, बचाना—to save, अपना सिर इस प्रकार हिलाया—shook his head in such a way as, ठेस लगी—was shocked, चक्कर खाकर—having spun round (or giddied), चेतना में आई—returned to (or came) her senses.

Exercise 7

बहुत पूर्व सुदर्शन नाम का एक राजा था। उसके कई पुत्र थे किन्तु सभी मूर्ख थे। वे न तो पढ़ सकते थे और न लिख सकते थे। राजा ने मन ही मन सोचा कि इन मूर्ख लड़कों का क्या करें। यदि ये नहीं पढ़े लिखेंगे तो शासन कैसे करेंगे ? जब राजा इस तरह निराशा में डूबा था तब विष्णु शर्मा नामक एक बड़े पंडित वहाँ आए। राजा ने अपनी व्यथा कथा उन्हें सुनाई। अन्त में उन्होंने राजकुमारों को पढ़ाने का भार अपने ऊपर लिया। विष्णु शर्मा ने राजकुमारों को कहानी के माध्यम से राजनीतिशास्त्र की शिक्षा देना चाहा। प्रायः उनकी कहानियाँ वनों, पहाड़ों, जंगली जानवरों से सम्बन्धित थीं। वे कहानियाँ एक पुस्तक में एकत्रित की गई हैं जिसका नाम 'हितोपदेश कथासार' है। नीति-शिक्षा के लिए यह एक अनुपम ग्रन्थ है।

Hints : बहुत पूर्व—long ago, मन ही मन—himself, क्या करें—what he should do with, शासन करना—to reign, निराशा में डूबा था—was plunged into disappointment, बड़े पंडित—a great scholar, व्यथा

कथा—woeful story, worry, भार—responsibility, माध्यम से—through the medium of, राजनीतिशास्त्र—political science, सम्बन्धित थी—were related to, नीति शिक्षा—moral lesson, एक अनुपम ग्रन्थ—a unique work.

Exercise 8

नर्मदा नदी के किनारे एक बहुत बड़ा बरगद का पेड़ था। उसके खोखले में एक कबूतर दम्पत्ति रहा करते थे। उसी पेड़ पर एक सर्प भी रहा करता था। वह कबूतर के सभी अंडों को खा जाया करता था। इस कारण से वे बड़े उदास रहते थे। यह घटना अनेक बार घटी। अन्त में उन्हें एक उपाय सूझी। उस देश का राजकुमार रोज सुबह नदी में स्नान करने आया करता था। वह अपने सोने के हार को किनारे पर रखकर नदी में गोते लगाता। एक दिन कबूतर ने हार को उठाकर साँप के खोखले में रख दिया। राजकुमार ने जो यह सब देख रहा था, अपने नौकरों को बुलाया। उसने पेड़ पर से हार को लाने की उन्हें आज्ञा दी। जब नौकर पेड़ पर चढ़े तो वहाँ उन लोगों ने साँप को देखा। उन्होंने साँप का वध कर डाला और हार लाने में सफलता प्राप्त की। वस्तुतः विवेक हमेशा बड़ा होता है।

Hints : बरगद का पेड़—banyan tree, खोखला—hollow, एक कबूतर दम्पत्ति—a pair of pigeons, एक उपाय सूझी—thought out a plan, an idea dawned upon them, सोने का हार—gold necklace, गोते लगाना—to dip, देखना—to watch, विवेक हमेशा बड़ा होता है—discretion always prevails.

Exercise 9

प्राचीनकाल में विक्रमादित्य नाम का एक राजा इस देश में राज्य करता था। वह बड़ा न्यायी था। आज भी लोग उसके न्याय की प्रशंसा करते हैं। एक दिन गड़ेरियों के कुछ बच्चे गाँव के निकट जंगल में खेल रहे थे। वहाँ उन्होंने एक टीला देखा जो पत्थरों से ढका हुआ था। उनमें से एक लड़का उस पत्थर पर बैठ गया। उसने अपने साथियों को बुलाया और कहा, 'मित्रों, अब मैं राजा विक्रमादित्य हो गया हूँ। तुम लोग अपने मुकदमे मेरे पास लाओ। मैं न्याय करूँगा।' उस लड़के ने अपने साथियों के मुकदमों का निर्णय किया। उसके निर्णय इतने न्यायोचित थे कि यह कहानी दूर-दूर तक फैल गई। जो झगड़ा करते थे, उस लड़के के पास जाते थे। प्रत्येक व्यक्ति उस लड़के के न्याय से सन्तुष्ट था। जब वह मिट्टी का ढेर खोदा गया तो लोगों को मालूम हुआ कि सचमुच वहाँ राजा विक्रमादित्य का न्याय-सिंहासन था।

Hints : प्राचीन काल में—in ancient time, न्यायी—just, गड़ेरिया—shepherd (शेपर्ड), गाँव के निकट—(near), in the vicinity of the village, टीला—mound, मुकदमें—cases, निर्णय किया—decided, निर्णय—judgement, decision. इतने, न्यायोचित, so judicious. दूर-दूर तक फैल गई, spread far and wide (climbed abroad). खोदा गया, was turned up or dug out. न्याय-सिंहासन, seat of judgement (judgement seat). मालूम हुआ, came to know.

Exercise 10

एक समय एक राजा था जिसके बारे में एक बड़ी रुचिकर कहानी कही जाती है। वह राजा बाज का बड़ा शौकीन था। वह बाज को हमेशा अपने कलाई पर बैठाए रहता था। वह कहीं भी जाता उसे हमेशा अपने साथ रखता था। एक बार वह सघन वन से भरी पहाड़ियों की ओर शिकार के लिए निकला। गर्मी का मौसम था। शिकार के पीछे दौड़ते-दौड़ते राजा को बड़ी प्यास लगी। उसके अनुचरों का कहीं पता नहीं था। पानी की तलाश में वह एक झरने के पास पहुँचा। जैसे ही उसने पानी पीना चाहा कि बाज ने पंख फड़फड़ाया और पानी को गिरा दिया। यह घटना तीन बार घटी। अंत में राजा ने क्रोधित होकर बाज को जमीन पर दे मारा। फलस्वरूप उसकी मृत्यु हो गई। किन्तु जब राजा जी भरकर पानी पी चुका तब उसके शरीर में बुरी तरह से खुजली होने लगी। राजा को अपने प्रिय बाज के प्रति अपने व्यवहार पर बड़ा पश्चात्ताप हुआ।

Hints : एक रुचिकर कहानी, an interesting story. बाज, falcon. कलाई, wrist. सघन वन ...... की ओर, towards the hills luxuriant with dense woods. प्यास, thirst. (प्यासा, thirsty). अनुचरों, **attendants.** फड़फड़ाना, to flap. दे मारा, struck against. जी भरकर, to one's heart's contents. खुजली होना, **to itch.** व्यवहार, behaviour, treatment. पश्चात्ताप करना, to repent.

Exercise 11

एक बार एक लोमड़ी सघन वन में शिकार के फेर में घूम रही थी। दुर्भाग्यवश इस प्रयास में उसने अपनी दुम खो दी। दुम कट जाने से वह बहुत दुखी हुई। वह सोचने लगी कि अब वह अपने समाज में कैसे जाएगी। तब उसके मन में एक विचार आया। उसने जंगल के सभी जानवरों की एक सभा बुलाई। वह बोली, 'मैं पहले से अधिक तेज भाग सकती हूँ। मेरी सुन्दरता भी अब बढ़ गई है। इसके अतिरिक्त हमारी दुम एक व्यर्थ की चीज है। मैं चाहती हूँ कि आप सभी अपनी दुम कटवा लें।' कुछ दूर पर एक वृद्ध भेड़िया यह सब ध्यानपूर्वक सुन रहा था। वह खड़ा होकर बोला, 'मैं समझता हूँ कि यदि आपको अपनी पूँछ पुनः मिलने की आशा होती तो आप हमें ऐसी नेक सलाह न देतीं।' इस पर सभी जानवर वहाँ हँसने लगे। लोमड़ी एक तमाशा बनकर रह गई।

Hints : सघन वन में, in the dense forest. शिकार के फेर में, after a prey. घूमना, to wander. प्रयास, attempt. दुम, tail. खोना, to lose. बहुत दुखी हुई, was much grieved. एक सभा बुलाई, called a meeting. लाभ, advantage. व्यर्थ की चीज, a useless thing, a thing of nought. कटवा लें, get your tail cut. कुछ दूर पर, at a stone's throw. भेड़िया, wolf. ध्यानपूर्वक, attentively. नेक सलाह, an honest piece of advice. तमाशा बनकर रह गई, turned a laughing stock. जंगली जानवर, beast.

Exercise 12

एक बार एक भगवद्भक्त एक छोटी यात्रा पर निकला। रास्ते में उसने एक गुफा के सामने एकत्रित लोगों की भीड़ देखी। पूछने पर पता चला कि उस गुफा में एक साधु रहते हैं जो वर्ष में एक बार बाहर निकलते हैं। वे जिसे स्पर्श कर देते हैं, वह रोगमुक्त हो जाता है। वह भगवद्भक्त भी उस विचित्र घटना को देखने के लिए रुक गया। निश्चित समय पर वह साधु गुफा से निकले। उन्होंने सभी लोगों को स्पर्श किया। फलस्वरूप सभी रोगमुक्त हो गए। जब सभी वहाँ से चले गए और साधु पुनः गुफा में जाने लगे तो भगवद्भक्त ने झट से उनकी चादर पकड़ ली और बोला, 'प्रभु ! सभी को तो आपने रोगविमुक्त कर दिया, क्या मेरा रोग नहीं दूर करेंगे ?' तब साधु ने हड़बड़ाकर कहा' 'छोड़ मेरी चादर। तुमने एक की चादर छोड़कर यहाँ दूसरे की पकड़ रखी है।' यह कहकर वह गुफा में लुप्त हो गए।

Hints : एक भगवद्भक्त, a devotee of God. एक छोटी यात्रा, a short trip. निकला, went out. गुफा, cave, एकत्रित, gathered. भीड़, crowd. पूछने पर, on enquiry. पता चला-it was learnt. रोगमुक्त हो जाता है-gets rid of the disease, विचित्र घटना, strange happening. निश्चित समय पर, at the appointed time. फलस्वरूप, consequently, as the result. झट से, hurriedly. चादर, sheet. रोगमुक्त हो गए, were recovered. हड़बड़ाकर, impatiently. लुप्त होना, to disappear or vanish.

Exercise 13

अरब के खलीफा (Caliph) हारू-अफ-रशीद अपनी उदारता के लिए प्रसिद्ध थे। एक रात्रि वेष बदलकर वे राजधानी के बाहर घूम रहे थे। इसी बीच उन्होंने एक पेड़ के नीचे बैठे हुए एक लड़के को देखा। लड़का बहुत उदास दिखाई दे रहा था। वे चुपके से उस लड़के के पास बैठ गए। उन्होंने उस लड़के से पूछा, 'इस देश का बादशाह कैसा है ?' लड़के ने बिगड़कर कहा, 'उसका नाम न लो। वह अत्याचारी और निष्ठुर है।' बादशाह शीघ्र महल को लौट आया। उसने नौकरों को उस लड़के को पकड़ने की आज्ञा दी। जब दूसरे दिन वह लड़का दरबार में सजा के लिए लाया गया तो उसका पिता भी वहाँ पहुँचा। उसकी रक्षा में पिता ने बादशाह से कहा, 'हुजूर ! मेरा लड़का एक माह में तीन दिन पागल रहता है। जिस दिन वह आपसे मिला वह तीन दिनों में से एक था।' इस उक्ति से बादशाह बड़ा प्रसन्न हुआ। उसने उस लड़के को छोड़ दिया।

Hints : उदारता, charity, generosity. वेष बदलकर, in disguise. राजधानी, capital. इसी बीच, in the meantime. बिगड़कर, being angry. उसका नाम न लो, do not mention his name. अत्याचारी और निष्ठुर, tyrant and cruel. सजा, punishment. उसकी रक्षा में, in his defence. हुजूर, your majesty, my lord. उन तीन ...... एक था, was one of those three days. उक्ति, remark. छोड़ दिया, renounced.

Exercise 14

डाक्टर राजेन्द्र प्रसाद भारत के प्रथम राष्ट्रपति थे। उन्होंने बहुत दिनों तक पटना उच्च न्यायालय में वकालत की थी। एक बार एक मुअक्किल अपनी विधवा चाची की जायदाद लेने के सिलसिले में उनकी सलाह लेने आया। उसने कहा, 'मेरी चाची को कोई संतान नहीं है। यदि आप मेरी सहायता करेंगे तो मैं सम्पूर्ण जायदाद का मालिक बन जाऊँगा।' राजेन्द्र बाबू थोड़ी देर तक चुप रहे और फिर बोले, 'मैं समझता हूँ कि भगवान ने आपको काफी जायदाद दी है। आप असहाय विधवा की सम्पत्ति क्यों लेना चाहते हैं ? मनुष्य को अपने भाग्य से संतोष करना चाहिए। आप अपनी चाची की सहायता कीजिए। ऐसे मुकदमें में मैं आपकी कोई सहायता नहीं कर सकता।' मुअक्किल उनकी बातों को सुनकर अवाक् रह गया। उसने उनके सम्बन्धी से जाकर कहा, 'आपने मुझे वकील के पास भेजा था या साधु के पास ?'

Hints : वकालत की थी, had practised. मुअक्किल, client. जायदाद, property. लेने के सिलसिने में, in connection with possessing. संतान, issue. मालिक, owner. सलाह लेना, consult. थोड़ी देर तक, for a while. चुप रहे, kept mum. असहाय, helpless. लेना, to grab. भाग्य, fate. संतोष करना, to satisfy. अवाक् रह गया, was stunned. सम्बन्धी, relative.

Exercise 15

टहलना स्वास्थ्य के लिए बहुत उपयोगी है। इसे प्रात:काल सूर्य उगने से पहले और संध्या को सूर्यास्त के बाद करना चाहिए। फेफड़े के उचित कार्य के लिए यह एक प्रभावशाली निदान है। यह हमारे शरीर को अतिरिक्त स्फूर्ति प्रदान करता है और चित्त को दिन भर प्रसन्न रखता है। हमारे जोड़ों तथा माँसपेशियों के लिए भी यह एक स्वास्थ्यवर्धक टॉनिक है। इससे रक्त संचार सामान्य हो जाता है। एक आदमी शुरू के जीवन में अनेक बीमारियों से ग्रस्त था। उसने प्रख्यात डाक्टरों से सलाह ली और उनसे इलाज भी कराया। किन्तु सब व्यर्थ। निराश उसने सभी दवाओं को छोड़ दिया। उसने सुबह शाम टहलने का निश्चय किया। वह खूब तड़के दूर खुले खेतों की ओर चला जाता और ताजी हवा का आनन्द लेता। प्रथम दिन से ही वह स्वयं को तरोताजा अनुभव करने लगा। अब उसे सभी बीमारियों से छुटकारा मिल गया। उसे ऐसा लगा मानो सूखी हड्डियों में जीवन आ गया हो।

Hints : उपयोगी, beneficial, useful. फेफड़े, lungs. उचित कार्य के लिए, for proper function. प्रभावशाली निदान, efficacious cure. अतिरिक्त स्फूर्ति प्रदान करता है, adds extra stimulus. प्रसन्न रखना, to keep cheerful. जोड़ों तथा माँसपेशियों, joints and muscles. एक स्वास्थ्यवर्धक टॉनिक, a wholesome tonic. रक्त संचार, blood-circulation. सामान्य, normal. ग्रस्त था, suffered. प्रख्यात डाक्टर, renowned physician. इलाज कराया, got treated. निराश, being disappointed. निश्चय किया, decided. खूब तड़के, very early. आनन्द लेना, to enjoy. तरोताजा, fresh. छुटकारा मिल गया, got rid of. ऐसा लगा मानो, felt as if. सूखी हड्डियाँ, dry bones. जीवन आ गया हो, life was breathed (charged) (into).

Exercise 16

विश्वामित्र नामक एक ज्ञानी मुनि आधुनिक बक्सर के निकट एक जंगल में रहा करते थे। एक दिन जब राजा दशरथ अपनी सभा में बैठे थे, विश्वामित्र वहाँ पहुँचे। उन्हें देखकर राजा सिंहासन से उठ खड़े हुए और मुनि को प्रणाम किया। उन्होंने उनका यथोचित सत्कार किया। अंत में राजा दशरथ ने हाथ जोड़कर उनसे पूछा, 'महामुनि ! कृपाकर अपने यहाँ आने का उद्देश्य कहिए।' विश्वामित्र ने कहा, 'मैं जंगल में रहता हूँ, जिसमें दो राक्षस भी रहते हैं। जब भी मैं यज्ञ प्रारम्भ करता हूँ, वे दोनों आकर विघ्न डालते हैं। उनमें से एक का नाम सुवाहु और दूसरा मारीच है। वे दोनों बड़े बलवान हैं और रावण के प्रति निष्ठावान हैं। इसलिए वे हम ऋषियों से नहीं डरते बल्कि हम लोगों को बहुत कष्ट देते हैं। यदि राम मेरे साथ चलेंगे तो वे उन दोनों राक्षसों को मार डालेंगे।' विश्वामित्र की बात सुनते ही राजा दशरथ का हृदय काँप उठा। वे घबड़ाकर हाथ जोड़कर कहने लगे, 'प्रभु ! मेरी प्रार्थना है कि आप राम को छोड़ दीजिए क्योंकि अभी वह एकदम बच्चा है और राक्षसों से लड़ने में असमर्थ है। जो राक्षस आपको कष्ट पहुँचाते हैं उन्हें मारने के लिए मैं आपको एक बड़ी सेना देता हूँ।'

Hints : मुनि, sage. सिंहासन से उठ खड़े हुए, arose from the throne. प्रणाम किया, saluted. यथोचित, properly. हाथ जोड़कर, with folded (or clasped) hands. राक्षस, devil, demon. विघ्न डालते हैं, create hindrance. निष्ठावान, loyal (to). बल्कि, rather. हृदय काँप उठा, trembled to his very core. एकदम बच्चा है, is a mere child, is too young to. देता हूँ, offer. यज्ञ, yajan. असमर्थ, incapable (of).

Exercise 17

जापान अनेक द्वीपों का देश है। यह चीन के उत्तर पूर्व में प्रशान्त महासागर में है। जापानी बड़े राष्ट्रवादी होते हैं और उन्हें अपने देश पर बड़ा गर्व है। इसे वे प्रभात सूर्य का देश (दाई नेपन्) कहते हैं। यहाँ भूकम्प बहुत आते हैं। यहाँ लगभग दो सौ ज्वालामुखी पहाड़ हैं। यही कारण है कि यहाँ की अधिकतर मकान लकड़ी के बने होते हैं। जापान की राजधानी टोकियो है जो संसार के सबसे बड़े नगरों में से एक है। यहाँ की आस-पास की भूमि बड़ी उपजाऊ है। यद्यपि जापान पहाड़ी देश है किन्तु यहाँ के लोग बड़े परिश्रमी होते हैं। जापान के वनों की लकड़ियों से नाना प्रकार की मूल्यवान वस्तुएँ तैयार की जाती हैं। जापान की बनी हस्तशिल्प वस्तुओं की विदेशों में बड़ी माँग है। जापान का व्यापार उसके निर्यात पर बहुत कुछ निर्भर करता है। कोयला और मिट्टी का तेल जापान को आयात करना पड़ता है। यहाँ के अधिकतर निवासी बौध हैं और इसकी जनसंख्या घनी है।

Hints : द्वीप, island. प्रशान्त महासागर, pacific ocean. राष्ट्रवादी, nationalist. प्रभात सूर्य का देश, a country (or land) of the rising sun. भूकम्प, earthquake. बहुत आते हैं, take place frequently, occur oftener. ज्वालामुखी पहाड़, volcanoes. आस-पास की भूमि, adjacent soil (land). ऊपजाऊ, fertile. पहाड़ी देश, a hilly country. परिश्रमी, industrious, laborious. लकड़ी, timber, wood. मूल्यवान, precious, costly. हस्तशिल्प वस्तुएँ, handiwork. माँग, demand. निर्यात, export. बहुत कुछ, to a great extent. मिट्टी का तेल, kerosene oil. आयात, import. घनी है, is populous.

Exercise 18

एक दिन सोलोमन (Solomon) के सामने दो औरतें आईं। उन लोगों ने उनसे न्याय करने को कहा। उनमें से एक की गोद में एक बच्चा था। उसने चिल्लाकर कहा, 'बच्चा निश्चय ही मेरा बेटा है।' दूसरी औरत ने कहा, 'ओ मेरे प्रभु, बच्चा मेरा है। इसने उसे मुझसे ले लिया है।' सोलोमन कैसे समझते कि बच्चा वास्तव में किसका है ? अन्त में उसे एक अनूठी उपाय सूझी। उसने एक तलवार मँगाई। राजा ने एक सेवक से कहा, 'लड़के को दो बराबर हिस्सों में काट दो। आधा एक औरत को दे दो और शेष दूसरी औरत को।' इस पर वह औरत जिसका वास्तव में बच्चा नहीं था चुप्पी साध ली। परन्तु दूसरी औरत जो वास्तविक माँ थी, चिल्ला उठी, 'मेरे मालिक ! जीवित बच्चे को उसे दे दो, किन्तु उसकी हत्या न करो।' राजा समझ गया कि बच्चा उसी का है। उसने उसके बेटे को उसे सौंप दिया।

Hints : गोद, lap. ओ मेरे प्रभु, O my lord !. ले लिया है, has snatched. अनूठी उपाय सूझी, struck out a novel plan. काट दो, bisect. चुप्पी साध ली, kept mum. जीवित, living. सौंपना, to hand over. शेष, remainder.

Exercise 19

एक सन्त पानी की जहाज से यात्रा कर रहे थे। यात्रा लम्बी थी। अत: यात्री उनके सत्संग का लाभ उठाते। वह एक बात अवश्य याद दिलाते थे कि संसार नश्वर है। सदैव मृत्यु को याद रखो। एक दिन समुद्र में भयंकर तूफान उठा। सभी जान के पीछे इधर उधर भागने लगे। वहाँ कुछ भी सुनाई नहीं देता था। सभी प्राण रक्षा के लिए चिन्तित थे किन्तु असहाय क्या करते। तब सभी प्रार्थना में लीन हो गए। सभी ने देखा कि संत सहज, अनुद्विग्न बैठे हैं। तूफान शान्त हुआ। एक यात्री ने संत से जाकर पूछा, 'क्या आपको मृत्यु से डर न लगा ?' सन्त ने कहा, 'मृत्यु का फंदा समुद्र में ही नहीं, पृथ्वी पर भी इसी भाँति सदैव झूलता रहता है। फिर डर किस बात का ? मृत्यु से केवल अज्ञानी, अविवेकी डरते हैं। फिर भी डरकर वे बचते नहीं।'

Hints : सन्त, hermit, saint. समुद्री यात्रा करना, to travel by water, was on the voyage (or passage). यात्रा (समुद्री), voyage, passage. उनके सत्संग का लाभ उठाते, the benefit of his divine (or holy) company. याद दिलाना, to remind. नश्वर, perishable, transitory. एक भयंकर तूफान उठा, a violent storm arose. जाने के पीछे, after life. इधर उधर, to and fro. चिन्तित थे, were worried. लीन हो गए, meditated on. सहज, unperturbed. अनुद्विग्न, unworried. फन्दा, death-trap. झूलना, to hang, to hover over. अज्ञानी, the ignorant. अविवेकी, the unwise. बचना, to escape.

Exercise 20

यद्यपि ओमर शक्तिशाली खलीफा थे, तथापि एक गरीब आदमी जैसा रहते थे। अपनी व्यक्तिगत आमदनी से ही वे अपने परिवार का पालन पोषण करते थे। वे मदीना की सड़कों पर बहुधा फटे और पेबन्द लगे कपड़े पहने घूमा करते थे। एक बार उन्होंने कहा—सभी चीजें ईश्वर की हैं। मैं केवल उसका नौकर हूँ। मुझे कीमती कपड़ों की जरूरत नहीं है। मुझे केवल दो पोशाक चाहिए—एक गर्मी के लिए और दूसरा जाड़े के लिए। मुझे सार्वजनिक खजाने का रुपये लेने का कोई अधिकार नहीं है। कहते हैं कि उनके कर्मचारियों को भी वैसा ही सरल जीवन व्यतीत करना पड़ता था। उन्होंने सभी से प्रतिज्ञा कराई कि अपने द्वार से गरीबों एवं अपाहिजों को बिना कुछ मदद के वे न जाने देंगे।

Hints : शक्तिशाली, powerful. व्यक्तिगत आमदनी, personal income. पालन-पोषण करना, to support. फटे एवं पेबन्द लगे कपड़े पहने, clad in shabby (worn out) and patched clothes. ईश्वर की हैं, belong to God. पोशाक, garments. सार्वजनिक खजाना, public treasury. अधिकार, right. कहते हैं, it is said, story goes that. कर्मचारी, employees. व्यतीत करना पड़ता था, had to lead. प्रतिज्ञा कराई, made all swear. अपाहिजों, the disabled, the handicapped, न जाने देंगे, would not let go.

Exercise 21

भारतवर्ष में धर्मात्माओं की बहुत सी कहानियाँ प्रचलित हैं। उनमें से युधिष्ठिर की भी कहानी है। वे अपनी सच्चाई के लिए बहुत प्रसिद्ध थे। उनके जीवन में वफादारी का भी एक ज्वलन्त उदाहरण मिलता है। अपनी जीवन-यात्रा की समाप्ति पर स्वर्ग जाते समय उनका प्रिय पालतू कुत्ता भी उनके साथ गया। स्वर्ग के प्रहरी ने उन्हें फाटक पर रोका और कहा, 'धर्मराज! आप इस कुत्ते के साथ अन्दर नहीं जा सकते।' युधिष्ठिर ने नम्रतापूर्वक कहा, 'मैं कुत्ते के साथ ही अन्दर जाऊँगा, अकेला नहीं।' युधिष्ठिर अपनी बात पर अड़े रहे। प्रहरी की समझ में नहीं आया कि वह क्या करे। अन्त में निर्णय युधिष्ठिर के पक्ष में ही हुआ। युधिष्ठिर के साथ उनके कुत्ते को भी स्वर्ग में प्रवेश मिला।

Hints : धर्मात्माओं, sages and seers. प्रचलित हैं, are rampant (prevalent). सच्चाई, truthfulness, verocity. वफादारी, loyalty. ज्वलंत उदाहरण, a bright example. पालतू, domestic, pet. प्रहरी, sentinel. रोका, halted. धर्मराज, Defender of faith, king of religion. नम्रतापूर्वक, politely, modestly. अड़े रहे, stuck to his word, abided his word. पक्ष में हुआ, went in favour of.

Exercise 22

एक बार एक लोमड़ी ने एक कौए को पनीर का टुकड़ा चोंच में लेकर वृक्ष की शाखा पर बैठते हुए देखा। 'वह तो मेरे लिए है', लोमड़ी ने कहा और वृक्ष के नीचे जा पहुँची। वह बोली, 'कौआ जी। नमस्कार। आज आप कितना अच्छा दिखाई दे रहे हैं। आपके पंख कितने चमकदार हैं! आपकी आँखें कितनी चमकीली हैं! मुझे विश्वास है कि आपकी बोली अन्य चिड़ियों की बोली से उसी तरह मधुरतर होगी, जिस तरह आपका रूप। आप केवल एक गाना सुनाएँ, जबकि चिड़ियों का राजकुमार कहकर मैं आपकी प्रशंसा करूँगी।' कौआ ने अपना सिर उठाया और जोर से काँव-काँव करना शुरू किया। फलस्वरूप पनीर का टुकड़ा जमीन पर गिर पड़ा। लोमड़ी ने झपटकर उसे उठा लिया। वह बोली, 'बस, इतना ही काफी है। तुम्हारे पनीर के टुकड़े के बदले मैं भविष्य के लिए तुम्हें एक सलाह दूँगी। खुशामदियों का विश्वास न करो। वे चुपके से तुम्हारी बुद्धि और धन दोनों ही चुरा लेते हैं।'

Hints : पनीर का एक टुकड़ा, a piece of cheese. चोंच, beak. शाखा, branch. पंख, wing, feather. चमकदार, bright. चमकीली, shining. मुझे विश्वास है, I believe, I am sure. बोली, note, voice. रूप, face, appearance. उठाया, raised. झपटकर, hurriedly. इतना ही काफी है, enough, no more. बदले में, in lieu of, in return of. खुशामदी, flatterer. बुद्धि और धन, wit and wealth. चुरा लेते हैं, to take away, to steal away. काँव-काँव करना, to caw.

Exercise 23

एक शेर जो इतना बूढ़ा और दुर्बल हो गया था कि शिकार को न जा सकता था, चुपचाप एक गुफा के द्वार पर पड़ा रहता था। एक बार एक गीदड़ वहाँ आया। उसे देखकर शेर ने कहा, 'मित्र, अन्दर आओ। मैं तुमसे बातचीत करना चाहता हूँ। यहाँ मैं बिलकुल अकेला हूँ। तुम्हारे जैसे बुद्धिमान जानवर से बात करके मैं बड़ा सुखी होऊँगा।' गीदड़ ने कहा, 'मुझे डर है कि यह मुलाकात मेरे स्वास्थ्य के लिए अच्छी न होगी।' शेर ने कहा, 'अरे, मैं इतना बूढ़ा और निर्बल हूँ कि तुम्हें कोई हानि नहीं पहुँचा सकता। पैर के चिह्नों को देखकर तुम जान सकते हो कि कितने लोग मुझसे मिलने के लिए आए।' चालाक गीदड़ ने उत्तर दिया, 'हाँ, मैं उन लोगों का निशान तो देखता हूँ, जो तुमसे मिलने के लिए गए लेकिन उधर से लौटने वालों का निशान नहीं देखता।'

Hints : मुलाकात, meeting. मेरे स्वास्थ्य ...... न होगी, will not suit my health. पैर के चिह्नों, footprints. जान सकते हो, can guess. गीदड़, jackal. निशान, mark.

Exercise 24

किसी समय एक व्यापारी के घर चोरी हो गई। उसने अपने नौकरों को बुलाकर पूछताछ की परन्तु चोर का कोई पता न लग सका। अंत में उसने चोर को पता लगाने का एक ढंग निकाला। उसने प्रत्येक नौकर को एक जैसी छड़ियाँ दी और कहा कि चोर की छड़ी कल तक एक ईंच बढ़ जाएगी। कल इसी समय तक छड़ियों को मेरे पास लाना। नौकर छड़ियों को लेकर अपने-अपने घर चले गए। जिस नौकर ने चोरी की थी उसने अपनी छड़ी को काटकर एक ईंच छोटा कर दिया ताकि जो बढ़ोतरी होगी वह पहले ही काट दी जाय। अगले दिन जब नौकरों की छड़ियाँ देखी गई तो चोर की छड़ी सबसे एक ईंच छोटी थी। उसे पकड़ लिया गया। उसने अपना अपराध मान लिया और व्यापारी का सारा धन ज्यों का त्यों मिल गया।

Hints : चोरी हो गई, a theft was committed, पूछताछ की, enquired (of), कोई पता न लग सका, could not be detected. एक ढंग निकाला, designed (chalked out) a trick (or a plan). एक जैसी, similar types. बढ़ना, to increase. काटकर एक ईंच छोटा कर दिया, cut and shortened the stick by an inch. बढ़ौतरी, increment. पहले ही, beforehand. सबसे एक ईंच छोटी थी, was the shortest of all by an inch. अपराध मान लिया, confessed his guilt (or crime). धन, wealth. ज्यों का त्यों, as it was, safe and sound.

Exercise 25

सावित्री राजा अश्वपति की एकलौती कन्या थी। वह सर्वाधिक सुन्दरी थी और उसका चरित्र भी बहुत ऊँचा था। एक दिन वह जंगल से होकर जा रही थी। वहाँ एक लड़के को वह पेड़ के नीचे देखी। उसे देखकर वह प्रथम दृष्टि में ही उस पर मोहित हो गई। घर जाकर उसने सभी बातें अपने माता-पिता से बताई। इतने में ही देवऋषि नारद वहाँ आ गए और बोले, 'यह युवक सत्यवान है और इस वर्ष के अन्त में यह मर जाएगा।' परन्तु सावित्री ने कहा, 'जो भाग्य में लिखा है वह अवश्य होगा। अत: मुझे किसी बात की चिन्ता नहीं है।' यह सुनकर माता-पिता चुप हो गए। उन्होंने सावित्री का विवाह उसकी इच्छानुसार सत्यवान से कर दिया।

Hints : एकलौती कन्या, the only daughter. सर्वाधिक सुन्दरी, the champion of beauty (the most beautiful). जंगल से होकर, through the forest. प्रथम दृष्टि में ही, at the first sight. मोहित हो गई, was charmed (fell in love). जो भाग्य में लिखा है, what is fated. उसकी इच्छानुसार, according to her wish (or will). देवऋषि, the divine sage.

Exercise 26

एक समय एक मुर्गा किसी पेड़ पर बैठकर बाँग दे रहा था। इसी बीच एक लोमड़ी की दृष्टि उस पर पड़ी। मुर्गे को देखकर लोमड़ी के मुँह में पानी भर आया। वह उसे मारने के लिए उपाय सोचने लगी। वह मुर्गे से बोली, 'क्या तुमने नई घोषणा नहीं सुनी ? जंगल में सभी पशु पक्षियों ने मिलकर एक विशाल सभा की थी। वहाँ सभी ने शपथ ली कि अब से कोई जीव किसी को नहीं मारेगा।' मुर्गे ने जोर से बाँग दिया। इस पर लोमड़ी ने पूछा, 'क्या बात है ?' मुर्गे ने कहा, 'कुछ शिकारी कुत्ते इस ओर आ रहे हैं।' यह सुनकर लोमड़ी भागने लगी। मुर्गे ने पूछा, 'क्यों भागती हो ? अब तो कोई डर की बात नहीं है, न ?' लोमड़ी यह कहते हुए नौ दो ग्यारह हो गई कि शायद तुम्हारे जैसा वे भी इस नवीन घोषणा को न सुने हों।

Hints : बाँग देना, to crow. दृष्टि उस पर पड़ी, eyes fell on him. पानी भर गया, was watered. उपाय सोचने लगी, began to contrive (to chalk out or design) a plan. नई घोषणा, new announcement, शपथ ली, swore, took oath, अब तो कोई डर की बात नहीं है, न ?, now there is no room of fear, is there (or I suppose) ?, नौ दो ग्यारह हो गई, took to her heels.

Exercise 27

किसी घने जंगल में एक लोमड़ी रहती थी। थोड़ी दूर पर एक गीदड़ भी रहता था। ये दोनों बड़े मित्र थे और एक दूसरे के लिए जान देने को तैयार थे। एक दिन तीसरे पहर कुछ शिकारी उधर आ निकले। उनके साथ बहुत-से कुत्ते थे। कुत्तों को देखकर लोमड़ी ने अपने मन में सोचा, 'हाय ! गीदड़ के प्राण संकट में हैं। मैं उसके प्राण कैसे बचा सकती हूँ ?' जब उसे और कोई उपाय न सूझा तो वह अपने बिल से बाहर निकली और कुत्तों के सामने एक ओर बड़ी जोर से भागी। कुत्तों ने उसका पीछा किया। बेचारी लोमड़ी भी बहुत दूर तक भागी। फलस्वरूप कुत्ते शिकारियों से बहुत दूर निकल गए। इतने में अंधेरा होने लगा और कुत्तों को बुलाने के लिए शिकारी अपना बिगुल बजाने लगे। बिगुल की आवाज सुनकर कुत्ते लौट आए और लोमड़ी की जान बच गई। गीदड़ भी बच गया और शिकारी उसको कोई हानि न पहुँचा सके।

Hints : थोड़ी दूर पर, at a stone's throw. बड़े मित्र, fast friends, bosom friends. तैयार थे, were ready. तीसरे पहर, afternoon. शिकारी, hunter. उधर आ निकले, passed by that way. संकट में, in peril. हाय, alas. बिल, den, lair, कोई उपाय न सूझा, thought no way out. बहुत दूर निकल गए, went far away. बिगुल, bugle, clarion, horn. बजाना, to trill. कोई हानि न पहुँचा सके, could do no harm.

Exercise 28

एक बरगद के खोखले में एक गिद्ध रहता था। उसी पेड़ की डाली पर बहुत सी चिड़ियों के घोंसले थे। गिद्ध बूढ़ा तथा अन्धा था। उसके बुढ़ापे पर तरस खाकर चिड़ियाँ उसको खाना दे देती थीं। गिद्ध चिड़ियों के बच्चों की रखवाली करता था। एक दिन एक बिल्ली वहाँ आई। उसने गिद्ध की खुशामद कर पेड़ पर चढ़ने की आज्ञा ले ली। बिल्ली चुपके से चिड़ियों के घोंसलों में जाती और उनके बच्चों को मुँह में उठा लाती। वह हड्डियों को गिद्ध के घोंसले में डाल देती थी। जब चिड़ियों को उनके बच्चे न मिले तो उन्होंने उनकी खोज की। उन्होंने हड्डियों को गिद्ध के खोखले में पाया। वे गिद्ध पर इतनी नाराज हुईं कि उन्होंने मिलकर गिद्ध को मार डाला। गिद्ध के मरने पर बिल्ली को कोई डर नहीं रहा और उसने धीरे-धीरे सब चिड़ियों को खा डाला।

Hints : खोखला, hollow. गिद्ध, vulture. तरस खाकर, taking pity on. चिड़ियों के बच्चे, young ones of the birds, broods. रखवाली करना, to look after. खुशामद करके, having flattered. आज्ञा ले ली, got the permission. उठाना, to pick up. हड्डियाँ, bones. डालना, to lay. खोज की, searched for.

Exercise 29

एक सिंह एक वृक्ष की छाया में गहरी नींद में सोया हुआ था। सारे दिन वह भोजन की खोज में इधर उधर भटका था। इसलिए बहुत थक गया था। एक चूहा अपने बिल से बाहर आया और उसके शरीर पर फिरने लगा। सिंह जग गया और

कुद्ध हो गया। उसने चूहे को पंजे में दबाया और कहने लगा, 'मुझे बताओ कि तुमने मुझे क्यों जगाया है ? मैं तुम्हें निश्चय ही मार डालूँगा।' बेचारा चूहा भय से काँपने लगा और उसने कहा, 'कृपया मुझे जीने दीजिए। मैं आपको जगाना नहीं चाहता था। यदि ईश्वर ने चाहा तो मैं आपकी इस कृपा का ऋण चुका दूँगा।' सिंह इस पर हँसा और उसने चूहे को छोड़ दिया। कुछ दिनों पश्चात् वह सिंह एक जाल में पकड़ा गया। उसने बहुत चेष्टा की किन्तु उससे बाहर नहीं जा सका। जब चूहे को उसके बारे में ज्ञात हुआ तो वह वहाँ आया। उसने जाल को कुतर कर शेर को स्वतंत्र कर दिया।

Hints : छाया में, in the shadow of. गहरी नींद में सोना, to sleep soundly. सारे दिन, the whole day, all day long. इधर उधर, to and fro. भटकना, to wander about. बहुत थक गया था, was much (very) tired. फिरने लगा, began to move about. जग गया, woke up. पंजे में दबाया, pressed into the paw. निश्चय ही, certainly. बेचारा, the poor. भय से काँपने लगा, began to tremble with fear (or out of fear). जीने दीजिए, let me live. जगाना, to awake, to arouse. कृपा, grace. ऋण चुकाना, to repay the debt. छोड़ दिया, set free, जाल में पकड़ा गया, was entrapped or was caught in a trap. बहुत चेष्टा की, tried his best (or utmost), left no stone unturned. कुतर डाला, nibbled away.

Exercise 30

एक बार एक गड़ेरिया जंगल में सो रहा था। रात अंधेरी थी उसकी भेड़ें उसके पास सो रही थीं। एक भेड़िया आया और एक भेड़ को लेकर चल दिया। रास्ते में उसे एक शेर आता दिखाई दिया। शेर ने भेड़िए से भेड़ छील ली और अपनी गुफा की ओर चल दिया। जब शेर कुछ दूर चला गया, तब भेड़िए ने पुकार कर कहा, 'ओ जंगल के राजा, तुझे मुझ गरीब का माल छीनने में शर्म नहीं आई ?' शेर ने उत्तर दिया, 'तुम्हें गड़ेरिए की भेड़ चुराते शर्म क्यों नहीं आई ?' शेर द्वारा टका सा जवाब पाकर भेड़िया चुप हो गया और वहाँ से चला गया।

Hints : गड़ेरिया, shepherd. भेड़ें, sheep, (or heads of sheep), भेड़िया, wolf. छीन ली, snatched (from). पुकार कर कहा, cried loudly. शर्म आना, to feel ashamed. टका सा जवाब पाकर, having received the blunt reply. मुझ गरीब, a poor beast like me.

Exercise 31

एक दिन एक लकड़हारा जब जंगल को गया, उसने एक अद्भुत दृश्य देखा। वहाँ एक छोटी लड़की खड़ी थी जिसके शरीर में असंख्य हीरों की कान्ति थी। वह लड़की को घर लाया। लड़की जब से लकड़हारे के घर आई, धन उसके ऊपर बरसने लगा। जब वह जंगल में लकड़ी काटने जाता, वह एक न एक बहुमूल्य वस्तु प्रतिदिन पा जाता। परिणाम यह हुआ कि वर्ष के भीतर ही लकड़हारा करोड़पति बन गया। लड़की जब उसको मिली थी तो वह छोटी थी किन्तु एक वर्ष में बढ़कर पूर्ण युवती हो गई। उसकी सुन्दरता की कहानी दूर-दूर तक फैल गई। कुछ दिनों बाद एक रात गोल बादल धीरे से आकाश से उतरा। वह लकड़हारे के घर के सामने रूक गया। चार परियाँ उससे उतरीं। उन्हें देखकर वह लड़की घर से बाहर आई। शोक भरे हृदय से उसने अपने माता पिता से विदा ली। वह लकड़हारे के घर में बहुत आनन्दपूर्वक रहती थी। इसलिए पृथ्वी उसे बहुत प्रिय थी।

Hints : लकड़हारा, wood cutter. अद्भुत, strange. असंख्य हीरों की कान्ति थी, was illuminating with myriad diamonds. बहुमूल्य वस्तु, precious thing. वर्ष के भीतर, within a year. करोड़पति बनना, to turn a millionaire. पूर्ण युवती हो गई, attained her full virginity. उतरा, descended. परियाँ, fairies. शोक भरे हृदय से, with heavy heart. विदा ली, took farewell.

Exercise 32

गर्मी के दिनों में कुमारी नाइटिंगल (Miss Nightingle) एक अस्पताल में दवा लेकर गई। वहाँ पर घायल सैनिक उसके आने से बहुत प्रसन्न हुए। कुछ दिनों तक वहाँ रहने पर वह स्वयं बीमार पड़ गई। जब वह अच्छी हुई तो इग्लैंड लौट

गई। वहाँ लौटने पर महारानी से लेकर गरीब किसान तक ने उसके स्वागत का विचार किया। परन्तु वह ऐसे सम्मान को पसन्द नहीं करती थी। अत: इग्लैंड पहुँचने पर वह इस तरह चुपके घर चली गई कि कोई उसे पहचान न सका। तथापि लोग उस पर अपनी कृतज्ञता प्रगट करना चाहते थे। इसलिए उन लोगों ने लाखों रुपये चन्दा जमा किए। उसकी इच्छानुसार उक्त धन से एक अस्पताल खोला गया। तुर्की के सुल्तान (The Sultan of Turkey) ने उसकी नि:स्वार्थ सेवा पर प्रसन्न होकर उसे एक बहुमूल्य आभूषण दिया। महारानी विक्टोरिया (Queen Victoria) ने उसे हीरे जड़े हुए हार से सम्मानित किया।

Hints : बीमार पड़ गई, fell ill. अच्छी हुई, recovered. कृतज्ञता प्रगट करना, to express one's gratitude. चन्दा जमा किए, collected in subscription, तथापि, however, nonetheless. नि:स्वार्थ सेवा, selfless service. एक बहुमूल्य आभूषण, a precious ornament. हीरे जड़े हुए हार, a necklace studded with diamonds. सम्मान, honour. उक्त, overmentioned.

Exercise 33

उस दिन श्रीमती यूब्राइट् (Mrs. Yeobright) ने निश्चय किया कि वह अपने एकलौते पुत्र क्लीम (Clym) से समझौता कर लेगी। अत: वह उसके निवास स्थान की ओर चल पड़ी। जब वह पहुँची तो किसी को वहाँ नहीं पाई। वह दरवाजा खटखटाई और आवाज दी। किन्तु कोई प्रत्युत्तर नहीं। निराश झुंझलाकर वह वहाँ से लौट गई। क्लीम घर में गाढ़ी निद्रा में मग्न था। जब वह जगा तो सभी हाल ज्ञात हुआ। यह जानकर कि माँ के आने पर दरवाजा न खोला गया और उसका अपमान हुआ, क्लीम अपनी पत्नी यूस्टेशिया (Eustacia) पर अत्यन्त क्रोधित हुआ। दोनों में बातें बिगड़ गईं। झगड़ा इतना बढ़ा कि यूस्टेशिया अपने पिता के घर चली गई। जब माँ को ढूँढने क्लीम बाहर आया तो अंधकार में कुछ दूरी पर उसे आवाजें सुनाई दीं। निकट जाने पर उसने देखा कि उसकी माँ को साँप ने काट लिया है। उसने झट से माँ को गोद में ले लिया। किन्तु अब माँ न रही।

Hints : एकलौता पुत्र, the only son. समझौता कर लेगी, would compromise (with). निवास स्थान, abode, residence. प्रत्युत्तर, response. निराश झुंझलाकर, being disappointed and irritated. आने पर, on the arrival. अपमान हुआ, burst out in anger. बातें बिगड़ गईं, the situation worsened. इतना बढ़ा, became so tense. काट लिया था, had bitten (envenomed). न रही, was no more.

Exercise 34

एक बार एक राजा ने अपने सभासदों की ओर लक्ष्य करके कहा, 'एक समय जल में आग लगी। इससे मछलियाँ बड़े वेग से भागीं।' यह सुनकर उसका सेवक बोला, 'हाँ महाराज ! वे भागती हुई किनारे के एक वृक्ष पर चढ़ गईं।' फिर राजा ने कहा, 'उन भागी हुई मछलियों में से बहुत सी लौट आईं और उस जलती हुई आग में विहार करने लगीं।' सेवक ने कहा, 'एक बात और करुणानिधान ! वे बड़ी भूखी थीं, अत: वे चिनगारियाँ खाने लगीं।' राजा ने कहा, 'मेरे मिथ्या कथन को तुम सत्य क्यों कहते हो ?' सेवक ने कहा, 'हे स्वामिन ! आपके अधीन होने से ही मेरा मन ऐसा हो गया। किसी कवि ने ठीक ही कहा है कि यदि राजा दिन को रात कहे तो सेवक को उसे चन्द्रमा और तारे भी दिखा देना चाहिए।'

Hints : सभासदों को लक्ष्य करके, addressing his courtiers. आग लगी, caught fire. एक बात और करुणानिधान, one thing more, my noble lord (or merciful lord). चिनगारियाँ, sparks. सुखपूर्वक विहार करने लगीं, began to enjoy themselves comfortably. मिथ्या कथन, false and faked statement. आपके अधीन होने से ही, only by being subordinate to you. ऐसा हो गया, turned so. किसी कवि ...... है, rightly has some poet remarked. चन्द्रमा और ...... देना चाहिए, should show the moon and stars as well.

Exercise 35

एक बार एक अमरीकन को लाटरी मिली। किन्तु उसकी प्रथम सूचना उसके लड़के को मिली। लड़के ने सोचा कि यदि पिताजी यह खबर अचानक सुनेंगे तो उनकी हृदय-गति रुक सकती है। बहुत विचार करने के बाद उसने वृद्ध पादरी के यहाँ जाने का निश्चय किया। वहाँ जाकर उसने अपनी सारी स्थिति उपस्थित की। पादरी ने कहा, 'यह कोई ऐसी समस्या नहीं

जैसी तुम सोचते हो। मुझे अपने पिता के पास ले चलो।' पादरी उसके पिता के यहाँ जाकर उसका मनोवैज्ञानिक उपचार करने लगा। अन्त में उसने तथ्य को उसे सही रूप से बताया। इस पर पिता ने कहा, 'यदि ऐसी बात है तो उसमें से आधा मैं आपको अवश्य दूँगा।' कहते हैं कि इस पर पादरी इतना प्रसन्न हुआ कि वह अपने को रोक नहीं सका। वह वहीं गिर पड़ा और मर गया।

Hints : लाटरी मिली, won a lottery. सूचना, information. हृदय-गति रुक सकती है, heart may fail (or cease its function). पादरी, clergy. सारी स्थिति उपस्थित किया, presented (or related) all situations. कठिन समस्या, a hard problem (or a hard nut to crack). ले चलो, lead me. मनोवैज्ञानिक उपचार करना, to treat on psychotherapy. तथ्य, fact. सही रूप में, in the true colours. इतना प्रसन्न हुआ, overwhelmed with so much joy (overjoyed so much). रोकना, to control.

Exercise 36

एक गाँव में एक अन्धा रहता था। एक दिन उस गाँव में आग लग गई। आग ने भयंकर रूप धारण कर लिया। बहुत से लोग घर छोड़कर भागने लगे। उसी गाँव में एक लंगड़ा भी रहता था। अंधे और लंगड़े दोनों ने भी जान बचानी चाही। अंधे ने लंगड़े से कहा, 'तुम्हारे पास आँखें हैं पर तुम चल नहीं सकते। मेरे पास पैर हैं पर आँखें नहीं। आओ, मेरे कंधे पर बैठ जाओ। तुम मुझे जो रास्ता दिखाओगे, उधर ही मैं चलूँगा। ऐसा करने से हम दोनों की जान बच जाएगी।' लंगड़े ने अंधे का सुझाव मान लिया। दोनों सकुशल गाँव से बाहर चले गए। सहयोग से कठिन कार्य भी सरल हो जाता है।

Hints : आग लग गई, fire broke out. भयंकर रूप ...... लिया, took a horrid shape. लंगड़ा, lame. जान बचानी चाही, wanted to save their life. जो रास्ता ...... चलूँगा, shall take the same course that you direct, (shall follow the ......). सुझाव, suggestion, proposal. मान लेना, to agree. सकुशल, safe and sound. सहयोग, co-operation.

Exercise 37

एक आदमी जो अपने पड़ोसी के खेत में अनाज चुराने जाया करता था। एक दिन अपने लड़के को भी साथ ले गया जो आठ वर्ष का था। पिता ने कहा, 'बोरा पकड़ो जब तक मैं पता लगा आऊँ कि कोई मुझे देख रहा है या नहीं।' थोड़ी देर बाद जब पिता लौटा तो लड़के ने उससे कहा, 'पिताजी, आपने सब ओर देखा पर एक तरफ नहीं देखा।' यह सुनकर उस आदमी ने डर के मारे बोरा गिरा दिया। वह घबराकर चारों ओर देखने लगा। उसने लड़के से पूछा, 'किस ओर लड़के ?' लड़के ने उत्तर दिया, 'आप आकाश की ओर देखना और यह सोचना भूल गए कि सर्वशक्तिमान ईश्वर आपको देख रहा है।' उस आदमी ने अपने लड़के की चेतावनी को समझा। वह चुपचाप वहाँ से घर लौट आया और कभी चोरी करने का विचार भी मन में न लाया। उसने यह शिक्षा याद रखी कि ईश्वर की आँख हमें प्रत्येक पल देखती है।

Hints : पड़ोसी, neighbour. अनाज, corn. बोरा, sack. पकड़ना, to hold. तरफ, direction. डर के मारे, out of fear. घबराकर, being puzzled (or confused). सर्वशक्तिमान ईश्वर, the Almighty God. शिक्षा, lesson. पल, moment.

Exercise 38

एक बार सन्त जॉनसन (Johnson) को एक गुलाम खरीदने की आवश्यकता पड़ी। जब वे बाजार पहुँचे तो उन्होंने एक स्थान पर एक आदमी द्वारा तीन गुलामों को बेचते हुए देखा। उनमें से एक सन्त ईसप भी थे। जॉनसन ने एक से पूछा, कि वह कौन सा कार्य कर सकता है ? उसने उत्तर दिया कि वह कोई भी काम कर सकता है। पुनः सन्त ने जब दूसरे गुलाम से पूछा तो उसने उन्हें बताया कि वह प्रत्येक काम कर सकता है। जब सन्त ईसप की बारी आई तब उन्होंने कहा, 'जब ये दोनों सभी कार्य कर ही लेंगे तो मेरे लिए शेष ही क्या रह जाता है ?' ईसप के कथन से जॉनसन अति प्रभावित हुए। उन्होंने पूछा, 'यदि मैं तुम्हें खरीद लूँ तो क्या तुम ईमानदारी से काम करोगे ?' सन्त ईसप ने कहा, 'आप मुझे खरीदें या न खरीदें, ईमानदार तो मैं हमेशा ही रहा हूँ।' इस पर जॉनसन ने उन्हें तुरन्त ही खरीद लिया।

Hints : आवश्यकता पड़ी, was in need of wanted to buy. गुलाम, slave, बारी, turn. शेष रज जाना, remain, what is left for me ?. टिप्पणी, remark. अति प्रभावित हुए, was immensely impressed with.

Exercise 39

सन् 1941 में बापू के एक बड़े भक्त ने उनसे पूछा, 'बापू, आप तो राम के बड़े भक्त हैं और राम के जीवन से आपको प्रेरणा भी मिलती है। ऐसा कहा जाता है कि राम ने बालि को धोखे से मारा। वे कंचन मृग के पीछे भागे थे फिर भी राम को आप आदर्श क्यों मानते हैं ?' बापू ने कहा, 'मेरे राम वे नहीं जो उस द्वन्द्व युद्ध में बालि को धोखा दिये थे। मेरे राम वे भी नहीं जिन्होंने मायामृग के पीछे दौड़ लगाई थी। मेरे राम वे हैं जिन्हें अयोध्या की गद्दी मिलने वाली थी परन्तु पिता के लिए जिन्होंने बनवास जाना सहर्ष स्वीकार कर लिया। मेरे राम वह हैं जो भरत के आग्रह को स्वीकार नहीं किए एवं जंगल में ही रहने का निश्चय किया। मेरे राम वे हैं जो एक धोबी को भी महत्त्व दिए और निष्कलंक सीता का परित्याग कर दिए।'

Hints : प्रेरणा पाना (मिलना), to derive inspiration from. धोखे से, deceitfully. कंचन मृग, golden deer (or stag). पीछे भागना, to run after, to chase. आदर्श, ideal. मानना, to account. द्वन्द्व युद्ध, duel. मायामृग, illusive (or delusory) deer. मिलने वाली थी, was to be coronated. बनवास, exilement, banishment. निष्कलंक, innocent, blameless. परित्याग करना, to abandon (or renounce).

Exercise 40

तब राजकुमारी ने दुखी होकर मुँह फेर लिया। वह हैरान थी कि सुन्दरता और ज्ञान के अतिरिक्त उसे और क्या चाहिए ? इसी बीच उसकी घूमती आँखें एक खिड़की की ओर जा पड़ी। उसने बाहर खड़े साधु को देखा। अचानक उसकी दृष्टि उन दो भिखारी बच्चों पर पड़ी जो सर्दी तथा भूख से काँपते सड़क पर चिल्ला रहे थे। राजकुमारी ने राजा से चिल्लाकर कहा, 'पिताजी, मुझे उन दो नन्हें बच्चों को अन्दर लाने की अनुमति दीजिए।' पहले तो राजा उसकी बात स्वीकार नहीं कर रहा था किन्तु अन्त में उसका अनुरोध मान लिया। राजकुमारी दौड़कर दरवाजे पर गई और हाथ पकड़कर उन दोनों को अन्दर लाई। जब वह आग से उन्हें गर्म करने की कोशिश कर रही थी तब साधु ने कमरे में प्रवेश किया। उसने कहा, 'यद्यपि मैं तुम्हारे सौन्दर्य और चातुर्य के सामने झुक नहीं सका, तथापि तुम्हारे हृदय की दयालुता के सामने झुकता हूँ।'

Hints : दुखी होकर, being displeased. मुँह फेर लिया, turned her face aside. हैरान थी, was vexed (or annoyed). और क्या चाहिए, what more she needed. घूमती आँखें, moving eyes. गर्म करना, to warm. झुक नहीं सका, could not submit. सौन्दर्य एवं चातुर्य, beauty and sagacity. तथापि, yet, however. दयालुता, compassion.

Exercise 41

माता भरत के वचन सुनकर बड़ी कोमलता से उठी और उन्हें हृदय से लगा लिया। उस समय माता के नेत्रों से आँसू गिर पड़े थे। वे भरत से बोली, 'मेरे पुत्र ! धीरज रखो। कुसमय जानकर शोक का परित्याग करो। अब ग्लानि से कोई लाभ नहीं क्योंकि काल की गति अमिट है। तात ! किसी को दोष मत दो। विधाता मुझसे ही सब प्रकार रुष्ट है। हे पुत्र ! पिता की आज्ञा से रघुनाथ ने भूषण, वसन सब त्याग दिया। हृदय में हर्ष, विषाद कुछ भी नहीं हुआ। और राजा के बारे में मैं क्या कहूँ ? वे तो जब तक जीवित रहे, राम का दर्शन करते रहे और वियोग होते ही प्राण त्याग दिए।' कौशल्या की बात सुनकर वहाँ खड़े सभी लोग फूट पड़े। अन्त में भरत ने कहा, 'हे माता ! मैं मन, वचन तथा कर्म से रामचन्द्र का दास हूँ। वे तो सबके हृदय में व्याप्त हैं। अतः वे सबकी प्रीति एवं कपट जानते हैं।'

Hints : बड़ी कोमलता से उठी, got up very tenderly. आँसू गिर पड़े, tears trickled down. धीरज रखो, bear up, have patience. कुसमय, adverse time. ग्लानि, repentence. कोई लाभ नहीं, no use. काल की गति अमिट है, time is indelible, destiny cannot be abated. दोष देना, to blame. विधाता, destiny. मैं क्या कहूँ, what may I say ?. वियोग होना, to part (or separate). फूट पड़े, burst into tears. प्रेरणा पाना (मिलना), to derive inspiration from. धोखे से, deceitfully. हृदय में व्याप्त, immonent in, (to pervade in).

Exercise 42

सवेरे मरजीना ने अलीबाबा को सारी कहानी सुनाई। उसने यह भी बताया कि चोरों का सरदार अभी बचा है। अलीबाबा ने मरजीना की बुद्धि की प्रशंसा की। रात के समय चुपचाप चोरों की लाशें दफना दी गई। थोड़े दिनों बाद सरदार फिर नगर में सौदागर का वेष बदलकर आया। धीरे-धीरे उसने अलीबाबा के लड़के से अपनी मित्रता बढ़ाई। एक दिन अलीबाबा ने सरदार को भोजन के लिए निमंत्रित किया। उस समय मरजीना ने सरदार को पहचान लिया। जब भोजन समाप्त हुआ तो शानदार पोशाक पहने मरजीना नाच दिखाने लगी। उसके हाथ में एक खंजर था। अचानक नाचते नाचते उसने सरदार के सीने में खंजर भोंक दी। अलीबाबा तथा उसका लड़का दोनों धक् से हो गए। अलीबाबा घबराकर बोला, 'मरजीना ! यह क्या किया ? मेहमान को मार डाला ?' मरजीना ने सप्रमाण सभी रहस्य खोल दिया।

Hints : सुनाई, narrated. सरदार, leader. अभी बचा है, was still alive. लाशें, corpses. दफना दी गई, were buried. सौदागर का वेष बदलकर, in disguise of a merchant. मित्रता बढ़ाई, grew (developed) friendship. भोजन के लिए, invited at table (or dinner). शानदार पोशाक पहने, being magnificently arrayed. भोंक दिया, thrust into. धक् से हो गए, were stunned. सभी रहस्य खोल दिया, unfolded (unveiled) all secrets.

Exercise 43

समय के सदृश बहुमूल्य कोई वस्तु नहीं। जिसने समय के मूल्य को पहचान लिया उसके लिए संसार में कोई वस्तु असाध्य नहीं। समय में महान शक्ति है। इसके सदुपयोग से हम स्वयं को महान बना सकते हैं। बहुत लोग आलस्य में पड़े रहते हैं और इस तरह समय नष्ट कर देते हैं। किन्तु समय किसी की प्रतीक्षा नहीं करता। जो इसे पहचानता है जीवन में सफलता एवं सुख पाता है। यह व्यक्ति अपनी शक्ति में विश्वास करता है। यदि वस्तुतः हम समय का उचित प्रयोग करना चाहते हैं तो हमें अपना कोई काम कल पर नहीं छोड़ना चाहिए। हमारा अधिकार आज सुरक्षित है। बीता हुआ कल बीत गया और आने वाला कल अनिश्चित है। अतः हमें वर्तमान में काम करना चाहिए। खेद का विषय है कि हम समय का महत्त्व नहीं समझ पाते। यही कारण है कि हमें पग-पग पर कठिनाइयों का सामना करना पड़ता है।

Hints : बहुमूल्य, valuable, precious. पहचान लिया, estimated. असाध्य, inaccessible, impossible. सदुपयोग से, by the best use of. आलस्य में पड़ा रहना, to lie idly. समय नष्ट करना, to kill (or waste) time. सुरक्षित है, is secured. अनिश्चित, uncertain. खेद का विषय है, it is a matter of regret (or sorrow). महत्त्व, importance. पग-पग पर, at every step.

Exercise 44

फारस (Persia) में वह युग सुल्तान स्टार्क (Sultan Stork) का था। उसके शासन में भी सभी अग्निपूजकों को देश से निकाल दिया गया। तब वे लोग भारत आए और यहीं बस गए। किन्तु सुल्तान के प्रति उनके मन में घृणा और बदला लेने की भावना थी। अतः वे लोग व्यापारियों का वेष बदलकर फारस के बाजार में जाने लगे। इन्हीं में से एक ऐसा व्यापारी था जो खुले बाजार में अनेक प्रकार की जड़ों एवं भस्मों को बेचता था। एक दिन सुल्तान जब बाजार घूम रहा था तो उसकी नजर उस पर पड़ी। निकट जाकर पाउडर के एक बोतल के बारे में उसने पूछताछ की। व्यापारी ने कहा, 'इसे खाकर आप जैसा वेष चाहें बदल सकते हैं।' यह सुनकर सुल्तान को बड़ा आश्चर्य हुआ। उसने जिज्ञासावश एक बोतल को खरीद लिया। वास्तविक वेष में आने के लिए उसने मंत्र भी जान लिया। अब सुल्तान फारस के बड़े अमीरों के घर छिपकर जाने लगा। एक बार एक पतंगा बनकर वह एक धनी आदमी के शृंगार-कक्ष में बैठा था। इसी बीच एक छिपकली आई और उसे निगल डाली।

Hints : अग्निपूजक, fire-worshipper. निकाल दिए गए, were expiated (or expelled) from. बस गए, settled. आए, immigrated. घृणा ..... भावना, feeling of contempt and vengeance. वेष बदलकर, having disguised in. जड़ों एवं भस्मों, roots and powders. बोतल, bottle, fial. जिज्ञासावश, out of curiosity. पतंगा, moth. छिपकर, lying in ambush. शृंगार-कक्ष, drawing-room (or chamber). छिपकली, lizard. निगल डाली, swallowed.

Exercise 45

बहुत दूर जाने के बाद भीम पहाड़ी पर चढ़ने लगे। वहाँ सम्पूर्ण पर्वत उलझी झाड़ियों तथा पेड़ों से भरा था। एक दो पग आगे जाने पर उन्होंने देखा कि एक वृद्ध बन्दर रास्ते पर पूँछ फैलाए पड़ा हुआ है। उन्होंने जोरों से डाँटा, 'कौन हो तुम ? हट जा मेरे रास्ते से।' पहले तो उस बन्दर ने कुछ भी उत्तर न दिया किन्तु एक क्षण बाद वह बोला, 'भाई, मैं बहुत वृद्ध तथा कमजोर हो गया हूँ। मेरी पूँछ एक ओर हटाकर चले जाओ।' भीम के क्रोध का पारावार न रहा। उसने बन्दर की पूँछ पकड़कर दूर फेंकना चाहा। किन्तु वह पूँछ एक इंच भी न हिल सकी। भीम ने लाख बल लगाया लेकिन सब व्यर्थ स्मरण होने पर वे बन्दर के पैर पर गिर गए और क्षमा माँगने लगे। वह बन्दर और कोई नहीं बल्कि हनुमान थे। महावीर ने उन्हें क्षमा कर दिया और आगे जाने से मना किया।

Hints : चढ़ना, ascend. उलझी झाड़ियाँ, entangled shrubs. फैलाए, stretching. जोरों से डाँटा, scolded harshly. हट जा, be off, hence away. एक ओर हटाना, to set aside. पारावार न रहा, knew no bounds. हिलाना, to shake. स्मरण होने पर, on recollection. और कोई नहीं, was no other than. मना करना, to forbid. किन्तु सब व्यर्थ, but all in vain.

Exercise 46

रात काफी बीत चुकी थी। बहुत दूर पर बीरबल ने एक महिला के दर्दनाक विलाप को सुना। वह उस आवाज की ओर धीरे-धीरे बढ़ने लगा। वहाँ उसने एक वृद्ध महिला को पाया जिसके केश बिखरे हुए थे और चेहरे पर झुर्रियाँ थीं। उसने पूछा, 'तुम कौन हो और क्यों रोती हो ?' वृद्ध महिला ने कहा, 'मैं इस देश के राजा की लक्ष्मी हूँ। किन्तु यह सोचकर कि महल का परित्याग कर रही हूँ, मुझे बहुत दुख हुआ है।' बीरबल ने पूछा, 'आप पुनः महल में कैसे चलेंगी ?' वृद्धा ने कहा, 'यदि तुम अपने पुत्र की बलि चढ़ा दो तो मैं प्रसन्नतापूर्वक लौट जाऊँगी।' बीरबल लौट गया और पुत्र को देवी के सामने बलि चढ़ा दिया। वह खून से लथपथ तलवार लिए दरबार में पहुँचा और राजा को सब किस्सा कह सुनाया। राजा बहुत प्रसन्न हुआ और उसे अपना मुख्य सचिव बनाया। जब बीरबल घर पहुँचा तो उसने अपने बच्चे को खेलते हुए पाया।

Hints : रात......चुकी थी, it was the dead of night. दर्दनाक विलाप, pathetic cry. केश बिखरे हुए थे, locks were dishevelled. झुर्रियाँ थीं, was wrinkled. लक्ष्मी, goddess of wealth. बहुत दुख हुआ है, have been deeply distressed. खून से लथपथ तलवार, blood stained sword. बनाया, appointed.

Exercise 47

प्राचीन काल में दासों को नाना प्रकार के कष्ट सहने पड़ते थे। इसलिए एक समय रोम नगर से जो आधुनिक इटली की राजधानी है, एक दास भाग गया। रास्ते में उसे एक वन तथा मरुस्थल मिला। थक जाने पर विश्राम करने के लिए वह गुफा में घुस गया। ज्योंही वह गुफा के अन्दर गया, उसे एक सिंह का गर्जन सुनाई पड़ा। वह भागना चाहता था कि सिंह एक पैर उठाए बाहर निकला। पैर में काँटा गड़ने के कारण वह अपना पैर जमीन पर नहीं रख सकता था। वह लंगड़ा-लंगड़ा कर दास के पास आया और अपने पाँव को उसके सामने रख दिया। दास ने उस सिंह का अभिप्राय समझकर सुगमता से काँटा निकाल दिया। सिंह प्रसन्न होकर अपना पंजा उसके शरीर पर रगड़ने लगा। उस दिन से वह सेवक की भाँति दास के साथ रहने लगा।

Hints : दास, slave. नाना प्रकार ...... पड़ते थे, had to undergo (suffer) many sorts of troubles. भागना, flee-fled-fled. मरुस्थल, desert. थक जाने पर, being tired. गर्जन, roar, उठाना, to hold up. लंगड़ा-लंगड़ा कर, limpingly. अभिप्राय, motive. निकाल दिया, extracted. पंजा, paw, रगड़ना, to rub. उस दिन से, thenceforth, since that day.

Exercise 48

एक दिन एक राजा जो प्रसिद्ध धनुर्धारी था शिकार के लिए मित्रों तथा अनुचरों के साथ निकला। जब वे लोग जंगल में घोड़ों पर सवार हुए जा रहे थे, राजा की दृष्टि एक सुन्दर हिरन पर पड़ी। राजा ने तुरंत उसका पीछा किया। परन्तु हिरन

इतना तेज भागा कि कोई उसे पा नहीं सका। अंत में वह घने वन में लुप्त हो गया। अब चारों ओर अंधेरा छाने लगा था। राजा के साथी बहुत पीछे छूट गए थे। वह घोड़े से उतर गया और ताजी मधुर हवा का आनन्द लेने लगा। राजा जल्दी ही महल को लौट जाना चाहता था। परन्तु अंधेरा इतना बढ़ गया था कि उसे लौटने का साहस नहीं हुआ। वह एक ऊँचे पेड़ पर चढ़ गया और चारों ओर देखने लगा। बहुत दूर उसे हजारों दीपकों के प्रकाश में झलकता हुआ एक सुन्दर नगर दिखाई दिया। राजा को आश्चर्य हुआ कि वह कौन सा नगर था। उसने अपने मन में उसे जीतने की ठान ली।

Hints : धनुर्धारी, archer. निकला, went out. पीछा किया, chased. घने वन में, in the dense forest. लुप्त हो गया, disappeared. बहुत पीछे छूट गए थे, were lagged (left) far behind. उतर गया, alighted, dismounted. साहस न हुआ, dared not. हजारों दीपकों के प्रकाश में झलकता हुआ, shining with the illumination of thousands lamps. मन में ठान ली, made up his mind, determined.

Exercise 49

उज्जैन में माधव नाम का एक ब्राह्मण रहता था। एक दिन अपने पति की रखवाली में अपने नवजात शिशु को छोड़कर उसकी स्त्री स्नान करने चली गई। इसी बीच राजा का निमंत्रण लेकर एक आदमी आया। अत: अपने बच्चे को पालतू नेवले की देख रेख में छोड़कर उसने जाने का निश्चय किया। ब्राह्मण के घर छोड़ने के पश्चात् एक सर्प निकला और धीरे-धीरे लड़के की ओर बढ़ने लगा। नेवले ने उसकी मंशा जानकर उस पर आक्रमण किया और उसे टुकड़े-टुकड़े कर दिया। जब ब्राह्मण घर आया तो उसने सबसे पहले नेवले को खून से लथपथ पाया। उसने सोचा कि अवश्य ही इसने मेरे लड़के को मार डाला है। अत्यन्त क्रोधित होकर उसने नेवले को पत्थरों से मार डाला। जब वह घर में प्रवेश किया तो देखा कि बच्चा मुस्करा रहा था। उसने वहीं एक मरा हुआ साँप पाया। किसी ने ठीक ही कहा है कि बिना सोच-विचार किए जल्दबाजी में कोई निर्णय नहीं लेना चाहिए।

Hints : रखवाली में, under the care of. पालतू नेवला, pet weasel. धीरे-धीरे बढ़ने लगा, began to creep slowly. मंशा, intension. टुकड़े-टुकड़े कर डाला, tore into many pieces. खून से लथपथ, stained with blood. अत्यन्त क्रोधित होकर, being blazed up. बिना सोच-विचार किए जल्दबाजी में, without deliberation and in haste.

Exercise 50

एक अर्द्धरात्रि को राजा जनक ने स्वप्न देखा कि उनका राज्य ऊजड़ गया है। वे फटे कपड़े पहने एक भिखारी की तरह मारे-मारे फिर रहे हैं। सुबह होते ही उन्होंने सभी ब्राह्मणों एवं ऋषियों की एक विशाल सभा बुलाई और अपनी शंका सबके सामने रखी। किन्तु वहाँ कोई भी राजा को उचित उत्तर नहीं दे सका। अंत में एक दिन ऋषि अष्टावक्र दरबार में पहुँचे। सभी हाल जानकर उन्होंने राजा से प्रश्न पूछने को कहा। राजा ने कहा, 'हे ऋषि ! यह सत्य है कि वह सत्य है ?' ऋषि ने जवाब दिया 'राजन ! न यह सत्य है, न वह सत्य है। जैसा कि आप देखते हैं आपका वह स्वप्न संसार झूठा था। किन्तु यह दृश्य संसार भी वास्तविक तथा सत्य नहीं है। एक दिन आएगा जब आप किस्से कहानी तक सीमित रह जाएँगे। आपके ये वैभवशाली महल खंडहर हो जाएँगे। अत: यह भी सत्य नहीं है।' राजा इस उत्तर से बहुत संतुष्ट हुए। उन्होंने ऋषि का उचित सम्मान किया।

Hints : एक अर्द्धरात्रि को, one mid-night. स्वप्न देखा, dreamt. ऊजड़ गया है, was deserted (had been ...). मारे-मारे फिर रहे हैं, was wandering from pillar to post. सुबह होते ही, as the day dawned. एक विशाल सभा, a mammoth meeting. न यह सत्य है, न वह सत्य है, neither of these is true. झूठा, false, delusive. दृश्य संसार, visible world. वास्तविक, real. सीमित रह जाएँगे, become confined to. वैभवशाली, palatial, stately. खंडहर हो जाएँगे, will be deserted, will turn into remains.

Exercise 51

एक बार एक बारहसिंगा, एक साफ झील में पानी पी रहा था। उस समय उसने अपने सींगों की परछाई पानी में देखी और उनकी सुन्दरता पर मुग्ध हो गया। किन्तु जब उसने अपनी टांगों को देखा तब कहा, 'कैसी शोक की बात है कि ऐसे

सुन्दर जानवर को ऐसी कुरूप टाँगें दी जायँ। यदि मेरी टांगें मेरी सींगों के अनुरूप होतीं तो मैं बड़ा सुन्दर जानवर होता।' वह अपने मन में यह कह ही रहा था कि शिकारी कुत्तों का शब्द उसे सुनाई पड़ा। घबराकर वह जंगल की ओर भागा। वह इतनी तेजी से दौड़ा कि कुत्ते उसे नहीं पकड़ सके। दुर्भाग्यवश उसकी सींग एक झाड़ी में फँस गई। उसने बहुत कोशिश की किन्तु भाग न सका। इसी बीच कुत्ते वहाँ आ पहुँचे। उन्होंने उसे फाड़कर टुकड़े-टुकड़े कर दिए। मरते समय वह बारहसिंगा बोला, 'वे टांगें जिनसे मैं घृणा करता था मेरी जान बचा देतीं यदि मेरी सुन्दर सींग मुझे धोखा न देतीं।'

Hints : बारहसिंगा, stag, antelope. साफ झील में, in a clear (or transparent) lake. सींगें, horns. परछाई, reflection. मुग्ध हो गया, was charmed. कैसी शोक की बात है, what a matter of regret. कुरूप, ugly. अनुरूप, in accordance (or correspondent) with. फँस गई, entangled. शिकारी कुत्ते, hounds.

Exercise 52

हिन्दुस्तान के डकैतों की चालें अनोखी होती थीं। जब वे किसी को लूटना चाहते थे तो उसे पूर्व सूचना देना अपना कर्त्तव्य समझते थे। एक बार एक धनी साहूकार को इसी प्रसंग की एक गुमनाम चिट्ठी मिली। अतः डकैती के एक दिन पहले ही उसने बोरिया बिस्तर सहित घर छोड़ दिया। संयोगवश उसी दिन एक स्त्री उस गाँव में आई। सन्ध्या को उसने साहूकार के घर में ही रात व्यतीत करने की सोची। उसे न तो किसी चेतावनी का ज्ञान था और न किसी डकैती का। वह सुख से सो रही थी। अर्द्धरात्रि को जब डकैत आए तो उनका शोर सुनकर वह जाग पड़ी। सभी हाल जानकर वह साहस बटोरी। अपने प्राण और इज्जत बचाने के लिए उसे तुरंत एक अनोखी चाल सूझी। उसने मेज पर से दवात ली और झटपट स्याही से अपने चेहरे को रंग ली। तब अपने लंबे केशों को खोले हुए, मुँह फैलाए वह सीढ़ी पर खड़ी हो गई। अचानक मशाल की रोशनी में डाकुओं ने उसे देखा। उसका चेहरा निपट डाइन जैसा लग रहा था। डाकू उसे देखते ही भयभीत हो गए और भाग खड़े हुए।

Hints : चालें, tricks. अनोखी, strange. वे अपना कर्त्तव्य समझते थे, they held (or took) it as their duty. साहूकार, grocer. गुमनाम चिट्ठी, anonymous letter. डकैती, robbery. साहस बटोरी, took heart. बोरिया बिस्तर सहित, bag and baggage. संयोगवश, by chance. इज्जत, honour, cap of respect. अनोखी चाल सूझी, struck out a novel trick. रंग ली, dyed. अपने लम्बे केशों को खोले हुए, having dishevelled her long hair. सीढ़ी, lift, stair. मशाल की रोशनी में, in the light of the torch. झटपट, hurriedly. निपट डाइन, sheer witch, भाग खड़े हुए, took to their heels. स्याही से, in ink. पूर्व सूचना, prior notice (or information).

Exercise 53

एक बार दिल्ली के निकट एक गाँव में तैमूर अपने सरदारों के साथ बैठा हुआ था। गाँव एकदम उजड़ा हुआ था। लोग कई महीने पहले अपना सामान लेकर चले गए थे। वहाँ किसी मनुष्य व जानवर को न पाकर तैमूर को आश्चर्य हो रहा था। थोड़ी देर बाद उसकी नजर उल्लुओं के एक जोड़े पर पड़ी। वे एक खंडहर पर बैठे थे और आपस में बातें करते मालूम पड़ते थे। तैमूर अपने वजीर की ओर घूमा और कहा, 'क्या तुमने मुझसे एक साल पहले नहीं कहा था कि तुम चिड़ियों की भाषा समझते हो ? वे उल्लू आपस में क्या बातें कर रहे हैं ?' वजीर ने उत्तर दिया, 'हुजूर ! उन उल्लुओं में एक पति है और दूसरी पत्नी। पत्नी अपने पति से पूछती है कि दौलत क्या है ? पति कहता है कि दौलत अन्धी है। पत्नी पूछती है कि यह कैसे ? इस पर पति जवाब देता है, 'अगर दौलत अंधी न होती तो लँगड़े के पास क्यों जाती ?' तैमूर का नाम तैमूर लंग था क्योंकि वह एक पैर से लँगड़ा था।

Hints : सरदार, knight. एकदम, totally, quite. खंडहर, remains, ruins. मालूम पड़ते थे, appeared, seemed. वजीर, secretary. समझना, to follow, to read. लँगड़ा, lame. एक पैर से, by one leg. जाती, to accept, to adopt.

Exercise 54

रात हो गई। चारों ओर निविड़ अंधकार छा गया। तोता जाने पत्तों में कहाँ छिपा था। महादेव जानता था कि रात को तोता कहीं उड़कर नहीं जा सकता और न पिंजरे में आ सकता है। फिर भी उस जगह से हिलने का नाम न लेता था। आज

उसने दिन भर कुछ न खाया। रात के भोजन का समय भी निकल गया। पानी की एक बूँद भी उसके कंठ में न गई। लेकिन उसे न तो भूख थी, न प्यास। तोते के बिना उसका जीवन निस्सार, शुष्क और सूखा जान पड़ता। आधी रात गुजर रही थी। सहसा वह कोइ आहट पाकर चौंका। उसने देखा कि एक वृक्ष के नीचे एक धुंधला दीपक जल रहा है और कुछ आदमी आपस में बातें कर रहे हैं। वे सब चीलम पी रहे थे। वह उनकी तरफ बढ़ा। किन्तु उसे आते देख, वे सभी भाग खड़े हुए।

Hints : निविड़ अन्धकार, dense darkness. पिंजरा, cage. शुष्क, निस्सार और सूना, dull, empty and desolate. आहट, sign. चौंका, startled, alarmed. धुंधला, dim, faint. तम्बाकू, tobacco. महक, smell. चीलम पीना, to smoke claypipe.

Exercise 55

जून महीने की एक शाम थी। गर्मी के मारे बुरा हाल था। लोग गर्मी से बचने के लिए अपने-अपने घरों से बाहर निकल आए। पड़ोस की एक बुढ़िया जो अकेले एक छोटी सी झोंपड़ी में रहती थी, गर्मी से बचने के लिए सामने के पेड़ के पास आ बैठी। एकाएक बड़ी तेजी से पश्चिम दिशा की ओर से काले बादल आकाश में छाने लगे। इसी बीच बुढ़िया की आँख लग गई। थोड़ी ही देर में आकाश बादलों से घिर गया। ज्योंही वर्षा की पहली बूँद बुढ़िया पर पड़ी वह चौंक कर उठी और अपनी झोंपड़ी की ओर भागी।

Hints : गर्मी के मारे, owing to outrageous heat. बुरा हाल, discomfort. बचने के लिए, with a view to get relief. एकाएक, all of a sudden, suddenly. तेजी से, rapidly. छाने लगे, began to cover. आँख लग गई, fell into a nap.

Exercise 56

एक समय एक मनुष्य घोड़े पर सवार होकर यात्रा पर निकला। कुछ दूर चलने के पश्चात् वर्षा होने लगी और वह व्यक्ति बारिश से बिल्कुल भीग गया। उसने अपने मन में कहा, 'मैं कैसा मूर्ख हूँ, जो ऐसे खराब मौसम में घर से बाहर निकल आया। अब मैं अवश्य बीमार पड़ जाऊँगा।' कुछ देर बाद डाकुओं के एक गिरोह ने उस पर आक्रमण किया और उसे लूटना चाहा। किन्तु बारिश के कारण उनकी बारूद भीग गई थी। अत: उनकी बन्दूकें बेकार हो गई। इस प्रकार डाकू उसकी कोई हानि न पहुँचा सके और उसकी जान बच गई। घर लौटते समय उस व्यक्ति ने अपने मन में कहा, 'मैं कितना मूर्ख था कि उसी वस्तु से अप्रसन्न था जिसके कारण मेरी जान बच सकी थी।'

Hints : यात्रा पर निकला, went out (or set out) on a trip. बिल्कुल भीग गया, was completely got wet. मैं कैसा मूर्ख हूँ, how foolish I am, खराब मौसम, wretched weather. गिरोह, band, gang. बारूद, gunpowder. बेकार हो गई, turned ineffective. अप्रसन्न, displeased.

Exercise 57

पूर्ण आशा के साथ मैं घोड़े पर सवार हो गया और पहाड़ियों की ओर चला। मुश्किल से मैं दस मील तक जा सका था कि दुर्भाग्यवश अपने साथियों से बिछड़ गया। वहाँ सम्पूर्ण वन चिड़ियों की निरन्तर ध्वनि से भरा था। एकान्त में पहुँचकर मैं घोड़े से उतर गया। मैं नीचे की ओर पैदल चला और अन्त में पहाड़ी के निचले भाग पर पहुँचा। बहुत पहले इस स्थान पर एक हत्यारे की फाँसी हुई थी। यद्यपि कि वहाँ न तो हड्डियाँ थी और न ही टूटी हुई जंजीरें। परन्तु वहीं एक चट्टान पर उसकी कहानी खुदी हुई थी। डर के मारे मैं वहाँ से भाग खड़ा हुआ। आतंक की भावना से मैं ग्रस्त था। फिर मैं पहाड़ी पर चढ़ा जहाँ एक टूटा हुआ पुल देखा। मैंने एक लड़की को सिर पर घड़ा लिए देखा। वह तेज हवा के प्रतिकूल आगे बढ़ने की कोशिश कर रही थी। स्पष्टत: यह कोई विशिष्ट दृश्य तो नहीं था। किन्तु मेरे लिए यह एक ऐसा दृश्य लगा जिसे विशिष्ट भाषा द्वारा ही प्रगट किया जा सकता है।

Hints : बिछड़ गया, was separated from. निरन्तर ध्वनि से, with incessant melody. नीचे की ओर, downward. पहाड़ी का निचला भाग, base (or foot) of the hill. हत्यारा, murderer. टूटी हुई जंजीरें, broken fetters. खुदी हुई थी, was engraved (or inscribed). डर के मारे, out of fear. आतंक की भावना से मैं ग्रस्त था,

I was engrossed with a feeling of terror, a feeling of terror had overpowered me. तेज हवा, violent (or wild) wind. प्रतिकूल, against. स्पष्टत:, obviously. विशिष्ट, significant, uncommon, विशिष्ट भाषा, extraordinary language. प्रगट किया जा सकता था, could be revealed (or expressed).

Exercise 58

दिन अच्छा नहीं था। सम्पूर्ण वातावरण में कुहासा छाया था। सूर्य का पता नहीं था। बहुत यत्न हुआ किन्तु यह निश्चित न हो सका कि शत्रु किस ओर कितनी दूर पर है। इतने में ही सर फिलिप सिडनी (Sir Philip Sidney) और उसके सिपाही स्पेन की बड़ी सेना के सामने आ पहुँचे। सिडनी को तनिक भी भय नहीं हुआ। वे अपने सैनिकों को उत्साहित करने लगे। शत्रुदल के एक सैनिक ने उनकी जाँघ में गोली मार दी। सिपाहियों ने तुरन्त उन्हें अस्पताल पहुँचाया। वहाँ सिडनी को ज्वर आ गया और उन्हें बड़ी प्यास लगी। एक सैनिक पानी लाया। जैसे ही सिडनी पानी का ग्लास होंठ से लगाना चाहते थे कि उनकी दृष्टि एक घायल सिपाही पर पड़ी। वह ग्लास को लालच भरी दृष्टि से देख रहा था। किन्तु उसे हिम्मत न पड़ी कि वह पानी माँगे। सिडनी ने उसकी ओर पानी का ग्लास देते हुए कहा, 'यह लो मित्र, तुम्हारी आवश्यकता मेरी आवश्यकता से अधिक है।'

Hints : कुहासा छाया था, was covered with fog. किस ओर, in which direction. और कितनी दूर पर, and on (or at) what distance. उत्साहित करना, to encourage. जाँघ में गोली मार दी, shot him into the thigh. ज्वर आ गया, was attacked (or down) with fever. लालच भरी दृष्टि से, with greedy eyes. हिम्मत न पड़ी, dared not. देते हुए, offering.

Exercise 59

चम्पतराय ने कहा, 'मैं मुगलों का बन्दी होकर बेड़ियाँ पहनकर दिल्ली के कारागार में नहीं रहना चाहता। अपनी तलवार से मेरा अन्त कर दो।' हिन्दू रमणी अपने पति पर हाथ उठाए, सपने में भी कल्पना नहीं की जा सकती। सारन्धा ने कहा, '....... नाथ ! आप क्या कह रहे हैं ? यह कैसे हो सकता है ?' चम्पतराय ने कहा, 'तुमने जीवनभर आन निभाने की शिक्षा दी। अब मुगलों का कैदी बनकर दिल्ली में तमाशा नहीं बनना चाहता।' चम्पतराय के सभी वीर साथी कट चुके थे। मुगल सैनिक चम्पतराय को पकड़ने के लिए झपटे। सारन्धा ने एक क्षण में अपना कर्त्तव्य निश्चित किया। उसका मुख लाल और तेजपूर्ण हो गया। उसके पहले कि किसी मुगल सैनिक का हाथ चम्पतराय पर लगे सारन्धा ने अपनी तलवार चम्पतराय की छाती में भोंक दी।

Hints : मुगलों का बन्दी होकर, being the captive of the Moghals. बेड़ियाँ पहनकर, locked in fetters (shackled). अपनी तलवार ...... कर दी, put me on your sword, shear me. आन निभाना, to carry on dignity. तमाशा नहीं बनना चाहता, do not want to be a laughing stock. कट चुके थे, were slain. झपटे, pounced upon. एक क्षण में, within a moment. लाल एवं तेजपूर्ण हो गया, blushed and glowed. भोंक दी, pierced into, thrust into.

Exercise 60

निरन्तर निर्धनता के जीवन से हेनचार्ड (Henchard) ऊब चुका था। अत: खूब तड़के अपनी पत्नी और बच्चों के साथ वह अंधेरे में गायब हो गया। बहुत दूर चलने के बाद वह एक छोटे से बाजार में पहुँचा। उस समय वह बहुत भूखा था। उसके पास पैसा भी नहीं था। अत: वह एक शराबखाने में गया और अपनी पत्नी तथा बच्ची को नीलाम करने लगा। बहुत सस्ते अपने परिवार को नीलाम करके उसने शराब से अपना पेट भरा। पश्चात् वह किसी अज्ञात स्थान को चल पड़ा। एक दो दिनों के बाद वह कास्टरब्रिज (Casterbridge) पहुँचा। वहाँ उसे एक फैक्ट्री में मजदूर का कार्य मिल गया। उसने कुछ पैसा बचाया और छोटे-छोटे ठेके लेना शुरू किया। कुछ दिनों में उसकी ख्याति इतनी बढ़ी कि वह कास्टरब्रिज का सर्वसम्मत से महापौर चुना गया।

Hints : निरन्तर निर्धनता, endless (or unending) poverty. ऊब चुका था, was vexed with. छोटा बाजार, a tiny market. शराबखाना, tavern, bar. नीलाम करना, to sell by auction. बहुत सस्ते, at a very cheap rate. एक दो दिनों बाद, after a day or two. अज्ञात, unknown. बचाया, saved. छोटे-छोटे ठेके लेना, to take petty contracts. ख्याति, fame, reputation. सर्वसम्मत से, unanimously. महापौर, mayor.

Exercise 61

लक्ष्मीबाई का विवाह झाँसी के राजा गंगाधर राव से हुआ था। उस समय भारत के एक बड़े भाग पर अंग्रेजों का अधिकार था। वे अपना राज्य बढ़ाते जा रहे थे। गंगाधर राव की मृत्यु के पश्चात् झाँसी को उन्होंने अपने राज्य में मिला लिया। लक्ष्मीबाई को यह बात अच्छी न लगी। भारत के लोगों में असंतोष फैल रहा था। देश को स्वतंत्र करने के लिए अनेक स्थानों पर लड़ाइयाँ होने लगीं। यह 1857 ई० का समय था। रानी लक्ष्मीबाई भी बड़ी वीरता से लड़ी। वह अंग्रेजी सेना के भीतर घुस गई। उसकी तलवार बिजली की तरह चमक रही थी। वह जिधर निकल जाती, मैदान साफ हो जाता। परन्तु अंग्रेजी सेना बहुत बड़ी थी। अन्त में रानी को गोली लगी और वह मैदान में गिर पड़ी। उनका घोड़ा उनके पास नीचे सिर किए खड़ा रहा।

Hints : अधिकार था, was in the possession of. मिला लिया, annexed (with). लड़ाइयाँ होने लगीं, fights began to occur. बिजली, lightening. जिधर, wherever. बढ़ाते जा रहे थे, were going on extending. असंतोष फैल रहा था, dissension was growing. मैदान साफ हो जाता, she swept the sea. गोली लगी, was shot by a bullet. नीचे सिर किए, lowering the head.

Exercise 62

कुन्दन अपने इलाके का एक अति कुख्यात डाकू था। जब बीस वर्ष का आजीवन कारावास काटकर वह बाहर निकला तब देश काफी बदल चुका था। सम्पूर्ण भारत ब्रिटिश शासन के प्रति विद्रोह पर था। कुन्दन घर की ओर बढ़ा। वह अत्यन्त भूखा तथा प्यासा था। वह जहाँ जाता दरवाजा बन्द हो जाता। अन्त में एक परोपकारी ने उसे अपने यहाँ शरण दी। उसने हृदय से उसकी आवभगत की। किन्तु जब अर्द्धरात्रि हुई तो कुन्दन उसका सामान लेकर चम्पत हो गया। पश्चात् वह पुलिस द्वारा पकड़ा गया। जैसे ही उस परोपकारी आदमी के सामने उसे लाया गया उसका सिर लज्जा से झुक गया। मन ही मन उसे बड़ी ग्लानि हुई।

Hints : इलाका, locality. कुख्यात, notorious. आजीवन कारावास, life imprisonment. काफी बदल चुका था, was immensely changed. विद्रोह पर था, was on a surge against, was resurgent against. परोपकारी, altruist, philanthropist. उसे शरण दी, gave him shelter. आवभगत की, took in, received him with hospitality. सामान, articles. लज्जा से सिर झुक गया, his head bowed down with shame. मन ही मन बड़ी ग्लानि हुई, repented himself sorely.

Exercise 63

अचानक विमान जोरों से हिला और अनियंत्रित हो गया। क्षणभर में वह दुर्घटनाग्रस्त होकर हिमालय की एक चोटी पर गिर गया। उसके मलवे चारों ओर फैल गए। सौभाग्य से राजा पहले ही जहाज से लुढ़क गया था और झील के पारदर्शी जल में गिर पड़ा था। अचेतावस्था में लहरों ने उसे किनारे कर दिया था। जब उसकी आँखें खुलीं तो उसने स्वयं को एक शानदार एवं विलासपूर्ण महल में पाया। जब वह पीछे की ओर मुड़ा तो उसने एक ऊँचे स्थान पर एक ध्यानमग्न सन्यासी को देखा। वह दौड़कर साधु के चरणों में गिर गया। साधु ने उसे सान्त्वना दी। घबराओ मत। तुम अपने महल को शीघ्र एवं सुरक्षित लौट जाओगे। किन्तु राजा अत्यधिक परेशान था। अपने विषय में जानने की उसकी उत्सुकता तीव्र हो रही थी।

Hints : अनियंत्रित हो गया, went uncontrolled. दुर्घटनाग्रस्त होकर, being crashed. मलवा, debris. फैलना, to scatter. लुढ़क गया, had rolled down. झील का पारदर्शी जल, the transparent water of the lake. अचेत, senseless. किनारे कर दिया था, had drifted to the bank. पीछे मुड़ा, turned about. शानदार एवं

विलासपूर्ण महल में, in a stately (or grand) and luxurious palace. ध्यानमग्न, in meditation (or trance). सुरक्षित, safe and sound. सान्त्वना दिया, consoled. अत्यधिक परेशान था, was immensely annoyed (or disgusted). उत्सुकता curiosity. तीव्र होना, to become profound.

Exercise 64

भारत में ऐसा कौन है जो गुरु नानक के नाम से परिचित न हो ? बुद्ध तथा चैतन्य की भाँति गुरु नानक ने सभी को सत्य, प्रेम तथा दया का मार्ग दिखाया। नानक गरीब माता-पिता की संतान थे। उनका जन्म लाहौर के पास एक गाँव में सन् 1469 में हुआ था। उनकी प्रारम्भिक शिक्षा गाँव की पाठशाला में हुई थी। बाल्यावस्था से ही वे बड़े सूझ बूझ वाले थे तथा शीघ्र ही उन्होंने संस्कृत तथा फारसी में प्रवीणता प्राप्त कर ली। वे इन भाषाओं में काव्य-रचना भी करने लगे। बचपन से ही नानक सांसारिक आकर्षणों से दूर रहते थे जिससे उनके माता-पिता को बड़ी चिन्ता हुई। उन्होंने अपने पुत्र का ध्यान सांसारिक वस्तुओं की ओर मोड़ने का भरसक प्रयास किया परन्तु इसमें वे असफल रहे। बत्तीस वर्ष की आयु में नानक सन्यासी हो गए तथा भारत के अन्दर तथा बाहर विभिन्न स्थानों का दर्शन करते घूमते रहे।

Hints : परिचित, familiar with, (or at home with). भाँति, like. मार्ग दिखाया, paved (or showed) the way for. प्रारम्भिक, primary. बड़े सूझ-बूझ वाले व्यक्ति, a man of great prudence (or was a great prudent). प्रवीणता प्राप्त करना, to be at home in, to obtain the mastery of. सांसारिक आकर्षण, earthly allurements, worldly (or mundane) charms. मोड़ना, to mould. भरसक प्रयास किया, tried their best, (left no stone unturned). दर्शन करते घूमते रहे, went about (or on) taking the vision of.

Exercise 65

गुजरात में मूलशंकर नाम का एक लड़का शिव की पूजा के लिए मंदिर गया। शिव-पूजा के पश्चात् वह मूर्ति के सामने बैठ गया। अचानक उसने देखा कि एक चूहा देवमूर्ति पर बैठकर पवित्र वस्तुओं को सुखपूर्वक खा रहा है। यह देखकर उस लड़के ने सोचा, 'अहो ! इस शिव में क्या शक्ति है जो एक चूहे को भी नहीं मना कर सकती।' तब अपने पिता के यहाँ जाकर उसने अपनी जिज्ञासा प्रगट की। किन्तु कोई सन्तोषप्रद उत्तर न मिला। फलस्वरूप उसका मन मूर्ति-पूजा से विरक्त हो गया। किन्तु ईश्वर के वास्तविक रूप का चिन्तन करने लगा। दूसरे दिन शिव को जानने के लिए उसने घर छोड़ दिया और मथुरा पहुँचा। वहाँ महर्षि विरजानन्द की देख रेख में उसने संस्कृत साहित्य का गहन अध्ययन किया। बहुत शीघ्र वह एक विलक्षण मेधावी हो गया। कुछ दिनों पश्चात् गुरु की कृपा से उसने शिव के स्वरूप को ज्ञात किया। गुरु ने उसे आदेश दिया कि वह सम्पूर्ण भारत भ्रमण करके आर्य जाति को अन्धविश्वास से मुक्त करें। पश्चात् यही व्यक्ति महर्षि दयानन्द के नाम से विख्यात हुआ। उन्होंने 'आर्य समाज' की स्थापना की।

Hints : पवित्र वस्तुएँ, pious offerings. मूर्ति, idol. देवमूर्ति, idol of the deity (divine idol). जिज्ञासा, curiosity. विरक्त हो गया, was detached from. वास्तविक, real, actual. चिन्तन करना, to meditate (or contemplate). देख-रेख में, under the guidance (or care) of. गहन अध्ययन करना, to study (or peruse) deeply (or thoroughly). एक विलक्षण मेधावी, a rare genius. कृपा से, by the grace of. अन्धविश्वास से मुक्त करना, to liberate from shams and hypocrisy.

Exercise 66

शिवाजी अपने आक्रमणों में सभी धर्मों के पवित्र स्थानों का आदर करते थे। हिन्दू मन्दिरों, मुस्लिम सन्तों और मस्जिदों के लिए वे धन तथा भूमि देते थे। वे ब्राह्मण विद्वानों को प्रेशन प्रदान करते थे और साधुओं तथा फकीरों के रहने के लिए झोंपड़ियाँ बनवाते थे। शिवाजी के आध्यात्मिक गुरु रामदास स्वामी महाराष्ट्र के बड़े सन्तों में से एक थे। एक सुन्दर कहानी कही जाती है कि शिवाजी नहीं समझ पाते थे कि स्वामी जी प्रतिदिन अपने भिक्षाटन के लिए क्यों निकल जाया करते थे यद्यपि उन्होंने उन्हें बहुत धनवान बना दिया था। अगले दिन उन्होंने अपने गुरु के चरण पर एक दान-पत्र रख दिया जिसमें अपना

समस्त राज्य गुरू को दान कर दिया। रामदास ने इसे स्वीकार कर लिया। उन्होंने शिवाजी को अपना प्रतिनिधि नियुक्त किया और जनता के सेवक के रूप में राज्य-शासन करने की आशा दी। उसी दिन से शिवाजी ने अपने पूज्य गुरु के सम्मान में केसरिया वस्त्र पहनना प्रारम्भ कर दिया।

Hints : पवित्र, holy. आध्यात्मिक, spiritual. दान कर दिया, donated. प्रतिनिधि, representative. केसरिया, saffron. दान पत्र, will (gift deed). भिक्षाटन के लिए जाना, to go for alms.

Exercise 67

अपने बाल्यकाल में महात्मा बुद्ध सिद्धार्थ गौतम के नाम से पुकारे जाते थे। वे कपिलवस्तु के राजा शुद्धोदन के पुत्र थे। उनका जन्म लुम्बिनी के वन में हुआ था। उनके माता का नाम माया था। सोलह वर्ष की अवस्था में उनका विवाह यशोधरा से हुआ। कुछ समय बाद उन्हें एक पुत्र हुआ जिसका नाम राहुल रखा गया। गौतम की जन्मतिथि विवादग्रस्त है किन्तु ईसा पूर्व 563 अधिक तर्कसंगत लगता है। अनेक रूढ़िकथाओं के अनुसार बाल्यकाल से युवराज का मन विलासिता से विरक्त था। वृद्ध मनुष्य, रोगी, मृतक तथा साधु-दर्शनों से उनकी संसार के प्रति यह उदासीनता और बढ़ गई। उन्होंने तीस वर्ष की अवस्था में सत्य की खोज के लिए गृह त्याग किया। गौतम जीवन तथा मृत्यु से हमेशा चिन्तित रहते थे। गृह-त्याग के पश्चात् वे अनेक साधुओं के सम्पर्क में आए। सत्य तक पहुँचने और मुक्ति-मार्ग प्रशस्त करने के लिए उन्होंने अनेक प्रयोग किए।

Hints : के नाम से, after (or by) the name of. एक पुत्र हुआ, was blessed with a son. विवादग्रस्त, controversial. तर्कसंगत, reasonable (logical). रूढ़िकथाएँ, myths, legends. युवराज, prince. विलासिता से विरक्त था, was detached from luxury. उदासीनता, melancholy, sadness. सम्पर्क में आए, came into contact with. मुक्तिमार्ग प्रशस्त करने के लिए, to pave the way for salvation (or deliverance).

Exercise 68

ज्योंही मैं उस लोक में गया मैंने अनुभव किया कि वहाँ प्रातःकाल हो गया है। वहाँ पर प्रकाश था लेकिन वह कहाँ से आया यह विदित नहीं हो पाया। न तो वहाँ सूर्य दिखाई देता था और न चन्द्रमा। वहाँ हवा चल रही थी। किन्तु वनस्पतियों का नितान्त अभाव था। वहाँ कोई पेड़ या लता न थी। वहाँ प्राणी भी न थे। मेरा राकेट यान धीरे-धीरे उतरने लगा। मैं अपने मित्रों के साथ यान से बाहर निकलकर एक छोटे जहाज में घूमने लगा। जल्दी ही एक सुन्दर नगर सामने आया।

Hints : लोक, world. वनस्पति, vegetables. अभाव, scarcity, lack of. नितान्त, altogether. लता, vine, climber. प्राणी, species (creatures). राकेट, rocket (space craft). उतरना, to land, to descend. घूमना, roam. सामने आया, appeared before (became visible).

Exercise 69

जिस समय श्रीकृष्ण बालक थे उस समय कंस ने उनका वध करने के लिए बहुत राक्षसों को भेजा। परन्तु उन्होंने अपनी कुशलता तथा पराक्रम से सबको मार डाला। उन्होंने केवल राक्षसों से ही नहीं अपितु अन्य आपत्तियों से भी गोकुल के निवासियों की रक्षा की। एक बार वर्षाकाल में यमुना का पानी तेजी से बढ़ने लगा। उस समय श्रीकृष्ण ने अपने प्राणों की चिन्ता न करके सभी लोगों की रक्षा की। इसी तरह एक बार महाअग्नि से उन्होंने गोकुलवासियों के हृदय में अपना स्थान बना लिया। उनके शील तथा सुन्दरता से सभी मुग्धचित्त हो गए थे। उनकी वंशी सभी जीवों पर जादू का काम करती थी। इस तरह अपने उत्तम गुणों एवं परोपकार की भावना से वे लोकप्रिय बन गए।

Hints : राक्षस, devil, demon. कुशलता तथा पराक्रम, skill and bravery. आपत्ति, calamity (or catastrophe). निवासी, natives, inhabitants (or dwellers). बढ़ना (जल का), to inflate. महाअग्नि, conflagration. स्थान बना लिया, occupied a place (or post). शील, modesty, politeness. सभी मुग्धचित्त हो गए थे, all were captivated (or ravished). काम करना, to exercise (or enchant). परोपकार की भावना, altruistic feelings (or philanthropic ideas). लोकप्रिय, popular.

Exercise 70

एक साधु के बारे में एक कथा कही जाती है कि वह सोना बनाने की विद्या जानता था। परन्तु उस विधि को वह गुप्त रखता था। उस विद्या को सीखने के लिए बहुत व्यक्ति भक्त बनकर आए। वे सभी रहस्य जानने का प्रयत्न करते। साधु सभी को एक ही उत्तर देता, 'दस वर्ष मेरे साथ रहो, मेरी सेवा करो, तब रहस्य बताऊँगा।' इस शर्त को मानने के लिए कोई तैयार न होता। फलस्वरूप सभी निराश होकर लौट गए। अन्त में एक ऐसा व्यक्ति आया जिसने उसकी सभी शर्तों को मान लिया। वह उनके साथ रहने लगा। सतसंग का प्रभाव उस पर ऐसा पड़ा कि वह एक सच्चा संत हो गया। दस वर्ष बाद साधु ने उसे सच्चा रहस्य बताने के लिए बुलाया। तब शिष्य ने उत्तर दिया, 'अब मैं स्वयं ही सोना बन गया। विलास एवं कठिनाइयों में फँसाने वाले सोने का मैं क्या करूँगा ?'

Hints : एक कथा कही जाती है, a story goes (or is told). विद्या, art, skill. विधि, method (technique). गुप्त, secret. भक्त, devotee (disciple). रहस्य, mystery, secret. शर्त, condition. सतसंग, saintly company. प्रभाव पड़ा, was impressed. एक सच्चा संत, a true saint. फँसाना, to entangle. to enmesh.

Exercise 71

एक घटना मुझे याद है जो मेरे मस्तिष्क पर अमिट प्रभाव डाली। एक बार हम लोग सूर्योदय का दृश्य देखने के लिए एक पहाड़ी की ओर बढ़े। पहाड़ के निचले भाग पर एक सामान्य झोंपड़ी के द्वार पर हम पहुँचे। वहाँ हमने एक गडेरिए को जगाया जिसने हमारी यात्रा का निर्देशन किया। फिर हम लोग अल्पाहार किए और तब वहाँ से चल दिए। यह गर्मी का समय था। सम्पूर्ण वातावरण यद्यपि कि चिड़ियों की ध्वनि से भरा था, नीरस एवं रंगहीन लग रहा था। किसी तरह बिना निराश हुए हम लोग पहाड़ की चढ़ाई जारी रखे। चोटी पर खड़ा होकर मैंने आकाश की ओर देखा। ऐसा लगा कि हम लोग अनंत की ओर जा रहे हैं। पास ही मेरा कुत्ता एक सुअर के बच्चे को तंग करने लगा। बेचारा वह डर के मारे सिकुड़ा पड़ा था। जब मैं पूर्व की ओर घूमा तो मैंने देखा कि सम्पूर्ण आकाश प्रकाश की किरणों से भर गया। ये सभी कार्य मुझे सर्वशक्तिमान के प्रतीक से लगे।

Hints : अमिट प्रभाव डाली, cast an indelible impression. निर्देशन किया, guided. अल्पाहार किया, took light refreshment. चिड़ियों की ध्वनि, notes (or melodies) of birds. नीरस एवं रंगहीन, dull and colourless. अनन्त की ओर, towards eternity (or infinite). सुअर का बच्चा, pig. तंग करना, to tease. सिकुड़ा पड़ा था, lay smitten (with). प्रकाश की ...... भर गया था, was bathed in the flash (or rays) of light. मुझे ...... लगे, appeared to me the symbols of Mighty Mind (or the Almighty God).

Exercise 72

21 जुलाई, 1969 की शुभ घड़ी में अमेरिका ने आर्मस्ट्रांग तथा एल्ड्रिन (Armstrong and Eldrin) को चन्द्रमा पर उतार दिया। वे जिस अन्तरिक्ष यान से वहाँ तक पहुँचे उसका नाम अपोलो-11 (Appollo-11) था। जब तक ये चन्द्रयात्री चन्द्रमा पर थे तब तक उनके साथी कालिन्स (Collins) अपोलो में बैठे चन्द्रमा का चक्कर लगाते रहे। चन्द्रमा के धरातल पर पैर रखते ही यात्रियों ने उसे काले आकाश की ओर देखा। उन्होंने बताया कि उस काले आकाश में हमारी गोल पृथ्वी जगमगा रही है। यह बड़ी सुन्दर लगती है। पृथ्वी से चन्द्रमा चमकता हुआ दिखता है। चन्द्रलोक से पृथ्वी बीस गुनी अधिक चमकीली दिखाई देती है। पृथ्वी से चन्द्रमा जितना बड़ा दिखता है, उससे चार गुनी बड़ी हमारी पृथ्वी वहाँ से दिखाई देती है। चन्द्रलोक का एक दिन और रात का समय पृथ्वी के एक माह के बराबर होता है।

Hints : शुभ घड़ी, auspicious moment (or hour). आ गई, approached. अन्तरिक्ष यान, space rocket. चन्द्रयात्री, cosmonauts. चक्कर लगाते रहे, continued (or went on) revolving round. धरातल, surface. बीस गुनी अधिक चमकीली, twenty times as bright as. बराबर होता है, is equal to.

Exercise 73

आधुनिक वैज्ञानिकों का विश्वास है कि पृथ्वी के अतिरिक्त अन्य ग्रहों पर भी जीवन संभव है। अपनी कृति 'लोकों का युद्ध' (War of the Worlds) में एच॰जी॰ वेल्स (H.G. Wells) ने कल्पना किया है कि एक नक्षत्र के लोगों ने पृथ्वी पर आक्रमण कर दिया है। पृथ्वी के लोग उनके नए नए हथियारों से जो अधिक परिष्कृत हैं, परिचित नहीं हैं। लोगों में आतंक व्याप्त हो जाता है। सभी अपनी जान के पीछे भाग रहे हैं। ऊँचे-ऊँचे भवन गिर रहे हैं। धुँआ उठ रहा है और नदियों का जल उबल उठता है। इस तरह सम्पूर्ण कथावस्तु भयानक एवं अंधकारपूर्ण है। पाठकगण स्वयं ही एक बार घटनाओं को यथार्थ मानकर काँप उठते हैं। अन्ततः उनकी शंका तब दूर होती है जब उन्हें ज्ञात होता है कि यह सर्वनाशकारी घटना सुदूर भविष्य के लिए मात्र एक अनुमान है।

Hints : ग्रहों, planets. जीवन संभव है, species are possible. कल्पना किया है, has imagined, हथियारों, weapons. परिष्कृत, refined and sophisticated. परिचित नहीं हैं, have no knowledge (not familiar, unknown to or not at home with). आतंक व्याप्त हो जाता है, terror mounts up. गिर रहे हैं, are razing to ground. उबलना, to boil. भयानक एवं अन्धकारपूर्ण, horrid and nebulous (or gloomy). सुदूर भविष्य के लिए, for the remote future.

Exercise 74

सन् 1191 में पृथ्वीराज ने मुहम्मद गोरी का सामना तराईन के मैदान में किया। राठौर नरेश जयचन्द ही ऐसा राजा था जो युद्ध में सम्मिलित नहीं हुआ। कारण था कि पृथ्वीराज ने उसकी बेटी का अपहरण कर उसकी प्रतिष्ठा को धक्का पहुँचाया था। राजपूतों ने दो ओर से मुस्लिम सेना पर भीषण आक्रमण किया। राजा के भाई गोविन्दराय ने सुल्तान को बुरी तरह घायल कर दिया। इससे मुस्लिम सेना में आतंक फैल गया और वह मैदान छोड़कर भाग गई। सन् 1192 में गौरी ने अपनी सेना को पुनः संगठित किया और तराईन के मैदान में तम्बू डाल दिया। तुरन्त करीब डेढ़ सौ राजपूत शासक लड़ने के लिए पृथ्वीराज के झंडे के नीचे एकत्र हो गए। सुबह से शाम तक घमासान युद्ध होता रहा। रक्त की नदियाँ बह चलीं। यह एक निर्णायक युद्ध था। अधिक सेना होते हुए भी राजपूत मुसलमानों द्वारा पराजित हुए। पृथ्वीराज की पराजय से राजपूत शक्ति को बड़ा धक्का पहुँचा।

Hints : सम्मिलित होना, to join. अपहरण करना, to confiscate. प्रतिष्ठा को धक्का पहुँचाना, to inflict the dignity. भीषण आक्रमण करना, to launch (to lodge) a horrid attack. पुनः संगठित किया, reorganised. तंबू डाल दिया, encamped. झंडे के नीचे एकत्रित हो गए, gathered under the banner of. सुबह से शाम तक, from dawn to dusk. घमासान युद्ध, a horrible battle (or fight). एक निर्णायक युद्ध, a decisive battle. बड़ा धक्का पहुँचा, was greatly (or deeply) shocked.

Exercise 75

वर्तमान युग अपनी गतिशीलता के लिए प्रसिद्ध है। विज्ञान और तकनीक के कारण जीवन अत्यन्त व्यस्त एवं गतिशील हो गया है। प्रातःकाल से लेकर रात्रि में सोने के समय तक हमारे कार्यों में जल्दबाजी ही रहती है। प्रत्येक व्यक्ति के लिए करने को इतना अधिक काम रहता है कि अवकाश के समय का प्रश्न ही मुश्किल से उठता है। ये सभी बातें अधिकांशत : शहरी जीवन के लिए लागू होती हैं जहाँ घर एवं कार्यालय दूर-दूर रहते हैं। प्रत्येक मनुष्य जिसे उस सड़क पर देखा जाता है, धन के पीछे भागा जा रहा है। वह अति शीघ्र उचित या अनुचित रूप से धनवान बनना चाहता है। फलस्वरूप पारस्परिक प्रेम तथा सम्बन्ध कुप्रभावित हो उठे हैं। इस प्रकार की स्थिति स्पष्टतः सराहनीय नहीं कही जा सकती। हमारी कोशिश होनी चाहिए कि इस दुरूह स्थिति में भी हम अपनी परम्परा तथा संस्कृति से दृढ़ता से चिपके रहें।

Hints : प्रसिद्ध है, is marked with. गतिशीलता, haste, rapidity. अत्यन्त व्यस्त एवं गतिशील, immensely busy and active. जल्दबाजी में, in hurry (or in haste). करने को ......रहता है, has so lot of work to discharge. अवकाश का समय, leisure. लागू होती है, are applied. शहरी जीवन, urban life. उचित या अनुचित

रूप से, by hook or by crook. पारस्परिक, mutual. कुप्रभावित, badly affected. सराहनीय, praiseworthy. दुरूह स्थिति, critical (or angerous) situation. परम्परा तथा संस्कृति, tradition and culture. दृढ़ता से, strongly, firmly. चिपकना, to stick with.

Exercise 76

श्रीराम के पवित्र चरणों का स्पर्श पाते ही सचमुच वह मूर्ति अहिल्या प्रगट हो गई। भक्तों को सुख देने वाले राम को देखकर वह हाथ जोड़कर सामने खड़ी हो गई। अत्यन्त प्रेम के कारण वह अधीर हो गई। उसका शरीर पुलकित हो उठा। मुख से वचन कहने में नहीं आते थे। वह बड़भागिनी प्रभु के चरणों पर गिर गई। उस समय उसके नेत्रों से आँसुओं की धारा बहने लगी। फिर उसने मन में धीरज धारण कर प्रभु को पहचाना और उनकी कृपा से भक्ति प्राप्त की। वह राम से बोली, 'हे नाथ ! आप सम्पूर्ण ब्रह्माण्ड के नियन्ता हैं। मैं आपकी शरण में हूँ, अत: कृपाकर मेरा भी उद्धार करें।

Hints : पवित्र चरणों, holy feet. प्रगट होना, to appear. भक्त, devotee. हाथ जोड़कर, with folded (or clasped) hands. अत्यन्त प्रेम के कारण, owing to profound love (or out of boundless love). अधीर, impatient. पुलकित होना, to thrill. धारा बहने लगी, began to stream. ब्रह्माण्ड, universe. नियन्ता, creator. उद्धार करना, to salvate.

Exercise 77

प्राचीन काल में भोज एक प्रतापी राजा थे। उनके काल में विद्या एवं कला का चरमोत्कर्ष था। राजा विद्वानों को संरक्षण देते तथा सम्मान करते थे। एक बार उन्होंने दो मालाएँ तैयार करवाई। एक कागज के फूलों की और दूसरी सुगन्धित प्राकृतिक फूलों की। दोनों ऐसी तकनीक से बनाई गई थीं कि देखने वालों को एक दूसरे में कोई अन्तर दिखाई नहीं देता था। राजा ने अपने दरबारियों से पूछा, 'इनमें से कौन माला प्राकृतिक फूलों की है ?' किन्तु बहुत सोचने के पश्चात् भी कोई दरबारी सही निष्कर्ष न निकाल सका। अन्त में जब कालिदास की बारी आई तो उन्होंने उन मालाओं को बाहर रखने का निवेदन किया। उस समय लोग वास्तविक माला आसानी से पहचान गए क्योंकि उस पर मधुमक्खियाँ भनभनाने लगी थीं।

Hints : एक प्रतापी राजा, a glorious king. उनके काल में, during his reign. चरमोत्कर्ष, climax. संरक्षण देना, to give patronage. मालाएँ, garlands. सुगन्धित, fragrant. तकनीक, technique. देखने वाला, onlooker, spectator. अन्तर, distinction. निष्कर्ष निकालना, to conclude. बारी, turn. भनभनाना, to hum.

Exercise 78

ईसा की सातवीं शताब्दी के पूर्वार्द्ध की बात है। प्रयाग में बहुत बड़े दान समारोह का आयोजन किया गया था। सम्पूर्ण भारत से विभिन्न धर्मों के पंडित, विद्वान और दीन-दुखी लोग दान पाने के लिए एकत्र थे। जब राजा दान की समस्त वस्तुओं को यहाँ तक कि राजकोष की सम्पूर्ण सम्पत्ति और अपने शरीर के समस्त आभूषणों को भी दान दे चुका तो एक व्यक्ति ऐसा रह गया जिसे दान देने के लिए उसके पास कुछ नहीं बना। गरीब याचक बोला, 'राजन ! आपके पास मुझे देने के लिए कुछ नहीं बचा। मैं वापस जाता हूँ।' राजा ने कहा, 'ठहरो, अभी मेरे वस्त्र शेष हैं जिन्हें मैंने दान नहीं किया है।' और पास खड़ी अपनी बहन से अपना शरीर ढंकने के लिए दूसरा वस्त्र माँगकर अपने वस्त्र उस याचक को दे दिए। जनसमूह ने हर्षध्वनि की, 'राजा चिरंजीव हो। आपका यश अमर रहे। जानते हो यह राजा कौन था ? यह राजा कोई और नहीं, दानवीर हर्षवर्धन था। हर्षवर्धन की बहुमुखी प्रतिभा और विलक्षण चरित्र का वर्णन करना बहुत कठिन है। वह एक साथ ही राजा और कवि, योद्धा और विद्वान, राजसी और साधु स्वभाव का था। ऐसे ही सम्राटों ने भारत को महान बनाया है।

Hints : बात, event. ईसा की सातवीं शताब्दी का पूर्वार्द्ध, before half of the seventh century. दान समारोह, ceremony of charity (or alms). आयोजन किया गया था, was held. विभिन्न, various. पंडित, scholars. विद्वान, learnedmen. दीन-दुखी, the poor and the aggrieved. दान पाने के लिए, to get alms. एकत्र थे, were assembled (or gathered). राजकोष, royal treasury. सम्पत्ति, wealth. दान दे चुका, offered in charity. देने के लिए कुछ भी नहीं बचा था। had nothing to give to. याचक, beggar. पास खड़ी, standing by (beside). हर्षध्वनि की, exclaimed with joy. चिरंजीव, long live. यश, glory, fame. और कोई नहीं, no other than. दानवीर, man (or champion) of charity. विलक्षण, distinctive, unique. योद्धा, warrior.

Exercise 79

बहुत पुरानी बात है। अटलांटिक महासागर (Atlantic Ocean) के मध्य में एक द्वीप था जिसका नाम था अटलांटिस (Atlantis)। उस देश के निवासी बड़े सशक्त और सम्पन्न थे। उनके पास एक बड़ा जहाजी बेड़ा भी था जिससे वे समुद्र के तटवर्ती क्षेत्रों पर दूर-दूर तक धावा बोलते थे। वे द्वीपवासियों की सम्पदा लूटकर लाते और युवा नर नारियों को कैद करके अपना गुलाम बनाते। उनके पास सब प्रकार की सुविधाएँ थीं। प्रकृति का नियम है कि वह सन्तुलन बनाए रखती है। छोटों को उठाती है और बड़ों को घटने के लिए बाध्य करती है। एक बार ऐसा हुआ कि वहाँ एक ज्वालामुखी पहाड़ फटने से प्रलय आ गया तथा सम्पूर्ण टापू समुद्र में समा गया। मनुष्य मात्र के लिए यह द्वीप, चाहे उसे लोग काल्पनिक ही मानें, एक ज्वलन्त उदाहरण है कि अत्याचार का फल बुरा होता है।

Hints : द्वीप, island. सशक्त एवं सम्पन्न, powerful and prosperous. जहाजी बेड़ा, war fleet. तटवर्ती क्षेत्रों, neighbouring areas. द्वीपवासियों, islanders. लूटना, to plunder. कैद करना, to capture. सुविधाएँ, amenities, facilities. सन्तुलन, balance (to balance). उठाना, to exalt. घटाना, to lower (or diminish). बाध्य करना, to force (or to compel). एक बार ऐसा हुआ, once it so happened. ज्वालामुखी पहाड़, volcano. फटना, to burst up. प्रलय आ गया, doomsday came (devastation befell). समा गया, sank into (or was swallowed by the sea). मानना, to assume, to suppose. एक ज्वलंत उदाहरण, a burning example. अत्याचार, tyranny, oppression.

Exercise 80

कठिन हो या सरल, पर्याप्त आय का हो या कम का, हाथ में जो काम आ जाए उसे अवश्य स्वीकार कर लेना चाहिए और जितनी योग्यता हो उसका निर्वाह करना चाहिए। एक बेकार बैठे रहने वाले आदमी की अपेक्षा किसी काम में लगे रहने वाले व्यक्ति को ऊँचा पद प्राप्त करने की संभावना अधिक रहती है। 'बहुत दिन हुए जब मैं तुम्हारी स्थिति में था तब आठ आने रोज की मजदूरी पर कुली के काम से कोई बेहतर काम मुझे नहीं मिला। मैं तुरंत उसे करने लगा। आज इस कारखाने का मैं एकमात्र स्वामी हूँ।' नवयुवक ने कहा, 'यह करीब चालीस वर्ष पहले की बात है। उस समय व्यापार की दशा कुछ और ही थी।' वृद्ध सज्जन ने उत्तर दिया, 'परिश्रमी मनुष्य को ऊँचे पद की आशा में बेकार बैठे रहने से कोई लाभ नहीं होता। जो काम उसे मिल रहा है उसे तुरन्त स्वीकार कर लेना चाहिए भले ही वह तुच्छ ही क्यों न हो। एक दिन आएगा जब वह अवश्य ही सफल होगा।'

Hints : कठिन हो ...... या कम का, whether difficult or easy of affluent or petty income. निर्वाह करना, to carry out. बेकार बैठे रहने वाला व्यक्ति, an idle man, a jobless person. लगे रहने, be engaged in, (at work). प्राप्त करना, to acquire. संभावना, possibility. मजदूरी, wages. कुली, coolie. बेहतर काम, better job. और ही थी, was something different. परिश्रमी, industrious, diligent. कोई लाभ नहीं, no use. भले ही, however. तुच्छ, trifle.

Exercise 81

मैं गोलकुंडा की एक निर्जन गुफा में पैदा हुआ था। किस प्रकार मैं गोलकुंडा के एक व्यवसायी के हाथ पहुँच गया, मुझे ठीक याद नहीं है। किन्तु इतना अवश्य याद है कि उस व्यवसायी के घर मैं बहुत दिनों तक नहीं रहा। धीरे-धीरे मेरी ख्याति भारत सम्राट शाहजहाँ के कानों में पहुँची। मेरे स्वामी ने उस समय अपने मन में विचार किया कि सम्राट की दृष्टि जब मुझ पर पड़ चुकी है तब किसी न किसी प्रकार वे मुझे अपने अधिकार में ले लेंगे। इसलिए यदि मुझे वे सम्राट के पास उपहार रूप में ले जायँ तो उनका मान भी रह जाएगा और मेरी जान भी बच जाएगी। ऐसा निश्चय कर मेरे स्वामी मुझे साथ लेकर

एक दिन राज्यसभा में उपस्थित हुए। शाहजहाँ के दरबार का वैभव देखकर मैं गर्व से फूल गया। मैंने मन ही मन सोचा, 'हाँ, यही स्थान मेरे रहने योग्य है।' आप कदाचित कहेंगे कि पत्थर के इस छोटे से टुकड़े को इतना गर्व और मुझ पर हँसेंगे। सम्राट शाहजहाँ मुझे पाकर अत्यन्त प्रसन्न हुआ। इसके बाद मेरे जीवन का वह अध्याय प्रारम्भ हुआ जब मैं एक राजा के सिर से दूसरे राजा के सिर पर घूमता रहा।

Hints : एक निर्जन गुफा में, in a lonely cave. ठीक, precisely (exactly). स्वामी, master. दृष्टि मुझ पर पड़ चुकी है, have come into the knowledge of. किसी न किसी प्रकार, by hook or by crook. अधिकार में लेना, to take into possession. उपहार, gift, (present). मान, honour, dignity. वैभव, glory (or splender) गर्व, pride (or conceit). फूल गया, elated with. कदाचित, perhaps. जीवन का अध्याय, chapter of life. आरम्भ हुआ, opened. घूमता फिरता, went about.

Exercise 82

उन दिनों यूरोप के वैज्ञानिकों में यह चर्चा थी कि बिजली की लहरें हवा में गुजारी जा सकती हैं। जगदीशचन्द्र बोस को इस बात में दिलचस्पी हो गई। वे बिजली की लहरों द्वारा एक स्थान से दूसरे स्थान तक समाचार भेजने की संभावना पर गंभीरतापूर्वक सोचने लगे। उन्होंने इन लहरों का क्रमवार प्रयोग किया। कहा जाता है कि उन्होंने बिजली द्वारा ध्वनि की लहरें प्रेषित करने की विधि का आविष्कार किया। अभाग्यवश उनके पास आवश्यक यंत्र खरीदने के लिए पूँजी न थी। यह सम्मान इटली के मारकोनी को ही जाना था। आज हम जो रेडियो सेट काम में लाते हैं, वह मारकोनी के आविष्कार का परिणाम है। यद्यपि बोस बेतार के तार के आविष्कर्त्ता न हो सके परन्तु अपनी दूसरी गंवेषणा द्वारा उन्होंने अपने ही बनाए वैज्ञानिक यंत्रों द्वारा प्रमाणित किया कि मनुष्य की तरह पेड़ पौधे भी दुख-सुख का अनुभव करते हैं।

Hints : यह चर्चा थी, it was talked (words climbed up). लहरें, waves. गुजारी जा सकती हैं, can be passed through. समाचार भेजने की संभावना पर, on the possibility of transmitting news. गम्भीरतापूर्वक, seriously. क्रमवार प्रयोग किया, made successive experiments. ध्वनि की लहरें, sound waves. विधि, method (or technique). आवश्यक यंत्र, requisite apparatus (or instruments). पूँजी, money. को ही जाना था, was conferable (was to be conferred on) Marconi of Italy ...... बेतार का तार, wireless telegraphy. आविष्कर्त्ता, inventor. प्रमाणित किया, proved. गंवेषणा, research (work). दुख-सुख, pain and pleasure.

Exercise 83

प्रिय मित्र ! तुम्हारा पालन पोषण एक ऐसे महानगर में हुआ है जिसका वातावरण मेरे लिए एकदम भिन्न है। लेकिन हम दोनों प्रकृति के एक ही लक्ष्य तक दो भिन्न रास्ते से पहुँचे हैं। इस कारण तुम्हारे प्रति मैं किसी ईर्ष्या या रूखाई की आशा नहीं करता। ऐसी स्थिति में मैं तुमसे मानसिक विकास की कथा कहता हूँ। मैं जानता हूँ कि तुम उस कड़वाहट से मुक्त हो जो मनुष्य के बीच खाई पैदा कर देती है और प्रेम तथा सौन्दर्य को विनष्ट कर देती है। तुम स्वार्थ एवं संकीर्णता से बहुत दूर हो क्योंकि तुमने प्रकृति की गोद में साधना किया है। प्रकृति का दुलार पाकर तुमने अपनी आत्मा को कृत्रिमता से विमुक्त कर दिया है। इस प्रसंग में संसार में तुम मेरे सर्वप्रिय एवं निकट के मित्र हो। मैंने उस पागल एवं वंचित माँ का गीत गाया है जो काँटेदार झाड़ी के पास अपने दुर्भाग्य पर पश्चाताप कर रही थी। तुम अनुभव करते होगे कि वस्तुत: एक कवि का जीवन प्रत्येक प्रशंसा एवं न्याय के योग्य होता है। ईश्वर तुम्हें सुखमय जीवन प्रदान करे।

Hints : पालन पोषण हुआ है, have been brought up. वातावरण, surroundings. लक्ष्य, goal, ईर्ष्या या रूखाई की आशा न करना, to expect no contempt or sternness. विकास, growth. कड़वाहट से मुक्त, free from bitterness. खाई पैदा करना, to create a gulf. नष्ट करना, to impair. स्वार्थ तथा संकीर्णता से दूर, far from selfishness and narrow mindedness. साधना करना, to devote. दुलार पाकर, being fondled. मुक्त करना, to liberate (or to salvate). कृत्रिमता, artificiality. सर्वप्रिय एवं निकट का मित्र, the most intimate and nearest companion. प्रशंसा एवं न्याय के योग्य होना, to deserve praise and justice.

Exercise 84

आत्मविश्वास की शक्ति से तुम असंभव को संभव कर सकते हो। अतः आस्था एक मूल्यवान चीज है। ईश्वर में विश्वास, अपने कार्य में विश्वास और अपनी शक्ति में विश्वास। तब तुम हमेशा एक विशाल चट्टान की भाँति अडिग रहोगे और कभी नहीं गिरोगे। अन्तर के प्रकाश का अनुसरण करना और निडर होकर अपने लक्ष्य की ओर जाना—सफलता की प्रथम गारंटी है। अपने जीवन का उद्देश्य खूब सोच समझ कर निश्चित करो और उसकी ओर बढ़ो। मैं मानता हूँ कि लोग तुम्हारी खिल्ली उड़ाएँगे और मुँह छिपाकर हँसेंगे किन्तु हिम्मत मत हारो। हमेशा याद रखो कि एक महान आदमी अन्यथा नहीं सोचता। इतिहास साक्षी है कि ऐसे लोग विजय को झपट जाते हैं। तब उनके आलोचक उनकी प्रशंसा करने लगते हैं। प्रबल विश्वास से अंधकार के बादल छँट जाते हैं और रास्ता साफ हो जाता है। इस तरह आत्मविश्वास, सुख, सफलता और स्वास्थ्य का जादूगर है। यह सफलता का मुख्य द्वार है।

Hints : आत्मविश्वास की शक्ति से, by the power of self-confidence. असंभव को संभव करना, to make impossible possible. आस्था, faith. एक विशाल चट्टान, a massive rock. अडिग, immovable. अन्तर के प्रकाश का अनुसरण करना, to follow the inward light. निडर होकर, fearlessly. गारण्टी, guarantee. खिल्ली उड़ाना, to mock at. मुँह छिपाकर हँसना, to laugh in one's sleeve. हिम्मत हारना, to break the heart, (to feel disheartened). अन्यथा, otherwise. साक्षी है, witnesses. झपटना, to snatch. विजय, victory. छँट जाते हैं, disperse. जादूगर, talisman. आलोचक, critic. द्वार, gate.

Exercise 85

हिन्दी के उपन्यासकार एवं कहानीकार प्रेमचन्द से कौन परिचित नहीं है ? उनका जन्म वाराणसी जनपद के लमही ग्राम के एक गरीब परिवार में हुआ था। बचपन में उनका नाम धनपत राय था। अपने जीवन के पूर्वकाल में वे उर्दू में नवाबराय के नाम से गल्प लिखा करते थे। बाद में उन्होंने हिन्दी में कहानियाँ एवं उपन्यास लिखने के लिए लेखनी उठाई। उनकी उच्च श्रेणी की कहानी कला होने के कारण फिल्म की पटकथा लिखने के लिए उन्हें मुम्बई बुलाया गया। किन्तु संसार से वे ऊब गए और वाराणसी लौट गए। वे बहुत दिनों तक शिक्षक भी रहे। कुछ दिनों तक उन्होंने जिला विद्यालय निरीक्षक के पद पर कार्य किया। उनके उपन्यासों में गोदान, गबन, कायाकल्प, निर्मला आदि बड़े प्रसिद्ध हैं। समाज के प्रत्येक कोने को वे सूक्ष्म अन्तर्दृष्टि से झाँक आए थे। उनकी कृतियों में उनके युग की चेतना प्रगट है। इसीलिए साहित्य में वे नवीन युग ला सके।

Hints : उपन्यासकार एवं कहानीकार, novelist and story-writer. अपने जीवन के पूर्वकाल में, in his early life. गल्प, fiction. लेखनी उठाई, wielded his pen. उच्च श्रेणी ...... के कारण, owing to his splendid (or outstanding) art of story-writing. पटकथा, theme. ऊब गए, was vexed with. ग्रामीण जीवन, rural life. सूक्ष्म अन्तर्दृष्टि, piercing insight (or sharp acumen). झाँक आए थे, had peeped into. उनके युग ...... प्रगट है, the temper of his age has been revealed. एक नया युग ला सके, could herald (or bring about) a new age (or epoch).

Exercise 86

हमारी बीमारियाँ हमारे पापों एवं त्रुटियों का प्रतिफल होती हैं। ये केवल उन्हें ही होती हैं जो इन्हें निमंत्रित करते हैं अथवा जिनका शरीर इन्हें आकर्षित करता है। बीमारियाँ उस व्यक्ति से दूर भागती हैं जिसका हृदय पवित्र और दृढ़ होता है। इस सत्य को हम जितना ही शीघ्र समझ लेंगे उतना ही शीघ्र अच्छे स्वास्थ्य की ओर बढ़ेंगे। यदि आप हमेशा चिन्ता, क्रोध, ईर्ष्या, संशय या लालच में डूबे हुए हैं और साथ ही पूर्ण स्वास्थ्य की भी कामना करते हैं तो आप एक असंभव चीज की कामना करते हैं। किन्तु एक बुद्धिमान व्यक्ति इस प्रकार के अवांछनीय विचारों को अपने मन में शरण नहीं देता। अतः हमेशा सुखमय और प्रिय विचारों को सोचें। आप पायेंगे कि आपको किसी भी दवा की आवश्यकता नहीं है। अनेक व्यक्ति यह शिकायत करते हैं कि उनका स्वास्थ्य अधिक कार्य करने के कारण खराब हो गया है। किन्तु वे नहीं जानते कि उनका स्वास्थ्य व्यर्थ के विचारों को मन में संपोषण करने से खराब हुआ है।

Hints : पापों एवं ...... होती हैं, are the results of our sins and errors. उन्हें ही होती है, come only to those. आकर्षित करना, to attract. दूर भागना, to flee far away. पवित्र और दृढ़, pure and immovable. समझना, to realise. ईर्ष्या, संशय या लालच, jealousy, suspiciousness or greed. डूबे हुए हैं, are plunged into. पूर्ण स्वास्थ्य, complete (or perfect) health. अवांछनीय विचारों, undesirable ideas. शरण देना, to give refuge. अधिक कार्य ...... कारण, owing to overwork. खराब हो गया है, has broken. व्यर्थ के विचारों, useless thoughts. सम्पोषण करना, to support.

Exercise 87

मैंने झटपट पत्र लिखा और उसे छोड़ने के लिए बाहर निकला। जब मैं सड़क पर जा रहा था तो मैंने एक व्यक्ति को देखा। निकट पहुँचने पर मैंने देखा कि वह शराब के नशे में धुत्त था। वह रास्ते के दोनों ओर पथिकों को गाली बक रहा था एवं मारता जा रहा था। जब मैं उसके निकट से गुजरा तो उसने मुझे भी गाली देना शुरू किया। फिर वह मुझपर अचानक टूट पड़ा। मैं उसके इस गुंडेपन को सहन न कर सका। मैंने उसकी गर्दन पकड़ ली और ऐसा थप्पड़ मारा कि उसके होश ठिकाने हो गए। अब उसे मालूम हुआ कि किसी जबर्दस्त से पाला पड़ा है। बाद में वह जोर से बड़बड़ाया और फिर अपनी राह ली।

Hints : झटपट, hurriedly. छोड़ना, to post. निकट पहुँचने पर, on approaching. शराब के नशे में धुत्त था, had deadly drunk. पथिक, passer-by. उसके निकट से गुजरा, passed by him. टूट पड़ा, pounced upon. गुंडापन, hooliganism, boisterous act. उसकी गर्दन पकड़ ली, caught him by the neck. थप्पड़ मारना, to slap. मालूम हुआ, came to know. होश ठिकाने हो गए, came to his senses. जबर्दस्त से पाला पड़ा है, had caught a Tartar. जोर से बड़बड़ाया, chattered (or growled) loudly.

Exercise 88

भारत के दो प्रमुख महाकाव्य रामायण और महाभारत हैं। इनकी रचना सैंकड़ों वर्षों के कालक्रम में हुई। अपने वर्तमान रूप में संभवतः दूसरी ई० में ही ये ग्रन्थ लिखे गए। महाभारत में लगभग एक लाख श्लोक हैं और यह संसार का सबसे बड़ा काव्य-ग्रन्थ है। भगवद्गीता बाद में महाभारत में जोड़ी गई। इसमें एक गूढ़ दार्शनिक सिद्धान्त का विवेचन किया गया है। रामायण में राम की कथा है। इसमें अनेक रूचिकर घटनाओं तथा साहसिक कार्यों का वर्णन है। इन दो महाकाव्यों ने सदियों से करोड़ों लोगों के विचारों को प्रभावित किया है। निस्सन्देह इनके संदेश सभी लोगों एवं युगों को उद्बोधित करते रहेंगे।

Hints : प्रमुख महाकाव्य, eminent epics. कालक्रम, duration of. वर्तमान रूप में, in their existing forms. श्लोक, verse. काव्य-ग्रन्थ, poetic work. जोड़ा गया, was added. एक गूढ़ दार्शनिक सिद्धान्त, a deep philosophic principle. विवेचन करना, to interpret (or expound). साहसिक कार्यों, adventurous deeds. प्रभावित किया है, have moved (or influenced). संदेश, message. उद्बोधित करना, to console (or give solace). निस्सन्देह, undoubtedly.

Exercise 89

स्वामी रामकृष्ण का जन्म बंगाल में सन् 1836 ई० में हुआ। उनके माता-पिता अत्यन्त धार्मिक थे। बचपन से ही रामकृष्ण ने अद्भुत चरित्र को दिखाया। उसी बीच उनकी ईश्वर में स्वाभाविक भक्ति हो गई। वे जीवन भर आत्मचिन्तन में लीन रहे। इस विषय में उनके अनेक अनुभव लोक में प्रसिद्ध हैं। वे इतने ज्ञानी तथा शुद्ध चित्त थे कि व्यक्ति द्वारा किए गए विभेद उनके द्वारा व्यर्थ हो गए। अपने आचरण से उन्होंने सभी चीजों को सिद्ध कर दिया था। स्वामी विवेकानन्द इन्हीं महापुरूष के शिष्य थे। केवल भारत में ही नहीं बल्कि पश्चिमी देशों में भी उन्होंने मानवता का ढिंढोरा पीटा।

Hints : धार्मिक, religious minded. अद्भुत चरित्र, miraculous (or strange) character. दिखाया, displayed. स्वाभाविक भक्ति, spontaneous (or natural) devotion. आत्मचिन्तन, self-meditation (or contemplation). लीन रहे, was busy in. शुद्ध चित्त, pure hearted. विभेद, distinction. किए गए, created. व्यर्थ, meaningless. आचरण, conduct. शिष्य, disciple. मानवता, humanity. ढिंढोरा पीटा, sounded (or beat) the clarion call.

Exercise 90

यदि आप सफलता प्राप्त करना चाहते हैं तो अकेले खड़ा रहना सीखिए। हमेशा याद रखें कि सभी शक्तियाँ अविचलित विचारों से सम्बन्धित होती हैं। जब सभी मित्र संवेगों के शिकार हो गए हों उस समय भी जो शान्त तथा अविचलित बना रहता है वही शक्तिशाली कहलाता है। इसके साथ ही यह भी सत्य है कि केवल वही व्यक्ति दूसरों को नियंत्रित कर सकता है जो स्वयं को नियंत्रित करना जानता हो। अत : यदि आप सफलता पाना चाहते हों तो डरपोक और संकीर्ण विचार वालों का साथ छोड़ दें। जो व्यक्ति शान्त, निर्भय, विचारशील एवं गम्भीर होता है वह निर्जन वन या मरूस्थल में भी अडिग बना रहता है। संवेग शक्ति नहीं होता, बल्कि यह शक्ति का दुरूपयोग होता है। यदि आप में शक्ति का अभाव है तो आप इसे अभ्यास के द्वारा सुलभ कर सकते हैं। न भूलें कि शक्ति के प्रारम्भ का अर्थ है बुद्धि का प्रारम्भ।

Hints : अविचलित विचारों, unshakable thoughts. सम्बन्धित होती हैं, are associated with. संवेग, passion. शिकार हो गए हों, are fallen victim to. शान्त तथा अविचलित, calm and immovable. बना रहना, remain. नियंत्रित करना, to command. डरपोक, fearful (timid). संकीर्ण विचारों वाले, narrow minded (men or persons). साथ, company. विचारशील, thoughtful, (considerate). गम्भीर, serious (reserved). दुरूपयोग, abuse (or misuse). अभाव, scarcity.

Exercise 91

गीता में भगवान श्रीकृष्ण ने उपदेश दिया है कि हमें निरन्तर कर्म करना चाहिए। संसार में कोई ऐसा कार्य नहीं है जो कुछ न कुछ अच्छा न करे। वैसे ही सभी कार्यों से हानि भी संभव है। इस तरह प्रत्येक कर्म अच्छे और बुरे का मिश्रण होगा। फिर भी हमें निरन्तर कर्म करने की आज्ञा दी गई है। स्पष्टत: अच्छे और बुरे कर्मों के उनके अनुसार फल होते हैं। अच्छे कार्य अच्छे फल प्रदान करते हैं और बुरे कार्य बुरे। किन्तु अच्छे और बुरे दोनों ही आत्मा को जंजीरों से बाँधते हैं। गीता में इसका उपाय दिया गया है कि हमें इनसे आसक्ति नहीं रखनी चाहिए। इस तरह अनासक्त कर्म हमारी आत्मा को बन्धन से बचा लेंगे।

Hints : उपदेश दिया है, has preached. निरन्तर, incessantly (or tirelessly), वैसे ही, similarly. मिश्रण, mixture or amalgamation. अच्छे और बुरे, good and bad (or evil). जंजीर, fetter, shackle. उपाय, remedy, solution. आसक्ति, attachment, (affection). अनासक्त कर्म, detached action. बन्धन, bondage.

Exercise 92

कुछ पश्चिमी इतिहासकारों द्वारा शिवाजी को लुटेरा कहा गया है। किन्तु सामान्यतया इसे पक्षपातपूर्ण एवं एकांगी विचार माना जाता है। मुगल बादशाह औरंगजेब शिवाजी का समकालीन था। वह एक धर्मान्ध व्यक्ति था। वह शंकालु स्वभाव का था और किसी पर विश्वास नहीं करता था। वह हिन्दुओं के बिल्कुल खिलाफ था। शिवाजी में हिन्दू धर्म के आदर्श कूट-कूट कर भरे थे। वे इस जाति को औरंगजेब के अत्याचार से मुक्त कराना चाहते थे। अत: उन्होंने उसके प्रति जीवन-पर्यन्त युद्ध का व्रत लिया। प्राय: वे छापामार युद्ध लड़ा करते थे। एक बार उनके सैनिकों ने अनेक बेगमों को पकड़ लिया। जब उन्हें शिवाजी के सामने लाया गया तो वे बड़े क्रोधित हुए। उन्होंने सैनिकों को आज्ञा दी कि उन्हें दरबार में ससम्मान लौटा दिया जाय। शिवाजी ने साम्राज्य स्थापना भी की थी। उनकी शासन-प्रणाली मुख्यत: ब्राह्मण धर्म पर आधारित थी।

Hints : लुटेरा, highwayman. पक्षपातपूर्ण और एकांगी, partial and one sided. समकालीन, contemporary. धर्मान्ध, fanatic. अत्याचार, oppression. शंकालु, of doubtful nature (or suspicious minded). कूट-कूट कर भरे थे, were deeply rooted. व्रत लिया, took a vow, swore. छापामार युद्ध लड़ा करते थे, waged gorilla warfare. स्थापना की, founded. शासन प्रणाली, method of administration. मुख्यत:, primarily (or fundamentally).

Exercise 93

अशोक हमारे देश के महान शासकों में से एक हैं। उसने एक महान आदर्श सामने रखा और उसे कार्यान्वित करने के लिए आजन्म प्रयत्न किया। उसने राजनीति से धर्म को मिलाया और शासन को नया रूप दिया। उसने सिद्ध कर दिया कि

कैसे एक राजा धर्म, न्याय तथा दया के पथ पर चलता हुआ प्रजा का महान कल्याण कर सकता है। वह कहता था कि धर्म की विजय ही वास्तविक विजय है। हमारे इतिहास में अशोक का नाम सदा अमर रहेगा। महान साहित्यकार एच०जी० वेल्स (H.G. Wells) अशोक के सम्बन्ध में लिखता है, 'विश्व-इतिहास के पृष्ठों में सहस्रों शासकों के नाम आते हैं, परन्तु अशोक का नाम इन सबमें उज्ज्वल तारे की भाँति अकेला चमकता है। आज भी बोल्गा (Volga) से लेकर जापान (Japan) तक उसके नाम का आदर है। चीन, तिब्बत और भारत में भी यद्यपि इस देश में उसके अनुयायी नहीं हैं, उसका स्थान सुरक्षित है। कान्स्टाइन शार्लेमन (Contestine Charlemagne) के नाम बहुतों ने सुने हैं परन्तु उनकी संख्या कहीं अधिक है जिनके हृदय में अशोक आज भी जीवित है।'

Hints : सामने रखा, placed before. उसे कार्यान्वित करने के लिए, to bring that into practice (to execute). आजन्म प्रयत्न किया, tried throughout his life, नया रूप देना, to give a new shape. प्रजा, subjects, gentry. कल्याण, welfare, (betterment). नाम आते हैं, are mentioned. उज्ज्वल .... चमकता है, shines alone like an illuminating star. नाम का आदर है, is held with great reverence (or esteem). अनुयायी, followers. उसका स्थान सुरक्षित है, his position (or post) is secure. जीवित है, is alive.

Exercise 94

अपने बाल्यकाल से ही मुहम्मद साहब मूर्ति पूजा से घृणा करते थे। उन्होंने कावा की 360 मूर्तियों की पूजा को व्यर्थ बताया। अरबों की मिथ्या देवभक्ति देखकर उन्होंने निश्चय कर लिया था कि मैं उन्हें धर्मान्धता एवं अज्ञानता से मुक्त करूँगा। उनको अपने विचारों में निष्ठा थी। उन्होंने अपने धर्म का प्रचार सार्वजनिक रूप से किया। तब तो वे आपत्ति में पड़ गए। चारों ओर से उनकी निन्दा होने लगी और उन पर अभियोग लगाए गए। जब उनकी स्थिति अति चिन्तनीय हो गई तो वे मक्का छोड़कर मदीना चले गए। वहाँ उनके उपदेशों का शानदार स्वागत हुआ। कालान्तर में उनके असंख्य अनुयायी हो गए। उन्होंने लोगों को समझाया कि केवल एक ही ईश्वर अर्थात् अल्लाह पूजा के योग्य हैं, असंख्य प्रचलित देव नहीं। इस तरह उनके उपदेश बड़े सरल थे। उन्होंने कहा कि मैं उस अल्लाह का पैगम्बर हूँ। उसका हुक्म सुनाने के लिए ही मैं संसार में आया हूँ। मुहम्मद साहब इतने कर्त्तव्यनिष्ठ थे कि अपने जीवन के अन्तिम दिनों तक वे मस्जिदों में उपदेश देते रहे। अंत में वे बीमार पड़ गए और 8 जून 632 को उनकी मृत्यु हो गई।

Hints : मूर्ति पूजा, idolatory. व्यर्थ, meaningless. मिथ्या देवभक्ति, false devotion (or piety). अज्ञानता, ignorance. निष्ठा, confidence. सार्वजनिक रूप से, openly (publicaly). प्रचार किया, preached. आपत्ति में पड़ गए, got into hot water (or landed into disaster). चारों ओर से, from all quarters. निन्दा करना, to criticise (or he had to run the gauntlet). अभियोग लगाए गए, was charged (or alleged). अत्यन्त चिन्तनीय, highly concerning. शानदार, warmly, heartily. कालान्तर में, in the course of time. समझाया, persuaded (or convinced). असंख्य प्रचलित देव, countless rampant deities (or deities in vogue). पैगम्बर, messenger. कर्त्तव्यनिष्ठ, true to his duty, diligent. अर्थात्, *i.e.* (id est) that is.

Exercise 95

टॉमस हार्डी (Thomas Hardy) का अपना एक अलग संसार है जो सौन्दर्य एवं उदासीनता से पूर्ण है। चारों ओर निराशा एवं क्रूर भाग्य के थपेड़े उनके पात्रों का रास्ता निर्दिष्ट करते हैं। प्रारब्ध को हार्डी ने एक बलशाली एजेन्ट माना है। वह मनुष्य को स्वेच्छया नचाता है और विनाश की ओर ले जाता है। मनुष्य एक कमजोर किन्तु उच्च आकांक्षाओं वाला प्राणी है, जब वह सफलता के पास पहुँचता है, तब भाग्य विपरीत कार्य करता है। अगर मृत्यु से बच गया तो वह दर-दर की ठोकरें खाने लगा। इस तरह मानव-जीवन एक दुखदाई धंधा है जिस पर दुर्भाग्य अट्टहास करता है। मनुष्य की असहायता, निराशा और उदासीनता को प्रगट करने के लिए हार्डी का वेसेक्स (Wessex land) प्रदेश बड़ा ही उचित सिद्ध हुआ है। सम्पूर्ण प्रदेश उजड़ा हुआ, कहीं-कहीं टीले और चरागाह हैं जहाँ से जीवन का खिन्न संगीत आ रहा है। और फिर वही स्याह रातें, दुखी एवं निराश।

Hints : अपना अलग संसार है, has his own separate world. उदासीनता, melancholy. पूर्ण है, is imbued with. क्रूर भाग्य के थपेड़े, the pangs of the cruel destiny. पात्रों, characters. निर्दिष्ट करते हैं, direct (guide). स्वेच्छा, voluntarily. विनाश की ओर, towards doom. उच्च आकांक्षा, aspiration (or ambition). दर-दर की ठोकर खाना, to suffer from bitter tribulation (or to go from pillar to post). एक दुखदाई धन्धा, a sorry business. अट्टहास करना, to laugh at. असहायता, helplessness. बड़ा ही उचित, very precise (or appropriate). उजड़ा, deserted. टीले, mounds. चरागाह, meadow, pasture. जीवन का खिन्न संगीत, sad music of life. स्याह राहें, gloomy paths. दुखी, miserable.

Exercise 96

शंकराचार्य दक्षिणी भारत में मालावार के नम्बूट्री ब्राह्मण थे। बचपन से ही उनमें विचित्र चिह्न दर्शनीय थे। बत्तीस वर्ष की अवस्था में उन्होंने सभी वेदों, पुराणों का अध्ययन कर उस पर मौलिक टीका किया। उनका ज्ञान अति विस्तृत और गहन था। उन्होंने सम्पूर्ण भारत का पर्यटन कर बौद्धों को शास्त्रार्थ में हराया। दर्शन के क्षेत्र में उन्होंने अद्वैतवाद का प्रतिपादन किया। उनके अनुसार आत्मा तथा परमात्मा में कोई भेद नहीं। सम्पूर्ण जगत की विचित्रता केवल माया की झलक है। किन्तु सच्चा ज्ञान होते ही वह लुप्त हो जाती है। उन्होंने अपने सिद्धान्तों को उपनिषदों का आधार दिया है। उन सबका अर्थ उन्होंने अपनी दार्शनिक धारणा के अनुसार किया। उस समय उत्तरी भारत में कुमारिल भट्ट एक प्रख्यात विद्वान एवं दार्शनिक थे। शंकराचार्य ने उनसे दार्शनिक शास्त्रार्थ किया और उन्हें हराया। कुमारिल ने शंकर के अनुष्ठान में खुलकर सहयोग किया। फलस्वरूप, उन दोनों के कारण पूर्वी भारत को छोड़कर बौद्ध धर्म का प्रायः समस्त भारत से लोप हो गया।

Hints : दर्शनीय थे, were visible. मौलिक टीका करना, to give novel interpretations (or comments). अति विस्तृत एवं गहन, very wide and deep. शास्त्रार्थ, discussion on the shastras. दर्शन के क्षेत्र में, in the domain of philosophy. अद्वैतवाद, monotheism. प्रतिपादन किया, expounded. विचित्रता, diversity. झलक, glimpse, illusion (mirage). कोई भेद नहीं, no distinction. सिद्धान्त, theories, (principles). अपनी दार्शनिक धारणा के अनुसार, according to his own philosophic concept. दार्शनिक शास्त्रार्थ किया, entered into a philosophic discussion (with). अनुष्ठान, mission. सहयोग किया, co-operated.

Exercise 97

आधुनिक मनोविज्ञान ने मनुष्य के विचार को काफी प्रभावित किया है। मनोवैज्ञानिकों ने मस्तिष्क को दो भागों में विभाजित किया है। प्रथम चेतन मन और दूसरा अवचेतन मन। चेतन मन केवल जाग्रत अवस्था में खुला रहता है। वह बाह्य प्रकृति का अवलोकन करता है एवं कार्यों का मूल्यांकन करता है। वह आशा, निराशा, आनन्द तथा दुख का अनुभव करता है। अवचेतन मन सर्वदा खुला रहता है। यह सोते, जागते हमेशा जाग्रत रहता है। कहते हैं कि यह क्षेत्र मनुष्य की अवदमित इच्छाओं का संग्रहालय है। व्यावहारिक जीवन की जागती अवस्था में जो इच्छाएँ पूर्ण नहीं हो पातीं वे अवचेतन मन में चली जाती हैं। जब हम सो जाते हैं, ये इच्छाएँ स्वप्न में आती हैं। मनोवैज्ञानिकों के विचार में यह प्रक्रिया मनुष्य को पागल होने से बचा लेती है। काफी हद तक वह मानसिक रूप से स्वस्थ हो जाता है।

Hints : मनोविज्ञान, Psychology. काफी, immensely. विभाजित किया है, have classified. चेतन मन, conscious mind. अवचेतन मन, unconcious mind. बाह्य प्रकृति, external phenomena (or appearances). अवलोकन करता है, watches. मूल्यांकन करता है, evaluates (assesses). क्षेत्र, sphere. अवदमित इच्छाओं का संग्रहालय है, is a reservoir (or storeroom) of suppressed desires. व्यावहारिक जीवन, practical life. चली जाती हैं, creep into. प्रक्रिया, process. पागल होने से बचा लेती है, saves man from being mad. मानसिक रूप से स्वस्थ, mentally healthy. जाग्रत, wakeful.

Exercise 98

इस भौतिकवादी युग ने संसार को गंदा और कुरूप कर दिया है। हमारे जीवन का लक्ष्य धन हो गया है। इस प्रवृत्ति से लोगों में स्वार्थ की भावना बढ़ गई है। पारस्परिक सहानुभूति और स्वाभाविक प्रेम समाप्त हो गए हैं। इसीलिए महात्मा गाँधी ने त्याग और निस्वार्थमय जीवन पर अधिक बल दिया। सत्य एवं अहिंसा धर्म के मौलिक आदर्श हैं। इन्हीं से हम ईश्वर का दर्शन पा सकते हैं। कुछ आदमी अपने वचनों एवं कर्मों में प्रतिकूल होते हैं। परन्तु महात्मा गाँधी के धर्म में हृदय की स्वच्छता मूल आधार है। वे जीवनभर सत्य पर चलने की कोशिश करते रहे। उन्होंने सभी धर्मों को निकट से देखा था। उनके विचार में सत्य, अहिंसा आदि सभी धर्मों के सामान्य सिद्धान्त हैं। प्रेम, सहानुभूति तथा क्षमा यह सत्य तक पहुँचने के साधन हैं। इन्हीं विचारों के कारण वे एक युग ला सके। जो प्रकाश इस अंधियारे विश्व पर उन्होंने फैलाया वह आज भी प्रासंगिक है।

Hints : भौतिकवादी युग, materialistic age. प्रवृत्ति, attitude, tendency. समाप्त हो गए हैं, are faded away. त्याग और निस्वार्थ, renunciation and selflessness. बल दिया है, has stressed on. मौलिक आदर्श, fundamental ideals. दर्शन पाना, to have a vision of. प्रतिकूल होना, to contradict (to differ). क्षमा, forgiveness. पहुँचने के साधन हैं, are means to approach. अंधियारे, dark. फैलाया, flashed. प्रासंगिक, relevant.

Exercise 99

साहित्य समाज का दर्पण है। सभी महान कलाकार अपने युग के साक्षी हैं। यद्यपि यह तो सत्य है कि महान साहित्य समय विशेष से नहीं बाँधा जा सकता। अनेक ग्रन्थ ऐसे भी हैं जो सार्वकालिक होते हैं। वे हमारे अन्तर के संसार में विचरते हैं और मृत्यु के पश्चात् जीवन की भी कल्पना करते हैं। उनमें से उपनिषद्, गीता, रामायण आदि को अति विशिष्ट उदाहरण के रूप में रखा जा सकता है। कुछ लोगों का विचार है कि साहित्य संस्कृति का साधन है। यह संस्कृति के द्वारा बनता है, संस्कृति इसके द्वारा नहीं। यह पूर्णतया सत्य नहीं है। जान कीट्स (John Keats) एक सौन्दर्यबोधी थे। उन्हें प्राचीन यूनानी (Greek) साहित्य में विराम मिलता था। फिर उनका साहित्य किस प्रकार उनके काल को प्रतिबिम्बित कर सकता है ? फिर भी आलोचकों ने उनकी प्रशंसा की है तथा उन्होंने कीट्स को शेक्सपीयर (Shakespeare) की कोटि में रखा है।

Hints : दर्पण, mirror. समय विशेष, particular time. सार्वकालिक होना, to belong to all times. विचरना, to move (or wander). अन्तर का संसार, the inner world. अति विशिष्ट ...... सकता है, can be cited as patterns (or uncommon examples). बनता है, is shaped by. पूर्णतया असत्य, totally (completely) untrue एक सौन्दर्यबोधी, an aesthete. विराम मिलना, to feel at home in. प्रतिबिम्बित कर सकता है, can mirror (or reflect). आलोचक, critic. प्रशंसा करना, to appreciate. कोटि में रखा है, have ranked him with.

Exercise 100

भारत के प्राचीन कवियों अथवा नाटककारों में राजशेखर का स्थान औरों से किसी भाँति हीन नहीं है। यद्यपि भारतीय समाज में उन्होंने कालिदास या भवभूति की तरह प्रसिद्धि एवं सर्वस्वीकार्यता न पाई तथापि इससे यह नहीं अनुमान करना चाहिए कि इनकी कविता या विद्वता दूसरों से निम्नकोटि की है। यथार्थ यह है कि जैसा लार्ड मैकाले (Lord Macaulay) ने एडिसन् (Addison) के जीवन-चरित्र में लिखा है, 'संसार में बहुधा वे लोग ख्याति लाभ नहीं करते हैं जो ऐसे कार्य करते हैं जिन्हें करने का दूसरे प्रयत्न नहीं करते, बल्कि ऐसे लोग प्रसिद्धि पाते हैं जो उन कार्यों को उत्तम रीति से करते हैं। जिन्हें अन्य लोग सामान्य ढंग से करते हैं।' दूसरा कारण यह है कि भारत में संस्कृत के विद्वानों की अपेक्षा प्राकृत भाषाओं के विद्वानों का सम्मान सदा से कम रहा है। राजशेखर संस्कृत के अतिरिक्त प्राकृत भाषाओं के भी ऐसे बड़े पंडित थे कि उनके पांडित्य की गहराई का मूल्यांकन करना सामान्य जनों के लिए कोई सरल बात नहीं थी। ऐसी दशा में राजशेखर के गुणों की पहचान कौन करता और उन्हें कवियों के बीच यथोचित स्थान कौन देता ? परिणाम यह हुआ कि गुण और विद्या के रहते हुए राजशेखर अन्य कवियों की भाँति उतना प्रसिद्ध न हो सके।

Hints : नाटककारों, dramatists (playwrights). किसी भाँति हीन नहीं हैं, is no way inferior to. प्रसिद्धि एवं स्वीकार्यता, celebrity and wide recognition. यह नहीं अनुमान करना चाहिए, it should not be concluded (or supposed) निम्नकोटि की है, is of inferior value (or order). यथार्थ यह है कि, the truth is that (or the fact ......). उत्तम रीति से करना, to do in the best way. सामान्य ढंग से करना, to do well. सम्मान सदा से कम रहा है, have always been in less esteem than. पांडित्य की गहराई का मूल्यांकन करना, to assess the depth of (his) learning. सरल बात, an easy task. पहचान करना, to apprehend. यथोचित स्थान देना, to assign a proper place. गुण और विद्या के रहते हुए, despite his merit and learning.

Exercise 101

मैं मनुष्य को एक घने अंधकार में देख रहा हूँ। जैसे अंधेरी रात में किसी घर का दीपक बुझ जाए, ऐसा ही आज मनुष्य हो गया है। पर जो बुझ गया है, उसे प्रज्ज्वलित किया जा सकता है। और मैं मनुष्य को दिशाहीन हुआ देख रहा हूँ। जैसे कोई नाव अनन्त सागर में राह भूल जाती है, ऐसा ही आज मनुष्य हो गया है। वह भूल गया है कि उसे कहाँ जाना है और क्या होना है। पर जो विस्मृत हो गया है उसकी स्मृति को उसमें पुन: जगाया जा सकता है। इसलिए अंधकार है, पर आलोक के प्रति निराश होने का कोई कारण नहीं है। वस्तुत: अन्धकार जितना घना होता है, प्रभात उतना ही निकट आ जाता है।

(साधना पथ-रजनीश)

Hints : घने अंधकार में, (engulfed) into the dense darkness. बुझ जाना, to extinguish. प्रज्ज्वलित किया जा सकता है, can be kindled. दिशाहीन हुआ, being misled (or confused). अनन्त, boundless. राह भूलना, to miss the way (or be distracted). और क्या होना है, and what more to be. जगाया जा सकता है, can be recalled (or quickened). आलोक, light. अंधकार ...... आ जाता है, the denser is darkness, the nearer is dawn.

Chapter 17

Vocabulary

A. Proverbs (मुहावरें), Idioms and Phrases

A bad man is better than a bad name.	बद अच्छा, बदनाम बुरा।
A bad workman quarrels with his tools.	नाच न जाने आँगन टेढ़ा।
A bird in hand is worth two in the bush.	नौ नगद न तेरह उधार।
A burnt child dreads the fire.	दूध का जला छाँछ फूँककर पीता है।
A drop in the ocean.	ऊँट के मुँह में जीरा। सागर में बूँद।
A little knowledge is a dangerous thing.	नीम हकीम खतरे जान।
All's well that ends well.	अन्त भला तो सब भला।
An empty vessel sounds much.	थोथा चना बाजे घना।
As you sow, so will you reap.	जैसी करनी वैसी भरनी।
Barking dogs seldom bite.	जो गरजते हैं, बरसते नहीं।
Birds of a feather flock together.	हम पंछी एक डाल के, चोर-चोर मौसेरे भाई।
Coming events cast their shadow earlier.	होनहार बिरवान के होत चिकने पात।
Morning shows the day.	पूत के पाँव पालने में ही देखे जाते हैं।
Diamonds cut diamonds.	लोहा ही लोहा को काटता है।
Example is better than precept.	कथनी से करनी भली।
Fortune favours the brave.	पुरुषसिंहमुपैति लक्ष्मी।
Half a loaf is better than no bread.	कुछ नहीं से थोड़ा अच्छा।
Ill got, ill spent.	पाप की परिणति प्रायश्चित।
It is no use to cry over spilt milk.	अब पछताए होत क्या।
It takes two to make a quarrel.	एक हाथ से ताली नहीं बजती।
To kill two birds with one stone.	एक पंथ दो काज।
Let bygones be bygones.	बीती ताहि बिसार दे।
Man proposes, God disposes.	मेरे मन कुछ और है कर्त्ता के कुछ और।
Might is right.	जिसकी लाठी उसकी भैंस।

407

Misfortunes never come alone.	दुख अकेले नहीं आता।
Money begets money.	धन से धन कमाया जाता है।
Out of the frying pan into the fire.	आकाश से गिरा खजूर पर अटका।
Penny wise and pound foolish.	सोना लूटे, कोयला पर छापा।
Self-praise is no recommendation.	अपने मुँह मियाँ मिट्टू बनना।
Something is better than nothing.	कुछ नहीं से हाँ भला।
Strike the iron while it is hot.	जब तक लोहा गर्म है, खूब चोट करो।
Tit for tat.	जैसा को तैसा।
To make a mountain of a mole hill/To raise storm in tea cup.	तिल का ताड़ बनाना।
To build castles in the air.	हवाई किला बनाना।
Too many cooks spoil the broth.	अनेक योगी, मठ ऊजाड़।
To add insult to injury.	जले पर नमक छिड़कना।
To add fuel to fire (or flame)/To fan the fire.	आग में घी डालना/आग को हवा देना।
To dance attendance on.	तलवा चाटना।
To drive a (hard) bargain.	अधिक मोलाई करना।
To make the best of a bad bargain.	प्रत्येक उपाय से कठिनाई का समाना करना।
A beggar description.	वर्णनातीत।
Beggars must not be choosers.	जो मिल जाय, ले लो।
To bell the cat.	बिल्ली के गले में घंटी बाँधना।
To make the best of both worlds.	दोनों हाथ लड्डू।
Between two fires/Between scylla and charybdis/Between the devil and the deep sea.	इधर कुँआ उधर खाई।
Blood is thicker than water.	खून का सम्बन्ध सबसे बढ़कर।
A bolt from the blue.	वज्रपात।
To burn one's fingers.	आ बैल मुझे मार।
Every cloud has a silver lining.	निराशा में भी आशा की किरण।
Every dog has his day.	कभी न कभी सौभाग्य सभी को मिलता है।
To have all one's eggs in one basket.	एक ही दाँव में सब लगा देना।
To fall in evil days.	दुर्दिन में फँसना।
To follow in the footsteps of.	पदचिह्नों पर चलना।
To gird up one's loins.	कटिबद्ध, कमर कसकर तैयार होना।
A snake in the grass.	छिपा शत्रु।
Hair-breath escape/narrow escape.	बाल-बाल बचना।
To have one's heart in one's mouth.	कलेजा मुँह को आना।

To take to one's heels.	नौ दो ग्यारह होना। (भाग खड़ा होना)
To show a light (or clean) pair of heels.	सिर. पर पैर रखकर भागना।
To cut no ice.	दाल न गलना।
A wolf in lamb's clothing.	भेड़ की खाल में भेड़िया।
Necessity knows no law.	भूखा क्या नहीं करता।
To be at a loss.	किंकर्त्तव्य विमूढ़ होना।
Even Homer sometimes nods.	कभी-कभी मुनि भी भ्रमित हो जाते हैं
The order of the day. युगधर्म	धियोऽपि पुंसाः मलिना भवन्ति। युगधर्म।
Every man has his price.	किसी का भी ईमान खरीदा जा सकता है।
One swallow cannot bring a summer.	एक चना भाड़ नहीं फोड़ता।
A live ass is better than a dead lion.	एक मरे शेर से एक जीवित गधा बेहतर है।
Borrowed garments never fit well.	उधार लिए कपड़े उपयुक्त नहीं होते।
Many men, many minds.	मुंडे-मुंडे मतिर्भिन्ना/अपनी-अपनी डफली अपना-अपना राग।
Great boast, small roast.	ऊँची दुकान का फीका पकवान।
Grapes are sour.	अगूंर ही खट्टे हैं।
An empty mind is a devil's workshop.	खाली दिमाग, शैतान का घर।
A guilty mind is always suspicious.	चोर की दाढ़ी में तिनका।
A nine day's wonder.	चार दिन की चान्दनी फिर अँधेरी रात।
All that glitters is not gold.	सभी चमकने वाले सोना ही नहीं होते।
Prevention is better than cure.	अग्र सोची सदा सुखी।
Chips of the same block.	एक ही थैली के चट्टे बट्टे।
Uneasy lies the head that wears a crown.	ताज तले, सिर भारी।
Authority forgets a dying king.	मरता को कोई नहीं पूछता।
A cry in the wilderness.	नक्कारखाने में तूती की आवाज।
No vice like avarice.	लालच बुरी बला।
Bone of contention.	विवाद की जड़।
A black sheep.	कुलांगार, कुलकलंकी।
A bed of roses.	पुष्प शैय्या (सुख की सेज)।
Broad daylight.	दिन दहाड़े।
A burning question.	प्रमुख (ज्वलन्त) प्रश्न (समस्या)
Crocodile tears.	दिखावटी (घड़ियाली) आँसू।
Clarion-call.	दुन्दुभी नाद।
A fancy price.	मुँहमाँगा दाम।
A fresh lease of life.	नव जीवन।

Gift of the gab.	भाषण का वरदान।
A good samaritan.	दयालु व्यक्ति।
A hard nut to crack.	टेढ़ी खीर।
A jack of all trades.	हरफनमौला।
A man of letters.	साहित्यिक (विद्वान) व्यक्ति।
A man of parts.	गुणवान व्यक्ति।
A man of oily tongue.	चिकनी चुपड़ी बात करने वाला।
Palmy days.	समृद्धि के दिन।
Part and parcel.	अविभाज्य अंग।
All in all.	सर्वे सर्वा।
At all costs.	किसी भी कीमत पर।
At a loss.	किंकर्त्तव्यविमूढ़।
By leaps and bounds.	दिन दूना, रात चौगुना।
Few and far between.	दुर्लभ।
For good/forever.	हमेशा के लिए।
In full swing.	जोर शोर से।
In no time.	पलक मारते।
In the same breath.	एक ही साँस में।
To one's heart's content.	जी भरकर।
To the last farthing.	पाई पाई भर।
Under one's breath.	दबी जुबान से।
And what not.	और क्या क्या नहीं ? सब कुछ।
Without rhyme or reason.	अकारण ही/व्यर्थ।
Bag and baggage.	बोरिया बिस्तर सहित।
Fast and loose (to play).	कथनी कुछ, करनी कुछ।
Weal and woe.	सुख दुख।
A bird's eye view.	सरसरी निगाह से।
A bolt from the blue.	वज्रघात/अचानक सदमा/शोक
A bull in a china shop.	अवांछित व्यक्ति।
A utopian scheme.	हवाई किला।
A white elephant.	खर्चीली वस्तु।
A flowery style.	अलंकारिक भाषा।
To dine with Duke, Humphrey.	भूखे रह जाना।
To make faces.	मुँह बनाना।
To catch the fancy of.	आकर्षित करना।

To smell a rat.	संशय करना।
Tight fisted.	कंजूस।
Of the first water.	उच्च श्रेणी का।
A wind fall.	अप्रत्याशित सौभाग्य।
To beat the breast.	छाती पीटना (शोक से)
To beat the air.	व्यर्थ प्रयास।
Above one's understanding.	समझ से परे।
To take into account.	आंकना, मूल्यांकन करना।
To bear in mind.	ध्यान में रखना।
On no account.	किसी हालत में नहीं।
What is he after ?	वह किस फेर में है ?
To take amiss.	बुरा मानना।
To run amuck.	सनक जाना, पागल हो जाना।
Animal spirits.	यौवन की चंचलता।
Away with you/Be off.	दूर भागो।
To have an axe to grind.	अपना उल्लू सीधा करना।
To go bad.	सड़ जाना।
His bark is worse than his bite.	बाहर से कड़ा, अन्दर से कोमल। अहानिकारक व्यक्ति।
To be the be-all and end-all.	चरमोद्देश्य।
To blow one's own trumpet.	आत्मप्रशंसा करना।
Not born yesterday.	कल का दूध पीता बच्चा नहीं।
A cat-and-dog life.	निरन्तर कलह का जीवन।
To catch a Tartar.	जबर्दस्त से पाला पड़ना।
To come to blows.	हाथापाई करना।
His days are numbered.	चन्द दिनों का मेहमान।
To go to the devil. (The dogs)	भाड़ में जाना।
To eat the humble pie.	अपमान का घूँट पीना।
To end in smoke.	टाँय-टाँय फिस होना।
To care a fig for.	बिल्कुल परवाह न करना।/किस खेत की मूली।
To fish in troubled water.	बहती गंगा में हाथ धोना।
To play to the gallery.	वाहवाही पाने का प्रयास, डींग हाँकना।
To get by heart.	जुवानी याद करना।
To get into hot water.	झंझट/परेशानी में पड़ना।
To be hand and glove with.	चोली-दामन का संबंध।
To greese the palm of.	घूस देना।

To make one's hair stand on end.	रोंगटे खड़े करना।
Hand to mouth.	कमाया खाया बराबर।
To harp on the same string.	एक ही राग अलापना।
To take heart.	हिम्मत बाँधना।
To one's heart of hearts.	अन्तर्मन से।
To pick holes.	छिद्रान्वेषण करना।
To laugh in one's sleeve.	मुँह छिपाकर हँसना।
To lead astray.	बहकाना।
To leave one in the lurch.	विपत्ति में छोड़ जाना।
To read between the lines.	गुप्त भाव को समझना।
To look down upon.	हेय दृष्टि से देखना।
To look a gift-horse in the mouth.	बिना परिश्रम उत्तम फल की आशा।
To mind one's own business.	अपना काम (देखो) दूसरों में दखलन्दाजी मत करो।
A miss is as good as a mile.	गलती गलती ही है।
Money makes the mare go.	दुनियाँ में मूल है रुपैया।
To move heaven and earth.	आकाश पाताल एक करना।
Now or never.	अभी या कभी नहीं।
Next to nothing.	नगण्य
To turn up one's nose at.	नाक भौं सिकोड़ना।
Well off.	खुशहाल।
To pave the way for.	पथ प्रशस्त करना।
To poison one's ears against.	किसी के विरुद्ध कान भरना।
The rank and file.	जन सामान्य।
To reduce or meet to dust/	धूल में मिल जाना। जलकर राख होना।
burn to ashes/to the dust.	धूल चाटना (धूसरित होना)।
Riff-raff/Tom, Dick and Harry.	ऐरू गैरू नत्थू खैरू।
Safe and sound.	पूर्णरूपेण सुरक्षित।
To take one to task.	डाँटना फटकारना।
To face the music.	डाँट फटकार सुनना/आलोचना का सामना करना।
An ugly customer.	बखेड़िया व्यक्ति।
To hold the upper hand.	पलड़ा भारी होना।
The schoolmaster is abroad.	शिक्षा का प्रसार होना।
Debunk.	बदनामी दूर करना।
To carry through.	कठिनाई से सुरक्षित निकालना।
To catch up away.	झपट से भागना।

To be sick of the whole business.	झंझट (धंधे) से ऊब जाना।
To get abroad.	समाचार फैलाना।
To get out of hand.	काबू से बाहर होना।
To get wind.	कान में भनक पड़ना।
To keep body and soul together.	गुजर बसर करना।
To keep pace with.	कदम से कदम (कंधे से कंधा) मिलाकर चलना।
Lame excuse.	झूठा बहाना।
A white crow.	दुर्लभ/अनहोनी।
To throw cold water upon.	हतोत्साहित करना।
With zest and zeal.	जोश खरोश के साथ।
Yes man.	जी हुजूरी वाला व्यक्ति।
To win laurels.	सम्मान प्राप्त करना।
To be a laughing stock.	हँसी का पात्र होना।
To have words with.	बाता बाती (झगड़ा) होना।
To eat one's words.	कथन/शब्द को वापस लेना।
Red-handed.	रँगे हाथों।
Nine times out of ten.	सर्वसामान्यतया, अधिकांशतः।

B. Groups, Cries of Birds and Beasts

1. Groups (समूह)

An *army* of *soldiers*
A *bale* of *cotton*
A *team* of *players, inspectors*
A *crew* of *ship, aircraft*
A *gang* of *robbers*
A *pack* of *hounds, cards*
A *hand* of *bananas*
A *bunch* of *keys, grapes* etc.
A *jury* of *judges*
A *galaxy* of *beauties, talent, milkyway* etc.
A *flock* of *sheep*
A *herd* of *cattle*
A *crowd* or *mob* of *people*
A *sheaf* of *corn*
A *company* of *men*
A *band* of *musicians, robbers*

A *bundle* of *goods, articles*
A *fleet* of *ships, boats of navel*
A *swarm* of *insects, birds*
A *cluster* of *honey, bees, stars*

2. Cries of Birds and Beasts

भुनभुनाना	To murmur
कानाफूसी करना	To whisper
आह भरना	To sigh
सुबकना	To sob
बड़बड़ाना, चिड़ियों की निरंतर ध्वनि	To chatter
प्रतिध्वनि करना	To echoe, to resound
कौंधना (बिजली)	To thunder
कूकना (Cuckoo)	To coo
गुटुरना (Dove, Pigeon)	To coo
काँव काँव करना (Crow)	To caw
रेंकना (Ass, donkey)	To bray
गुर्राना (Bear)	To growl
मक्खी (Fly)	To buzz
मधुमक्खी (Hive-bee)	To hum
म्याऊँ म्याऊँ करना	To mew, to purr
मिमियाना (Goat)	To bleat, (Duck = to quack)
रंभाना (Cattle, Cow)	To low, to moo
हुँआ हुँआ करना (Jackal, Fox)	To howl
चिंघाड़ना (Elephant)	To trumpet
गर्जना (Lion, Gun)	To roar
टर्र टर्र करना (Frog) (Raven काग)	To croak
भौंकना (Dog)	To bark
फुफकारना (Snake)	To hiss
कुकड़ूँ कूँ करना (Cock)	To crow
किड़किड़ाना (Squirrel)	To squeak
हिनहिनाना (Horse)	To neigh
चूँ चूँ करना, चहचहाना (Bird)	To twitter, to chirp
टिक टिक करना (Clock)	To tick
किरकिराना, चरमर करना (Door, shoes)	To creak
गड़गड़ाना (Cloud)	To rumble

किटकिटाना (Teeth)	To clatter
सनसनाना, साँय साँय करना (Wind)	To whistle, to swish
खनखनाना (Pot, jewel)	To tinkle
झनझनाना (Coin)	To jingle
झनझनाना (Fetters)	To clink
(Monkey, apes) खों खों करना	To gibber, to chatter
गुर्राना (Pigs, camels)	To grunt
चीं चूँ करना (Larks लावापक्षी)	To sing
उल्लू का बोलना (Owl)	To hoot

3. Names of Young Ones of Animals

Ass	गधा	Foal
Bear	भालू	
Fox	लोमड़ी	Cub
Tiger	बाघ	
Wolf	भेड़िया	
Stag	बारहसिंगा	
Deer	हिरण	Fawn
Cat	बिल्ली	Kitten
Cow	गाय	Calf
Dog	कुत्ता	Puppy
Duck	बत्तख	Duckling
Goat	बकरी	Kid
Hen	मुर्गी	Chicken
Horse	घोड़ा	Colt
Hare	खरगोश	Leveret
Sheep	भेड़	Lamb

C. Names of Persons and Things

1. Names of Flowers

कमल, lotus. कमलिनी, lily. केतकी, pandanus. गुलदाऊदी, chrysanthemum. गुलमेंहदी, balsam. गुलबहार, daisy. गुलाब, rose. गेंदा, marigold. चमेली, jasmine. चम्पा, magnolia. धतूरा, belladonna. नरगिस, narcissus. वनफशा, sweet violet. सूर्यमुखी, sunflower. पंखुड़ी, petal.

2. Names of Fruits

अखरोट, chestnut. अन्ननास, pine-apple. अनार, pomegranate. अंगूर, grape. अंजीर, fig. आम, mango. ईख, sugarcane. ककड़ी, cucumber. कटहल, jack-fruit. काजू, cashewnut. किशमिश, currant. केला, banana. खजूर, date. खरबूज, musk melon. तरबूज, water melon. खीरा, cucumber. गाजर, carrot. बेर, berry. जामुन, blackberry. जैतून, olive. नारियल, coconut. नारंगी, orange. नाशपाती, pear. नींबू, lemon. पपीता, papaya. बादाम, almond. मुनक्का, raisin. मूँगफली, groundnut. ज्वार बाजरा मक्का, maize. शकरकन्द, sweet potato. सेब, apple. अमरूद, guava. चना, chick-pea. दाल, gram (red gram अरहर, green gram मूँग), गेहूँ, wheat. चावल, rice. भूसी, flake.

3. Names of Vegetables and Spices

आलू, potato. इमली, tamarind. कद्दू लौकी, pumpkin. कुम्हड़ा, squash (gourd). धनिया, coriander. पालक, spinach. पुदीना, mint. प्याज, onion. फूलगोभी, cauliflower. बन्दगोभी, cabbage. बैंगन, brinjal. भिन्डी, lady's finger. मिरचा, chilli. मूली, radish. लहसुन, garlic. सेम, bean. अजवाइन, king's cumin. शलजम, turnip. साग, spinach.

4. Names of Animals

ऊँट, camel. कस्तूरी मृग, musk-deer. कुतिया, bitch. खच्चर, donkey. खरगोश, rabbit. खरहा, hare. गधा, ass. गिलहरी, squirrel. गैंडा, rhinoceros. जेवरा, zebra. घोड़ी, mare. चीता, panther. छछुन्दर, mole. जंगली सूअर, boar. टट्टू, pony. तेंदुआ, leopard. नेवला, mongoose, weasel. पिल्ला, puppy. बकरा, he-goat, बकरी, she-goat. बकरी का बच्चा, kid. बछड़ा, calf, बछिया, heifer. बछेड़ा, calf. बछेड़ी, filly. बिल्ली का बच्चा, kitten. वनमानुष, chimpanzee. बाघ, tiger. बारहसिंगा, antelope. बारहसिंगी, hind. भालू, bear. भेड़िया, wolf. भेड़ी, ewe. मेमना, lamb. लंगूर, ape. शिकारी कुत्ता, hound. सिंह, चीता, lion. सूअर, hog-pig. सूअरी, swine. हिरण का बच्चा, fawn.

5. Names of Birds

अवाविल, swallow. उल्लू, owl. कठफोड़वा, wood-pecker. कबूतर, pigeon. पड़ुक, dove. काग, raven. कोयल, cuckoo. गरूड़, eagle. गिद्ध, vulture. गौरैया, sparrow. चमगादड़, bat. चील, kite. तीतर, partidge. नीलकंठ, magpil, jav. पंख, feather, wing, plume. बत्तक, duck. बुलबुल, nightingale. वया, weaverbird. वटेर, quail. बाज, falcon, hawk. मुर्गी का बच्चा, chicken. मोर, peacock. मोरनी, peahen. लावा, lark. शुतुर्मुर्ग, ostrich. सारस, crane. सुग्गा, parrot. हंस, swan. तोता, macaw, parrot.

6. Reptiles and Insects

अजगर, boa. कछुआ, tortoise. केंचुआ, earthworm. केकड़ा, crab. खटमल, bed-bug. गिरगिट, chameleon. गेहुँअन साँप, cobra. गोजर, centipede. गोवरैला, beetle. मगर, crocodile. घोंघा, snail. चीलर, body-lice. चींटी, ant. छिपकली, lizard. जुगनू, firefly, glow-worm. ढील, जूँ, lause. जोंक, leech. झींगुर, cricket. टिड्डी, locust. तितली, butterfly. दरियाई घोड़ा, hippopotamus. दीमक, white-ant. टिड्डा, grasshopper. बर्रे, wasp. बिच्छू, scorpion. मक्खी, fly. मकड़ा, spider. मच्छर, mosquito. मधुमक्खी, bee. मेंढक का बच्चा, tadpole. रेशम का कीड़ा, silkworm. शंख, conch.

7. Organs

जीभ, tongue. पलक, eyelid. भौं, eyebrow. पपनी, eyelash. पुतली, eyeball. दाढ़ी, beard. मूँछ, mustache. नख, nail. अनामिका, ring-finger. तर्जनी, index-finger. अंगूठा, thumb. पैर का अंगूठा, toe. कोहनी, elbow. घुटना, knee. होठ, lip. कलाई, wrist. नस, nerves, sinews. पसली, rib. फेफड़ा, lung. छाती, chest. उर, breast. पुठा, muscle. मंसूड़ा, gum. मुट्ठी, fist. मूत्राशय, urinary bladder. रीढ़, backbone. रोमकूप, pore. ललाट, forehead. हथेली, palm.

D. Inflexions of Some Verbs

Present		Past	Past participle
Advise	सलाह देना	Advised	Advised
Agree	सहमत होना	Agreed	Agreed
Appear	प्रगट होना	Appeared	Appeared
Arise	उठना	Arose	Arisen
Awake	जागना	Awoke	Awaken
Bear	सहन करना	Bore	Borne
Beat	पीटना	Beat	Beaten
Become	होना	Became	Become
Begin	शुरू करना	Began	Begun
Bend	झुकना, झुकाना	Bent	Bent
Bind	बाँधना	Bound	Bound
Bite	दाँत से काटना	Bit	Bitten
Bleed	रक्तस्राव होना	Bled	Bled
Blow	बहना (हवा का)	Blew	Blown
Boast	डींग हाँकना	Boasted	Boasted
Borrow	उधार लेना	Borrowed	Borrowed
Break	तोड़ना	Broke	Broken
Bring	लाना	Brought	Brought
Broadcast	प्रसारित करना	Broadcast	Broadcast
Build	निर्माण करना	Built	Built
Burn	जलाना, जलना	Burnt	Burnt
Burst	फटना	Burst	Burst
Buy	खरीदना	Bought	Bought
Carry	ढोना	Carried	Carried
Cast	डालना	Cast	Cast

Catch	पकड़ना	Caught	Caught
Cost	लागत होना	Cost	Cost
Choose	चुनना	Chose	Chosen
Chide	डाँटना, फटकारना	Chid	Chidden
Cling	चिपकना	Clung	Clung
Creep	रेंगना	Crept	Crept
Cry	चिल्लाना	Cried	Cried
Cut	काटना	Cut	Cut
Dare	साहस करना	Dared	Dared
Deal	व्यवहार करना	Dealt	Dealt
Defeat	हराना	Defeated	Defeated
Dig	खोदना	Dug	Dug
Do	करना	Did	Done
Draw	खींचना	Drew	Drawn
Dream	स्वप्न देखना	Dreamt	Dreamt
Drink	पीना	Drank	Drunk
Drive	हाँकना	Drove	Driven
Drown	डूबना (जीव का)	Drowned	Drowned
Dwell	निवास करना	Dwelt	Dwelt
Dry	सुखाना	Dried	Dried
Eat	खाना	Ate	Eaten
Fail	असफल होना	Failed	Failed
Fall	गिरना	Fell	Fallen
Feed	खिलाना	Fed	Fed
Feel	अनुभव करना	Felt	Felt
Fell	काटकर गिराना	Felled	Felled
Fight	लड़ना	Fought	Fought
Fill	भरना	Filled	Filled
Find	पाना	Found	Found
Flee	भागना	Fled	Fled
Flow	बहना (द्रव का)	Flowed	Flowed
Fly	उड़ना, उड़ाना	Flew	Flown
Forbid	मना करना	Forbade	Forbidden
Forsake	त्यागना	Forsook	Forsaken
Found	स्थापना करना	Founded	Founded

Freeze	जमना	Froze	Frozen
Get	पाना	Got	Got (Gotten)
Go	जाना	Went	Gone
Grow	उगना, उगाना	Grew	Grown
Hang	लटकना/टाँगना	Hung	Hung
Hang	फाँसी देना	Hanged	Hanged
Has/Have	रखना	Had	Had
Hear	सुनना	Heard	Heard
Hide	छिपना, छिपाना	Hid	Hidden
Hit	चोट करना	Hit	Hit
Hold	पकड़ना, थामना	Held	Held
Hunt	शिकार करना	Hunted	Hunted
Hurt	चोट पहुँचाना	Hurt	Hurt
Injure	घायल करना	Injured	Injured
Keep	रखना	Kept	Kept
Kneel	घुटने के बल झुकना	Knelt	Knelt
Knit	बुनना	Knit, Knitted	Knit, Knitted
Know	जानना	Knew	Known
Lay	डालना	Laid	Laid
Lead	नेतृत्व करना	Led	Led
Lean	झुकना	Leaned	Leaned
Leap	छलांग करना	Lept, Leaped	Lept, Leaped
Learn	सीखना	Learnt	Learnt
Leave	छोड़ना	Left	Left
Lend	उधार देना	Lent	Lent
Let	अनुमति देना/दो	Let	Let
Lie	लेटना	Lay	Lain
Lie	झूठ बोलना	Lied	Lied
Lift	उठाना	Lifted	Lifted
Light	प्रकाशित करना	Lighted, Lit	Lighted, Lit
Live	रहना	Lived	Lived
Look	देखना	Looked	Looked
Lose	खोना	Lost	Lost
Loose	ढीला करना	Loosed	Loosed
Make	बनाना	Made	Made

Mean	अर्थ बताना	Meant	Meant
Meet	मिलना	Met	Met
Melt	पिघलना	Melted	Melted
Owe	ऋणी होना	Owed	Owed
Obey	आज्ञा मानना	Obeyed	Obeyed
Obtain	प्राप्त करना	Obtained	Obtained
Pay	चुकाना	Paid	Paid
Permit	अनुमति देना	Permitted	Permitted
Praise	प्रशंसा करना	Praised	Praised
Pray	प्रार्थना करना	Prayed	Prayed
Preach	उपदेश देना	Preached	Preached
Prefer	प्राथमिकता देना	Preferred	Preferred
Prepare	तैयार करना	Prepared	Prepared
Prevent	मना करना, रोकना	Prevented	Prevented
Prey	शिकार करना	Preyed	Preyed
Promise	प्रतिज्ञा करना	Promised	Promised
Prove	प्रमाणित करना	Proved	Proved
Pull	खींचना	Pulled	Pulled
Pursue	पीछा करना	Pursued	Pursued
Push	धक्का देना	Pushed	Pushed
Put	रखना	Put	Put
Say	कहना	Said	Said
Search	खोजना	Searched	Searched
See	देखना	Saw	Seen
Seek	ढूँढना	Sought	Sought
Seem	प्रतीत होना	Seemed	Seemed
Sell	क्रय करना	Sold	Sold
Sew	सींना	Sewed	Sewed/Sewn
Shake	हिलाना	Shook	Shaken
Shine	चमकना	Shone	Shone
Shoot	गोली मारना	Shot	Shot
Shrink	सिकुड़ना	Shrank	Shrunk
Shut	बन्द करना	Shut	Shut
Sing	गाना	Sang	Sung
Sink	डूबना (वस्तु का)	Sank	Sunk

Sit	बैठना	Sat	Sat
Slay	कत्ल करना	Slew	Slain
Sleep	सोना	Slept	Slept
Slip	फिसलना	Slipped	Slipped
Smell	महकना	Smelt	Smelt
Speak	बोलना	Spoke	Spoken
Spin	कातना	Span	Spun
Spoil	बर्बाद होना/करना	Spoiled	Spoiled
Spread	फैलना/फैलाना	Spread	Spread
Spring	कूदना	Sprang	Sprung
Stand	खड़ा होना	Stood	Stood
Stay	ठहरना	Stayed	Stayed
Steal	चुराना	Stole	Stolen
Stick	चिपकना	Stuck	Stuck
Sting	डंक मारना	Stung	Stung
Stop	रुकना	Stopped	Stopped
Strike	मारना	Struck	Struck
Study	अध्ययन करना	Studied	Studied
Succeed	सफल होना	Succeeded	Succeeded
Suffer	कष्ट सहना	Suffered	Suffered
Swear	कसम खाना	Swore	Sworn
Swim	तैरना	Swam	Swum
Take	लेना	Took	Taken
Taste	स्वाद लेना/चखना	Tasted	Tasted
Teach	पढ़ाना	Taught	Taught
Tell	बताना/कहना	Told	Told
Tear	फाड़ना	Tore	Torn
Think	सोचना	Thought	Thought
Throw	फेंकना	Threw	Thrown
Travel	यात्रा करना	Travelled	Travelled
Trust	विश्वास करना	Trusted	Trusted
Try	प्रयत्न करना	Tried	Tried
Understand	समझना	Understood	Understood
Vanish	गायब होना	Vanished	Vanished
Wait	इन्तजार करना	Waited	Waited

Walk	टहलना	Walked	Walked
Wear	पहनना	Wore	Worn
Weave	कातना/बुनना	Wove	Woven
Wed	विवाह करना	Wedded	Wedded
Weep	रोना	Wept	Wept
Win	जीतना	Won	Won
Wind	चाबी देना	Wound	Wound
Wish	इच्छा करना	Wished	Wished
Wound	घायल करना	Wounded	Wounded
Wring	निचोड़ना	Wrung	Wrung
Write	लिखना	Wrote	Written